Also by John B. Boles

The Great Revival, 1787–1805:
The Origins of the Southern Evangelical Mind

America: The Middle Period.
Essays in Honor of Bernard Mayo (edited)

Maryland Heritage:
Five Baltimore Institutions Celebrate the Bicentennial (edited)

Religion in Antebellum Kentucky

Dixie Dateline:
A Journalistic Portrait of the Contemporary South (edited)

Black Southerners, 1619–1869

Interpreting Southern History:
Historiographical Essays in Honor of S.W. Higginbotham
(co-edited with Evelyn Thomas Nolen)

Masters and Slaves in the House of the Lord:
Race and Religion in the American South, 1740–1870 (edited)

A University So Conceived: A Brief History of Rice

The Irony of Southern Religion

The South Through Time: A History of an American Region

Autobiographical Reflections on Southern Religious History (edited)

A Companion to the American South (edited)

Origins of the New South, 1877–1913, Fifty Years Later: The Continuing
Influence of a Historical Classic (co-edited with Bethany L. Johnson)

Shapers of Southern History:
Autobiographical Essays by Fifteen Historians (edited)

Unto a Good Land: A History of the American People
(co-authored with David E. Harrell, Jr., Edwin S. Gaustad,
Sally Foreman Griffith, Randall M. Miller, and Randall B. Woods)

University Builder: Edgar Odell Lovett and the
Founding of the Rice Institute

Seeing Jefferson Anew: In His Time and Ours
(co-edited with Randal L. Hall)

JEFFERSON

Watercolor of west front of Monticello.
By Jane Pittman Braddick Peticolas, 1825.

Jefferson

ARCHITECT OF AMERICAN LIBERTY

John B. Boles

BASIC BOOKS

New York

Published by Basic Books, an imprint of Perseus Books, LLC,
a subsidiary of Hachette Book Group, Inc.

Books published by Basic Books are available at special discounts
for bulk purchases in the United States by corporations, institutions, and other
organizations. For more information, please contact the Special Markets Department
at Perseus Books, 2300 Chestnut Street, Suite 200, Philadelphia, PA 19103,
or call (800) 810-4145, ext. 5000, or e-mail special.markets@perseusbooks.com.

Interior book design by Cynthia Young

Library of Congress Control Number: 2017934233
ISBN: 978-0-465-09468-4 (hardcover)
ISBN: 978-0-465-09469-1 (e-book)
LSC-C
10 9 8 7 6 5 4 3

For Parker, Bailey, Sonia, and Nicolas

"grandchildren . . . furnish me great resources of happiness."
—THOMAS JEFFERSON TO CHARLES THOMSON,
DECEMBER 25, 1808

Contents

A Note on Capitalization

Thomas Jefferson usually did not begin written sentences with capital letters. However, Julian P. Boyd, founding editor of the *Papers of Thomas Jefferson* (Princeton, 1950–),[1] silently capitalized the initial letters of Jefferson's sentences, and subsequent editors continued this practice until Volume 30, published in 2003. The editors of the following volumes rendered his writings exactly as Jefferson wrote them. I have decided to adopt the practice of the volumes I am citing; hence, in the letters from volumes prior to the thirtieth (which begins with January 1798), capitalization follows modern standards as established by Boyd. In citations of letters written after that date, I follow the usage of the editors and replicate Jefferson's almost capital-free style. I have only corrected Jefferson's sometimes idiosyncratic spelling when necessary for clarity.

Introduction

THOMAS JEFFERSON puzzles us. By birth, education, and demeanor an aristocrat, he was the most thoroughgoing democrat of the Founding Fathers. As learned and bookish a man as any other of his era, he himself only wrote one book (accidentally) and merely attempted, halfheartedly, to write an autobiography. The most widely traveled and cosmopolitan of the Founders, he never journeyed south of his home state of Virginia or farther than fifty miles west of Monticello. A hesitant, ineffective orator, he was a sensational conversationalist. Known around the globe for penning the words "all men are created equal," he was a lifelong slaveholder. Critical of the very existence of mulattoes, he nevertheless had a long-term intimate relationship with a mixed-race slave woman, Sally Hemings, and fathered five children by her. Labeled a deist and sometimes charged with atheism, he came to believe himself a Christian, though of a special sort. Ridiculed as dreamy and philosophical to a fault, he was an effective political leader. Often praising the unique delights of his mountaintop rural retreat at Monticello, he in fact lived much of his adult life in Philadelphia, New York, Paris, and Washington, DC, and became a connoisseur of cities. He defies those trying to grasp him, down to the smallest details: famous as an oenophile, he preferred to dilute his wine with water.

How can one make sense of such a tangle of apparent contradictions? Surely not simply by picking and choosing one side or the other of these various binaries—aristocrat or democrat, unqualified lover of freedom or unrepentant slaveholder, true wine lover or snobbish dilettante. Jefferson's complexity renders him easy to caricature in popular culture. Particularly in recent years, Jefferson, long the hero of small *d* as well as capital *D* democrats, has seen his reputation wane due to his views on race, the revelation of his relationship with Sally Hemings, and his failure to free his own slaves. Once lauded as the champion of the little man, today he is vilified as a hypocritical slave owner, professing a love of liberty while quietly driving his own slaves to labor harder in his pursuit of personal luxury. Surely an interpretative middle ground is possible, if not necessary. If we hope to understand the enigma that is Thomas Jefferson, we must view him holistically and within the rich context of his time and place. This biography aims to provide that perspective.

We should begin by acknowledging that Jefferson lived in a world fundamentally different from ours. It was pre-Darwinian, which is only one reason most people, in general, did not expect much change in their lives. Jefferson's society was, compared to today, remarkably undemocratic, even though it was more democratic than any other society of the time. Women, blacks, and propertyless white males could not vote. Rigid expectations governed what women could and could not do; blacks were hardly considered persons, and racial slavery was commonplace throughout the nation; class distinctions were assumed to be practically immutable. A new democratic age was dawning, but its implications were poorly understood, as were the consequences of new modes of trade and production that would soon remake the American economy and society.

Many of Jefferson's assumptions reveal him to be a man thoroughly of his own time, which sometimes surprises us because we imagine him as so ahead of it. In many ways he was, but not in all, and it is the partiality of his escape from the prevailing beliefs of his age that so disappoints us. His expectations about his own patriarchal responsibilities, his fears of monarchy, his worries about the survival of the new nation, and his apparent belief that only Providence could eradicate some evils shaped many of his responses to the world as he found it. Like others of his class, he cared about his reputation and hence was thin-skinned in the face of criticism; he was relentlessly, and sometimes misleadingly, polite, as the code of gentlemen required; he believed reason essential to correct judgment about most things; he supposed his views to be not only correct but representative of the best interests of the people and that they, when not misled, agreed with his policies. As much as we might wish, Jefferson was not a modern man.

Though the most democratically minded of any of the Founders, he still expected elite white men who shared his views to lead government. He believed that all people of all races possessed basic natural rights but accepted the existence of stark inequalities in society. He knew slavery to be wrong but was also certain that for reasons of inherent inequalities between the races as well as a legacy of mutual hatred, whites and blacks could not live together in harmony. Hence emancipation would necessitate colonization—sending the newly freed slaves away from the United States to start a colony, perhaps even a nation, of their own. Yet he never found—or, really, looked for—a way to achieve this end financially or socially; whites would not give up the economic advantage of slave ownership, and where would funding come from for the immense expense of colonization? The internal struggle engendered by his belief in the inherent natural rights of all peoples and his entanglement in the moral, political, financial, and legal web of slavery demonstrates the complicated task of trying to do right in a world that does wrong. He could not imagine a world in which blacks and whites coexisted without conflict, a failure that haunted him in life and still haunts his legacy in death. The most elegant defender of liberty in the nation's history did not defend the liberty of those whose lives it would have most transformed. Later generations (and leaders, including Abraham Lincoln) would employ his ideas and his language as they labored to secure freedom and equality for all. Tragically, Jefferson, who best articulated the nation's loftiest aspirations, could not perceive or refused to recognize the full implications of his principles. He was the architect of American liberty almost despite himself.

We should not expect him to have embraced the values of a cosmopolitan, progressive person of the twenty-first century. How could he possibly have done so? Instead, we should try to understand the constraints—legal, financial, personal, intellectual—under which he lived. To understand certainly does not mean to approve or even forgive; rather, it means to comprehend why Jefferson made the kinds of decisions he made and saw the world as he did. He was a gentle, well-educated, idealistic man who sought—by his lights—to do right. Yet at times he acted in ways we now find abhorrent. Appreciating how this can be so is the task of the Jefferson scholar, the student of history, and perhaps every American citizen.

Jefferson puzzles us too because he does not fit neatly into modern categories. Although he spent almost four decades in appointed or elected government positions, he did not identify himself as a career politician. He made signal contributions to the craft of architecture but was never a professional architect. Devoted to science and claiming it as his first love, he lived in an era before "scientist" was an occupation. His reading was varied and idiosyncratic. He imbibed philosophy, starting with the ancients, but never worked out a philosophical system of his own. He long pondered religion but never found systematic theology attractive and attempted instead to simplify his religious beliefs and rejected proselytization of any form. He claimed as his home a tobacco plantation and loved gardening but never became a skilled or profitable planter. He enjoyed the study of the law but found legal practice unfulfilling. Despite his enormous learning and curiosity about practically every single thing in the world—and his notable accomplishments in many fields—he was not a match for any available vocation. He was at once an anomaly and a representative figure of his age. Jefferson happened to live at a moment in history when societies across the globe were undergoing fundamental changes in governance, and the resulting challenge attracted his energies and interests as did nothing else. This scholarly introvert found himself drawn onto the world's stage, where he helped shape a new nation that he hoped would become a model for all others.

Yet Jefferson was a homebody at heart. As he repeatedly told just about everyone he corresponded with, he loved the quiet of his library, the privacy of his quarters, gentle conversation with like-minded persons, the beauty of his gardens, tinkering with the inventions of others in his study—and he always contrasted these scenes of domesticity with the disharmony of the political world. Although he became skilled at governing and thought comprehensively about the future of the American nation, he never liked the give-and-take of politics, despised contentiousness, and wanted to be loved by all. Still, he made brilliant and implacable enemies, who saw him as an impractical idealist, a dissembler who concealed his real values and secretly conspired and hungered for power. Despite the challenges of the major offices he held—governor of Virginia, secretary of state, vice president, and president—and despite an adulthood plagued with debt, tragedy, and death, Jefferson retained his fundamental optimism.

The issues of race and slavery are so important to us today that they almost overwhelm our view of Jefferson. Of course we must face squarely where he stood on each. But we impoverish our understanding of the man if we do not examine as well his manifest contributions to a variety of fields, especially his commitment to political liberty and intellectual and religious freedom. Indeed, to put Jefferson in the context of his own times is to see that, for him, race and slavery were generally not of central importance. The views on race he presented in *Notes on the State of Virginia*, for instance, existed alongside longer passages about everything from caves to mammoths and from religion to the Virginia constitution.

This book attempts a full-scale biography. I have strived to present Jefferson in all of his guises: politician, diplomat, party leader, executive; architect, musician, oenophile, gourmand, traveler; inventor, historian, political theorist; land owner, farmer, slaveholder; and son, father, grand-father. Fully grounded in modern scholarship, the portrait of Jefferson that follows is admittedly sympathetic but critical when appropriate. In our time it is the fashion to demythologize our ancestors, to eagerly point out their faults and minimize their accomplishments—in short, to cut them down to size. Can we recognize the failures of those who came be-fore us and yet acknowledge their contributions? I have tried to do just that: to humanize and contextualize Jefferson without either deifying or demonizing him. Jefferson challenges us more thoroughly than any other Founder, but in the end, he is the most attractive, most elusive, most com-plicated, most intellectual, most practical, most idealistic, most flexible, and most quintessentially American Founder of them all.

PART I

Colonial Virginia,
1743–1770

"A Hard Student"

T O BEGIN TO COMPREHEND Thomas Jefferson, we must start years before his birth. His surname appears several times in the early records of the colony of Virginia. The first Jefferson was a delegate to the initial legislative assembly in the colony in 1619, but there is no solid evidence he was related to the future president.[1] In his brief autobiography, written when he was seventy-seven, Jefferson mentioned his family's belief that the first Jefferson in the New World came from Wales, near Mount Snowdon, but again, we have no genealogical proof.[2] The first reference to a Jefferson whom we can link to Thomas was, in fact, a man of the same name who lived in Henrico County in the late seventeenth century. This Thomas Jefferson appears in records for serving as a juror and surveyor, among other such minor functions. By the end of his life he had become a middling farmer, possessing land and a few slaves. He died in 1697, leaving a son also named Thomas, who in turn had a son, born in 1708, named Peter.

Peter Jefferson's son Thomas, born on April 13, 1743, would become president of a country that did not yet exist. As Thomas later recalled, his father's education was "quite neglected," but "being of sound mind, sound judgment and eager after information, he read much and improved himself."[3] For his time and place, Peter Jefferson's education was probably slightly better than average. Among his friends was William & Mary professor Joseph Fry, and he accumulated a library far superior to those of most men of his rank, suggesting that Peter's mind was capacious and well employed.

Family lore tells of his massive size and tremendous strength, portraying him as an almost mythical figure. Supposedly he could stand between two 1,000-pound barrels of tobacco lying on their side and, grasping each with one hand, set them upright simultaneously. As a surveyor in the western reaches of the colony, he overcame extreme cold, hardship, and danger from savage animals to lead his assistants in laying out their lines.[4] He was apparently as comfortable with the rigors of the outdoor world as with the pleasures of reading Shakespeare in his study.

Peter inherited land on Fine Creek, beyond the falls of the James River, and as a young man whose surveying experience acquainted him with the best lands to the west, he was soon purchasing acreage outright and investing in speculative projects. In July 1735 he acquired 1,000 acres on the south side of the North Fork of the James River, later called the Rivanna River (land that would become Monticello). He was clearly ambitious. Notably, he had become fast friends with William Randolph, five or six years his junior, who lived twelve miles or so across and eastward down the James at a much larger, finer plantation home named Tuckahoe.

Tuckahoe had been built by Thomas Randolph, now dead, son of William, one of the famous founding Randolphs, planter-aristocrats whose ancestral home, Turkey Island, lay south of Richmond. Upstream of Tuckahoe, and just west of Fine Creek, lived one of young William's uncles, Isham Randolph, on a large plantation named Dungeness. Isham had made his fortune in tobacco, slaves, and trade. Peter visited Dungeness in the late 1730s, surely in the company of William. There he met and courted Isham's teenaged daughter, Jane; she and Peter would wed on October 3, 1739, when she was nineteen years of age, Peter thirty-one.[5]

Isham Randolph was wealthy, worldly, and highly educated. He had attended the College of William & Mary, took French lessons for a few weeks from learned surveyor and diarist William Byrd, and spent many years as a merchant captain in London. In that city in 1718, he married Jane Lilburne, and shortly thereafter the first of their many children, a daughter they named after her mother, was born; she was baptized on February 20, 1719, at St. Paul's, Shadwell. By the early 1730s she and her parents and siblings had moved to Virginia, where Isham established Dungeness, a smaller version of the great English manor houses.[6] Owing to his time in London, Isham had an international network of acquaintances, and as the result of his friendship with the naturalist Peter Collinson, leading American botanist John Bartram visited Isham at Dungeness.[7] All this goes to show how Jane had broader cultural and intellectual horizons than most of her contemporaries in colonial Virginia. And she saw in Peter Jefferson far more than a rough-hewn frontiersman.

Following his original purchase of 1,000 acres on the south side of the Rivanna in 1735, the very next year Peter acquired 200 acres across the river from William Randolph for, as the family enjoyed retelling, the price of "Henry Weatherbourne's biggest bowl of arrack punch!"—a transaction presumably initiated in a tavern.[8] Peter may have begun clearing fields and even erected a small, temporary dwelling within a year or two—Jefferson recorded in his "Autobiography" that his father "was the 3d or 4th settler of the part of the country in which I live, which was about 1737."[9] Shortly before or after his marriage to Jane, Peter moved to his Rivanna property, naming the homesite "Shadwell" in honor of his wife's baptismal location. Their first four children were born there: Jane in 1740, Mary in 1741, Thomas in 1743, and Elizabeth in 1744. The next year Goochland County was subdivided and Albemarle County came into existence. On February 28, 1745, a small group of the new county's citizens met near the present-day town of Scottsville and inaugurated the county government; among them was Peter Jefferson.[10] Meanwhile he was purchasing more land, enlarging his fields, buying slaves, expanding his home and outbuildings at Shadwell, and fulfilling a range of civic responsibilities. Of all this his son Thomas remembered nothing.

William Randolph had married early, but in 1742 his wife died, leaving him with three small daughters and an infant son. Newly alert to the precariousness of life, William soon drew up a will, naming Peter one of the executors. Several years later, in failing health, Randolph added a codicil, requesting that "my Dear and loving friend Mr. Peter Jefferson do move down with his family to my Tuckahoe house and remain there till my son comes of age with whom my dear son and his sisters shall live."[11] Randolph died suddenly in late 1745, and, perhaps surprisingly, early in 1746 Peter and Jane, with their then five small children, moved the approximately fifty miles to Tuckahoe and assumed responsibility for the four orphaned Randolph children. This journey, which took the family several days, Jefferson did recall: his first memory was of being carried on a pillow by a slave on horseback.

Perhaps we can explain the move easily: Peter no doubt felt honor bound to his friend, and William had been a first cousin of Jane's. Tuckahoe was a commodious house; the families could to a degree be segregated, and the Randolph slaves could oversee the Randolph children at night. Jane may well have felt more comfortable on the estate than in her smaller residence at Shadwell. While they dwelled at Tuckahoe she gave birth to four more children. Peter, with the help of seven overseers, managed the Tuckahoe plantation, and as an absentee owner (with a local overseer or two) he kept his personal slaves on the Rivanna, clearing fields, growing crops, and improving his properties. Peter and Jane received no remuneration for their duties to the Randolph children, but the Tuckahoe estate paid all their living expenses.[12] The Rivanna estate's output was pure profit.

We know little of Thomas Jefferson's life during the Tuckahoe years. William Randolph had instructed that his son Thomas (and no doubt Thomas's sisters) be educated at home by tutors, and it was probably Jane Jefferson who had a little one-room school built near the house and arranged to have a teacher available for both the Randolph and the Jefferson children. The future president remembered being placed at "the English school" at age five, and Peter Jefferson's account book shows payment to a teacher in 1750 and 1752.[13]

The Oxford-educated Joshua Fry had come to Virginia in 1720 and in 1732 been appointed professor of natural philosophy and mathematics at the College of William & Mary; in 1737, however, he resigned this position and moved his family to Goochland County, where he became a good friend of Peter Jefferson. Fry was an accomplished surveyor; soon he and Peter were associated in various projects. Steady population growth and the need for fresh land on which to grow tobacco sent settlers westward, so land surveyors were in strong demand. In 1746 the colonial government contracted with some forty men, led by Fry and Peter Jefferson, to survey a boundary line from the headwaters of the Rappahannock River to those of the Potomac.

The success of this project led the colonial government to hire Fry and Jefferson in 1749 to extend the famous "dividing line" between Virginia and North Carolina. For this work the colonial council handsomely rewarded them; it also directed the two to compile a map of the populated portions of Virginia. The resulting Fry-Jefferson Map, completed in 1751 and promptly published in London, would be reprinted in subsequent decades.[14] Peter's adventures in the West ignited a fascination with the frontier in his son Thomas that would never subside.

While his family was at Tuckahoe, Peter enlarged and refined his house at Shadwell, and possibly for that reason, his family decided to return there in early 1752. The Jeffersons were now members of the gentry, possessing approximately 2,650 acres at the Shadwell estate alone. Situated on a small ridge overlooking the Rivanna River to the south, the house sat in the middle of a ten-acre square, encompassing slave quarters, a kitchen separate from the main house, stables, storage sheds, orchards—in effect, a little village that constituted a working plantation. Contrary to what some earlier biographies suggested, the Jeffersons lived comfortably and corresponded directly with merchants in London, and their house reflected the most current styles. While geographically in the Piedmont, Shadwell was culturally a part of the earlier-settled Tidewater region to the east.

THOMAS JEFFERSON was nine when his family returned to Shadwell. How much interaction he had with Peter is unclear. He certainly looked up to his imposing, energetic father, who surely instructed him in such manly sports as horseback riding, hunting, and shooting, although only horseback riding remained a lifelong practice. Peter probably taught his son at least the rudiments of surveying—throughout his life Thomas Jefferson would be interested in and a student of maps.[15] The son learned from his mother as well. Jane ran the household efficiently and, especially when guests were present, with an elegance appropriate to the family's rank in Albemarle society.[16] She taught the children good manners, instructed them in dancing and music, and made sure they knew how to behave at table with guests. Still, Peter insisted that, while Jane might adequately supervise his daughters' education, his oldest son, Thomas, required more formal schooling.

Soon after the family moved back to Shadwell, Peter dispatched young Jefferson to the Latin school operated by the Reverend William Douglas, located between Shadwell and Tuckahoe. Jefferson boarded with the Reverend Douglas's family during the week, although on weekends he visited both his cousins at Tuckahoe and his family at Shadwell. A Scot, Douglas possessed a good-sized library and was no doubt well meaning, but Jefferson did not find him a very capable teacher, recalling him as "but a superficial Latinist, less instructed in Greek, but with the rudiments of these languages he taught me French."[17] Even so, Jefferson continued under Douglas's tutelage until his father's death on August 17, 1757.

IT COULD NOT HAVE BEEN entirely unexpected. Peter Jefferson's good friend Dr. Thomas Walker had been summoned first on June 25, and throughout July and mid-August the physician came another fourteen times.[18] We do not know the nature of Peter's illness. Upon his death he left Jane with eight children, including two-year-old twins Anna and Randolph, but, importantly, with no debts.[19]

Peter willed the Shadwell house and plantation, one-sixth of his slaves, and all the household goods to Jane; he specified that each of his children should receive an education and designated a particular slave to go to each of his six daughters. He likewise left slaves to his two sons, directing that when Thomas turned twenty-one, he and his brother should divide equally the slaves not otherwise distributed. While the other children inherited young slaves, Peter gave Thomas his trusted slave valet, Sawney, who was roughly Peter's age. He probably intended Sawney to serve a quasi-fatherly role in helping Thomas daily navigate the next decade or so of his life. Peter owned a total of about 5,000 acres in Albemarle County and provided that Thomas and Randolph (who was only two) could choose between two roughly equal estates. Jefferson opted for one adjoining Shadwell south of the Rivanna (which became Monticello), leaving Randolph later to take possession of the other estate in southern Albemarle, which Peter had named Snowdon after the ancestral home in Wales. Until Thomas came of age, the executors, especially John Harvie, a frequent business partner of Peter's, would oversee the workings of the plantations and payment of all accounts.[20] To Thomas, Peter also gave his books and surveying instruments.

Reverend James Maury delivered Peter's funeral sermon. In 1749 or slightly earlier Maury had joined with Dr. Walker and Joshua Fry to found the Loyal Land Company, with the goal of speculating west of the Allegheny Mountains. Irish born but of Huguenot stock, he had come to Virginia as an infant, graduated from the College of William & Mary, returned to England for ordination in the Anglican Church, and become a rector in Louisa County in 1754. He established a school at his home about fourteen miles northeast of Shadwell. Peter must have been aware of his son's unhappiness with Reverend Douglas, because Maury took over Thomas's education. He was to have a major influence on Jefferson, who fondly remembered him as "a correct classical scholar."[21]

JEFFERSON BOARDED with the Maury family and grew very close to them, especially James Maury Jr. Another student, Dabney Carr, became Jefferson's closest friend, and during this period Jefferson also met James Madison (not the future president but the boy who would become Episcopal bishop of Virginia and president of the College of William & Mary) and John Walker. He enjoyed walking and playing in the woods with the other schoolboys, and his proficiency with the violin grew.[22] Still, classmates remembered him for his studiousness.

At Maury's school Jefferson developed a profound love of learning, particularly coming to adore the Greek language, and probably embarked on his lifelong commitment to reason in both intellectual and religious life. Maury may have taught him to accord slaves spiritual equality with whites, perhaps planting the seed from which grew Jefferson's oft-stated opposition to slavery.[23] It was also almost certainly at Maury's direction that Jefferson began his literary commonplace book, a compilation of quotations and paraphrases from literary sources that he added to for more than fifteen years and referred to for the rest of his life. The earliest entries predate any surviving correspondence and hence are the first indicators of his thoughts and reflections. Perhaps unsurprisingly for a youth who had just lost his beloved father, death was a prominent theme in the earliest entries,[24] as was stoicism in the face of loss. Horace, Cicero, and other ancient stoics would remain sources of counsel throughout Jefferson's life.

Jefferson's idyllic stay with Maury lasted less than two years. Over the Christmas holidays in 1759, Thomas found himself in the stately home of his uncle Peter Randolph, one of his guardians (and an executor of his father's estate). Peter suggested to the then sixteen-year-old that he matriculate at the College of William & Mary. Randolph must have been persuasive, because a few days later, writing from Shadwell, Jefferson addressed a carefully reasoned letter to John Harvie, evidently the primary executor of his father's estate. In this, the earliest extant Jefferson letter, the aspiring student laid out his reasons for requesting both permission and funds to attend the colony's only college.

> I was at Colo. Peter Randolph's about a Fortnight ago, and my Schooling falling into Discourse, he said he thought it would be to my Advantage to go to the College, and was desirous I should go, as indeed I am myself for several Reasons. In the first place as long as I stay at the Mountain [Shadwell] the Loss of one fourth of my Time is inevitable, by Company's coming here and detaining me from School. And likewise my Absence will in a great Measure put a Stop to so much Company, and by that Means lessen the Expences of the Estate in House-Keeping. And on the other Hand by going to the College I shall get a more universal Acquaintance, which may hereafter be serviceable to me; and I suppose I can pursue my Studies in the Greek and Latin as well there as here, and likewise learn something of the Mathematics. I shall be glad of your opinion.[25]

Harvie may have smiled at the suggestion that going to college would be an economy, but he gave his quick approval, and two months later Jefferson, probably accompanied by Sawney, was off to Williamsburg. Admission was hardly stiff, requiring only proficiency in Greek and Latin. Jefferson was then a tall, lanky boy with reddish hair and skin prone to freckle. Though rather shy and physically awkward, he was voraciously curious about the world.

JEFFERSON ARRIVED in Williamsburg on or just before March 25, 1760, the date he began to pay for room and board at the college. The food was apparently execrable, but the college did at least provide a salaried stocking mender for students' convenience. This was probably Jefferson's first visit to the capital city, then still hardly more than a village. Although the oldest and most populous of England's mainland colonies, Virginia had no substantial city like Philadelphia or Boston. Boasting a permanent population of about 1,500, Williamsburg doubled in size for the several months that the General Court and the General Assembly were in session. Nevertheless, it was the largest city Jefferson had seen, and he soon knew intimately the bustle of Duke of Gloucester Street, friendly ordinaries or inns like the Raleigh Tavern, Bruton Parish Church (which he attended occasionally), and even the Governor's Palace. Williamsburg had bookstores and a variety of shops, one could attend occasional concerts and theatrical performances, and the church had a small pipe organ. But the center of Jefferson's life for two years was the College of William & Mary.

The college, chartered in 1693, had four divisions: an Indian school, a preparatory grammar school, a divinity school, and a school of philosophy. Jefferson matriculated into the last, which was more or less a tiny liberal arts college with courses in natural philosophy (science) and mathematics. The total enrollment before the American Revolution averaged less than sixty students. The grammar school had a single master, as did the Indian school, and the divinity and natural philosophy schools had only two faculty members each. Just two years before Jefferson's arrival, the normal residency requirements for a bachelor's degree had gone up from two years to four, comparable to the standard at Cambridge and Oxford.[26] At about the same time, there was turmoil in the faculty ranks, and the resulting removals had made way for one William Small in 1758. This Scottish-educated professor only remained in Williamsburg for six years before returning to England, where he became a prominent member of the so-called Lunar Society of scientists and inventors in the vicinity of Birmingham.[27]

For most of Jefferson's stay at the college, he took lessons only from Small. As Jefferson wrote in his autobiography sixty years later, "It was my great good fortune, and what probably fixed the destinies of my life that Dr. Wm. Small of Scotland was then the professor of Mathematics, a man profound in most of the useful branches of science, and with a happy talent of communication, correct and gentlemanly manners, & an enlarged & liberal mind."[28] Small also assumed the role of professor of moral philosophy. He ended the practice of rote teaching and student recitation and introduced lecturing at the college. As the only nonminister among the college's faculty, he emphasized rational thought, not revelation or tradition, thus reinforcing the teachings of James Maury.

Only twenty-six when Jefferson arrived in Williamsburg, Small was "the first truly enlightened or scientific man" Thomas had ever met.[29] Small was also discretely antislavery. Jefferson did not earn a formal degree and seems to have left the college sometime around April 25, 1762, when he stopped paying board. But he continued to study privately with Small, who, single and lonely in Williamsburg, obviously found in Jefferson an ideal student and a brilliant, intellectually curious companion. Jefferson later wrote that Small had been "to me as a father," and "to his enlightened & affectionate guidance of my studies . . . I am endebted for every thing."[30]

Small introduced his young protégé to Williamsburg's other two luminaries: eminent professor of law George Wythe and suave royal governor Frances Fauquier. Soon Jefferson was a regular member of their Friday dinner parties, "a partie quarree" where, Jefferson recalled, he "heard more common good sense, more rational & philosophical conversations than in all [the rest of] my life."[31] Though he was only a teenager, both Small and Wythe were young men themselves, and Jefferson was a sophisticated son of the local gentry class, possessing polished manners, fashionable clothes, and the gift of conversation. Small, Wythe, and Fauquier in effect made up the real university in which Jefferson obtained his education. Wythe, born in Hampton County, Virginia, in 1726, had learned Greek and Latin from his Quaker mother, who probably also instilled in him a cautious opposition to slavery. Wythe became the most learned practitioner of law in pre-Revolutionary Virginia. He understood law as grounded in the widest possible historical context, particularly that of antiquity, and he emphasized clarity of expression. Privately a religious man, he had little patience with public rituals and believed reason pointed to moral character as the essence of spiritual life.[32] Jefferson would study law under Wythe's direction for three years, likely passing the bar in late 1765.[33]

The fifty-four-year-old Fauquier had come to the colony in 1758. Urbane, witty, and intellectually restless, he had become a fellow of the Royal Society in 1753. Jefferson probably picked up his lifelong habit of keeping meteorological records from Fauquier's practice of maintaining a weather diary. Fauquier gathered about him the ablest, liveliest men (and women) in Williamsburg for social events at the Governor's Palace and invited Jefferson to these occasions. The governor, who played the violin, viola, and cello, liked to organize amateur ensembles at his soirées, adding Jefferson with his violin to the evening musicales.[34] Decades later Jefferson recalled Governor Fauquier as "the ablest man who had ever filled that office,"[35] by which he may have been referring to the combination of learning and culture in a working politician.

Jefferson did not spend all his time with these men. For his first two years in Williamsburg, he lived at the college with other young students; thereafter, for several months he boarded elsewhere in the town. College classes took place in the Wren Building, which would have been the largest building Jefferson had ever seen. Jefferson knew all the other boys enrolled in the college and became especially good friends with John Page and John Walker; his boon companion from Maury's school, Dabney Carr, was there too. The list of names of fellow students reads like a roll of famous Virginia families, and Jefferson would interact with most of these students and their relatives for the rest of his life.

Perhaps his desire to fit in with the other boys, most of them from families wealthier than his, led Jefferson during his first year in Williamsburg to maintain "a little too showy style of living." After that first year, he curtailed his spending.[36] His fellow students remembered not his extravagance but his diligence in his studies. Classmate John Page envied his study habits, for he "could tear himself away from his dearest friends, and fly to his studies."[37] Another student remembered, "Even when at school he used to be seen with his Greek Grammar in his hand while his comrades were enjoying relaxation in the interval of school hours."[38] According to family members, he "habitually" studied fifteen hours a day, taking a break at twilight to run for two miles before reading deep into the night.[39] By all the evidence he placed high demands upon himself; he admitted in 1819, "I was a hard student."[40]

KNOWING HE DID NOT WANT to be primarily a planter, Jefferson gravitated toward the law and therefore to Wythe. He did not love this field as much as he did science and mathematics, yet neither of the latter suggested an available profession. One could not find work as a professional scientist in colonial Virginia. Moreover, he already sensed that his emerging skepticism toward orthodox Anglicanism meant that he could hardly become a clergyman, and the ineffective medicine of the day did not attract him. But he saw that one could combine planting, the law, and government service. Two of Jefferson's prominent Williamsburg relatives, Peyton and John Randolph, were eminent in law, having both studied and become barristers at the Inns of Court in London. Yet Jefferson did not study with either of them. He chose Wythe, who combined independent reading, practical experience, and knowledge of the twelve-member General Court, the colony's highest court, which met twice annually in Williamsburg and served as the governor's council. It was, in effect, the upper house of the General Assembly.

Wythe considered a solid grounding in the technicalities of the law mandatory. That meant a long and daunting regimen of reading. The bulk of a lawyer's work in Virginia then dealt with land claims and disputes— the colony's economy was overwhelmingly agricultural—so Wythe also directed his students to become intimately familiar with the land record office in the capital city. Recognizing Jefferson's scholarly predilections, Wythe no doubt gave him an unusually extensive reading list.

On Christmas Day in 1762—just two days after Albemarle County officials had established the town of Charlottesville, along Three-Notch-d Road only several miles from Shadwell—Jefferson, while on his way home from Williamsburg, wrote a long, playful letter to his college friend John Page. The nineteen-year-old filled it with posturing about his supposed girlfriend Rebecca Burwell (he spelled her name a variety of ways, including in Greek written backward), whose love he desired but was unsure how to acquire. He compared his plight with that of Job—an indication of how overblown his adolescent rhetoric was. Unpersuasively playing the lackadaisical student, Jefferson explained that he was thinking of Rebecca "too often I am sure to get through Old Cooke this winter; for God knows I have not seen him since I packed him up in my trunk in Williamsburg. . . . Well, Page, I do wish the Devil had old Cooke, for I am sure I never was so tired of an old dull scoundrel in my life."[41] "Cooke" was Sir Thomas Coke, whose four-volume *Institutes of the Laws of England* was a notoriously difficult text. Wythe considered it the essential bedrock of law. Jefferson eventually came to hold the volumes in the same esteem.

In Coke, Jefferson found evidence for a view of early English history that he had already acquired, a reverence for the Saxon past before the Norman conquest. The earliest Saxons who peopled the island had—according to what became known as the Whiggish interpretation of English history—maximized liberty in a prefeudal age through an elected monarchy, annually elected parliament, land held without military or labor obligations owed to feudal lords, and basic equality before the law. Coke subscribed to this view, seeing the Magna Carta as an embodiment of true Saxon belief in the primacy of parliamentary authority. Jefferson would throughout his life hold to this romanticized portrait of original Saxon liberties, which he would soon enough come to see King George III trampling upon.[42]

Over the next nine months, while at Shadwell living in his mother's house, Jefferson presumably continued to work his way through Wythe's reading list. In another letter to Page he bemoaned again his inability to court Rebecca, and perhaps not yet fully habituated to the rigors of reading law and missing the camaraderie of the society of Williamsburg, he lamented his situation: "we rise in the morning that we may eat breakfast, dinner and supper and go to bed again that we may get up the next morning and do the same."[43]

In letters he wrote later to students aspiring to study law, Jefferson laid out his exhausting schedule: from dawn till 8:00 a.m., one should study science, religion, and ethics; from 8:00 till noon, one should read foundational books in law covering everything from origins to comparative studies to practical tomes; then from noon to 1:00 p.m., politics, with the balance of the afternoon devoted to history, ancient through modern; after dinner, one should spend a couple of hours reading various genre of literature.[44] At Shadwell Jefferson might have followed a schedule something like this, but he certainly did not after he returned to Williamsburg. Yet Shadwell was not all drudgery. Jefferson's mother, Jane, with whom he got along well, was the mistress of the plantation, and also present were most of his other siblings, including his eldest sister, Jane, of whom he was especially fond. His mother was content to let the executors manage the plantation and all financial affairs, which Jefferson happily accepted.

He might have returned to Williamsburg earlier but for rumors of smallpox in the capital, and in a letter to John Page he also fantasized about traveling to Europe, but he would not realize that dream for more than twenty years. In early October though, he was back in Williamsburg, and at Wythe's direction. As Jefferson wrote Page again, "The court is now at hand, which I must attend constantly."[45]

ANOTHER PHASE OF his legal education had begun. Whether it was Wythe's idea or Jefferson's—probably it was Wythe's—Jefferson was preparing to practice before the General Court, not in the lesser county or hustings courts. At the time fewer than ten lawyers constituted the bar of the General Court, so Jefferson would be joining an elite group. He had the accoutrements of a wealthy man, having brought a horse and a slave named Jupiter to Williamsburg. (Sawney drops out of the records after 1762.) Jupiter, born the same year as Jefferson, was the son of Sal, who had nursed Thomas as well as Jane Jefferson's other children; Jupiter would be a trusted slave until his death in 1799. He performed all sorts of errands for Jefferson, and on occasion, finding himself without pocket change, Jefferson even borrowed small sums of money from him.[46]

Though Wythe made certain his student studied both the history and philosophy of the law as well as the practical aspects of appearing in court, Jefferson did not restrict himself narrowly to the regimen he later recommended to others. He visited with William Small and other social luminaries, attended concerts and the theater, enjoyed dancing and horseback riding, and read not only incessantly but broadly.

We know from the books he purchased from the offices of the *Virginia Gazette* that in addition to law texts, Jefferson bought Latin, Greek, and Italian dictionaries, as well as books of history (more than on any other subject), philosophy, belles lettres (including poetry), anatomy, and agriculture, among other subjects. His purchases included works by John Milton and Cicero; David Hume's six-volume *History of England*; the Latin prose collection *Satyricon*; *Sheridan on Elocution*; and the two-volume edition of Yorick's sermons (the pseudonymously published sermons of Laurence Sterne). The accounts of the *Gazette* show that no one else in the city bought as many books as Jefferson did in this period.[47]

Yet his main studies didn't suffer, and Jefferson passed the bar exam in 1765. At that point, unless trained as a barrister in London at the Inns of Court, an aspiring lawyer had to wait a year after his licensure to practice in the county courts before he could appear in the General Court. Jefferson chose not to take cases in the lower courts and simply to wait out the year.

Jefferson left Williamsburg and spent most of the following months at Shadwell. His mother maintained a pleasant home, and he was absolutely devoted to his sister Jane, with whom he shared a love of botany and music; he considered her his equal in every way. She died suddenly of unknown causes on October 1, 1765, a loss that affected Jefferson deeply.[48] Only the earlier marriage of his sister Martha to his close friend Dabney Carr on July 20 served partially to redeem the year. Jefferson had come of age the previous year but did not assume responsibility for his own accounts and those of his mother and siblings until 1765.

Very little is known of Jefferson's activities in 1766, when he returned once again to Williamsburg. He continued to buy books from the *Virginia Gazette* office and to read voraciously. He still considered himself a student. According to a letter he wrote long afterward, during these years he persisted "in the habit of abridging and common-placing what I read meriting it, and of sometimes mixing my own reflections on the subject."[49] Remarkable in his literary commonplace book from this time is his near infatuation with Henry St. John, 1st Viscount Bolingbroke (1678–1751), the British political philosopher whose four-volume *Philosophical Works* contained many rationalist critiques of religious orthodoxy. Jefferson copied far more words from Bolingbroke than from any other writer. The viscount confirmed and elaborated ideas initially introduced to him by Maury, Small, and Wythe. Baptized and reared in the Anglican Church, Jefferson had boarded for several years in the homes of clergymen and on occasion as a student at the College of William & Mary had attended Bruton Parish Church. Yet his teachers and his reading sent him in a new direction.

In his commonplace book Jefferson recorded passages such as "We must not assume for truth, what can be proved neither à priori, nor à posteriori."[50] He had doubts about the Trinity, about the expiatory death of Jesus, and about scripture's portrayal of Jehovah, preferring a "natural religion" to "the god of Moses, or the god of Paul."[51] He concluded, "It is not true that Christ revealed an entire body of ethics, proved to be the law of nature from principles of reason, and reaching all the duties of life." In his view, "a system thus collected from the writings of ancient heathen moralists of Tully, of Seneca, or Epictetus, and others, would be more full, more entire, more coherent, and more clearly deduced from unquestionable principles of knowledge."[52] Jefferson had not turned against religion but was both questioning and searching. He had become a deist who found—at this point in his life—his favorite ethical teachers among the philosophers of antiquity. He believed in one God but not in the Trinity or in the divinity of Jesus.

Because such rationalistic views were unpopular and dissent against the established Anglican Church was actually illegal, Jefferson kept his emerging heterodoxy private. He outwardly conformed, even to the point of serving on the local vestry.[53] Here, in the necessity of keeping his personal views concealed, was the seed of Jefferson's advocacy for religious freedom, for him not just an abstract principle but a consequence of having unorthodox beliefs.

Jefferson was at Shadwell during the first months of 1766, where, on March 30, in tiny, precise handwriting, he made the first entry in what became his Garden Book, noting, "Purple hyacinth begins to bloom."[54] He would add to the book for more than a half century. In the late spring and early summer, he took his first trip beyond the borders of the colony of Virginia. He had expected to travel with Frank Willis, a college friend, but poor communications resulted in Willis leaving earlier. The primary purpose of the trip was to visit the eminent Dr. William Shippen Jr., of Philadelphia, for inoculation against smallpox. That Jefferson chose this course indicates not a little bravery and a commitment to science uncommon at the time because the medical procedure was itself dangerous.

Before Dr. Edward Jenner discovered vaccination in 1796, the only known means of warding off smallpox was inoculation. This risky procedure involved taking a tiny bit of material from smallpox sores on people who had mild cases and placing it beneath the skin of the one being inoculated. This was typically done by dipping a piece of string into the existing sore and then dropping it into a tiny incision on the new patient. The hope was that the latter would get a similarly mild case of the disease, after which he would be immune for life. The procedure was sometimes deadly and required several weeks of treatment; one had to be quarantined and cared for until the disease had run its course. Jefferson's inoculation involved no complications that we know of. Later in life, he would have his entire family and some of his slaves inoculated, so convinced was he of the procedure's worth.

The inoculation took up only a portion of his journey. Jefferson traveled through Maryland and Delaware in a one-person carriage en route to Pennsylvania and afterward to New York City.[55] He wrote to his confidant John Page a long, descriptive letter of his visit to the Maryland statehouse, where he was appalled by the informality of governance in Annapolis, the "noise and hubbub" in the chamber, and the apparent confusion among the members about what was transpiring.[56]

Perhaps without fully realizing it, Jefferson had inadvertently become a close student of government. He was coming of age at just the moment when politics—and, above all, the proper relationship between the mother country and her colonies—was evolving into the central concern of the day. We know from later writings that he had already witnessed several political events in Williamsburg that reflected rising tensions between the colony and England, but a comment in his Maryland letter about "the rejoicings here on the repeal of the stamp act" are the first extant words from Jefferson about the train of events that would lead to the American Revolution.[57]

After Jefferson's northern sojourn, he returned to his preparations for the practice of law. Yet international political events had already begun to influence his life. The next decade would prove remarkably eventful both for him and for the emerging nation.

2

Young Legislator

AS HIS STUDIES PROGRESSED, Jefferson became interested in political affairs and the workings of representative government in Williamsburg. He was already an observer of the proceedings of the General Court. At the opposite wing of the capitol met the House of Burgesses, the colony's legislative body, and Jefferson knew many of the men who sat in it. As early as the spring of 1765, excitement was building over what many saw as an unwise decision by Great Britain to begin raising revenues in the colonies by a mechanism long used in England itself, a stamp tax. Early word of the proposed tax had reached the colonies in late 1764, where the idea met with instant opposition. Late that year the House of Burgesses had issued a written protest, but this and remonstrances from other colonies had no effect; in the spring of 1765 the British parliament formally passed the Stamp Act. Toward the end of the May 1765 session of the General Assembly, Patrick Henry spoke, armed with six resolutions objecting to the tax. Jefferson, at the door to the chamber, "heard the splendid display of Mr. Henry's talents as a popular orator," as he recalled more than a half century afterward. "They were great indeed; such as I have never heard from any other man. He appeared to me to speak as Homer wrote."[1]

We have no transcript of Henry's remarks, but apparently in the midst of his tirade against the king, he used the word "tyranny." Aghast, the senior members of the assembly feared that such language would be counterproductive. Two of the resolutions failed to pass, and another passed by only one vote. Jefferson remembered Attorney General Peyton Randolph storming out of the hall and saying, "By God, I would have given 100. Guineas for a single vote."[2] Henry, thinking his purpose accomplished, went home. The next day, cooler heads, led by Speaker John Robinson,

Peter and Peyton Randolph, George Wythe, and others, toned down the four successful resolutions. But the original versions had already gone out, so people across the colonies came to believe that all six had passed in their original form. Henry had changed the temper of the debate.[3]

Jefferson had first met Henry while visiting Captain Nathaniel West Dandridge's home during the Christmas holidays of 1759, and he held a conflicted opinion of the man: "his passion was fiddling, dancing and pleasantry. He excelled in the last, and it attached every one to him." Though put off by Henry's "idle disposition"—he called him "the laziest man in reading I ever knew"—Jefferson found him likable. He could not deny Henry's personal magnetism and, later on, his remarkable public eloquence.[4]

By the time of Henry's ascendance in opposition to the Stamp Act, Jefferson, though not a politician, had exercised leadership and drawn on personal connections to secure various ends. One revealing episode occurred several years before, when he realized that the Rivanna River could not accommodate the boats that took tobacco down the James and beyond. In either 1764 or 1765, Jefferson paddled downstream in a canoe, discovering that loose rocks obstructed navigation; consequently he began a subscription fund to underwrite clearing the river. Jefferson also convinced his neighbor, Dr. Thomas Walker, a member of the House of Burgesses, to push through the assembly an act authorizing an undertaking, privately funded, to remove the obstructions. Jefferson spearheaded the effort, monies were raised, and by the 1770s the Rivanna had been made navigable at almost every point from its confluence with the James up to Shadwell.[5] His success suggested his natural talent for persuasion and problem solving.

UNTIL 1767 JEFFERSON had primarily been a student and an observer of politics—and, in many ways, still a dependent. Yet his passage into full adulthood was swift. At age twenty-four, he still lived in his mother's house; yet he was now keeping the estate's accounts and distributing its income to his mother and siblings. In addition, he was helping manage Shadwell's farms, becoming more of a practical than a dilettantish gardener. His notations in his Garden Book in 1766 had referred to flowers; in 1767 he began to make entries regarding asparagus, lettuce, cucumbers, onions, and peas (his favorite vegetable). On August 3 he noted that he had grafted cherry buds "into stocks of large kind at Monticello," his first mention of the name, Italian for "little mountain," of the home he was already planning to build across the Rivanna from Shadwell.[6] In 1767 Jefferson entered the practice of law, ending his apprenticeship to Wythe. He began to prepare for the construction of his own separate residence, apart from Shadwell, and that year he started keeping a detailed memorandum book of his expenditures.

Although Jefferson would only try cases before the General Court, which sat in May and October in Williamsburg, he did travel to the county courts in the Piedmont to seek legal business. His first solicitation for hire occurred on February 12, 1767, when one Gabriel Jones of Augusta County enlisted his help in a land controversy. As in the vast majority of Jefferson's cases, this one never resulted in a hearing before the General Court.[7] In most instances, disputants settled out of court, gave up, moved, died, or for a number of reasons did not persevere all the way to Williamsburg. The House of Burgesses set the fees for lawyers, whether they practiced at the highest level before the General Court or in various county courts, and they were scandalously low. Because of the extraordinary backlog before the General Court and its unhurried pace, most cases took years to resolve. Jefferson could, on the side, pick up fifty shillings or so for drawing up wills and other documents, but an even bigger problem than the low fees and the court delays was clients' unwillingness or inability to pay.

As a result, despite being quite busy, Jefferson earned little. The most careful scholar of Jefferson's legal career concludes that over the duration of his seven-year legal practice (the Crown closed the colonial courts after 1774), he averaged an income of less than £200 annually. It is true that Jefferson never liked personal disputation (which was primarily why he chose not to take cases in the more boisterous county courts), and his voice broke and became husky when he spoke long and loudly. But money concerns ultimately drove him to end his formal legal career. In late 1773 he decided to quit his practice, arranging in August 1774 to turn over to Edmund Randolph all his ongoing cases and the associated fees.[8]

WHILE THE MAJORITY of Jefferson's cases in private practice involved land purchases, transfers, or disputes, several were of wider interest. One involved a controversy in Norfolk in 1768 and 1769 over smallpox inoculation. A group opposed to the practice protested against two doctors and their willing patients, and a riot ensued. Jefferson represented the side of science and modern medicine in the resulting suit, but in 1770 the court, headed by a judge himself opposed to inoculation, ruled against Jefferson's clients.⁹ Another case revealed Jefferson's evolving attitudes toward slavery. In April 1770, he took on, without fee, support of a plea by one Samuel Howell, a mulatto servant, who was suing for freedom from his indenture. Howell's grandmother was a mulatto, born after 1705 as the offspring of a white woman and a black man, and thereby bound by the local church wardens to serve to the age of thirty-one. Before she reached that age, she conceived and gave birth to Howell's mother, who was likewise declared an indentured servant and bound to service. She in turn conceived Samuel in 1742, and his grandmother's owner declared him a servant as well. Howell was protesting this third-generation penalty for the original act of miscegenation.¹⁰

Speaking before the court, Jefferson offered a painstaking analysis of the entire corpus of colonial laws dealing with interracial sex, servitude, and related issues. He argued that while there existed laws stipulating that such persons as Howell's grandmother and mother be indentured for a set number of years, no legislation specifically carried the penalty on to the third generation. Amid his analysis of the existing legislation, Jefferson made a daring declaration of principle: "Under the law of nature," he stated, "all men are born free, every one comes into the world with a right to his own person, which includes the liberty of moving and using it at his own will. This is what is called personal liberty, and is given him by the author of nature, because necessary for his own sustenance."¹¹ These were radical views in slaveholding Virginia, and before the opposing attorney could even respond to Jefferson's plea, the judge interrupted him and immediately settled the case against Samuel Howell.¹²

This was the second rejection of an attempt by Jefferson to ameliorate some of the worst aspects of slavery and perhaps whittle away at its influence; he dared not attack the institution head-on. The year before, he had been elected to the House of Burgesses. Soon after, he "made," as he put it in his autobiography, "one effort in that body for the permission of the emancipation of slaves, which was rejected."¹³ By the terms of a 1723 statue, "no negro, mullato or indian slaves shall be set free upon any pretence whatsoever, except for some meritorious services, to be adjudged and allowed by the governor and council."¹⁴ Jefferson believed that individual owners should have the discretion to free such slaves as they wished. He took his concern to his cousin, Colonel Richard Bland, "one of the oldest, ablest & most respected members" of the House, and persuaded him to introduce a bill to liberalize manumission procedures. Jefferson seconded Bland's motion, and when Bland endeavored to argue it, he was, in Jefferson's words, "denounced as an enemy of his country, & was treated with the grossest indecorum."[15] The bold effort, however limited, failed completely.[16]

IN 1768, JEFFERSON had begun construction of his own home, a love affair—even obsession—with building and renovation that would continue for four decades. Jefferson was both architect and contractor, poring over architectural and planning books in search of inspiration. At first he seems to have consulted books by English designers including James Gibbs and Robert Morris, both highly influenced by the great Italian Renaissance architect Andrea Palladio. Soon Jefferson was consulting Palladio's work itself. Palladio laid down precise rules regarding proportion and balance, rules Jefferson adopted. He had early on decided to build with brick and to break with English and Virginian tradition and site the house atop the small mountain he had taken to calling Monticello.

Typically, Virginia plantation houses (like William Byrd's Westover or George Washington's Mount Vernon) sat on slight rises that afforded a gentle down-slope view toward a river, but Jefferson chose, for aesthetic—certainly not practical—reasons, to construct his home upon this 867-foot-high mountain, which rose about 500 feet above the surrounding countryside. On May 15, 1768, he contracted with one Mr. Moore to level out a 250-foot-square area at the summit.[17] Then on October 2, 1769, he paid one man for forty-six days of labor and another for twenty-two days spent digging a well some sixty-five feet deep. That the diggers averaged less than a foot and a half a day suggests the difficulty of driving through the rocky soil to water.[18] In July of the next year the first of several brick makers, George Dudley, began producing bricks on site.[19] Jefferson filled many pages calculating the number of bricks he would need and how many gallons of water would be required to make them. As it turned out, the latter amount was far more than the well could provide, so barrels of water were hauled up from the Rivanna.

For several years his memorandum book included notations about slaves digging out cellars, building terraces and roundabouts, planting fruit trees on the southern ridge of Monticello (in March 1769, for example, he had transplanted pears, apples, cherries, nectarines, pomegranates, peaches, apricots, and walnuts, setting them out in orderly rows), sawing lumber, and assisting with the brickmaking.[20] Jefferson also calculated the efficiency of moving dirt in wheelbarrows, the speed of the well diggers, the amount of labor various slaves could perform in a single day, and so on. At first he focused on building just one room, with a cellar below (what became the South Pavilion). When he noted on November 26, 1770, "Moved to Monticello," he took up residence in that single room.[21]

The main house wasn't finished until a few years later, though nothing was ever really "finished" at Monticello. This initial version of the house was a rectangular structure of two stories, much smaller than the structure that sits there now. It was Georgian, or neoclassical, in style, without a dome but with a portico.[22] Over the course of decades, Monticello, in its evolving design, its elevated location with a view to the west, its combination of practical convenience and aesthetic principle, its creative borrowing from design books and Jefferson's later travels to England, France, and Italy, its dependence on slave labor, became in diverse ways a brick-and-mortar manifestation of Jefferson's philosophy and attitude toward life and art.

TOWARD THE END of 1767 Jefferson's friend Governor Frances Fauquier suffered several bouts of sickness. He died on March 3 the following year. Appointed to succeed him was Norborne Berkeley, Baron de Botetourt, who arrived in Williamsburg late on October 21, 1768, to a warm greeting from the twelve members of the governor's council and other dignitaries. He read his commission and took the oath of office, and after dining together at Raleigh Tavern, all enjoyed a festive "illumination" of the city. The next day Governor Botetourt dissolved the current General Assembly (which was not in session) and called for a new election that fall. In mid-December 1768, the voters of Albemarle County assembled at the Charlottesville courthouse to reelect Dr. Thomas Walker and to elect the newcomer Thomas Jefferson as their two burgesses.[23]

The election of a person only twenty-five years old, who had not worked his way up by first serving as a justice of the peace (though at the time he was serving as a vestryman), testifies to the respect Jefferson commanded in the county. His appearance on county court days soliciting legal work, his leadership in opening the Rivanna to navigation, the good name of his family all surely counted in his favor, as did Jefferson's manifest ability. Candidates for political office did not publicly campaign until the nineteenth century, but in Jefferson's time they certainly did other things to win votes. Jefferson attended a militia muster on December 3 and apparently shared some expenses with his opponent in providing rum and cakes for the occasion. He also paid a ferryman to make sure voters could easily cross the Rivanna River on election day.[24]

Monticello, first elevation, probably before March 1771, by Thomas Jefferson.

Source: Coolidge Collection of Thomas Jefferson Manuscripts,
Massachusetts Historical Society. Used by permission.

The new assembly would not meet until May of the following year, but Jefferson left early for Williamsburg. He obviously enjoyed this latest sojourn in the city, frequenting the coffeehouse and attending concerts and plays.[25] He seems to have particularly enjoyed the coffeehouse, where he read newspapers, shared in the talk about tobacco and horses, and learned the latest political news from the other colonies and London.

At about 10:00 a.m. on May 8, 1769, the ninety or so members of the House of Burgesses took their oaths of office in the council chamber, then returned to the assembly chamber to await the governor's arrival. Botetourt rode down Duke of Gloucester Street in his lavish state carriage drawn by six white horses. Once he was in the council chamber, the assembly members greeted him. He then directed them to elect a Speaker. They unanimously chose Peyton Randolph, who had filled that role in the previous assembly. Botetourt formally approved their choice, then, with appropriate pomp and ceremony, addressed the assemblymen, flattering them that "the real interests of those you have the honour to represent . . . are most certainly consistent with the prosperity of Great Britain, and"—in a un-subtle warning—"so they will forever be found when pursued with tem-per and moderation."[26]

In polite response to Botetourt's remarks, the members resolved to de-liver to him a brief address thanking him for his comments and selected the new member from Albemarle County to draft a set of resolutions for presentation to the governor. Jefferson's first state paper is most notable for its reverence.[27] The language carried no hint of revolutionary fervor. One member, Robert Carter Nicholas, deemed Jefferson's draft of the ad-dress that would follow and build upon these resolutions too similar to the resolutions themselves. Nicholas agreed to rewrite it—tinkering that annoyed Jefferson—and the revised version was presented to the gover-nor.[28] This exchange of addresses completed the opening ceremonies, and the House of Burgesses set about its work.

Jefferson was placed on two rather minor committees: "privileges and elections" and "propositions and grievances." In his first legislative session he mostly observed and absorbed. The assembly quickly became em-broiled in long-standing issues that would prove extraordinarily import-ant, both for the colony and for Jefferson. On its first day in session, Speaker Randolph announced that he, as directed by the last assembly, had written to the various colonial governments in response to actions of the British parliament and received letters in return. These he proposed to place on a table, along with sundry other correspondence between the colonies, for the members to read. Jefferson soon saw firsthand that the elevated words exchanged between the governor and the assembly did not wholly fit the realities of the political moment.

IN THE FACE OF MASSIVE protest in the colonies, Parliament had backed down on the Stamp Act in 1766, although in the accompanying but little-noticed Declaratory Act, it had firmly stated its right to pass laws, on any subject, that were binding on the colonies. Reeling from the expenses of the just-concluded Great War for Empire (the so-called French and Indian War), England badly needed revenue. Taking the colonists at their word—that is, that they objected to "internal taxes" (those raised within the colo-nies) as opposed to "external taxes" (those related to the control and regulation of trade)—Chancellor of the Exchequer Charles Townshend pushed through Parliament in 1767 a series of new duties on a wide range of goods imported into the colonies, along with measures to enforce and collect them. Townshend's legislation included a proposed suspension of the New York legislature for its unwillingness to provide housing and food for British soldiers stationed there, as required by the Quartering Act of 1765. Colonists were outraged, believing the duties aimed more at raising revenue than regulating trade and interpreting the suspension of the New York General Assembly as an outright attack on the legitimacy of colonial governments. In February 1768 the Massachusetts House of Representatives sent a circular letter to the other colonial legislatures beseeching them to support their protest of British actions by boycotting the listed goods. This letter was among those Randolph laid before the Virginia assembly during Jefferson's first session.

Britain's actions had angered most of the assemblymen. By this time they knew that Crown officials had denounced the incendiary circular letter from the Bay Colony and instructed the various colonial governors to summarily dissolve any legislature that approved it. Undaunted, the assembly resolved itself into a committee of the whole in order to consider and ultimately approve unanimously a series of four resolutions. The first stated forthrightly that "the sole right of imposing taxes on the inhabitants of this his Majesty's colony and dominion of Virginia is now, and ever hath been, legally and constitutionally vested in the House of Burgesses." The other three resolutions defended the privilege of petitioning the king for redress of grievances, insisted that all trials for treason be held in the colonies, and stated the assembly's intention "that an humble, dutiful and loyal address be presented to his Majesty, to assure him of our inviolable attachment to his sacred person and government," in trust that he would intervene on behalf of their traditional rights and privileges.[29] When Botetourt learned what was happening, he called the burgesses to his council and announced that he had heard of their "resolves and augur[ed] ill of their effect. You have made it my duty to dissolve you, and you are dissolved accordingly."[30]

The Virginians expected as much and politely left the capitol building, marching together to the Apollo Room of the nearby Raleigh Tavern, where they promptly elected Peyton Randolph as their moderator. Then they proceeded to form themselves into what they called the "Association" and adopted a series of eight resolutions, whereby they pledged to neither import nor buy any goods taxed by Parliament. To improve the chances that nonimportation would succeed in forcing Parliament to rescind the Townshend duties, they pledged themselves to "promote and encourage Industry and Frugality, and discourage all Manner of Luxury and Extravagance," adding a moral imperative to the political document.[31]

Nonimportation proved surprisingly effective up and down the colonies. In 1770 a new prime minister, Lord Frederick North, repealed all the duties except those on tea, kept as a matter of principle. Having achieved almost complete success, the nonimportation effort came to an end, and peaceful relations between the colonies and the mother country resumed. Though this turn of events convinced Jefferson of the utility of commercial boycotts, he did not believe that the critical issues of governance had been settled.

IN 1769, WHEN JEFFERSON officially became a burgess, he was twenty-six, still unmarried, and living with his mother. His surviving correspondence from the early 1760s, sparse as it is, brims with references to young women, especially Rebecca Burwell. He pretends to have fallen irrevocably in love with her but hardly approaches her, and when he does, he is too tongue-tied, bashful, and indecisive to impress. The letters include rumors and questions about other young women he was interested in and other couples' engagements. The shy and self-conscious young Jefferson's missives almost play at courtship, as though his words are performing for him. After the marriages in 1765 of his closest friends, John Page and Dabney Carr (Carr to Jefferson's sister Martha), he seemed to fear being left behind in the matrimonial competition.

In this context arose a scandal, made public years later. His longtime friend Peter Walker (son of Dr. Thomas Walker) had married Elizabeth (Betsy) Moore in June 1764, and for years Jefferson was close to the couple. Apparently, one day in 1768, when Peter was away from home, Jefferson visited Betsy and made an inappropriate advance. What actually happened is unclear. Fifteen years later, while Jefferson was in France, Betsy told her husband about the event. Almost two decades after that, Peter protested to Jefferson and made noises about a duel. Intermediaries quieted things down, helped along by a letter Jefferson wrote in 1805 to a third party confessing that "when young and single, I offered love to a handsome lady. I acknowledge its incorrectness."[32]

The year 1770 found Jefferson unmarried and lonely, maybe pining for domestic felicity and wifely affection; he called the now-married Dabney Carr "the happiest man in the universe."[33] On February 1, when all the family members happened to be elsewhere, Shadwell—the Jefferson family home—burned to the ground. Jane and Jefferson's other siblings crowded into a nearby overseer's dwelling until a small new house could be constructed for them. Jefferson had his single room up on Monticello, but the conflagration intensified his efforts to complete the main house. The fire struck him particularly hard because, as he bemoaned to John Page, it meant the loss "of every pa[per I] had in the world, and almost every book."[34] The papers included his case notes and briefs, and the General Court would be sitting just two months later. Better news was on the horizon, however, for in early October he visited the Forest, the Charles City County home of a wealthy merchant and lawyer, John Wayles. There Jefferson met Wayles's widowed daughter, twenty-one-year-old Martha Wayles Skelton.[35]

PART II

REVOLUTIONARY AMERICA, 1771–1784

3

"Inspire Us with Firmness"

JEFFERSON DID NOT RECORD when he first met John Wayles, but it must have been early in his Williamsburg years. Wayles was a wealthy merchant and an industrious and successful lawyer. By the time Jefferson would have met him, Wayles lived at the Forest, a plantation home some sixteen miles outside Richmond. Jefferson had probably seen Wayles at courthouses and perhaps at the high General Court in Williamsburg, although Wayles was not qualified to serve on it. Wayles was also a debt collector for a large English tobacco firm, a delicate position among Virginia aristocrats who thought it ungentlemanly to approach them about their debts. Perhaps he managed to perform that job and retain his social standing because he was "a most agreeable companion, full of pleasantry & good humor, and welcomed in every society."[1] Wayles occasionally went to the offices of the *Virginia Gazette*, so it's possible Jefferson, there to browse through the newest delivery of books, fell into conversation with the older lawyer. Or they could also have met on June 22, 1770, when the two were among 162 other Virginia men who signed a strengthened nonimportation agreement.[2]

In May 1746, Wayles had married a well-connected widow named Martha Eppes. A little more than seven months later, Martha gave birth, prematurely, to twins, a stillborn daughter and a son who lived only hours. Quickly pregnant again, Martha gave birth to another girl on October 31, 1748, only to die five days later. Wayles soon remarried, needing a new wife to help with the baby, kept alive by nursemaids. He had four more daughters with his second wife, before she too passed away. In 1760 he again remarried, but his third wife lived hardly a year.

At that point, Wayles turned to a mulatto slave woman, Elizabeth (Betty) Hemings, who had served in his house for years. She would be his concubine for the rest of his life, bearing him six additional children, whom he never formally acknowledged but whose lineage was widely recognized. While his eldest daughter Martha, named for her mother, his first wife, appears not to have had good relationships with her white stepmothers, she nonetheless learned to manage a household. She became known for her skill at conversation, dancing, and music; she sang sweetly and was accomplished on the spinet, or harpsichord, and the fortepiano. Family lore described her in many ways: of slight build, "small" or "low" in stature, "with a lithe and exquisitely formed figure," with auburn hair, hazel eyes, "pretty," "distinguished for her beauty," graceful in her movements, vivacious, fond of reading (like Jefferson, she enjoyed the Anglican novelist Laurence Sterne).[3]

At eighteen, Martha married Bathurst Skelton, a well-established young planter, and they moved to their home, Elk Hill. Less than a year later, Martha gave birth to a boy, whom they named John, but Bathurst died ten months after that, leaving Martha, at only twenty, a widow with an infant son. Death was ever-present in colonial Virginia, and the bereaved had to quickly recover from their grief and move on with life. No doubt Martha did so, and after her mourning period she surely accompanied her father to Williamsburg to shop or socialize. Jefferson likely noticed her there. They may have even taken music lessons from the same Italian teacher, one Francis Alberti, Jefferson on the violin and Martha on the harpsichord.[4] But Jefferson most certainly noticed her when he visited her father's plantation in October 1770.

No CORRESPONDENCE between Jefferson and Martha survives, and neither kept a diary. But on the evidence of expense notations in Jefferson's memorandum book, he apparently visited the Forest twice more in December 1770 and at least eight times in 1771.[5] Now older and more assured, with a career and a home of his own, Jefferson vigorously courted Martha. She had other suitors as well. A family story relates that on one occasion two hopefuls showed up at the Forest. Before they entered the house, they heard the sounds of her "harpsichord and voice, accompanied by Mr. Jefferson's voice and violin," promptly sized up the situation, and silently withdrew.[6] The courtship moved rapidly.

In February Jefferson wrote to a friend on an unrelated matter, and after referring to a mutual acquaintance who was "wishing to take to himself a wife," he revealed, "I too am in that way." But he added that the recent fire at Shadwell and the loss of all his belongings had placed an obstacle in his path. After all, his bride-to-be already had a young son to care for, and Monticello still only boasted a small house.[7] Jefferson remained undeterred. Further evidence of his intentions appear in a letter he wrote in June to his merchant factor in London (who purchased his annual tobacco crop and acquired items for him in England), Thomas Adams, seeking to alter a recent invoice: "I wrote therein for a Clavichord. I have since seen a Forte-piano and am charmed with it. Send me this instrument then instead of the Clavichord. Let the case be of fine mahogany, solid, not veneered . . . and the workmanship of the whole very handsome, and worthy the acceptance of a lady for whom I intend it."[8] He added, "I desired the favor of you to procure me an architect. I must repeat the request earnestly and that you would send him [on] as soon as you can."[9] By architect Jefferson meant a master builder, one who could realize his plans for Monticello.[10]

Correspondence between Jefferson and Robert Skipwith, who married Tabitha ("Tibby") Wayles, Martha's half sister, in or around July of that year, reveals much about Jefferson. In July, Skipwith, who must have gotten to know Jefferson through mutual visits to the Forest, requested that his future brother-in-law provide him with a reading list "suitable to the capacity of a common reader." Jefferson replied in August. After a brief essay on reading and a defense of novels, he supplied the inventory for a complete library, practically a lifelong educational program. Then Jefferson invited Skipwith to "Come to the new Rowanty," a literary allusion to Monticello, where he could access Jefferson's growing library and they could enjoy elevated conversation. "Come then and bring our dear Tibby with you; the first in your affections, the second in mine." Then, in a further literary allusion, he added, "Offer prayers for me too at that shrine [Martha] to which, tho' absent, I pay continual devotion. In every scheme of happiness she is placed in the fore-ground of the picture, as the principal figure. Take that away, and there is no picture for me."[11] Skipwith soon replied, thanking Jefferson for the catalog of books and acknowledging the pleasant idyll he had painted of the two couples living near each other.[12] Alas, sometime before February 1773, Tibby died.

Martha may well have had concerns about the cramped living arrangements at Monticello, which might have complicated her agreement to marry Jefferson. Then, tragically, little John died in June 1771 of unknown causes. Meanwhile Jefferson was busy with his legal career and had the General Court to attend in October that year. He was also reelected to the House of Burgesses (he recorded paying in November for "cakes had at election").[13] The two discussed an appropriate marriage date and settled on New Year's Day 1772. Jefferson's memorandum book shows him purchasing drapes and a bed for his single-room accommodation at Monticello, and on December 23, Jefferson, with Francis Eppes (a friend since his college days) cosigning, paid fifty pounds for a bond in preparation for buying a marriage license.[14] A week later he paid forty shillings for the actual license. (Eppes had married another of Martha's stepsisters, Elizabeth, and their son would, in 1797, marry Jefferson's daughter Maria.)

No list of wedding guests exists, but surely Martha's family attended, and Jane Jefferson must have come down from Shadwell; Dabney and Martha Carr probably came from their home in Goochland County. Martha's father, John Wayles, gave her away, and the Reverend William Coutts read the marriage rites from the Anglican *Book of Common Prayer*. Jefferson's memorandum book shows that he paid a fiddler generously for the occasion and gave tips to a number of slaves for helping out, including Betty "Hemmins," Wayles's black mistress.[15] Jefferson was twenty-eight years old, Martha was twenty-three, and in Jefferson's later, bittersweet words, he and the "cherished companion of [his] life" were to live together for "ten years in unchequered happiness."[16]

THE NEWLYWEDS LINGERED at the Forest until at least January 18, when they set off westward, in a two-person carriage, for Monticello. They stopped for a day or so at Tuckahoe, a few miles west of Richmond, then set forth for Albemarle County. They had begun their journey in a light snowfall that became heavy after Tuckahoe. Some eight miles from Monticello, on January 25, the snow was so deep that they had to get out of their carriage and continue afoot, trudging along, cold and tired, as day turned to night. As their daughter Martha Jefferson Randolph later described it, "They arrived late at night, the fires all out and the servants retired to their own houses for the night. The horrible dreariness of such a house at the end of such a journey I have often heard both relate." An early biographer with access to Jefferson's grandchildren added a critical detail: "Part of a bottle of wine, found on a shelf behind some books, had to serve the new-married couple both for fire and supper."[17] The next morning Jefferson recorded the blizzard in his Garden Book, using the plural pronoun: "the deepest snow we have ever seen. in Albemarle it was about 3 f. deep."[18] After a brief stay, the couple retreated to Martha's home, Elk Hill, about thirty miles away to the southeast.

Jefferson was soon busy again with legal business (although he did not attend the General Assembly meeting that February) and with the construction on the main house at Monticello. Martha, who had overseen her father's household and borne (and buried) a child, was unflappable; she knew how to run a household and supervise slaves, make soap and candles, and maintain the inventory of the pantry. The account book she kept shows her quickly taking charge of the domestic scene, buying cider, eggs, chickens, a quarter of beef, mutton, peas, sugar, and other provisions. She even purchased three bushels of hops that fall because she took pride in the brewing of small beer (that is, beer with low alcohol content); over three months in late 1772 she recorded brewing seven casks.[19] Martha could be tart. A granddaughter recalled her mother saying that Martha possessed a "vivacity of temper," along with a "little asperity [that] sometimes shewed itself to her children."[20] Jefferson, by contrast, was almost famously reserved.

Martha became pregnant soon after the move. They may have anticipated her having trouble breastfeeding. On June 10, Jefferson paid a Dr. Carter for "breast pipes," a device meant to elongate inverted nipples.[21] On September 27, at 5:00 a.m., their first child, Martha—she would be called Patsy—arrived.[22] As feared, Martha had trouble breastfeeding, and the infant struggled; at six months, they procured Ursula, Martha's trusted former slave housekeeper from the Forest, whose supply of "a good breast of milk" allowed the baby to thrive. At Martha's bidding, Jefferson purchased Ursula and her children on January 21, 1773, and she would remain the family's primary cook until her death in 1800.[23] Patsy, after her shaky start, developed a hearty constitution.

THROUGHOUT 1772 and into the spring of 1773, the tensions between England and the colonies lessened, and Jefferson focused his attention on Martha, Patsy, and Monticello. Yet, during this relative lull, the persisting tax on tea still rankled the colonists. When the British customs schooner *Gaspee* ran aground in the harbor of Providence, Rhode Island, on June 9, 1772, eight boatloads of protestors from the city attacked and eventually burned the ship. Irate Crown officials subsequently ruled that those caught and arrested would be brought to England for prosecution. This attack on the traditional concept of trial before one's peers outraged colonists up and down the coast. Back in Virginia, the new royal governor, Lord Dunmore, would have preferred not to deal with the assembly but had to call it into session in March 1773 to address an issue involving forged paper currency.

When the assemblymen began to arrive in Williamsburg, they had more than forgery on their minds. A group of younger, more radical burgesses, including Jefferson, Patrick Henry, Richard Henry Lee, Francis Lightfoot Lee, and Dabney Carr, "not thinking our old & leading members up to the point of forwardness & zeal which the times required," met in a private room at the Raleigh Tavern before the formal assembly sat.[24] They intended to discuss the disturbing implications of the Providence crisis. Agreeing that insistence on the trial of Americans before American courts was "a common cause to all" colonists, they resolved to create a committee of correspondence to facilitate intercolonial communication and "to produce an unity of action."[25] The younger burgesses decided to present their plan to the full assembly the next day, March 12. Though asked to make the presentation, Jefferson never liked public speaking and successfully urged that the newly elected Carr do so instead. Carr spoke effectively, arguing for the appointment of eleven men to a committee of correspondence. The assembly approved, and although not pleased, Dunmore did not prorogue (suspend) the assembly until a shortened session had dealt with the forgery matter and several other noncontroversial issues. Then he called for another session to meet in June, but later prorogued that and all subsequent meetings until May 1774. He seemed not to grasp what was brewing. The committee of correspondence, once established, initiated the intercolonial effort that led to ever stronger unity and eventually to revolution.

BEFORE JEFFERSON could return from Williamsburg, Dabney Carr suddenly fell desperately ill and died on May 16—a major blow to his dear friend. Jefferson had Carr's body disinterred from its initial grave and reburied at a spot on the hillside of Monticello where the two men as boys had lain under a great oak tree to read and converse.[26] Martha's absence compounded Jefferson's grief: she had gone with their child to be with her gravely ill father, who himself died on May 28. Both deaths had significant implications. Jefferson took responsibility for Martha Carr and her six children, essentially raising the Carr children at Monticello.[27] Then, in 1774, through his wife, Jefferson inherited more than 10,000 acres of land and 135 slaves (in addition to the 52 he already owned), along with Wayles's substantial debts. Jefferson sold about half the land, expecting that the bonds he received would suffice to repay the money owed, but the English creditors rejected them (they were in depreciated Revolutionary currency). The inherited debt burdened Jefferson for the remainder of his life.[28] And within a few years, as another portion of her inheritance, Martha Jefferson brought Elizabeth (Betty) Hemings, whom she had known most of her life, and her children to Monticello, where they would occupy privileged positions in the household.

In late 1773 and early 1774, as Jefferson was in the process of divesting himself of his law practice, he, his again pregnant wife, and their infant daughter spent time at the Forest and at Elk Hill. In January 1774, he inaugurated his Farm Book, wherein he kept detailed records of every aspect of plantation affairs for Monticello. His Garden Book reveals that at the time he was busily engaging carpenters, cabinetmakers, and brick makers, determined to make progress on his house. In March he began to level out a terrace and added a stone wall in preparation for a long, rectangular garden on the south side of the mountain. He planted fruit trees and experimented with new kinds of vegetables, as he and Martha awaited the birth of their second child. The quietness of this period was disturbed on February 21, when, shortly before midnight, an earthquake "shook the houses so sensibly that every body run out of doors"; an aftershock occurred the next day. These were the first recorded earthquakes in Virginia history.[29]

Then another tragedy: perhaps frightened by the shaking earth, Jefferson's mentally disabled sister Elizabeth and her caretaker slave, Little Sal (sister to Jefferson's Jupiter), attempting to cross a rain-swollen Rivanna in a small, flat-bottomed boat, either capsized or simply fell out. Both drowned. Jefferson noted in his memorandum books that Elizabeth's body was found on February 24.[30] The river continued to rise, and he noted on March 6 that it was nearly at a record flood stage. A superstitious man might have wondered if these were geological or meteorological omens, especially after a disastrous late frost struck his crops on May 5.[31] But in the midst of this torrent of misfortune, there was a brief happy lull. On April 3, just before noon, a second daughter was born and named Jane Randolph, after Jefferson's mother. Martha developed a breast abscess, and presumably Ursula again stepped in to nurse the baby.

THE POLITICAL CALM in Virginia came to an end before the middle of 1774. Events elsewhere shifted Jefferson's attention from the personal to the imperial. On sending the assemblymen home in March 1773, Governor Dunmore had insultingly admonished them to promote among their constituents "a love of agriculture and attention to their private affairs, by which you will render a most essential service to them and to your country."[32] But on May 5, 1774, the date Dunmore had called for a new session of the House of Burgesses after repeated prorogations, the men from the far-flung counties had far more than private affairs to reflect upon. England had engaged for many months in efforts to impose order on and extract revenue from its empire. When the assembly met, the governor addressed them, making no allusions to portentous recent events. Instead, he condescendingly requested that the assemblymen handle their routine business with "prudence and moderation."

But Virginia was abuzz with developments in Boston the previous year. When in May 1773 Parliament passed the Tea Act, authorizing the East India Company to sell cheaper tea directly to colonists via its own agents, colonists quickly smelled a ploy to establish a tea monopoly. On December 16, 1773, hundreds of colonists disguised as Mohawk Indians boarded three tea ships in Boston harbor and dumped their cargo overboard. Parliament passed a series of so-called Coercive Acts (or, from the colonial perspective, Intolerable Acts) the next spring, in 1774. Among other things, these closed the port of Boston until the tea was paid for. On May 19, Virginia published accounts of this action, called the Boston Port Act.

With the assembly in full session, the news from Boston could not have broken at a more combustible moment. British actions had taken an ominous turn: first there had been taxation without representation, then contempt for trial by a jury of one's peers, then a government-backed attempt to establish a commercial monopoly, and now the closing of a great city's port and the imminent destruction of its economy. For a decade or more, largely because of overproduction, tobacco prices had been falling, diminishing Virginia planters' profits. The planters, with no real understanding of broad economic forces, assumed malevolent British merchants were behind the drop in prices. Did the British intend to force credit-dependent planters into subservience and debt slavery? As an anonymous planter had warned in an October 1771 essay in the *Virginia Gazette*, "We all know that we are slaves to the power of the merchants: For who can truly say he is free, when there is a fixed price set upon his tobacco, and goods he purchases, at rates he does not like?"[33]

Hence the colony was primed to react strongly to the slightest whiff of economic interference or oppression by Great Britain. As Jefferson recalled, a small group of men, who believed the issue too critical to be "left to the old members" and agreed "that we must boldly take an unequivocal stand in the line with Massachusetts," decided to meet on their own in the library of the capitol building and devise a way to "arous[e] our people from the lethargy into which they had fallen as to passing events." Jefferson apparently came up with the idea of appointing "a day of general fasting & prayer [as] most likely to call up & alarm their attention." His retelling of these events makes clear that he saw fasting and prayer as gimmicks to ramp up public sentiment against British action and in support of colonial rights. He described how the group "rummaged" through John Rushworth's seventeenth-century *Historical Collections* to find inspiration from their Puritan forebears. When they found some useful piece of history or law, they "cooked up a resolution" in modern language "to implore heaven to avert from us the evils of civil war, to inspire us with firmness . . . and to turn the hearts of the King & parliament."[34]

The group drafted on May 24 a "Resolution of the House of Burgesses Designating a Day of Fasting and Prayer," which they persuaded older and more devout member Robert Carter Nicholas to introduce to the full house. In order "to oppose, by all just and proper Means, every Injury to American rights," the resolution set aside June 1, 1774, for meetings at all Virginia churches, including Bruton Parish in Williamsburg, for sermons and prayers, along with appropriate fasting, all to support the opposition cause.[35] The resolution was printed as a broadside and reprinted several days later in the Williamsburg papers. In response, Governor Dunmore told the assembly that their words made "it necessary for me to dissolve you; and you are dissolved accordingly."[36]

The dismissed assemblymen once more walked to the Apollo Room of the Raleigh Tavern. There, the full eighty-nine in attendance, with Peyton Randolph serving as moderator, drafted, and on May 27, signed, another declaration of Association. The assemblymen now pledged to abstain from purchasing all East India commodities and recommended that the various committees of correspondence invite the other colonies to send delegates to "meet in general congress" at some agreed upon location, where they would consider future action. The declaration's language reflected an escalation of tensions. It raised measures "to secure our dearest rights and liberties from destruction, by the heavy hand of power now lifted against North America" and stated that "a determined system is formed and pressed for reducing the inhabitants of British America to slavery, by subjecting them to the payment of taxes, imposed without the consent of the people or their representatives."[37] On May 30, styling themselves "the late

House of Burgesses," they decided to send letters to all of their "Sister Colonies," acting on behalf of the "Preservation of the Common Rights and Liberties of British America." They also sent notices throughout Virginia calling all assembly members to gather in Williamsburg on August 1 to "conclude finally on these important Questions."[38] Accordingly, on May 31 a more aggressive group of twenty-four former members—including Jefferson, George Washington, Edmund Pendleton, Peyton Randolph, and Robert Carter Nicholas—signed and posted a formal letter to all the other former members of the House of Burgesses warning, "Things seem to be hurrying to an alarming Crisis."[39] With that, the various delegates went home.

JUNE AND JULY found Jefferson back at Monticello, where he pondered the simmering political crisis. Sometime before July 23, he and fellow Albemarle burgess John Walker sent a letter to their constituents in St. Anne's Parish, asking them to gather on that date at the new church on the Hardware River for "fasting, humiliation and prayer devoutly to implore the divine interposition on behalf of an injured and oppressed people." The letter announced that the Reverend Charles Clay would preach that day.[40] Jefferson would later say of this and similar ceremonies, "the effect . . . thro' the whole colony was like a shock of electricity, arousing every man."[41] Jefferson was using religion more to appeal to the people than as an expression of his own beliefs. The two burgesses chose a date just three days before the county election, at which both Jefferson and Walker won reelection to the disbanded assembly.[42] The voters also approved a set of resolutions—surely authored by Jefferson—that called for a complete ban on imports from England. The first paragraph stated the resolutions' foundational principle: the people were bound only by the laws they or their representatives had adopted, and "no other legislature whatever may rightfully exercise authority over them." Thus they declared themselves not subject to Parliament. The resolutions named Jefferson and Walker as the county's deputies to attend the called-for special meeting on August 1 in Williamsburg and instructed them to vote in conformity with the desires of the freeholders of Albemarle County.[43]

Shortly after the election, Jefferson set out for Williamsburg, bringing with him a lengthy text described as a "draught of instructions to be given to the delegates . . . which I meant to propose at our meeting." But he had no sooner left Monticello than a severe case of dysentery forced him to return home and miss the August 1 meeting. Yet he sent on, probably in the hands of his slave Jupiter, his planned remarks. One copy was intended for Patrick Henry, who he hoped would speak on behalf of his proposed instructions; another was for the presumed chair of the meeting, Peyton Randolph.[44] Jefferson's manuscript, though perhaps not as polished as he would have wished, was quickly published (without his prior knowledge) as a pamphlet. Destined to become famous in the colonies and infamous in London, the publication marked Jefferson's entry into the intercolonial arena as "the pen of the American Revolution."[45]

4

"These Are Our Grievances"

PATRICK HENRY APPARENTLY did not read the long manuscript, but Peyton Randolph immediately recognized its import. Upon receiving it, he read the proposed resolutions aloud to a sizable group of the colony's delegates gathered at his home. Randolph's nephew Edmund Randolph "distinctly recollect[ed] the applause bestowed on the most of them" by those in attendance.[1] Peyton Randolph later made the resolutions available to all members by laying them on the table of the meeting room. Yet, as Edmund Randolph's memory suggested and Jefferson's autobiography confirmed, the resolutions were "too bold for the present state of things," and the convention never actually voted on them, even though many of the younger delegates agreed with them. Most Virginians simply had trouble contemplating a real break with England. Jefferson said it best: "tamer sentiments were preferred, and, I believe, wisely preferred, the leap I proposed being too long, as yet, for the mass of our citizens."[2]

The deputies—they were careful not to label themselves burgesses—did, however, elect seven of their most distinguished members to attend the proposed Continental Congress set to meet in Philadelphia that September. In the "Instructions by the Virginia Convention to Their Delegates in Congress," the deputies were more respectful of the king and Parliament than Jefferson had been, making clear their "Faith and true Allegiance to his Majesty King George the Third" and expressing their approval of a "constitutional Connexion with Great Britain." Only then did they raise concerns, stating, "British Subjects in America are entitled to the same Rights and Privileges as their Fellow Subjects possess in Britain."[3] The colonists remembered how their response in 1765 had caused Parliament to repeal the Stamp Act; they hoped for a similar result now.

The seven Virginia delegates—Peyton Randolph, Richard Henry Lee, George Washington, Patrick Henry, Richard Bland, Benjamin Harrison, and Edmund Pendleton—were all older and better known than Jefferson, so even if he had been present at the Williamsburg convention, he may not have been chosen to go to Philadelphia. But his proposed resolutions would make it to Philadelphia and far beyond. They were published as a pamphlet by friends and supporters in Williamsburg, with one of them adding a brief preface and suggesting the title *A Summary View of the Rights of British America*. On August 6 George Washington recorded in his account book that he had bought a copy, and Patrick Henry, and probably the other deputies as well, took copies with them to Philadelphia. Soon there was a Philadelphia edition, and printers in New York, Boston, and Norfolk may have put out their own as well. There were even two London editions by the end of the year.[4] Jefferson's words, even though not officially adopted in Williamsburg, would have an outsize impact on the discussion emerging in the colonies about the nature of political sovereignty and the position of the colonies in the British Empire.

The text of *A Summary View* is a mishmash of tendentious history valorizing England's Saxon era, ponderous analysis, soaring rhetoric, and elegant phraseology. Parts of it clearly inspired Jefferson's readers; other parts—such as his attack on slavery and the slave trade—troubled some. Overall, much of his language was more radical than many of the delegates at the convention were ready to accept. Edmund Randolph wrote that Jefferson tended "to run before the times in which he lived."[5] *A Summary View* recapitulated prior arguments, reshaped current ones, and prefigured subsequent colonial debate. It was not an academic treatise but a call to action. Jefferson was creating the concept of an American people and at the same time working through the principles of governance that should apply to the colonies in the context of an imperial system.[6]

Jefferson began the manuscript by instructing the Virginia delegates to prepare an address for the king that laid out the "united complaints of his majesty's subjects in America." They must do so, moreover, "in the language of truth, and divested of those expressions of servility which would persuade his majesty that we are asking favors and not rights." Calling the king "no more than the chief officer of the people," Jefferson argued that, in the same way that the early Saxon settlers of the "island of Britain" owed no legislative allegiance to their mother country when establishing themselves in their new land, so too did the colonial governments possess their own sovereignty independent of Britain.[7] The establishment of their own laws and regulations was a right "which nature has given to all men."[8] Thus the colonists were not transplanted Englishmen but a separate, unique, sovereign people.

After defending this position based on an idealized and in part imaginary account of Britain's history before the Norman conquest, Jefferson argued that "the exercise of a free trade with all parts of the world" was also colonists' "natural right." Accordingly, the so-called navigation laws that had long regulated colonial maritime commerce violated the colonists' rights. Jefferson reiterated his basic point: "The true ground on which we declare these acts void is that the British parliament has no right to exercise authority over us."[9] Not all the delegates would so categorically dismiss parliamentary authority.

Jefferson warmed to his theme. British "exercises of usurped power" extended to the internal affairs of the colonies. He admitted that earlier and apparently random incidences of parliamentary regulation had been overlooked or excused because they were rare and that the colonists were predisposed to look favorably on Britain. But the situation of the previous three or four years was different. "Scarcely have our minds been able to emerge from the astonishment into which one stroke of parliamentary thunder has involved us, before another and more alarming is fallen on us." Then his hammer blow: "Single acts of tyranny may be ascribed to the accidental opinion of a day; but a series of oppressions, begun at a distinguished period, and pursued unalterably thro' every change of ministers, too plainly prove a deliberate, systematical plan of reducing us to slavery."[10]

Jefferson proceeded to itemize the usurpations: the Stamp Act, the Declaratory Act, the Townshend duties, the suspension of the New York legislature, the Boston Port Act. He admitted that the perpetrators of the Boston Tea Party had done wrong, but theirs were the understandable actions of "An exasperated people." To punish all the citizens of Boston for the deeds of a tiny group was, in Jefferson's words, "administering justice with a heavy hand indeed!"[11]

In laying out a list of British actions that had provoked Americans to protest, Jefferson borrowed a strategy that English protestors had employed when writing the Declaration of Rights in 1689, which had officially ended the reign of James II and launched that of William and Mary. That famous document, known to educated Americans and lawyers in 1774, had included, in thirteen clauses, specific instances of royal misconduct so egregious as to justify repudiation of the king.[12] Jefferson offered the long train of unhappy events as the cause of the colonial protest and called on the king to use his authority to override these examples of Parliamentary overreach.[13]

Jefferson stressed that Parliament had voided laws duly considered and passed by the various colonial assemblies. In one of the most controversial passages of his manuscript, which did not find significant support among his fellow deputies, he singled out Parliament's rejection of Virginia's effort to curtail the importation of slaves. Many viewed this limitation more as a boycott than a condemnation of the institution of slavery. Yet Jefferson wrote that "the abolition of domestic slavery is the great object of desire in those colonies where it was unhappily introduced in their infant state." Here he clearly privileged his private opinion over popular sentiment in Virginia, perhaps trying to convince the other members to support ending slavery.[14] He continued with other examples of American laws overridden, questioning, still boldly, whether it was "possible then that his majesty can have bestowed a single thought on the situation" of the people in America. Yet nowhere was British action more high-handed, in his view, than in the dissolving of colonial legislatures. Jefferson stated that in such cases, "power revert[ed] to the people," where true sovereignty lay.[15] Even worse, if possible, was Britain's sending troops to the colonies and requiring the local citizens to house them. As Jefferson wrote, "Let [the king] remember that force cannot give right."[16]

At this point, the text reached the peak of its rhetorical power. "These are our grievances which we have thus laid before his majesty with that freedom of language and sentiment which becomes a free people, claiming their rights as derived from the laws of nature, and not as the gift of their chief magistrate. Let those flatter, who fear: it is not an American art." Jefferson insisted that Americans rightfully understood kings to be "the servants, not the proprietors of the people." Then he irreverently exhorted the king, "Only aim to do your duty, and mankind will give you credit. . . . No longer persevere in sacrificing the rights of one part of the empire to the inordinate desires of another." He added, unpersuasively, that the manuscript conveyed the advice of well-meaning American counsel, "on the observance of which may perhaps depend your felicity and future fame, and the preservation of that harmony which alone can continue both to Great Britain and America the reciprocal advantages of their connection."[17]

Then Jefferson pulled back a bit. He was trying, in the end, to figure out how the colonies fit into the empire. They were exempt from parliamentary authority, so did some kind of relationship to the king bind them to Britain? Was he imagining something like the idea of the British Commonwealth that emerged more than a century later? As he wrote, "It is neither our wish nor our interest to separate from her." Calling once again for the king to hold back parliamentary regulations and interference in colonial affairs, Jefferson argued aphoristically that "the god who gave us life, gave us liberty: the hand of force may destroy, but cannot disjoin them." He entreated the king to stop parliamentary abuse, redress the "great grievances" of the colonists, and thereby reestablish "fraternal love and harmony thro' the whole empire."[18] However radical he was, Jefferson was not yet willing to suggest that independence was the only solution.

ON SEPTEMBER 5, 1774, a total of fifty-six deputies or delegates from twelve colonies assembled in Philadelphia at Carpenters' Hall and promptly chose Peyton Randolph as president of the Congress. The delegates agreed that each colony would have one vote and to proceed in secrecy until a decision was reached. On October 18, the Congress approved and announced what it called a "Non-importation, Non-consumption, Non-exportation Agreement," closely based on the earlier Association measures passed in Virginia.

The Continental Congress labeled the proposed economic sanctions the Continental Association. They called for banning the import (effective December 1, 1775) of a long list of goods, including slaves (the August Virginia convention had also called for an end of the Atlantic slave trade) and tea. The sanctions also called for the end of exports of colonial-produced goods, including tobacco, on September 10, 1775. The colonies were to establish committees in each county and town to guard against violations. The committees of correspondence in each colony would keep one another apprised of events. The delegates concluded by declaring that the sanctions would remain in effect until the repeal of the hated parliamentary acts.[19] They fully expected that outcome.

Jefferson thought the conclusions of this First Continental Congress too weak, but he understood there was a diversity of opinion in Virginia and in the colonies as a whole and that the more radical members would need to be patient as the more conservative ones were brought along. Early in 1775 Jefferson and John Walker were reelected as delegates to the Second Virginia Convention, called to meet in March in the tiny village of Richmond in order to avoid Williamsburg and the royal governor.

GOVERNOR DUNMORE underestimated the degree of anger in Virginia. He thought a few extremists objected to recent British actions and that the general population was relatively content.[20] He had recently received instructions from Lord Dartmouth, the British secretary of state for colonial affairs, not to allow the importation of powder and arms and to prevent the colonial assembly from electing delegates to the next Continental Congress. By the time the Virginia delegates were assembled in Richmond, they knew that the king had reacted angrily to news of the protests in America. At the Richmond meeting, Patrick Henry did more than anyone else to shift opinion toward rebellion. Speaking "as man was never known to speak before," reported one awestruck contemporary, Henry roused the delegates to the immediate need to prepare for military defense of the colony's liberties.[21] Richard Henry Lee seconded his resolution, but others, like Edmund Pendleton and Robert Carter Nicholas, cautioned against moving so precipitously, warning that the colony was nowhere near ready for war.

Jefferson and George Washington, Virginia's most respected military leader, supported the Henry faction. Henry, sensing that the convention might be hesitating, rose again to speak. His rhetorical brilliance overwhelmed everyone, Jefferson included. Henry said the colonists had done everything they could: they had sent petitions and remonstrances to no effect. "There is no longer any room for hope. . . . If we wish to be free . . . we must fight!" In an atmosphere charged with excitement, Henry then delivered his soon-to-be-famous peroration: "Gentlemen may cry peace, peace—but there is no peace. The war has actually begun. . . . Why stand here idle? . . . Is life so dear, or peace so sweet, as to be purchased at the price of chains and slavery? Forbid it, Almighty God! I know not what course others may take; but as for me . . . give me liberty, or give me death!"[22]

The conservatives held firm, but they no longer had the votes to control the convention. A committee of twelve, including Jefferson, was formed to establish, arm, and train colony militia units of both infantry and "troops of horse" in each county. Precise instructions outlined the kind of weapons they should be provided, including tomahawks, and specified that horses should be trained to tolerate the noise and flash of gunfire.[23] The convention also moved to support local manufactures and greater wool production, owing to the colonial boycotts of British goods. It passed a resolution asking that a committee look into Governor Dunmore's new land policy and suggested that no one either purchase or accept land grants until after the investigation was completed.[24] Finally, recognizing that Peyton Randolph, one of the colony's seven delegates to the Second Continental Congress, could take ill or, should Dunmore call the assembly into session, have to remain in Virginia, the convention elected Jefferson as his alternate.[25]

While the convention was in session, Dunmore issued a proclamation instructing its members not to elect or send delegates to the Second Continental Congress—which the Virginians ignored. After the convention came to an end, on April 20 and 21, Dunmore had royal marines seize, under the cover of night, the gunpowder stored in the public magazine. The marines moved the matériel to the HMS *Magdalen*, positioned in a nearby tributary of the York River. Dunmore inflammatorily announced that if he or other officials were harassed, he would "by the living God, declare Freedom to the Slaves, and reduce the City of Williamsburg to Ashes."[26] Fearing public reprisal, he then barricaded himself inside the Governor's Palace. Then, on April 29, news arrived of gunfire exchanged between Massachusetts militiamen and British troops at Lexington and Concord. Eight days later, Jefferson would write his former teacher, William Small, then in England, that "within this week we have received the unhappy news of an action of considerable magnitude between the king's troops and our brethren of Boston. . . . This accident has cut off our last hopes of reconciliation, and a phrenzy of revenge seems to have seized all our ranks."[27] These tumultuous events formed the backdrop for the Second Continental Congress as its members converged on Philadelphia on May 10, 1775.

Jefferson was not among the initial arrivals. Governor Dunmore had summoned the Virginia assembly to meet on June 1 in order to present a set of conciliatory proposals from Prime Minister Lord North. Dunmore opened with a conciliatory speech, causing Jefferson and Randolph to fear that he would soften the opposition. In response to the proposals, Jefferson authored resolutions, passed on June 10 even though moderates had, in Jefferson's words, thrown "a dash of cold water on [them] here & there, enfeebling [them] somewhat." The final compromise document won almost unanimous support.[28] Jefferson transformed his remarks in support of the resolutions into a written address to Governor Dunmore, presented to him on June 12. Meanwhile, Dunmore had grown so frustrated by the onrush of events and the tenor of the debate that during the night of June 8, he had moved himself and his family to the HMS *Fowey*, a twenty-four-gun warship resting securely in the York River.[29] From that point, Dunmore attempted to govern the colony from aboard ship.

North had proposed that Parliament would tax the colonies no more (except with regard to maritime trade) if they would make voluntary contributions to support the expense of administrating the government and defending the colonies. Compared to *A Summary View*, the language of the resolutions rejecting North's proposal was prosaic, though still forceful. By approving Jefferson's resolutions, the assembly rejected North's proposal because, in Jefferson's words, "it only changes the form of oppression, without lightening its burthen." The resolutions went on to enumerate the reasons for the rejection and concluded by referencing the Second Continental Congress then in session. Because North's proposal involved all the colonies, the Virginia assembly could offer only its own opinion. "Final determination we leave to the General Congress now sitting."[30]

THE VERY DAY THE resolutions passed, June 10, Jefferson made ready to depart for Philadelphia. He was to replace Peyton Randolph, who had been recalled to Virginia to preside over the final assembly ever to meet in the colony. When Jefferson arrived in Philadelphia on June 20, he was almost the youngest delegate to the Congress. Among the others were many of the most famous American colonials of the time, including, above all, Benjamin Franklin, known internationally for his experiments with electricity. Three days before Jefferson arrived, the Battle of Bunker Hill had erupted in Boston: actual war was underway. Earlier in the month the Congress had named the American forces defending Boston the Continental Army, and following John Adams's recommendation, on June 15 it appointed George Washington commander in chief. Washington, twelve years older than Jefferson and far wealthier, had been a military hero in Virginia since a militia engagement against the French in 1754, and his martial fame had spread throughout the colonies. On June 26 Jefferson wrote to his brother-in-law Francis Eppes that "the war is now heartily entered into, without a prospect of accommodation but thro' the effectual interposition of arms."[31]

Almost immediately after Jefferson's arrival, the Congress sketched out a "Declaration of the Causes and Necessity of Taking Up Arms," but some members objected to the text. Jefferson and John Dickinson joined the committee that had drafted it. Dickinson, eleven years Jefferson's senior, had gained renown from his publication in 1767 and 1768 of a series of essays collectively known as *Letters from a Farmer in Pennsylvania*; as for Jefferson, *A Summary View* had recommended him to the committee. Both prepared drafts, read each other's versions, and in some fashion produced—with Dickinson probably playing the leading role—a document acceptable to the Congress. In many ways, it followed the structure of *A Summary View* and reflected Jefferson's ideas throughout, but Dickinson made the statement blunter and more forceful, if not as elegant. Certainly some of the most stirring words were Dickinson's. Congress adopted the new version on July 6, 1775, and four days later it was published in Philadelphia.[32]

On July 8, the Congress, practically caving into the demands of its most conservative members, also approved a separate document, authored by Dickinson and addressed to the king, that became known as the Olive Branch Petition. As Jefferson recalled, "The disgust against this humility was general," but in deference to Dickinson and the document's supporters, Congress accepted it.[33] The king would simply ignore it. The next item on the agenda, however, would prove influential: the Congress had to devise a reply to Lord North's conciliatory proposal and charged Franklin, John Adams, Richard Henry Lee, and Jefferson with the task. Aware that Jefferson had previously prepared Virginia's response and in fact had brought a copy with him to Philadelphia, the others turned to him. The reply to Lord North was essentially a more moderate version of what Jefferson had written in Williamsburg in June. The committee and the Congress accepted the message as written, with only the most minor revisions, and adopted it on July 31.[34]

JEFFERSON'S WORK AT the Congress was largely over; he had little to do with the explicitly military measures. He could look back over the previous six weeks with a degree of satisfaction: he had done important work in his first appearance on the national stage. During the last few days of July, Jefferson busied himself with paying all his accumulated bills.[35] Then, on August 1 he left for Virginia, but before going to Monticello he stopped for a week in Richmond to attend the remainder of the Virginia convention, now in effect the ruling body of the colony. Already in session for two weeks, it had passed a set of measures that created a colony-wide militia system.[36] While Jefferson was in attendance the convention voted on delegates to the next Congress, and he was among those elected.

Immediately thereafter Jefferson left for Monticello and reunion with his wife and two girls. Because his correspondence with Martha did not survive, we cannot know exactly how the two of them coped during their long period apart. While he was gone on public business, Martha reared the girls with the help of slave women and managed the farm, all while living in a house still only partially complete and constantly under construction. For the first time in months, on September 21, Jefferson made an entry in his Garden Book. But yet another death in the family disrupted his and Martha's lives. Just seventeen months old, their daughter Jane died.[37] Domestic bliss instantly turned to grief and mourning, making it excruciatingly difficult for Jefferson to depart on September 25 for the renewed session of the Continental Congress.

Jefferson's attitudes and resolve toward Britain had hardened significantly over the previous months. On August 25, having just arrived at Monticello from Richmond, he wrote to his Loyalist relative John Randolph in London, "I am one of those too who rather than submit to the right of legislating for us assumed by the British parliament, and which late experience has shewn they will so cruelly exercise, would lend my hand to sink the whole island in the ocean."[38] These were fighting words.

5

"Pen of the American Revolution"

A POWERFUL SENSE OF DUTY pulled Thomas Jefferson toward Philadelphia, but he also worried about the days to come: Would there be war? His journey overland was uneventful. Once he arrived, he found little of interest in the everyday business of the Congress meeting in the newly built Carpenters' Hall. Still, the work was extremely time-consuming, with Jefferson, heavily involved in committee work, often laboring at his desk into the night. He was lonely and consumed with anxiety about his wife's fragile health and her possible safety should conflict erupt. Hearing no news for months, he could only imagine the worst. On November 7 he wrote brother-in-law Francis Eppes that he had not received "the scrip of a pen from any mortal in Virginia since I left it, nor been able by any enquires I could make to hear of my family." The distress was almost more than he could stand. "The suspense under which I am is too terrible to be endured. If any thing has happened, for god's sake let me know it."[1]

Virginia's open conflict with Great Britain had begun in September when Dunmore directed troops to attack in the Hampton Roads area. On November 7, the governor had issued a proclamation giving freedom to all "indented servants, Negroes or others (appertaining to Rebels)" who would take up arms on behalf of "his Majesty's Troops." The residents of Norfolk believed the city could be burned to the ground at any time.[2] Jefferson sent warnings to his wife to stay as far inland as possible; as he informed Eppes on November 21, he had written "to Patty [his pet name for Martha] to keep yourselves at a distance from the alarms of Ld. Dunmore."[3] His earlier hopes for compromise had turned to anger. Writing a few days later to John Randolph in London, Jefferson assumed, "You will have heard before this reaches you that Ld.

Dunmore has commenced hostilities in Virginia." But Jefferson directed his real anger at King George. "It is an immense misfortune to the whole empire to have a king of such a disposition at such a time. We are told and every thing proves it true that he is the bitterest enemy we have."[4] In Jefferson's mind, the colonies and the Crown had reached the point of no return.

The Congress adjourned on December 13, though Jefferson compiled directions for a rump committee that would remain in Philadelphia to handle emergency matters. He left for Monticello on December 28, having secured an extended leave. Jefferson may have seen, just before leaving Philadelphia, an incendiary publication by recent British expatriate Thomas Paine that appeared on December 23. Paine had launched a series of addresses titled "The Crisis," and his pungent writing style had the same electrifying effect on his readers as Patrick Henry's oratory did on his listeners. "These are the times that try men's souls," Paine wrote, then laid out in vivid prose the rationale for rebellion.[5] His was a new style of political discourse that eschewed scholarly quotations and classical allusions, speaking to the common man, not elites.

Two months later Jefferson received copies of Paine's even more strident call to arms, *Common Sense*; published in pamphlet form on January 10, 1776, it sold phenomenally well throughout the colonies.[6] "O ye that love mankind!" Paine exclaimed. "Ye that dare oppose, not only the tyranny, but the tyrant, stand forth! Every spot of the old world is overrun with oppression. Freedom hath been hunted round the globe. Asia, and Africa, have long expelled her. Europe regards her like a stranger, and England hath given her warning to depart. O! receive the fugitive, and prepare in time an asylum for mankind."[7] Paine had elevated the colonies' cause to saving freedom for the entire world. He knew that some colonists still hesitated to blame the king out of (in Paine's view) misplaced reverence. Trying to jolt them from that perspective, Paine wrote bluntly that the king was no more than a "crowned ruffian," a "royal brute."[8]

While much evidence suggests that Paine's uncompromising language took Virginia by storm, perhaps even more people in the colony became convinced of Britain's iniquity as a result of Dunmore's attack on, and burning of, Norfolk on January 1.[9] Letters arriving at Monticello gave news about military actions in the other colonies as well; Jefferson's friend Thomas Nelson Jr., still in Philadelphia, tried to convince him to bring his wife and daughter with him when he returned.

JEFFERSON'S MOTHER JANE had been ill for some time, and he had apparently brought her to Monticello for care and nursing. His memorandum book noted on March 31, "My mother died about 8. oclock this morning in the 57th year of her life."[10] Some scholars have suggested that this brief notice perhaps reveals that Jefferson and his mother were not particularly close. Yet Jefferson was always reticent about deeply personal matters; his notation about the death of friend Dabney Carr in 1773 was similarly terse.[11]

When time came for Jefferson to return to Philadelphia, a severe migraine kept him at Monticello for six weeks, making this the second time that, at a very stressful moment, illness delayed his attendance at an important event.[12] He was loath to go anyway, since he knew another Virginia convention was to convene in early May. He would have much preferred to participate in that assembly, which would soon begin drafting a new plan of government for the colony. Nothing seemed more important to Jefferson. Back in Philadelphia he wrote to Thomas Nelson Jr. that again his wife had been unable to travel with him and that he wished the Virginia convention would "recall" its congressional delegates to Williamsburg. He mentioned to Nelson that before he had journeyed north, he had taken "great pains to enquire into the sentiment of the people on [the issue of independence]" and reported, "In the upper counties I think I may safely say nine out of ten are for it."[13] Indeed, groups from every colony sent more than ninety addresses, declarations, and petitions to Philadelphia, spelling out their protest and advocating separation from Britain.[14]

On May 16, 1776, the Virginia convention passed resolutions calling for independence. After condemning the king for "carrying on a piratical and savage war against us by tempting our slaves by every artifice" to turn "against their masters," the Virginians unanimously resolved that their delegates to the Continental Congress be instructed "to propose to that respectable body to declare the United Colonies free and independent states, absolved of all allegiance to, or dependence upon, the crown or parliament of Great Britain." They then exhorted the colonies to join into a confederation and seek alliances with other nations. They also proposed an appropriate plan of government for the colony of Virginia—not yet calling it a state.[15] Delegate Thomas Nelson set out for Philadelphia with a copy of the resolutions and the plan of government for the Congress, but even before he arrived (after a slight delay), the *Pennsylvania Evening Post* printed them. Jefferson was especially interested in the call for the creation of a Virginian system of government. As he had written earlier to Nelson, "It is a work of the most interesting nature and such as every individual would wish to have a voice in. In truth, it is the whole object of the present controversy."[16]

In Philadelphia, the Virginia resolutions engendered spirited debate as, aside from Massachusetts, no other colony had made such a radical move. Richard Henry Lee of the Virginia delegation had introduced a possibly incendiary resolution, which John Adams quickly seconded: "Resolved, That these United Colonies are, and of right ought to be, free and independent States, that they are absolved from all allegiance to the British Crown, and that all political connection between them and the State of Great Britain is, and ought to be, totally dissolved." Realizing that some of the middle colonies in particular were not quite ready for such a bold and irreversible move, the Congress decided on June 8 to postpone the final vote until July 1. In the meantime, it appointed Benjamin Franklin, John Adams, Roger Sherman, Robert R. Livingston, and Jefferson to a committee "to prepare a Declaration to the effect of the said first resolution."[17]

Congress simultaneously established two more key committees, one to develop a "Model Treaty" to shape how the new nation would interact with other nations (Adams and Franklin were named to this committee) and another to begin drafting a plan of government for the new nation (Sherman and Livingston). The committee appointed to draft the declaration unanimously elected Jefferson, at thirty-three its youngest member, to write the document. As Adams later explained, Jefferson had "a happy talent of composition" and a "peculiar felicity of expression."[18] He was also well liked, more so than the prickly and vain Adams, who was as blunt and thin-skinned as he was learned in history and law. Franklin, though popular, suffered terribly from gout and was essentially disabled. Just as determinative was Jefferson's status as a Virginian, representing the largest colony and indeed all the southernmost colonies. But before turning his attention to the declaration, Jefferson had another project in mind.

THE VIRGINIA CONVENTION had assembled in Williamsburg in early May, and its president, Edmund Pendleton, had appointed a constitutional committee of more than two dozen members, with George Mason taking the leading role. Jefferson soon learned of this, for on May 24 Pendleton wrote to him, "Mason seems to have the Ascendancy in the great work."[19] The news surely heartened Jefferson, for he had great respect for Mason, but probably also made him regret even more his own absence from Williamsburg. He decided to draft a constitution to send to the delegates, and by early June he had prepared three versions. Together, they make clear Jefferson's evolving ideas about proper governance.

Each of the three versions began with a long list of grievances against the king for recent actions: suspending colonial legislatures, keeping standing armies in the colonies, taxing colonists without their consent, transporting people to England for trial, closing ports, and so on.[20] Then Jefferson outlined his plan for a new government in Virginia—a plan embodying his political philosophy.

His views on specific aspects of government differ slightly across the three versions, but in each he advocated a bicameral legislature, an elected lower house, and an upper senate with members appointed by the lower house. He wanted to broaden the franchise by allowing all (white) males "of full age and sane mind," who either owned a town lot or a minimum of fifty acres of land or had paid taxes for two years, to vote and to hold office. He suggested that those who owned fewer than fifty acres of land be granted unappropriated or forfeited tracts owned by the state to bring them above the threshold.[21] He also proposed that the number of representatives from each county should be proportionate to the number of eligible voters, which would end the overrepresentation of the Tidewater counties. Jefferson's proposed governor, whom he called the administrator, would be a weak executive, appointed by the house for a one-year term (though he could be reappointed three years after the end of each term). Among other limitations, the administrator could not veto legislation or prorogue or dissolve the legislature, and the lower house would appoint his advisory privy council as well as both the treasurer and attorney general.

Jefferson described a legal system comprised of county courts, a general court and high court of chancery, and a court of appeals. The state and its inhabitants could not simply take, but had to purchase, land held by Indians. He proposed that any new territories to the west "shall be free and independent of this colony and of all the world"—that is, Virginia would never have dependent colonies of its own. "No person hereafter coming into this colony shall be held within the same in slavery under any pretext whatever"—thus Jefferson called for a ban on new slave imports. He called as well for easing the process of naturalization for immigrants. Importantly, he made clear his stance on the state's role in religion, writing, "All persons shall have full and free liberty of religious opinion; nor shall any be compelled to frequent or maintain any religious institution."

The third version of the document provided, "None of these fundamental laws and principles of government shall be repealed or altered, but by the personal consent of the people on summons to meet in their respective counties on one and the same day by an act of Legislature to be passed for every special occasion." Had Jefferson's draft been accepted, it would have been the most progressive constitution in the world.[22]

The grounding of political authority in the people, the broadening of the franchise to include practically every adult white male, the creation of a strong lower house and a weak executive, the ending of the importation of slaves, the proposal to disestablish the Anglican Church and provide for complete religious freedom—these were ideas far in advance of public opinion. Jefferson entrusted a copy of the third version to George Wythe on June 13 to take to the Williamsburg convention. Yet by the time Wythe arrived, the constitutional committee had made much progress on its own. And, in any event, its members would not have accepted Jefferson's version; much of it was simply far too radical.[23]

Jefferson would soon find that his list of the grievances against the king was about the only passage accepted almost verbatim; his plan for the courts was largely incorporated too. The final constitution was much more conservative than his, although more democratic than might have been expected.

BEFORE HE LEARNED the fate of his proposals, Jefferson had reason to be hopeful. On June 6, the *Pennsylvania Evening Post* published a truly remarkable declaration of rights authored primarily by Mason in late May.[24] Mason originally introduced ten "rights," and the committee added eight more (though Mason himself seems to have written five of these). One or more members apparently leaked the draft, which was then published in Philadelphia and elsewhere.[25] The committee intended this declaration of rights to be the foreword to the Virginia constitution, but because the latter was not completed and approved until much later, on June 29, the declaration has often been understood as a stand-alone document.[26]

Jefferson was much impressed by what became known as the Virginia Declaration of Rights. The first "right" resonated strongly with his views: "That all men are born equally free and independent, and have certain inherent natural Rights, of which they cannot, by any compact, deprive or divest their posterity; among which are, the enjoyment of life and liberty, with the means of acquiring and possessing property, and pursuing and obtaining happiness and safety."[27] Clearly, these words stuck in his mind, although the ideas were not new to him. (Actually the full Williamsburg convention later weakened the potential antislavery implications of this first "right" in its final version.[28]) Mason's second "right" emphatically insisted that "all power is vested in, and consequently derived from, the people," a concept Jefferson had earlier asserted in his *A Summary View*. The third "right," showing the influence of John Locke, stated, "That government is, or ought to be, instituted for the common benefit, protection, and security of the people, nation, or community . . . and that whenever any government shall be found inadequate or contrary to these purposes, a majority of the community hath an indubitable, unalienable, indefeasible right, to reform, alter, or abolish it."[29] Jefferson was convinced that what Locke would have called a right to revolution was an inherent right of Virginians. Overall, he fully accepted the first three rights in the document.

The other rights were exactly those that Jefferson believed the king had infringed upon. Perhaps most important to him was the ninth "right," though he believed the declaration did not go nearly far enough: "That as Religion, or the Duty which we owe to our divine and omnipotent Creator, and the Manner of discharging it, can be governed only by Reason and Conviction, not by Force or Violence; and therefore that all Men shou'd enjoy the fullest Toleration in the Exercise of Religion, according to the Dictates of Conscience, unpunished and unrestrained by the Magistrate."[30] Jefferson agreed that reason and conviction should govern one's religious opinions, but he wanted complete religious freedom, not mere toleration. The full Virginia convention did strengthen the concept, owing to the influence of a young James Madison. In his first participation in a deliberative body, Madison objected to the toleration clause and replaced the existing language following "all men" with "are entitled to the free exercise of religion."[31] In Madison, Jefferson found a like-minded intellectual and political partner. Their friendship and collaboration would last five decades, though no issue they addressed together would be more important than this first, concerning religious freedom in Virginia.

But Jefferson and Madison's partnership still lay in the future. In June 1776, with his draft constitution on its way to Williamsburg and Mason's declaration of rights fresh in his mind, Jefferson turned to the great task set him by the Congress: to draft a declaration that explained and legitimated the colonies' decision to sever their relationship with Britain.

IT IS EASY TO OVERLOOK both how frantically busy Jefferson and the other Philadelphia delegates were and the fact that the colonies were already at war with England. The delegates attended committee meetings in the morning and deliberations of the whole Congress in the afternoon; then, after dinner, they performed more committee work into the evening. Congress was in effect the government for all the colonies, with responsibilities ranging from provisioning the Continental Army to establishing a postal system. The delegates were exhausted and growing testy. Jefferson himself had already served on an astounding thirty-four committees. While trying to find time to write the declaration, he also wrote reports on the disappointing colonial attempt to invade Canada and on the so-called Cedars Cartel, an agreement for the exchange of prisoners.[32] Hanging over the delegates was the threat of a British invasion. By the second week of June, they were aware that a British flotilla of 132 ships was headed for New York City. On July 1—just before beginning to consider the final draft of the declaration—Congress learned that a squadron of fifty-three British ships had arrived off the coast of Charleston.

As if this were not enough to worry Jefferson almost to the point of distraction, he was desperately concerned about the health of his again pregnant wife. Then, on June 30 he wrote Edmund Pendleton that "the situation of my domestic affairs renders it indispensably necessary" that he be relieved and another delegate sent in his place. "The delicacy of the house will not require me to enter minutely into the private causes which render this necessary." Apparently Martha had suffered a miscarriage.[33] Overworked, rushing to meet deadlines, fearful of invasion, and distraught over Martha's health, Jefferson nevertheless managed to sit in his parlor and compose, on a slant-topped writing box, a draft of the Declaration of Independence.

It is possible that the committee members suggested the basic outline of the document. John Adams claimed twenty-six years later that within a couple of days of its appointment, the committee had "proposed the Articles of which the Declaration was to consist."[34] But Jefferson may have already decided, before the committee even formally met, on a three-part structure, involving a brief philosophical preamble or introduction, a list of grievances, and a brief statement of the united colonies' right to join the established nations of Europe as a full-fledged nation-state.[35]

In any event, within several days of starting, Jefferson had produced a draft, which he apparently showed to the other committee members, except for Franklin, who was too ill to attend meetings. The committee made some suggestions (we have no record of the specifics), and after addressing them, Jefferson sent the revised version to Franklin.[36] We do not know what changes Franklin made, if any, though it has been suggested—with no actual proof—that the phrase "self-evident" in the preamble was his. Jefferson submitted the cleaned-up copy, incorporating the suggestions of the committee, to Congress on Friday, June 28. On Tuesday, July 2, in the middle of an oppressive heat wave, congressional consideration got underway. Acting together, Congress made thirty-nine changes, mainly excisions, shortening the document by a little over a quarter. Even so, a full 90 percent of the words in the final Declaration of Independence were Jefferson's. He is rightly credited as its author.

How DID JEFFERSON approach his task? Whether or not the committee had helped shape the document, he had ready material at hand. Jefferson was a student of political philosophy and legal history, and for him, as for many of the delegates, the basic ideas of John Locke, Algernon Sidney, John Trenchard and Thomas Gordon (authors of the essays in *Cato's Letters*), and other writers were ingrained in his mind.[37] Jefferson had effectively rehearsed the application of these ideas to the American situation in his *A Summary View* and, more recently, in his proposed constitution for Virginia. And fresh in his memory were the newspaper reports of the Virginia Declaration of Rights. Given this background, Jefferson fashioned in very short order the document the committee approved and, after revisions, the Congress accepted on July 4 as the Declaration of Independence.

The first three clauses of Mason's Virginia Declaration of Rights provided Jefferson with the most proximate inspiration. Jefferson's preamble made more elegant and memorable the content of Mason's clauses: "We hold these truths to be self-evident; that all men are created equal; that they are endowed by their Creator with inherent and unalienable rights; that among these are life, liberty, and the pursuit of happiness." Congress retained almost every word, except for one salutary revision: "inherent and inalienable" became "certain unalienable." Various reprintings of the declaration have ended the sentence with the word "happiness." Jefferson had not done so; he did not intend his text to limit the self-evident truths in this way. To him, the clauses that followed were also self-evident: that governments derive their powers from the consent of the people, that governments are instituted to promote the people's basic rights, and that, if

Draft of first page of the Declaration of Independence, in Jefferson's hand.

Source: Manuscript Collection, Library of Congress. Used by permission.

they fail to do so, the people have the right to alter or abolish them. With consummate artistry, Jefferson summarized years of thinking and political philosophizing in about two hundred words. The whole is organized as a rational argument. In view of the unalienable rights of the people and the fact that governments are supposed to promote those rights, it logically follows that when governments do not, they deserve to be changed.[38]

In the tradition of the 1689 Declaration of Rights, Jefferson next turned to a lengthy enumeration of the injustices the colonies had suffered and now justified the people's right to reject British governance. Jefferson understood that the colonies, founded at different times, for different purposes, and now boasting different economies and religions, nevertheless constituted a unitary "people." He drew on his proposed draft of the Virginia constitution, rearranging and adding to the list of grievances, which he offered in order of ascending degree of egregiousness. Jefferson wrote in essence as a lawyer, marshalling the best evidence to advance his purpose to a jury made up of a "candid world." The final charges were, in order, plundering the coasts, burning towns (Falmouth, Maine; Charlestown, Massachusetts; Norfolk, Virginia), sending foreign mercenaries to America, and inciting both slaves and Indians against the colonists.

The last drew a long harangue from Jefferson that unfairly blamed the king for the spread of slavery into the colonies. Jefferson labeled the transportation of human beings from Africa to the colonies a "cruel war against human nature itself, violating . . . [the] most sacred rights of life & liberty in the persons of a distant people."[39] Jefferson assumed that slaves—African men and women—had rights identical to those of the rest of the American people. Moreover, when he later referred in this passage to enslaved men and women using the generic word "men," he clearly meant both genders, as he did in writing earlier that all "men" are created equal. He was referring to the equal possession of inherent rights, not equality of any other kind.

In his autobiography Jefferson complained that Congress struck the section on slavery "in complaisance to South Carolina and Georgia" and also in deference to some northern colonies involved in the slave trade.[40] But Congress might have removed the passage in recognition of the contradiction inherent in slaveholding colonies clamoring for liberty for themselves while ignoring the plight of their bondspeople, not to mention the colonists' role in slavery's rise and continuance. This was the third rejection, by either a court or a deliberative body, of Jefferson's language attacking the slave trade or slavery itself as a violation of the natural rights of man. Had the passage on slavery remained, it could have supported Jefferson's later attempts to promote abolition and the colonization or re-settlement of the freed people.[41]

Jefferson had also added a complaint about the British people, pointing out that the colonists had addressed them again and again by way of petitioning Parliament to repeal unfair and unjust legislation, but to no effect. While the drafting committee left most of Jefferson's language intact, Congress almost completely eliminated this complaint, though it added several phrases that did strengthen one charge against the king: that he had sent "large Armies of foreign Mercenaries" to suppress the Americans.

John Adams, the colonies' foremost constitutionalist, preferred Jefferson's original draft and felt that Congress "obliterated some of the best of it."[42] Benjamin Franklin, commiserating with Jefferson over the agonies of seeing one's writing heavily edited, related a humorous story about a hatter whose design for a sign to advertise his business underwent drastic changes, with all the text cut, leaving only an image of a hat. Franklin explained that he had "made it a rule, whenever in my power, to avoid becoming the draughtsman of papers to be reviewed by a public body."[43] Most scholars, however, agree that the congressional edits improved the Declaration of Independence.

In addressing the conclusion of Jefferson's draft, Congress added new language, essentially reprinting the congressional resolution of July 2 declaring the colonies absolved of the former allegiance to Britain. The delegates—on the whole more explicitly religious than Jefferson was at this time—also added "appealing to the supreme judge of the world" to the first sentence of the last paragraph and "with a firm reliance on the protection of divine providence" to the final sentence, resulting in a total of four references to God in the document. The first, in Jefferson's language, referred to "Nature's God" and the second to the unalienable rights with which people were "endowed by their Creator." The last insertion concerning divine providence was the only change to the soaring language at the end of Jefferson's masterwork: "And for the support of this declaration, with a firm reliance on the protection of divine providence, we mutually pledge to each other our lives, our fortunes, and our sacred honor."[44]

THUS THE DECLARATION OF INDEPENDENCE was neither entirely the work of one person, nor primarily a committee project, nor the result of congressional deliberation—it was the result of all these, with Jefferson playing an essential role; the document's basic argumentative strategy and literary elegance show his hand. It represented a remarkable synthesis of the delegates' and much of the public's views. No delegate sought originality of thought. Rather, as Jefferson wrote more than a half century later, "the object" was "not to find out new principles, or new arguments . . . but to place before mankind the common sense of the subject. . . . it was intended to be an expression of the American mind, and to give to that expression the proper tone and spirit called for by the occasion. All its authority rests then on the harmonizing sentiments of the day."[45]

Once adopted by Congress on July 4, the Declaration of Independence was quickly printed in Philadelphia and reprinted in newspapers throughout the colonies. It was read out loud in public spaces, General George Washington proclaimed it to the army, and it was soon published in England and France. But its fame was not immediate, and its importance was not instantly recognized. In the summer of 1776, the revolution that the declaration announced appeared unlikely to succeed against the military power of Britain. The afternoon following its adoption, Jefferson went to a store on Second Street to pay for a thermometer he must have selected and taken with him a day or so before. Several times on July 4, he recorded the temperature, noting the day's high at 1:00 p.m.: seventy-six degrees.[46]

6

Revolutionary Lawmaker

ONE MIGHT IMAGINE that Jefferson experienced the fortnight surrounding July 4, 1776, as a moment of triumph, but he did not. It had been excruciating for him to sit in Congress while his draft was edited, and there was no immediate recognition of the historical nature of his and the Congress's accomplishment. Personal concerns depressed him even more. By the end of June, he knew that his wife was gravely ill, apparently from a miscarriage or difficult delivery, and was with her sister and brother-in-law, the Eppeses, at the Forest. Eager to return to her, Jefferson had asked his alternate to the Virginia convention, Dr. George Gilmer, to implore that body not to reelect him. Jefferson subsequently learned in a letter from Edmund Randolph that although unable to attend the convention, Gilmer had sent Randolph a memo expressing Jefferson's desire. But the convention—perhaps doubting the authenticity of the request—reelected Jefferson anyway in late June.

Jefferson quickly sent Edmund Pendleton, president of the Virginia convention, a plea that a substitute replace him because, as he delicately put it, his wife's illness made it essential that he be relieved from duty in Philadelphia.[1] The Virginia delegation was already down two members, and Richard Henry Lee was absent, so Jefferson was needed for a quorum. Jefferson could only impatiently await Lee's return. On July 23 he wrote in distress to his brother-in-law at the Forest that he had "received no letter this week, which lays me under great anxiety."[2] Finally he sent Lee a cry for relief: "For god's sake, for your country's sake, and for my sake, come. I receive by every post such accounts of the state of Mrs. Jefferson's health, that it will be impossible for me to disappoint her expectation of seeing me at the time I have promised, . . . I pray you to come. I am under a sacred obligation to go home."[3] Still, Lee did not arrive promptly in

Philadelphia; Jefferson, though almost beside himself with worry, nevertheless found the composure to continue his work as a delegate. He had an ability to compartmentalize his personal life, to a degree, and therefore to concentrate on his public duties.

During these harrowing days he completed work on a congressional committee that developed a set of procedures for the Congress itself. He would later expand on these efforts to adapt them to the needs of the US Congress.[4] He handled requests from Virginia as well. One was that the Congress mediate a dispute between Virginia and Pennsylvania over border issues; another was for a designer for a new state seal. He heard concerns about conflicts with Indians in the West and listened to a constant stream of issues regarding the military situation, about which Jefferson had little expertise.[5] In this earliest phase of the revolution, military conflict was confined to the Northeast. Meanwhile Pendleton was trying to get him to leave the Congress and return to Virginia to take an important judicial post and to "exercise Your talents for the nurture of Our new Constitution."[6]

But Jefferson was trapped in Philadelphia; the work of Congress continued to press upon him. He, John Adams, and Benjamin Franklin struggled in vain with an artist in Philadelphia to develop a prototype for the seal of the new nation and ended up agreeing on only two mottos, "E Pluribus Unum" and "Rebellion to Tyrants Is Obedience to God." The design the artist suggested was far too elaborate. Jefferson's ideas probably did not help. He proposed that one side show the children of Israel wandering in the wilderness, led by a cloud by day and a pillar of fire by night; on the reverse, the images of Hengest and Horsa, "the Saxon chiefs," in Adams's words, "from whom we claim the Honour of being descended and whose Political Principles and Form of Government we have assumed."[7] Jefferson also spent a large amount of time calculating the value, in gold and silver, of foreign coins circulating in the colonies. This endeavor resulted in his helping draft a report describing stable values for the different currencies.[8]

Finally Richard Henry Lee arrived in Philadelphia, and after settling up his accounts in the city, a hugely relieved Jefferson resigned from Congress on September 2, left Philadelphia the very next day, and rushed back to Monticello, arriving six days later.[9] He and Martha must have been overjoyed by the long-delayed reunion. And Jefferson was soon back at work on Monticello: he contracted with a bricklayer and began to purchase building materials. A few weeks after his return, he made arrangements to go to Williamsburg and assume his duties, on October 7, in the new state government. George Wythe, serving in the Congress in Philadelphia, offered his Williamsburg home to Jefferson and his family. (Wythe returned to Williamsburg in early December; Jefferson leased another house for the remainder of the session.) For the next three years, as the revolution proceeded through both major setbacks and victories but mainly bypassed Virginia, Jefferson alternated primarily between Monticello and Williamsburg, focusing largely on what he saw as the failures of the existing state constitution. His goal, as he later described it, was the eradication "of every fibre . . . of antient or future aristocracy."[10] These years as constitutional reformer would be among the most important of Jefferson's career.

WHEN THE JEFFERSONS arrived in Williamsburg, awaiting them was word of an exciting appointment. From Philadelphia John Hancock had sent a letter containing a copy of a resolution, passed by Congress on September 26, appointing Jefferson to serve, along with Silas Deane and Benjamin Franklin, as a commissioner to France. Their mission would be outlined later on. In his cover letter, Hancock, referring to this "most important and honourable" appointment, simply assumed that Jefferson would "render [the nation] the great Services which she so fondly expects from you on this Occasion." Richard Henry Lee had written a separate letter stating that in his "judgement, the most eminent services that the greatest of her sons can do America will not more essentially serve her and honor themselves, than a successful negotiation with France."[11] Jefferson greatly admired Franklin, and the opportunity to go to Paris, famed for its architecture, intellectual scene, music, art, food, and wine, must have appealed extremely. And yet, there was important business to attend to in Williamsburg, and—more important—with her delicate health, his wife simply could not travel across the ocean. After three agonizing days of consideration, Jefferson felt compelled to decline the coveted appointment.[12]

He then turned to the task of designing a new government for his beloved state. Several months before, he had begun a correspondence with Pendleton over the matter, and although Jefferson's program was longer and more radical than Pendleton's conservative agenda, their debate was friendly. Jefferson, for example, explained why he believed the members of House of Delegates (the former House of Burgesses), rather than voters, should elect the new senate. Jefferson stated that he aimed to "get the wisest men chosen, and to make them perfectly independent." In his experience direct election would prevent that from happening. The argument revealed that Jefferson's fears of unrestrained popular sentiment leavened his commitment to democracy. "I have ever observed that a choice by the people themselves is not generally distinguished for it's wisdom. This first secretion from them is usually crude and heterogeneous. But give to those so chosen by the people a second choice themselves, and they generally will chuse wise men." He went on to explain that he did not think those selected as senators needed to "possess distinguished property." As he wrote, "My observations do not enable me to say I think integrity the characteristic of wealth. In general I beleive the decisions of the people, in a body, will be more honest and more disinterested than those of wealthy men."[13]

The House of Delegates that Jefferson entered that October largely comprised the same men who had formed the convention that had drafted the new state constitution, with one important exception: Patrick Henry, who had been elected governor. For all his talents, Henry was not an adept legislator, a job that often required a capacity for legal research and always demanded careful attention to language, as well as the ability to collaborate and compromise. Unlike Henry, Jefferson possessed these skills and qualities. Deeply learned in the law and a gifted researcher, he was a master of precise language, effortlessly pleasant and soft-spoken, tolerant of opposing viewpoints, and extraordinarily hardworking. He was, in some respects, a born legislator.

Jefferson came to the House of Delegates with a wide-ranging project in mind: revising the laws of the state. He quickly became a legislative force. He did best in committees, not on the floor, and learned to identify like-minded colleagues—Wythe, George Mason, and, later, James Madison—and work with them to achieve his purposes. While many of Jefferson's ideas were way ahead of his time, he never had the unrelenting demeanor of a radical. Rather, as befit the gentlemanly ideal of the time, he was polite almost to a fault.[14]

Jefferson's first big moment in the House came on October 12, 1776, when it gave him permission to draft two bills, one to abolish entail and the other to produce a general revision of the laws of the state. Two days later Jefferson submitted a bill that would end the medieval concept of entail, which maintained property holdings by limiting inheritance to the owner's lineal descendants or to a particular class of them.[15] Jefferson later added a bill outlawing primogeniture (together with entail, a key foundation of the aristocratic order), but the practice would not come to an end in Virginia until 1785, when James Madison pushed through legislation to that effect; Jefferson was then in Paris serving as the US minister to France.

The legislature passed Jefferson's bill for the overall revision of the state's laws on October 26, and on November 4 it appointed a committee of five "to repeal, amend, or revise the laws in force, to introduce others, and then to report the whole for the action of the legislature."[16] The committee members were Jefferson, Wythe, Pendleton, Mason, and Thomas Ludwell Lee. The group first met in early January 1777, deciding then to repeal laws obviously out-of-date or no longer applicable and to leave the rest. Soon thereafter Lee became ill and died, and Mason, protesting that he was insufficiently learned in the law, resigned from the committee, leaving most of the work to Jefferson, Pendleton, and Wythe, with Jefferson essentially assuming responsibility for those portions assigned to Lee and Mason.

The group delivered its complete body of work to the House of Delegates on June 18, 1779, as ninety folio pages covering 126 proposed acts. The delegates would take a decade to consider and act on all of them, and much of what they eventually accepted passed under the direction of Madison. (As before, many of Jefferson's proposed revisions were simply more advanced and progressive than the members of the House, and the public they represented, could accept.)

Jefferson himself immediately began pursuing issues of particular importance to him, all of them represented in the broad bill of revision. He wanted, for instance, to provide for the democratic disposition of western lands and to ease and shorten the naturalization process, since he welcomed immigrants who would contribute intellectually to their new nation.[17] In 1779 Jefferson and like-minded delegates managed to pass a bill establishing a state land office and allowing settlers to obtain titles to up to four hundred acres at very low cost, but Jefferson's original hope to provide free land to immigrants and native settlers was voted down.

Settling the West with lower- and middle-class whites was essential to Jefferson's larger goal of creating a nation of landholding white farmers. By wealth and education Jefferson was effectively an aristocrat on the American stage, but no other Founder was so ideologically supportive of a democratic society. Sturdy farmers, independent on their own land, sufficiently educated to know their rights and needs, and possessed of the right to vote, were—in Jefferson's mind—the surest guarantee of the liberties of the people and freedom of the nation. But still, Jefferson restricted his view of citizenship to whites only. Though opposed to slavery, he could not imagine blacks as citizens participating in the governance of the American nation. Later he would suggest colonizing emancipated blacks, preferably in the Caribbean, where as a separate people they could develop their own independent nation.

Just as important as settling the West was the provision of free public education for the masses. Jefferson desired a system that could identify and promote "natural geniuses," which in turn would create a true meritocracy independent of family status and wealth. The result was a bill to support the "more general diffusion of knowledge." Jefferson wrote the bill, whose self-justification explained that "the most effectual means of preventing" the perversion of the government into tyranny was to "illuminate, as far as practicable, the mind of the people at large."[18] Jefferson called for a state-supported system of universal education for all white male and female children for three years. The best male students would then go on to more advanced schools for three to seven years. His proposed system would also, after a rigorous winnowing process, eventually pay for ten male students each year to attend the College of William & Mary. In Jefferson's mind, this system would provide free elementary schooling for the masses and elevate ten natural geniuses a year to receive the education necessary to become state leaders.[19] He presented this bill to the House of Delegates in 1778 and again in 1780, but it took no action.

Jefferson drew up another, associated bill intended to transform the College of William & Mary from an Anglican institution into a secular, state-supported university, governed by a board with members appointed by the General Assembly, not the church. While he hoped to stabilize and increase the college's funding, he wanted more than anything to modernize and secularize its curriculum.[20] As might be expected, nothing came of this proposed bill, but in 1779, after Jefferson became governor and hence a member of the college's board, he pushed through several reforms that closely approximated the curricular changes he sought.

Another major ambition of Jefferson's on his arrival in the House of Delegates was the reform of the penal code. In eighteenth-century Virginia, dozens of crimes called for capital punishment. Jefferson had read, in the original Italian, jurist Cesare Baccaria's famous work on penal reform, titled *On Crimes and Punishments* and published in 1764. The book solidified his belief that the death penalty was inappropriate for most crimes and that punishment should not only be proportionate to the offense committed but strive both to deter and to reform. Jefferson's draft bill on punishment called for replacing capital punishment with hard labor.[21] This was far more lenient than the existing system, which, if conviction did not impose the death penalty, called for whipping, pillorying, branding, and so forth. Yet other sections of the bill were shockingly retrograde, as even Jefferson recognized when he drafted them, noting, "This needs reconsideration."[22] Later, in 1796, Virginia's legislature passed a reform of criminal punishments and authorized construction of a penitentiary.

The general revision of the laws also contained a bill, written by Jefferson, that would prevent the future importation of slaves into the state. At the time, there already existed in Virginia a statute preventing the importation of slaves (except those previously purchased by residents of the state who had traveled with their owners outside Virginia), which was one of the first outright bans in the world.[23] The bill Jefferson wrote mostly summarized existing law but gave it teeth by adding that slaves imported in the future would be free after one year and requiring slaves subsequently manumitted by their owners to leave the state after one year.[24] In his 1821 autobiography Jefferson claimed that he had intended, once the General Assembly brought up this bill, to offer amendments that provided for a general emancipation tied to colonization. No such amendment was presented, however; as Jefferson put it, "It was found that the public mind would not yet bear the proposition."[25] The bill, with some revisions, was put forward by Madison in late 1785 and passed; of course, it included no language about general emancipation.

Jefferson also authored a series of five bills to establish and organize five different courts of law. When the General Assembly finally acted on the court issues in 1792, it watered down every reformist aspect of Jefferson's plans.[26] Meanwhile his 1776 proposal to move the state capital from Williamsburg to Richmond failed, perhaps because the war still seemed distant. In May 1779, he would present almost exactly the same bill, and this time—with the war having shifted southward—it passed on the grounds that the new location was nearer the center of the state and would be easier to defend against a possible invasion.[27]

THE BILL THAT JEFFERSON in retrospect considered both the most difficult to win approval for and the most important dealt with a concern long dear to him: religious freedom. Its ultimate passage, in 1786, proved one of the signal accomplishments of his life. A number of factors converged to give this issue special significance to him. The Anglican Church had for decades been established in Virginia, supported by taxes, serving purposes both religious and civil (caring for the county poor, for example). Only marriages by its offices were considered official, and it also had the authority to issue harsh punishments for heresy, denial of the Trinity, and blasphemy. At the least, occasional attendance at its services was compulsory, and Catholics and members of other faiths suffered civil disabilities. These old laws had been mostly ignored for years, but as Jefferson understood, attitudes toward enforcement could change, and he believed that a person's religious freedom should not depend on the whims of the age. Jefferson dedicated himself to eliminating the potential for abuse arising from Virginia laws concerning religious belief and practice.

The religious establishment did not hesitate to defend its position with zeal. The recent growth in the number of dissenters in Virginia, particularly Baptists, had resulted in their increased persecution; their religious services were disrupted and their ministers thrown in jail. As Madison wrote to a college friend in 1774, describing the local situation, "That diabolical Hell conceived principle of persecution rages among some and to their eternal Infamy the Clergy can furnish their Quota of Imps for such business. This vexes me the most of any thing whatever. . . . There are at this [time?] in the adjacent County not less than 5 or 6 well meaning men in close Goal [jail] for publishing their religious Sentiments."[28] Over the course of the next several years, dissenters—again, especially Baptists—sent scores of petitions to the legislature protesting their oppression and calling for religious freedom and disestablishment of the Anglican Church. Shortly before November 1776, Jefferson received a petition from dissenters in Albemarle and Amherst Counties, imploring him to call on the House of Delegates "to put every religious Denomination on an equal footing, to be supported by themselves independent one of another." On Christmas Day 1776, he received another petition from the Virginia Association of Baptists.[29]

Altogether many thousands of signatures were offered in support of the principle of religious freedom. The largest petition was the so-called Ten Thousand Name Petition sent by Baptists and calling for removal of the yoke of oppression.[30] As Jefferson wrote in his autobiography, "The first republican legislature which met in 76. was crowded with petitions to abolish this spiritual tyranny. These brought on the severest contests in which I have ever been engaged."[31] The petitions put additional pressure on Jefferson and Madison to address the issue of religious persecution in the state. They wanted to make a reality what the June 12, 1776, Virginia Declaration of Rights had proposed but the state constitution had left out: "That Religion, or the duty which we owe to our Creator, and the manner of discharging it, can be directed only by reason and conviction, not by force or violence; and, therefore, all men are equally entitled to the free exercise of religion, according to the dictates of conscience."[32]

Though the dissenters brought the matter to a head, Jefferson had long been convinced of the necessity of religious freedom as a right, not a consequence of mere toleration. His proposed constitution for Virginia, drafted in late spring 1776, had included the statement "All persons shall have full and free liberty of religious opinion; nor shall any be compelled to frequent or maintain any religious institution."[33] Just before completing the draft he must have read a pamphlet by an eminent dissenting minister from England, Richard Price, titled *Observations on the Nature of Civil Liberty* . . . , which was published in 1776 in London and quickly reprinted in America. Price was an old friend of Benjamin Franklin, who approved of Price's "rational Christianity"; Joseph Priestley, the famed chemist committed to reforming Christianity, had sent Price's newest pamphlet to Franklin in February.[34] Franklin probably discussed the work, and also its author, with Jefferson. We do know that on July 29 Jefferson sent a copy to Richard Henry Lee.

Price addressed a number of topics in his lengthy pamphlet, and his comments about religious freedom must have caught Jefferson's eye. In one of his most striking passages, Price wrote, "RELIGIOUS LIBERTY signifies the power of exercising, without molestation, that mode of religion which we think best; or of making the decisions of our own consciences respecting religious truth, the rule of our conduct, and not any of the decisions of our fellow-men."[35] These words resonated with Jefferson's prior thinking on the matter.

Jefferson's papers for 1776 also contain detailed but undated notes and quotations from John Locke's "A Letter Concerning Toleration" (1689), which he recorded as he prepared to defend his bill for religious freedom. His notes contain such paraphrases of Locke as "no man has *power* to let another prescribe his faith" and "[a church] is a *voluntary* society of men."[36] Jefferson likewise took notes on the history of the establishment in England, the acts of Parliament dealing with religion, and the concepts of episcopacy and heresy. From his reading in early Saxon history he determined that at that time, only voluntary contributions, not taxes, supported the church. He was preparing for a major battle in the Virginia legislature.[37]

Why did Jefferson invest this issue with such urgency? He certainly understood that his unorthodox ideas about religion—for example, his disbelief in the Trinity and miracles and his refusal to accept Jesus as divine—put him at risk, but he probably had little or no fear of actual punishment. In the process of thinking these matters through, he may have become somewhat more respectful of traditional Christianity—and less enamored of the ancient philosophers—by the mid-1770s. He had experienced a number of deaths of family and friends over the previous years: his favorite sister, his closest friend, his mother, an infant daughter (a newborn son would die in June 1777 even before he was named). Such events often cause people to turn to the consolations of religion and the hope for reunification with loved ones in a life after death.[38] Both Richard Price and John Locke, from whom Jefferson borrowed much, were devout Christians as well as supporters of religious freedom, and their larger body of writings led him to rethink some of his earlier positions.

Indeed, by late 1776, Jefferson's recent references to God and the creator in public documents have a more reverential tone than his instrumental invocation of religion in the May 1774 resolution calling for a day of fasting and prayer in Virginia, which, he frankly recalled, he and his fellow burgesses had "cooked up" to generate support among the people for anti-British politics.[39] Targeting a different audience in his *A Summary View* a few months later, Jefferson wrote, "The god who gave us life, gave us liberty at the same time." Then, in his June 1775 draft of the "Declaration of the Causes and Necessity of Taking Up Arms," he had written, "We do then most solemnly, before god and the world declare . . . we will exert . . . all those powers which our creator hath given us, to preserve that liberty which he committed to us." And in the Declaration of Independence, of course, he referred to the "Creator" and "nature's god."[40] He seems to have grown less dismissive of religion.

Even if he had moderated his views on the established religion of this time, Jefferson's support for religious freedom was, fundamentally, a matter of principle. On October 11, 1776, he was named to a nineteen-member legislative committee on religion, to which all the petitions calling for disestablishment were referred; James Madison joined the committee several days later. Various controversies led the legislature to suspend the committee on November 9 and turn the matter over to the entire House of Delegates, which, on November 19, approved a series of resolutions, apparently written by Jefferson, repealing all legislation setting forth punishments for heresy, disavowal of the Trinity, blasphemy, and nonattendance; they also ended the taxation of religious dissenters and discontinued the church tax completely. Then on November 30—while Jefferson was briefly absent—the House rescinded all these resolutions except the one exempting the tax on dissenters.

Jefferson hurried back and, with Mason's help, got new resolutions passed that repealed all existing laws requiring religious conformity but left the Anglican Church as the established church of the state.[41] During the debates, Jefferson, who seldom gave speeches in the House, addressed his colleagues with great passion. The notes he made for this occasion outline his argument. He sketched the history of Parliamentary support of the church in England, discussed the issue of heresy, traced the long history of religious oppression in Europe, and stated, "Most men imagine that persecution is unknown to our laws." He then referred to the existing oppression, though admitted that persecution almost never meant death. "Happily," he said, "the Spirit of the times is in favor of the rights of Conscience." Yet conscience was "tender," and its free exercise should not rest on the attitudes of the moment.

He continued in the same vein, saying that men could not "surrender" their religious rights; that they are "answerable only to God"; that religion is an "*unalienable* right"; that "God requires everyone to act according to their *Belief*, that Belief was founded on evidence offered to . . . [the] mind." If the civil laws required certain beliefs, then "Religion is no longer *free*." As he put it, "Coercion was exercised by *fallible men*." He went on to argue that putting all denominations on an equal footing would strengthen religion, because the ministers would thus have to be "Industrious. Exemplary." He insisted that religion would not decline without tax support because—here he quoted scripture—"the Gates of Hell shall not prevail [against the church]." He stated forthrightly, "Uniformity was no more necessary in *Religion* than in *Philosophy*." In fact, religious diversity was advantageous to society because "difference in Religious opinion supplies the place of a *Censor Morum* [censor of morals]."[42] Nearly every phrase of Jefferson's remarks either looked back to his earlier writings or forward to his proposed bill for establishing full religious freedom.

Jefferson apparently wrote the bill in early 1777 but decided not to present it to the legislature. At that time, the issue of complete disestablishment was tangled up with concern over the established church's traditional role in caring for orphans, the destitute, and so on. How would these semigovernmental functions be handled if not by the church, utilizing tax revenues and funds earned from glebe lands? The issue became messier when proposals arose for a general tax on all citizens, with the revenues distributed proportionately to the various denominations in the state. Even some dissenters who had previously opposed a tax to support the Anglican Church accepted the principle of a state religious tax if the monies were distributed to the churches of taxpayers' choice. Patrick Henry, as governor, also supported the general assessment. Still, no individual believer would be able to direct his contributions to whichever particular congregation or preacher he chose.

Given the contentious nature of these issues, Jefferson delayed his bill until 1779, when it was brought to the House on June 12. But by that time he no longer could rely on Madison's support, since the latter had not won reelection in 1777.[43] Nor could he advocate for it in the House himself, since he was elected governor on June 1. Not until Madison returned to the House (from the Continental Congress) in 1784 did the bill gain traction. After a long process of give-and-take—with Jefferson in Paris serving as the American minister to France—Madison finally won its passage on January 16, 1786.[44] The resulting Virginia Statute for Religious Freedom was one of the most important intellectual and political victories of the entire revolutionary era and one of three accomplishments Jefferson wanted memorialized on his tombstone.

As with a number of his seminal written documents, Jefferson began his "bill for establishing religious freedom" with an exquisitely crafted philosophical preamble seven times longer than the act itself. It is a powerful manifesto in support of intellectual freedom in general, not merely freedom of religion. It begins by stating that whereas "Almighty God hath created the mind free . . . all attempts to influence it by temporal punishments, or burthens, or by civil incapacitations . . . are a departure from the plan of the holy author of our religion . . . [who chose] to extend it by its influence on reason alone."[45] The bill then spoke of the oppressive actions of "fallible and uninspired men . . . [who] hath established and maintained false religions over the greatest part of the world." It condemned efforts to "compel a man to furnish contributions of money for the propagation of opinions which he disbelieves and abhors" as "sinful and tyrannical," even in the form of a general assessment.[46] Jefferson made clear that a person's religious beliefs should not bring down adverse political consequences: "our civil rights have no dependance on our religious opinions, any more than on our opinions in physics or geometry." Hence a would-be politician need not subscribe to a specific form of religion. In sum, government should remain separate from religion: "to suffer the civil magistrate to intrude his powers into the field of opinion and to restrain the profession or propagation of principles on supposition of their ill tendency is a dangerous fallacy, which at once destroys all religious liberty." On the contrary, "truth is great and will prevail if left to herself; . . . she is the proper and sufficient antagonist to error . . . errors ceasing to be dangerous when it is permitted freely to contradict them."[47]

After the extensive preamble, the bill as enacted stated, "No man shall be compelled to frequent or support any religious worship, place, or ministry whatsoever, nor shall be enforced, restrained, molested, or burthened in his body or goods, nor shall otherwise suffer, on account of his religious opinions or belief; but that all men shall be free to profess, and by argument to maintain, their opinions in matters of religion, and that the same shall in no wise diminish, enlarge, or affect their civil capacities."[48] Here Jefferson quite explicitly meant that Jews, Muslims, Hindus, and even "infidels" were not to be discriminated against and had the full rights of citizenship—even though he was elsewhere critical, for example, of actual Muslim beliefs. He understood that religious freedom must encompass unpopular creeds.[49] Jefferson also knew, since this was to be a legislative statute, that subsequent legislatures might be tempted to change it. To prevent that possibility, the bill closed by claiming that "the rights hereby asserted are of the natural rights of mankind, and that if any act shall be hereafter passed to repeal the present or to narrow its operation, such act will be an infringement of natural right."[50] Virginia was the first state in the young nation to pass such a bill.

Jefferson, in Paris, was thrilled to learn by way of a letter Madison wrote on January 22, 1786, that the bill had passed both chambers of the General Assembly.[51] Between 1776 and 1778, he had authored the Declaration of Independence, the Virginia Statute for Religious Freedom, a bill to promote the "general diffusion of knowledge," and a partner bill to the last that revised the charter of the College of William & Mary. The latter two bills together anticipated Jefferson's later work in establishing the University of Virginia in 1819. In the space of three years, in short, he had either written the documents or proposed the ideas that, at the end of his life, he considered his greatest accomplishments.

DURING HIS TIME in the Virginia legislature, Jefferson did most of his research and drafting in the comfort of his home at Monticello. His was the only library in the state that would have facilitated the great intellectual projects he labored on. Jefferson's memorandum book gives some insight into these years at his mountaintop retreat. His political activity aside, his records are sprinkled with notations related to the ongoing construction of Monticello. The house was approaching completion, although the Jeffersons still spent time at Elk Hill and the Forest. Martha must have enjoyed the temporary respite from the seemingly eternal construction. As always Jefferson's memorandum books recorded purchases of books and household supplies.[52] His Garden Book, meanwhile, shows renewed attention to his extensive variety of vegetables and the grafting of a wide assortment of fruit trees. It also reveals his plans for improving the roundabout walkway completed in 1772 and for new fencing, as well as providing general comments about livestock.[53] On many evenings, Jefferson played his violin accompanied by Martha at her keyboard, and no doubt their voices often blended in song;[54] Jefferson wrote in 1778 that music was "the favorite passion of my soul."[55] For her part, Martha was constantly involved in food preparation—the slaughtering of beeves, the butchering of hogs, the brewing of beer—along with chores like making candles and soap. Of course, Martha herself did not actually butcher pigs or make soap; she merely supervised the slaves who did that work.

One major tragedy and one especially happy occasion marked these three years. The former was the death of Jefferson's unnamed son only two weeks after his birth on May 28, 1777. Jefferson was home for most of Martha's next pregnancy, and on the first day of August 1778, she delivered a healthy baby girl, named Mary but called Polly as a child and Maria from adolescence on.[56] The three years from mid-1776 to mid-1779 were among the most pleasant of Jefferson's entire life, and though he was never not busy with his legislative duties, events during this time brought him almost unbroken joy. Despite his political career, Jefferson was a decidedly domestic person.

These years were also marked by war. The Continental Army under the command of George Washington managed to keep the British forces at bay in the north, and the British soon learned that the logistics of waging war thousands of miles away against a dispersed population with no great capital city like London or Paris posed unexpected difficulties. After 1778, the British shifted their efforts to Georgia and the Carolinas. The conflict Jefferson had helped instigate did not touch him directly before 1779, but he kept closely apprised of developments elsewhere in the colonies. Soon enough, the war came to Virginia, and he was called on to serve.

7

The Fight for Independence

W HEN THE WAR FINALLY did arrive in Virginia, it did so in an unusual way. In September 1777 British general John Burgoyne led his army south from Canada, planning to cut a swath through New York and thereby isolate the Northeast from the remainder of the rebelling colonies, but his campaign suffered a major defeat on September 19 at the hands of General Horatio Gates. After several more weeks of skirmishes and maneuvers along the Hudson River, on October 17 Burgoyne surrendered at Saratoga, handing over his arms and nearly 6,000 British troops. Historians often consider the battle a major turning point in the war, because it prompted France to sign treaties of commercial and military assistance with the new American nation. By the terms of the surrender convention at Saratoga, Burgoyne's troops, pledged not to reenter combat, were to remain in Boston. Yet after a year these so-called Convention troops proved not only a severe drain on the scarce food supplies of New England but a tempting target for the British navy. Consequently the American Congress, sitting in Philadelphia, discussed relocating these prisoners of war—who by this time numbered a little over 4,000, owing to escapes and exchanges—southward. When John Harvie, a member of the Congress, offered his land along Ivy Creek, about five miles north of the village of Charlottesville, as a site for their encampment, the decision was made.[1]

Departing in the middle of one of the coldest winters in decades, the troops marched almost seven hundred miles on execrable roads, taunted by rebels along the way, and arrived at their designated camp in mid-January 1779. They found their log cabin barracks only partially constructed and a severe shortage of food.[2] Despite much grumbling over their conditions, the soldiers quickly set about building huts, finishing the cabins, and chinking cracks with Albemarle County clay to keep out the bitter winds. As was customary, the officers were allowed to rent private quarters nearby, within loose supervisory reach of their men; the Virginia state cavalry guarded the captives rather casually, at a distance. Nearly half the prisoners were not British but rather hired German soldiers, called Hessians because a large number of them came from the German state of Hesse-Cassel. The Hessians had little attachment to the British cause, and many of their officers in particular were highly educated, skilled professionals.

As a member of the Virginia House of Delegates, Jefferson had had nothing to do with the decision to move the captured troops to the vicinity of Charlottesville, but he quickly took an interest in this development, because he saw in their relocation a variety of opportunities. Almost immediately he helped several of the officers procure private homes to rent. British general William Phillips (soon joined by his wife) rented Colonel Edward Carter's estate Blenheim, some seven miles south of Monticello, and with Jefferson's help, Major General Friedrich von Riedesel, the German commander, arranged the lease of Colle, the estate of Jefferson's friend Philip Mazzei. Riedesel's colorful wife, Baroness Frekerika Charlotte Louise von Riedesel, also soon joined him, along with three small daughters. As unlikely as it may seem today, it was common until the American Civil War for the spouses of senior officers to move to the theaters of war to be near their husbands. And Jefferson's friendly relations with members of the enemy officer corps was a feature of life then, when aristocratic gentlemen from different nations, even those at war with each other, believed that a common interest in things like science and music transcended political differences.

Within weeks the Convention troops had much improved their barracks, planted gardens and fenced enclosures for chickens, pigs, cows, and sheep, and constructed a church along with a theater for putting on comedies, including some that mocked their American captors. Moreover, they established a commissary and a coffeehouse, and an enterprising local citizen opened several houses of entertainment that offered billiards along with alcohol. The prisoners of war purchased food from nearby farmers and in effect turned their large camp into a reasonably pleasant small city, one actually larger in population than any in the state. Jefferson may well have employed skilled craftsmen from among their number to assist with the ongoing construction at Monticello.[3]

Just when it seemed the troops had overcome their initial poor living conditions, rumors arose that they were to be moved further south and into the interior. Jefferson wrote Governor Patrick Henry offering a justification for keeping them near Charlottesville. The present site, according to Jefferson, was healthy, well watered, and easy to provision. In addition, the soldiers' purchase of goods benefited the local economy. The location was also at a safe distance from possible British incursions along the Chesapeake and its waterways. Jefferson further offered idealistic support for his request: "It is for the benefit of mankind to mitigate the horrors of war as much as possible. The practice therefore of modern nations of treating captive enemies with politeness and generosity is not only delightful in contemplation but really interesting to all the world."[4]

Jefferson had personal reasons for defending the presence of the Convention army. He was an intensely social person who valued intelligent conversation with lively minds, and he found this with more than a few of the British and German officers. He also was a passionate lover of music, and all of a sudden, he unexpectedly found himself in the vicinity of several skilled musicians. Soon Jefferson was regularly inviting them to join his family for evening musicales at Monticello. He became especially fond of a young German officer (and violinist) named Baron de Geismar, and when he found that Geismar desperately desired to return home to see his aged father, Jefferson wrote Richard Henry Lee, a delegate to the Congress in Philadelphia, to attempt to arrange an exchange. Lee reported that there were difficulties involved (mainly raised by prickly British officials), but eventually the exchange occurred. When the thankful Geismar returned to his homeland, he left his sheet music for Jefferson.[5]

Aside from drawing on the prisoners' musical talents, Jefferson also on occasion hired soldiers with various other skills. His account books show him twice paying a tailor for work, and he even employed three of the soldiers' wives for three days' labor weaving lace. He also paid a surgeon who stayed at Colle for attending Mrs. Jefferson.[6] The Jeffersons enjoyed social visits with Generals Phillips and Riedesel and their families.

In the end, the British and Hessian troops were not relocated. Jefferson was. On June 1, 1779, the General Assembly elected him governor of the state, requiring him to move to Williamsburg. In the new year, he would move again, to the new capital of Richmond. He remained on cordial terms with the two enemy generals, arranging in June for both families to travel together to Berkeley Springs, and in July he commissioned a

Williamsburg silversmith to make eight silver spoons for the baroness.[7] In August, when the Jeffersons were back at Monticello for several weeks, General Phillips invited them to join him in his box at the barracks theater to see a play.[8] But these pleasantries soon came to an end.

THE VIRGINIA STATE constitution limited governors to three one-year terms, so Patrick Henry's administration concluded at the end of May 1779. The General Assembly met in recognition of this event, and on June 1, in a close election between Jefferson, John Page, and Thomas Nelson— three friends—narrowly chose Jefferson as governor on the second ballot. The very next day, speaking before the assembly, Jefferson accepted the honor, stating, "In a virtuous and free state, no rewards can be so pleasing to sensible minds, as those which include the approbation of our fellow citizens."[9] Over the next few weeks he received numerous letters of congratulation and well wishes, but he sensed that the future months would be difficult. In a reply to a note from Richard Henry Lee, he wrote, "In a virtuous government, and more especially in times like these, public offices are, what they should be, burthens to those appointed to them which it would be wrong to decline, though foreseen to bring with them intense labor and great private loss."[10] And when he replied to a letter of congratulation from the Hessian general Riedesel, Jefferson quipped, "Condolences would be better suited to the occasion."[11] Though he had been spared the rigors of waging war while at Monticello and even enjoyed the company of the garrisoned enemy troops and officers nearby, he was aware of the manifold difficulties facing the state and the threat of active British forces nearby.

As an assembly member since 1776, Jefferson understood the problems involved in trying to raise troops to send to the Continental Army, then under the overall control of George Washington. He had also experienced the disheartening difficulty of summoning sufficient militia forces from the counties. Moreover, there were dire shortages of every kind of military matériel. While in the assembly, Jefferson had become knowledgeable about the simmering military crisis in the state, which had failed to boil over only because the British forces had initially concentrated on the northern states. In line with the political philosophy behind the movement for independence, the Virginia state constitution had created the office of governor with strictly limited powers.[12] In effect, the governor was little more than the chair of the eight-member Executive Council, and he could not act without the approval of this council. When Jefferson spoke of his actions as governor, he used the plural "we." Ironically, Jefferson had agreed earlier with the weak executive created by the 1776 state constitution, but experience would change his mind.

Securing the Executive Council's approval proved such a cumbersome process that it crippled the governor's ability to respond quickly to the state's needs. When all or most of the members of the council were not together or in easy communication, nothing at all got done. Time and again Jefferson's decision making was delayed for these reasons. This flaw in the instrument of government would be corrected by the assembly, but only after the successful British invasion and the end of Jefferson's second term in mid-1781. The two events together forced not only an election but an emergency reconsideration of the nature of the gubernatorial office that significantly strengthened the power and autonomy of the governor.

ON MAY 8, 1779, just weeks before the end of Governor Henry's term, a flotilla of twenty-eight British ships sailed into the Chesapeake and entered the Virginia Capes, anchoring near Norfolk. The Virginia naval forces were essentially nonexistent, and British marauders wreaked havoc along the multiple waterways of the region, burning ships, military stores, and homes. Owing to poor intelligence, Henry did not call for a full mobilization of militia until May 14, and when troops did begin to assemble, only about a quarter had arms. The British departed of their own accord on May 24, never having intended their incursion as a full-scale invasion. But the call-up revealed how utterly unprepared the state was for war. It was clear to leaders, including Jefferson and Washington, who thought not just locally but continentally, that the state's geography put it at special risk. The Chesapeake and its broad, navigable rivers reached far into the interior, and the flat coastal plains stretched as deep as 150 miles inland before mountainous terrain posed any sort of obstacle to invading forces. Virginia was eminently vulnerable.

The state's leaders, especially Jefferson, were also mindful of the possibility of British-inspired Indian attacks on the western frontier. When Jefferson took office, he saw how crucial supporting the efforts of American forces fighting the British in South Carolina, Georgia, and then North Carolina was to Virginia's safety. If defeated or contained in those states, the British would not be able to march northward and attack Virginia from the south. He also aggressively supported George Rogers Clark in his efforts to take northern and western British strongholds in places like Kaskaskia and Detroit and thereby bring to an end the devastating Indian raids on the Virginia frontier. Jefferson, moreover, wanted to send militia and supplies westward for the same reason.

Jefferson needed to improve fortifications along several of the major rivers as well. He had been the strongest advocate of moving the state capital from defenseless Williamsburg, located between both the James and the York Rivers and hence within easy reach of British naval forces, to Richmond, farther upstream. "Our miserable navy" so dismayed Governor Jefferson that he thought it almost better to destroy existing ships ("burn our whole navy" were his actual words) and start over again—and this at a time when he believed "that our only practicable defence is naval."[13] On top of everything else, Jefferson had to do everything possible to send men, arms, and supplies northward to Washington's Continental forces.[14]

After his election, Jefferson took up residency in the Governor's Palace in Williamsburg, which no doubt brought back memories of happier days in the city in the early 1760s, when he was a student prodigy at the college and enjoyed dinners and musicales at the invitation of the royal governor. But now he led the state in a time of war. His wife and family probably didn't join him until autumn. Meanwhile the paperwork was overwhelming; he spent hours corresponding with local leaders across the state, trying to persuade them to recruit militia, provide supplies, and generally support the government's needs. Three years into a conflict that still had not disrupted their everyday lives, the public was nevertheless war weary. Citizens were loath to pay taxes in support of a war that in many ways was itself a revolt against taxation. The state had already turned to printing money to meet its needs, and the resulting inflation only grew worse as the months went by. A constant refrain among the state's leaders was that greed and personal interest seemed always to trump the needs of the government, leading even the popular Patrick Henry to complain to Jefferson, "Do you remember any Instance, where Tyranny was destroyed and Freedom established on its Ruins among a people possessing so small a Share of Virtue and public Spirit? I recollect none; and this more than the British Arms, makes me fearful of our final success."[15] Jefferson exhausted himself in trying to bolster support for the cause, but to little avail.

VIRGINIA ENDURED ANOTHER invasion scare in late 1779. General Washington wrote Jefferson on December 11 that he had "received advice from New York that a very large embarkation had taken place (said to amount to 8000) and that the fleet containing them was at the Hook on the point of sailing. Their destination *reported* to be for Chesapaek bay, on a combined operation in the 1st place against the French squadron there, and afterwards to attempt the rescue of the Convention troops."[16] The state's Board of War had a month earlier warned that preparations should be made against a naval assault, and on December 22 Jefferson received a report from the governor of Maryland saying much the same thing that Washington's did: a British naval expedition was headed toward the Chesapeake. But neither of these reports rested on concrete evidence. Although Jefferson put precautions into effect, he hesitated to summon the militiamen, who were thoroughly tired of getting called up only to find there was no battle to fight.[17] The assembly was so little concerned that it adjourned on December 24. Had there been an invasion attempt, posterity could blame both Jefferson and the assembly for indecision and incompetence, but in fact the British ships were on their way to Charleston. Jefferson's caution proved justified, a lesson he learned perhaps too well.

The new year brought little relief to the beleaguered state or its governor. In some far western counties (and even in sections of the north and east) citizens were protesting the incessant calls for taxes and men. Resistance to the American cause began to proliferate, to such an extent that Jefferson wrote George Rogers Clark in March, "There is reason to apprehend insurrection among some discontented inhabitants (Tories) on our South-Western frontier. I would have you give assistance on the shortest warning to that quarter, should you be applied to by the militia officers."[18] This problem persisted, however, spreading to additional counties, and proved a source of constant irritation to Jefferson. The shortage of revenue in Virginia, and indeed throughout the colonies, threatened the nation's ability to raise provisions and supply its dwindling forces. Even the usually unperturbable James Madison wrote Jefferson, "Believe me Sir as things now stand, if the States do not vigorously proceed in collecting the old money and establishing funds for the credit of the new, . . . we are undone."[19]

In April 1780, the state government finally made the move from Williamsburg to Richmond, then hardly more than a village. Jefferson rented a house that belonged to an uncle by marriage. Eventually his family joined him, and they subsequently divided their time between Richmond, Elk Hill, Tuckahoe, and Monticello. Two months after the transfer of the government came devastating news from South Carolina. Earlier Jefferson had, after a great struggle with the House, arranged to send hundreds of Virginia troops, along with much-needed supplies, to aid in the defense of Charleston; the troops began their march southward on March 8. But on June 9 word arrived that about a month earlier, on May 12, British general Sir Henry Clinton had taken the city, capturing the American garrison of more than 5,000 men. The Virginia fighting force was annihilated. For the young nation, it was the worst defeat of the entire war.

The General Assembly had reelected Jefferson governor on June 2, and two days later he had formally accepted the appointment in a brief message to the assembly.[20] The news from Charleston was not an auspicious beginning to his second term. Morale across Virginia sank even lower, revenues dried up, and militiamen became even less willing to go south. Jefferson worked to recruit men to send to General Gates, who had replaced the defeated (and captured) General Benjamin Lincoln in command of the southern armies, recognizing that it was still better to fight British forces in the Carolinas than in Virginia. As he had written General Washington shortly after the surrender of Charleston, "There is really nothing to oppose the progress of the enemy Northward but the cautious principles of the military art."[21] The shortage of men, weapons, wagons, and rations was utterly distressing. Martha Jefferson became involved in trying to support a drive among her countrywomen to raise funds. She wrote to Madison's mother, reporting that Washington's wife had sent her news of a movement among Pennsylvania women to support the patriot cause; Martha sent Mrs. Madison "papers to be disposed as you think proper" to advance their own effort.[22]

In early September, more terrible news made its way to Virginia: General Charles Cornwallis had inflicted a crushing defeat on General Gates at Camden on August 16, forcing Gates to retreat into North Carolina. Jefferson voiced doubts about his ability to lead Virginia if the conflict should reach the state. He wrote Richard Henry Lee on September 13, 1780, that he had determined to retire "after the present campaign" (presumably before the scheduled end of his term) in the hope that someone better qualified could be chosen governor. "Such a one may keep us above water even in our present moneyless situation."[23] In fact, the problem was not Jefferson's lack of military experience but the constitutional limits to his powers and the fears and fatigue of the people of Virginia. Longtime friends like George Mason and John Page implored him not to resign. Jefferson did not, and news on October 12 of a stunning American victory five days earlier over the British forces at King's Mountain (on the border of North Carolina) soon buoyed his spirits. The result forced

Cornwallis to retreat back into South Carolina, where he established winter quarters.

The victory proved crucial for Virginia. A British force of over 2,000 entered Chesapeake Bay on October 20, and the next day began landing at Portsmouth. Jefferson acted with alacrity, calling up troops, moving supplies away from the coasts, and arranging a defense of the iron foundry at Westham, near Richmond.[24] Assuming the British object was the Convention troops garrisoned near Charlottesville, he ordered the Virginia commandant there, James Wood, to prepare immediately to move them to Maryland (Jefferson decided only to send the British troops away).[25] But the commander of the invasion, Major General Alexander Leslie, learned of the defeat at King's Mountain and that Cornwallis would not soon be supporting him. As a result, during the night of November 15–16, the British pulled out of Portsmouth and headed for Charleston. Virginia was saved, but the respite would be brief.

ON DECEMBER 9 Washington sent Jefferson another vague alert of a possible invasion attempt: "Another embarkation is taking place . . . supposed to be destined Southward."[26] The governor could not summon Virginia's militia on such indeterminate news. In the event, on December 30 a British fleet arrived in the Chesapeake Bay, commanded by the hated turncoat Benedict Arnold. A member of the Virginia navy sighted twenty-seven sails but initially could not tell whether they were British. The information eventually reached Jefferson, who asked local militia to gather.[27]

Finally, on January 2, 1781, it became clear that British troops had landed. Jefferson promptly notified the assembly and asked the Executive Council for advice, meanwhile issuing orders to call up militia from across the state. Plans were quickly put into place to secure military stores and make other preparations. But by now Arnold was at Jamestown. Given the high tides and strong winds blowing up river, he did not land there, instead proceeding toward Richmond. Arnold made landfall at the storied Byrd family plantation Westover and began marching overland toward the state capital. Jefferson learned very early on January 4 that the British were coming; he awakened his fragile wife and small children and sent them upstream to Tuckahoe. Then he returned to Richmond, seeing that military matériel was moved, arms were saved, and the militia was in position; he also attempted to hide official papers.[28] For two days and nights, in unrelenting cold rain, he moved incessantly about the capital city. At one point his horse collapsed under him, and he had to hoist the saddle over his shoulder and find a nearby farmer to supply him with another mount.[29]

Arnold's forces arrived in the city at about noon on January 5, after facing negligible resistance from what militia had arrived in time. (Later Jefferson would be charged with negligence in not more promptly calling forth the militia, but it's very likely, given their normal delay in mobilizing, that even an immediate alert would not have resulted in an effective defense.) The invaders set about plundering and burning warehouses and private homes. British troops were sent to Westham to destroy the state foundry. A British officer stormed into Jefferson's home on Shockoe Hill and, placing a gun on the chest of Jefferson's dependable slave George Granger, demanded to know where Jefferson and the family silver were. Granger bravely and effectively lied, saying that the governor had fled to the mountains and taken all the silver with him. The disgruntled officer and his men left, but only after breaking into Jefferson's wine cellar.[30] With the raid having accomplished what Arnold intended—to damage state morale more than anything else—the British fell back on January 8, returning to a defensive position in Portsmouth.

As 1781 BEGAN, Virginia's prospects seemed bleak. Jefferson was in constant communication with General Nathanael Greene (who had replaced Gates) and other officers, following with intense interest the movement of Cornwallis and dreading his expected turn toward Virginia. Yet spirits soared when, in February, General Washington sent a heralded young French general, the Marquis de Lafayette, with 1,200 regular troops from New England and New Jersey to help the Virginians.[31] Lafayette proved a significant aid to the cause of liberty in Virginia, and he and Jefferson began a friendship that would span two continents and more than four decades.

The spring found Jefferson frantically busy. He acted, as it were, as governor, as quartermaster general, as communicator to Generals Washington and Greene, as chief executive, and as ombudsman. Out went letters to suppliers of clothing, hats, socks, and shoes; of pots and kettles; of wagons and saddlery; of horses and food. He wrote letters to the men overseeing the lead mines in Fincastle County to increase their output; he wrote to the operators of the foundry in Fredericksburg; he wrote to countless militia captains to try to promote the recruitment of volunteers. He had to deal with what he called "a Spirit of Disobedience" among war-weary and tax-resistant Virginians.[32] He kept Washington informed of events in Virginia, wrote regularly to the Speaker of the assembly, and answered complaints about the failure of various supplies to show up as expected. He wrote Lieutenant John Banister in Dinwiddie County to have him arrest and court-martial a soldier who had summarily and insultingly taken an ox from a farmer. Jefferson understood that the army at times might need to seize property, but as he lectured Banister, "It is our duty to lay the practice under strict rules, to guard it against oppression and wanton injury, and to reprobate every thing like insult which might make the sufferer feel the act of violence more deeply."[33]

Jefferson found himself having to justify American ways to Lafayette and also to Major General Von Steuben, who had come from Germany to assist the American cause. Baron Friedrich Wilhelm Ludolph Gerhard Augustin Von Steuben, after having first trained American militiamen at Valley Forge during the winter of 1777 and 1778, had come south at Washington's behest to train the Virginia militia. Von Steuben, accustomed to the Prussian model of unchallenged governmental authority, found it difficult to understand why he or state officials could not simply order civilians to work for them or force slaves into military service. As Jefferson not so patiently explained, "The Executive have not by the laws of this State any power to call a freeman to labour even for the Public without his consent, nor a Slave without that of his Master."[34] Anticipating that Lafayette, too, would find nearly incomprehensible the shortages and delays in Virginia, Jefferson gave him some historical context: "Mild Laws, a People not used to war and prompt obedience, a want of the Provisions of War and means of procuring them render our orders often ineffectual, oblige us to temporize and when we cannot accomplish an object in one way to attempt it in another."[35]

Amid his intensive work on behalf of the state, Jefferson learned in early March that the Continental Congress had adopted the Articles of Confederation, creating a national government for the states. Moreover, he had been elected a councilor of the American Philosophical Society, a pleasure he could only look forward to enjoying in the future.[36] Any momentary elation quickly gave way to the kind of excruciating sadness that seemed so often to mark Jefferson's life. As though he—a deeply affectionate husband and father—could hardly bear to mention it, his account book for April 15 succinctly records, "Our daughter Lucy Elizabeth died about 10 o'clock A.M. this day."[37] Jefferson, trying to balance duty with attention to his wife, sent a note to a senior member of the Executive

Council explaining his intended absence from the day's meeting: "The day is so very bad that I hardly expect a council, and there being nothing that I know very pressing, and Mrs. Jefferson in a situation in which I would not wish to leave her, I shall not attend to-day."[38] With that exception, Jefferson kept drudging on.

While he had frequently looked to bolster the American war effort elsewhere, Jefferson was among the first to realize that Virginia—as the most populous and wealthy state—would ultimately be the key to either victory or defeat. An ominous turn came in March, when reinforcements under the control of General William Phillips (exchanged in November 1780 for American general Benjamin Lincoln, captured in May of that year with the fall of Charleston and now back leading an army) joined up with Benedict Arnold in Portsmouth. Von Steuben believed if he led an attack into North Carolina against Cornwallis, Arnold and Phillips would go to Cornwallis's assistance, but Jefferson thought it too risky to allow him to draw so many Virginia forces away and thus leave the state practically undefended.

In late April, the British moved toward Richmond. Jefferson had most of the state's supplies transported to Point of Fork, at the junction of the Rivanna and the James—presumably beyond the reach of British forces. Then Phillips's men began to march away from Richmond and back toward Portsmouth, but suddenly changed course again and returned to take Petersburg. Unexpectedly, Phillips died of either typhus or malaria in that city on May 13. Meanwhile, Cornwallis, harassed by Nathanael Greene, had been moving northward; he entered Virginia and took command of the British forces in the state on May 20.[39]

The need for troops grew so grave that a desperate Jefferson, then in Monticello, wrote to the Speaker of the House to say that "further experience" convinced him "that something is necessary to be done to enforce the calls of the Executive for militia to attend in the field."[40] But the assembly was crumbling, with many of its members no longer showing up, and in fact it had already decided to move from Richmond to Charlottesville by the time Jefferson's letter arrived. Due to consistently poor attendance, it also agreed to drop the number required for a quorum.

Just as problematic was the failure to constitute a quorum in the Executive Council. By late May, the state government was evaporating. The same day that he wrote to the Speaker, Jefferson—who had several assemblymen as his guests—addressed a letter to General Washington, begging him to bring his Continental forces to rescue Virginia.[41] In the meantime, Jefferson, though technically compliant with the limited powers of his office, stretched those restraints to their breaking point in an attempt to save the state from total collapse. Here he came to recognize that in periods of severe crisis (and, as he would later come to understand, great opportunity), an executive had to at least temporarily exceed his authorized powers for the good of his state or nation. If necessary, he came to believe, the executive could seek retroactive sanction for decisions made in an emergency.[42]

WHILE JEFFERSON was beseeching Washington, Cornwallis decided to send two separate forces northwestward, one under the command of Colonel John Graves Simcoe to seize the supplies at Point of Fork, the other commanded by Lieutenant Colonel Banastre Tarleton to Charlottesville to capture the governor and rump legislature. On June 4, Simcoe destroyed the guns, cannon, powder, and other supplies supposedly stored safely at Point of Fork. Tarleton, with about 250 men under his control, headed rapidly for Charlottesville and Monticello. Jefferson had let it be known that he did not intend to stand for reelection when his second term expired on Saturday, June 2. Arguing that someone with more military experience was needed, he strongly favored an old friend, militia commander Thomas Nelson Jr. The assembly, hastily gathered in Charlottesville, rather characteristically dithered, eventually deciding to choose his successor the following Monday.[43]

But Tarleton took no notice of these developments. Early in the night of June 3, his raiders paused at the Cuckoo Tavern in Louisa, about forty miles east of Charlottesville, for a quick meal. An alert member of the Virginia militia, Jack Jouett, saw them and guessed their destination. Jouett slipped away, mounted his horse, and began a breakneck race over back trails and shortcuts to Monticello.[44] He arrived at dawn, and Jefferson, appearing unruffled by the news, proceeded to have breakfast prepared for the assemblymen staying with him before sending them toward Charlottesville. He had a carriage brought up for his wife and two children to take them to safety, first to Blenheim and shortly afterward to Enniscorthy, John Coles's estate.

Jouett rushed to Charlottesville to warn the disbelieving assemblymen there, and they hurriedly decided to move beyond the Blue Ridge Mountains and reconvene later at Staunton. Those who tarried were captured. Tarleton's forces had met a small company of Virginia militia stationed east of Charlottesville, intended to slow down just such an incursion and warn the assemblymen, but the militia panicked and scattered at the sight of the approaching British. Most of Tarleton's men then headed directly toward Charlottesville, which they ransacked, while Captain Kenneth McLeod and a smaller contingent headed for Jefferson's mountain home. A young American lieutenant, Christopher Hudson, who happened to be in the region, heard about the British troop movements and rushed toward Monticello, unaware of Jouett's prior warning. He arrived to discover the place practically empty, except for a calm Jefferson, who was hiding his papers. Hudson insisted that the British were just minutes away.[45]

Family legend says that Jefferson accidentally spied the Redcoats approaching the base of Monticello through his small telescope. In any event, at the last moment, it seems, Jefferson mounted his favorite horse, the redoubtable Caractacus (named for the first-century British chieftain who fought against the invading Romans) and rode down from Monticello. He headed toward Blenheim, joining his family that evening.[46] Within minutes of Jefferson's departure McLeod and his men arrived. The troops found two of Jefferson's slaves, one named Caesar and the other Martin Hemings, the latter Jefferson's butler for years. They had been stowing away silver and other valuables. The British pressed them about Jefferson whereabouts, even putting a pistol to Hemings's breast and threatening to fire, much as had happened to George Granger in Richmond. According to the family lore, Hemings stared back and said, "Fire away, then." The officer put down his gun, and the men actually respected the house, though they did help themselves to some wine.[47] In contrast, Cornwallis's army of about 7,000 camped out for ten days in early June at Jefferson's Elk Hill plantation, stripping it bare and trampling the fields. Not all of Jefferson's slaves were as loyal as Caesar and Hemings. Altogether, twenty-seven or so ran away to join the British forces, although more than half soon died of disease.[48]

By June 14, Jefferson had transferred Martha and their two daughters to his farthest farm, Poplar Forest. While there, Jefferson suffered a fall from his horse and was housebound for six weeks.[49] Not until late July did he and his family return to Monticello, his term as governor having expired.

WHEN TARLETON departed Charlottesville, the assembly was in tatters and Cornwallis's forces loomed as an ever-present threat. Finally, by June

7, enough members of the lower house had gathered in Staunton to call an official meeting, and several days later the upper house did likewise. Not enough members of the Executive Council were present for it to officially meet. In no apparent rush, the lower house set the election date for a new governor for June 12, and in the meantime the delegates—many of whom now considered the executive office far too weak—considered a motion put forward by George Nicholas to appoint "a Dictator" to govern temporarily. Patrick Henry, of all people, supported this proposal, which only lost by a few votes.[50] Jefferson never forgave Henry for this antidemocratic turn. Finally, on June 12 the legislature elected Jefferson's preferred candidate, Thomas Nelson Jr., the next governor. That same day, Nicholas moved "that at the next session of the Assembly an inquiry be made into the conduct of the Executive of this State for the last twelve months."[51] Nicholas provided no specifics, but presumably he meant that Jefferson had not employed the militia as promptly and effectively as he might have.

Nothing in Jefferson's entire political life wounded him so deeply. He had worked too tirelessly, neglecting the health and comfort of his ailing wife, to face such charges with equanimity. He was also acutely sensitive to unmerited criticism. Even after his exoneration by the legislature, he wrote James Monroe that the charges "had inflicted a wound on my spirit which will only be cured by the all-healing grave."[52] And though no informed and impartial observer could hold him responsible for the British incursion into Virginia, he was painfully aware that it had occurred on his watch.

Back at Monticello by late July, Jefferson sent Nicholas a curt letter, asking for the particulars of the charges against him. Nicholas, apparently in over his head, responded that he was not really accusing Jefferson of anything in particular.[53] By now, if not earlier, Jefferson had come to believe that Henry was behind the charges and using the naïve Nicholas to hide his hand.[54] (Jefferson had long suspected Henry of laziness and opportunism; the following year, in a private later, he referred to him as "being all tongue without either head or heart."[55]) Jefferson determined to attend the session to defend himself and made the preparation of his defense his highest priority. In August he received a June 15 letter from Thomas McKean, president of the Congress, offering him a position as a minister for the negotiation of a peace treaty in Paris. Jefferson declined the appointment by referring to "a temporary and indispensable obligation of being within the state till a later season of the present year than the duties of this appointment would admit."[56] That obligation was the legislative inquiry into his role as governor. He explained more carefully to Edmund Randolph his decision to put personal matters above national service, writing about how important he believed it was to clear his name. Jefferson—who believed "the approbation of our fellow citizens," which he feared he had lost, to be the highest reward of public services—was convinced his public days were finished. "I have taken my final leave of every thing of that nature, have retired to my farm, my family and my books from which I think nothing will ever more separate me."[57]

In late November a vacancy opened up in Albemarle's representation at the assembly, and Jefferson sought and won election with one cause in mind. On November 27 his friend John Harvie sent him a copy of the resolution, just formally passed, appointing a committee to conduct the inquiry. Harvie added that in his recent conversation with other legislators, he found nothing but praise for Jefferson: his administration was unanimously viewed as "honorable to the Cheif Magistrate, and preservative of the Rights of the people, and the Constitution of the Land. In short I think Sir in no period of your life, has your Character shown with a Superior Lustre."[58] Soon Jefferson was in Richmond, and on December 11 and 12 he read aloud before the assembly the charges as he believed them to be and answered them in order and in detail. His public accuser, George Nicholas, did not attend and made no new charges; neither did anyone else. On the second day of Jefferson's testimony, John Banister, of the investigative committee, reported that they had no information to support the "groundless rumors," and the Senate unanimously adopted a resolution in praise of Jefferson's gubernatorial conduct.[59]

Jefferson, to all rational observers, had gotten his vindication, although critics in the future would continue to hurl charges of incompetence and cowardice at him. Meanwhile, following Tarleton's raid in early June, Cornwallis found the possibility of moving inland stymied by Lafayette's troops positioned near Jamestown. In August the British general began to solidify his position near Yorktown, a few miles away on the York River, by which he assumed he could receive provisions and reinforcements. Washington, in New York, learned that a large French fleet under the command of the admiral Comte de François-Joseph-Paul de Grasse was headed for Virginia, where it proceeded to block the mouth of the Chesapeake. Together with the French commander Comte de Jean-Baptiste-Donatier de Vimeur Rochambeau, who had 5,000 troops also in New York, Washington with his 5,000 Continentals made a quick march to Virginia, where they linked up with Lafayette and other French troops brought by de Grasse. Suddenly Cornwallis found himself surrounded, outnumbered, and with no chance for help or escape by sea. On October 19, 1781, Cornwallis, taking the measure of his dire situation, surrendered his entire army of 8,000. Ironically, had Jefferson agreed to serve a third term, he would have received immense praise for this victory. Within months the British government collapsed, and Lord Frederick North resigned. And in France, John Jay, John Adams, and Benjamin Franklin secretly hammered out a treaty with the British that effectively ended the war. Jefferson, back at Monticello, expected as a private citizen to settle into family life and absorb himself in his books, his garden, and his curiosity about all things.

8

A Congress
"Little Numerous, but Very Contentious"

J EFFERSON'S LAST PERIOD of sustained intellectual activity had occurred in the months just before he assumed the governorship, when
he had worked to revise the state's legal code. Perhaps the March
1781 notice of his election as an officer of the American Philosophical
Society only intensified his desire to return to the pleasures of his books.
A more direct invitation to the scholarly life came that same month,
when he received a forwarded letter from the Marquis François de
Barbé-Marbois, secretary of the French legation in Philadelphia, posing
a series of questions about the state of Virginia. In his reply to Barbé-
Marbois, Jefferson said that his "present occupations disable[d him]
from compleating" his answers but that he hoped to formulate a response shortly.[1] This was exactly the kind of task Jefferson loved and was
superbly equipped to carry out—were he not consumed with his duties
as governor. As he fled Monticello in early June, he may well have looked
forward to crafting answers to Barbé-Marbois's queries. And in late June
and July, laid up by the fall from his horse, Jefferson had the leisure to
begin drafting his reply. Toward the end of the year Jefferson sent Barbé-
Marbois what he himself termed "a very imperfect" response, little more
than a promise of the ultimate version.[2] The pleasure of preparing this
document strengthened his resolve to retire from politics for good, but
he could not foresee that it would, several years later, result in his only
published book.

While Jefferson directed most of his reading to scientific or governmental purposes, throughout his life he derived great satisfaction from the
immensely popular "translations" by Scottish poet James Macpherson of

the epic poetry of a third-century Celtic bard or warrior named Ossian. In fact, no original poems and no Ossian had ever existed. The three volumes of poetry that Macpherson published in the 1760s were by turn elegiac and romantic, with a vibrant sense of cultural regeneration. No doubt Jefferson read this verse, as he did various Saxon tracts, as supportive of the cause of American settlement in the New World. Ossian's intense descriptions of natural phenomena also influenced him stylistically. Writing to one of Macpherson's relatives seeking more information about the ancient bard—Jefferson did not yet accept that Macpherson was the true author—Jefferson said that Ossian's poems "have been, and will I think during my life continue to be to me, the source of daily and exalted pleasure. . . . I am not ashamed to own that I think this rude bard of the North the greatest Poet that has ever existed."[3]

Jefferson's extravagant appreciation of Ossian was widely shared at the time, and it was one of several intellectual fascinations that, over the course of his life, would link him to an international community of scholarly men and women. Jefferson had also long been accustomed to entertaining visitors at Monticello, but April 1782 brought an unusually gifted visitor, the Marquis de Chastellux, a major general in the French army under the Comte de Rochambeau, who had served as the main liaison between the French commander and General George Washington. Chastellux, some nine years Jefferson's senior, was also a noted man of letters and a member of the Académie Française. In a detailed and perceptive account of his trip to Charlottesville, Chastellux described Monticello as in the "Italian style" and "quite tasteful," observing, "It may be said that Mr. Jefferson is the first American who has consulted the Fine Arts to know how he should shelter himself from the weather."[4]

Fascinated by his accomplished host, Chastellux provided one of the earliest written portraits of Jefferson.

Let me then describe to you a man, not yet forty, tall, and with a mild and pleasing countenance, but whose mind and attainments could serve in lieu of all outward graces; an American, who, without ever having quitted his own country, is Musician, Draftsman, Surveyor, Astronomer, Natural Philosopher, Jurist, and Statesman; a Senator of America . . . ; a Governor of Virginia . . . ; and finally a Philosopher, retired from the world and public business. . . . A gentle and amiable wife, charming children, extensive estates to improve, the arts and sciences to cultivate— these are what remain to Mr. Jefferson, after having played a distinguished role on the stage of the New World, and what he has preferred to the honorable commission of Minister Plenipotentiary in Europe.[5]

Over several days Jefferson took Chastellux about Monticello. In the evenings, over a bowl of punch, they discussed philosophy, natural history, and the poetry of Ossian, talking deep into the night. Their conversation ranged extensively, "for no object has escaped Mr. Jefferson; and it seems indeed as though, ever since his youth, he had placed his mind, like his house, on a lofty height, whence he might contemplate the whole universe."[6] Jefferson spoke ecstatically of the Natural Bridge of Virginia—a great natural arch in Rockbridge County that Jefferson so loved he bought it and its surrounding acreage—and would have accompanied his French guest there except that "his wife was expecting her confinement at any moment, and he is as good a husband as he is a philosopher and citizen."[7] So they parted, not realizing that in a few years they would meet again in Paris.

SOME SEMBLANCE of order returned to Monticello in 1782; for example, after having made only one entry in his Garden Book for the whole of 1780 and 1781, Jefferson jotted a number of observations the year after, recording the transplanting of fruit trees, a sighting of wild geese flying to the northwest, and even notes on the taxidermy of birds.[8] And, as suggested by Chastellux's comments, Martha Wayles Skelton Jefferson gave birth to a baby girl on May 8, whom they named Lucy Elizabeth after her sister, who had died thirteen months before.[9] Yet Martha did not recover from the labor. Jefferson was seldom away from her as she deteriorated; this prolific correspondent wrote only one substantive letter over the following three months.

In that letter after Lucy's birth, Jefferson poured out his anguish to James Monroe. "Mrs. Jefferson has added another daughter to our family. She has been ever since and still continues very dangerously ill." Distraught, Jefferson explained his decision to completely withdraw from the world of politics. "Before I ventured to declare to my countrymen my determination to retire from public employment I examined well my heart to know whether it were thoroughly cured of every principle of political ambition, whether no lurking particle remained which might leave me uneasy when reduced within the limits of mere private life. I became satisfied that every fibre of that passion was thoroughly eradicated."[10] He continued, describing his public service over the last thirteen years, during which his private affairs had "run into great disorder and ruin." Now he owed his family more "attention and instruction." He mentioned his "constant sacrifice of time, labour, loss, parental and friendly duties," for which he had been rewarded only with the forfeiture of the "small estimation" in which his countrymen had once held him. Obviously, the attempted censure still rankled deeply, in part because reputation—the public reflection of a person's character—was then considered a measure of a man's worth and in part because he was unusually sensitive to criticism.

This was the letter in which he said that the "injuries" caused by the charge against him "had inflicted a wound on my spirit which will only be cured by the all-healing grave."[11] These bitter words were a cry from the heart of a man driven almost mad by worry, exhaustion, and the devastating sadness prompted by the approaching death of his beloved wife. The stark facts recorded in Jefferson's account book on September 6—"My dear wife died this day at 11H–45' AM"—give no hint of the impact of the event on him.[12] But other sources do. His eldest daughter recalled years later that for the four months of his wife's illness, Jefferson "was never out of her calling; when not at her bedside, he was writing in a small room which opened immediately at the head of her bed." Along with his sister Martha Carr (whom Jefferson's children always called Aunt Carr), Jefferson sat up with his wife and "administered her medicines and drink to the last."[13] At the final moment the children were apparently not in the room. Along with Jefferson and Aunt Carr, six of the slaves closest to the family, including Betty and Sally Hemings, must have also ministered to Martha during her final hours. Edmund Bacon, Jefferson's overseer for almost two decades, recorded in his memoirs that the slaves in attendance at her death "have often told my wife that when Mrs. Jefferson died they stood around the bed. Mr. Jefferson sat by her, and she gave him directions about a good many things that she wanted done. When she came to the children, she wept and could not speak for some time. Finally she held up her hand, and spreading out her four fingers, told him she could not die if she thought her four children were ever to have a stepmother brought in over them. Holding her other hand in his, Mr. Jefferson promised her solemnly that he would never marry again."[14]

Martha's eyes followed Jefferson when he entered and left the room, and she seemed only to listen for his voice.[15] Just before the end she took up a pen and began writing some lines from Laurence Sterne's *Tristram Shandy*, which both she and her husband knew well: "Time wastes too fast: every letter I trace tells me with what rapidity life follows my pen.

The days and hours of it are flying over our heads like clouds of windy day never to return—more every thing presses on—"

Then she faltered. Jefferson picked up the pen and completed the quotation: "And every time I kiss thy hand to bid adieu, every absence which follows it, are preludes to that eternal separation which we are shortly to make!"[16]

As his daughter Patsy recalled (she must have learned the details from Aunt Carr), "A moment before the closing scene, he was led from the room almost in a state of insensibility, by his sister Mrs. Carr, who, with great difficulty, got him into his library, where he fainted, and remained so long insensible that they feared he would never revive."[17]

In an age when—and among a class for whom—emotions were suspect and reason supposedly supreme, Jefferson's emotional collapse indicated both the depth of his love for Martha and the state of his own mental health. As Patsy recounted years later, "The scene that followed I did not witness; but the violence of his emotion, when almost by stealth I entered his room at night, to this day I dare not trust myself to describe. He kept [to] his room three weeks, and I was never a moment from his side. He walked almost incessantly night and day, only lying down occasionally," when he was completely exhausted. Patsy, who turned ten during these agonizing days, remembered that after three weeks he left the room only to ride "incessantly on horseback, rambling about the mountain. . . . In those melancholy rambles, I was his constant companion, a solitary witness to many a violent burst of grief."[18] The bond between father and daughter grew far stronger and endured throughout their lives.

Jefferson had grieved deeply before, but no earlier tragedy affected him to the same degree. Everyone who knew him recognized the toll his wife's death had taken, and he never fully recovered. After his own death, "in the most secret drawer of a private cabinet which he constantly resorted to," was found that fragment from *Tristram Shandy*, wrapped around several locks of Martha's hair.[19] Friends grew concerned; Edmund Randolph confided to James Madison, "I ever thought him to rank domestic happiness in the first class of the chief good; but I scarcely supposed that his grief would be so violent, as to justify the circulating report, of his swooning away, whenever he sees his children."[20]

Jefferson wrote his first substantial letter after his wife's death to sister-in-law Elizabeth Wayles Eppes, assuring her that his three daughters were doing well despite "the immeasurable loss we have sustained." He admitted that he found life almost unbearable, made sustainable only by "the infidelity of deserting the second charge left me," the care of his children. He reported that he could not yet entertain the idea of visiting her family at Eppington, having promised her that he would not come until he "could support such a countenance as might not cast a damp on the cheerfulness of others."[21]

MEANWHILE, JEFFERSON'S closest friends were conspiring to bring him back into the affairs of the world. Madison knew that concerns over Martha's health had prevented Jefferson from accepting Congress's appointment as a negotiator of the peace in France in August 1781; now that this concern was lifted, Madison asked again, privately noting that "the death of Mrs. J. had probably changed the sentiments of Mr. J. with regard to public life." Henry Laurens, who had been appointed in Jefferson's stead, was currently being held as a prisoner of war in the Tower of London; Madison made a motion that Jefferson be appointed to replace him.[22] The motion, as Madison related it, "was agreed to unanimously and without a single adverse remark."[23]

Promptly Robert R. Livingston sent a letter to Jefferson informing him of his appointment, and this time Jefferson replied the very next day, accepting and pledging "to employ in this arduous charge, with diligence and integrity, the best of my poor talents."[24] No doubt he welcomed the idea of a change of residence, of leaving Monticello behind at least for a while. As he explained to Chastellux the same day he accepted the appointment, "Your letter recalled to my memory, that there were persons still living of much value to me." Referencing the "catastrophe" that had occurred in September, he said, "Before that event my scheme of life had been determined. I had folded myself in the arms of retirement, and rested all prospects of future happiness on domestic and literary objects. A single event wiped away all my plans and left me a blank which I had not the spirits to fill up."[25] But now the prospect of going to Paris to work with Benjamin Franklin and John Adams and enjoy lively conversation with people like Chastellux, gave Jefferson a fresh reason for living.

At the time, he was staying near Richmond, at the home of a longtime friend, Archibald Cary. He had taken his daughters and the children of his sister Martha Carr there to have the little ones inoculated against smallpox, with Jefferson himself serving as their nurse. Then he made arrangements to send the infant Lucy and four-year-old Polly to live with their aunt, Elizabeth Eppes, while he prepared to take Patsy with him to Philadelphia, from which they would embark for Paris; he was emotionally dependent upon Patsy and also wanted to closely supervise her education. He arranged for trusted friends to handle his business affairs, and on December 19, 1782, he and Patsy departed north. He planned to spend at least several weeks in the nation's capital, poring over state papers and readying himself for his duties as Minister Plenipotentiary for Negotiating Peace. He hoped to make the transatlantic voyage in the same vessel with Chastellux and French general Rochambeau. But that was not to be.

While Jefferson was in Philadelphia, word arrived that the final treaty in Paris had been signed and was en route to the Congress for approval. On April 4 he was informed that significant progress in negotiations "render[ed] it unnecessary for you to pursue your Voyage."[26] One can hardly imagine his disappointment, despite the good news concerning the treaty. After sending John Jay and his fellow negotiators a letter of congratulation, Jefferson settled up his financial affairs, and he and Patsy journeyed back to Monticello by way of Baltimore and Richmond, arriving at the mountaintop on May 15, 1783. Fate had foiled another trip to France.

BUT HIS SOJOURN in Philadelphia had nevertheless proven fruitful. The dark spell of grief and even self-pity had been broken. He rediscovered what excited him about life, recovered the stoicism that had first served him well almost three decades before when his father died, found a true intellectual colleague in Madison (they lived in the same boardinghouse), and resolved to put aside the allures of premature retirement. Never frivolous, Jefferson found an even greater seriousness of purpose. It was as though he, now more mature and resilient, had been reborn to a life of learning and public service.

He likely discussed his new outlook not only with Madison but with political leaders in Richmond. They were only too happy to oblige Mr. Jefferson. On June 6, 1783, the assembly elected him a delegate to the Congress of the Confederation, and, as Edmund Randolph soon wrote Madison, "Mr. Jefferson was placed at the head of the delegation, not without his approbation, as I have been informed."[27] Once again, after a two-year absence, Jefferson was in harness.

Before he departed again for Philadelphia, Jefferson became convinced that a special convention, called just for that purpose, was about to revise the state constitution—an event Jefferson believed should have taken place in 1776. Aware that his constitutional proposals in the summer of 1776 had arrived in Richmond too late to have much influence, Jefferson promptly set about drafting a new constitution that, in his view, corrected some of the weaknesses of the current document.[28] Because he considered the present constitution's consolidation of legislative, judicial, and executive functions in one elected body potentially despotic, he separated them. Other important changes included increasing the governor's term to five years and limiting him to only one term. His proposals demoted the Executive Council to merely an advisory body, which the governor could call for consultation as he wished, and although its members could meet on their own, their advice was merely that. The governor would also have sole direction of the "whole military of the state, whether regular or militia," but the execution of his orders would be left to "General officers" appointed by the legislature.[29]

Jefferson's most significant proposal was a bold abolitionist clause: the new General Assembly would not have the power "to permit the introduction of any more slaves to reside in this state, or the continuance of slavery beyond the generation which shall be living on the 31st. day of December 1800; all persons born after that day being hereby declared free."[30] This gradual approach to emancipation was probably modeled on the 1780 constitution of Pennsylvania, which provided that all slaves currently in the state (most of whom were children) would be freed upon reaching the age of twenty-eight.[31] However, Jefferson was again disappointed in his attempts at constitution making: in the end the state did not call a special convention. (The constitution was not replaced until 1830.) Even had the convention met, Jefferson's proposal to end slavery would have gone nowhere. Afterward, he increasingly grounded his hopes for emancipation in the younger generation, having lost faith in his own.

Soon Jefferson began working out the details of his return to Philadelphia. He wrote Madison in late August to inquire if he and Patsy might again stay in the comfortable boardinghouse run by Mary House and her daughter Elizabeth Trist, and in late September he again placed his two youngest daughters with their Aunt Eppes. If Congress chose to meet in a different location, Jefferson asked Madison to find him a small room, but in either case, he expected to set up Patsy in a boarding home in Philadelphia, where he would arrange tutors for her in a variety of subjects. Jefferson understood that Madison had recently been disappointed in his romance with Catherine "Kitty" Floyd, and, in the role of a kind uncle, he counseled the younger man (Jefferson was forty to Madison's thirty-two), "Firmness of mind and unintermitting occupations will not long leave you in pain"—a comment that perhaps reveals how Jefferson himself had overcome his bereavement.[32]

The summer and early fall of 1783 saw Jefferson back at Monticello with his daughters. He had the leisure to return to his reply to Barbé-Marbois's queries about Virginia. He may have consulted several of the books in his library, but he certainly wrote letters to persons he believed to be in possession of useful information. The topic obviously fascinated him, and though he had turned to it now and again when he had a leisure moment—it was apparently often on his mind—he had little sustained time to devote to the project over the next few months. Placing Monticello in the charge of a steward, Jefferson and Patsy left home on October 16, 1783, riding in a phaeton pulled by two horses, with Jefferson's slave James Hemings accompanying them on horseback. Surely because Jefferson wanted to supplement the report he was preparing for Barbé-Marbois, the three took a western route, up the Shenandoah Valley. They stopped to tour some famous caverns, and for the first time Jefferson visited Harpers Ferry, where he saw the confluence of the Shenandoah and Potomac Rivers about which he later wrote so rapturously.[33] Armed with new knowledge about his home state, Jefferson pushed on, arriving in Philadelphia on October 29.

Congress had recently fled the city for Princeton, New Jersey, due to a riot by troops disgruntled over not receiving back pay. Before going on to Princeton, Jefferson temporarily arranged for Patsy to stay at the boarding establishment run by Mrs. House and Mrs. Trist—Patsy and Elizabeth Trist became lifelong friends and correspondents. Jefferson hurried to Princeton, but the day he arrived, Congress adjourned, planning to recon-vene three weeks later in Annapolis. Jefferson returned to Philadelphia during the adjournment. Probably at Mrs. Trist's suggestion, he arranged for Patsy to live with Mary Johnson Hopkinson, the widowed mother of a close and like-minded friend, Francis Hopkinson. Eleven-year-old Patsy was soon comfortably ensconced in her new home, and Jefferson arranged for her to take private dancing, music, and drawing lessons.[34]

For the next six months, during which Jefferson was to play an im-portant role in Congress, Patsy remained with Mrs. Hopkinson, and Jefferson closely supervised her education because he wanted her to be improved "chiefly . . . in acquiring a little taste and execution in such of the fine arts," which she could not have found in rural Virginia.[35] Fortuitously, Barbé-Marbois had helped him find a French teacher for Patsy. Jefferson's expectations for her were unusually rigorous, and as self-directed as he had been and remained, he prescribed a demanding schedule for his daughter. Still, her curriculum seems excessive, and his cautions against her disappointing him strike today's reader as troubling. His first letter to Patsy in Philadelphia set the tone: after admonishing her to always obey Mrs. Hopkinson and "consider her . . . as your mother," he laid out his expectations for her daily routine:

> from 8. to 10 o'clock practise music.
> from 10. to 1. dance one day and draw another.
> from 1. to 2. draw on the day you dance, and write a letter the next day.
> From 3. to 4. read French.
> From 4. to 5. exercise yourself in music.
> From 5. till bedtime read English, write &c.

He also expected her to write him every post, write relatives back in Virginia every week, and always check her spelling. "I have placed my happiness on seeing you good and accomplished, and no distress which this world can now bring on me could equal that of you disappointing my hopes." Could he have demanded any more? Yes. "If you love me then, strive to be good under every situation and to all living creatures . . . which will go far towards ensuring you the warmest love of your affectionate father."[36]

Perhaps because Jefferson himself realized his demands were excep tionally high, he attempted to justify them to Barbé-Marbois. "The plan of reading which I have formed for her is considerably different from what I think would be most proper for her sex in any other country than America. I am obliged in it to extend my views beyond herself, and consider her as possibly at the head of a little family of her own. The chance that in marriage she will draw a blockhead I calculate at about fourteen to one, and of course that the education of her family will probably rest on her own ideas and direction without assistance."[37] One might be prompted to ask whether this committed democrat was really so critical of Virginia manhood, or if, like many fathers, he was simply uncertain that any man would truly be worthy of his daughter. His exhortations to Patsy went beyond intellectual growth to include proper womanly behavior. He warned her in explicit detail about being clean and tidy in her dress, explaining that slovenliness was "disgusting" to men.[38]

Yet whatever his demands and harsh advice in the body of his letters, Jefferson's valedictory always expressed his love unconditionally, as in "accept yourself assurances of the sincere love with which I am my dear Patsy, Yours affectionately."[39] Despite his requests that Patsy write often, she only wrote him eight letters over the next six months, and he only wrote her the same number in return. She did not send him regular examples of her drawing and in other little ways launched small rebellions. But overall, Patsy proved an uncommonly obedient and affectionate daughter who spent her entire life adoring her father, and the feeling was mutual.[40]

THOUGH HE PUT much stock in his fatherly duties, during this period Jefferson was primarily a legislator. The Congress he joined, established by the Articles of Confederation, was not the distinguished body he had been a part of in 1775. Now he was its most prominent member and also its most active. In his first few months, he served on every significant committee and drafted a total of thirty-one reports.[41] As he remembered the 1783–1784 Congress in his autobiography, it "had now become a very small body, and the members very remiss in their attendance," making it hard to accomplish anything. As he put it, "Our body was little numerous, but very contentious."[42] Any act of significance required the positive votes of nine states, but in most cases only seven had representatives present, and sometimes illness or other causes for absence absolutely prevented governmental action.

In Annapolis, Jefferson and James Monroe, newly elected from Virginia, took rooms in a private home for several months before renting a small house in February. By that time, the poor accommodations in both Princeton and Annapolis had prompted a discussion of where to locate a permanent capital city, a discussion Jefferson soon engaged in. After pondering the proposed options, he noted that he favored Georgetown, on the Potomac.[43]

A more pressing matter was the ratification of the treaty of peace between England and the United States; a letter from the American negotiators in Paris and a copy of the definitive treaty was laid before the Congress on November 26.[44] By the terms negotiated, the nation had six months— until March 3—to accept the treaty or it would become void. Yet Congress did not have delegations from enough states to accept it.

On December 20 the Congress received a letter from General Washington informing its members that he was coming to Annapolis and wanted to resign his commission. The letter asked in what form he should tender his resignation. Congress acted by voting to invite Washington to address its members on December 23 following a "public entertainment to be given" for him the preceding evening. To plan the occasion it appointed a committee headed by Jefferson. Everyone understood the importance of the occasion: the nation's victorious military leader, rather than seeking to seize power, was voluntarily stepping down in recognition of the primary authority of the people's elected Congress. On Monday, December 22, Jefferson's committee presented a proposal for an elaborate and appropriate ceremony, which the Congress promptly accepted.[45]

That evening a public dinner was held, thirteen toasts were lifted, and thirteen cannon shots were fired. The next day, December 23, Washington addressed the Congress, saying that he now had "the honor of . . . presenting myself before them to surrender into their hands the trust committed to me. . . . Having now finished the work assigned me, I retire from the great theatre of Action; and bidding an Affectionate farewell . . . take my leave of all the employments of public life."[46] As he drew his commission from his pocket and handed it to the president of the Congress, Thomas Mifflin, witnesses reported that not a single attendee remained unmoved. Following Washington's farewell comments, Mifflin read his own remarks, prepared for him by Jefferson (years later Madison said that they had "the shining traces of his pen"[47]): "Having defended the standard of liberty in this new world: having taught a useful lesson to those who inflict and to those who feel oppression, you *retire from the great theatre of action* with the blessings of your fellow citizens."[48] The formal subordination of military authority to civilian authority resonated far and wide. Jefferson remarked later that "the moderation and virtue of a single character has probably prevented this revolution from being closed as most others have been by a subversion of that liberty it was intended to establish."[49]

Yet Jefferson soon turned again to worry over the impending deadline for accepting the peace treaty. He was concerned about how Congress's flight from Philadelphia because of a mutiny must have looked to European powers, a situation that appeared all the worse owing to that body's inability to function. Others in Congress began to argue that only seven states would be sufficient to accept the treaty, but Jefferson strongly opposed this position, fearful that Britain might reject as insufficient such a partial acceptance. For weeks the internal debate went on. But suddenly the situation changed. On January 13, 1784, delegates from Connecticut and New Jersey arrived, and the next day a delegate from South Carolina who had been ill was well enough to attend.[50] Nine states were now available to vote, and the treaty was approved unanimously on January 14.[51] The actual instrument of ratification was essentially a report Jefferson had prepared on December 16, but he also authored the official ratification document of January 14 and the accompanying proclamation announcing it.[52] Jefferson, the primary author behind the Declaration of Independence in 1776, now had the honor of authoring the ratification of the treaty that ended the resulting war.

Jefferson was "fantastically industrious"[53] in what proved to be the last legislative position he ever held, even though for the first half of it he was often ill, writing to his daughter in January that his health had been so bad for weeks that "I have just been able to attend to my duty in the state house, but not to go out on any other occasion." And he reported to a young friend that to his "habitual ill health, [I] have lately added an attack of my periodical headach" and thus "am obliged to avoid reading writing and almost thinking."[54] Even so, he did a prodigious amount of work during these months. Of course there were the committee meetings to attend and reports to write, but he also maintained his customarily huge stream of correspondence, writing to others about what needed to be done in Congress and receiving letters on a variety of subjects ranging from giant animal teeth and so-called white Negroes to hot-air balloons and making brandy from potatoes.

THE NEXT MAJOR issue that confronted Jefferson had a long history, dating back to 1781, when as governor he had sent a document to the Congress describing Virginia's cession of its western lands. But Congress had not immediately accepted the cession; there were complaints about the legitimacy of Virginia's land claims and stronger objections that the terms of the cession required the voiding of previous claims based on supposed purchases from the Indians. The Virginia cession had been intended to privilege small settlers, not large land speculators, and of course the latter balked. So the munificent offer of millions of acres of land remained unaccepted when Jefferson took his seat in the Congress. In early February 1784, after interminable squabbling and negotiation, Virginia made its final offer to cede the land. Jefferson then drew up the form that provided the means of conveyance by way of a deed; Congress at first demurred, but on March 1 a Pennsylvania delegate changed his mind, and the motion passed.[55] Almost a month earlier, on February 4—just after the Congress had learned of Virginia's offer—Jefferson, David Howell, and Jeremiah Townley Chase had been appointed to a committee "to prepare a plan for temporary government of western territory." On March 1, the day Congress voted to accept the land cession from Virginia, the committee on the western territory produced its report, authored by Jefferson.[56] There had been much discussion of this issue, so although the report bore the unmistakable mark of Jefferson's mind and pen, to a degree it synthesized attitudes present in the Congress.

The far-reaching report called for the division of the territory being ceded by Virginia (and future cessions all the way south to the Florida panhandle, then under Spanish control) into an unspecified number of individual states. These were to be two degrees of latitude in width, measured north to south, set forth in two ranks between the Mississippi River and the Appalachian Mountains. The settlers in each state would gather together and establish temporary governments based on existing governments in any of the earlier states. When a new state achieved a population of 20,000, it should call a convention to establish a permanent constitution. The report specified that the newly formed states should become a permanent part of the nation, subject to its laws; they should pay their fair portion of taxes, establish republican governments, and accept as a citizen no one who held a hereditary title. The document also stipulated that "after the year 1800 . . . there shall be neither slavery nor involuntary servitude in any of the said states, otherwise than in punishment of crimes, whereof the party shall have been duly convicted to have been personally guilty."[57] Considered most important was the guarantee that new territories would not be subservient colonies of the existing nation but would receive self-rule with an orderly road to statehood. Abolishing slavery was the paramount issue to no political leader of the time.

Congress adopted the report on April 23 as the Ordinance of 1784, but not before making two significant changes. It omitted the proscription against hereditary titles and, following a resolution passed four days earlier, removed the restriction against slavery; the motion for the latter (offered by the North Carolina delegate and seconded by the delegate from South Carolina) passed by just one vote. No southern state accepted the prohibition on slavery, not even Virginia, whose other two delegates also voted to strike the clause.[58] Jefferson's distress over this occurrence was painfully obvious in his letter to Madison detailing the vote. "!Virginia! voted against it," he wrote almost in shock.[59] This fateful decision left the Old Southwest open to the expansion of slavery.

The same year Jefferson, as the member of yet another committee charged with disposing of western lands, authored the "Report of a Committee to Establish a Land Office." This document suggested a method of surveying and dividing the territory, in effect placing a geometric grid upon it before land sales began. The report had its first reading before Congress on May 7, 1784, with no vote taken, but it failed to pass when voted upon after its second reading on May 28. By then Jefferson had been elected treaty commissioner to France and was no longer in Congress. Finally, on May 20, 1785, a revised version of the bill passed as the Land Ordinance.[60] The land was divided into townships six miles square, one-square-mile (640 acre) lots were offered for sale, and land was set aside to be sold to support public education.

Two years later, Congress essentially replaced the Ordinance of 1784 with the Northwest Ordinance of 1787, which kept much of what Jefferson had originally proposed. Since the later act dealt only with the territory north of the Ohio River, it reinstituted a prohibition against slavery. The hand of Jefferson was still evident despite the revisions, compromises, and new political realities.[61]

Jefferson viewed the western territories in the context of nationalism. He expected commerce between the future western states and the older eastern states to bind the nation together in mutually advantageous trade. He was quick to promote river navigation and canal building to further such commerce. Whatever he might have once thought about the primacy of agriculture, he was alert to social and economic change and revised his views accordingly. As he wrote Washington shortly after delivering the report on western lands, "All the world is becoming commercial. Was it practicable to keep our new empire separated from them we might indulge ourselves in speculating whether commerce contributes to the happiness of mankind. But we cannot separate ourselves from them. Our citizens have had too full a taste of the comforts furnished by the arts and manufactures to be debarred the use of them. We must then in our own defence endeavor to share as large a portion as we can of this modern source of wealth and power."[62] No other politician was more convinced of the promise of the West—at the time, he was thinking only of the lands east of the Mississippi River—than Jefferson.

He made another of his concerns known during his time in Congress, too. Jefferson had long opposed hereditary privilege, as evidenced by his proposals, in the Virginia legislature, to do away with entail and primogeniture. The issue arose again in early 1784. The previous year a group of army officers had organized the Society of Cincinnati, open to officers who had served a minimum of three years in the Continental Army or Navy. Among its provisions was a version of primogeniture by which membership passed down to the eldest son after the death of the original member. This feature elicited great criticism, resulting in provocative pamphlets and fiery words. George Washington, appointed temporary president of the group and always alert to the effect of his public actions, asked Jefferson if he, in full frankness, would give him his opinion on the society. Jefferson condemned in no uncertain words the implications of hereditary organizations.[63] Subsequently Washington used his considerable influence to convince the society, in his words, to "discontinue the hereditary part in all its connexions, *absolutely*."[64]

Then there was another perennial problem: money. In addition to raising sufficient funds to operate the government, the lack of a mint and a standardized currency was proving a source of immense difficulty for the young nation. In the early 1780s Americans still used a wide variety of European coins of differing values, and these circulated amid much confusion over their comparative value. In September 1776 Jefferson had made elaborate calculations and notes on the comparative values of more than a dozen coins in common usage and then prepared a report for Congress relating these values to a popular Spanish coin called the dollar.[65] But the issue persisted, compelling Jefferson to author a report in April 1784 advocating a monetary system based on the dollar as the basic unit (pegged to both gold and silver). The various coins had values based on a decimal ratio to the dollar, which represented an even one hundred cents. Here was the first monetary system ever based on the decimal system. Jefferson left Congress before action could be taken, but he passed on copies of his report to several colleagues. Congressman David Howell of Rhode Island helped to get it published in the *Providence Gazette*. The following year Congress took up the topic, reprinted the newspaper version of Jefferson's informal report, and soon adopted it largely unchanged.[66]

JEFFERSON WAS A capacious thinker, and while in his most theoretical mode he might have preferred a largely agricultural society populated with small, landholding farmers, he understood the complicated globalized world in which he lived, including the necessity of trade or commerce not only within a nation but between nations. He, among others in Congress, had been appalled to learn from Britain's July 2, 1783, order-in-council that the United States was excluded from trade with the British West Indies. This confirmed that Britain intended to restrict US trade in a variety of ways and to continue dominating US commerce, both imports and exports. Jefferson, long committed to free trade, certainly wanted both to wean the United States off dependence upon Britain and to reward France for its wartime support by increasing trade with that nation.[67] To do so involved gaining congressional authority over trade conducted by US citizens and persuading European nations to open up to American merchants. On this topic, Jefferson was a committed nationalist, not a supporter of states' rights.[68]

He had chaired a congressional committee in December 1783 that produced a report consisting of instructions for the US ministers in Europe for negotiating treaties of "amity and commerce with the commercial powers of Europe."[69] The instructions centered on the idea of an anti-mercantilist system of free trade, with the American commissioners given authority to negotiate such treaties as they thought appropriate. And the instructions directed explicitly "that these U.S. be considered in all such Treaties and in every case arising under them as one Nation."[70] Individual states had no authority to seek trade agreements. Several weeks later, having received a letter from Benjamin Franklin reporting that commissioner John Jay was returning to the United States, Congress almost immediately elected him as secretary for foreign affairs. To replace Jay it appointed Jefferson as minister plenipotentiary, to augment the ambassadorial team of Franklin and John Adams "for the purpose of negotiating *treaties* of Commerce." On the same day Congress adopted a slightly revised version of the instructions that Jefferson's committee of 1783 had drafted.[71] Jefferson had in effect created his own job.

THE ALACRITY WITH which Jefferson prepared for his new mission reveals his excitement at the prospect of finally going to Paris. The very day of his election he wrote to ask William Short to join him as private secretary and to bring Jefferson's slave James Hemings with him to Philadelphia; James would go to Paris with the Jefferson entourage. Later Jefferson wrote what must have been understood as good-bye letters to his sister Martha Jefferson Carr; to his sister-in-law Elizabeth Wayles Eppes; to his middle daughter Polly, who along with his youngest, Lucy, was staying with the Eppeses; to his other sister-in-law Anne Wayles Skipwith; to his unmarried sister Anna Scott Jefferson; and to a number of friends and political associates. On May 9 he wrote to Francis Eppes and Nicholas Lewis to take charge of his business affairs in Virginia, as he had done in early 1783 when he first thought he was going to France. The house at Monticello would be practically shut up for the duration of his French service. Jefferson sold James Monroe all his books and house furnishings in Annapolis.[72] Then he left for Philadelphia.

Once there, Jefferson paid all his accounts, including Mrs. Hopkinson for boarding Patsy. He purchased books, trunks, and an unfinished portrait of Washington, which he would have completed in Paris. He also bought a large panther skin to present to the Comte de Buffon, who had written disparagingly about the size of animals in North America. He also took time to buy two tickets so he and Patsy could see a balloon ascension in Philadelphia, all the rage then. He paid three years of dues to the American Philosophical Society.[73] He received from Charles Thomson, secretary to the Continental Congress, a detailed set of commissions and instructions for negotiating treaties of amity and commerce, portions of which he had, of course, written himself.[74]

As Jefferson finalized his plans, he had reason to worry again about the viability of the new nation. The trusted Thomson had written from Annapolis on May 19, "Unless a different spirit prevail from what has of late appeared there is reason to apprehend a dissolution of the Confederacy." Two days later Samuel Hardy—the delegate from Virginia who had nominated Jefferson for the post in France—reported that a recent controversy over the eligibility of the Rhode Island delegation had brought forth a "great diversity of sentiment, and more altercation than I have ever seen either in Congress or any other place."[75] Fear for the new nation's survival was never far from Jefferson's mind. Yet he was nevertheless preparing to go to France in part to "convert all Europe to the commercial principles of the American Revolution."[76] It was a bold mission indeed; Jefferson saw himself as an advocate for the entire nation, not just the southern states.[77]

On May 28, forty-one-year-old Jefferson and eleven-year-old Patsy set out. They went by way of Trenton, Princeton, and Brunswick, arriving in New York City on May 30. Jefferson had composed a detailed list of questions concerning the form of government for each state he expected to visit; the costs of various categories of labor; the role of shipbuilding; the infrastructure for navigation; the nature of the fisheries, exports, imports, and manufactures; the freight costs to various destinations; the amount of debt owed Great Britain; and how the state had handled persons and property as specified by the treaty with Great Britain. He subsequently received answers to his queries from New York, Connecticut, Rhode Island, Massachusetts, and New Hampshire.[78] Father and daughter spent six days in New York City, where, among other things, Jefferson borrowed a copy of *Don Quixote* and bought a Spanish dictionary. He had every intention of making good use of his time aboard ship.[79]

From New York City they traveled through Connecticut, stopping in New Haven, where Jefferson visited Ezra Stiles, president of Yale College.

They discussed their respective colleges, Yale and William & Mary, their respective states, and new developments in science. Stiles confided to his diary that Jefferson was "a most ingenuous Naturalist and Philosopher, a truly scientific and learned Man, and every way excellent."[80] Then they were on their way again: Hartford, New London, into Rhode Island and Providence, arriving in Boston on June 18. Jefferson found that Abigail Adams and her daughter Nabby were about to leave for France, and he would have liked to make the Atlantic voyage with them. But he still had preparations to make, and the Adamses could not delay their ship, so his hopes were dashed. After three days in Boston, Jefferson arranged for Patsy to stay there several more days with the family of Judge John Lowell while he extended his travels of inspection through other Massachusetts cities and into New Hampshire. He returned to Boston in time to meet with a delegation of the General Court of Massachusetts on the state's commerce.[81]

By this time he had made a reservation to cross the Atlantic aboard the *Ceres*, owned by Nathaniel Tracy, a learned merchant, philanthropist, and Harvard graduate, who was making the voyage himself. There were only six other passengers besides Jefferson, Patsy, and James Hemings. Just before the break of dawn on July 5, 1785, the *Ceres* lifted anchor for England, whose mainland it would reach twenty-one days later.[82] The sojourn in France would prove transformative not only for Jefferson and Patsy but for the Monticello slaves who joined them in Paris.

PART III

PARIS, 1784–1790

9

"On the Vaunted Scene of Europe"

J EFFERSON NORMALLY suffered terribly from seasickness, but the voyage to France was so smooth that he was barely ill, although Patsy was sick for two days. According to her, the sun shone the whole trip, and the ocean "was as calm as a river."[1] During the passage Jefferson read at least volume one of his Cervantes, then put it aside, perhaps because he thought his Spanish good enough to suffice. As was his wont, each day at noon he recorded the ship's latitude and longitude, as well as the wind direction and temperature, and noted the distance traveled in the last twenty-four hours. He wrote about sightings of a variety of seabirds as well as sharks, a spouting whale, and a terrifying Portuguese man-of-war. After only nineteen days at sea they spotted, at 10:00 p.m., the famous Scilly lighthouse on the westernmost finger of Cornwall. Two days later, on July 26, 1784, they landed at West Cowes, a small port city on the Isle of Wight, off the English coast.[2] Following a visit to the custom house to pay their fees, Jefferson arranged transport to the mainland city of Portsmouth for himself, Patsy, and James Hemings. Patsy had developed a cold and a fever over the last few days at sea, so the party tarried several days at Portsmouth, Jefferson paying a British military doctor from the nearby naval garrison for two visits to her.[3]

While Patsy recuperated, Jefferson toured the immediate region. On July 31, having booked passage on a small ship, he, Patsy, and James, along with all their baggage and his phaeton (which he had shipped from America), set forth at about 6:00 p.m. across the English Channel, bound for Le Havre de Grace. The overnight voyage was miserable. Their cabin, as Patsy remembered it, was "not more than three feet wide and about four feet long." She and her father had to crawl into the tiny room, and with only a short bench to lie on, they slept fitfully in their clothes. The sea was rough, and it rained violently, so they had to keep the windows closed; they spent the entire night in the dark, with Patsy seasick.[4] Upon their arrival, their troubles continued. While Jefferson could read French and thought he could speak it, he was utterly flummoxed by the patois he encountered on the docks at Le Havre. Luckily a helpful Irishman came to their aid.

Through his services they found accommodations in a nearby hotel, but Jefferson—taken advantage of by the dockworkers—ended up paying as much to have his baggage carted to the hotel as it had cost him to ship it from Boston.[5] He engaged a "broker" to handle the customs officials. He then hired horses to pull his phaeton and gave James money to pay for a horse on which to ride separately to Paris via Rouen. Then he and Patsy began their journey toward the French capital.[6] Every twelve miles or so they stopped at a relay station for fresh horses. Each time, they were swarmed by beggars, an unsettling annoyance that nevertheless did not prevent them from enjoying their travel. As Patsy put it, they were in "the most beautiful country I ever saw in my life, . . . a perfect garden."[7] This disjunction between the beauty and fecundity of the land and the poverty of most of the populace would shape Jefferson's ultimate evaluation of France.

IT TOOK THEM FIVE days to reach Paris. They lingered a bit in Rouen, where Patsy enjoyed the cathedral and Jefferson inspected the famous Marly waterworks that provided water for the gardens at Versailles. But Jefferson was eager to get to the capital. His friend St. John de Crèvecoeur had written that he hoped Jefferson would "be pleas'ed with our Social Scène, which is the Shining Side of our Nation." He recommended to him the Duc de La Rochefoucauld, "the pearl of all the Dukes," to whom Crèvecoeur was writing a letter of introduction on Jefferson's behalf.[8] Jefferson also looked forward to reuniting with his fellow commissioners, Benjamin Franklin and John Adams.

Finally, on August 6, 1784, they arrived. Jefferson took accommodations at the Hôtel d'Orleans rue Richlieu on the Right Bank, not the more commercial Hôtel d'Orleans rue Petits Augustins on the Left Bank, where he had intended to stay. Little wonder he was confused. Jefferson had never seen such a large city; with a population of 600,000, Paris was fifteen times the size of Philadelphia, the largest city in the United States. Even before moving to the correct hotel on August 10, Jefferson took pains to buy more stylish clothes for Patsy—if he knew anything about Paris, it was the importance placed on fashion.[9] He soon improved his own wardrobe as well. Throughout his time in Paris he wore his hair long, tied into a ball at the back; he also kept it stylishly powdered and scented with pomade.

Jefferson spent his initial weeks in Paris preparing for his diplomatic work, but he also had to establish his residence, find Patsy a school, and handle a variety of mundane matters. He dined on August 15 with Thomas Barclay, the American consul general to France, as well as John and Abigail Adams, along with their teenaged children, Nabby (short for Abigail) and John Quincy Adams.[10] They would all enjoy each other's company over the next ten months. By that point, Jefferson already had begun to frequent the book stores and stalls along the Seine; he confessed in 1789 that he suffered "grievously under the malady of Bibliomanie." Years later Jefferson described his Parisian collecting habits: "I devoted every afternoon I was disengaged, for a summer or two, in examining all the principal bookstores, turning over every book with my own hands, and putting by every thing which related to America, and indeed whatever was rare & valuable in every science."[11] On August 20 he engaged a *valet de chambre* (valet), Marc, who, once Jefferson rented a house, would serve as *maître d'hôtel* (butler) until Jefferson fired him in June 1786 for what amounted to embezzlement. On August 26, thanks to the good offices of the Marquis de Chastellux, who persuaded the Comtesse de Brionne to act as Patsy's sponsor, Jefferson enrolled his daughter in the prestigious Abbaye Royale de Panthemont, a convent school also on the Left Bank.[12] Moreover, he paid for Patsy's special instruction at the school in drawing, dancing, Italian, and the harpsichord.

Already aware of what he later called "the infidelities of the post-offices both of England and France,"[13] Jefferson began encrypting his correspondence with most Americans, especially officials like John Jay and friends such as James Madison. Everyone seemed to have trouble at times correctly deciphering the codes, which usually consisted of a grid containing over 625 random letters.[14] Jefferson also kept exact copies of important correspondence, which meant hours of tedious work performed by a clerk. Since the 1770 fire at his ancestral home of Shadwell had destroyed many of his papers, Jefferson had made the production of copies a habit.

He had earlier learned from Benjamin Franklin of a copying press patented in 1780 by James Watt—the pioneer of steam technology—and in fact had ordered a Watt press in 1783, but it did not arrive before he left for France. So on August 16 he gave money to Franklin's son William Temple

Franklin to order him another press, which finally arrived in Paris in May of the following year. He would use the press for almost twenty years (until he adopted a new invention, the polygraph, in early 1804) and actually designed a portable version that he took with him when traveling. Watt's copying press, which Franklin and George Washington also used, employed a special kind of ink that reproduced itself on a dampened sheet of extremely thin paper firmly pressed on the initial page after the original writing had dried. The reproduced handwriting had to be read through the thin copying paper because the transferred ink created a mirror image of the original handwriting.[15]

Jefferson always had in mind not only his own reputation but that of his nation. He knew that government officials of his rank were expected to entertain various dignitaries, from France and other nations. Consequently, on October 16, 1784, he rented a house, the Hôtel Landron, on the Right Bank, at the cul-de-sac Taitbout.[16] According to the custom in Paris, it came unfurnished, and Jefferson had to spend dearly to acquire furniture, china, drapes, and more.

The house, which required four servants to run, was far more expensive than his earlier quarters. He knew beforehand that his income was not nearly sufficient. Still, the house did not signal that he was living extravagantly; in comparison, John Adams was renting a larger house in Auteuil, on the outskirts of Paris, that could sleep forty.[17] Meanwhile Nabby Adams wrote in her journal that the Spanish ambassador had a hundred servants in his house; the English ambassador employed fifty.[18] This was the reality of the diplomatic scene in Paris.

On November 11, Jefferson wrote James Monroe privately of his financial stress. Long concerned over his personal debts, Jefferson had hoped to apply all the proceeds from his plantations at Monticello and elsewhere to pay off what he owed and thereby live in Paris on his salary alone. But he discovered that Congress had reduced his salary by 20 percent and ceased to pay living expenses, as it had done earlier for Franklin. The necessity of establishing his residence—which was, in essence, the US embassy—threatened to bankrupt Jefferson. He explained to Monroe that he was living at about the level he and Monroe had several years previously when both had been delegates to Congress at Annapolis. "Be assured," he wrote to Monroe, "we are the lowest and most obscure of the whole diplomatic tribe." He asked his friend to discreetly check if Congress would at least reimburse him for what he called his "outfit."[19] But Jefferson got no assistance, so he sacrificed his own assets.

Jefferson's status changed in the spring of 1785. John Adams was appointed the American minister to England, so he and his family moved to London—a great personal loss to Jefferson. As Jefferson confided to Adams toward the end of May, "The departure of your family has left me in the dumps."[20] The feeling was mutual. Abigail wrote Jefferson, "I think I have somewhere met the observation that nobody ever leaves paris but with a degree of tristeness. I own I was loth to leave my garden. . . . I was still more loth on account of the increasing pleasure, and intimacy which a longer acquaintance with a respected Friend promised, to leave behind me the only person with whom my Companion could associate with perfect freedom, and unreserve."[21] Abigail said much the same in a letter to her sister: "I shall really regret to leave Mr. Jefferson; he is one of the choice ones of nature."[22] At the same time the Adamses departed, Franklin at last received approval of his request to retire in Philadelphia, with the result that Congress appointed Jefferson the American minister to France. While he had liked and gotten along perfectly with the popular Franklin—unlike Adams, who was constantly angry at Franklin, believing he received too much credit, and complained unceasingly about his behavior—Jefferson had been more comfortable visiting in the Adams home.

JEFFERSON RECEIVED HIS commission from the US Congress on May 2 and had to formally present himself and his credentials at the Court of Versailles on May 17. The new position meant a change in social obligations. On May 22 he hired as his valet Adrien Petit, who came over from the Adams family; Petit would later become his *maître d'hôtel* in 1786 after Marc was dismissed. Jefferson also realized that he now needed a larger, more advantageously located house. On October 17 he moved into the Hôtel de Langeac. The twenty-four-room building boasted lovely oval-shaped rooms, including Jefferson's bedroom overlooking the gardens, where he grew Indian corn, watermelons, and sweet potatoes. The home's second floor even had piped-in water and two flush toilets.[23] The grand salon, illuminated by a skylight, as well as the handsome dining room, made it an appropriate location for the formal dinners that Jefferson frequently hosted. Still, he seemed to prefer the informal Sunday evening family dinners with his daughters (Polly would come to Paris in 1787) and one or two intimate friends. Jefferson now employed six servants, including a *cuisiniere* (cook), until James, who took French cooking lessons at Jefferson's insistence, assumed those duties in 1787.

Jefferson came to prefer French food and considered the money for James's training well spent. Before eventually returning to Monticello, Jefferson bought a complete set of French cooking utensils, along with—showing still broader preferences for European foods—a waffle iron and a macaroni machine, the products of which he introduced to American cuisine.[24] He also became a fan of vanilla ice cream, writing out his own recipe so that he might enjoy it and serve it to guests in the United States.[25] Much later, diners at the White House would benefit from Jefferson's preferences as a gourmand. And of course he also became expert in French wines.

The Hôtel de Langeac's location at the corner of rue de Berri and the Champs Élysées (near the present-day Arc de Triomphe) was then at the western fringe of Paris, adjacent to one of the custom gates, the Grille de Chaillot, where tolls were collected from those who entered the walled city. The walls were tax barriers, not the defensive structures of medieval times, which had been torn down in the seventeenth century and replaced by a circular greenspace.[26] A short journey further west brought Jefferson to the Bois de Boulogne, the former royal hunting park. Whenever possible Jefferson took lengthy walks at midday, and like John Adams, he loved to stroll through these wooded acres. Over the course of his public life, he often felt the need to retreat from the pressures of his office and find a quiet place to work. He found such a place shortly beyond the Bois de Boulogne, where a community of lay brothers called the Hermites operated a boardinghouse for guests. Especially in 1787 and 1788, Jefferson frequently rented a room there for solitude to study and write. As his daughter recalled long afterward, "Whenever he had a press of business, he was in the habit of taking his papers and going to the hermitage, where he spent sometimes a week or more till he had finished his work."[27]

JEFFERSON WAS ON official assignment in Paris and worked tirelessly to advance American interests. But he was also an infinitely curious, humane, and cosmopolitan American eager to engage what he considered the most civilized city on the globe. Paris during the 1780s was undergoing a building boom, and many of today's landmark structures were finished while Jefferson lived there.[28] In the seventeenth century the city had already become recognized as the most beautiful in Europe, with great public gardens like the Tuileries, extensive street paving, and nighttime illumination by means of thousands of candle-lit lanterns on the main city streets.[29]

When Jefferson and Patsy first arrived in Paris, their hotel was adjacent to the most exciting new structure, the Palais Royal. The older palace at the location had been remodeled and opened that year as a *U*-shaped four-story arcade, two blocks long and surrounding a courtyard; the entire bottom floor featured a colonnaded walkway, behind which were restaurants, luxury stores, bookshops, art galleries, cafes, the editorial offices of dozens of newspapers, and a variety of amusements high and low. It seemed the beating heart of the city. Everyone of style and substance came to visit, to shop, to attend concerts, to discuss philosophy and politics, to court, to see and be seen. As with Dr. Johnson's London, no one could tire of the Palais Royal. Jefferson loved the crowds, the bookshops, the music and art, and he even briefly joined a chess club there.[30] Other Americans had similar experiences, whether it was New York financier Gouverneur Morris enjoying lemonade and ice, John Quincy Adams describing the "vast fund of entertainment," Nabby Adams gushing over the pleasant walks through the Palais, or artist John Trumbull judging it "magnificent, and in good taste."[31]

Near the Palais Royal sat a more utilitarian building that Jefferson also greatly admired, the circular Halle aux Bleds, the city's grain market. This structure's great dome set it apart: wooden beams, with panes of glass between them, arched across the immense court below. The result was a courtyard filled with sunlight. Jefferson called it a "wonderful piece of architecture . . . the most superb thing on earth."[32] He likewise enjoyed the huge Church of Sainte Geneviève (now known as the Pantheon), then under construction and completed in 1789.

But Jefferson absolutely fell in love with a smaller domed building, the Hôtel de Salm, a construction project underway just south of the Seine across from the Tuileries Gardens, where he loved to walk and rent a chair so he could relax among its trees.[33] The palace, the last great one built in the city and designed for a young German prince, went up between 1782 and 1787. It was gleaming white, set amid gardens on the edge of the Seine (and near the home of Lafayette). Jefferson was entranced by its horizontal look and its low, flattened dome.[34] As he wrote to Lafayette's aunt, Madame de Tessé, "I was violently smitten with the hotel de Salm, and used to go to the Thuileries almost daily to look at it."[35]

The dome of the Hôtel de Salm inspired Jefferson to fundamentally redesign Monticello, then a two-story Georgian structure. He would turn it into a low horizontal building that camouflaged its actual three-story height and cap it with the dome that became perhaps its most recognizable

Detail of The Building of the Hotel de Salm, 1786.

Source: De Agostini Picture Library/G. Dagli Orti/Bridgeman Images,
New York City. Used by permission.

feature. Jefferson's interest in architecture expanded beyond contemplation of Monticello. As he walked and rode about Paris, he admired the gardens surrounding the Luxembourg Palace and the Jardin du Roi, the public buildings, the handsome domestic architecture that adorned the main boulevards, the book stalls along the Seine near the Ile de la Cité, and the many bridges. Gouverneur Morris once remarked in his diary that during a ride with Jefferson, the latter had specifically requested that they go across the "Bridge of Neuilly, which I had crossed four Times without re-marking it and which he says is the handsomest in the World."[36]

While Jefferson appreciated painting and sculpture and saw as much of each as he could, he considered architecture the most valuable art for the United States. The nation's rapid growth would necessitate a great amount of construction. Thus it was "desireable to introduce taste into an art which shews so much."[37] He came to greatly admire the magnificent east facade of the Louvre Palace, its classical form designed during the reign of Louis XIV by Claude Perrault and intended as the front of the palace. Jefferson called this 548-foot wing the Galerie du Louvre. Later, when Pierre Charles L'Enfant was engaged to design the new capital city in the United States, Jefferson wrote him suggesting as models not only examples from classical antiquity but also some of "the celebrated fronts of Modern buildings which have already received the approbation of all good judges." He went on to single out the Galerie du Louvre, along with his adored Hôtel de Salm.[38]

In March 1785 Jefferson received a letter on behalf of officials in Richmond announcing that they had started to construct several public buildings to house government offices and asking for architectural advice. He confided to James Madison the following month that he had decided to model the capitol building in Richmond after a Roman temple in Nîmes called the Maison Carrée, built just before the beginning of the common era; Jefferson called it "one of the most beautiful, if not the most beautiful and precious morsel of architecture left us by antiquity." He based this judgment on engravings he had seen.[39] When he eventually saw it in person, he wrote Madame de Tessé that he sat "gazing whole hours at the Maison quarree, like a lover at his mistress."[40] To assist the Richmond builders, Jefferson had a scale model constructed. Justifying his choice to Madison, Jefferson asked, "How is taste in this beautiful art to be formed in our countrymen, unless we avail ourselves of every occasion when public buildings are to be erected, of presenting to them models for their study and imitation?"[41] Thus did Jefferson introduce the temple form of classical architecture to the United States.

IN TERMS OF PERSONAL enjoyment, at least, music had long been Jefferson's favorite art form. Within weeks of arriving in Paris, he bought tickets to comic operas (at the Comédie-Italienne and the Comédie-Française), and on September 8, 1784, he first attended the *concert spirituel*, held about every other week in one of the large pavilions flanking the Tuileries. These concerts, featuring a fifty-eight-piece orchestra, usually included a symphony by Franz Joseph Haydn and a variety of shorter pieces.[42] Jefferson would return again and again. He continued to attend the operas, seeing many of the most prominent productions; he particularly liked the popular composer Niccolò Piccini but also heard works by Wolfgang Amadeus Mozart, George Frideric Handel, and Christoph Willibald Gluck. He also attended organ concerts at Notre-Dame Cathedral, even employing its accomplished organist, Claude Balbastre, to give Patsy harpsicord lessons at the Hôtel de Langeac. Of all the attributes of Paris, Jefferson most treasured its musical riches. As he explained to an Italian friend, "Were I to proceed to tell you how much I enjoy their architecture, sculpture, painting, music, I should want words. It is in these arts they shine. The last of them particularly is an enjoyment, the deprivation of which with us cannot be calculated. I am almost ready to say it is the only thing which from my heart I envy them, and which in spight of all the authority of the Decalogue I do covet."[43]

The musical sensation of the time was Pierre Beaumarchais's *Le mariage de Figaro, ou la folle journée*, which Jefferson saw on August 4, 1786. The play, whose author had surreptitiously funneled supplies to the American rebels during the revolution, was a risqué satire of the aristocracy and a subtle critique of the monarchy. For French audiences, it was both controversial and irresistible. Jefferson saw it in the new Théâtre Français building called the Odéon, which had opened in 1782, with a bust of Voltaire by Jean-Antoine Houdon in the lobby.[44] Even the Adams family saw *Figaro*; the proper Nabby Adams did not completely approve of its "low wit."[45] For his part, Jefferson had simply fallen in love with Paris. He exulted in the opportunity to savor his experience, blurting out to a correspondent, "Behold me at length on the vaunted scene of Europe!"[46]

Paris was also Jefferson's entrée into the world of fine art. Before coming to the city, he had seen notable works of art only as black-and-white engravings in books. Now, finding himself in a city filled with real art and artists, he enthusiastically embraced the artistic scene, attending exhibitions and frequenting galleries. Jefferson typically did not view art collections alone. The American artist John Trumbull spent weeks living at the Hôtel de Langeac and accompanied Jefferson to galleries, helping him develop a more sophisticated understanding of and appreciation for what he saw. Jefferson met other artists, including Jean-Antoine Houdon, Jacques-Louis David, Hubert Robert.[47] He also bought art, often copies of famous works, to bring back to Monticello. His choices evinced his politics and intellectual concerns. He avoided portraits of kings, selecting instead those of great men (explorers, scientists, American Founders), history paintings, biblical scenes, and depictions of antiquity.[48] He brought back from Paris what became one of the more extensive private art collections in America.

JEFFERSON FOUND THE social scene in Paris scintillating if a bit artificial. On the surface he could seem shy, but he was a marvelous conversationalist: soft-spoken, remarkably well read, genuinely interested in nearly every possible topic, and irenic in demeanor. He never sounded shrill, angry, or confrontational; he seldom bluntly disagreed with anyone, and his dislike of contentiousness sometimes misled interlocutors into thinking he agreed with them when he was simply being polite. In fact, throughout his life, this characteristic led some people to believe him two-faced, because they mistook his tactful nodding for accord.

Jefferson's savoir faire quickly made him a favorite among the intellectuals and cultural elite of Parisian drawing rooms. If he did not have the colorful fame of Franklin, the fur-capped scientist who had tamed lightening, Jefferson was seen as an exemplar of the philosopher as statesman.[49] A young American, seeing Jefferson at the court of Versailles, wrote his father, "I observed that although Mr. Jefferson was the plainest man in the room, and the most destitute of ribbands crosses and other insignia of rank that he was most courted and most attended to (even by the Courtiers themselves) of the whole Diplomatic corps."[50] Jefferson had become a celebrity of sorts, the darling of the French enlightened who loved the idea of America.

At the time, Paris was the intellectual center of the Western world. Although several of the greatest minds had died only a few years before Jefferson's arrival—Voltaire and Jean-Jacques Rousseau both in 1778, Anne-Robert-Jacques Turgot in 1781, and Denis Diderot in 1784—the city still hosted a galaxy of savants, known then as now as philosophes and literati. With introductions by Franklin and recommendations from Lafayette and Chastellux, Jefferson soon became known to all the important thinkers and writers, many of them admirers of the American Revolution and the idea of the new nation. He was invited to their homes and often invited them to his. He grew especially close to the Marquis de Condorcet and the Duc de La Rochefoucauld (and his remarkable mother, the Duchess d'Anville), Pierre Samuel Du Pont de Nemours (whose friendship with Jefferson lasted thirty years), the Abbé Morellet, and, most of all, Lafayette (and also his aunt, Madame de Tessé). With these men and their impressive women relatives—who were every bit their intellectual equals—Jefferson discussed philosophy, the arts, science, and government.[51]

More fashionable perhaps were the public salons of such women as Madame d'Houdetot, Madame Necker, and Madame Helvétius, who on a regular day of the week had an entourage of writers, thinkers, and artists gather for playful and serious conversation about ideas. Jefferson attended these events occasionally but never became infatuated with them, as did

Franklin; nor was he utterly disgusted by them, as were John and Abigail Adams.

Abigail was especially repulsed by Madame Helvétius. Describing an evening at this woman's salon, she recorded that after dinner the madame "threw herself upon a settee, where she showed more than her feet. She had a little lap-dog, who was, next to the Doctor, her favorite. This she kissed, and when he wet the floor she wiped it up with her chemise. This is one of the Doctor's most intimate friends, with whom he dines every week, and she with him."[52] Franklin, by contrast, reveled in these encounters, often with women sitting on his lap and patting and kissing him, drawing John Adams's complete contempt. Jefferson too found this behavior off-putting and was reserved at the salons he attended.

The hosts and the roster of philosophes with whom Jefferson consorted were not only sympathetic to the United States but in a position to assist it. Jefferson courted them assiduously and to good effect. As Gouverneur Morris wrote to financier Robert Morris, "I feel it a Duty also to mention that he [Jefferson] commands very much Respect in the Country and which is merited by good Sense and good Intentions."[53] Although Jefferson could hardly have been more unlike Franklin in the diplomatic venue of Paris and its fashionable salons, in his own way he proved immensely popular and effective.

IO

At Home in Paris

THE ABBAYE ROYALE de Panthemont, the most prestigious convent school in Paris, was headed by the powerful and worldly Madame Béthisy de Méziéres. Jefferson soon found himself paying extra so that Patsy could take her meals at the abbess's table. There were about sixty students, of all ages, and instruction included reading, math, geography, and history, as well as music, drawing, and dancing; Jefferson also secured private tutors for Patsy in the last three. Students were not strictly confined within the gates of the convent. Patsy went home to be with her father almost every Sunday, and he occasionally took her to concerts and special dinners. The students went on excursions to the Palais Royal, the Tuileries, and even Versailles. She also attended events with the wives and mothers of several of Jefferson's eminent friends. The convent was home to wealthy spinsters, widows, and women estranged from their husbands, so the girls had, in a way, contact with the larger world.[1]

As Patsy wrote to her adult friend Elizabeth Trist in Philadelphia, at first she was unhappy at the school because she could not speak French, but she quickly became fluent. During the first month or two, until she felt at home, Jefferson visited her every evening. "At present I am charmed with my situation," she soon reported.[2] She was evidently popular with the other students, who called her "Jeffy." The students wore crimson-colored frocks "laced behind with the tail like a robe de cour hoocked on muslim cufs and tuckers."[3] Later her father asked her, when coming home for the weekend, to wear her normal dresses rather than her uniform. Jefferson reassured several worried relatives and friends who feared Catholic influence that the convent did not proselytize and that several other students were Protestant too.

Jefferson continued to send his daughter didactic letters, with constant admonitions about avoiding laziness, dressing neatly, and studying hard, and ending with professions of his love. Patsy took the fatherly advice good naturedly and came to respond with more and more independence. In March 1787, when Jefferson was traveling to the south of France, Patsy chided him for not writing. "You promised to write me every week. Until now you have not kept your word the least in the world, but I hope you will make up for your silence by writing me a fine, long letter by the first opportunity."[4] Several days later a letter did finally arrive, but it was less about his adventures and more concerned with exhortatory advice, with lines like "No laborious person was ever yet hysterical."[5] Patsy couldn't let that stand unanswered. "As for the hysteria, you may be quiet on that head, as I am not lazy enough to fear [hysterics]." In a moment of filial affection, she continued, "You say your expectations for me are high, yet not higher than I can attain. Then be assured, my dear papa, that you shall be satisfied in that, as well as in any thing else that lies in my power; for what I hold most precious is your satisfaction, indeed I should be miserable without it." She couldn't stop there—now for the coup de grâce: "You wrote me a long letter, as I asked you; however, it would have been much more so without so wide a margin."[6]

Patsy was beginning to think for herself and was confident enough to express her opinions to her father. A few weeks after complaining about his wide margins, she wrote, "I wish with all my soul that the poor negroes were all freed. It grieves my heart when I think that these our fellow creatures should be treated so teribly as they are by many of our country men."[7] Jefferson generally criticized French women for openly expressing political opinions, but he must have agreed with Patsy's sentiments (she had probably heard him say much the same). Throughout their correspondence their love for each other glowed. Patsy absolutely adored her father, a sentiment he reciprocated. And to the end of her life, she valued the education she had received in Paris, employing her learning in supervising the education of her children and grandchildren.

JEFFERSON'S DEDICATION extended to his younger daughters as well. Because he did not know how long he would serve in Paris, he had left two-year-old Lucy and six-year-old Mary (or Polly) with their aunt Elizabeth Wayles Eppes; he wanted them to enjoy life in a household filled with children and also receive loving maternal supervision. Then, on January 26, 1785, he received a shocking letter from one Dr. James Currie.

After several sentences about random topics—as though he dreaded getting to the point—he wrote, "I am sincerely sorry my dear friend now to acquaint you of the demise of poor Miss L. Jefferson, who fell a Martyr to the complicated evils of teething, Worms and Hooping Cough. . . . Miss P. Jefferson got early over it and is now in good health."[8] Had Jefferson received an earlier letter sent in mid-September by Mrs. Eppes reporting that her daughter Lucy and son Bolling were quite ill with whooping cough, he might have been somewhat prepared for the news.[9]

Jefferson was devastated. Not only would he never see the child again, but he had not been there as she suffered. No doubt Lucy's death brought back his grief over her mother's death, just months after Lucy's birth. As Jefferson wrote to his sister, "It would be difficult to find a fibre of the human heart whose sufferings are unknown to me. My losses have left me little more to lose."[10] He seemed almost beyond despair. He wrote stoically to Francis Eppes on February 5, "It is in vain to endeavor to describe the situation of my mind; it would pour balm neither into your wounds nor mine; I will therefore pass on from the subject."[11] But he manifestly could not simply pass on. His sense of loss, helplessness, and failed parental responsibility—his guilt—continually agitated him. In the same letter he wrote, "Present me affectionately to Mrs. Eppes, who will kiss my dear, dear Polly for me. Oh! could I do it myself!"[12]

Grief almost overcame him on May 6 when he finally received two letters written on October 13 and 14, respectively, by Elizabeth Eppes and then Francis Eppes, reporting on the death of Jefferson's Lucy (and their own Lucy). The letters could only have intensified his pain. The kindly meaning Elizabeth wrote, "Your dear angel was confined a week to her bed, her sufferings were great though nothing like a fit. She retain'd her senses perfectly, called me a few minutes before she died, and asked distinctly for water." Mr. Eppes wrote that the two Lucys "both suffered as much pain, indeed more than ever I saw two of their ages experience."[13] Five days later a resolute Jefferson wrote Mr. Eppes, "I must have Polly. As would not have her at sea but between 1st of Apr. and Sep. this will allow time for decision—is there any woman in Virga. could be hired to come."[14] Sure enough, time did allow Jefferson to firm up his resolution to bring Polly to Paris, but how would he accomplish it?

Three months later Jefferson spelled out his desiderata for Polly's voyage across the Atlantic. She would have to sail between May and August to avoid tropical storms. The vessel must have made at least one such trip before but be no older than four or five years. He proposed that they try to find "some good lady passing from America to France" to accompany her, or even a "careful gentleman" would suffice. But if the escort were male, "some woman who has had the small-pox must attend her. A careful negro woman, as Isabel, for instance, if she has had the small-pox, would suffice under the patronage of a gentleman." He added that the slave woman could be returned to Virginia after Polly was delivered. Jefferson could meet them at the coast of either France or England. "I would rather live a year longer without her than have her trusted to any but a good ship and a summer passage."[15]

IN HIS TIME AT the Hôtel de Langeac, Jefferson did not live by himself. Even before he met the new secretary of the commission, Colonel David Humphreys, Jefferson was prepared to value him on George Washington's warm recommendation.[16] Despite his military demeanor, Humphreys was an aspiring poet and a friend of John Trumbull. Jefferson initially found Humphreys a place to board, but as soon as he acquired his first house in Paris, he asked Humphreys to join him there. Humphreys continued to live in Jefferson's home until he was transferred to London in 1786; he took meals with the family and often accompanied Jefferson to dinner at the Adamses. He became a respected and valued member of Jefferson's staff.

No young man became closer to Jefferson than William Short, who also became a longtime occupant of the Jefferson home. Born in 1759, Short was a Virginian of good family, a graduate of the College of William & Mary who had studied law under the tutelage of George Wythe. But Short soon found that a legal career in Virginia was not to his liking; Jefferson, realizing this and appreciating Short's ability, diligence, and personality, had asked him in early May 1784 to join him in Paris as his assistant. Short eagerly accepted.[17] Because at first there were no government funds for his salary, Jefferson initially paid Short out of his own pocket. (Humphreys was the secretary to the commissioners as a group.) Short arrived in Paris in November 1784 and immediately took up residence in Jefferson's rented home; when Jefferson moved the following year to the larger Hôtel de Langeac, Short went with him. Soon he was on the government payroll and served Jefferson and the nation with skill and aplomb, becoming, in the process, virtually a member of Jefferson's family.

Short was an exceedingly pleasant, even charming man: handsome, a suave conversationalist, and a skilled dancer. At the beginning of his posting in Paris he lived for several months (with Jefferson's blessing) with a

William Short, by Rembrandt Peale, 1806.

Source: Muscarelle Museum of Art at the
College of William & Mary. Used by permission.

French family in order to become fluent in French.[18] After moving in with
Jefferson, he was present at most family meals; he became friendly with
Patsy, and later Polly, and looked in on them at the convent when Jefferson
was out of town.[19] Short's fluency in French made him especially valuable.
When Jefferson was away from Paris, he appointed Short chargé d'affaires
in temporary command of the legation.

HUMPHREYS AND SHORT were employees and genuine residents of
Jefferson's home, but Jefferson also entertained a number of guests, none
more important than the young artist he first met in London in 1786,
John Trumbull. Born in Connecticut in 1756 into a prominent family,
Trumbull went to London in 1780 to study with fellow American painter
Benjamin West. Jefferson and Trumbull liked one another instantly and,

when in London, discussed the current negotiations with Jean-Antoine Houdon to sculpt George Washington. Jefferson grew fascinated with the young artist's planned historical series featuring American military leaders and the British surrenders at Saratoga and Yorktown.[20] As Trumbull wrote in his autobiography, "[Jefferson] had a taste for the fine arts, and highly approved my intention of preparing myself for the accomplishment of a national work. He encouraged me to persevere in this pursuit, and kindly invited me to come to Paris, to see and study the fine works there, and to make his house my home, during my stay."[21] Accordingly Trumbull traveled to Paris in early August 1786 and took up residence at the Hôtel de Langeac. For the next few weeks he toured the city, often accompanied by Jefferson, meeting the leading Parisian artists and visiting numerous galleries.

Jefferson's interest in Trumbull's proposed American history series was serious, in part because he recognized Trumbull's ability.[22] Jefferson apparently proposed to Trumbull that he broaden his ambition and paint a scene of the signing of the Declaration of Independence. Jefferson sketched out the shape of the room and the position of the main actors for Trumbull, who, they agreed, should also consult John Adams upon returning to London. Trumbull began the painting in London in the spring of 1787, adding Adams to the scene after meeting with him. He then returned to the Hôtel de Langeac in the winter of 1787 and 1788 to paint Jefferson's portrait directly onto the small canvas. He also made three miniatures of Jefferson, one for the artist Maria Cosway, one for Angelica Church (the mother of one of Patsy's friends), and one for Patsy.[23]

The much enlarged version of Trumbull's *Declaration of Independence* (which now hangs in the US Capitol rotunda) would turn out to be his masterwork. On the twelve-by-eighteen-foot canvas, he showed American statesmen in their everyday clothes—not in the ornate costumes of a European court. With its striking depictions of Adams, Benjamin Franklin, and Jefferson (along with the lesser known figures Robert R. Livingston and Roger Sherman), it shows Jefferson handing over the completed document to a seated John Hancock. It has become one of the most iconic paintings in American history.[24]

For the remainder of his stay in Paris, Jefferson kept in regular correspondence with Trumbull, and the young artist gladly performed a number of tasks for Jefferson back in London, including making arrangements for the construction of a harpsichord for Patsy. But no favor he ever rendered Jefferson matched the unanticipated one he performed just after

Maria Cecilia Louisa Cosway,
by Valentine Green, 1787. Color mezzotint.

Source: National Gallery of Art, Washington, DC. Used by permission.

mid-August in 1786. That month, Jefferson invited Trumbull back to Paris to accompany him to the city's impressive grain market, the Halle aux Bleds. There Trumbull spied British friends of his who were also artists, Richard and Maria Cosway. Richard, an eccentric, foppish man and accomplished portraitist and miniaturist, had married but seemed often completely uninterested in Maria, twenty-seven that summer, an accomplished portraitist and musician in her own right. With a towering coiffure of curly blonde hair, blue eyes, fair skin, a tiny but graceful figure, sensuous lips, and a soft, melodious, Italian-accented voice, she found in Jefferson an almost immediate admirer.[25] He did not want the day to end, canceling other obligations so that the foursome could dine together and continue sightseeing far into the evening.

Jefferson was absolutely captivated. The next few weeks were a whirl-wind of activity. At first, he and Maria were usually accompanied by oth-ers, but soon they conspired to be alone as they toured most of the treasured locales that still make Paris such a romantic city. In the company of this petite, beautiful, and artistic woman, Jefferson saw Paris, perhaps life itself, with new passion, but this carefree interlude could not last long.[26] On the evening of September 18, while the two were strolling along a promenade beside the Seine that stretched westward from near the site of today's Place de la Concorde (then the location of the great equestrian statue of Louis XV), Jefferson playfully jumped over a low fence, stum-bled, and badly sprained his right wrist. Maybe he broke a bone, for even after seeing two surgeons, he was to suffer severe pain in the wrist for months. For weeks he wrote laboriously with his left hand.[27] He did not see Maria again until the morning of October 5, when he met her and her husband as they were entering their carriage to leave the city. And though Maria would return to Paris in August and September 1787, they hardly saw each other then. Clearly the magic of that first encounter had dissi-pated, partly because neither tried very hard to recapture it.

What was the nature of their 1786 romance, and why did the ardor cool? Historians have puzzled over this month in which Jefferson seems to have cast aside his usual measured approach to life. If the reasons for Jefferson's attractions to Maria Cosway appear obvious, his hesitations re-quire explanation. The mature Jefferson proved attractive to and became friends with many women. They were all married, and the relationships were always proper, even though the correspondence was often light, ban-tering, and teasing. To Abigail Adams, for one, he made slightly risqué al-lusions to Laurence Sterne. Jefferson always acted the gallant, often even shopping for Abigail and Nabby Adams, and he did favors for all of the women he was close to. But his interest in correct behavior became fastid-ious in Paris, because he found typical French behavior between the sexes outrageously improper and destructive of both conjugal happiness and wholesome family life. This aspect of Parisian life he found least attractive and most often condemned.

In fact, a constant theme in his letters about Parisian society was its casual attitude toward the marriage bond. To his Italian friend Charles Bellini, who was teaching at the College of William & Mary, he wrote a letter praising French art, music, and the amiableness of life, but he sin-gled out for reprobation the sexual looseness among married persons in France. "Conjugal love having no existence among them, domestic happiness, of which that is the basis, is utterly unknown. . . . Much, very much inferior this to the tranquil permanent felicity with which domestic society in America blesses most of it's inhabitants."[28] Later in 1785, he warned the traveler John Banister Jr. against many of the wicked habits young men could pick up when visiting France, where they might learn such evils as to "consider fidelity to the marriage bed as an ungentlemanly practice and inconsistent with happiness."[29] To Anne Bingham, a wealthy socialite from Philadelphia whose intellect Jefferson appreciated, he mocked the "empty bustle" of the aristocratic Parisian women who slept late, played cards, and went on endless rounds of visiting, treading "like a mill-horse, the same trodden circle over again," with nothing to show for their lives but feelings of "ennui."[30]

So while Jefferson surely found Cosway attractive, his cultural and moral objections to high society mores in Paris may have led him to stop just short of launching into an actual affair. Another factor, surely, was his promise to Martha. As for Maria she may have felt similarly restrained, though perhaps more so because she was a devout Catholic. After their parting on October 5, Jefferson struggled for several days to write out with his left hand a long farewell letter, dated October 12, regarded as perhaps the most famous missive in the entire corpus of his correspondence. Cast in the form of a dialogue between his head and his heart, it ran to an incredible 4,000 words across twelve sheets of paper.[31]

The letter begins with a mention of Maria and Richard riding away in their carriage and concludes with another mention of her husband— Jefferson's way of recognizing that she was a married woman. Within this frame, Jefferson's "heart" rapturously recreates many of their excursions and describes her as having distinguishing "qualities and accomplishments, belonging to her sex [gender]": "music, modesty, beauty, and that softness of disposition which is the ornament of her sex and charm of ours." The letter fantasizes about her coming to Virginia and the delights they had already and would in the future enjoy together. But the "head" constantly brings the unruly heart down to earth, chiding, "I often told you [that] you were imprudently engaging your affectations under circumstances that must cost you a great deal of pain."[32]

The heart monopolizes the text, as though Jefferson wanted to reassure Maria of his genuine affection for her, but in the end the head triumphs, with Jefferson in effect announcing that although it had been wonderful while it lasted, their flirtatious moment was over. It is not clear that Maria truly understood what Jefferson meant to convey in this long, artfully constructed letter. There is no record of a reply from her. In any event, Jefferson had promised his wife never to remarry, he found adulterous dalliances wrong, and he may well have assumed that a life of celibacy lay ahead. As he wrote to his old friend Elizabeth Trist that winter, "I am burning the candle of life without present pleasure, or future object. A dozen or twenty years ago this scene would have amused me. But I am past the age for changing habits. I take all the fault on myself."[33]

WHEN TRAVELERS FROM America arrived in Paris, they usually contacted Jefferson, and he often assisted them in various ways: helping them make contacts, preparing their passports, directing them to historical and artistic sites, offering them temporary residence. He saw this service as an unofficial part of his diplomatic duties. In 1786 he met the intrepid traveler John Ledyard, a native of Connecticut who as a member of Captain James Cook's third voyage had visited the northwest coast of North America. Jefferson found him fascinating, and discovering that Ledyard had put some thought into establishing a fur-trading company in the American Northwest, Jefferson persuaded him to walk across Russia and the Nootka Sound ending at the Northwest coast. Jefferson tried to secure permission from the empress of Russia for the expedition and attempted to raise funds as well, but when Ledyard, "of fearless courage, & enterprise," set forth, Russian officials turned him back.[34] Not long afterward, in 1789, Ledyard died after accidently poisoning himself during a trek up the Nile. Jefferson had feared that Ledyard would never come back from his plunge into Africa, though he reported, "If he returns, . . . [he] has promised me to go to America and penetrate from Kentucke to the Western side of the Continent."[35]

Jefferson had many other well-known and famous visitors: John Paul Jones, who was seeking employ in the Russian navy; young American tourists like John Banister Jr., Thomas Shippen, and John Rutledge Jr. (for whom Jefferson prepared a detailed itinerary for a journey through the Netherlands, Germany, and onward to Italy); and talented financier and business agent Gouverneur Morris, who would later be a member of the Constitutional Convention and still later (1792–1794) minister plenipotentiary to France.[36] None, however, caused Jefferson more trouble than John and Lucy Paradise.[37] John was superbly educated, sweet natured, and a true lover of learning, yet also totally inept in the normal business of life. He met a beautiful young Virginia heiress, Lucy Ludwell, in London, and they married in 1769. Unfortunately Lucy, with an uncontrollable temper and extravagant tastes, lived almost beyond the edge of eccentricity. Theirs was a marriage destined for disaster, and they were already headed toward bankruptcy when they met Jefferson first in London in 1786 and later in Paris. He ended up investing what can only be described as an unreasonable amount of time and energy trying to help them. But there could be no happy ending for the Paradises; John died on December 12, 1795, a shadow of the man he once had been, and nine years later Lucy at last returned to Virginia and took up residence in Williamsburg, where she quickly became noted as a colorful and unpredictable character. Three city alderman eventually ruled her insane in January 1812 and removed her to the Eastern Lunatic Asylum in the city, where she died on April 24, 1814, ending the sad tale of their lives.

AMID ALL HIS SOCIAL activities, Jefferson's mind was never free of worry about his daughter Polly. He still wanted to bring her to Paris but had not yet determined how. Beginning at the end of the summer of 1785, he made plans only to be disappointed again and again. The task was complicated by the fact that Polly was comfortable living with her aunt and several cousins in the Eppes household. Having learned that her father wanted to see her again, Polly wrote him a letter that he must have found upsetting: "Dear Papa, I want to see you and sister Patsy, but you must come to Uncle Eppes's house."[38] Jefferson realized that the difficulty involved more than simply finding safe passage and an appropriate chaperone. He had to persuade Polly herself.

He began by explaining that he understood her hesitation: "I know, my dear Polly, how sorry you will be, and ought to be, to leave [your aunt and uncle] and your cousins but your [sister and m]yself cannot live without you, and after a while we will carry you back again to see your friends in Virginia." He laid out the inducements for coming: "You shall be taught here to play on the harpsichord, to draw, to dance, to read and talk French and such other things as will make you more worthy of the love of your friends." Then he made his strongest argument: "But above all things, by our care and love of you, we will teach you to love us more than you will do if you stay so far from us." And if all this was not tempting enough, "when you come here you shall have as many dolls and playthings as you want for yourself."[39] Still, he was anxious about the ocean voyage. As he confessed to Elizabeth Eppes, "No event of your life has put it into your power to conceive how I feel when I reflect that such a child, and so dear to me, is to cross the ocean, is to be exposed to all the sufferings and risks, great and small, to which a situation on board a ship exposes every one. I drop my pen at the thought—but she must come. . . . kiss dear Polly for me, and encourage her for the journey."[40]

An inveterate worrier, Jefferson imagined all kinds of possible dangers in Polly's coming to Paris. He even seriously considered that she might be captured by "Algerine" pirates and told Francis Eppes that she should travel only in an English or French vessel that had a "*Mediterranean* pass" to lessen the chances of such a disaster.[41] Polly did her best, in her own way, to mitigate his fears of her traveling. In May 1786 he got a note from Mr. Eppes enclosing a letter from Polly: "I long to see you . . . [but] I am very sorry that you have sent for me. I don't want to go to France, I had rather stay with Aunt Eppes."[42]

But Jefferson would simply not give up. Realizing that the Eppeses might consider his pressure on Polly excessive, he restated his rationale: Mary must come to reestablish her ties with her father and sister.[43] Finally Jefferson received a letter from Francis Eppes on November 28 reporting that eight-year-old Polly would at last be coming in the summer of 1787— the ship and season met all of Jefferson's requirements.[44] Jefferson advised him that if the ship went to London, he should "address" Polly to Abigail Adams, who would gladly receive her, and if to any French port, she should be addressed to the American agent there.[45] Now there was nothing to do but wait.

That itself might have been the most excruciating aspect of the entire episode for Jefferson. Every letter that arrived from family members back in Virginia carried the same message: Polly was adamantly against leaving.[46] Jefferson's sister Martha Carr reported that Aunt Eppes had informed her that "Pollys aversion to going to France Increases dayly, and that she fears she must at last be draged like a calf to Slaughter."[47] Still, in this matter as in so many others, Jefferson persisted doggedly, and he was also fanatically devoted to the idea of family domesticity and the importance of the family circle for childrearing. He would have Polly, and that was that. He reminded Patsy, in his usual demanding way, that she would have new responsibilities as the older sister. "When [Polly] arrives, she will become a precious charge on your hands. The difference of your age, and your common loss of a mother, will put that office on you. Teach her above all to be good . . . to be always true . . . never to be angry . . . and teach her industry and application to useful pursuits."[48]

A plan arrived from Mrs. Eppes. She intended to have all the children play aboard the ship for a few days until Polly got acclimated.[49] Then a day or two later, when Polly was asleep or napping, the other children would be hurried off the ship as it raised anchor—and Polly would be on her way.[50] To his great relief Jefferson received, on June 30, a hurriedly written note from Abigail Adams, dated June 26, conveying most welcome news: "I have to congratulate you upon the safe arrival of your Little Daughter, whom I have only a few moments ago received." But Abigail described a rather fragile child: in effect having been stolen away from her beloved aunt and cousins in Virginia, only to become extremely attached to the friendly ship's captain, she again collapsed into tears when handed over to Abigail.[51]

Abigail also informed Jefferson that "the old Nurse whom you had expected to have attended her, was sick and unable to come. She has a Girl about 15 or 16 with her, the Sister of the Servant you have with you." Here Abigail misjudged the actual age of Polly's nurse, whose name she never gave. It is not clear why Abigail thought her older than she was, for she was apparently neither large nor overly developed for her age, fourteen. The letter Abigail sent the next day clarified, "The Girl who is with her is quite a child, and Captain Ramsey is of opinion will be of so little Service that he had better carry her back with him. But of this you will be a judge. She seems fond of the child and appears good naturd." Then the letter reported that Polly had so bonded with Abigail, as she had with Captain Ramsey, that "you will find it I imagine as difficult to seperate Miss Polly from me as I did to get her from the Captain."[52]

What happened next is inexplicable. Jefferson wrote Abigail immediately after receiving news of Polly's arrival that he was sending his *maître d'hôtel*, Adrien Petit, to retrieve Polly and escort her back to Paris.[53] In other words, he sent his French-speaking servant, a complete stranger to Polly, to meet her, take her away from the Adams family, and bring her across the channel to Paris. How could he have devised such an insensitive plan? He lamely explained to Abigail that he had just gotten back two weeks prior from a long trip to the south of France and found himself overwhelmed with work.[54] It has even been suggested, unpersuasively, that he might have been expecting a visit that summer from Maria Cosway. Whatever the explanation, it was callous on the part of this usually tender, considerate, and devoted father.

Jefferson's decision shocked not only Polly but both John and Abigail Adams. Abigail admitted that had she known Polly would so soon be called for, she would have delayed notifying Jefferson of her arrival. She reported that when Petit appeared, Polly "was thrown into all her former distresses, and bursting into Tears."[55] She described in some detail what a sensitive, pleasant child she was, "the favorite of every creature in the House." Referring again to Polly's nurse (whom Abigail always called "the Girl"), Abigail said, "The Girl she has with her, wants more care than the child, and is wholly incapable of looking properly after her, without some superiour to direct her." If this were even partially true, Mrs. Eppes may have sent the young slave woman more as a companion than as a care-taker. Regardless, Abigail informed Jefferson that she would insist on Petit staying a few days so that Polly could become at least somewhat comfort-able with him.[56]

They apparently left four days later, and John Adams wrote Jefferson the day of their departure, "I am extreamly sorry, that you could not come for your Daughter in Person, and that we are obliged to part with her so soon. In my Life I never saw a more charming Child."[57] The dreary trans-atlantic passage from Virginia for Polly was at last over on July 15, and the next day Jefferson wrote a worrying Abigail, "I had the happiness of re-ceiving yesterday my daughter in perfect health. . . . She had totally for-gotten her sister, but thought, on seeing me, that she recollected something of me."[58] Now Jefferson had to work at making his family, or rather what remained of it, whole again. He soon wrote his sister Mary Jefferson Bolling that Polly had joined the same convent school as Patsy and would be visiting him "once or twice a week." Several days later he wrote more extensively to Aunt Eppes that Polly was "established in the convent, per-fectly happy." Before Polly went to the convent, Patsy came to stay with her for a week at the Hôtel de Langeac, taking her sister several times to visit the school until Polly was comfortable there. Almost immediately, Jefferson said, she became "a universal favorite with the young ladies and the mistresses."[59]

With both daughters in Paris, Jefferson's references to them in letters cease. They regularly visited their father, often had Sunday meals with him, and occasionally went to plays or on other such outings. He regu-larly gave money to Patsy, presumably to share with her sister. Patsy had grown quite tall and gangly, like her father. She also had his elongated face, coloring, and red hair. And like him she was gregarious and comfort-able around everyone. Polly, by contrast, was petite, like her mother, with dark hair, and at first she was much shier than Patsy. She was the more at-tractive of the two. As for Polly's shipboard companion, Jefferson never even considered returning her to Virginia. He instantly realized who she was by Abigail's reference to her as James Hemings's sister—"the Girl" was

Sally Hemings, daughter of Betty Hemings, and hence half sister of Jefferson's deceased wife Martha. The day after receiving Abigail's initial letter, Jefferson prepared passports for Petit, Polly and "Sally Hemings."[60] Jefferson had not expected Sally, but accustomed as he was to having light-skinned Hemings slaves in most of the household and skilled positions at Monticello, she must have immediately seemed acceptable for his Paris household. Probably Jefferson was sensitive enough to understand that Polly needed a familiar friend, certainly at first, and he must have realized he had need of what at the time would have been called a lady's maid to serve his daughters. Sally's brother James had been in Paris from the beginning, and so it may have required practically no decision at all to allow her to stay. Because she would be interacting so closely with his family, Jefferson paid an eminent physician to inoculate Sally against smallpox in early November.[61] The two Hemingses completed Jefferson's Paris household.

By the time Polly and Sally arrived, Jefferson had finished paying for lessons in French cooking for James. He also had apparently let his prior French chef go. In October he began regularly paying James a generous salary for assuming the cooking duties.[62] Even before then, Jefferson had often given James spending money, and James had hired a French-language tutor for himself. So when Sally arrived, James could speak French, had a secure position in the household, knew the city, and could help his younger sister quickly adapt to her new surroundings. That James had gone to Paris in the first place must have been somewhat of a surprise to others at Monticello, for James's older brother Bob had been Jefferson's valet for the previous dozen years. Bob had been with Jefferson in Philadelphia, Richmond, and Annapolis, but in Maryland Jefferson had paid for Bob's training as a barber and purchased the necessary tools for him.[63] Since he now possessed that remunerative skill and probably was married, Bob may well have preferred not to go to France. For that reason, and also because James was "likely"—that is, generally promising as a slave—and perhaps had an aptitude for cooking and service, Jefferson had brought him, and not his older brother, to Paris.

As no doubt both James and Sally quickly learned, slavery was illegal in Paris. Visitors who brought their slaves to the country were supposed to register them; after a certain period they had to send the slaves home or free them. If their masters did neither, slaves could petition the Admiralty Court, where they invariably won their freedom. Jefferson was careful always to call his enslaved help servants, not slaves; in fact, most slave-holders even in the US did the same, both because it sounded less harsh and because that was the term for bondspeople in the King James Bible. Jefferson paid both James and eventually Sally a salary. Even before he put James on salary, he gave him free board and clothing. By sleight of hand, Jefferson tried to transform James and Sally into servants—and essentially treat them as such—for the duration of their stay in France.

Exactly how Sally would fit into the household was not at first clear. When Jefferson first realized that she was in London with Polly, he was so happy to finally have his younger daughter with him that he probably gave little thought to Sally's role. But of course his daughters were mostly at the convent and needed a maid only during the day or two a week they visited their father. It is not clear what Sally did most weekdays, and at first Jefferson did not pay her. He probably expected James to share some of his income with her. Jefferson abhorred idleness, so Sally was surely given certain tasks, perhaps sewing and mending for the two girls and for Jefferson himself. She also might have helped serve the meals James prepared or assisted with Jefferson's laundry and private rooms. Sally learned French, came to know and freely move about the city, and gained in confidence and poise. After late 1788 or so, when Patsy began going out socially, Sally probably accompanied her in the role of a lady's maid, for Jefferson bought her new clothes so that she would be dressed appropriately to appear with Patsy. Sally became known to several of the girls' school friends. A French classmate, Marie de Botidoux, wrote Patsy, after she had returned to Virginia, to say hello to "Mlle Sale," and Patsy, in a letter to her chum Kitty Church, reported that Sally sent her regards.[64]

In subtle and at first imperceptible ways, Sally's presence changed the ambience of the Jefferson household, not least because there now was a permanent female resident. Jefferson must have felt almost at ease with Sally. After all, he had known her as a small child (though he might have forgotten what she looked like). He knew her mother Betty, who had cared for his wife Martha after her biological mother had died, and Martha had brought Betty to Monticello. He knew Sally's father, John Wayles, who also was, of course, Martha's father—it was no secret that Wayles had a black family with Betty. She and her children, the half brothers and sisters of Martha, had all been employed at Monticello and treated as a caste apart from and above the other slaves. So Jefferson would have seen Sally as, in the loose parlance of southern slaveholders, "family."

He could not have been unaware that the maturing Sally was decidedly attractive. She had very light skin; long, straight black hair; and a noted resemblance to Martha herself. If he did not at first, certainly within a year or so he would have seen her not as an underaged minor but as a young woman. Men of that era often courted and married women of fifteen, sixteen, or seventeen years of age; Patsy Jefferson herself married only a few months after she turned seventeen. It was not deemed inappropriate for men to take wives thirty or more years their junior.[65] We do not know when precisely, but at some point he did notice Sally. He had promised his wife that he would never remarry, but he was only forty-five in 1788, and his dalliance with Maria Cosway reveals a reemergence of sexual interest in women. Now he found himself in frequent and close contact with Sally Hemings.

A teasing letter that Jefferson sent Maria Cosway in 1788 may have indicated a subconscious desire making its way to the surface. By that time Cosway was much more interested in Jefferson than he was in her—her letters are far more frequent and have an almost plaintive tone, while Jefferson often delayed for months in answering them. He wrote her, however, on April 24, 1788, from Paris, having just returned from a seven-week trip through the Netherlands, parts of Germany, and Strasbourg. He mentions lingering over a painting by Adriaen Van der Werff that he had seen in Düsseldorf: "His picture of Sarah delivering Agar to Abraham is delicious. I would have agreed to have been Abraham though the consequence would have been that I should have been dead five or six thousand years."[66] The reference was to a story in Genesis. Sarah, too old to become pregnant, brought and presented to her husband, Abraham, a young slave woman, Hagar, to become his concubine and bear his child. The painting depicts an elderly, fully clothed Sarah presenting to Abraham, who is sitting up in bed, a half nude, voluptuous slave maiden (she is blonde and white). The implication is that sex between them is acceptable, in fact moral, because his wife, no longer able to give him a child, has dutifully provided him a substitute wife (the standard meaning of concubine in the eighteenth century).[67] Did Cosway take this as just another example of Jefferson's mildly risqué teasing, akin to some of his references to Laurence Sterne? Did Jefferson believe that fate, as it were, was presenting him with an acceptable substitute wife in the person of Sally Hemings?

We simply cannot fully know what happened between Jefferson and Sally. It seems probable that genuine affection—if not love itself—arose between them. Many more educated, older, and more experienced women in Paris found Jefferson attractive and charming; why would Sally have been immune from such feelings, particularly after she came to know him? The overwhelming majority of cases of interracial sex in the South at this time consisted of white slaveholders raping enslaved women who were usually incapable of resisting, but that horrendous fact does not preclude the possibility of an exception. Mutual affection between individuals of unequal status can develop in certain circumstances. That appears to have happened with Jefferson and Sally Hemings.

If their relationship changed in late 1788 or early 1789, both would have been discreet. While the French staff would have found such liaisons almost expected, Jefferson was always a very private man regarding intimate matters; he had taken pains to destroy all his correspondence with his mother, his closest friend Dabney Carr, and especially his wife. And because he disliked French sexual mores, he would have thought it inappropriate to publicly display affection for someone French society would have considered his servant. Moreover, after late April 1789, his daughters returned to their father's home after they withdrew from their school.[68] In that context, Jefferson would have been extraordinarily careful to keep hidden any romantic involvement with Sally.

I I

Tourist

BEFORE 1784 JEFFERSON had journeyed between Albemarle County and Williamsburg, with stops at plantations along the way. He had been to Philadelphia and Annapolis, and on his way to the capital city in 1783, he and Patsy had traveled up the Shenandoah Valley. As a young man he had made a short trip to New York City, and then later, on the eve of going to France to take up his diplomatic post, Jefferson and Patsy had traveled up the East Coast all the way to Boston. But Jefferson had never been farther south than Virginia or more than fifty miles west of Monticello.

Yet he had collected and read every book he could on travels through North America, harbored a deep interest in the voyages of explorers such as Captain James Cook, and, following after his father, developed a love of maps. Seemingly every living thing intrigued him—as he wrote Patsy in 1790, "There is not a sprig of grass that shoots uninteresting to me, nor any thing that moves."[1] He was a very close observer and inveterate note taker, always on the lookout for useful human inventions and practices, for new crops and better breeds of livestock. Fascinated by architecture as well as gardening, by vineyards as well as bridges and canal locks, he had a sponge-like approach to the world.

Jefferson's observations and commentary always had a comparative dimension: Why did vineyards grow better on one hillside than another? Why were English farms more productive than French? Why were (white) southerners in the United States noticeably different from northerners? Regarding the last, he noted that northerners tended to be cool, sober, and laborious while southerners were often fiery, voluptuary, and indolent. He suggested that the cause of these differences was climate, specifically "the warmth of the [southern] climate which unnerves and unmans both body and mind."[2]

This insatiably curious man made three extensive trips while serving his nation in France. On February 27, 1786, he had a surprise visitor to Paris. Colonel William S. Smith, secretary to the American legation in London, delivered to Jefferson an express letter from John Adams, dated February 21. Adams had been convening a series of meetings with the ambassadors from Portugal and Tripoli. He believed the negotiations so promising that he pressed Jefferson to come to London as quickly as possible so the two Americans could pursue a commercial treaty with Portugal and an end to piratical raids by Tripolitans.[3] The next day, as protocol dictated, Jefferson sent a letter to Charles Gravier, Comte de Vergennes, the French foreign minister, asking for a brief audience to explain the necessity of his leaving Paris for several weeks. Vergennes gave him permission to go.[4] Jefferson and Smith left Paris on March 6 and arrived in London on March 11.

Despite considerable effort, Adams and Jefferson were unable to come to terms on a most-favored-nation trade treaty with Portugal; the Portuguese minister would have accepted their proposal that Portugal receive both unprocessed wheat and flour from America, but Portuguese milling interests sank the deal. After repeated meetings with the Tripolitan minister, Abdrahaman, including far more puffs from the hookah and sips of overstrong coffee than desired, Adams and Jefferson determined that his demand for annual tributes of tens of thousands of guineas far exceeded what the nation was able, much less willing, to pay.[5] Contrary to many subsequent accounts, Jefferson never interpreted the discord with the Barbary pirates as rooted in a conflict between Christianity and Islam; he saw the issue purely as a matter of extortion.[6]

Likewise the British rebuffed the American ambassadors' attempts to settle several outstanding aspects of the peace treaty of 1783; the English foreign minister did not even deign to reply to their offers. When they finally had an audience with King George III, his royal majesty contemptuously turned his back to them. As Jefferson described it decades later, "I saw at once that the ulcerations in the narrow mind of that mulish being left nothing to be expected, . . . confirm[ing] me in my belief of their aversion to have anything to do with us."[7] The diplomatic potential of Jefferson's trip to London came to nothing.

Jefferson wrote to his boyhood friend John Page about what he took to be the British attitude toward Americans: "That nation hates us, their ministers hate us, and their king more than all other men."[8] He jokingly commented to Abigail Adams that the British diet was the source of their antipathy toward America.[9] Jefferson's account books show that he did, however, often dine at restaurants in London, including the venerable London Tavern and the famous Dolly's Chop House in Paternoster Row, which had been a favorite of Benjamin Franklin, James Boswell, and John Wilkes.

Jefferson saw that there was so much more to do in London, and England more generally, than conduct impossible negotiations with recalcitrant diplomats. Also in London he attended the theater, seeing England's most famous stage actress, Sarah Siddons, for example, at Drury Lane, playing the role of Portia in *The Merchant of Venice* and later as Lady Macbeth.[10] He attended the opera at Haymarket, saw plays at Covent Garden, and went to a musical revue at Sadler's Wells in Islington. London was a larger city than Paris, dotted with stores of every imaginable kind, and Jefferson was an indefatigable shopper—despite his chronic indebtedness and his frequent complaints about the same. Some of his purchases were immediately practical: cotton stockings, books, and a walking stick, along with maps and guide books and a good reading lamp. As an amateur architect, draftsman, and scientist, he bought a protractor, a circular drawing pen, dividers, a pentagraph, a damping box, and special paper for his letterpress, as well as a thermometer, telescope, microscope, hydrometer, theodolite, and "little electrical machine." And of course he purchased books at a variety of shops, making several visits to Lackington's famous bookstore on Chiswell Street.[11] Always a tinkerer who loved to work with his hands, he also purchased "a chest of tools."[12]

Jefferson eagerly anticipated seeing the gardens on the outskirts of London and beyond. He had collected and read a number of British horticultural books long before arriving in England, including Thomas Whately's *Observations on Modern Gardening* (1770) and volumes by Joseph Heely (1777) and William Shenstone (1773) that described the latter's innovative gardens at Leasowes.[13] Jefferson was impatient to begin exploring, and even though Adams intended to travel with him, Jefferson went out alone for several days to visit nearby gardens, then returned to London to pick up his companion. Both Jefferson and Adams made notes on their tour of English gardens, and both carried with them Whately's *Observations on Modern Gardening* as their much-consulted guide book. Adams's journal mainly contained casual comments about the beauty of the gardens, which he found extravagant.[14] Jefferson, by contrast, was traveling for a purpose. With Whately's guidebook in hand, he made no-tations "directed chiefly to such practical things as might enable me to es-timate the expence of making and maintaining a garden in that style."[15] He had Monticello in mind.

Jefferson loved natural beauty and mechanical wonders alike, and he wished to make Monticello a working plantation that would not compro-mise its aesthetic values. He noted that Wooburn Farm combined beauty with practicality: the farm, the kitchen garden, and the ornamental gar-dens, "all are intermixed, the pleasure garden being merely a highly orna-mented walk through and round the divisions of the farm and garden kitchen."[16] On the whole Jefferson preferred attractive vistas of trees, shrubs, water, and rolling hills, without the intervention of the architec-tural "follies" common in European gardens. At Stowe he noted the use of a ha-ha (a moat or deep ditch that served as a fence without obstructing the view) to contain the sheep and cattle, and he later employed a ha-ha (or, as he wrote, a "ha! ha!") at Monticello for the same purpose.

Both Adams and Jefferson preferred the natural style of most of the English gardens over the geometrical precision of baroque European gar-dens, like those at Versailles.[17] One explanation might be that many of the ornamental trees, shrubs, and flowers then on display in English gardens had in fact been introduced from America through the offices of such seed exporters as John Bartram.[18] (Jefferson was himself an active agent in the international brotherhood of botanical enthusiasts, and he often asked friends back in the United States to send seeds and seedlings to Europe so that he could share them with foreign gardeners.[19]) Before finishing their garden tour, Adams and Jefferson traveled to Stratford-on-Avon to visit the birthplace and tomb of William Shakespeare. Both were great admir-ers, though Jefferson merely marked in his account book the slight fee he paid to see the sights. On this occasion Adams was more detailed, briefly describing the home, commenting that they saw an old chair in which Shakespeare reputedly sat, and noting, "We cutt off a Chip according to the Custom."[20]

Jefferson and Adams returned to London by way of Oxford, where they toured several of the colleges. Jefferson spent about two more weeks in the city before departing on April 26 for Dover, in preparation for crossing the channel. During his final days in London, he continued to shop and see such landmarks as the Tower of London and Buckingham House (now Palace). Jefferson also stopped briefly at Canterbury Cathedral on the way to Dover. Spending a day at Dover, he purchased tickets for himself and Adrien Petit, his valet, and after a voyage of only three hours, they made landfall at Calais. Not so long afterward, they were back in Paris.

Jefferson captured his six-week experience in England in a long letter to John Page. He commented that the soils of that country were less fertile than those of France but, because they were better manured, were more productive. Correspondingly, the "labouring people" in France were poorer than their counterparts in England. Jefferson did not care for the architecture of London, though he did believe that the "mechanical arts in London are carried to a wonderful perfection." But the gardens—that's where England most impressed. "The gardening in that country is the article that surpasses all the earth. I mean their pleasure gardening. This indeed went far beyond my ideas." And he revealed his love of shopping there in a comment more than a year later to Madame de Corny about "the splendor of their shops, which is all that is worth seeing in London."[21]

JEFFERSON'S PRIMARY goal in Europe was not to admire the local gardens but to advance American trade interests, and to that end he saw the need to become better acquainted with the facilities, practices, and preferences of France's ports on the Mediterranean. On September 7, 1786, he wrote to John Banister Jr. that he planned, in a couple of months, to make a tour to "Lyons, Toulon, Marseille &c. the canal of Languedoc, Bourdeaux &c." He had no way of knowing that eleven days later he would fall and severely injure his wrist while cavorting with Maria Cosway. As he told William Stephens Smith, the injury "has defeated my views of visiting the South of France this fall." On December 16 he was able to write James Madison that he hoped to set out soon and to "try the use of some mineral waters there, by immersion," which he had been told would accelerate the healing. Two days later he spelled out to James Monroe the revised twofold purpose of his upcoming trip: "to try the mineral waters there for the restoration of my hand, but another is to visit all the seaports where we have trade, and to hunt up all the inconveniences under which it labours, in order to get them rectified."[22]

There were other delays, including some business regarding a possible treaty with Morocco, and then he wanted to await the beginning of the French Assembly of Notables in February. He was required to appear before the new French foreign minister, the Comte de Montmorin, following the unexpected death of Vergennes on February 13. Finally Jefferson was able to depart Paris for the south on February 28, 1787. It was not a mere pleasure trip but rather one of inspection and personal education. He quickly learned, once he got to the springs and tried four days of the water treatment, that it was ineffective—but because the trip was not wholly about business, he charged none of his expenses to the government, paying for the entire journey out of his personal funds.

For most of the first two weeks of his travels, he wrote to William Short, he was "pelted with rain, hail, snow," with only "now and then a few gleamings of sunshine."[23] Jefferson seemed unusually sensitive to the damp cold, and as he pushed ever further toward the warmth of the Mediterranean, his outlook improved. Once in Provence, he wrote to Short, "If I should happen to die at Paris I will beg of you to send me here, and have me exposed to the sun. I am sure it will bring me to life again."[24]

He traveled in a one-person carriage, with stops every ten or twelve miles for fresh horses. At first he intended to hire a valet for the day in every city where he stopped, but he met such a useful servant in Dijon, a man named Petitjean, that he employed him for the entire trip. Jefferson traveled light, with only one small trunk; he also had with him a thermometer, a measuring tape, and his portable letterpress. His account book brims with entries for meals, coffee, carriage repairs, maps and guidebooks, entrance fees ("seeing things," as he put it), barbers, and laundry. Determined to make the trip as a private citizen, he did not wear the finery associated with his diplomatic position and often walked beside his carriage, talking with strangers he met along the way and interviewing French farmers working in the fields. He observed seemingly everything, alert to both beauty and utility.

Jefferson covered about 1,200 miles in slightly more than three months. Heading southeast from Paris at first, he turned south on reaching Dijon and then passed through towns and cities, including Châlon, Tournis, Mâcon, Lyons, Vienne, Tain, Orange, and Nîmes. At the last he turned east to Arles, Aix, Marseilles, and Nice (then part of the Duchy of Savoy in Italy), continuing on into the Italian republics of Piedmont and Sardinia, where he visited Turin, Milan, and Genoa. The press of time did not allow him to continue to Rome, and thus he had, alas, "a peep only into Elysium,"[25] before circling back toward France. Next, by way of Les Baux and Nîmes, he journeyed westward to Montpellier and on to Béziers. From there he traveled via the Canal of Languedoc all the way to the Atlantic coast and turned northward, eventually reaching Nantes, with a short loop to Lorient on the coast, and from there eastward to Paris. It was a long, hurried, tiring trip, but Jefferson fully enjoyed it and made what he considered useful observations in his journal along the way.[26]

On entering a city, Jefferson bought a city map and guidebook, when available. If there was a wall around the city, he walked along the top of it with his map in hand; if there wasn't, he sought out the largest church or cathedral, not to admire it but to climb the steeple for a bird's-eye view of the entire city. He tried to work in the mandatory tourist sites as quickly as possible, avoiding tour guides, who tended to give excess information, and often went to theaters, public markets, and the like to mingle with "inhabitants from high to low."

He was zealously committed to learning practical details about crops. He took dense notes on various vineyards, attending to the differences in soil type, the angle of the hillside toward the sun, the intermixture of fruit trees with vines and of different kinds of grapes, the spacing of the grape vines, and the cultivation of various nuts and fruits, of thyme and lavender. He particularly liked a white wine called Hermitage, produced at Tain. (He would later purchase more than five hundred bottles of it for serving in the White House.[27] Surprisingly, though an oenophile, Jefferson normally diluted the wine he drank with water.) He described fencing methods, the shape of farm wagons, the design of plows; he drew a diagram of a yoke, remarked on his first sighting in France of a butterfly and first hearing of a nightingale, and explained the operations of the locks in the Canal of Languedoc. Near Orange he first saw olive trees, which were common from there southward. Jefferson was extraordinarily impressed by the olive tree—he called it "assuredly the richest gift of heaven. I can scarcely except bread." Olive trees grew easily even in poor soil and with little rainfall, and their product was both valuable and healthy. (He would later urge their cultivation in the southern states in part because they were so much less labor intensive than rice, but they never caught on.[28])

As for the farmers themselves, he commented on what they ate, what they fed their cattle, and how they dressed; he disapproved of how farming families were not spread out but lived in villages, thereby losing, in his view, a sense of independence.[29] Again and again he remarked on the surprising poverty of farmers, especially the spectacle of women performing the kinds of hard labor that he thought only men fit for. As he wrote in his journal, "I observe women and children carrying heavy burthens and labouring with the hough," which was "an unequivocal indication of extreme poverty." He gave example after example of similar outrages, noting in one instance that "the women here smite on the anvil, work with the mawl and the spade." He saw that one of the two hands on the barges pulled along the Canal of Languedoc was always a woman and that women operated the lock gates, "operations . . . much too laborious for them." Everywhere he saw "numbers of people in rags, and abundance of beggars."[30] These examples were, in his mind, further evidence of his conclusion that farmers were far better off in America than in France. Even though Jefferson, like most elite individuals from America, was accustomed to great gulfs between the lives of commoners and the upper classes, the gap he witnessed in France astonished him.[31] As if in a nostalgic haze, from a distance the plight of the working poor in Virginia—and that of the slaves—seemed less severe to him.

In a letter written before he completed his tour, Jefferson urged the Marquis de Lafayette to make a similar trip, to better understand the laborers on his own property and perhaps improve the quality of their lives. As Jefferson advised, "You must be absolutely incognito, you must ferret the people out of their hovels as I have done, look into their kettles, eat their bread, loll on their beds under pretense of resting yourself, but in fact to find if they are soft. You will feel a sublime pleasure in the course of this investigation, and a sublimer one hereafter when you shall be able to apply your knolege to the softening of their beds, or the throwing a morsel of meat into their kettle of vegetables."[32] Jefferson concluded that monarchical government was to blame for the shocking discrepancy in living standards between the richest and the poorest.

During his travels in Provence. Jefferson found his visits to Roman ruins surprisingly rewarding. As he wrote to William Short, "The remains of antiquity . . . are more in number, and less injured by time than I expected, and have been to me a great treat."[33] He thought the ruins in Nîmes outranked those anywhere else, in large part because of the Maison Carrée, with which he was smitten, but he also loved the Temple of Diana as well as the amphitheater.[34] At Orange he was impressed, as are visitors today, by the grandeur of the great theater and the "sublime triumphal arch," though he was dismayed to see that workers were taking its stones in order to pave a road. He called the Pont du Gard, that magnificent three-story aqueduct that brings water to the city of Nîmes, "a sublime antiquity" and rode across its lower level in his carriage.[35]

Jefferson had not necessarily intended to go into Italy, but as he pondered the reasons for the French preferring Italian over American rice, he thought perhaps it was because the Italians had a different process for husking. So he took an arduous trip over the southern Alps, riding a mule, to investigate the Italian husking machines, only to discover that they were identical to those in America. In fact, the Italians cultivated a slightly different species of rice. Understanding that it was a capital offense to smuggle out seed rice, Jefferson did so anyway, on his person no less.[36] (To his dismay, though he sent the seeds to South Carolina, growers there preferred to continue with their own.) He also went into elaborate detail describing the making of parmesan cheese. His sojourn in Italy was short, but he did find time to be disgusted by the cathedral in Milan. The extravagantly, even excessively decorated Gothic structure was, he concluded, "a worthy object of philosophical contemplation, to be placed among the rarest instances of the misuse of money."[37] He saw not the beauty of a Gothic cathedral but the expenditure of vast sums better spent on behalf of the poor.

Jefferson's final project during his travels was to explore the Canal of Languedoc, as he called it. Perhaps the greatest engineering feat in French history at that point, the canal had been completed in 1681. It stretched some 150 miles from the small town of Sète (Jefferson spelled it Cette) on the Mediterranean to the Garonne River at Toulouse, connecting the Atlantic with the Mediterranean. The canal employed a series of eighty-six locks that lifted the waterway to a maximum height of 620 feet, over a low mountain range.[38] When Jefferson got to the Canal of Languedoc (now called the Canal du Midi), he had the wheels taken off his small carriage and the carriage set on a horse-drawn barge. He could walk along the tow paths and, when tired, sit in his carriage seat, observing what passed by. He found this a wonderfully pleasant way to travel. He took special care in preparing an extremely detailed list of the locks, the distance between each, the amount of lift each provided, and so on.

Moving along the canal, Jefferson came to appreciate the nightingale. He penned a letter to Patsy, back in Paris, writing, as he put it, "from the Canal of Languedoc, on which I am at present sailing, as I have been for a week past, cloudless skies above, limpid waters below, and on each hand a row of nightingales in full chorus."[39] (Always a Virginian, while he could enjoy this delightful bird, he found its song inferior to that of mockingbirds.) Jefferson went on to reassure Patsy that he would soon be back in Paris and predicted that they could soon begin to expect the arrival of "our dear Polly": "It will be a circumstance of inexpressible comfort to me to have you both with me once more."[40] He arrived back in Paris on June 10 and the very next day saw Patsy. A month later Polly joined them.

JEFFERSON TOOK ONE last major trip while in Europe, and it too began for reasons of official business. John Adams had been authorized to make credit arrangements with Dutch bankers; the resulting loans had been essential to the operation of the American government. The need for additional loans was nevertheless great, and since Adams was returning to the United States (he had just been elected vice president), he wanted Jefferson to join him in Amsterdam both to meet the leading bankers and to participate in forging new arrangements. Jefferson received a letter on March 2, 1788, from Abigail Adams, reporting that her husband hoped to meet him at The Hague, from where they could go on together to the Netherlands to confer about financial matters. Jefferson promptly wrote John Adams that he would set out the next day, assuming his carriage was repaired and ready for use.[41] They met on March 9 in The Hague.

The next day, the two American ministers rode in Jefferson's carriage to Amsterdam. There followed an intense series of meeting with bankers, and together (though Adams was more experienced at these kinds of negotiations) they worked out satisfactory arrangements, with Jefferson writing John Jay to that effect on March 16.[42] Adams returned to London and soon to the United States, but Jefferson stayed another two weeks in Amsterdam to finalize the details. He spent most of his days working, with little leisure to visit galleries and the opera, but he managed to sneak some time away to enjoy these and other pursuits. As usual, he also managed to work in some shopping. On March 30 he traveled to Utrecht and then to the Rhine and into Germany.

Even during his busy days in Amsterdam, Jefferson did not neglect his note taking. He recorded how the wooden joists in houses were constructed in a diamond-shaped fashion for added strength; he commented on the practice of making windows in such a way that they could be opened to admit a fresh air but not rainfall; he described an ingenious means of fastening a flag staff to a vessel; he admired a folding table that collapsed to a strikingly narrow width; he noted a device for drawing light boats over a low dam; and he sketched a Dutch wheelbarrow that was notably easy to load and unload. Nothing escaped his inquiring mind.[43]

Jefferson looked forward to traveling through Germany; among other things, he hoped to again meet the Baron de Geismar, who had, as a prisoner of war near Charlottesville, come to Monticello in 1778 and 1779 to play his violin with Jefferson and his wife. As Jefferson traveled southward and heard that the locals cured ham with smoke, he noted that even "well informed people" in the region believed they were the only ones who did so.[44] Actually, in many places, particularly near Frankfurt, he saw practices that reminded him of those he was familiar with in the German-settled regions of the United States. He even remarked to a correspondent, "The neighborhood of this place is that which has been to us a second mother country. . . . I have been continually amused by seeing here the origin of whatever is not English among us. I have fancied myself often in the upper parts of Maryland and Pennsylvania."[45]

He did manage to meet Geismar in Frankfurt. The German officer took Jefferson to the garrison at Hanau, where he saw several other officers he had known from their barracks days near Charlottesville.[46] From Frankfurt Jefferson traveled along the Neckar to Mannheim and Heidelberg, both of which he enjoyed, Mannheim because it had been a planned city with a rational grid of streets and Heidelberg for its beauty and for the spectacular ruins of a castle in the heights beyond the city. In his account book Jefferson recorded, "This chateau is the most noble ruin I have ever seen. . . . The situation is romantic and pleasing beyond expression."[47] He was a little more expansive in a letter to Maria Cosway, even though their passion was cooling, suggesting the ruins at Heidelberg would compare well with the pyramids and that they were certainly "the most magnificent ruin after those left us by the antients."[48] He measured every aspect of the giant wooden wine barrel in the castle—still a favorite of tourists today—and sketched in the margin of his book the intricate pathways up the hills. Much later, he added, "The paths on some parts of these mountains give me the idea of making paths on Monticello and Mont Alto"—the higher mountain immediately to the west of Monticello.[49]

Because Jefferson did not read German, he was almost completely ignorant of German literature; he had not read Goethe, for example. And because at this time Gothic architecture was not widely appreciated, he showed no interest in the cathedrals of Cologne and Worms, not to mention the massive Romanesque basilica at Speyer, though he did remark that the mighty steeple of the cathedral at Strasbourg, which he climbed to get a view of the city, was "the highest in the world, and the handsomest." He more appreciated Amand Koenig's bookstore in Strasbourg, calling it "the best shop of classical books I ever saw." He would continue to buy books from this shop as long as he was in Paris.[50]

IN HIS TRAVELS Jefferson saw things to emulate (a folding ladder at Bergen, a version of which he later designed for Monticello), things to improve (near Nancy, in France, the awkwardness of the moldboard plow used by local farmers, which set him down the path of designing his own celebrated version), and things to condemn (in France, women doing difficult field work; in Germany, "the fear . . . of slaves . . . visible in the faces of the Prussian subjects," owing to their authoritarian government).[51]

Thus Jefferson's travels strengthened his nationalism. In his three tours of Europe, he ended up discovering more reasons to appreciate the United States. He was surely thinking of his European experiences when he wrote William Shippen back in the United States about the prospect of Shippen's son traveling through France, Italy, the Netherlands, and Germany. Your son will "return charged, like a bee, with the honey of wisdom, a blessing to his country," Jefferson wrote. And after having seen "the best parts" of these European nations, Jefferson counseled Shippen, his son would come home to the United States "satisfied that no part of the earth equals his own country."[52]

"A Powerful Obstacle . . . to Emancipation"

WHEN AMERICANS TRAVEL abroad, they are often viewed as unofficial spokespeople for and experts on their homeland. In Jefferson's case, he was indeed an expert, almost certainly more knowledgeable than anyone else. Not only was he quickly recognized in Paris for the breadth and depth of his learning, but word soon got around that he had prepared an informal document answering questions about Virginia put to him in 1780 by the Marquis de Barbé-Marbois, secretary of the French legation in Philadelphia. Writing in English, Jefferson had worked on his response in spare moments in the latter half of 1781 and forwarded a short manuscript reply to Barbé-Marbois in December 1781. He continued to work on the manuscript after his arrival in Paris, expanding it perhaps threefold, and hired a small private press in the city to print about two hundred copies to share with carefully selected friends. At first, he had not planned to publish the text as a book, but the project took on a life of its own, and in 1787, an official version was published. It was the only book Jefferson ever wrote.

Jefferson often expressed his views on America in many other forums and at many other times, of course. He wrote letters on the subject to correspondents in France and in the United States and commented on manuscripts by French authors attempting to write about his nation. To him, explanation was often simply impossible without comparison. Though he loved Paris and many of the other parts of Europe he visited, he never lost his distinct preference for all things American. He constantly compared French women active in public society unfavorably with the wholesome housewives of America. His travels in France and Germany led him to comment on the unseemliness of women performing hard manual labor. He never grew comfortable with the hordes of beggars in Paris and along the roads through the countryside. In a long letter to Italian friend Charles Bellini, a language professor at the College of William & Mary, Jefferson reported that from his perspective "as a savage of the mountains of America," the stark social stratification in France did not strike him "advantageously I assure you. I find the general fate of humanity here most deplorable. The truth of Voltaire's observation offers itself perpetually, that every man here must be either the hammer or the anvil."[1] Political freedom and opportunities for upward mobility (for whites) were in his view much greater in America, a point he made repeatedly to American correspondents curious about Europe. Jefferson found himself explaining America to Europeans and France to Americans.[2]

As part of the former task, he tried to shape the relevant entries in the enormous *Encyclopédie méthodique*, which, when finally finished in 1832, consisted of 216 volumes. Intended as a revised and updated version of Denis Diderot's famous *Encyclopédie* published between 1752 and 1772, the project was naturally of great interest to Jefferson, and he subscribed both for himself and other like-minded Americans. A young French scholar, Jean-Nicolas Démeunier, was assigned to write articles on the United States as a whole and briefer articles on the individual states. Sometime in very late 1785, he asked Jefferson to read and comment on the former. There followed an extensive correspondence and several meetings between the two.

While most of Jefferson's comments and corrections dealt with population, commerce, the nature of specific laws and governmental practices, and other rather technical matters, he commented more pointedly on two topics of great importance to him. First, believing that in his treatment of George Washington and the Society of the Cincinnati, Démeunier had slighted his fellow Virginian, Jefferson went into elaborate detail on the society's origins and rationale, attempting to salvage Washington's reputation by offering a more positive view of the Cincinnati than he actually held. Shortly thereafter, on November 4, 1786, he wrote a long letter to Washington restating his earlier opposition to the society on the grounds that a hereditary aristocracy had the potential "to destroy the fabric" of the American system. His experience in France had reinforced his understanding of "the mass of evil which flows from this fatal source," and he believed "this germ of destruction" must be removed from American soil.[3]

The second topic was slavery. Embarrassed by the contradiction of the so-called land of liberty being a slaveholding nation, Jefferson attempted to persuade European readers that American slavery would not last forever.[4] In his answers to Démeunier's first round of questions, he estimated that in the five southern states there were approximately 650,000 slaves and in the northern states, another 50,000. Outside the South, he advised Démeunier, "effectual measures have been taken for their future emancipation." He admitted that no such actions had yet been launched in the southern states but reported, "The disposition to emancipate them is strongest in Virginia. Those who desire it, form as yet the minority of the whole state, but it bears a respectable proportion to the whole in numbers and weight of character, and it is constantly recruiting by the addition of nearly the whole of the young men as fast as they come into public life. I flatter myself it will take place there at some period of time not very distant." He admitted that the situation was different elsewhere in the South: few were "disposed to emancipate" in Maryland and North Carolina, and in South Carolina and Georgia there was "not the smallest symptom of it."[5] Still, he strove to make clear his belief that the liberal principles of the revolution would eventually destroy slavery, a view shared by most of the Founders.[6] Jefferson's hope seems misplaced today, but he was writing before the spread of cotton cultivation across the Deep South following the invention of the cotton gin in 1793 and shortly after Vermont (1777), Pennsylvania (1780), Massachusetts and New Hampshire (1783), and Rhode Island and Connecticut (1784)—all states with few slaves—had either abolished slavery or set underway programs of gradual abolition.[7] An ever-sanguine Jefferson believed that through education and reflection the American public would grow to recognize the injustice of slavery. And he was deeply committed to the principle that the only authority for ending such a long-entrenched institution was the approval of the nation's citizens as expressed electorally. Leaders in a democracy, understanding that sovereignty resided in the people, could not simply impose a change because they thought it just—a majority of voters had to agree.[8] When, in February 1788, Jefferson was asked to join a French society supporting the abolition of the slave trade, he declined, stating that as a "public servant," he felt that without express authority he could not lend his name to the cause, even though personally "nobody wishes more ardently to see an abolition not only of the trade but of the condition of slavery."[9]

Jefferson did ask his personal secretary William Short to attend the meetings of the Société des Amis des Noirs, as it was known.[10]

DESPITE THE TIME and effort spent assisting Démeunier, Jefferson was not entirely pleased with the article eventually published in the *Encyclopédie méthodique*. Perhaps this helps explain why he went to such great pains to expand on and corroborate his original 1781 reply to Barbé-Marbois's queries, with the result being his extraordinary if accidental book, *Notes on the State of Virginia*. Everything else Jefferson wrote about America is epiphenomenal to this work, which had no precedent at the time and is remarkably revealing of Jefferson's attitudes on a wide range of subjects.[11] There is nothing quite like it in the balance of the corpus, and how it took its final shape deserves careful attention.

Jefferson had sent his initial and admittedly limited response to Barbé-Marbois's questions in December 1781. But frustrated by the disparaging remarks about America made by several French naturalists, Jefferson—having more leisure now that his gubernatorial term had ended and with the library resources of Monticello at hand—decided to expand and clarify his reply.[12] The preeminent French naturalist of the time, the Comte de Buffon, had suggested that owing to climate, the fauna of North America were smaller than their counterparts in Europe, even arguing that domesticated animals brought to the New World had offspring smaller in size than their counterparts in Europe. Believing this an affront to the American nation, Jefferson determined to mount an extensive defense of the animals of North America. Even in the tragic year of 1782, during which his beloved wife died, he wrote letters to several men who had seen "big bones," or mammoth bones, seeking information.[13] He continued this line of inquiry in 1783 and also began asking his correspondents, who included Virginian amateur naturalists and explorers Thomas Walker and Arthur Campbell, precise questions about the heights and weights of a wide range of American animals.[14]

In the late eighteenth century, science primarily meant accurate observation, measurement, and categorization—not theory. Jefferson wanted evidence to refute Buffon. He did not just depend upon correspondence but traveled and examined natural phenomena for himself. This is why, when he and his daughter Patsy journeyed to Philadelphia in October 1783, they went by way of the Valley of Virginia; Jefferson could thus examine several of the limestone caves and visit the confluence of the Shenandoah and Potomac Rivers at Harpers Ferry. The expanded version of his answers to Barbé-Marbois contained information gathered on this detour. By early 1784, as Jefferson wrote to the Marquis de Chastellux, he had found in his original answers to Barbé-Marbois that "some things should be omitted, many corrected, and more supplied and enlarged."[15] As a result, his text had "swelled to nearly treble bulk," but in fact he kept adding information until mid-1784 and slightly beyond.

Because friends and others had begun hearing about his project and requesting copies, sometime in the spring of 1784 Jefferson discussed a small private printing with a Philadelphia printer but found the estimated cost prohibitive. He decided to wait until he arrived in Paris, where he hoped to find a much less expensive English printer.[16]

Probably through the assistance of Benjamin Franklin, Jefferson did find a capable printer, Philippe-Denis Pierres, who agreed to publish—for about a quarter the cost of the Philadelphia printer—a private edition of Jefferson's manuscript, in English, which Jefferson titled *Notes on the State of Virginia*. He did not, however, include his name on the title page, which showed the year 1782 (when most of the additions had been completed), not 1785, when this first "edition" was actually printed. On May 11, 1785, he reported to James Madison that the printing of two hundred copies had been completed the previous day.[17] Jefferson made clear that they were to be distributed mainly to close friends upon their pledging not to show them around freely. He thought he might give copies selectively to students at the College of William & Mary too.[18] Jefferson feared—as did all his friends—that his criticisms of slavery and the Virginia constitution would bring harsh censure on him and "produce an irritation which will revolt the minds of our countrymen against reformation in these two articles, and thus do more harm than good."[19] But despite his best efforts, when one of the recipients, Charles Williamos (who, incidentally, turned out to be a British spy), died, an eager bookseller acquired his copy. The bookseller had arranged what Jefferson at the time called "a surreptitious translation" into French, though years later he said he "never had seen so wretched an attempt at translation. Interverted, abridged, mutilated, and often reversing the sense of the original."[20]

Jefferson was thankful when a friend, the Abbé Morellet, offered to retranslate the book into French; Jefferson accepted his offer, although he was not completely satisfied with the result, which, when finally published in early 1787, was riddled with typos, errors, and awkward translations; it was also printed on poor-quality paper. The title page bore Jefferson's initials but not his name; nor did it give the translator's name. Jefferson considered the edition "mutilated."[21] But now he faced another dilemma: what to do about a possible pirated English edition.[22] Madison urged him in May 1786 to arrange a proper English publication, warning that with the French version soon to be available, it "will inevitably be translated back and published in that form." Not only would his language be injured, but "the ideas themselves may possibly be so perverted as to lose their propriety."[23]

Three months later Jefferson received a letter from John Stockdale, a London bookseller he often patronized, stating his interest in publishing an English edition of *Notes on the State of Virginia*. He repeated the offer several times, but Jefferson ignored him.[24] Finally, fearing a badly flawed and embarrassing English edition, he wrote Stockdale on February 1, 1787, accepting his offer but insisting that a new map be inserted, which he claimed would be "worth more than the book."[25] The map, which Jefferson had meticulously prepared, depicted Virginia, Maryland, Delaware, and Pennsylvania.[26] On February 13 Stockdale replied; he would be glad to receive Jefferson's final copy, would publish it without changes of any sort, and proposed a print run of five hundred copies.

On February 27 Jefferson promised to send, the next day, his corrected copy, "which I will pray you to print precisely as [the pages] are, without additions, alterations, preface, or any thing else but what is there."[27] But Jefferson had an agonizing time getting the map produced accurately in Paris, and this delay in turn delayed the publication of the book, which did not finally appear until July, several months after the French edition. It included his latest text and three appendices: a commentary by his friend Charles Thomson on the version of *Notes* written in about 1784 (to which Jefferson had made several changes in response); Jefferson's 1783 draft of a constitution for the state of Virginia (which, of course, had come to no practical effect); and a copy of Virginia's Act for Establishing Religious Freedom, which had passed in 1786. Jefferson sent copies of the official version of his *Notes* to trusted associates and arranged to have copies sent to the students at the College of William & Mary. Since they were the political leaders of the next generation, Jefferson believed that educating them about the evils of slavery would help bring about, or at least further the cause of, emancipation—by now he realized that he could not expect much on this score from his own generation. As Jefferson understood, the College of William & Mary was a small island of relative liberalism on the issue.[28]

NOTES ON THE STATE OF VIRGINIA is presented as a series of replies to Barbé-Marbois's questions, though Jefferson rearranged and reframed the original questions as he saw fit. The Stockdale edition began with a discussion not of slavery but of the geographical setting of Virginia, in which Jefferson's inquiry reached all the way to the Mississippi, and even beyond—a discussion Charles Thomson deemed "a most excellent Natural history not merely of Virginia but of No. America."[29] From borders, rivers, and mountains, Jefferson moved to climate, population, and the state's counties and towns, then to its constitution and laws, and, finally, to its society, from colleges and religion to manners and historical writing about Virginia's people. Throughout, Jefferson drew on facts he had collected from sources far and wide to refute popular French theories disparaging the climate, flora and fauna, and aboriginal people of North America. Simultaneously, he laid out his philosophical positions on religion, constitutionalism, slavery, and—in what would prove the most enduringly controversial aspect of Notes—the nature of African Americans.[30]

While Jefferson's prose was clear, at times he wrote in a more romantic vein, bringing not only reason but emotion to the topic, just as he did in his "head and heart" letter to Maria Cosway. In fact, Jefferson had been contemplating a possible official English publication of Notes at the same time he was describing to Cosway his love for his "dear Monticello": "Where has nature spread so rich a mantle under the eye? . . . With what majesty do we there ride above the storms! How sublime to look down into the workhouse of nature, to see her clouds, hail, snow, rain, thunder, all fabricated at our feet! And the glorious Sun, when rising as if out of a distant water, just gilding the tops of the mountains, and giving life to all nature!"[31] Similar paeans appeared in the Stockdale edition of Notes, indicating, perhaps, that Jefferson was not only an Enlightenment rationalist but a proto-romantic.

> The passage of the Patowmac through the Blue ridge is perhaps one of the most stupendous scenes in nature. You stand on a very high point of land. On your right comes up the Shenandoah, having ranged along the foot of the mountain an hundred miles to seek a vent. On your left approaches the Patowmac, in quest of a passage also. In the moment of their junction they rush together against the mountain, rend it asunder, and pass off to the sea. . . . For the mountain being cloven asunder, she presents to your eye, through the cleft, a small catch of smooth blue

horizon, at an infinite distance in the plain country. . . . This scene is worth a voyage across the Atlantic.[32]

No site in Virginia thrilled Jefferson more than the great Natural Bridge, in Rockbridge County, which he had purchased in 1774. In *Notes*, he called it "the most sublime of Nature's works" and described it in precise mathematical and geometrical terms. Crossing over it, he wrote, "you involuntarily fall on your hands and feet, creep to the parapet and peep over it. . . . It is impossible for the emotions, arising from the sublime, to be felt beyond what they are here: so beautiful the arch, so elevated, so light, and springing, as it were, up to heaven, the rapture of the Spectator is really indescribable."[33] *Notes on the State of Virginia*, though it has a hodge-podge character, contains many of Jefferson's most quotable—and quoted—words.

The longest reply to Barbé-Marbois in *Notes* is that to Query VI, "Productions Mineral, Vegetable and Animal." Jefferson dutifully listed lead mines, iron and coal deposits, and related information and included a four-page account of the most commonly grown vegetables. But the topic of animals really engaged him, and here he went far beyond simple lists. Jefferson carefully addressed and argued against each aspect of Buffon's thesis. He also spent an inordinate amount of time on what he called the mammoth, the name he gave to a creature, actually a mastodon, whose large bones had been excavated in the United States. He was aware that mammoth bones had been found in Europe too, so he was determined to expound on the size of the American skeletons. He showed through detailed descriptions of the bones, especially the teeth, that the American version was not, as some European naturalists had claimed, either an elephant or a hippopotamus but in fact a mammoth. He estimated the weight of the American version to be "six times the cubic volume of the elephant." He called it "the largest of all terrestrial beings," so living in the American climate clearly had not made it puny. Jefferson assumed that the American mammoth was not extinct but still roamed somewhere in the far northwest of the continent. As he put it, "Such is the oeconomy of nature, that no instance can be produced of her having permitted any one race of her animals to become extinct; of her having formed any link in her great work [the "chain of being"] so weak as to be broken."[34]

Not until 1796 did French naturalist Georges Cuvier convincingly demonstrate that many animals such as the mammoth had indeed died out.[35] In 1793, Jefferson hoped that the explorer André Michaux—who was to be sponsored by the American Philosophical Society—would find traces of the giant creature somewhere in the remote Northwest. By 1803, Jefferson had evidently come around to Cuvier's view, since the mission statement he wrote out for Meriwether Lewis mentioned that Lewis should seek evidence of animals now extinct.

In *Notes*, Jefferson also took spirited objection to Buffon's harsh criticism of American Indians as cowardly and having "no vivacity, no activity of the mind," smaller sexual organs, a "lack [of] ardor for their females," and no "state of society." Jefferson rebutted these claims point by point, defending Indians' bravery, attraction to their wives, devotion to their children, and oratorical abilities (he gave a moving account of a speech by Mingo chieftain Logan). He concluded that their "vivacity and activity of mind is equal to ours in the same situation."[36] His disparaging remarks on America aside, Jefferson generally found Buffon "the best informed of any Naturalist who has ever written."[37] But he had barely contained contempt for another French naturalist and philosophe, the Abbé Raynal, who applied Buffon's ideas about the degeneration of common domesticated animals in America to the descendants of the initial European immigrants. Raynal professed astonishment that "America has not yet produced one good poet, one able mathematician, one man of genius in a single art or a single science." Jefferson retorted, "When we shall have existed as a people as long as the Greeks did before they produced a Homer, the Romans a Virgil, the French, a Racine and Voltaire, the English a Shakespeare and Milton, should this reproach still be true," the cause of this failure should then be sought. But Jefferson emphasized that the young nation had already produced Washington, Franklin, and astronomer David Rittenhouse, all of whom he hailed as great men worthy of the world's acclaim.[38]

Jefferson's interest in Native Americans led him to devote a discrete chapter of *Notes* to "aborigines" that was less a defense of Indians than a simple description of their tribes, societies, habits, and so forth. He provided charts accounting for the tribes and subtribes known to him in great detail. Yet the most fascinating aspect of his discussion is his account of his archaeological examination of an ancient burial mound near Monticello, in the floodplains of the Rivanna River. He does not give the date of his investigation, but his excavation techniques were revolutionary, and experts in the field came to see him as the "father of American archaeology." After some preliminary digging in the mound, which was forty feet in diameter and about seven and a half feet tall, he discovered skeletal remains of men, women, and children all jumbled together. He then decided to cut a trench crosswise through the mound, all the way to the underlying earth. He took careful notice of what he called the strata of bones, from the lowest level, which he deemed the most ancient, up through the highest and newest.[39] In his use of the terms "stratum" and "strata," he pioneered the archaeological principle of stratigraphical excavation.

JEFFERSON FEARED THAT his highly critical section in *Notes* on the constitution of Virginia would generate a major controversy. In fact, it was one of the two parts of the book that caused him to worry about its widespread distribution in the state; the other was his discussion of the institution of slavery. Jefferson's fundamental opposition to the Virginia constitution stemmed from how it was drafted and approved amid the early stages of the Revolutionary War. He believed the process of its creation was flawed: the regularly elected delegates to the assembly had drafted and passed the constitution; Jefferson believed that a specially elected convention should have been called for the sole purpose of proposing a constitution, which would then be submitted to a formal public vote. Hence he viewed the 1776 constitution as more akin to conventional legislation than a formal foundational document.

In 1783 he had reason to believe that a special convention would be called to reconsider the state's constitution, and again he prepared a text to propose, only to be disappointed when the rumored convention never happened. Almost a cry from the heart, his comments in *Notes* kept alive his contention that the constitution was not legitimate. He was caustic about the refusal to correct the situation and singled out particular features for criticism, including the limited franchise and the concentration of legislative, executive, and judicial powers in the primary legislative body.[40] He included his 1783 draft of a new constitution as an appendix to show how the current version could be improved. He wrote the broader constitutional commentary in *Notes* just months after the hoped-for convention of 1783 did not materialize, a time when he was also still stinging from the threatened legislative censure in 1781 of his gubernatorial administration. About the June 1781 suggestion to appoint a temporary dictator to govern the state during wartime, he now wrote that mere consideration of such a proposal had been "treason against the people; was treason against mankind in general." He could only hope that his countrymen would come to their senses and "apply, at a proper season, the proper remedy; which is a convention to fix the constitution, to amend its defects."[41]

WHAT JEFFERSON WROTE in the next section of *Notes*, titled "Laws," brought him and his legacy sustained condemnation later on, though this was not the section Jefferson expected to be controversial. Whereas Jefferson considered Indians to have originated in Europe and to have gradually, sometime in the distant past, migrated across Asia to America,[42] he believed Africans represented a separate people. As he theorized, an entirely different climate had helped make them distinct from Europeans and those of European stock.[43] What might otherwise have seemed a digression was relevant because, in discussing the laws of Virginia, Jefferson mentioned an act he and his mentor George Wythe had proposed in 1779 dealing with prohibiting the future importation of slaves into Virginia. At that time, he and Wythe hoped that when the act came up for discussion, an amendment would be offered calling for the emancipation of all slaves after a certain date, after which the former slaves would be resettled in another land to start a society of their own. Jefferson felt it necessary to explain why he and Wythe had deemed it essential that freed persons be removed from the country (he would get to his views on the institution of slavery later in the text). He began by mentioning "deep rooted prejudices entertained by the whites; ten thousand recollections, by the blacks, of the injuries they have sustained." Then he listed "the real distinctions which nature has made . . . which are physical and moral." These distinctions, he said, "will divide us into parties, and produce convulsions which will probably never end but in the extermination of the one or the other race."[44] This horrifying scenario of genocidal conflict provided the segue to what modern readers view as the most disturbing words in the entire Jefferson corpus.

In five pages, Jefferson revealed that he found almost every aspect of Africans inferior, from the "eternal monotony" of skin that failed to show blushes to kinky hair and the unfavorable contrast with the supposedly "more elegant symmetry of form" of whites. That blacks were less physically attractive was proven, he said, by "their own judgment in favour of the whites, declared by their preference of them, as uniformly as is the preference of the Oran-ootan for the black women over those of his own species."[45] He continued in the same vein: "They secrete less by the kidneys, and more by the glands of the skin, which gives them a very strong and disagreeable odour"; "They seem to require less sleep"; "They are more ardent after their female; but love seems with them to be more an eager desire, than a tender delicate mixture of sentiment and sensation. Their griefs are transient." They seem "in memory . . . equal to whites; in reason much inferior."[46] Perhaps most damning, coming as it did from a lover of art, music, and other cultural pursuits, was this: "But never yet could I find that a black had uttered a thought above the level of plain narration; never see even an elementary trait of painting or sculpture. In music they are generally more gifted than the whites with accurate ears for tune and time, and they have been found capable of imagining a small catch. Whether they will be equal to the composition of a more extensive run of melody, or of complicated harmony, is yet to be proved."[47]

When he tried to sound balanced, the effort seemed forced. Although he admitted, "They are at least as brave, and more adventuresome," he added, "but this may perhaps proceed from a want of forethought, which prevents their seeing a danger till it be present." Countering the charge that they had a tendency toward theft, he did at least admit that the reason was their situation, not any "depravity of the moral sense." Then again, "Whether further observation will or will not verify the conjecture, that nature has been less bountiful to them in the endowments of the head, I believe that in those of the heart she will be found to have done them justice." To this he appended a disclaimer. "The opinion, that they are inferior in the faculties of reason and imagination, must be hazarded with great diffidence." As Jefferson put it, "Let me add too, as a circumstance of great tenderness, where our conclusion would degrade a whole race of men from the rank in the scale of beings which their Creator may perhaps have given them . . . I advance it therefore as a suspicion only, that the blacks, whether originally a distinct race, or made distinct by time and circumstance, are inferior to the whites in the endowments both of body and mind."

The point of all this was to support his final conclusion: "This unfortunate difference of colour, and perhaps of faculty, is a powerful obstacle to the emancipation of these people." As a result, "when freed, he is to be removed beyond the reach of mixture"—that is, resettled elsewhere.[48] Jefferson spelled out the preparation he believed necessary for humane colonization. He proposed that the slave children

> should continue with their parents to a certain age, then be brought up, at the public expence, to tillage, arts or sciences, according to their geniuses, till the females should be eighteen, and the males twenty-one

years of age, when they should be colonized to such place as the circumstances of the time should render most proper, sending them out with arms, implements of household and of the handicraft arts, seeds, pairs of the useful domestic animals, &c. to declare them a free and independent people, and to extend to them our alliance and protection, till they shall have acquired strength.[49]

While Jefferson never articulated his hopes in more detail, apparently he expected the freed slaves, appropriately assisted and in a hospitable climate, would create a functional and sustainable nation of their own.

Jefferson was by no means an outlier in holding the position that colonization was a prerequisite for the popular acceptance of emancipation. The view was common in America for the next half century and beyond, shared by such prominent figures as James Madison, John Marshall, Henry Clay, and Abraham Lincoln, who believed in colonization as a solution to slavery at least until mid-1864.[50] Even most abolitionists supported colonization until about 1830 because they otherwise feared bloody violence between the races.[51] Colonization was not primarily a subterfuge for perpetuating chattel slavery—because it would require immense effort and resources. Rather, most of its adherents viewed it as the only realistic approach, however impractical, to ending what they deemed an abomination.[52]

While Jefferson posed his comments as tentative, never in the thousands of letters he wrote afterward did he suggest that his views had significantly evolved or changed—even after he became acquainted, in 1791, with the accomplishments of black mathematician Benjamin Banneker or, still later, when he found himself surrounded at Monticello by talented and manifestly skilled mixed-race slaves.[53] While he later wrote many marginal comments in his personal copy of *Notes*, correcting the text and adding bibliographical citations, he never amended or updated the passages on blacks. Perhaps just as surprising and dismaying, he neither expected nor received much contemporary criticism.[54] His friend Charles Thomson, who read the text in the 1785 private printing, was astute enough to see that the passage on black inferiority could give the misleading sense that Jefferson sought to justify slavery. Thomson thus suggested he remove the passage from a more public printing, even though he said, "I am much pleased with the dissertation on the difference between the Whites and blacks & am inclined to think the latter a race lower in the scale of being."[55]

Why did these words, so explosive to us today, not elicit more outrage in 1787? As Jefferson showed in 1776, he had a genius for synthesizing commonly accepted ideas and restating them in memorable terms. He did that nobly in the Declaration of Independence and, here, deplorably, in his characterization of Africans in *Notes on the State of Virginia*. This voraciously curious reader was summarizing commonplace late-eighteenth-century French and European scientific conjecture, which regularly described Africans as inferior, their blackness, reputed smell, and resemblance to and even sexual preference for the orangutan taken for granted.[56] A decade later some of his Federalist opponents did attack him for his disquisitions on race, but their motivation was more political than moral. Adherents of some religious groups such as Baptists, Methodists, and Quakers accepted the spiritual equality of blacks in the eyes of God, but even among those whites at the time opposed to slavery, actual physical equality of the races was a decidedly minority view.[57]

ON TWO OTHER general topics addressed in *Notes*—religious liberty and manners, though he discussed the latter in the context of his then controversial view of slavery—Jefferson was far more progressive and forward thinking. After a short survey of the legislative support for a state religion in Virginia, which he bluntly called a "summary view of that religious slavery, under which a people have been willing to remain, who have lavished their lives and fortunes for the establishment of their civil freedom," he emphasized, "The error seems not sufficiently eradicated, that the operations of the mind, as well as the acts of the body, are subject to the coercion of the laws." In some of the most direct language on the subject he ever employed, Jefferson wrote, "The rights of conscience we never submitted, we could not submit. We are answerable for them to our God. The legitimate powers of government extend to such acts only as are injurious to others. But it does me no injury for my neighbour to say there are twenty gods, or no god. It neither picks my pocket nor breaks my leg."[58] Jefferson was advocating for the full freedom of religious conscience and complete intellectual freedom. Later on he would be charged as an opponent of Christianity for these very words.

Jefferson believed religion thrived best in a situation of complete liberty. "Reason and free enquiry," he wrote, "are the only effectual agents against error. Give a loose to them, they will support the true religion, by bringing every false one to their tribunal, to the test of their investigation. They are the natural enemies of error, and error only." He repeated this point: "It is error alone which needs the support of government. Truth can stand by itself."[59] State interference and coercion were attempts to produce uniformity of opinion, and uniformity was undesirable even to the true believer: "Difference of opinion is advantageous in religion" because the competing sects served to monitor one another. In a free society, reason and "good sense" counter any sect "whose tenets would subvert morals." And now, he argued, while the spirit of freedom was still strong following the revolution, it was time to enact legislation guaranteeing religious liberty.[60] The summer before the English-language publication of *Notes on the State of Virginia*, he took comfort not only in the passage of his religious freedom bill in Virginia but in its spreading fame and influence across Europe.[61] He reprinted the act as an appendix in the book.

Barbé-Marbois's original question about both customs and manners Jefferson changed to one about manners alone, and this he placed near the end of *Notes*. The result, less than two pages long, was the second section Jefferson feared would be so controversial that it might actually prove counterproductive to his intent: the gradual abolition of slavery. Writing of the "unhappy influence on the manners of our people produced by the existence of slavery among us," Jefferson lamented, "The whole commerce between master and slave is a perpetual exercise of the most boisterous passions, the most unremitting despotism on the one part, and degrading submissions on the other." He wrote, "Our children see this and learn to imitate it. . . . The parent storms, the child looks on, catches the lineaments of wrath, puts on the same airs in the circle of smaller slaves, gives a loose to his worst of passions, and thus nursed, educated, and daily exercised in tyranny, cannot but be stamped by it with odious peculiarities. The man must be a prodigy who can retain his manners and morals undepraved by such circumstances."[62] The system of human bondage teaches legislators to "trample on the rights of others," turning them "into despots," and it thereby "destroys the morals" of the slaveholding class and the natural love of country among the slaves. It also destroys the respect for "industry," for work itself, among whites, since in "a warm climate, no man will labour for himself who can make another labour for him." How, Jefferson asked, can "the liberties of a nation be thought secure" in such a situation?[63] Although he recognized the cruelty meted out to bondspeople, he was more concerned about slavery's harm to whites and their political institutions.

Still, Jefferson did believe slavery a terrible evil inflicted on Africans and founded part of his support for colonization on the possibilities of divinely sanctioned retribution. "Indeed I tremble for my country," he wrote, "when I reflect that God is just: that his justice cannot sleep for ever: . . . a revolution of the wheel of fortune, an exchange of situation, is among possible events: that it may become probable by supernatural interference! The Almighty has no attribute which can take side with us in such a contest." As Jefferson suggested several times in *Notes*, he trusted that the nation would in good time grow beyond slavery. In fact, he thought "a change already perceptible, since the origin of the present revolution. The spirit of the master is abating, that of the slave arising from the dust, his condition mollifying, the way I hope preparing, under the auspices of heaven, for a total emancipation, and that this is disposed, in the order of events, to be with the consent of the masters, rather than by their extirpation."[64] For Jefferson, however, the ultimate solution remained the permanent colonization of the freed slaves in a more appropriate (warmer) climate, probably in the Caribbean. Like most of his white Virginia contemporaries, he could not, in the end, imagine a peaceful multiracial society.[65]

Jefferson had only one more strong set of principles to advocate, which he did in a section titled "Manufactures." Here he defended the dominance of agriculture in the American economy and argued that it should be complemented only as absolutely necessary by trade and limited manufacturing. "Those who labour in the earth," he wrote in one of his most famous phrases, "are the chosen people of God, if ever he had a chosen people, whose breasts he has made his peculiar deposit for substantial and genuine virtue." In them was kept alive the "sacred fire" of liberty, and on the whole they avoided the "Corruption of morals" that was so common to mankind. Husbandmen, as he called farmers, represented the healthier parts of any society, and "the mobs of great cities add just so much to the support of pure government, as sores do to the strength of the human body." He argued that the nation should continue to concentrate on agriculture, with only small-scale and local industry: "let our workshops remain in Europe." That would best guarantee the "happiness and permanence of government."[66] Jefferson was surprisingly brief in his remarks on this topic given how important the idea of a yeoman republic was to his political philosophy, but much of his political activity in coming years grew out of this sentiment.

With that evocation of the agricultural ideal, Jefferson concluded what had begun, years earlier, as his response to a series of twenty-one questions about Virginia asked by the secretary to the French legation at

Philadelphia. Jefferson's final version of his reply, though it took on aspects of a concise encyclopedia, also soared to rhetorical heights on subjects to which Jefferson was most committed (and, on the nature of Africans, to rhetorical lows). It is an essential compendium of Jefferson's beliefs concerning nature, philosophy, race, government, slavery, religion, agriculture, and the destiny of his nation, and many of the positions revealed in this brief text shaped his actions over the remainder of his life.

13

"Liberty Is to Be Gained by Inches"

J EFFERSON HAD NO ILLUSIONS that his primary diplomatic assignment in Paris—to negotiate treaties of commerce with European nations—would be easy or even successful. After all, he and the other
two treaty commissioners, John Adams and Benjamin Franklin, were essentially attempting to explode the existing system of European maritime
commerce. According to the ascendant theory and practice of mercantil-
ism, a mother country and her colonies prospered to the extent that they
kept all commerce within the empire. Leakage to other nations, in the
form of either imports or exports, was considered harmful to the empire
and hence restricted. The new American nation was, by these standards,
cut out of international trade except on terms favorable to individual
European nations, which presumed the right to restrict trade to their own
ships. As decided by the Congress, the American position was that commerce between all nations should be open and free, under the assumption
that all would prosper as a result.

This was an idealistic position, but also one that would clearly benefit
the United States, which needed markets in Europe for its major products: tobacco, wheat, rice, whale oil, salted fish, and deer skins. From the
American point of view, free trade would benefit Europe too because US
merchants would purchase manufactured and specialty goods from the
nations that bought America's raw products. Of even greater importance
than Europe itself, however, were the markets for American goods, especially foodstuffs and lumber products, in Europe's West Indian colonies.
Importantly, as the instructions to the commissioners—which Jefferson
had helped draft before he knew he would be one of them—made explicit, they were to negotiate treaties with the understanding that the several American states would be considered "one nation," not a collection of

independent potential trade partners. The Articles of Confederation had not explicitly banned states from seeking their own commercial agreements, a flaw the commissioners hoped to correct.

The Europe to which Jefferson journeyed had for decades been relatively free of the bloody internecine warfare that so marked the previous century. The intellectual movement known as the Enlightenment was fully underway, and while the American Revolution had sparked a democratizing current, most of Europe was under the sway of powerful if relatively enlightened autocratic leaders: Catherine the Great in Russia, Frederick the Great in Prussia, Emperor Joseph II on the Hapsburg throne in Vienna, and of course Louis XVI in France. Altering the reigning European commercial system must have seemed a daunting challenge.

JUST AS JEFFERSON WAS preparing to go to France in 1784, the permanent secretary of the Congress, Charles Thomson, sent him "all the necessary papers," along with twenty commissions to deal with an enumerated list of European nations and principalities. Included were "Instructions for Negotiating Treaties of Amity and Commerce by the United States in Congress Assembled," which laid out the underlying principles for trade treaties.[1] In fact, Jefferson brought with him a complete draft of a model treaty, of which he was the principal author.[2] The model treaty provided that merchant vessels of nonbelligerent nations could trade without interference with one or more of the nations that might be at war. It also stated that, between nations enjoying commercial relations, "the most perfect freedom of conscience and of worship is granted to the citizens or subjects of either party within the jurisdiction of the other without being liable to molestation in that respect for any cause other than an insult on the religion of the others."[3]

The United States already had commercial treaties with France, the United Netherlands, and Sweden, and although the commissioners in France might seek to modify these, their main charge was to negotiate new treaties with England, Hamburg, Saxony, Prussia, Denmark, Russia, Austria, Venice, Rome, Naples, Tuscany, Sardinia, Genoa, Spain, Portugal, the Porte (the central government of the Ottoman Empire), Algiers, Tripoli, Tunis, and Morocco. Jefferson particularly desired increased trade with France as a means of reducing the influence of England in the United States.

The commissioners found the work frustrating.[4] Because the colonists had traditionally bought most of their manufactured items from England

and sold practically all their raw products to the same nation, and because England's merchants not only provided convenient credit arrangements but knew the American market and American tastes intimately, merchants from other European countries were very far behind. If European manufacturers and merchants neither produced nor provided items for American consumers and, at the same time, simply paid in cash for American products, then American shippers took those payments and proceeded to England to buy manufactured items for their home markets, thereby maintaining US economic subservience to England. It didn't help that European merchants, shippers, and manufacturers were wedded to their traditional practices; entrenched interests on the Continent were generally unwilling to explore and experiment with the American trade. As a result, despite their combined diplomatic efforts, Adams, Franklin, and Jefferson had little to show for all their efforts to forge commercial treaties.

By late 1785 neither Adams nor Franklin was still in Paris, and Jefferson was the American minister. He continued to try to promote French importation of American products like whale oil and rice. The French government had "farmed out" the import market for tobacco to a group of wealthy individuals, collectively called the Farmers-General, who, in return for collecting the taxes and import duties on the tobacco, reaped huge profits and enjoyed monopoly control. To make matters worse, they had contracted with American financier Robert Morris for a three-year monopoly of tobacco imports from the United States; this double monopoly, as it were, depressed prices and disincentivized or even prevented American producers from seeking independent markets and higher prices. Jefferson did effect some reform in the tobacco trade by making it possible for the Farmers-General to purchase 7,000 to 12,000 hogsheads of tobacco annually from America in addition to that controlled by Morris, but it represented a small return on his investment of time and effort.[5]

Another major issue facing the commissioners was the piratical activities of the Barbary powers (Morocco, Algiers, Tunis, and Tripoli) on the north coast of Africa. The pirates raided maritime commerce entering the Mediterranean and sometimes even ventured into the Atlantic. They not only stole cargo but also captured ships and enslaved their sailors, holding them for exorbitant ransoms. England was powerful enough to intimidate the pirates and thus prevent them from interfering with its trade, but they extorted huge annual tributes from most other nations, especially smaller ones, in exchange for assurance that they would not molest their ships.[6]

Seeing the infant US government as unable to protect its commerce, the Barbary pirates targeted it. Jefferson had not been in France two months when he learned that Moroccan raiders had captured the American brig *Betsy* and taken its sailors prisoner. Jefferson was outraged, above all, by the idea of a ransom. He thought it beneath the dignity of the nation to be subject to a tribute, which, after some delicate inquiries, he learned would amount to several hundred thousand dollars annually. "Surely our people will not give this," he wrote James Monroe. "Would it not be better to offer them an equal treaty. If they refuse, why not go to war with them? . . . We ought to begin a naval power, if we mean to carry on our own commerce. Can we begin it on a more honourable occasion or with a weaker foe?" He believed that John Paul Jones, the naval hero of the American Revolution, could crush the pirates with only a handful of ships.[7] However, Jefferson could act only according to the wishes of Congress, which was not ready to create a navy, and John Adams opposed the military option altogether. Instead, Congress proposed a budget for ransoms and tributes that provided a fraction of what was necessary. Adams believed that the profits gained from increased commerce in the Mediterranean would justify paying higher tributes, but Jefferson opposed this on principle and because he feared the tributes demanded would constantly escalate.

In 1785 Jefferson and Adams sent the US consul general to Paris, Thomas Barclay, to Morocco, the most cooperative of the Barbary powers, and for the relatively small sum of $30,000, he freed the *Betsy*'s crew. Yet all other efforts to make treaties or negotiate reasonable tribute payments with the Barbary powers failed. Jefferson, always protective of his country's reputation, understood that Barbary disrespect hurt it in the eyes of various European nations. Nothing less than the honor of the United States was at stake.[8]

Jefferson believed that in the long run it made both economic and political sense to spend the money to equip a naval force sufficient to thwart the Barbary menace. But Congress was loath to appropriate sufficient funds. Not until 1805, when Jefferson was president, did a naval force under the command of Stephen Decatur end the Tripolitan pillaging of American maritime commerce.[9]

JEFFERSON HAD FOUND the problem of the Barbary pirates aggravating, but he proved an exemplary diplomat while in France, even if his achievements do not rival those of his predecessor, Benjamin Franklin. Jefferson's successes came despite his considering the French diplomatic corps pompous and the formal court at Versailles extravagant, inefficient, and excessively mired in ritualistic behavior. The secret to his success lay in his personality and ability: he was polite, patient, a good listener, and attentive to detail, with an enormous capacity for work. Yet while Jefferson was respected in Paris and widely admired as the author of the Declaration of Independence, except for minor improvements in gaining markets for American whale oil and tobacco, he made little progress in opening Europe to US trade.

Jefferson's final diplomatic chore in France was the completion of a bit of unfinished business. After France and America had signed their treaty of amity and commerce in 1778, a proposed consular convention—an agreement stipulating policies regarding consular staffs in both nations—had never been finalized amid the ongoing American Revolution. Since then, France had sought the completion of a consular agreement far more avidly than had the United States, but Jefferson was sufficiently adroit to find a happy compromise between the two nations. He admitted to French foreign minister Armand Marc, Comte de Montmorin, "We do not find the institution of Consuls very necessary." But after a discussion of how commerce between nations and the needs of merchants grow, he graciously acknowledged to Montmorin, "That this government [the French] thinks them useful, is sufficient reason for us to give them all the functions and facilities which our circumstances will admit. Instead therefore of declining every article which will be useless to us, we accede to every one which will not be too inconvenient."[10]

Jefferson managed to rein in the powers and immunities for consular officials that France had been pushing for, bringing the consuls to a great degree under US law. On November 14, 1788, he and Montmorin signed an agreement, "not indeed such as I would have wished," Jefferson later admitted in his autobiography, "but such as could be obtained with good humor & friendship," an indication of why he was so effective in diplomacy.[11] Jefferson knew that this first consular convention was an experiment, and so the treaty specified that the agreement would be "in full force during the term of twelve years to be counted from the day of the exchange of ratifications."[12] After studying the careful document Jefferson had drafted, Secretary of Foreign Affairs John Jay grudgingly recommended it to the Congress recently elected under the terms of the 1787 Constitution. The Consular Convention became, on July 29, 1789, the first treaty ratified by the new US government. The vote was unanimous.[13]

FROM HIS FIRST appearance on the national stage, Jefferson had intended to help create a true union out of the thirteen states that had won their independence.[14] Naturally, he could not directly attend to this broad ambition while working as a diplomat in France. Although often frustrated by the delays in the Congress and, relatedly, by its frequent failure to maintain a quorum, he was probably taken aback to receive a letter, on May 24, 1784, from the Congress's permanent secretary, Charles Thomson, expressing his concern that without a reformation, "there is reason to apprehend a dissolution to the Confederacy."[15]

Jefferson apparently never replied to this letter, perhaps thinking it stemmed from nothing more than the kind of momentary annoyance he himself had often experienced when dealing with Congress. But he did take notice of a letter from James Monroe on April 12, 1785, reporting that a congressional committee was considering amending the confederation to give the Congress complete authority over "the entire regulation of the commerce of the Union." Jefferson desired such a change, believing it the last improvement the confederation constitution needed until—and this may have been almost a throwaway line—"the states shall by new compact make them more perfect."[16] Which is to say, Jefferson did not think the Articles of Confederation needed more than some minor corrections. Even when he heard from James Madison later that year that Congress desperately needed the ability to force the various states to pay their quotas of taxes, Jefferson still had no firm sense of how strongly nationalists in the US believed that crisis impended.[17] In fact, before he received Madison's letter on tax collections, Jefferson wrote him suggesting more progressive tax assessments: "exempt all from taxation below a certain point, and . . . tax the higher proportions of property in geometrical progression as they rise."[18]

Stationed abroad, Jefferson wrote on January 24, 1786, "The Confederation is a wonderfully perfect instrument, considering the circumstances under which it was formed." He did admit that it needed three slight "alterations": a provision for forming new states out of the western territories, a fairer method of apportioning the taxes required from the various states, and, most important, a means of forbidding the individual states from entering into commercial treaties with other nations.[19] Jefferson was clearly so removed from the American scene, and so convinced of the evils of Europe's monarchical governments, that he continued to make what his associates in Philadelphia and elsewhere viewed as unrealistic assessments of the situation in his home country. The distress he perceived abroad inured him to problems arising in the United States. He believed, after all, that the average person in France lived poorly. The common people were good, the climate genial, the soil fertile, but nevertheless, "of twenty millions of people supposed to be in France I am of opinion there are nineteen millions more wretched, more accursed in every circumstance of human existence, than the most conspicuously wretched individual of the whole United States." To Jefferson, the only explanation for the difference was that the French lived under "a bad form of government."[20] Thus, by comparison, any problems in the American government seemed to him fairly trivial and easy to fix.

But many thoughtful people in the United States saw the matter in more urgent terms. Jefferson received two letters from John Jay in 1786, the second more fearful than the first. The first simply reported that "the Construction of our federal Government is fundamentally wrong." The second enumerated the problems: the "inefficacy of our Government becomes daily more and more apparent," there was a general "reluctance to taxes," and, most important, "a Spirit of Licentiousness has infected Massachusetts," which Jay feared could spread.[21] Jay was referring to an uprising by farmers in western Massachusetts, known today as Shays's Rebellion, over what they believed to be unfair taxation. Perhaps because his friend John Adams advised him not to be "alarmed" by the "late Turbulence in New England," Jefferson found it hard to believe that this rebellion in a portion of one state jeopardized the security of the nation.[22] But he misread how seriously many in the United States took the threat. In fact, from his vantage in France, where an inert, passive people refused to resist obvious governmental oppression, the image of hale and hearty Massachusetts farmers standing up for their rights struck Jefferson as absolutely invigorating. In this context Jefferson wrote Madison, "I hold it that a little rebellion now and then is a good thing, and as necessary in the political world as storms in the physical. . . . It is a medicine necessary for the sound health of government."[23]

The notion of the usefulness of periodic rebellion was not, as many have thought since, a consistent aspect of Jefferson's political philosophy. Rather, he voiced this belief in a private comment and at a particular moment. The notion did stem from one consistent aspect of his political philosophy, however: Jefferson considered the threat of governmental repression a greater danger than rebellion from below. His sojourn in France had strengthened this view. And in this particular case, Madison was less frank about his worries with Jefferson than he was with others.

Madison had written to Edmund Pendleton on February 24, 1787, "The late turbulent scenes in Massts . . . have done inexpressible injury to the republican character in that part of the U. States; and a propensity towards Monarchy is said to have been produced by it in some leading minds." Some people with a more localistic orientation, he continued, were contemplating dividing the nation into "three more practicable and energetic Governments."[24] The next day he confided to Edmund Randolph, "Our situation is becoming every day more & more critical. . . . [T]he existing Confederacy is tottering to its foundation. Many individuals of weight particularly in the Eastern district are suspected of leaning towards Monarchy. Other individuals predict a partition of the States into two or more Confederacies."[25] Madison wrote Jefferson in less alarmist fashion.

The prospect of division did, of course, worry Jefferson, but not because of Shays's Rebellion. He believed that John Jay's 1786 negotiations with Spanish minister Diego de Gardoqui, in which Jay had indicated willingness to suspend American claims to navigation of the Mississippi River in exchange for a commercial treaty with Spain (favorable to the northeastern states but detrimental to the western ones), were far more potentially harmful than a localized farmers' revolt in Massachusetts. If accepted, the Jay-Gardoqui agreement would have fatefully alienated the entire western section of the nation from the eastern portion. This was the domestic issue that worried Jefferson. He stated flatly to Madison, "The act which abandons the navigation of the Missisipi is an act of separation between the Eastern and Western country." Fortunately, in Jefferson's mind, because of congressional opposition the negotiations broke off, and the danger passed.[26]

SOON AFTER, VARIOUS correspondents notified Jefferson of a convention to meet in Philadelphia during the summer of 1787 to address the failures of the confederation. Madison wrote that delegates were being chosen, but "what may be the result of this political experiment cannot be foreseen." He added that the problems facing the government were "truly alarming" and that, as a result, some sort of new government was needed. "I think myself that it will be expedient in the first place to lay the foundation of the new system in such a ratification by the people themselves."[27] Not until six days after he returned to Paris from his trip to the south of France, on June 10, 1787, did Jefferson see this letter, and he apparently did not instantly recognize the import of the words "new system." Then, in June, Madison sent a limited update, but he could only list the delegates, not relate any of the discussions, for the convention acted to "restrain even a confidential communication of our proceedings."[28] The secrecy bothered Jefferson and surely sparked his curiosity.

Learning nothing definitive, Jefferson began suggesting to various correspondents later that summer the kinds of changes he both hoped and expected to see: making "the states one as to every thing connected with foreign nations, and several as to every thing purely domestic"; separating the executive and judicial powers from the legislative; and strengthening only somewhat the powers of the executive, in view of the evils of anything approaching monarchical power.[29] He looked forward to the result of the convention, confiding to John Adams, "I have no doubt that all their other measures will be good and wise. It is really an assembly of demigods."[30] By December 13, 1787, when he received a relatively brief letter from Madison dated September 6 that gave a concise outline of the new government, revealing how extensive the proposed changes were, Jefferson had already seen a copy of the Constitution, sent to him by Adams. Madison accurately termed the proposal a "government," not a set of amendments. He mentioned that the people of Virginia "are said to be generally discontented," probably intending thereby to suggest to Jefferson the absolute necessity of reforming the structure of the national government.[31] Two months before Jefferson saw the finished document, he had written, "Happy for us, that when we find our constitutions defective and insufficient to secure the happiness of our people, we can assemble with all the coolness of philosophers and set it to rights, while every other nation on earth must have recourse to arms to amend or restore their constitutions."[32] But at first he was decidedly not happy with the proposed Constitution.

The precise chronology of what happened next is important if we hope to fully understand Jefferson's reactions. A few weeks after he received a copy of the completed document, and about a week after he received the initial short letter from Madison, he received a fifteen-page letter, posted on October 24, 1787, from Madison that laid out the rationale for every aspect of the Constitution. It is a tour de force only Madison could have written, and it anticipated and answered questions he assumed Jefferson would have.[33]

Jefferson must have gotten the copy of the Constitution sent by Adams before November 13, for on that day he wrote his initial and unfavorable responses. To Adams he expressed astonishment: "How do you like our new constitution? I confess there are things in it which stagger all my dispositions. . . . Their President seems a bad edition of a Polish king. He may be reelected from 4. years to 4. years for life. Reason and experience prove to us that a chief magistrate, so continuable, is an officer for life."[34] Any form of government that even hinted, however slightly, of kingly authority and duration was anathema to Jefferson. As he wrote to George Washington in the spring of 1788, "I was much an enemy to monarchy before I came to Europe. I am ten thousand times more so since I have seen what they are."[35] Jefferson most feared what he saw as a tendency of the people in times of perceived crisis to turn to a form of government with a powerful executive at its center, which to him was detestable.[36]

That same day he dashed off a letter to William Stephens Smith, Adams's son-in-law, again railing against the idea of a president reelectable for life. He thought that the creation of the office was a gross overreaction to the farmers' protest in western Massachusetts. He minimized the danger suggested by that event, asking, "What county can preserve it's liberties if their rulers are not warned from time to time that their people preserve the spirit of resistance? Let them take arms." Then he wrote what would become a famous, and infamous, passage referring to the protesting farmers. "The remedy is to set them right as to facts, pardon and pacify them. What signify a few lives lost in a century or two? The tree of liberty must be refreshed from time to time with the blood of patriots and tyrants. It is it's natural manure. Our Convention has been too much impressed by the insurrection of Massachusetts."[37] These ill-considered words, written upon his first look at the Constitution and reflecting his fear of a potentially monarchical president, were later turned against Jefferson by those seeking to portray him as a dangerous and bloodthirsty radical ready to tear down the established government. Yet after Jefferson read Madison's persuasive letter on December 19, he began to moderate his opposition to the proposed Constitution. He had originally intended to buttress the existing form of government by reminding his correspondents of its several failures that only needed addressing by its citizens. This was but one of several occasions over the course of their long collaboration when Madison cooled Jefferson's intemperate private rhetoric.

What a pity that Jefferson, Adams, Madison, and others could not have met in this period and taken minutes. For this all-important debate, letters had to suffice, even though months often elapsed between their exchange. On November 10 Adams sent Jefferson a brief letter from London that contained two crucial sentences: "What think you of a Declaration of

Rights? Should not such a Thing have preceeded the Model?"[38] Jefferson instantly agreed, and it is surprising that this had not been one of his own initial objections. After all, he was certainly familiar with the notion of a bill of rights introducing a constitution, since that was the form of the 1776 Virginia constitution. Shortly after receiving, on November 26, the letter from Adams, Jefferson wrote William Carmichael, the American chargé d'affaires in Madrid, complaining that the drafters of the document had "fenced the people by no declaration of rights."[39] Adams and Jefferson did diverge on another pressing matter. Whereas Jefferson believed the president under the new system had too much power and could remain in office for too long, Adams believed the president had too little power and was not likely to stay in office long enough. Adams thought Jefferson was too "Apprehensive of Monarchy."[40]

Madison's dissertation on the merits of the Constitution arrived on December 19. Jefferson must have read it immediately. The very next day he replied to Madison, writing, "I have much to thank you for." Jefferson admitted that he liked the "general idea of framing a government which should go on of itself peaceably, without needing continual recurrence to the state legislatures." He approved of the separation of powers, as well as the power of the federal government to levy taxes. He approved, too, of the ingenious compromise in the national legislature between the small and big states. But Jefferson made clear his worries about the absence of a bill of rights, which had more recently become one of his primary concerns, and about the absence of any limitation on the length of time a president could serve. He claimed that a bill of rights "is what the people are entitled to against every government on earth . . . and what no government should refuse." And he wrote explicitly that he did not just dislike but "greatly disliked" the potential for a president's continual reelection.[41] He went on to tell Madison what Madison no doubt already knew: "I own I am not a friend to a very energetic government. It is always oppressive. The late rebellion in Massachusetts has given more alarm than I think it should have done." Nevertheless, he wrote, "it is my principle that the will of the Majority should always prevail. If they approve the proposed Convention in all it's parts, I shall concur in it chearfully, in hopes that they will amend it whenever they shall find it work wrong."[42]

Jefferson received a stream of letters from various correspondents, but mainly Madison, throughout the winter, spring, and summer of 1788. These consisted of periodic updates on the progress of the Constitution in the various state legislatures and especially in Virginia, where Patrick

Henry fought it ferociously, perhaps even favoring, according to Edward Carrington, a Virginia delegate to the Articles of Confederation congress, a "dismemberment of the union."[43] George Mason was also a powerful foe, mainly because of the absence of a bill of rights. Washington and especially Madison led the fight for the new government, Washington lending his reputation and character, Madison his brilliance. Both obviously assumed Jefferson would eventually come around. And he did, though grudgingly. He wrote Madison in February that he hoped nine states would ratify, so the Constitution would go into effect, but he also hoped four would reject it, thereby forcing the government, in search of greater support, to add a bill of rights. "We shall thus have all it's good, and cure it's principal defect," Jefferson wrote.[44] By now he had abandoned his active opposition to the proposed tenure of the president because he had realized that no other prominent political figure in the United States seemed to share his concern.[45]

Clearly the fact that men Jefferson deeply respected supported the new Constitution began to erode his opposition, and on May 27, 1788, he wrote Carrington, "I learn with great pleasure the progress of the new Constitution. Indeed I have presumed it would gain on the public mind, as I confess it has on my own. At first, tho I saw that the great mass and groundwork was good, I disliked many appendages. Reflection and discussion have cleared off most of these." He stated that he had come to accept the reality that his concerns about the reelectability of the president had found no traction in the United States.[46]

When Jefferson finally learned that Virginia had ratified the Constitution, meaning the requisite nine states had voted in favor, he graciously sent Madison a note saying, "I sincerely rejoice at the acceptance of our new constitution by nine states. It is a good canvas, on which some strokes only want retouching," referring to the need for a bill of rights. He told Madison that since a majority had rejected his concern about the presidency, "I readily therefore suppose my opinion wrong." Jefferson sincerely believed in the judgment of the people, in this instance and most others. It was a bedrock principle of his political faith.[47] He was even more positive in his remarks several weeks later to William Carmichael, whom he wrote that the want of a bill of rights "will pretty certainly be remedied" and to whom he expressed great satisfaction in the almost total certainty that Washington would be elected the first president.[48] Washington himself had written Jefferson in late August explaining, "It is nearly impossible for any body who has not been on the spot to conceive (from any description) what the delicacy and danger of our situation have been," which may have helped Jefferson to set aside his earlier skepticism of the need for a completely new form of government.[49] By spring 1789 he was praising not only the process but the product as well.[50] He now had the enthusiasm of a convert.

Jefferson was gratified when Madison, on June 8, 1789, introduced a series of legislative articles to the first Congress of the new government; Madison did so probably less because he believed them necessary and more because he hoped they would head off efforts to call another convention to reconsider what was now the US Constitution. But whatever the reason, the House of Representatives adopted twelve of the articles on August 21. They were proposed formally as a joint resolution of the Congress on September 25, and by December 15, 1789—shortly after Jefferson and his family returned from France—three-fourths of the states had ratified ten of them, and they became the first ten amendments to the Constitution. While Jefferson was not totally satisfied with the wording of each amendment in the Bill of Rights, his major concerns were met, and his commitment to the Constitution from this point onward was unwavering. He had moved from critic to defender, changing his mind as he learned more about the matter, as he did many times throughout his long life.

JUST AS REFORMERS IN the United States began to plan for a convention to consider amendments to the Articles of Confederation, France too began a fateful process of governmental change, one whose outcome was, at least at first, utterly unpredictable. Either by his good luck or misfortune—it could be viewed in either light—Jefferson was present for the initial events that would lead to the French Revolution. In February 1787, economic necessity led Charles Alexandre, Vicomte de Calonne, the French finance minister, to call for the first meeting of the Assembly of Notables since 1626. Decades of warfare, extravagant government spending (exacerbated by debts France incurred to support the American Revolution), corruption, and the fact that the nobility and the church mostly avoided paying taxes now threatened the nation with bankruptcy. Calonne handpicked 144 "princes, prelates, noblemen, and magistrates" for the assembly and laid his proposals for fiscal reform before them.[51] Jefferson had long believed that the people of France deserved a better system of government. He was by nature an optimistic man, and his faith in both reason and the common people (at least in America) knew no bounds. So he was hopeful about this development in France, even though he understood that the obstacles to real change were far greater than in his own nation. The monarchy, the nobility, and the church would, with very few exceptions, fight to maintain their status.

Jefferson had notified John Jay in early January of Calonne's upcoming action but admitted that no one knew what the Assembly of Notables would discuss. A week later he wrote to Carrington that the meeting was widely considered the most important event in French civic life in the eighteenth century so far. Jefferson delayed his long-planned trip to the south of France to witness the opening of the assembly, writing to Carrington, "I wait to see the causes declared for which they are convened."[52] He attended the opening session, describing the "short but affectionate speech" of the king, the brief talk given by the keeper of the seals, and the hour-long presentation by Calonne on the state of the nation's finances. Five days later Jefferson began his journey; he remained optimistic about the results of the meeting.[53] But Calonne's honest accounting of the state's appalling financial situation so upset the assembly that the king was forced to remove him. The assembly, ill disposed to search for solutions to the multitude of problems facing the nation, dissolved on May 25.

The collapse of the Assembly of Notables was an enormous disappointment to the people of France. When they learned more about excessive government expenditures, that one consequence would be new taxes, and that none of the discussed reforms would be acted upon, they unleashed a torrent of criticism of the government. Jefferson could not help but find the upheaval fascinating. He wrote to John Adams in late August, "From the separation of the Notables to the present moment has been perhaps the most interesting interval ever known in this country." Ever the supporter of local democracy, he believed that the newly proposed provincial assemblies might well prove "to be the instrument for circumscribing the power of the crown and raising the people into consideration."[54]

While a tiny minority of the nobility were progressive friends not only to Jefferson but to the idea of America, few if any members of the clerical hierarchy could contemplate giving up any power or tax advantages. The government's predicament only worsened when Prussia invaded Holland to put down a reform movement led by the so-called Patriots. The French government (and Jefferson) had sided with the Patriots against the Stadtholder, the Prince of Orange. In Jefferson's view, the Patriots had failed in part because they had pushed too hard and too fast for reform, thereby alienating potential supporters.[55] When the king of Prussia took offense at a perceived Patriot slight against the Stadtholder's wife, who was his sister, and invaded Holland, the French government was too debilitated to step in.[56] The Patriots' overreach was the kind of action Jefferson often feared, as for example when he explained the wisdom of Virginian antislavery reformers choosing to move more slowly than they might have wanted. He was soon warning French reformers about maximalist actions, because the result, he feared, would be a violent counterreaction.

In the spring of 1788 Jefferson remarked to a correspondent, "The gay and thoughtless Paris is now become a furnace of Politics. All the world is run politically mad." To another correspondent the ever-optimistic Jefferson wrote that France "is at present in a crisis of very incertain issue. I am in hopes it will be a favourable one to the rights and happiness of the people: and that this will take place quietly." In July he wrote his old friend Bishop Madison, "This country is making it's way to a good constitution. The only danger is they may press so fast as to produce an appeal to arms, which might have an unfavorable issue for them."[57] But the looming financial crisis overtook the slow pace of reform; on August 16, the nation ceased payments from the national treasury, effectively declaring bankruptcy. Jefferson understood the unprecedented nature of this event, and his optimism began to waver.

The French king, Louis XVI, was not, relative to the United States, a progressive, but realizing the nation needed revenue and that the people were already hard-pressed to contribute more, he inclined toward raising more taxes from the undertaxed first and second estates: the clergy and nobility, respectively. Jefferson believed this the correct step.[58] While he recognized that the nation was "extremely agitated," he wrote Monroe that he thought "it probable this country will within two or three years be in the enjoyment of a tolerable free constitution, and that without it's having cost them a drop of blood."[59]

Jefferson continued to expect the best as 1789 began. He understood that a nation burdened for so long with an undemocratic government could not be remade into a replica of America overnight, but he believed that with patience France could move in that direction. As he wrote in March, "I beleive this nation will in the course of the present year have as full a portion of liberty dealt out to them as the nation can bear at present, considering how uninformed the mass of their people is."[60] Given the severe social stratification that kept the great majority of French peasants and workers illiterate and downtrodden, almost unable to imagine the possibility of improvement in their lives, he did not expect anything like American democracy to emerge quickly. Here, as always, he believed progress would come incrementally.

In July 1788 a ferocious hailstorm had hit the north of France, destroying much of a wheat crop already stunted by drought, and the winter that followed was uncharacteristically cold. Many of the poor were left hungry and freezing. As Jefferson witnessed, "Great cold carries off men here, as it does cattle with us, and for the same reasons, the want of being housed and fed." As late as March 1789, he reported that the Seine was completely frozen, with loaded carriages being driven over it.[61] Since the government remained unable to act in any useful way, unrest began to mount. The Estates General, the country's highest representative body, met in May 1789. When the nobility and the church held firm to their privileges, weeks of stalemate ensued. Finally, the third estate, representing the people at large, took over, renamed the representative body the National Assembly, and, on June 17, 1789, seized power in the name of the French nation. The French Revolution had begun.

In a flurry of letters throughout the spring and early summer, Jefferson described and responded to these events. He kept hoping that the Estates General would somehow evolve into a bicameral legislature, in which the first and second estates would make up one house and the third estate the other, although he soon lost patience with the intransigent nobility. Still he expected a good outcome, as the violence was mostly under control, and he continued to believe that "should this revolution succeed, it is the beginning of the reformation of the governments of Europe." After all, France was both the most powerful and the most populous nation on the Continent (it had approximately seven times the population of the United States), so in his mind this was an event of world-transforming power.[62]

The storming of the Bastille on July 14 seemed, briefly, to change everything. The beheadings of several officials by the insurgents shocked Jefferson, who wrote about "dangerous scenes of war." As troops massed in the city, he told Madison, "The insurrection now became universal."[63] But within a few weeks, with relative calm restored, Jefferson could report that the National Assembly was working on a constitution and a declaration of rights, and his incorrigible optimism returned. As he told various correspondents, he never felt personally endangered by the unrest and could move about the city unmolested. Then, on August 25 he received an emergency request from the Marquis de Lafayette: Would Jefferson host a dinner at his home for Lafayette and seven other aristocratic patriots who hoped to prevent a civil war and produce a useful form of government? Though embarrassed—Jefferson was, after all, the official American minister to the French Crown, not a private citizen—he assented.[64] At the dinner he appears to have been a neutral observer, a calming influence, and when he informed the king's minister the next day of how he happened to have hosted such a meeting, the minister told him he knew about it and approved of his role.

Jefferson sent John Jay a letter two days later outlining what he believed, based on the dinner Lafayette had arranged, the forthcoming constitution would look like. It would provide for a hereditary king but also create a legislature that would have some restraining power over his authority, and it would have a judicial system similar to that of England. Jefferson felt this was a sensible response to the demands from below for change. As he later wrote Thomas Paine, he believed the final result would be "a good constitution, which will in it's principles and merit be about a middle term between that of England and the United States."[65]

Jefferson saw this constitution as the first stage in a long evolution as the French nation grew into an understanding that sovereignty resided in the people, not in the divine right of kings, the nobility, or the church. He knew there still existed the possibility of great civil unrest, owing to a shortage of bread, or governmental bankruptcy, or the flight of the king from Versailles. But he was still, in September 1789, hopeful.[66] Jefferson consistently displayed patience in matters large and small. Writing to his old friend the Reverend Charles Clay soon after returning to Virginia from Paris, he reminded him that "the ground of liberty is to be gained by inches, that we must be contented to secure what we can get from time to time, and eternally press forward for what is yet to get. It takes time to persuade men to do even what is for their own good."[67]

As Jefferson prepared to leave France that fall, thinking he would be returning in five or six months, he had reason to believe that the French people had begun moving toward a better form of government with a minimum of violence and death. Since he thought moderates like Lafayette led the reform movement, in his view France was headed down a path to constitutional monarchy, not unlike that of England. If reformers moved deliberately and carefully, the French nation could likely follow the American example and navigate the frothy waters of revolution successfully and without terrible violence. Jefferson never completely abandoned this benign image of the French Revolution and its potential. But in the event, the revolutionaries lacked the patience Jefferson believed they would muster. He neither foresaw the profound social revolution that resulted nor witnessed the deadly Terror that came in its wake.

In late 1788 Jefferson had begun planning to return to Virginia for five months or so. He wanted to set his financial affairs aright but primarily to reestablish his daughters in a wholesome Virginia household, that of the Eppeses, so that they could begin to learn the domestic skills so necessary, he believed, for conjugal happiness. In Paris, Polly and Patsy had acquired a first-rate education in academic subjects, as well as in music, art, and dancing, but Jefferson knew that they needed to learn about cooking, the management of a household, and such mundane things as the planning of a garden. As early as July 1787, he had written to Aunt Eppes that after Patsy's French schooling, "she will need however your finishing to render her useful in her own country. Of domestic economy she can learn nothing here; yet she must learn it somewhere, as being of more solid value than every thing else."[68] He wrote again to Eppes a year later, "She will have to learn from you things which she cannot learn here, and which after all are among the most valuable parts of education for an American."[69] He intended to return without his daughters to France after this sabbatical, but only for six months or a year—at the most two—during which he planned to travel more extensively in Europe, in Italy, Sicily, and Greece.[70] Presumably he intended to leave Sally behind when he left Virginia.

By mid-1788 he had begun thinking about how to gradually close down his home in Paris and put his diplomatic affairs in order. He expected to have William Short named chargé d'affaires while he was in Virginia. In November he requested permission to return to the United States but had no sense of how long it would take to receive approval. His preparations were interrupted late that fall when both Patsy and Polly fell ill with typhoid, the latter contracting an extremely severe case from which she probably never completely recovered. The girls stayed at the Hôtel de Langeac during their illness and recuperation.

A family rumor has it that later, in April 1789, Patsy sent her father a note requesting permission to convert to Catholicism and join the convent, whereupon Jefferson went directly to the school, paid his fees in total, and removed both girls to the safety of his home.[71] A notice in a London newspaper the following month even announced that the "nuns . . . seduc[ed] Miss Jefferson . . . to change her religion."[72] Whether this story has any basis in fact, we cannot know. Jefferson may simply have removed them in advance of returning to the United States; he knew it could happen at any time. John Jay finally sent the written permission in June, but Jefferson did not receive it until August 23, 1789, nine months after he had made the request.[73] By late 1788 Jefferson had already permitted Patsy to begin attending balls and other fashionable events; during this period he spent generously to provide her (and, to a lesser degree, Sally) with fancier clothing. Patsy so enjoyed this social interlude—and perhaps a brief infatuation with the dashing Short—that she may have regretted returning to rural Virginia.[74] But as Jefferson's dutiful daughters, of course neither she nor Polly really had any say in the matter.

James and Sally Hemings, in contrast, did. They could have petitioned the Admiralty Court and stayed in France as free people. Both spoke French and would have had opportunities, James as a skilled cook and Sally as a seamstress or lady's maid—it had become quite the fashion to hire African or mixed-race servants.[75] Moreover, in France, they would be free, as would any children either ever had. Jefferson wanted them to return, and he was an enormously persuasive man. Yet James drove a hard bargain—he wanted his liberty. Jefferson agreed that if James returned to Monticello for at least long enough to teach his brother Peter how to cook in the French style, Jefferson would free him there. James accepted, even making out a list of the kinds of cooking utensils he would need in Virginia, and Jefferson did eventually live up to his word.

Sally also agreed to return, understanding that she would not be free and that she and Jefferson could never marry (even had she been free and white, Virginia law prevented a man from marrying the sister of his deceased wife[76]). Clearly they now trusted one another, and she must have sensed that with him, she and any potential offspring would have the best life possible, everything considered. No doubt Sally wished to return to more familiar surroundings and see her mother and other siblings again. It is possible, if not likely, that she also expected a degree of tenderness, care, and support from Jefferson. She evidently extracted from him not only a promise to treat her with consideration but also to free her children when they reached maturity. So it was that in October 1789, aboard the *Clermont*, Jefferson, his two daughters, and the two Hemingses began their voyage back to America, Jefferson having made sure that Sally's cabin gave her easy access to that of Patsy and Polly. None of them would ever see France again.

PART IV

Philadelphia and New York City, 1790–1801

14

From Paris to New York

FTER MONTHS OF WAITING to return to Virginia, Jefferson finally learned that John Trumbull had booked passage for his party on the *Clermont*, bound for Norfolk. Jefferson, his daughters Martha and Maria (Patsy and Polly), and James and Sally Hemings set forth from Paris on September 26, 1789, arriving in Le Havre, after delays caused by the pitiful condition of the roads, amid torrential rain and raging winds. The atrocious weather forced a ten-day postponement in crossing the English Channel, during which time, in addition to exploring the region, Jefferson purchased "a chienne bergere big with pup"—a Belgian shepherd—the breed of dog he considered most intelligent.[1] The dog would give birth to two pups on the voyage to Virginia, and she and her offspring introduced the breed to America.

From Le Havre they took the packet ship *Anna* across the channel to Cowes.[2] Boarding the *Clermont* on October 22, they at last reached the open sea on October 29. Jefferson and his party were the only passengers, and the return trip was peaceful, allowing him time to reflect on his experiences in France over the previous five years. The music, art and architecture, food, wine, friendships, conversations, travels—all had given him, for the most part, pure delight. He had finally published his account of America, *Notes on the State of Virginia*; he had come even more deeply to despise monarchical forms of government; and he had witnessed the opening scenes of a revolution, still largely peaceful, that he hoped would transform not only France but eventually all of Europe. Though he certainly looked forward to seeing relatives and friends in Virginia and enjoying the part of the world he loved best, he must have looked forward to returning to France to be on hand as it fulfilled its revolutionary goals. Jefferson believed he best served his own nation by representing it on the grand

European stage, and his diplomatic appointment still had two years left. But almost 4,000 miles away, and without his knowledge, on September 25 President George Washington, elected the previous April, had nominated him as secretary of state, and the Senate quickly approved the appointment the next day—the same day Jefferson and his family left Paris.[3]

After only twenty-six days on the open water, the *Clermont* entered Lynnhaven Bay at the mouth of the Chesapeake and landed in Norfolk in the early afternoon of November 23. The party had been ashore hardly more than an hour when fire broke out aboard the ship, practically gutting it, but miraculously the crew salvaged all of their baggage.[4] Amid the confusion Jefferson managed to find and read the local newspapers, which reported, to his surprise and dismay, the news of his appointment. Two days later the officials of the city welcomed Jefferson and thanked him for "the many eminent services you have rendered . . . the State," adding, "Our fervent wishes are, that you may be as happy in the important Station you are now called to by a grateful Country, as you have been successful in your negotiations." Jefferson responded noncommittally, not explicitly saying he would accept his new appointment.[5] His life had just gotten much more complicated.

Soon Jefferson and his daughters began a slow, sentimental journey by carriage toward Richmond, visiting friends and family along the way. In Richmond Jefferson renewed old acquaintances and received a welcome and congratulations from the General Assembly. He also caught up on national politics. He wrote William Short to report that North Carolina had at last ratified the Constitution and that the House had passed the amendments introduced by James Madison, though the Senate had not, yet. Jefferson added, rather ominously, "Antifederalism is not yet dead in this country. The gentlemen who opposed it retain a good deal of malevolence towards the new government. [Patrick] Henry is it's avowed foe."[6] He was pleased to see that the new Virginia capitol building, modeled after the Maison Carrée of Nîmes, was taking shape. On reaching Eppington, all three Jeffersons were happy to see the Eppes family again. There, on December 11, Washington's letter caught up with the visiting diplomat-on-leave.

In fact, there were two letters; the most recent, dated November 30, referenced an enclosed earlier letter of October 13, which stated Washington's request that Jefferson let him know his decision "as soon as you shall find it convenient." This earlier letter began as follows: "In the selection of Characters to fill the important offices of Government in the

United States I was naturally led to contemplate the talents and dispositions which I knew you to possess and entertain for the Service of your Country.—And without being able to consult your inclination . . . I was determined, as well by motives of private regard as a conviction of public propriety, to nominate you for the Department of State." To give him an opportunity to consider the offer, Washington explained that he had deferred nominating a successor to Jefferson at the Court of Versailles.[7] The appointment placed Jefferson in an agonizing position. Several days later, he replied to the president, clarifying that the duties of the office, seemingly much broader than foreign affairs, exceeded his expertise and capabilities. He also foresaw unwanted public criticism, whereas he felt competent and comfortable in his present position. Writing frankly, Jefferson told Washington he would prefer to return to France but would defer to the president's wishes.[8]

Jefferson must have been considerably preoccupied as he and his daughters progressed toward Monticello, reaching the cherished site on December 23. The enslaved laborers and house staff knew the Jeffersons were on their way, having been informed of their imminent arrival. As the carriage—driven by James Hemings, with the three Jeffersons and Sally Hemings inside—approached the foot of the little mountain, the estate's bondsmen rushed to meet it. Martha Jefferson (Patsy) remembered long afterward that they shouted with excitement and joy, surrounding the carriage; in her words, they "almost drew it up the mountain by hand." Even more dramatic—or romanticized—was the account of an elderly slave named Wormeley, who recalled the exuberant slaves actually unharnessing the horses and pulling and pushing the loaded carriage to the door of Monticello despite the protestations of Jefferson himself. Once in front of the house, they lifted him from the steps of the carriage and carried him above their heads to the entryway.[9] Many of the younger slaves could hardly have known him at all, but others may have remembered kindnesses and felt genuine affection for him. Or perhaps they understood that his return buttressed the stability of their situation at Monticello. Either way, it was a homecoming no one present ever forgot.

The following months found Jefferson extremely busy. Monticello was in disrepair, and he had much to do to turn its fortunes around. He spent a good bit of time arranging bonds and other financial matters related both to his inherited debts from John Wayles and the final details of the apportionment of his and his siblings' inheritance from their parents. Meanwhile, letters came in expressing hope that he would accept

Washington's appointment. Madison even traveled to Monticello, in part to assure Jefferson that the domestic duties should not be burdensome but that expectations could be adjusted if they turned out to be. Madison later intimated to Washington that most of Jefferson's hesitancy stemmed from the position's responsibility for overseeing the domestic scene.[10]

Amid these concerns, just before mid-January, the leading citizens of Albemarle County prepared a welcome-home address for Jefferson, which, after briefly outlining his services to his state and country, concluded with an appeal that he accept the position of secretary of state—almost certainly reflecting Madison's hand. On February 12, at Monticello, Jefferson formally acknowledged the wishes of his neighbors with a statement about his gratitude to his fellow citizens and his dedication to serve according to "the will of my country."[11] The brief address summarized Jefferson's bedrock political principles: "to shew by example the sufficiency of human reason for the care of human affairs and that the will of the majority, the Natural law of every society, is the only sure guardian of the rights of man."[12] But he did not explicitly mention the new appointment.

Yet how could he not bend to the desires of his president? After conferring with Madison, Washington had written Jefferson again on January 21; Jefferson received the letter shortly after the Albemarle welcome. In it, Washington acknowledged that he did not wish to ignore Jefferson's inclinations but pointed out that he considered "the successful Administration of the general Government as an object of almost infinite consequence to the present and future happiness of the Citizens of the United States," that he believed the Department of State was a "*very* important" position, and that he knew "of no person, who, in my judgement, could better execute the Duties of it than yourself." He said that the duties would not be as onerous as Jefferson might think and that if Jefferson could see his way toward accepting the position, Washington hoped he would come to New York immediately, where the new nation had moved its capital on March 4, 1789.[13] Jefferson replied a few days later, admitting that he could "no longer hesitate to undertake the office to which you are pleased to call me," although he had to attend to local matters before he came north.[14]

Another surprise delayed him. Shortly after their return to Monticello, seventeen-year-old Martha—his treasured Patsy—announced her betrothal to twenty-one-year-old Thomas Mann Randolph Jr., whom she had known all her life yet had seen only sporadically over the previous ten years.[15] She had played with him as a child, but they must have had a whirlwind courtship in the few weeks following her return from France. The announcement surely shocked Jefferson, who had expected his daughter to live with her Aunt Eppes for a year or so as she learned the rudiments of housekeeping and farm management. Now she would, in effect, have to learn on the job. But Jefferson did not disapprove. He had spent several of his early childhood years at Tuckahoe, the ancestral Randolph home, when his parents had moved there, and had known Thomas Mann Randolph Sr. almost his entire life. He liked that the younger Randolph had a scholarly mien, took a particular interest in science and natural history, aspired to a life of political service, was a good horseman and distinguished in appearance, and had a promising career before him.[16] Patsy, inexperienced romantically, may simply have been swept off her feet by this handsome suitor with many qualities in common with her father, to whom she was uncommonly devoted.[17] Perhaps, already missing the sophistication of Paris, she also sensed in the Scottish-educated Randolph a dollop of European urbanity.[18]

They could not have known each other very well; we have no evidence backing a family story that they met in Paris during Randolph's studies at the University of Edinburgh. It is somewhat puzzling that Jefferson assented to their engagement so promptly, without giving the matter much thought. At the same time, her age would probably not have been much of a factor, and Jefferson had, after all, once expressed fear that she might end up marrying a blockhead. Perhaps Randolph exceeded Jefferson's expectations for Patsy's suitors. Had both father and daughter gotten to know young Randolph better, they might have recognized his quick temper, extremely thin skin, contentiousness, and proneness to what we today term depression. But these troubles lay in the future. The marriage took place on February 23, 1790, at Monticello. Jefferson had hurried to make a transfer of property—land, slaves, and farming equipment—to his daughter beforehand; Randolph Sr. had similarly given his son a small plantation before the wedding. Jefferson paid for both the marriage license and the minister's fee.[19]

Whatever pleasure he took in the match, Jefferson surely felt a deep sense of loss at the nuptials, for Patsy had played an important role in his life since the death of her mother. Soon after the wedding, he wrote Patsy, "The happiness of your life depends now on the continuing to please a single person. . . . Cherish then for me, my dear child, the affection of your husband."[20] Though their relationship had changed, it is fair to say that no one ever replaced Jefferson in his daughter's heart.

Six days after the ceremony, Jefferson left for New York and his new public role. Stopping in both Richmond and Petersburg to tie up some loose financial ends, he then journeyed to Alexandria, where he received another welcoming address.[21] A massive snowstorm prevented travel by phaeton, so he continued by public stage, creeping along on one of the most miserable trips of his life.[22] He stopped in Philadelphia for two days, in large part to visit the gravely ill Benjamin Franklin, then on his deathbed. After several more days of fatiguing travel, Jefferson reached New York on Sunday morning, March 21, 1790. That afternoon, after Washington had returned from church, Jefferson reported to the president.

SHORTLY AFTER ARRIVING, Jefferson found a small house near his State Department offices. His staff was small—two clerks, two assistants, and a part-time translator—and his duties varied, including everything from judging patents to, later on, establishing the mint. Jefferson was shocked to discover, during his first social visits in New York City, that table conversation was mainly political, and "a preference of kingly over republican government was evidently the favorite sentiment. . . . I found myself, for the most part, the only advocate on the republican side of the question."[23] To his consternation, the Senate, pushed by Vice President John Adams, contemplated adopting as the formal title for Washington "His Highness the President of the United States and Protector of Their Liberties." And Jefferson learned, probably from Madison, that during the constitutional convention, now Secretary of the Treasury Alexander Hamilton had passionately praised the British system of government "as the best in the world."[24]

This news concerned Jefferson, but he trusted Washington's instincts, and of course Madison—who more than anyone else had been responsible for the Constitution and had coauthored the *Federalist* with Hamilton to defend it—was a major voice in the House of Representatives. Jefferson had not known Hamilton previously, had no reason to be suspicious of him, and expected to like him, not only for his work on the *Federalist* but because he had been Washington's most trusted adjutant during the American Revolution. Hamilton's Department of Treasury was much larger than the State Department, but there was at the time no conception of a cabinet. Hamilton and Jefferson were merely advisors to the president, who held all formal executive authority.

Notwithstanding the worrisome monarchical chatter at society dinner tables, Jefferson anticipated harmony at the highest rungs of government and set himself the task of reading up on the governmental business of the previous few months. He quickly discovered that one of his initial responsibilities was preparation of a report on standardizing weights and measures. He had immediately scotched a proposal to have American coins minted in England, wanting to wean the United States off things British; following his advice, a US mint would be established in 1792. The issue of weights and measures appealed to Jefferson's scientific side, and he poured himself into the project, despite enduring one of his periodic migraines in May. He could only work on his calculations—and write—at night.

At issue was the lack of uniformity in weights and measures not just within and among the thirteen states but in the broader Atlantic world, where most American commerce took place. Jefferson wanted to establish new standards that would foster economic and mercantile efficiency. Drawing on his wide reading and advice from people as diverse as Madison and Philadelphia astronomer David Rittenhouse, Jefferson proposed as the base standard of measurement a rod of such a length (approximately 58.723 current inches, as it turned out) that its oscillation time as a pendulum, with the pivot at the one-third point, would be one second at latitude forty-eight degrees. He next divided this rod into 587.2 equal parts, each called a line. Ten lines would make an inch, ten inches would make a foot (slightly shorter than the common English foot), and 10,000 feet would make a mile, almost double the length of the common mile. As for weights, one ounce would be the weight of one cubic inch of rainwater, and again this would be scalable up (and down) to different measures: pints and quarts, for example. Jefferson worked every measurement out to eighteen decimal places and forwarded his report to Congress on July 4.[25] But his changes, however elegantly rational, were far more sweeping than Congress had anticipated and hence were not accepted. The same Congress had already rejected the idea of a census as "a waste of trouble and supplying materials for idle people to make a book."[26] France, in 1799, would become the first nation to introduce a decimalized metric system of measurements.

Jefferson soon had another domestic concern: patents. The Constitution had given the new government the "power to promote the Progress of Science and useful Arts, by securing for limited Times to Authors and Inventors the exclusive Right to their respective Writings and Discoveries," and Congress responded on April 10, 1790, by establishing a Board of Arts consisting of the secretary of state, the secretary of war, and the attorney general, who together would consider patent applications. As expected,

Jefferson played the most active role on the board, insisting on the utility and novelty of proposed inventions and subjecting them to rigorous inspection. While he appreciated the importance of improving preexisting inventions—he was a tinkerer himself—meriting a patent, he believed, required more than improvement. He was more interested in promoting intellectual creativity and public utility than economic gain.[27] He did not seem particularly aware of the notion that inventors should hold a monopoly on their inventions; he was more concerned with the advantages the inventions offered to the public. After a few years, however, patents came to be seen as promoting ingenuity and progress precisely by protecting the potential commercial gain of the inventor and investor.

The first foreign affairs matter to land on Jefferson's desk was the question of how large the new government's diplomatic establishment should be. Both Jefferson and Washington faced opposition in the Congress from members who doubted the usefulness of a diplomatic corps in the first place. Jefferson wrote proposals to Washington and appeared in front of a congressional committee to defend the necessity of a limited establishment. Washington quickly, and Congress eventually, accepted Jefferson's recommendations, which initially called for one minister (to France), with lesser officials, chargés d'affaires, sent to four or five other nations. If and when England indicated an openness to honest negotiation, a minister to the Court of St. James would be appointed. Senator William Maclay of Pennsylvania, an inveterate foe of spending any money on a diplomatic corps, left a memorable description of Jefferson's appearance before the congressional committee: "I looked for gravity, but a laxity of manner seemed shed about him. He spoke almost without ceasing. But even his discourse partook of his personal demeanor. It was loose and rambling, and yet he scattered information wherever he went, and some even brilliant sentiments sparkled from him."[28] In spite of himself, Maclay was impressed.

THE FIRST POTENTIAL diplomatic crisis Jefferson faced got started in the summer of 1789, thousands of miles from New York. Decades earlier Spain had laid claim to the western coast of North America, including Vancouver Island. The viceroy of New Spain decided in 1789 to send a naval expedition to Nootka Sound, the most desirable anchorage on the northwestern coast of Vancouver, and there seized two anchored British ships. When London learned of this act in January 1790, calls for war immediately followed, led by Prime Minister William Pitt. Soon both England and Spain were preparing for war, while France—bound by the so-called Family Contract as an ally of Spain—dithered. Not until June did Jefferson and Washington begin hearing about the impending war from correspondents who conveyed rumors that England planned to seize all the Spanish territories west of the Mississippi River.[29]

Jefferson instantly understood that should Britain go to war with Spain, it would almost certainly take the trans-Mississippi territory, a possibility that represented a serious threat to the future of the American nation.[30] Jefferson recommended caution to Washington, hoping to play the neutrality card to the nation's advantage. But if necessary, he indicated, war against Britain would be justified. Washington asked his various advisors how the nation should respond if Britain requested permission to move troops through US territory. Jefferson said the United States should attempt to delay as long as possible. He and others feared that if Spain resisted British demands and asked France for assistance, treaty obligations would force the United States to assist France as well.

Jefferson sent a message to Spain via chargé d'affaires William Carmichael, suggesting that Spain cede to the United States its territories east of the Mississippi in return for US support of its territory west of the Mississippi. Included in the message was a threat that the United States would side with Britain to guarantee access to the mouth of the Mississippi. Jefferson contacted Gouverneur Morris in London to intimate that the United States would remain neutral toward Britain if it did not attempt to conquer territories adjacent to the new nation. In short, Jefferson saw both danger and opportunity and was not above playing one nation against another to win concessions for his country.

Jefferson did not know—as we do now—the extent to which Alexander Hamilton betrayed US thinking to the British through his connections with Major George Beckwith, an informal agent of the Crown. The anglophile Hamilton even suggested to Beckwith that if Jefferson proved uncongenial to their interests, the British should communicate through Hamilton instead of the secretary of state.[31] Hamilton was as aggressive and imperial as Jefferson was conciliatory and respectful of limits, but while their contrasting styles and aims soon brought conflict to Washington's administration, they proved irrelevant to the Nootka Sound controversy. France decided not to come to Spain's aid, Spain decided to negotiate with Britain, and the terms of the so-called Nootka Convention of October 28, 1790, defused the issue.[32] Jefferson's policy of studied delay had worked.

TODAY IT IS A COMMONPLACE to say that Jefferson and Hamilton were the chief protagonists in the nation's first great internal political dispute, which concerned how to pay the nation's debts and whether to establish a national bank. Yet the Jefferson-Hamilton controversy actually began with Madison. The differences between Madison and Hamilton revealed themselves in April 1789 when Madison introduced to Congress a resolution that would institute graduated tariffs on all goods imported into the nation. Goods carried by American ships had the lowest tariffs; those carried by the ships of nations that had commercial treaties with the United States had higher fees. The highest tariffs were levied on goods on ships of nations that had no commercial treaties with the nation. In effect, this privileged French trade over British, as Britain had not deigned to consider signing a commercial treaty with its former colonies. Hamilton, backed by New England merchants, fiercely opposed Madison's proposed tariff schedule, which failed in Congress as a result.[33]

In January 1790 Hamilton began to introduce his brilliantly conceived fiscal plan, starting with the "Report on Public Credit." An admirer of everything British, including the Bank of England and the nation's merchant empire, Hamilton sought to strengthen the United States by stabilizing its economy and winning the support of wealthy men and the merchant community. He understood securing the nation's credit to be essential, and accomplishing that would require the United States to pay its debts—foreign debts, debts owed by the states to the central government, and the various state debts incurred during the revolution. He proposed doing this by issuing new bonds and paying holders 4 percent interest. By replacing old bonds with new ones and pledging to honor the latter, the new securities, which were transferable, could provide needed capital for the emerging economy. Most of the funds to guarantee interest payments would come from excise taxes placed on imports—and since most of the nation's imports came from Britain, Hamilton opposed any tariff system that might discourage that trade.

There was little opposition among Washington's other advisors or in Congress to paying off foreign debts (totaling $12 million) or, in principle, to paying off the domestic debt ($40 million). There was opposition, though, to Hamilton's proposal to pay the present holders of bonds, not the original holders. Incensed, Madison and others considered the notion grossly unfair, since the original bondholders had mostly been soldiers, farmers, and regular people who had subscribed to the bonds as an act of patriotism. But after years of nonpayment, many of these people of slender means had sold their bonds at greatly reduced prices to speculators and men of wealth. Moreover, once word got out about Hamilton's plan, speculators became more aggressive, roaming the backcountry and buying up bonds from the uninformed at a fraction of their face value.

Madison argued that in the interests of fairness, the original bondholders should be identified and paid. Hamilton strenuously objected that this would be a logistical and accounting nightmare. Nor did he want the newly funded securities scattered far and wide among small bondholders; rather he needed them concentrated in the hands of a relatively few capitalists and merchants who would use the assets to fire the national economy. And he recognized that because wealthy men would benefit greatly from his plan, they would throw their powerful support behind the new government.[34]

By this time Madison and Hamilton were fully at odds, but Jefferson was still too new to his office to engage in the controversy. Then, for weeks in the late spring of 1790, he was incapacitated by a severe headache and otherwise engrossed in nighttime work on his weights and measurements report. Still, he must have become aware of the issue, since he had long championed the idea that the nation should pay its debts, especially its foreign ones, and maintain its credit. But the third leg of Hamilton's program, assumption of the states' debts (totaling $25 million), proved even more controversial than the bond issue, as it positioned Massachusetts and New York (and, strangely, South Carolina), which had large, unpaid revolutionary debts, against Maryland, Virginia, North Carolina, and Georgia, which had paid off most of theirs. Hamilton did not want two sets of debtors—those expecting payments from their states and those expecting payment from the national government. Instead, he wished to consolidate power in the central government. To southerners, his proposal clearly favored the delinquent northern states at the expense of the more responsible southern states.[35] Opposition was instant and vociferous, with a frightening regional dimension.

THE ISSUE OF SLAVERY quickened the approaching regional battle when, on March 16, 1790, a House committee reported on two antislavery petitions it had received the previous month: one from Quakers in New York, the other from the Pennsylvania Society for Promoting the Abolition of Slavery, signed and transmitted by Benjamin Franklin. The committee, upon careful consideration and cognizant of the Constitution's language prohibiting interference with slave imports before 1808, declared that the federal government could not emancipate any slaves born in the nation before that year and, moreover, could not try to change how states regulated their slave populations. But the committee did say that the federal government could levy taxes on slave imports, insist on relatively humane conditions aboard slaving vessels, and otherwise regulate the slave trade after 1808.

This rather cautious report generated fiery opposition from southern congressmen. South Carolina's William L. Smith defended slavery in a passionate address, foreshadowing almost every defense later mounted by southerners. He and others claimed, in effect, that attacking the institution would provoke the southern states to leave the nation. All of a sudden, members from South Carolina were talking of disunion and civil war.[36] The vehemence of the opposition thoroughly shocked Madison and others from both the North and the South. While himself mildly antislavery and an opponent of the Atlantic slave trade, Madison, along with other prominent government figures—including Washington and Hamilton—stepped back from the precipice when they realized this issue could rend the nation.[37]

After listening to more than a week of harangues, Madison confided to Benjamin Rush, "The Gentlemen from S. Carolina & Georgia are intemperate beyond all example and even all decorum."[38] To fellow Virginian Edmund Randolph, he made even stronger comments, calling the speeches of several of the southern members "shamefully indecent."[39] In his view, the union was too fragile to withstand such controversy. A letter from one of his constituents in Virginia exemplified the danger many saw in the antislavery debates. "It has disturbed the Minds of our people," wrote Adam Stephen from Berkeley County, Virginia, "and lessened their Confidence in Congress."[40] All the Founders remembered that during the ratification debates, spokesmen (including Patrick Henry) in some regions had wanted not one unified nation but rather two or three separate ones. Senator Maclay described the southerners using "base, invective, and undecorous language" and remarked, "Many of them do not hesitate to declare that the Union must fall to pieces at the rate we go on. Indeed, many seemed to wish it."[41] From this explosive debate all the Founders took one lesson: public advocacy of emancipation could threaten the United States' survival. As a result, none of those who might have been inclined to do so took up the abolitionist banner.

THE DEBATE OVER the assumption of debts transpired within this context of heightened concern for the survival of the union. Jefferson was at first a bystander, preoccupied with other reports (one on coinage, another on commercial policy). Moreover, he was simultaneously sending detailed instructions to William Short about his belongings in Paris, paying off his French servants, and trying to persuade Adrien Petit—his former house manager in Paris—to travel to America to perform similar duties for him there. The extant Jefferson correspondence contains only three references to the assumption issue, and in each instance Jefferson took a neutral stance.[42] Then, according to his later writings, he became caught up in the debate after a chance encounter with Hamilton.[43]

As Jefferson related it, in mid-June 1790 he met Hamilton outside the door of President Washington's home and was taken aback by how "haggled, and dejected" the Treasury secretary looked. Hamilton asked if they could speak, and Jefferson agreed, whereupon the former poured out his concern that the assumption bill was not going to pass. If it did not, he feared, the northernmost states would be most upset, even to the point of "*secession* . . . and the separation of the States.*" Hamilton argued that the members of the administration should work together and asked Jefferson to convince some southern members of Congress to support assumption. Jefferson explained that he was not knowledgeable enough about the subject to do so but felt that "if its rejection endangered a dissolution of our Union at this incipient stage, I should deem that the most unfortunate of all consequences, to avert which all partial and temporary evils should be yielded."[44]

Perhaps recalling the dinner he had hosted for the Marquis de Lafayette and other revolutionary leaders in Paris in 1789, Jefferson suggested to Hamilton that he invite both him and Madison to dinner, believing that as sensible men, they could come to some sort of agreement. Jefferson surely realized that various congressmen were already talking about the matter, that both Madison and Hamilton were doubtless in contact with supporters and considering options, and that this dinner would not be the first time any of these matters were broached. Jefferson later summarized the dinner discussion as follows. As Jefferson had assumed, neither man wanted to risk disunion, and while Madison could not agree to support assumption, he would agree not to oppose it aggressively, and either he or Jefferson would consent to speak to some of the southern recalcitrants. Presumably Hamilton suggested that, since assumption would be a "bitter" "pill" for the southern states to swallow, they should receive something in return.[45] Hamilton had in mind the settlement of a long-festering controversy: the location of the nation's capital.

Jefferson had long thought the best place would be on the banks of the Potomac River, near Georgetown. His fellow southerners—Madison and Washington included—also preferred that site, and at the dinner Jefferson hosted, Hamilton agreed to help get the deal done. The final terms stipulated that after ten years in Philadelphia—a period of transition—a new permanent capital would be laid out on the banks of the Potomac. Jefferson, probably anticipating reactions from southerners angry about assumption, wrote James Monroe—expecting him to share Jefferson's comments with others—that although he still had reservations about assumption, "in the present instance I see the necessity of yeilding for this time to the cries of the creditors in certain parts of the union, for the sake of union, and to save us from the greatest of all calamities, the total extinction of our credit in Europe," which would bring financial collapse.[46] By late July assumption was approved, as was the location of the new capital city.[47]

Congress adjourned on August 14, 1790, and after making arrangements to move to Philadelphia along with the federal government in December of that year, Jefferson began his journey southward, accompanied by Madison. The two Virginians tarried several days near Georgetown, scouting locations for the new capital. After spending the night at Mount Vernon, they continued on toward their respective homes, with Madison reaching Montpelier on September 18; Jefferson, hurrying onward, arrived at Monticello the next day. His first few months as secretary of state had been both eventful and productive, and as he prepared to enjoy his family and the delights of his mountaintop home, he had few premonitions of the troubles immediately ahead.

15

Jefferson Versus Hamilton

ONTICELLO USUALLY offered Jefferson respite from his labors
and what he found to be the discomfiting intrigues of politics.
But in October 1790 all was not peaceful even at Monticello.
While home he traveled to Tuckahoe to seek a rapprochement between
Thomas Mann Randolph Sr. and his son and namesake, Jefferson's son-in-
law, regarding the latter's intended purchase of Edgehill, a 1,500-acre farm.
Father and son had earlier agreed to the purchase, but for reasons unknown the recently remarried father had reneged, and Jefferson had counseled his son-in-law to accept his father's decision. Meanwhile Jefferson
attempted to recover the deal, with no success initially. He handled these
complicated family interactions with great delicacy.[1]

But his time in Monticello had to end, and on November 8, 1790,
Jefferson began his trek to Philadelphia, with a stopover at Mount Vernon
to visit briefly with the president. Before leaving Monticello, "in consideration of the affection I bear to Thomas Mann Randolph the younger and
Martha Randolph my daughter," he deeded to them eight slaves.[2] Martha
and her husband were then living at the estate, so the slaves—two mothers, five children, and a young girl—did not have to move.

Jefferson had already rented a house on Market Street in Philadelphia,
less than a block from the State Department offices. But, as was typical, he
had asked his landlord to make a number of changes and additions, which
Jefferson paid for, including construction of a large room across the back
for his library. These improvements remained unfinished when Jefferson
arrived, requiring him to take a room at Mary House's boardinghouse,
which he knew well and where James Madison lived. Jefferson soon
enough moved into a room at his own house before the renovations were
done, living amid clutter and noise. To make matters worse for this lover

of order and quiet, on November 30 a huge shipment arrived at the wharf—his furniture, books, and household goods from Paris, eighty-six packing crates in total. Fifteen of the packing boxes contained books, each separately wrapped. For more than six weeks Jefferson unpacked, supervised workmen, survived the din and confusion, and somehow kept up an intense schedule. He seldom had social engagements in the evening; instead, he worked.[3]

In his rare moments of leisure, Jefferson walked around Philadelphia, which he found the most pleasant and cosmopolitan of American cities. He probably attended the May 1792 meeting of the American Philosophical Society, at which botanist Benjamin Smith Barton named a small flowering plant *Jeffersonia diphylla* in recognition of Jefferson's contributions to natural history. Later he would plant an oval bed of his namesake flowers in front of Monticello.[4] He had two intimate Virginia friends in the city: Madison and newly elected senator James Monroe. Over the next few months Jefferson would find time for research and extensive correspondence concerning such scientific matters as the Hessian fly that had afflicted the American wheat crop and the physiology of the opossum (he wanted to know whether its pouch disappeared after its babies were weaned).[5] Yet in every moment not spent walking the city, visiting with friends, or pursuing his private interests, he found himself oppressed by his State Department duties.

Ever since the American boycotts of British imports in the 1770s, Jefferson had believed in the efficacy of commercial discrimination as a tool of diplomacy. His ultimate goal was free trade, but in the meantime, he believed the United States needed to liberate itself from the commercial domination of Britain. He also held that out of fairness to France for its assistance during the American Revolution, the United States should seek to promote trade with that country before other nations. In the winter of 1790 and 1791 Jefferson issued a series of reports reflecting this view and thus his favorable attitude toward France and hostility toward Britain. When it became clear from Gouverneur Morris's informal mission to Britain that John Bull was not about to withdraw quickly from outposts in the Northwest, agree to reciprocal commercial relations, or even send a minister to the United States, Jefferson wrote directions for Washington to send to Morris, putting an end to his efforts in London.[6] The United States would not promote a better relationship with Britain until it demonstrated some respect for the new nation.

Jefferson also prepared a report for Washington on the tonnage law, which he saw as an attempt to discriminate against some nations and favor others.[7] Jefferson sent a message to Congress addressing the issue of pirate attacks on American shipping in the Mediterranean, recommending a military response, but as when he was in Paris, Congress timidly chose to pay tribute, thus limiting American trade in the region.[8] In early 1791 Jefferson issued a "Report on the Cod and Whale Fisheries," a deeply researched history of the industry that also attempted to force open the British markets to American cod and whale fishermen by proposing prohibitions on British imports. In this case Jefferson was motivated not only by nationalistic support of the New England fisherman but also by a belief that the industry would prove a training ground for a potential American navy.[9]

On all these initiatives Jefferson found in James Madison a strong ally, in Alexander Hamilton a determined foe. The overwhelming preponderance of American trade was with England, which thus generated the vast majority of import duties—and since the monies these duties produced were necessary to finance Hamilton's funded national debt, he opposed every measure that might threaten trade relations with Britain. As Jefferson and Madison saw it, Hamilton's economic system rendered US commercial policy hostage to Britain.

CONGRESS TOOK NO ACTION on any of these bills, in part because Washington indicated no strong position on them, in part because of the opposition from Hamilton's supporters, and in larger part because the legislature was preoccupied with two measures Hamilton had submitted in December 1790.[10] One was a request to levy a new internal tax, the other a proposal to establish a national bank. Amid the debates over these proposals, and mainly owing to that over the bank, Congress had neither time nor energy to invest in any other matters. The bank controversy shaped American politics for months and ended up transforming Jefferson's relationship with Hamilton. Here was the precipitating cause of the conflict between these two Founding Fathers, which would cast a long shadow down the centuries.

On December 13, 1790, Hamilton proposed an excise tax on distilled liquors. He intended to use the resulting funds to pay the interest on the newly acquired public debt. Spirited discussions on the rate aside, even Madison supported the bill. It easily passed, as Congress understood the importance of the new government's meeting its financial obligations.[11] The bank bill was another matter. Hamilton had researched the theory and practice of banking and studied the organization and structure of the Bank of England.[12] The result was a brilliantly conceived and persuasively argued report, issued on December 14, 1791, on the necessity of establishing a national bank—though it did not convince Madison and Jefferson. The bank Hamilton proposed would help in the collection of taxes and the management of the public debt, among other tasks, disbursing and transferring government funds. It could make short-term loans to the government, and its notes could serve as a form of legal tender, in effect expanding the currency in circulation.

The bank's total capital would be $10 million, more than that of all the other banks in the nation combined, but only $2 million of that amount would come from the national government. Private investors would supply the rest by providing specie and buying bonds; three-fourths of this private investment would take the form of government-backed securities. In short, a small number of wealthy investors in government bonds—the very persons who had disproportionately reaped the benefit of the government's funding of the national debt—would control the bank, and these investors, concentrated in the Northeast, would benefit disproportionately from the profits of the national bank and hence become strong supporters of the central government. The bank would be a powerful engine of economic development.[13]

Hamilton's proposal was so skillfully conceived and so carefully presented both to Congress and the public, and the bank would serve so many useful functions, that its eventual passage was assured, even though the final vote had worrisome sectional overtones: in the House, for example, representatives from northern states voted 33–1 in favor, while their southern colleagues voted 19–6 in opposition.[14] The most persistent opponent in the House was Madison, who feared the consequences of concentrating all the banking functions in one institution. He also worried that the bank's privileging of paper notes might lead to American gold and silver ending up in Britain, and he feared as well an ever-rising public debt. Moreover Hamilton's proposal to site the bank in Philadelphia could, as Madison saw it, compromise the government's planned move to the shores of the Potomac. None of these arguments gained much traction, so Madison developed an argument that the Constitution, which strictly limited the powers of the national government, did not provide for a national bank. (Madison had argued exactly the opposite in *Federalist* 44, but his authorship of that essay was not then known—except by Hamilton.)[15]

When presented with the bank bill, Washington asked both Attorney General Edmund Randolph and Jefferson for their views on it. Randolph simply argued that the bill was invalid because the Constitution limited government functions to explicitly enumerated powers. Jefferson arrived at the same conclusion but offered considerably more detail. Probably influenced by Madison's arguments and certainly recognizing that Hamilton's bank represented a far-reaching system that would strengthen the central government and concentrate its powers in the hands of a small number of wealthy men in one section of the country, Jefferson believed Hamilton aimed to replicate the early-eighteenth-century British government under First Lord of the Treasury Robert Walpole. From Jefferson's as well as Madison's perspective, Walpole—often called England's first prime minister—had perverted the British government into a corrupt system controlled by self-interested, money-hungry men.[16]

The government Hamilton envisioned, Jefferson thought, had little to offer agricultural interests; it bought political support for itself, making the greed of a few, not the idealism of the many, the glue holding the nation together. In Jefferson's eyes, the bank threatened American republicanism; nothing less than the soul of the nation was at stake. This called for marshalling every possible argument against the bank, and the most effective was that rooted in the still-new Constitution. Jefferson's resulting recommendation on the bank, made privately to Washington, has been characterized as the strict constructionist argument: "I consider the foundation of the Constitution as laid on this ground that 'all powers not delegated to the U.S. by the Constitution, not prohibited by it to the states, are reserved to the states or to the people.'" [Here he referenced the proposed Twelfth Amendment, soon to be ratified as the Tenth.] "To take a single step beyond the boundaries thus specially drawn around the powers of Congress, is to take possession of a boundless field of power. . . . The incorporation of a bank, and other powers assumed by this bill have not, in my opinion, been delegated to the U.S. by the Constitution."[17]

Jefferson's earlier attitude toward the treaty-making powers of American commissioners in Paris and toward the Articles of Confederation government (not to mention his actions, as president, to acquire the Louisiana Purchase) imply that he was not as bound to this strict view as his comments here might suggest. His argument to Washington was almost provisional, a contingent political claim to stop the bank. At the end of his report, he wrote, "If the pro and con hang so even as to balance his judgment a just respect for the wisdom of the legislature would naturally decide the balance in favour of their opinion."[18]

As Jefferson understood, Washington was having trouble making up his mind. The president sent the Randolph and Jefferson opinions to Hamilton, asking for his response. The result was a comprehensive, well-argued defense of the constitutionality of the bank directed squarely at both Madison and Jefferson; indeed, Hamilton even quoted, without attribution, Madison's words in *Federalist* 44. Jefferson had argued that the government could only do those things necessary to achieve its purposes; Hamilton correctly rebutted that Jefferson had implied that the Constitution meant *absolutely* necessary, whereas by the common sense of the language it only meant "needful, requisite, incidental, useful, conducive to." Washington concluded that Hamilton made the more convincing case; two days later, on February 25, 1791, he signed the bill establishing the Bank of the United States.[19]

Because Jefferson's written opinion was private, Madison continued as the face of opposition to Hamilton's system. Owing to his temperament and respect for Washington, Jefferson hesitated to bring his dissent into the open. Over the next few months, however, he did write letters to correspondents across the South and West subtly suggesting that it would be advantageous if, in upcoming elections, agricultural interests were better represented in the next Congress.

THEN, ENTIRELY BY ACCIDENT, Jefferson's true beliefs were revealed and became widely known. In February 1791 Thomas Paine published *Rights of Man*, a spirited defense of the French Revolution, and a copy appeared in Philadelphia in mid-April. John Beckley—clerk of the House of Representatives and a strong supporter of Madison and Jefferson—got his hands on it and promptly made arrangements to reprint it. First, though, he loaned the copy to Madison, who, before a trip out of the city, passed it to Jefferson, to read in a day or two before conveying it to the local printer. Jefferson skimmed the text, then sent the book, along with a hurriedly penned private note, to that printer, Jonathan Bayard Smith. He intended his note as a polite formality, writing that he was "extremely pleased to find [the book] will be re-printed here, and that something is at length to be publicly said against the political heresies which have sprung up among us. [I have] no doubt our citizens will rally a second time round the standard of Common sense."[20] Jefferson thought no more about this inconsequential little note until, a week later, the *Rights of Man* was printed in Philadelphia, and Smith, without asking permission, included Jefferson's comments in the front of the book.

John Adams quickly sensed that by so-called political heresies Jefferson meant Adams's recent book, *Discourses on Davila*, a turgidly written attack on the popular ideas of equality, progress, and democratic rule. Jefferson and Adams were still on friendly terms although they differed on fundamental questions of aristocracy and democracy. But pro-Hamilton forces, seeing a way to cast Jefferson as a malcontent in the eyes of Washington, vilified him for his comments, which they tried to extend to apply to Washington as well. The comments received much greater publicity than they would have otherwise through a series of letters published the following month under the pseudonym "PUBICOLA" in a Boston newspaper—written with filial defensiveness by Adams's son John Quincy.[21] Suddenly the irenic Jefferson had become, in the eyes of Hamilton and his supporters, the chief agent of the opposition; they portrayed him as hostile to Washington and the government itself. Soon supporters of Jefferson joined the fray, attacking the pro-Hamiltonian writers in the nation's newspapers.

Jefferson wrote Washington, explaining that while he differed strongly with Adams, he believed him "one of the most honest and disinterested men alive," and that though they diverged on certain political matters, they did so privately "as friends should do." Jefferson made clear that he never intended his comments to become public, though he did in fact have in mind Adams's *Discourses on Davila* when he wrote the note, and he admitted to Washington that he "certainly never made a secret of my being anti-monarchical, and anti-aristocratical: but I am sincerely mortified to be thus brought forward on the public stage."[22] Yet the damage was done, and finally, in July, Jefferson felt he had no choice but to write Adams, repeating much of what he had said to Washington. Adams soon replied, accepting Jefferson's account but denying that he and Jefferson had ever strongly disagreed—and denying even more emphatically that he had ever advocated subverting the American system by installing a king, as Jefferson had implied.[23] Still, the political terrain had shifted with the publication of Jefferson's unguarded letter.

In late May 1791, even before Jefferson wrote his explanatory letter to Adams, he and Madison had set forth on a long-planned botanical excursion to Lakes George and Champlain, thence by the Connecticut River and Long Island back to New York City. They enjoyed the scenery and went fishing. Jefferson conducted research on the Hessian fly and interviewed Unquachog Indians on Long Island as part of his long but intermittent study of Indian vocabularies. The two men's political enemies saw the trip as an effort to generate political support in the North and identify political allies.[24] In fact, Jefferson and Madison's correspondence reveals that they engaged in no political activities. At the most they may have inadvertently gleaned a sense of the region's politics, but if they met with any political leaders, the meetings were quick and inconsequential.[25] Although no one was yet thinking of political parties, Jefferson and Madison were beginning to ponder ways to ensure that their viewpoints could reach potential voters and thereby, from their perspective, protect the system of government intended by the Constitution's framers.

Both considered John Fenno's *Gazette of the United States*, founded in 1789 primarily to offer news in support of both the Constitution and the new government, little more than a mouthpiece for Hamiltonian views. It was, after all, heavily subsidized by printing contracts from the Treasury Department. Madison and Jefferson wanted another newspaper, hopefully with a national circulation, to counter Fenno's influence. As they envisioned it, this paper would offer balanced international news as well as interpretations of domestic events more in line with their thinking. (In truth, newspapers at this time were purveyors of particular views and did not envision themselves as neutral providers of information.) In February Madison had approached a fellow Princetonian and poet, Philip Freneau, with the proposal that he should edit such a paper, to be called the *National Gazette*. Freneau was hesitant, even after Jefferson offered him a part-time paid position as interpreter for the State Department.[26] After immense pressure from Madison, Freneau finally accepted Jefferson's offer on August 4 and also agreed to take on the editorship. The first issue of the *National Gazette* appeared on October 31, 1791. Freneau proved more combative than Madison had anticipated. The infighting within Washington's administration was now in the open. Jefferson tried to remain above the fray; he never wrote for the *National Gazette*, unlike Hamilton, who often wrote under a pseudonym for the press. Yet Jefferson's subsidy of Freneau soon became known, opening him to stinging criticism from Hamilton.

In September, before Freneau's first issue appeared, Jefferson left Philadelphia for Monticello, staying there a full month. Among other things, he enjoyed meeting his first grandchild, born on January 23, 1791.[27]

Both mother and daughter were healthy, and the parents had wanted Jefferson to name her; the new grandfather suggested the name Anne. From that moment Jefferson seldom neglected the infant, of whom he would prove inordinately proud. A comment about her, when she was about a year old, reveals his playfulness toward her: "Dear little Anne, with whom even Socrates might ride on a stick without being ridiculous."[28]

But surely also on his mind during this supposed respite was a disheartening conversation he'd had with Hamilton in mid-August 1791, just prior to leaving for Monticello. Hamilton had allowed that, in his opinion, the existing form of government was "not that which will answer the ends of society, by giving stability and protection to it's rights, and that it will probably be found expedient to go into the British form." As Jefferson recalled, Hamilton added, "However, since we have undertaken the experiment, I am for giving it fair course, whatever my expectations may be."[29] The most important issue for Jefferson was the survival and prosperity of the new government, and now he believed that Hamilton could not be trusted to protect the new nation's promise with the vigor Jefferson thought necessary.

By this point Jefferson understood Hamilton as his bête noire. Just as he ruminated on this August 1791 meeting, he must have thought about an equally unsettling earlier dinner. As he recalled the event years later, while Washington was at Mount Vernon in April or May 1791, Jefferson, at the president's request, had hosted a dinner for Hamilton, Attorney General Edmund Randolph, and Vice President Adams to consider some pressing issue. After the business had concluded, the men sat drinking wine and engaging in a wide-ranging conversation. Adams opined that "if some of it's defects & abuses were corrected," the British constitution "would be the most perfect constitution of government ever devised by man. Hamilton, on the contrary asserted that, with it's existing vices, it was the most perfect model of government that could be formed; & that the correction of it's vices would render it an impracticable government." Jefferson must have shuddered. Then Hamilton, noticing three portraits hanging in Jefferson's dining room, asked whom they depicted. Jefferson replied Francis Bacon, Isaac Newton, and John Locke, who he said constituted the "trinity of the three greatest men the world had ever produced." Hamilton thought for a moment, then said, "The greatest man . . . that ever lived was Julius Caesar." Jefferson noted this statement with alarm, remarking that while Adams "was honest as a politician as well as a man,"

Hamilton was "honest as a man, but, as a politician, believ[ed] in the ne-cessity of either force or corruption to govern men."[30] Not long after this revealing dinner, Jefferson wrote to Thomas Paine of his fears about the political attitudes developing in the nation. "We have a sect preaching up and panting after an English constitution of kings, lords, and commons, and whose heads are itching for crowns, coronets and mitres."[31]

During his September visit to Monticello, Jefferson decided that thirteen-year-old Maria (Polly) should return with him to Philadelphia to finish her formal schooling, so on October 12 the two of them set out, ar-riving in Philadelphia ten days later, just in time for the opening of the new session of Congress. Jefferson was better prepared for Polly now than he had been earlier in the year, for in July his former house manager in Paris, Adrien Petit, had arrived in Philadelphia and quickly set the house-hold in order. Jefferson enrolled Polly in the boarding school of Mary Pine, just around the corner from his house, which meant she could visit her father often.[32] Her presence no doubt reminded him of his time with Patsy in the city ten years before.

Two MONTHS BEFORE, on August 26, 1791, Jefferson had received a letter from Benjamin Banneker, a free black man living near Baltimore. He was a literate, self-taught mathematician and astronomer who had recently re-tired from working with Andrew Ellicott to survey the boundaries of the new District of Columbia. Banneker had completed the calculations for an ephemeris, a chart showing the location in the sky of the various heav-enly bodies throughout the course of the year, often seen in almanacs. Previously acquainted with Banneker's surveying skills, Jefferson had rec-ommended that Ellicott employ him, but he had never met the man.[33]

Although born free in Baltimore County, Maryland, in 1731, Banneker had experienced racism his entire life and was well aware of the severe plight of slaves. On August 19 he had posted his lengthy, carefully crafted letter to his nation's secretary of state. As he wrote, he assumed that he had no need to tell Jefferson that as a race, blacks had "long labored un-der the abuse and censure of the world, and that we have long been looked upon with an eye of contempt, and that we have long been con-sidered rather as brutish than human, and Scarcely capable of mental en-dowments." But because he had been informed that Jefferson was "a man far less inflexible in Sentiments of this nature, than many others, that you are measurably friendly and well disposed toward us, and that you are willing and ready to Lend your aid and assistance to our relief," he took it upon himself to plead with Jefferson to work for the end of slavery.[34] Banneker movingly described the conditions under which his black brethren suffered, reminded Jefferson of his noble words in the Declaration of Independence about all men having been created equal, and urged him to free his own slaves and work for the emancipation of all others. Enclosed with the letter was a manuscript copy of "an Almanack which I have calculated for the Succeeding year . . . the production of my arduous Study in this my advanced Stage of life."[35] Clearly he intended this gesture to persuade Jefferson of the substantial intellectual ability of blacks, and Banneker indicated that a Philadelphia publisher would soon print the almanac.

Jefferson understood Banneker's plea as a response to the passages in *Notes on the State of Virginia* about the alleged inferiority of blacks.[36] He promptly replied, thanking Banneker for his letter and the almanac, and writing, "No body wishes more than I do to see such proofs as you ex-hibit, that nature has given to our black brethren, talents equal to those of the other colours of men, and that the appearance of a want of them is owing merely to the degraded condition of their existence both in Africa and America." He continued in this vein, saying how much he hoped to witness the development of a system to improve the conditions of both the bodies and the minds of blacks. He concluded by announcing that he had "taken the liberty" of sending the manuscript of Banneker's almanac to the Marquis de Condorcet, secretary of the academy of sciences in Paris, to show the European elite the necessity of correcting "the doubts" "entertained" about the abilities of blacks.[37]

Jefferson that very day sent a letter to Condorcet enclosing Banneker's manuscript. Jefferson introduced the man as "a very respectable Mathematician. . . . I have seen very elegant solutions of Geometrical problems by him. Add to this that he is a very worthy and respectable member of society." Remarking that Banneker was a free man, not a slave, Jefferson told Condorcet that he would be "delighted to see these instances of moral eminence so multiplied as to prove that the want of talents ob-served in them is merely the effect of their degraded condition, and not . . . intellect."[38] Although readers today might dismiss Jefferson's letter to Banneker as a polite but meaningless gesture, Banneker, other blacks, and white supporters of emancipation saw it differently. Jefferson was widely considered an enemy of slavery and his letter was seen as an im-portant, positive defense of the black race. Friends of Banneker quickly published their two letters bound together as a pamphlet, and subsequent editions of Banneker's almanac quoted Jefferson's reply.[39] Jefferson himself believed Banneker's accomplishments both genuine and significant.

Later, Jefferson came under fire for his approbation of Banneker and his scientific accomplishments. In 1796 and 1800 New England Federalists cited Jefferson's letter to Banneker as evidence both of his antislavery sentiments and his gullibility in believing the almanac to be Banneker's own work, suggesting the astronomer had received heavy assistance from white friends. Southern Federalists also attacked Jefferson for his favorable comments to Banneker.[40] Jefferson seems to have come to regret the whole affair, which only brought him grief. In a letter to Joel Barlow in October 1809, eighteen years after his correspondence with Banneker, Jefferson indicated that he may have been misled about the legitimacy of Banneker's sole authorship and used by Banneker's friends through their unauthorized publication of his reply. He also slighted Banneker, writing, "[As] to what we know ourselves of Banneker. we know he had spherical trigonometry enough to make almanacs, but not without the suspicion of aid from Ellicot, who was his neighbor & friend, & never missed an opportunity of puffing him. I have a long letter from Banneker which shews him to have had a mind of very common stature indeed."[41] This sour tone, so different from that of the 1791 letter, may reflect his political experience during the intervening years rather than his original opinion of Banneker. Nevertheless, it is difficult to determine the extent, if any, to which Jefferson ever moderated the views on blacks expressed in *Notes on the State of Virginia.*

WHEREAS DOMESTIC ISSUES had occupied much of 1791, the new year would usher in a series of diplomatic concerns. On one international development, the American leadership basically agreed. In August 1791 the slaves in the Caribbean sugar colony of Saint-Domingue, inspired by the charismatic black military leader François-Dominique Toussaint-Louverture, had successfully rebelled against their oppressive French masters. In September the new French ambassador, Jean Baptist de Ternant, sought assistance from the United States, and because both Washington and Jefferson were then at their Virginia plantations, he went to Hamilton and Secretary of War Henry Knox, requesting $40,000 and permission to buy arms. Hamilton was glad to render aid, and when Knox wrote Washington, the president quickly approved.[42] Though the American leadership thereby sided with the colonial overseers, none of them desired a crushing French victory over the black rebels. For the next several years

Jefferson received regular reports from a range of correspondents on the progress of the rebellion and the futility of French resistance. Though Jefferson, like many others, worried about the spread of the slave rebellion to America, his primary concerns were geopolitical. Would the English take advantage of weakened French forces to seize the island and thereby increase their power and influence in the West Indies to the detriment of US trade? How would Spain respond? Would it attempt to conquer Saint-Domingue too? Would the slave rebels, perhaps out of necessity, engage in piratical raids against American maritime commerce?

Jefferson did not support a French attempt to suppress the rebellion; he understood that an uncompromising policy by either side would be counterproductive. He wrote to the Marquis de Lafayette in mid-1792, cautioning, "No future efforts you can ever make will ever be able to reduce the blacks." In a similar situation in Jamaica in 1739, British officials had set aside a remote section of the island as an autonomous region for the rebel slaves, and in response the latter agreed to cooperate in maintaining the slave economy in the British portion of the island. Jefferson suggested that the French do likewise.[43] Such a negotiated peace would guarantee the freedom of the rebels and lessen possible dangers to US interests. Jefferson would eventually view Haiti, as Saint-Domingue soon came to be known, as a potentially hospitable location for freed American slaves.

Late in 1791, a long-festering issue again almost erupted into crisis. The problems posed by the British presence in the Northwest became acute when in October a British ambassador at last arrived in Philadelphia. George Hammond, a twenty-eight-year-old Oxford graduate, came to the American capital brimming with confidence.[44] He instantly found a confidant and supporter in Hamilton; Jefferson, by contrast, was quite hostile. Jefferson discovered that Hammond was neither ready nor authorized to negotiate on commercial issues; rather he was determined to press the Americans to settle debts with British creditors as the 1783 treaty specified. Hammond expected to conduct face-to-face negotiations with Jefferson, while Jefferson insisted rather coldly on official written communications. Jefferson made clear he wanted the British to leave their northwestern outposts and—reflecting pressure from southern states—to offer reimbursement for the slaves carried away from the South during the American Revolution. Hamilton imparted to Hammond that Jefferson was rigid on British-related matters. He also suggested that as his opponent had little influence in the administration, Hammond should deal with him instead.[45]

Finally, on March 5, 1792, Hammond presented a lengthy response to the American demands, charging that the United States had violated the treaty provisions first and had done so repeatedly. Jefferson wrote a rebuttal of more than 17,000 words, augmented with appendices and supporting documents. It was a tour de force of lawyerly disputation unconstrained by diplomatic niceties. Yet nothing ever came of it because Hamilton insinuated to Hammond that it represented only Jefferson's position, not that of the government, and that President Washington had not even read it, which was an outright falsehood. But advised by Hamilton, both Hammond and the British government brushed off the report and never responded. Jefferson would leave office with these issues with Britain unresolved.

Jefferson had more ambitious hopes for diplomacy with Spain. Two large matters were at stake: settling the southern boundary of the United States with Florida at the thirty-first parallel (the Spanish claimed up to the thirty-second parallel) and, far more important, securing the right to navigate the Mississippi River. For more than a decade Jefferson deemed paramount protecting the river as an avenue of commerce for the western territories. With the support of the administration and Congress, he sent instructions to the chargé d'affaires in Madrid, William Carmichael, and to the more senior negotiator, William Short, now minister to The Hague, to pursue negotiations with Spanish officials. Long delayed, the instructions arrived in Madrid in the spring of 1793, by which time Spain, now allied with England, was willing to rebuff the new nation thousands of miles away.[46] A breakthrough would not come until the diplomatic scene in Europe changed in 1795.

In that year the American ambassador to England, South Carolina's Thomas Pinckney, was sent to Madrid. The Spanish foreign minister, Manuel de Godoy, after some effective pressure from Pinckney (and with Spain no longer supported by England), agreed—in the Treaty of San Lorenzo, signed on October 27, 1795—to a border at the thirty-first parallel and granted the right of US boats to navigate the Mississippi and the right of deposit (that is, the right to unload riverborne cargo and temporarily store it until it could be reloaded onto seaworthy ships for further transport) at New Orleans itself.[47] Thus Jefferson's efforts yielded fruit after his tenure as secretary of state came to end. Jefferson would remain committed to American access to the Gulf of Mexico by means of the Mississippi, knowing how essential river-borne commerce was to farmers west of the Appalachians. Another threat to this commerce, in 1801, led to the unexpected bonanza of the Louisiana Purchase two years later.

DESPITE THEIR GROWING mutual animosity, Jefferson and Hamilton could work together toward a common aim, which was always Washington's desire. The president hated the infighting and tried to ignore or even deny it; out of respect for him, Jefferson especially made an effort to limit its public display. Yet this became ever more difficult. And since Jefferson normally preferred to avoid conflict when at all possible, he grew steadily more exhausted by his duties, more frustrated by the opposition and intervention of Hamilton, and more eager to retire to Monticello.

When in late 1791 Hamilton issued his "Report on Manufactures," calling on the national government to massively intervene in the economy, attract immigrants as workers, promote female and child labor, invest in transportation infrastructure, collect import duties, and provide bounties to certain industries—policies aimed at stimulating and directing economic development—the ambitions behind the document frightened Jefferson. He was far less concerned about the growth of industry than the implied transformation of the role and power of the central government: Hamilton was calling for nothing less than centralized control of the national economy.[48] Although far too radical for Congress, Hamilton's proposal gave Jefferson yet another reason to fear for the future of the nation.

Overworked and weary of intrigue, Jefferson decided sometime very early in 1792 to resign his office. He had an afternoon visit with Washington on February 28, primarily to propose a speeding up of the mail service. But during the meeting he proposed transferring the postal service from the Treasury Department to the State Department, as Treasury was growing so large it threatened to "swallow up the whole Executive powers." Jefferson pointed out that he was not seeking self-aggrandizement, because he intended to resign at the end of the president's term. Washington, called away before they finished, requested that Jefferson join him the next day for breakfast, when he returned to Jefferson's comment about retiring. As Washington explained, he himself was planning to retire, owing to his age and his desire to disabuse the public of the idea that, having "tasted the sweets of office," he was unwilling to return to private life. But for that very reason he would hate to see other "great officers of the government"—meaning Jefferson—leave as well, lest this suggest that the government was unraveling.[49]

Jefferson responded that he had only entered into government service during the revolution out of a sense of duty, that he had subsequently declined several appointments, that he had intended to retire completely from government after his gubernatorial term in Virginia, that he had accepted the appointment to France for what he expected to be a limited time, and that he had very reluctantly accepted Washington's call to become secretary of state. Now he was determined to retire permanently to Monticello and his books and family. But Washington did not relent. The conversation ended only after Jefferson explained his objections in relation to Hamilton and his vision of a vastly expanded government. Jefferson, assuming that Washington would be leaving at the end of his term, was determined to do likewise.

The political atmosphere was about to become even more poisonous. Freneau's *National Gazette* was relatively nonpartisan at first, despite its provenance. But once Freneau got his footing, his judgments became far more slashing. He began to refer to those who supported Jefferson in the great debate of the time as "republicans" and those who supported Hamilton as "anti-republicans," characterizing the latter as a pro-aristocratic party. The attacks on Hamiltonian policy only inspired Fenno to reply in kind in the *Gazette of the United States*, and Hamilton—a master polemicist—wrote a number of pieces pseudonymously for the paper. The resulting press war hardened attitudes.

Fenno and other Hamilton supporters portrayed Jefferson as the mastermind of their opposition, with lesser lights like Madison and Monroe doing his bidding; in actuality Madison was still more openly and aggressively partisan, while Jefferson still preferred to stay in the background. Political activists began to mobilize supporters for candidates associated with either the Jeffersonian or the Hamiltonian position, and although neither side would have admitted to direct politicking, organized oppositional groups had obviously emerged. While both Jefferson and Hamilton attended to the functions of their respective offices, all around them swirled partisan insults and attacks.[50]

IN THIS CONTEXT, Jefferson sent a long letter to Washington voicing his concerns over the future of the nation. He justified the letter on the grounds that the "public mind is no longer so confident and serene," owing to "the public papers."[51] What followed was a litany of complaints and the principal charge: "the ultimate object of all this is to prepare the way for a change, from the present republican form of government, to that of a monarchy, of which the English constitution is to be the model." The only hope Jefferson saw was if, in the elections later that year, true republicans could take control of Congress. Jefferson pleaded with Washington to serve beyond the limit of his first term. "The confidence of the whole union is centered in you. . . . North and South will hang together, if they have you to hang on."[52]

Jefferson, almost obsessed with his fear of monarchy, had another searching conversation with Washington on July 10, only to learn that while Washington would consider staying on, he was dismissive of Jefferson's more extreme fears. The president told Jefferson that the "suspicions against a particular party . . . had been carried a great deal too far. There might be *desires*, but he did not believe there were *designs* to change the form of government into a monarchy." Washington saw the newspaper tirades against the so-called Hamiltonian system as veiled attacks against himself and reported that on his travels he found the people generally contented. In short, he minimized Jefferson's worries of a monarchical plot.[53]

At the end of the month Washington sent Hamilton a letter summarizing Jefferson's arguments (but not mentioning his name), and on August 18 Hamilton wrote Washington a closely argued response in which he refuted each charge. He apparently convinced Washington on every count.[54] Washington, almost like a father trying to settle an argument between two sons, wrote to Jefferson, referring to "internal dissentions" that were "harrowing and tearing our vitals." He called for "more charity for the opinions and acts of one another in Government matters." Otherwise he frankly feared that "the fairest prospect of happiness and prosperity that ever was presented to man, will be lost—perhaps for ever!" As he wrote, "My earnest wish, and my fondest hope therefore is, that . . . there may be liberal allowances—mutual forebearances—and temporizing yieldings on *all sides*."[55] Jefferson believed that Washington simply didn't grasp the severity of the matter. So he took pen in hand and wrote, this time from Monticello on his usual late-summer visit, yet another long missive stating even more explicitly his opinion of Hamilton.[56]

Within weeks came what Jefferson saw as another example of Hamilton's autocratic tendencies. During the summer of 1792, hard-pressed farmers in western Pennsylvania had protested the 1791 excise taxes as an unfair hardship. Hamilton had written to Washington on September 1 urging strict observance of the laws, collection of the taxes, and the use of draconian force, including the military if necessary, to suppress the opposition. Attorney General Randolph convinced Hamilton to take a more measured approach, and Washington insisted on getting Jefferson to sign off on the proposal, which Jefferson moderated even more and Washington accepted. Jefferson saw Hamilton's initial instinct to use military force as auguring his attitude toward dissent.[57] Although the farmers' protests quieted later that year, they would spring forth again soon enough.

Jefferson, who had arrived at Monticello on July 22, regretfully left about two months later. In the interim Martha gave birth to his first grandson, Thomas Jefferson Randolph. During the slow journey northward to Philadelphia, he stopped on September 30, as he often did, to spend the night at Mount Vernon. During a conversation the next morning about Jefferson's resolution to resign from office, Jefferson sensed that Washington was trying to convince him to continue, as Washington planned to do, despite growing uncertainty. Washington again "expressed his concern at the difference which he found to subsist between the Sec. of the Treasury and myself, of which he said he had not been aware." Jefferson's letters and prior conversations had failed to convince Washington of Hamilton's perfidy, and clearly Washington did not understand how stark the differences were between the two men.[58]

Back in Philadelphia, Jefferson encountered a barrage of newspaper attacks, some of the harshest from Hamilton, writing pseudonymously. Among the charges were that an overweening ambition to become president himself motivated all of his actions. On October 17 Jefferson sent Washington various extracts from his writings to counter this charge.[59] Washington, tiring of the controversy between his two leading aides, replied the next day with exasperation: "I regret—deeply regret—the difference in opinions which have arisen, and divided you and another principal Officer of the Government; and wish, devoutly, there could be an accommodation of them by mutual yieldings. . . . Why then . . . should either of you be so tenacious of your opinions as to make no allowances for those of the other?"[60]

But Jefferson and Hamilton were long past reconciliation, even though they could still work together when duty required. The remainder of the year brought Jefferson few pleasures, though he could anticipate retirement in March 1793 and took pleasure in the results of the fall 1792 election, which promised a different cast for the new Congress. As he wrote Thomas Pinckney near the end of the year, "The elections for Congress have produced a decided majority in favor of the republican interest. . . . I think we may consider the tide of this government as now at the fullest, and that it will from the commencement of the next session of Congress retire and subside into the true principles of the Constitution."[61]

IT IS REMARKABLE that the partisanship of the time did not result in complete political dysfunction. When Jefferson and Washington were not at odds, for instance, they shared—more than anyone else—in the exciting project of designing, promoting, and bringing into being a new capital city. This project—along with their common interest in agricultural reform—provided a foundation of mutual support and sympathy.

The Congress had passed in August 1790 a Resident Act that authorized the president to choose a site, up to ten miles square, along an eighty-mile stretch of the Potomac River. Jefferson, stretching the interpretation of the law to the limit, convinced Washington to imagine an entire city, not just a collection of several government buildings. Jefferson pushed for choosing a site that covered the entire one hundred square miles and suggested to Washington that it straddle the Potomac, with half in each of Maryland and Virginia.[62] Jefferson wrote Washington with ideas for a capitol building, a president's house, squares, gardens, public walks, and a market. He proposed a grid of streets, with broad boulevards and avenues at least one hundred feet in width, and recommended the Parisian practice of forbidding building above a certain height.[63] Known as a lover of rural life, Jefferson was also, by this time, a connoisseur of cities.

Washington, Jefferson, Madison, and others inspected the region along the Potomac, near the small towns and villages of Georgetown, Carrollsburg, and Alexandria. That November Washington chose a location between Rock Creek and the eastern branch of the Potomac. Even before passage of the Resident Act, a French engineer whom Washington had known during the revolution, Major Pierre Charles L'Enfant, had approached him about designing a capital city, and Washington now turned to the brilliant if arrogant Frenchman in March 1791.[64] L'Enfant's ideas were even more ambitious than Jefferson's. Probably influenced by Versailles, his plan superimposed upon Jefferson's grid an imaginative system of large squares and radiating axes but kept Jefferson's idea of a large capitol building, a broad central mall, and a stately house for the president. Everything else L'Enfant blew up in size and grandeur, though Jefferson seems to have been enthralled with the result, as was Washington. In the absence of significant federal funding, the project would have to pay for itself through the sale of town lots, which slowed the pace of development and demanded that the entire undertaking gain and maintain local support—restrictions against which the headstrong L'Enfant chaffed.

There were constant problems with landowners and workmen: L'Enfant refused to submit his plans and schedule to the commissioners who were overseeing his work by law, and Jefferson had to effectively play the role of project supervisor, representing the interest and direction of President Washington. L'Enfant recognized that Jefferson knew architecture and had traveled widely in Europe, so asked him to "procur for me what Ever map may fall within your reach, of any of the differents grand city now Existing such as for Example, as London, madry, paris, Amsterdam, naples, venice"—indications of the scale L'Enfant had in mind. Jefferson provided him with some dozen city maps. He also suggested styling the capitol building after some notable building of antiquity, while the president's house might have a more modern design. For the latter, he invoked several of his favorite examples in Paris, including the renowned east facade of the Louvre (which Jefferson called the Galerie du Louvre) and his beloved Hôtel de Salm.[65] What L'Enfant thought of these ideas is unknown. Later that year, in September, the three commissioners met in Georgetown and decided to name the capital city Washington and the federal territory Columbia.[66]

Ultimately L'Enfant's overbearing nature and refusal to accept the supervision of the three commissioners forced Washington to ask Jefferson to dismiss the talented Frenchman, and there followed several superintendents, including master surveyor Andrew Ellicott.[67] All of the complications and irritations—including shortages of funds and material, weather-related delays, and personality conflicts between builders, local landowners, and the commissioners—bound Washington and Jefferson together. They worked in close tandem to achieve their larger purpose. With L'Enfant gone, Washington accepted Jefferson's proposal to hold an invited competition for the design of the capitol building and the president's house. The winners, announced in mid-1792, were James Hoban for the executive mansion and Stephen Hallet and Dr. William Thornton for the capitol building, with Jefferson serving all along as what architects call "clerk of the works."[68]

The project was truly a labor of love for both Virginians, and although Jefferson could not be present on September 18, 1793, when the cornerstone of the capitol building was laid, he would, in 1801, be the first president to start his term in the new executive mansion.[69] Jefferson and

Washington experienced many frustrations throughout the process, but they maintained their lofty ambitions for what they saw as a capital city of symbolic and world-historical importance. Amid the fear and loathing that threatened to tear not only the administration but the nation apart, they trusted each other's judgment and shared a common vision. Their unity of purpose became in itself a powerful symbol of the strength and permanence of the nation.

16

The Specter of the French Revolution

I N 1793, JEFFERSON may have made one of his great inventions. On April 8 of that year he received a letter from Thomas Pinckney, dated January 31, in which the American minister to Britain revealed that he had somehow misplaced the key to the secret code in which Jefferson communicated with him. For months Pinckney had lamented this loss. Jefferson had long used various codes to maintain the confidentially of his correspondence, a practice he had inaugurated as the American minister to France. He continued the use of complicated ciphers as secretary of state, even employing codes when communicating private political information (or gossip) to intimates like James Madison and James Monroe. Perhaps around this time, or perhaps later on, when he was president, he sought to develop a simpler yet more secure method. He struck upon the idea of an arrangement of thirty-six flat disks, imprinted on their outer edges with the letters of the alphabet, randomly arranged, the whole held together by a rod inserted through the center of each disk. The sender and receiver would need exactly identical versions of the cipher wheels. The sender would rotate the various disks, in order from the left, lining them up so that the letters across one row spelled out the intended message when read from left to right. Then the sender locked the disks together so that they could rotate as a whole without changing their position relative to each other.

Scanning the thirty-six disks along the twenty-five other possible positions, the letters appeared completely at random, but by sending the correspondent any one of these random lines of nonsense, the latter could rotate the various disks until he matched the line sent, then lock and rotate the entire assemblage until he found the one line that read across as a correct sentence: that was the intended message. The cipher wheel produced an almost unbreakable code. It was later independently discovered by a French cryptologist in about 1890 and again by an American military cryptologist at the beginning of World War I; the US military would employ it until the mid-1940s. Although he apparently never used it, this device has earned Jefferson the title "father of American cryptography."[1]

Also in 1793, the year Jefferson celebrated his fiftieth birthday, he had reason to believe that one of his oldest dreams, sending an expedition to explore the trans-Mississippi West, might at last come true. An accomplished French botanist, André Michaux, who had been traveling in the United States since 1785, appeared in Philadelphia in the spring of the previous year. He apparently had heard that Jefferson and like-minded members of the American Philosophical Society were contemplating a scientific exploration from the Missouri River all the way to the Pacific. In December Michaux evidently met with some members of the society and proposed they sponsor him to make such a journey.[2]

Jefferson quickly wrote to Benjamin Smith Barton on January 2, 1793, asking him to learn more about Michaux's plan.[3] A few weeks later Michaux responded with a list of six requests for things he needed or wanted assurance on, and after some negotiation, he and Jefferson reached an agreement. On or about January 22 Jefferson drew up the terms for the society's sponsorship of Michaux's travels and began planning a subscription campaign to raise the necessary funds. Among the subscribers, in addition to Jefferson, were Washington, Adams, Hamilton, Madison, and most of the other political and social leaders in Philadelphia.[4] Jefferson, as an officer of the society, took charge of all arrangements—this of course in addition to his governmental duties.

Jefferson's friend David Rittenhouse wrote in early April that Michaux had just visited and asked "that instructions be prepared for him if he goes"; Rittenhouse urged Jefferson, "This I hope you will do."[5] Jefferson sent Michaux at the end of the month a detailed list of objectives. The "chief" purpose of his journey, as Jefferson put it, was to "find the shortest and most convenient route of communication between the US. and the Pacific ocean, within the temperate latitudes" and to learn about "the country through which it passes, it's productions, inhabitants, and other interesting circumstances."[6] He cautioned Michaux to stay far enough north to "avoid the risk of being stopped" by agents of the Spanish settlements. Jefferson was more specific about the kinds of information desired: data on the country's "soil, rivers, mountains, it's productions animal,

vegetable, and mineral . . . the names, numbers, and dwellings of the inhabitants, and such particularities as you can learn of their history, connection with each other, languages, manners, state of society and of the
arts and commerce among them."7

The list reflected Jefferson's interests in the physical and social aspects
of the West and, at the same time, the debates he had engaged with in
Notes on the State of Virginia about the size of American animals; he asked
Michaux to investigate the existence of the mammoth, along with that of
the "Lama, or Paca of Peru."8 Jefferson concluded that Michaux, upon his
return, should be prepared "to give . . . a full narrative of your journey and
observations, and to answer the enquires" the members of the American
Philosophical Society "shall make of you."9

WITH HIS ILLIMITABLE curiosity, Jefferson had great hopes for Michaux's
expedition. He could not foresee that international developments would
intervene and greatly intensify the political storms already buffeting
Philadelphia. His old friend the Marquis de Condorcet, in the last letter
(dated December 21, 1792) he ever sent Jefferson, reported that one
"Genest" would be the new French minister to the United States. Two
weeks later Thomas Pinckney sent similar news from London; Jefferson
did not receive these letters until May and April, respectively.10 Edmund-
Charles Genet, only thirty years old when he arrived, would prove a cata-
strophically destructive force in American politics. Jefferson already knew,
at the start of the year, that France was in turmoil. He had worried about
the declaration of war by Prussia in June 1792, heard that the guillotine
was in grisly use in Paris, and briefly exulted in the French victory over
Prussian troops at Valmy in September. But he had not yet learned that
King Louis XVI had been put on trial in December, condemned to death
the following month, and executed on January 21, 1793.

Jefferson had been receiving a steady stream of distressing letters from
Gouverneur Morris—which he discounted to some degree because of
Morris's royalist sympathies—and even more worrisome missives from
William Short. Jefferson obviously did not witness the violence and bloodshed in Paris and held tenaciously to the hopeful expectations for the
French Revolution that had become fixed in his mind by 1789.11 He was
almost in a state of denial regarding matters in France, or, perhaps more
accurately, he was willing to tolerate dreadful means for such an important
end. In words that still have the capacity to shock, he supported the revolution as a herald of democracy in Europe, a cause so noble that it justified

thousands of deaths. He saw those who lost their lives in the maelstrom as comparable to martyrs in warfare for a just cause. Jefferson often wrote hyperbolically in private messages to intimate friends, almost as if to rid himself of intense emotions. In an outburst to Short he wrote, "The liberty of the whole earth was depending on the issue of the contest, and was ever such a prize won with so little innocent blood? My own affections have been deeply wounded by some of the martyrs to this cause, but rather than it should have failed, I would have seen half the earth desolated. Were there but an Adam and an Eve left in every country, and left free, it would be better than as it now is."[12]

Jefferson was not bloodthirsty, and Short probably read this language—as extravagantly dismissive of human causalities as the biblical account of Noah's flood—symbolically. But Jefferson believed that most Americans felt similarly about the sacredness of the cause of the French Revolution. At the very least, many others shared his view that the success of the American experiment was tied to that of the French. Neither he nor most Americans yet understood how news of the horrors of the Reign of Terror, including the beheading of the king, would tilt American support away from the revolution and shift power to partisans of England.

Jefferson did prove more balanced in his comments regarding the ongoing revolt of enslaved blacks on the island of Saint-Domingue, arriving at the view that at least partial French defeat was inevitable. Increasingly he read events there as a warning to the southern states. As he wrote his son-in-law, "I think it cannot be doubted but that sooner or later all the whites will be expelled from all the West India islands. What is to take place in our Southern states will depend on the timely wisdom and liberality of their legislatures. Perhaps the measures they ought to begin to think of may be facilitated by having so near an asylum established."[13] In other words, they should consider the gradual abolition of slavery, and one solution might entail sending newly freed slaves to the Caribbean.

AT THE START OF 1793, Jefferson expected he would shortly be back in Monticello, finally done with politics. He had notified his landlord on December 9 that he intended to relinquish the lease on his Philadelphia house in mid-March, and by the beginning of the year he was packing up his furniture and books for shipment back to Virginia.[14] He had also begun ordering materials for the repair and renovation of Monticello and sending building instructions to his son-in-law. But as others learned that he planned to resign his position, his closest advisors argued that to do so would be unwise. They made the decisive point that if he left now, in the face of Hamilton's criticism and the constant barrage of newspaper attacks, it would look as though the opposition had driven him from office. Jefferson still harbored resentment over the 1781 charges that he had abandoned the office of governor of Virginia when things went badly (which later enemies turned into a charge of cowardice). So, despite his desperate longing for Monticello and its delights—which now included his two grandchildren, Anne Cary Randolph and Thomas Jefferson Randolph—he decided to remain in office.[15]

Jefferson told Washington in a February 7, 1793, conversation that he was "willing . . . to continue somewhat longer, how long I could not say, perhaps to summer, perhaps autumn."[16] Sometime over the next couple of weeks he finalized his plans to remain in the capital, although, through a private arrangement with the subsequent renter of his present house, he did not move out until April 11. Having sent many crates of furnishings south, he on that date moved into a much smaller, three-room house about three miles outside the city.[17]

Jefferson had reasons besides reputation to stay in office. As he came to see it, issues domestic and foreign threatened the very existence of the republic in early 1793. In fact, Jefferson's investment in an emerging congressional inquiry into how Hamilton managed the affairs of the Treasury may have clinched his decision. Certainly Jefferson became more involved in the congressional charges against Hamilton than he admitted to Washington or anyone else. Perhaps he justified this as a fitting response to Hamilton's pseudonymous authoring of numerous newspaper critiques of him. Whatever the reason, Jefferson showed himself in this affair more willing to engage in aggressive politics than his public persona ever suggested. The battle began on December 24, 1792, when congressman William Branch Giles of Virginia—an intemperate and almost rabidly partisan member of the House—demanded Hamilton provide a detailed accounting of and rationale for a whole series of economic decisions.[18]

With surprising speed, even for him, Hamilton produced reports responding to every inquiry. These revealed that he had moved funds around rather cavalierly and ignored what he considered minor rules and expectations of transparency. They also showed that Hamilton himself was scrupulously honest with government funds and never worked against the financial interests of the nation as he interpreted them—which, of course, led to decisions that benefitted a rather small number of wealthy, powerful investors, businessmen, merchants, and manufacturers.[19] This fact and all of its implications formed the basis of Jefferson's deepest suspicions, not Hamilton's technical observance of accounting laws or personal honesty.

Giles and many of his Virginian colleagues, unsatisfied with Hamilton's reports, began to prepare a set of resolutions to censure him; Giles introduced nine such resolutions on February 27, and strong evidence indicates that Jefferson himself authored the original drafts of each. Usually even tempered, Jefferson revealed his fury with Hamilton and his profound fear of the influence of his policies on the nation. Although cooler heads had softened each of the resolutions that Giles offered, Congress rejected them easily—not even all the Virginian congressmen supported them.[20] Hamilton emerged victorious, stronger in Washington's mind than ever before, and Jefferson clearly took on the intellectual leadership of the anti-Hamilton faction, supplanting Madison. Nothing had been resolved, and everyone must have realized that the partisan rancor would persist.[21] Those politicians favoring the Jeffersonian position began self-identifying as Republicans in 1792 and 1793, and the Washington-Hamilton forces adopted the Federalist label in 1794.

By now Jefferson evinced a visceral personal dislike of Hamilton. In a letter to Madison, he even cast doubt on Hamilton's reputed military courage.[22] The tone of his comments suggests Jefferson's thorough exhaustion if not disillusionment with politics, and when Madison scolded him in early June 1793 for going forward with his plan to retire, Jefferson responded with a sharpness never before seen in his communications with his closest friend. "The motion of my blood no longer keeps time with the tumult of the world. It leads me to seek for happiness in the lap and love of my family, in the society of my neighbors and books, in the wholesome occupations of my farm."[23]

IN THE MEANTIME, more disturbing reports from France continued to arrive, including news of the execution of the king and many other worthies. The locus of partisan political conflict in Philadelphia was about to shift from domestic to foreign affairs. Washington even broached the idea that since Jefferson was contemplating leaving the State Department, he might consider returning to Paris as the American minister. Washington pressed him, arguing that the post was important, the issues were compelling, and Jefferson "possessed the confidence of both sides and might do great good." Yet Jefferson declined, in part because he dreaded another

Atlantic crossing and in part because the arrival of Minister Genet meant he perhaps could do more good working with him in the United States. Washington protested that Jefferson had pressured him into remaining "in public service and refused to do the same," but Jefferson parried that the president was indispensable whereas the secretary of state was not. A displeased Washington finally accepted Jefferson's refusal.[24]

France, and Genet, would dominate Jefferson's year. In early March, Jefferson reprimanded the US minister to France, Gouverneur Morris, who wanted to delay repayment of American debts incurred during the American Revolution because he disapproved of France's new leadership. Jefferson instructed the royalist Morris that despite recent political events in France, America still had to repay the French government. In his insistence that the US treaty was with the French nation, not a particular leader or form of government,[25] Jefferson established an enduring American foreign policy principle.

Related was the question of how the United States should receive the newly appointed minister from France. Morris had already written Washington a dismissive note about the "upstart" Genet,[26] whom Hamilton would have liked to ignore as a rebuke to France. At a meeting with Washington on March 30, Hamilton made this case, while Jefferson emphasized that the United States should welcome Genet. Washington essentially agreed with Jefferson, though he thought the French minister should not receive "too much warmth or cordiality."[27] Though less hostile to France than Hamilton, Washington was cautious about offending England unnecessarily. Hamilton believed Jefferson's (and Madison's) continuing hostility to England stemmed from peevishness or sentiment, not reason. Hamilton had privately the year before complained that Jefferson and Madison "*have a womanish attachment to France and a womanish resentment against Great Britain.*"[28] Hamilton was as convinced that Jefferson was a dangerous Jacobin revolutionary as Jefferson was certain Hamilton was a plotting monarchist.

More important than how to respond to Genet was the appropriate stance the United States should take toward France. Washington understood that the American people still felt widespread goodwill for France's assistance during the American Revolution. Even so, the young United States was militarily weak and could scarcely risk hostilities with a powerful European nation. Word at the end of March that France had declared war on England raised questions about what this would mean for the United States. Would treaty obligations with France dating from the

Revolutionary War entangle the infant nation in a large-scale European conflict? Washington sent his cabinet members—his chief advisors had by now informally evolved into his cabinet—a note on April 18, requesting that they convene at his home the next morning to consider the "delicate situation" concerning "the measures which will be proper for them to observe in the War" between the European powers.[29]

At the meeting Washington laid out thirteen questions; though they were in the president's handwriting, Jefferson recognized Hamilton's influence in the wording. Should the United States issue a formal declaration of neutrality? Should it receive a minister from the newly proclaimed Republic of France? And with any qualifications? What was the standing of the existing treaties with France? How should the United States treat the shipping interests of the warring nations and their privateers? Hamilton wanted an explicit declaration of neutrality that would, in practice, mostly favor England. He also wanted to interpret previous treaties with France as essentially null.

The cabinet members agreed on one thing: that the United States should not interfere in any European war. But Jefferson strongly resisted any proclamation that officially used the word "neutrality." He supported noninvolvement but argued that "neutrality" had a specific meaning in international law; as a result, the warring nations should approach the United States seeking formal relationships of neutrality to guarantee protection of neutral ships. Moreover, believing a proclamation of neutrality the opposite of a declaration of war, which was the prerogative of Congress, Jefferson insisted that Congress should be consulted in the drafting of any formal document. After much discussion and exchange of written opinions, Washington issued a statement on April 22 that made clear the United States' noninvolvement in the war. In deference to Jefferson, the word "neutrality" did not appear in the document, but everyone then and since has called it the Neutrality Proclamation.

The treaties with France were held to be valid but not applicable because they dealt with assisting France if it was attacked—and France had declared war on England. (Jefferson had made the point that even had the treaties required the United States to join the war, it could refrain on the principle, established in international law, that any nation could unilaterally void treaties as a means of self-defense.) The French minister would be received, US debt payments to France would continue, and Jefferson relented in his argument that Congress, not the president, should issue statements about nonintervention.[30]

GENET CHOSE TO BEGIN his tenure in America in Charleston, South Carolina. He arrived there on April 8, sent most of his baggage and his legation staff directly to Philadelphia by sea, and decided to wind his way overland to the capital city.[31] He appeared, despite his youth, the perfect minister to the United States, which he assumed to be a veritable hotbed of pro-French sentiment. And indeed this seemed to be the case in Charleston, where he was welcomed extravagantly.

The impulsive Genet, misreading the crowds, promptly began commissioning privateers, one of which he christened the *Citoyen Genet*, to raid British shipping. He also presumptuously established a court under the auspices of the local French consul to condemn the British prizes (that is, to claim the captured British ships and the property on them) he expected the privateers to bring in. Of course he had no legal authority to do any of this. All along his journey to Philadelphia, he met with exultation and huzzahs for the French cause.[32] Constantly feted and assuming that this popular appeal reflected practically unanimous American support for France, including within the American government, he arrived in Philadelphia on May 16 under the impression that the United States was ready to do his bidding.[33]

Philadelphia's leading citizens greeted Genet on May 17 with a grand celebration, at which Genet gave a speech in flawless English. Little changed over the following weeks; he reported to his superiors in France, "I live here in the midst of perpetual fetes."[34] Small wonder he concluded that the American people wanted their nation to give France all the support Genet asked for. The day after the celebratory ball on May 17, Jefferson formally presented Genet to President Washington, who received him with the ceremonial courtesy of which he was a master. As for Jefferson, he was taken with Genet, as were many others in those first weeks.[35]

Although Jefferson knew the fiercely anti-French Hamilton was lurking in the background, seeking an opening to attack Genet and diminish the French in the eyes of the populace, he dared hope that the goodwill between the United States and this representative of France would continue. "This summer is of immense importance to the future condition of mankind all over the earth," Jefferson wrote on May 23 to Harry Innes, a federal judge in Kentucky, "and not a little so to ours."[36] But the spell was broken that very day when Washington objected to the wording of a letter Jefferson had prepared for him to send to the leaders of the Republic of France. Jefferson had mentioned France's recall of its previous minister "to our republic." Washington complained about the phrase on the grounds that though the United States certainly had a republican form of government, its leaders had never referred to the nation in a formal document as a republic. Washington believed that Jefferson was trying to subtly link the United States with France, which did explicitly call itself a "republic." Washington, obviously outraged, stated, "If any body wanted to change into a monarchy he was sure it was only a few individuals, and that no man in the US. would set his face against it more than himself."[37] From Jefferson's perspective, Washington's response was yet more evidence of the fractured political scene in the United States.

The problem Genet immediately ran into and never seemed to comprehend, despite Jefferson's patient and repeated attempts to explain both the American system of government and existing American foreign policy, had to do with neutrality. Distracted by the adulation he received since his arrival, Genet simply could not accept that the policy reflected the true opinion of the American people. He continued trying to arm privateers and recruit sailors to man them; he pressed the United States to speed up repayment of its debt to France; and he intentionally misled Jefferson about the disembarkation from Philadelphia's harbor of a British vessel, the *Little Sarah*, captured by the French, armed, and rechristened the *Petite Democrate*. There was more: it became known that Genet had spoken disrespectfully of President Washington and threatened to go over his head and appeal directly to the American people.[38]

Genet's brazenness offended all but his most incorrigible defenders. It frustrated and outraged Jefferson and played right into Hamilton's efforts to vilify the secretary of state and France. Over the course of July 1793, Hamilton—under the pseudonym "Pacificus"—published seven blistering essays in the *Gazette of the United States*, excoriating Jefferson, Genet, and all who did not enthusiastically support the policy of neutrality. Jefferson, recognizing how politically damaging the Pacificus essays could be, implored Madison, "For god's sake, my dear Sir, take up your pen." Madison, as "Helvidius," responded with five essays that appeared in the *National Gazette* in August. An all-out war had erupted within the ranks of Washington's administration. Jefferson finally realized how irresponsible, uninformed, and politically inept Genet was.[39]

Washington sought advice from his cabinet on how to minimize the Genet problem. His secretaries agreed unanimously that he should be recalled and debated how to effect this. Hamilton wanted to do it in the most public way possible, to humiliate France and especially Jefferson. Washington, the coolest head in the room, thought it wiser to send all of

Genet's incriminating correspondence to Gouverneur Morris in Paris, along with a temperate but frank recounting of his behavior. Morris would assure France of US support and depend on the good sense of French officials to recall their minister.[40] A week later the cabinet met again and assented to this plan.

JUST ONE DAY BEFORE the first of these two meetings, Jefferson sent Washington a letter proposing to resign at the end of September 1793. As Jefferson wrote, he was "every day more and more convinced that neither my talents, tone of mind, nor time of life fit me" for his present position.[41] Amid the Genet controversy, Jefferson's thoughts were increasingly turning once again to Monticello. If Jefferson needed any reinforcement of this resolution, it came on August 2, when, at yet another cabinet meeting over Genet, Secretary of War Henry Knox unwisely mentioned a recent newspaper article that disparaged Washington, whereupon the president threw what can only be called a temper tantrum. As Jefferson put it, he "got into one of those passions when he cannot command himself" and subsequently declared "that *by god* he had rather be in his grave than in his present situation." Washington ended up attacking "that rascal Freneau"— editor of the anti-administration *National Gazette*—and the meeting petered out.[42]

Within a few days Washington went to Jefferson's house on the Schuylkill River and implored him to stay until the end of the year, asking if he could not handle his private affairs during a short visit to Virginia. As if to explain his recent fit of anger, he said he believed "the views of the Republican party were perfectly pure" but that the political machinery of the federal government was nevertheless in danger of breaking down. He supposed there "was a party disposed to change it into a monarchical form, but that he could conscientiously declare there was not a man in the US. who would set his face more decidedly against it than himself." Jefferson responded that no man in America would suspect Washington of any other disposition. The language Washington used— "the Republican party"—suggested the solidifying of oppositionist elements into political parties. Again Washington returned to the topic of Jefferson's remaining in office for the duration of the year, but Jefferson gave him no firm answer.[43] Five days later Jefferson wrote Washington that, provided he could go back to Monticello for several weeks in the fall, he would consent to remain in office until December 31. A relieved Washington agreed.[44]

Meanwhile Jefferson, realizing that Genet still had supporters, wrote a long letter to Madison, explaining exactly how he had tried to reason with the ambassador to no effect. He had ultimately realized that because the "man was absolutely incorrigible, I saw the necessity of quitting a wreck which could not but sink all who should cling to it."[45] Jefferson prepared a long letter to Gouverneur Morris, outlining the conduct of the irresponsible diplomat and enclosing his most inflammatory correspondence; the final draft was approved and sent on August 23. Jefferson, with Washington's consent, effectively made the case against Genet and clearly differentiated America's rejection of him from the nation's friendship with France. Jefferson subsequently informed Genet on September 7 that President Washington had requested that the French government recall him.[46]

As expected, Genet railed against this decision and made all kinds of blustering arguments against the Constitution and the American government, believing that Jefferson and others had betrayed him. More radical elements among the hundreds of Francophone whites from Haiti now living in Philadelphia joined him in his distemper.[47] Throughout the late summer and early fall, Genet wrote Jefferson continuously to express his views. At the same time, Hamilton and his allies were working to whittle away at popular support for France and generate opposition toward their political enemies. Not until February did Genet's replacement, Jean Fauchet, arrive. On February 22, 1794, Fauchet asked Washington to arrest Genet and return him to France, where the Jacobins—who disapproved of the now former ambassador—were currently in power. Genet requested, and a merciful Washington granted, political asylum, allowing him to remain in America.[48]

As one short-term result of the Genet affair, botanist Michaux's proposed exploration of the trans-Mississippi West was aborted. Michaux had encountered Genet in May 1793 and informed him that he would serve France in any way the minister thought appropriate. Genet thereupon recruited Michaux for one of his more outlandish schemes: to gather American volunteers in the western states, head southward, join up with a hypothetical French fleet, and help seize Spanish-controlled New Orleans. Overflowing with enthusiasm for the French Revolution, Michaux agreed to participate in this radical endeavor. In late August Spanish diplomats in Philadelphia heard rumors of a French-inspired plot in the West and complained to Jefferson. Jefferson told Washington what he knew about Genet's maneuvering (Genet had vaguely talked about hoping to inspire a movement against the Spanish authorities in Louisiana; Jefferson had told him in no uncertain terms that this was inappropriate and he should desist, but as usual the headstrong Genet went ahead) and wrote to the governor of Kentucky asking him to thwart any and all actions by American citizens against Spain.[49] But before Genet could realize his harebrained plot, the recall campaign was already moving forward. Genet's replacement, Fauchet, promptly cancelled all commissions Genet had given out, hence terminating any plans underway in the West. Michaux, his reputation tarnished, silently withdrew from his western adventure, made his way back to Charleston, and resumed his botanical studies for the French government. He returned permanently to France in 1796.

THE SUMMER OF 1793 was a time of intense political pressure: for most of the period Genet did not know that his recall was underway (he was notified on September 7); Jefferson and his allies were reeling from the newspaper attacks upon them by Hamilton and his supporters; independently organized "democratic societies" were actively working on behalf of policies more consonant with those of Jefferson than Hamilton; Washington was almost beside himself with frustration at the division in the country and in his administration. Then a totally unforeseen malady practically extinguished these partisan fires by halting most activity—political and otherwise—in Philadelphia. The unusually mild winter of 1792 and 1793 gave way to a very wet spring, perhaps contributing to the descent of a large number of mosquitoes on the city. The epidemic began slowly. The first deaths occurred in early August, with the final symptoms terrible: victims became feverish, turned a pallid yellow, and started vomiting black blood from internal hemorrhaging; both their vomit and stool had a horrible odor.

As the deaths multiplied, the city's leading doctor, Benjamin Rush, made the diagnosis on August 19: the dreaded yellow fever. The epidemic would rage for more than two months, finally subsiding at the end of October after the first frosts eliminated the mosquitoes. At its height, in the early weeks of October, more than a hundred people died every day. In total, the city of 50,000 lost 5,000 citizens. About half of the population fled to the countryside, including just about every government official; commerce came to a standstill, and the wharfs were abandoned.[50] Philip Freneau resigned and returned to New Jersey, making the *National Gazette* a casualty of the yellow fever epidemic. The Hamiltonian press campaign against Jefferson also collapsed.

Jefferson first wrote of the epidemic to Madison on September 1, reporting, "A malignant fever has been generated . . . , which gives great alarm. About 70. people had died of it two days ago. . . . It has now got into most parts of the city and is considerably infectious. . . . [E]very body who can, is flying from the city. . . . I have withdrawn my daughter from the city, but am obliged to go into it every day myself."[51] The role of the mosquito as the vector by which the disease spread was unknown. Luckily, by bringing Polly to his home on the Schuylkill River, Jefferson kept her relatively safe. Washington was scheduled to leave for Mount Vernon on September 9, Knox was departing the city then too, and Hamilton himself had contracted a milder form of the fever.

Jefferson wrote to Madison on September 8 that he would decamp as well, except "I had before announced that I should not go till the beginning of October, and I do not like to exhibit the appearance of panic. Besides that I think there might serious ills proceed from there being not a single member of the administration in place."[52] Less than a week later Jefferson reported to Madison, "The fever spreads faster. Deaths are now about 30. a day. It is in every square of the city. All flying who can. . . . All my clerks have left me but one. . . . I shall therefore set out in 3. or 4. days and perhaps see you before you get this."[53] Five days later, on September 17, Jefferson and his daughter embarked for Monticello.[54]

Jefferson would stay at Monticello for a month, leaving on October 25—Maria stayed behind—but not for Philadelphia. He had received a letter from Washington asking that he, along with Hamilton and Knox, meet with the president "by the first of November" in the vicinity of Philadelphia, and Washington had suggested Germantown, which had remained almost unaffected by the yellow fever. Jefferson overtook Washington in Baltimore, and they journeyed on together, arriving on November 1.[55] As the cold set in, the epidemic quickly drew to an end. Over the next two or three weeks, the various clerks and other government officers arrived, and shortly after the middle of the month, the cabinet members began meeting at the president's home, planning his address to the new Congress that would convene on December 2. The major issues were the recall of Genet and the Neutrality Proclamation. The debate, as usual, pitted Hamilton's effort to maximize the criticism, implicit and explicit, of France against Jefferson's attempt to maintain good relations with that nation; on both matters Washington sided with Jefferson.[56] In subsequent meetings, Hamilton was as combative as ever. At the final meeting Washington again backed Jefferson against the opinions of

Hamilton, Knox, and Attorney General Edmund Randolph, the first time Jefferson had ever seen the president so resolute.[57]

As THE CITY RETURNED to normal, Jefferson was counting the days till the end of the year and his resignation, although Washington tried one more time, on December 21, to change his mind. By December 8 Jefferson was asking his son-in-law to arrange horses to arrive for him at Fredericksburg in mid-January.[58] A week later Jefferson wrote to Maria that he hoped "to be with you all about the 15th. of January no more to leave you."[59] The very next day he presented to Congress his last report. Congress had first requested it in 1791, but for various reasons Jefferson had delayed. Now, in his last major act as secretary of state, he delivered the final version of his "Report on Commerce." It represented his long-held commitment to free trade, though it reflected more recent events in its emphasis on reciprocal agreements between nations. Jefferson saw commerce as a potential tool of foreign policy, never realizing that trade with the United States was a rather insignificant issue for most European countries. And the one nation to whom it was relatively important, Britain, was so economically powerful as to be, in the end, little influenced by American policies.[60]

On the last day of 1793, Jefferson penned his resignation letter to Washington: "I now take the liberty of resigning the office into your hands. Be pleased to accept with it my sincere thanks for all the indulgences which you have been so good as to exercise towards me. . . . I carry into my retirement a lively sense of your goodness, and shall continue gratefully to remember it. With very sincere prayers for your life, health and tranquility, I pray you to accept the homage of the great & constant respect & attachment with which I have the honor to be Dear Sir Your most obedient & most humble servt."[61] Jefferson truly meant these words of respect and affection. The president responded the very next day, admitting how much he hated to receive the letter, but adding, "I cannot suffer you to leave your Station, without assuring you, that the opinion, which I had formed, of your integrity and talents, and which dictated your original nomination, has been confirmed by the fullest experience; and that both have been eminently displayed in the discharge of your duties."[62] Jefferson settled all his outstanding accounts, paid his servants (including Adrien Petit, who returned to France), and departed Philadelphia on January 5, 1794, arriving at Monticello less than two weeks later, believing his years of public service at an end.[63]

17

"Totally Absorbed in My Rural Occupations"

S EVERAL PURCHASES JEFFERSON made as he was tying up his affairs in Philadelphia hint at new emphases in his life. On December 18, 1793, he arranged to buy a ton of nail rod from a Philadelphia ironmonger, in preparation for a nail-making manufactory at Monticello that he hoped would provide much-needed income.[1] He also bought unspecified toys and "sundries" for his two daughters.[2] Jefferson would be returning to his beloved family: his younger daughter Maria and his married daughter Martha, her husband, and two small children. Buttressing Monticello's finances and attending to family matters would dominate Jefferson's thoughts and actions over the three years from 1794 to 1796. After the aggravations of national and international politics, he looked forward to a new phase in his life.

IN EARLY LETTERS written after he resumed life at Monticello, Jefferson remarked time and time again on his withdrawal from the world of politics and his near total immersion in the challenges of farming.[3] As he told John Adams, "I return to farming with an ardour which I scarcely knew in my youth, and which has got the better entirely of my love of study." To James Madison he claimed, "I find my mind totally absorbed in my rural occupations."[4] This fanatical letter writer confessed that "instead of writing 10. or 12. letters a day, which I have been in the habit of doing as a thing of course, I put off answering my letters now, farmer-like, till a rainy day, and then find it sometimes postponed by other necessary occupations."[5]

But a letter to George Wythe "on the use of the Middle voice in Greek" suggests he was exaggerating his retreat from intellectual pursuits.[6] And another letter to Madison indicates Jefferson may also have missed keeping up with the political news of the day and still felt profound concern about decisions made in the capital.[7] Over the course of 1794 he would receive more than two dozen letters from Madison and James Monroe combined, and this correspondence, along with that from other political insiders, ensured he was never quite as insulated from national affairs as he pretended he wanted to be. In fact, over 1794 and 1795, Jefferson may have even surprised himself with his persistent interest in politics. The political scene had irrevocably become an integral part of him. Yet on the surface, at least, he focused his attention mostly on making Monticello profitable.

He arranged in the first months of 1794 for the establishment of a large garden, with many dozens of different plants, including six kinds of beans, various peas, and a surprisingly extensive range of other vegetables. He tried various species to maximize both taste and yield. According to his Garden Book, he also planted hundreds of trees: among others, shade trees, fruit-bearing trees, and 2,400 cuttings of weeping willows, a fast-growing tree he desired mainly for the firewood it produced. That December he replaced the rail fences that subdivided his fields with 1,157 peach trees: in his view a more aesthetically pleasing method of delimiting his fields, with, of course, the added benefit that the trees produced peaches.[8] The estate's population of livestock grew. He used workhorses for pulling plows and wagons and for threshing wheat (before he acquired a workable threshing machine) but employed mules too, preferring them and oxen to horses, as draft animals at least. Still, the most numerous farm animal remained the humble hog; although Jefferson preferred beef and mutton, he did like cured hams. He had introduced sheep to Monticello in the early 1790s, prizing them both for their meat and their wool, and once home again, he took great care to improve the breed of his flock, though, curiously, he did not do the same for his cattle.[9]

Chickens and guinea fowl were abundant beyond count. Jefferson always allowed his cattle and hogs to roam at will in his woodlands and open fields, which lessened his feeding costs but also made it impossible to aggregate the manure that otherwise could have fertilized the fields under cultivation. While wheat and tobacco were the marketable crops, he devoted many acres to growing corn for both human and animal consumption. Even so, Jefferson augmented the homegrown food by buying additional corn along with pickled herring by the barrel. No doubt his slaves often caught fish to supplement their diet. Monticello's slaves also bottled apple cider and peach brandy for the estate.

In 1794, Jefferson's total land holdings constituted more than 10,000 acres, about half of which were at Monticello; of that half, about 1,200 acres were under cultivation. Of his approximately 152 slaves, about 90 lived at Monticello. They slept, grouped by family, in individual log cabins that ranged from twelve by fourteen to twelve by seventeen feet, with dirt floors, wooden chimneys, and sparse furnishings.[10] While he still planted tobacco on his Bedford County property, he had shifted to wheat at Monticello in 1790. The change stemmed from his expectation that European demand would grow in the relatively peaceful times and from his long-standing antipathy toward tobacco cultivation, which exhausted the soil.[11] When he inspected his tobacco fields closely in early 1794, Jefferson found them in worse condition than he had imagined.

Assuming the remedy was crop rotation, Jefferson developed a complicated seven-year system. He divided his approximately 1,200 acres in tillage into four farms of 280 acres, with each further divided into seven fields of 40 acres that would follow the rotation plan in succession. Beginning with one field, wheat would be planted the first year; corn and potatoes in the second; then peas, vetch (like peas, a leguminous plant), and wheat again; then red clover, usually, for the final two years.[12] The rotation would begin in the second year for the next field, and so on.

Despite his careful plans, Jefferson never managed to make the Monticello farm truly prosperous. For one, he was not in residence at Monticello for enough time over the twelve years between about 1797 and 1809 to directly oversee the operation. The climate also introduced complications, including occasional droughts, periods of torrential rains that flooded fields, uncommonly late frosts, a freakishly cold summer, and a windstorm that blew down much of the wheat and corn. His wheat was occasionally afflicted by a rust, or then a smut, and there was an infestation of Hessian flies. In fact, he gave up on wheat in 1798, again becoming a tobacco planter, in part due to rising prices for the latter crop.[13]

JEFFERSON KEPT APPRISED of new agricultural methods and technologies. For example, he was eager to get plans for a grain drill, a plow-type device pulled by a mule that could plant small grain. After repeated tries, he decided that one created by Thomas C. Martin worked well.[14] Jefferson tinkered with and improved the planter over the years. He was much more invested in obtaining a workable threshing machine for his wheat harvests. With his quantitative mind and his concern for efficiency, once Jefferson began cultivating wheat, he predictably focused on the time- and labor-intensive method of threshing that then prevailed. Since biblical times, harvested wheat had been placed on a hard surface or floor; then people with flails (sticks or handles with a series of smaller sticks attached to one end) struck the wheat repeatedly, or horses and cattle walked over it, their hoofs cracking open the hard shell, or chaff, that surrounded the edible part of the wheat seed. Then a fork-like tool was used to toss the trampled-upon wheat stalks and broken chaff into the air so the wind could blow them away—a process called winnowing—leaving the edible wheat grains on the floor.[15]

In 1786 a Scottish mechanical engineer named Andrew Meikle devised a bulky machine to perform this task. In 1792 Jefferson wrote to the American minister to England, Thomas Pinckney, asking him to procure a model of Meikle's threshing machine. In February 1793 Pinckney reported that he had found and inspected one and employed a skilled mechanic to make a scale model of it, which he sent later in the year to Jefferson. Once it arrived, Jefferson engaged a local mechanic to make a full-size replica, even as Jefferson experimented with its design and gearing until he developed a portable version that a wagon could carry from field to field. On August 22, 1796, Jefferson put his version to work in one of his fields, reporting that the horse-powered machine increased output a hundredfold.[16]

While perfecting his threshing machine, Jefferson tried, during his 1795 harvest, to rationalize the deployment of his slave workers in the field, carefully arranging their tasks by order of difficulty and assigning workers by gender and age. He determined that Great George, the trusted patriarch of his workforce, should travel among the workers on a single-mule cart with a grindstone so that he could keep the workers' scythes sharp.[17] This system, in tandem with the new portable threshing machine that obviated the transport of sheaves to the central threshing floor at Monticello, significantly improved the efficiency of the 1796 wheat harvest.

The agricultural invention for which Jefferson is most famous actually had little impact on American farming practices, perhaps because of the innate conservatism of most farmers. When traveling through France in 1788, he had noted with dismay how backward the plows were, pulled by oxen wearing collars rather than yokes.[18] As Jefferson pondered the problem, he realized that optimally the plow should have a point to cut through the grass; then, as it is pulled forward, it should peel the soil back and lay it over. Jefferson concluded that to meet the least resistance, a plow should have the shape of a curved wedge. As he developed the geometry of his design over the next couple of years, he relied on Newtonian calculus, which he had taught himself, to perfect the shape.[19] From his readings about agricultural practices, Jefferson realized the advantages of deeper plowing and hence the advantages of a plow that could be pulled more easily. Over the next few years Jefferson had a model made according to his specifications.

By 1794 he believed he had finished the design and had begun using a wooden version at Monticello to good effect. He wrote to one agricultural reformer that he had "imagined and executed a mould-board which may be mathematically demonstrated to be perfect, as far as perfection depends on mathematical principles."[20] His designs supposedly made it simple for craftsmen to duplicate his plow, for which Jefferson never sought a patent. He sent a detailed, heavily mathematical description of the design to another reformer, the Scottish Sir John Sinclair, in 1798; the American Philosophical Society published a version of this letter in 1799 in its *Transactions*, giving wide notice of the so-called mouldboard of least resistance.[21] It became acclaimed in England and France as well, prompting the Société d'Agriculture du Département de la Seine eventually to bestow upon Jefferson its gold medal in 1805.

PERHAPS JEFFERSON INTUITED in 1793, even before leaving Philadelphia, that despite advances in crop rotation and improvements in machinery, his farming operations alone would never return the profits necessary to both pay off his debts and support his extended family. In search of products that could be manufactured at Monticello, he first considered potash, or potassium carbonate, widely used in England in soap, glass, and various dyes and at the time a major US export. Potash was also valued as a fertilizer, since it added potassium, a nutrient, to the soil; Jefferson could not only sell it but use it in his fields. He knew about potash from his reading and from his time overseeing the US patent office, for the first patent issued, in 1790, had been to one Samuel Hopkins for an improved method of making the substance.[22]

At the time, potash was produced by leaching wood ashes in huge pots (hence "pot-ash"), then boiling the water until it evaporated. Jefferson's Farm Book includes detailed notes on the process, especially regarding the number of acres of trees required both to produce the ashes and to boil away the water, plus the equipment needed, particularly the huge pots or kettles. In one instance, he noted that the process would require 150 acres of trees a year. Because it would involve the destruction of his forested lands, as well as expensive equipment and certain rare skills, Jefferson finally abandoned the idea of potash production.[23] Another long-term industrial project, begun in the 1770s and extending on and off into his presidency, was the rebuilding of a gristmill on the Rivanna that a fierce rainstorm had washed away in 1771. Thousands of hours of slave labor went into this effort, which resulted in, among other things, a long feeder canal to minimize the danger of future floods. For decades, however, this project represented only an expense, not a money maker or a community asset.[24]

Jefferson next turned to producing nails, a decision made sometime in 1793 that led to his initial order of nail rod just weeks before leaving office. He had, when touring England with John Adams in 1786, noted village nail-making shops and probably realized then that he could replicate the relatively small-scale manufacturing process in rural Virginia.[25] Here was a potential source of income—there was a steady demand for nails—that would conveniently employ slave boys between the ages of ten and sixteen; Jefferson imagined that work in his nailery would provide training in the skills and discipline that would enable the very best young workers to move into other skilled jobs at Monticello. Indeed, one of the boys, Joe Fossett, would later become the estate's chief blacksmith; others became carpenters, coopers, the head gardener at Monticello, and Jefferson's butler.[26] (Girls of the same age were put to the spinning wheel.)

In the first months of 1794 Jefferson moved the former blacksmith shop from Shadwell to Mulberry Row, on the uppermost roundabout road between the main house at Monticello and his extensive gardens. On April 29 forty bundles of nail rod arrived from Philadelphia. Jefferson must have already chosen which young slaves would work in the nailery and given them some preliminary training, because on May 21 he made his first delivery of finished eight- and ten-penny nails (two and three inches in length, respectively).[27] Jefferson quickly became almost obsessed with his nailery.[28]

Initially boasting one forge and soon two, the smoky, noisy nailery housed ten or a dozen boys, who cut and hammered the rods into the proper shape and length. Jefferson kept detailed records on wastage, the number of nails made daily by each worker, the nails produced per pound of nail rod, and so on. He hoped to incentivize the young slaves through praise, rewards (new clothes), and more generous rations of food.[29] George Granger, the slave who supervised the operation, himself received one-sixth of the annual profits. Jefferson, who generally considered himself a kind master, also gave his slaves a modicum of autonomy.[30] Outside the nailery, too, he similarly granted slaves more independence and attempted to incentivize them with rewards. In his absence several of his overseers did, however, whip his slaves, despite Jefferson's theoretical opposition to the practice.[31]

Given the violent nature of white society at the time—teachers cruelly whipped schoolboys, husbands could legally flog their wives, indentured servants were often harshly punished, and soldiers and sailors could receive a shocking number of lashes—contemporaries may have viewed the whipping of slaves as more benign than we today can understand. At the same time, Jefferson rarely sold slaves, finding the practice shameful, and he made an effort not to separate mothers from their small children, which he believed a paramount evil.[32] He only sold his slaves out of what he considered economic necessity.

For two years the nailery was the financial success Jefferson had hoped it would be, bringing in more than enough revenue to pay the total food bills for Monticello. But by early 1796 British importers began to force Richmond merchants to "decline" nails from domestic manufacturers like Jefferson—further evidence, as if he needed it, of how British domination of American trade harmed the nation's economy in general and crippled small, local industries.[33] Thereafter Jefferson had to retail his nails himself, making private deals with local stores in nearby towns and across the mountains in the valley. He distributed nail cards showing his wares and their prices, but the nailery, though it continued as a modest source of revenue for about two decades, never again returned the profits it had in those first two years.

To a degree perhaps unusual for a man so accomplished and possessing such a wide range of interests, Jefferson was decidedly domestic. Writing to an old friend in late 1795, he described himself in the "retirement I doat on, living like an Antediluvian patriarch among my children and grand children, and tilling my soil."[34] He loved having family nearby; he treasured the hours he could spend in reading and scholarship; he enjoyed riding about his mountain property and inspecting everything, from budding flowers and the clamorous nailery to construction on Monticello. Nothing brought him more pleasure than the company of his daughters and his grandchildren, and his hospitality extended to any of his kin and the many visitors who had reason to come to Monticello (and often stayed for weeks). Jefferson once recorded that he had so much company that "every corner of every room has been occupied."[35]

Martha, her husband, and two children often stayed at Monticello, and Maria still lived at the estate. Jefferson was a homebody, ranging no farther than ten miles from Monticello for the first three years of his retirement, with the exception of one trip to Richmond. He avoided travel partly due to a health issue that arose in early September 1794—Jefferson always called it rheumatism, but it was surely osteoarthritis. When he learned that September from Secretary of State Edmund Randolph that President George Washington wanted to appoint him a special envoy to Spain, Jefferson, in turning down the request for personal reasons, explained his delayed reply by saying he had been in bed for ten days "in constant torment." Two months later he wrote Randolph, "I am still confined in a great measure by the remains of my rheumatism, being unable to go out, either on horseback or in a carriage, but in a walk, and small distances."[36]

Jefferson took great interest in his two grandchildren, Anne and toddler Thomas Jefferson, always called Jeff. After Thomas Mann Randolph Jr. came down with a mysterious malady in 1794—apparently a form of depression—and decided he needed to travel for his health, Jefferson welcomed Martha and the children for extended visits to Monticello. The following year, Martha, her husband, and baby Ellen returned to their own plantation, Varina, for several months, leaving Anne and little Jeff at Monticello. Jefferson loved the children, played with them, and informed their mother of their antics.[37] Of course, Maria served as a nanny, and slave women provided substantial assistance, so Jefferson himself performed little or no actual child care.

Barely six months later, when Martha, her husband Tom, and infant Ellen were on their way to the Sweet Springs in western Virginia for Tom's health, the baby suddenly died of unknown causes. The parents—oddly—continued on but had the baby sent back to Monticello for burial. Jefferson recorded paying a minister $2 "for reading service" over her grave.[38] Tragedy, frequently in the form of loved ones dying young and unexpectedly, haunted Jefferson, spreading personal sadness across the life of this congenitally optimistic man.

Tom's depression would prove another perennial concern, eventually disabling him both physically and emotionally. Even in the early stages, his deteriorating condition greatly worried Jefferson, who gently offered words of encouragement. In the summer of 1794 Jefferson had written,

Thomas Mann Randolph Jr.
Unsigned and undated portrait.
Source: Virginia Historical Society. Used by permission.

"We are sincerely anxious about the state of your health. . . . I wish it's form were more determinate, so that it's character should be precisely known."[39] Jefferson felt a father's affection for his son-in-law, and neither he nor Martha could foresee that Tom's difficulties would result in the breakdown of their marriage. Members of Tom's extended family had significant problems of their own—including, possibly, incest, resulting in a stillborn infant—and these traumas also entered Jefferson's orbit of concern.[40] In 1808 Martha mentioned "the Randolph character" in worrying about the behavior of her son Jeff, and years later one of her daughters, remarking on the squabbling of her two youngest siblings, referred to "the Randolph" in them.[41]

No doubt Jefferson's recognition of his son-in-law's problematical nature contributed to his pleasure when, in September 1796, John Wayles

Eppes asked him for eighteen-year-old Maria's hand. Maria had played with John in his parents' home while she was living with the Eppeses during the first two years of her father's time in France, and they had been close almost their entire lives. Jefferson also knew John well and loved him as a son. (A month after this good news, there was still more: Martha gave birth to another healthy daughter, whom she named Ellen Wayles Randolph after the baby who had died two years before.) Once a date for the wedding was picked, Jefferson could hardly control his enthusiasm, writing to Maria, "I learn, my dear M. with inexpressible pleasure that an union of sentiment is likely to bring on an union of destiny between yourself and a person for whom I have the highest esteem. . . . I deem the composition of my family the most precious of all the kindnesses of fortune."[42] Maria and John would marry four months later on October 13, 1797, at Monticello.[43]

LIKE MOST SOUTHERN planters, Jefferson euphemistically referred to his slave workforce as family, and at Monticello his use of the word carried a strong element of truth. It was common knowledge that Betty Hemings, the matriarch of the Hemings family, had been the concubine of John Wayles, the father of Jefferson's wife. Betty and all her children—the half brothers and sisters of Martha Wayles Skelton Jefferson—lived at Monticello in privileged positions and were never, as a rule, whipped. Jefferson's favorite male slaves, Bob and James Hemings, had been with him in Philadelphia and France. And then there was Sally, the young, strikingly attractive Hemings daughter to whom Jefferson had become closely attached in Paris. That she decided to return to Monticello with Jefferson rather than remain in Paris suggests that she found him attractive too.

According to Hemings family lore, Sally was pregnant when she returned from Paris with Jefferson in 1789, but she might not have been showing. Although we have no incontrovertible evidence that she was pregnant, scholars today generally presume that she was but that the baby, born in 1790, did not survive.[44] When Jefferson left Monticello in February of that year to begin his term as secretary of state, Sally stayed in Virginia. She never joined him in either New York or Philadelphia, though not because slavery was illegal in both states: Jefferson's household included other slaves in both cities. We cannot know whether their relationship cooled after the return from France, or had not yet fully developed, or—more likely—Jefferson was wary of drawing attention to their attachment.

The best evidence suggests that after Jefferson retired from the State Department and returned permanently—or so he thought—to Monticello, Sally became again a fixed presence in his life.

That Jefferson remained on good terms with the other members of the extensive Hemings clan suggests that the relationship with Sally was consensual, founded on shared tenderness and love, even though they apparently both worked to keep it hidden from Jefferson's white family. Could they have really done so, or did family members, including Jefferson's daughters, simply fail or refuse to acknowledge it? Regardless, we do know for certain that Sally gave birth in 1795 to a daughter, Harriet, and then in 1798 to a son, Beverley. She went on to have a total of six children (one of whom died in infancy), and Jefferson was at Monticello approximately nine months before each birth. When he had not been there regularly, from 1790 to early 1794, Sally bore no children. While Jefferson did not treat her children as he did his white daughters and grandchildren, he did eventually see to it that all were freed from bondage. The sexual attraction between Jefferson and Hemings was likely mutual, to a degree, despite the differences in education and power. This would not have been unusual, and certainly in Charlottesville and the rest of the antebellum South, such unequal interracial relationships existed and could last for decades.[45] By law such couples could not marry, and the etiquette of the time required that the relationship—particularly for public men—be kept secret or, at the very least, quiet. Jefferson was nothing if not discreet.

If he ever felt a glimmer of guilt over their relationship, he might have found a medical justification to assuage his conscience. While Jefferson had a history of migraine headaches and occasional gastrointestinal problems, he had been quite healthy for his first fifty years, but in 1794, shortly after he returned to Monticello, he began to suffer periodically from what he called rheumatism, which incapacitated him for weeks at a time and caused him to fear that he did not have much longer to live.[46] The ailment become chronic. He wrote to his closest friend Madison that his "health [was] entirely broken down within the last eight months": "my age requires that I should place my affairs in a clear state; these are sound if taken care of, but capable of considerable dangers if longer neglected."[47] He had already lived three years longer than his father, and his childhood friend Thomas Mann Randolph (father of his son-in-law) had died in 1793 just before his fifty-second birthday. Jefferson did have in his library a number of medical books on which he often based his lifestyle and habits.[48] For example, he drank wine moderately (diluting it with water), ate meat sparingly, and exercised frequently, either by walking or riding a horse, although his "rheumatism" prevented jogging any more. He possessed, in the original French, the collected works of a Swiss medical writer, Samuel Auguste David Tissot, which he had purchased in Paris in 1788, along with a one-volume English translation of Tissot's well-known *Advice to the People*.[49] After reading Tissot Jefferson adopted the practice of bathing his feet in cold water every morning.

Tissot developed a bizarre theory that scholarly men who spent long hours at their desks, poring over their books, and lived according to a strict routine and discipline were prone to intellectual exhaustion related to an excessive buildup or retention of the so-called seminal fluid. For married men the cure was obvious. For the unmarried, preferable to masturbation was a moderate dose of sexual intercourse, ideally with a younger woman. Supposedly the health benefits were superior if the woman was attractive, and Tissot also theorized that the man's seminal fluid was healthy for the female recipient as well.[50] Jefferson could well have concluded that his intimacy with Sally not only brought physical and emotional pleasure but was both natural and prophylactic. Yet clearly he needed no medical tome to recognize his interest in her. Their covert relationship would continue until his death more than three decades later.

ON THE EVE OF HIS retirement, Jefferson had written a letter to one of his longtime women friends in which he discussed his goals for the near future. He was about "to be liberated from the hated occupations of politics," explaining, among other things, "I have my house to build."[51] The rebuilding and expansion of Monticello ended up taking fifteen years, in large part because Jefferson would be called away again. Another reason was that he invested money first in his nailery and his new crop-rotation system, and so proceeded, with the house, in a pay-as-you-go mode. For many years Monticello was under perpetual construction, a major inconvenience for its inhabitants. On one occasion, Maria fell through the uncompleted flooring into the basement, luckily incurring only minor injuries.[52]

When originally designing Monticello, Jefferson taught himself architecture by studying the illustrative plates in books, especially those depicting the buildings of the sixteenth-century Italian architect Andrea Palladio. The resulting house was a two-story Palladian structure, with a two-story portico planned for the east front. He came back to this home from Paris in late 1789 but brought with him vastly expanded architectural knowledge and sophistication. As the visiting Duc de La Rochefoucauld-Liancourt wrote about Monticello in 1796, "The taste and arts of Europe have been consulted in the formation of its plan."[53] Along with a fresh appreciation of classical buildings, Jefferson had become enthralled with the great glass-and-wooden dome over the Halle aux Bleds, the grain market of Paris, and the low, horizontal palace under construction, the Hôtel de Salm, with its flattened central dome. He also discovered oval and octagonal rooms, bedrooms with beds in small niches, and the uses of skylights. Moreover, he noted that modern homes were no longer three or four stories high, appropriate as that might have been on crowded city streets. Rather, as he wrote to Senator John Brown of Kentucky, now "all the new and good houses are of a single story. That is of the height of 16. or 18. f. generally, and the whole of it given to the rooms of entertainment; but in the parts where there are bedrooms they have two [tiers] of them of from 8. to 10 f. high each, with a small private staircase. By these means great staircases are avoided, which are expensive and occupy a space which would make a good room in every story."[54] These architectural principles shaped his thought as he mulled, in Paris and later Philadelphia, the renovation of Monticello. By 1794, too, with his growing family and frequent visitors, he realized he needed a larger home.

While he kept the original siting of Monticello unchanged, he understood that to expand the house he would have to tear down much of the existing structure, widen the foundations, and then launch the new construction. He spent much of 1794 and 1795 gathering the stones, bricks, wooden beams, and other materials he deemed necessary for the project, finally writing to his oldest daughter in February 1796, "We are just beginning our demolitions." He had discovered "that they will be very troublesome" because of "the rotten state in which we found some of our timbers."[55] Once begun, construction creeped along. Jefferson met with continual difficulties in finding and retaining the best craftsmen; then starting in 1797, he was increasingly away, first in Philadelphia and, after 1800, in Washington, DC, which generated repeated delays. As he explained, the workmen "must suspend their works during my absence, as I am my own [architect], and my plan too little like what they have seen to trust them with it's execution in my absence."[56]

Monticello was chaos; for months on end much of the house had no roof. Jefferson wrote in the spring of 1796, "We shall this summer . . . live under the tent of heaven."[57] The experience must have tried the patience even of Jefferson, who of course loved designing and building, and driven the others on the estate almost mad. As one disgruntled visitor remarked in 1802, Jefferson "is a very long time maturing his projects," adding there was both "something grand & awful in the situation" of the apparently eternal construction.[58] As Jefferson had warned an earlier visitor, "The noise, confusion and discomfort of the scene will require all your philosophy and patience."[59] The result, when substantially finished in 1809, would be the home that still stands today.[60]

The three main first-floor rooms—the parlor, the dining room, and Jefferson's bedroom—had the high ceilings then the fashion in Paris. Narrow, twenty-four-inch stairways led to a mezzanine level of small bedrooms, then further up to a third story. Ingeniously designed, the house appeared, from the exterior, to be one story tall, but the large windows actually extended to the second-floor bedrooms, although on that mezzanine level they only reached four feet up from the floor. The three third-floor bedrooms had tiny octagonal windows hidden from view by the balustrade. Throughout, beds were tucked into alcoves, both for added wintertime warmth and to save space. A low dome, designed in the style of the Halle aux Bleds (but without the glass between the beams), graced the west side of the home, but the beautiful room directly below the dome, not visible from the first floor, never found a formal use; probably the grandchildren used it for a playroom. Throughout the house were all manner of gadgets combining utility, efficiency, and beauty: dumbwaiters built into the sides of the dining room fireplace; a rotating serving door whereby slaves could turn plates of food into the dining room; double glass doors leading from the east hall into the parlor that open as one; a weather vane atop the east porch whose directional pointer can be read from below; a seven-day clock in the entrance hall whose cannon-ball-size weights extended through a hole in the floor; niches in the outside brick walls that allow insertion of scaffolding to give painters easy access to the upper woodwork; an indoor toilet in Jefferson's bedroom with a bucket-and-chain conveyor system connected to an underground tunnel to remove waste. The completed house is a spectacular collage of architectural styles that nevertheless evince a skilled eye for proportion and beauty. More than the home of any other American political leader, Monticello embodies the central aspects of its owner's personality, preferences, and infatuations.

IN THE FIRST MONTHS of his retirement, Jefferson appeared as happy as he had anticipated he would be. He enjoyed the challenge of reforming his agricultural operations, he loved having his family members—especially the grandchildren—around, he looked forward to rebuilding his home to the standards of the latest architectural fashions, he relished his library, he took pleasure in riding his horse around his fields, humming and singing softly to himself as he rode, and he found recreation in such time-honored rural sports as fishing and hunting.[61] And all the while he professed relief at being away from the tussle and turmoil of national politics.

But this seemingly idyllic situation included multitudes of frustrations and delays; family, financial, and health worries; and likely periods of loneliness, far as he was from his close political colleagues. Some years later he wrote his younger daughter Maria, trying to convince her to visit him more often at Monticello. He counseled against the evils of social isolation, referring to his early retirement days after leaving the State Department. "From 1793. to 1797. I remained closely at home, saw none but those who came there, and at length became very sensible of the ill effect it had upon my mind, and of it's direct & irresistible tendency to render me unfit for society, & uneasy when necessarily engaged in it. I felt enough of the effect of withdrawing from the world then, to see that it led to an antisocial & misanthropic state of mind, which severely punishes him who gives in to it."[62] While this letter may contain some element of retrospective justification, Jefferson very likely came to realize the costs of his relative isolation. He gradually began to reengage with the world of politics, perhaps without sensing where this could lead.

Reports of events across the nation and the world reached him through letters and greatly concerned him. Farmers in places like western Pennsylvania, upset by the excise tax on whiskey, which hurt their only exportable product, were ramping up their protests. Two democratic societies in western counties supported the movement, which came to be called the Whiskey Rebellion. Alexander Hamilton urged Washington into action, with the result that in August 1794, the president had called for the raising of a militia. Weeks later Washington headed a military force of almost 13,000—an army larger than any he had commanded during the American Revolution—and with Hamilton at his side began moving west. The farmers' protest quickly dissolved, and no pitched battles took place. Washington was on the scene only briefly, but Hamilton, relishing the moment, stayed in the region. Because fully formed political parties that could serve as the focus of political opposition did not yet truly exist, Washington saw the attacks on administration policy as personal assaults on himself and the current form of government—hence what Jefferson considered his overreaction.

The use of military force to quell a public protest and Washington's November 19 address to Congress on the dangers the protest had represented—he harshly attacked the democratic societies for fomenting opposition—dismayed Madison and the Republican partisans.[63] Jefferson was incensed.[64] In his view, the brazen attempt to suppress freedom of assembly and expression epitomized the problems facing the nation. He wrote Madison at the end of the year, "The denunciation of the democratic societies is one of the extraordinary acts of boldness of which we have seen so many from the faction of the Monocrats."[65]

On the very day that Washington addressed Congress, special envoy John Jay had signed a treaty with England ostensibly to head off a possible war between the two nations. The British agreed to withdraw from northwestern posts and to refer to a commission the ongoing dispute over payment of prerevolutionary American debts to British claimants—irked by these unpaid debts British authorities used them as an excuse not to fulfill all the obligations of the prior treaty. But the treaty did not address the issue of southern slaves taken by the British during the Revolutionary War—whom the southern states wanted returned—and allowed US merchants only very limited commercial access to West Indian ports. When its provisions became known in the United States after March 1795, opposition exploded.[66] Many Republicans believed Jay had sacrificed southern and western interests for those of the Northeast. Jefferson found himself caught up in the controversy, especially after Hamilton began publishing article after slashing article under the pseudonym "Camillus."[67] The Senate debates over the treaty were unusually contentious, and after that body approved it on June 24, 1795, the Republicans in the House of Representatives tried to negate it by refusing to authorize the funds necessary to put it into effect. The battle raged for months, into 1796.

From remote Monticello, Jefferson made clear that he shared the opinions of Madison and other Republican leaders. He remained hopeful, as he wrote in November 1795, that "the popular branch of our legislature will disapprove of it, and thus rid us of this infamous act, which is really nothing more than a treaty of alliance between England and the Anglomen of this country against the legislature and people of the United States."[68] Jefferson believed that the great majority of Americans sided with the Republican position.[69] In part to stay abreast of the raging political storms, Jefferson subscribed to the *Philadelphia Aurora* at the end of the year, evidence that he was becoming more involved with events beyond his little mountain.

The first American political parties had emerged in rudimentary form, though it would take several years for them to mature. Consistent subscription to either the administration or anti-administration position primarily took place in either the Senate or the House, not yet on the hustings across the nation.[70] Madison was the clear political leader of the Republicans, although Hamilton and his supporters—the Federalists—believed that Jefferson directed all oppositional activities from behind the scenes. Yet in every significant way, Madison headed the Republican Party; throughout 1796, as the political cauldron boiled, personal and domestic matters preoccupied Jefferson at Monticello. While Madison remained in the thick of the political process—pondering, for example, who might succeed Washington as president, assuming he would not seek another term—he and others purposely did not keep Jefferson apprised of their political machinations.

ONE OF JEFFERSON'S more local preoccupations in this time resulted from an unsolicited letter from John Stuart of Greenbrier County in April 1796. Stuart had served in the Virginia House of Delegates during the revolution and knew of Jefferson's scientific interest in the fauna of America, past and present. He sent Jefferson some "Bones of a Tremendious animal of the Clawed kind lately found in a Cave by some Saltpetre manufacturers about five miles from my house." He reported that some previously found bones had been lost, including a claw even larger, but hoped the ones he was enclosing would "afford you some amusements."[71] Excited by the package, Jefferson wrote about its contents both to his friend Archibald Stuart in Staunton and also to John Stuart himself, saying to the latter, "This animal is certainly hitherto unknown, and seems, from the dimensions of the bones, to have the same preeminence over the lion, which the big Buffalo or Mammoth has over the elephant. They furnish a victorious fact against the idle dreams of some European philosophers who pretend that animal nature in the new world is a degeneracy from that of the old."[72]

Over the next few months Jefferson corresponded widely about the bones and carefully studied comparable finds described in works of natural history. He reported to his astronomer friend David Rittenhouse in Philadelphia that given the size of some of the bones sent to him, their "bulk entitles it [the leg bone] to give our animal the name of the Great-claw, or Megalonyx."[73] Jefferson assumed he was examining the claw of a large lionlike creature. Ten days later another shipment of bones arrived from John Stuart, who related an anecdote, in his accompanying missive, that some hunters of the previous generation had one night heard the terrible roaring of some mysterious animal that frightened even their dogs; Stuart thought it possible this was the beast itself.[74] Archibald Stuart wrote Jefferson that there were Indian carvings on a rock near him depicting giant animals that had presumably gone extinct. Later that fall Jefferson, thanking John Stuart for additional bones, reported that he could not "help believing that this animal as well as the Mammoth are still existing."[75] The American Philosophical Society subsequently published Jefferson's "Memoir on the Discovery of Certain Bones of a Quadruped of the Clawed Kind in the Western Parts of Virginia" in its *Transactions* in early 1799.[76]

ON SEPTEMBER 15, 1796, a letter arrived at Monticello, though it brought no old bones and posited not a single naturalist theory. Its author, William Cocke, had served with Jefferson in the Virginia House of Delegates in 1777 and 1778 but had since lived in Kentucky and, later, Tennessee. Cocke announced to Jefferson that he had the pleasure of informing him that the "people of this State [Tennessee], of every description, express a wish that you should be the next President of the United States, and Mr. Burr, Vice President."[77] The letter came as a total surprise, and Jefferson apparently took it as an innocent compliment. He replied cordially six weeks later, stating that he did not wish to leave his retirement.[78]

Jefferson appeared to devote no more thought to this exchange, unaware that Madison and others were pressing to have electors chosen or elected in the various states, who would cast their votes for Jefferson in the upcoming presidential election (determined then by the electoral college, not the popular vote). Due to pressure from Hamilton, who wanted to forestall the efforts of other possible candidates—aside from his preferred candidate, Thomas Pinckney, whom he supported over John Adams—to garner support, Washington had waited until September 17 to issue his Farewell Address. Until its publication two days later in the Philadelphia press, the supporters of all would-be candidates had hesitated to publicly declare themselves out of deference to the nation's first president. Neither Madison nor any of his operatives ever mentioned to Jefferson their plans; in fact, Madison took care not to visit Monticello over the summer of 1796 so as to avoid any possible discussion of the topic.[79] Jefferson was obviously aware that an election was in the offing, and although he assumed that Adams would probably be elected president, he had no idea who would be his vice president. (At the time, there was no joint ticket; the president and vice president were elected separately.) Then he received a letter from Madison on December 5—the first from his closest political confidant in more than six months—reporting, "It is not possible yet to calculate with any degree of certainty whether you are to be left by the Electors to enjoy the repose to which you are so much attached, or are to be summoned to the arduous trust which depends on their allotment." Madison made clear that in the eyes of most Americans, the "principals" in the election were Adams and Jefferson.[80] Five days later Madison wrote a surprised Jefferson, "You must reconcile yourself to the secondary as well as the primary station, if that should be your lot," though the electoral results were still up in the air.[81]

Jefferson had already written Madison of his fond wish that Madison himself would stand for the election, but since he had not, Jefferson replied, "There is nothing I so anxiously hope as that my name may come out either second or third. These would be indifferent to me; as the last would leave me at home the whole year, and the other two thirds of it." He announced his wish, should he and Adams receive the same number of electoral votes: "I pray you and authorize you fully to solicit on my behalf that Mr. Adams may be preferred. He has always been my senior from the commencement of our public life, and the expression of the public will being equal, this circumstance ought to give him the preference."[82] Madison wrote additional letters on December 19 and December 25, when he still could not absolutely confirm the election results, although it looked to him as though Jefferson had been elected vice president. Madison, fearful Jefferson might decline the position, urged, "It seems *essential* that you should not refuse the station which is likely to be your lot." He was unaware that Jefferson had no intention of rejecting the public will.[83]

Days later the results were clear: Jefferson had indeed been chosen as vice president. He happily wrote to Madison, "I can particularly have no feelings which would revolt at a secondary position to Mr. Adams." Jefferson could not imagine that his new position would be onerous; his only constitutionally prescribed duty was to preside over the Senate. Moreover, he was pleased that Adams's election would serve as "perhaps the only sure barrier against Hamilton's getting in."[84] On January 21, he learned that he had also just been selected as the next president of the American Philosophical Society; in accepting the honor, he called it "the most flattering incident of my life." Three months later, on March 3, that position was made official, and the next day, he took the oath of office as vice president.[85] In this unexpected way, Jefferson's retirement came to an end. He could little anticipate, in early 1797, that more than a decade of public office lay ahead of him.

18

The Vice Presidency

JEFFERSON WAS RELIEVED to have been elected vice president instead of president. He wrote a few months after the fact that while the vice presidency was "honorable and easy," the presidency was "but a splendid misery."[1] This sentiment underlay his December letter to James Madison, urging him, in case of a tie, to work for John Adams's election as president. Madison later showed the letter to a select few to indicate Jefferson's cooperative spirit. Jefferson naturally wanted to reach out to Adams more directly. In his study in Monticello on December 28, 1796, when the election results seemed clearer, he had drafted a letter to his old colleague in France seeking to minimize their personal differences and wish Adams good luck in his new office.[2]

Perhaps sensing that the initial draft might be too effusive, Jefferson sent it to Madison first. Madison decided not to forward the letter, writing Jefferson that it might annoy the notably vain and "ticklish" Adams and even embarrass Jefferson's own supporters, should significant differences arise between the Republicans and Adams's policies. Moreover, those who had worked hard on Jefferson's candidacy would likely neither understand nor appreciate his overtures of friendship toward Adams. Madison added that he knew from other sources that Adams was already aware of Jefferson's collegial intentions, so no further action was needed.[3]

Preparing once more to assume public office, Jefferson hurriedly addressed a series of business issues. He let certain friends know that he required no formal notification of his election; the regular mails would suffice. He explained to Madison that he intended to limit his work to vice presidential duties set out in the Constitution—namely, presiding over the Senate. Recalling the bitter squabbles in Washington's administration, Jefferson made clear that "both duty and inclination" "shut the door" to the notion that he would participate as much as he had as secretary of state.[4] He wrote his old teacher George Wythe that he had become "entirely rusty in the Parliamentary rules of procedure" and asked him to send any notes he might have on how best to proceed.[5] (Wythe—then seventy years old—replied that he no longer possessed the relevant memorandum he had once prepared and had in fact forgotten what he once knew about the subject.[6])

Jefferson was optimistic about the approaching political season. He wrote James Sullivan, a supporter in Boston, that under the government created by the Constitution—blending aspects of monarchical and republican forms—the citizenry would naturally divide itself, to some extent, into two groups. Jefferson remained as confident as always that "the great mass is republican." He believed the popularity of the monarchical form of government stemmed from the "preponderant popularity of a particular great character." (Of course Jefferson saw a would-be monarchist lurking behind every bush.) But now that George Washington had retired and Alexander Hamilton had retreated to private life, he had "no doubt we shall see a pretty rapid return of general harmony, and our citizens moving in phalanx in the paths of regular liberty, order, and a sacro-sanct adherence to the constitution . . . [provided] a war with France can be avoided."[7] Jefferson held that patience and moderation, especially in foreign policy, would soon bring about the ascendancy of republicanism.

Jefferson left Monticello on February 20, 1797, and appeared in Philadelphia on March 2, two days before the inauguration. The evening of his arrival he made a cordial visit to Adams, and the next morning Adams returned the favor, visiting Jefferson at the Madisons'. Finding Jefferson alone, Adams admitted to anxiety about relations with France, a concern occasioned by news that France—still rankled by the 1794 Jay Treaty—had refused to accept Charles Cotesworth Pinckney as the American ambassador. Adams, who fervently wished to maintain peaceful relations, had initially imagined sending Jefferson on a special mission to Paris, although he assumed this would be inappropriate given the vice president elect's duties in the Senate. Jefferson, who had no desire to endure another ocean voyage, agreed. Adams then expressed his hope of appointing a three-person commission: moderate Elbridge Gerry of Massachusetts and James Madison would join Pinckney in Paris. Jefferson doubted Madison would accept, but Adams was insistent. Jefferson agreed to take up the issue with Madison, and with that, the brief meeting ended.[8]

Jefferson's inauguration, conducted separately from Adams's, took place on Saturday morning, May 4, at Congress Hall, in the Senate's upper chamber, with neither Washington nor Adams present. Once officially in office, Jefferson promptly swore in eight newly elected senators, then gave a brief address. He opened by apologizing for his incomplete knowledge of parliamentary procedure but promised to preside over the business of the Senate with impartiality. Given the tenor of the nation's politics, he declared, "with the greatest truth," his "zealous attachment to the constitution of the United States," proclaiming "the Union of these states as the first of blessings, and as the first of duties the preservation of that constitution which secures it." Jefferson closed by stating his hope that some unforeseen calamity would not thrust him into the presidency and, finally, with a brief tribute to George Washington.[9]

With these ceremonies completed, Jefferson led the senators downstairs to the Senate's lower chamber, where a small assembly of dignitaries had gathered. Washington, tall and erect and dressed in formal black, entered to sustained applause, followed by the short and portly Adams, attired in a pearl-colored suit, a ceremonial sword on his side. Jefferson, dressed in a long, blue frock coat and almost as tall as Washington, entered next. Both Washington and Adams had heavily powdered their hair; Jefferson had tied his lightly powdered hair in a queue with a black ribbon. It was the last time these three giants shared a stage. Before taking his oath, Adams gave an inaugural speech so moderate and balanced in tone that it pleased the Republicans as much as it provoked the High Federalists (those whose allegiance was to Hamilton) in the audience. Adams implied that he wanted to avoid war with France and unite the nation. His remarks made it seem that a relatively short spasm of partisanship had passed. Jefferson would write his son-in-law a week later, concerning France, "I hope and believe that the present administration will adopt friendly arrangements."[10]

But there would be no going back. Two days after the inauguration, Adams and Jefferson dined with Washington, and as the two left together, Jefferson reported that Madison had declined to go to France. Adams, embarrassed, said that Madison's response was immaterial; on broaching the idea with his cabinet—all carryovers from the previous administration and more loyal to Hamilton than to him—Adams had encountered unexpected opposition. According to Jefferson's private note on the matter, Adams "never after that said one word on the subject, or ever consulted me as to any measures of the government."[11] At the time of their morning meeting at the Madisons', Adams may not have recognized the level of Hamilton's influence in his administration, but he did soon enough.

Jefferson spent only a few more days in Philadelphia, arranging his finances with a private banker, attending a meeting of the American Philosophical Society and a farewell banquet for Washington, and, interested as always in rare animals and freaks of nature, viewing an elk as well as the first Bengal elephant exhibited in America. Jefferson left the capital city on March 13 for the weeklong trip back to Monticello.[12] He had expected to remain there until the new Congress convened in December, but soon Adams received confirmation that the French Directory had formally rejected Pinckney and proclaimed harsh decrees against American commerce. Adams called Congress into special session to deal with the expanding crisis.[13] Jefferson returned to Philadelphia on May 11, but not before suddenly becoming aware of another source of inflamed passions. This time the blame fell squarely on him.

MORE THAN A YEAR earlier, amid the controversy over the Jay Treaty, Jefferson had written a personal letter to an old friend and former neighbor, Philip Mazzei, in Italy. Much of the letter discussed family and mutual friends. But in its long middle paragraph, he had deplored the state of American politics, referring to the rise of an "Anglican, monarchical and aristocratical party," in place of the former "noble love of liberty and republican government," whose adherents hoped to "draw over" the nation the "substance, as they have already done the forms, of the British government." This was boilerplate Republican language. But Jefferson then turned personal, and in only a slightly veiled reference to Washington, whom he believed Hamilton had misled, Jefferson wrote, "It would give you a fever were I to name to you the apostates who have gone over to these heresies, men who were Samsons in the field and Solomons in the council, but who have had their heads shorn by the harlot England."[14] Jefferson, who would never have spoken so derisively of Washington in public, meant this as a most private comment.

In a stunning breach of discretion and an act of astonishingly bad judgment, Mazzei made copies of that single paragraph and shared them with friends. Somehow the paragraph, sloppily translated into French, got into the hands of a Paris newspaper editor, who, on January 25, 1797, published it in the *Gazette nationale ou le moniteur universel*. Three months later a US merchant brought a copy of the incriminating issue to New York City and passed it on to Noah Webster, editor of New York's *Minerva*, who promptly had it translated back into English and published in the May 2 edition of his newspaper. Within days it was reprinted up and down the Northeast, including in William Cobbett's highly influential *Porcupine's Gazette.* Jefferson first became aware of the breach while reading a newspaper on May 9, on his way to Philadelphia. This was exactly the ammunition the High Federalists needed to attack Jefferson as a pro-French traitor to America, a fanatical Jacobin with the audacity to smear the sacred name and reputation of George Washington. Any possibility that a calmer political climate would prevail vanished. For the next few months—and, later, during the campaign of 1800—Jefferson endured vicious attacks in language that knew no moderation. He had made a colossal blunder.

The Hamiltonians' suspicions that Jefferson was the mastermind of pro-French radical opposition to their policies seemed proven beyond a doubt, and in their minds his private statement to Mazzei revealed as fraudulent his carefully constructed personae as the mild-mannered, philosophically inspired spokesman of high principles.[15] They considered him and his supporters a threat to the nation. Jefferson never referred to the letter—neither denying authorship nor attempting to explain it—but it would haunt him and his reputation. The Federalists took his silence as an admission of guilt, and in the controversy that soon arose over events in France, Jefferson found himself thrust, against his will, into the role of leader of the opposition to administration policies. In an ironic twist, Jefferson, almost completely uninvolved in his own election in 1796, now found himself supplanting Madison as leader of the Republican Party.

Within two days of arriving in Philadelphia in May 1797, he sent a shrewd letter to Elbridge Gerry of Massachusetts, a moderate Federalist who claimed friendship with both Jefferson and Adams. After commending Gerry for his kind feelings for the president and saying that he too esteemed Adams, Jefferson warned that he expected "nothing will be left untried to alienate him [Adams] from me. These machinations will proceed from the Hamiltonians by whom he is surrounded, and who are only a little less hostile to him than to me."[16] Jefferson's sensitive political antennae had perceived the coming fights within the administration. He imagined his enemies suspected he would try to influence Adams's policies, but Jefferson told Gerry—expecting him to share the letter's contents—that the Federalists would soon learn that he considered his "office as constitutionally confined to legislative functions."[17] Subtly reinforcing Gerry's own policy views, Jefferson confided, "I do sincerely wish with you that we

could take our stand on a ground perfectly neutral and independent towards all nations . . . [and] with respect to the English and French particularly."[18] He went on to complain of the powerful merchant class's
influence on administration policy, saying, among other things, that this
group also "possess[ed] our printing presses" and hence had inordinate
and unhealthy power over public opinion.[19] But Jefferson nonetheless
made clear his belief that the good sense of the citizenry would eventually
triumph.[20]

SHORTLY AFTER ADAMS took office, Jefferson learned that the French
Directory had not only rejected Pinckney but also a key provision of its
1778 treaty with the United States. France would henceforth treat US
ships carrying British goods not as neutral but rather as liable to seizure.
Adams addressed the Congress on May 16, condemning French actions,
calling for a new effort at negotiation, and urging, at the same time, for a
strengthening of American naval defenses and military capabilities. Adams
wanted peace and saw these defensive measures in part as a means of improving his bargaining position with the French Directory. Hamilton, too,
wanted to work for peace.

In Jefferson and his supporters, by contrast, were aghast at what they incorrectly saw as warmongering on the part of the president. Vigorous
Republican opposition made certain that Congress eventually passed only
limited defense measures. It funded harbor defenses, slated the navy for
expansion, and equipped an 80,000-man militia force but established no
standing army, which Adams had also called for. After much debate Adams
selected a new three-person team of negotiators, comprised of Pinckney,
Gerry, and John Marshall of Virginia (already a decided opponent of
Jefferson). Jefferson and the Republicans still feared the administration's
militaristic tone. Adams was actually more eager to reestablish negotiations and avoid war than Jefferson and his supporters realized. But
Jefferson worried as well that the Hamiltonians would use the pretext of
war to suppress internal dissent.[21]

In May and June 1797, tensions rose and passions raged as congressmen debated the war measures. Jefferson conveyed his fears in letters to
Madison. Determined to solidify Republican support, he reached out to
Aaron Burr, who had been active on behalf of the Republican position
in New York. Of aristocratic birth and extraordinarily able but ambitious to an off-putting degree, Burr had served as a senator since 1791.
Knowing that Burr had felt slighted in the election of 1796, Jefferson

wanted to emphasize his continued support for him. Though fully engaged in political battle, Jefferson could hardly wait to return to Monticello, to "exchange the turbulence and hatred of faction for the delights of domestic affection and tranquility."[22] He left Philadelphia by stage on July 6, arriving at his mountaintop retreat on July 11.

FOR ALMOST THE NEXT five months Jefferson remained at Monticello, among other things making ready for the much-anticipated October marriage of his younger daughter, Maria, to her cousin John Eppes. "When I look to the ineffable pleasures of my family society," Jefferson wrote his older daughter, Martha, "I become more disgusted with the jealousies, the hatred, and the rancorous and malignant passions of this scene [in Philadelphia]. . . . Tranquility is now my object."[23] Jefferson pushed his slaves and hired workers to prepare Monticello to accommodate the wedding.

Alas, not even surrounded by family at Monticello could Jefferson escape the surging political passions of the moment. Shortly before leaving the capital, he had learned of a charge by Maryland's often inebriated, always dyspeptic attorney general, Luther Martin, that Jefferson had fabricated the famous "Logan's Lament" described in *Notes on the State of Virginia*, unfairly representing Captain Michael Cresap as a villain who had mercilessly slaughtered Chief Logan's family. Martin, who had married Cresap's daughter, intended to defend his father-in-law's reputation and damage Jefferson's. Jefferson never replied to Martin publicly, but he did check the facts of his depiction of Cresap. Over the next few years he wrote a couple dozen letters to various people he believed had been in position either to have heard Logan's famous speech or to know firsthand the details of the armed conflict between Logan's people and white militiamen. Jefferson did not plan to correspond directly with Martin; rather, donning the historian's mantle, he aimed "to correct the statement where it is wrong and support it where it is right."[24] Jefferson came to see that he had accidentally collapsed several military incidents into one and slightly misrepresented Cresap's exact role but also confirmed beyond question the authenticity of his account of Logan's speech and the appropriateness of the blame he directed at Cresap for cruel raids against the Indians. In a second edition of his *Notes*, Jefferson would make the necessary corrections, giving both positive and negative accounts of Cresap's role.

Another intrusion on Jefferson's eagerly sought tranquility came in the form of a presentment issued by a federal grand jury in Richmond—that is, a charge based on its own reconnaissance—against the Republican congressman who represented Albemarle County, Samuel J. Cabell. The charge alleged that in circular letters to his constituents, Cabell had attacked the Adams administration in "a time of real public danger"—the supposed threat of war with France—and, in so doing, increased the danger of foreign influence and jeopardized the peace of the nation. A Federalist judge, James Iredall, had egged the grand jury on, thereby—in Jefferson's view—threatening the freedom of a legislator to communicate with his constituents. Perhaps even worse, such a charge would intimidate constituents who desired an exchange of views with their representatives.

Jefferson assumed he could find no relief in the Congress or in the federal judiciary, both controlled by the Federalist Party. For that reason, sometime before August 3, 1797, he drafted a petition to the Virginia legislature to impeach the grand jurors; after making several slight changes based on comments from Madison, he arranged for its anonymous presentation to the House of Delegates. As he argued, legislators' "communications with their constituents should of right, as of duty also, be free, full, and unawed by any. . . . [F]or the Judiciary to interpose in the legislative department between the constituent and his representative . . . is to put the legislative department under the feet of the Judiciary," which ran counter to a basic principle of representative government. When no other body existed to protect this critical freedom, state governments must be "stationed as sentinels to observe with watchfulness and oppose with firmness all movements tending to destroy the equilibrium of our excellent but complicated machine of government."[25] The Virginia delegates debated and passed the petition but never handed down any penalties, and the case never came to trial. Jefferson had made clear, however, that he saw "the states as a last bastion of defense against powerful Federalist adversaries who he believed to be subverting the Constitution and marshalling the resources of the federal government to destroy opposition."[26] Borrowing without quoting from the Federalist, Jefferson sought to defend a basic democratic right from the encroachment of the federal government—not, as some have suggested, to claim state power to deprive a category of people of their rights.

Controversy continued to dog Jefferson. That summer a good friend of his, Dr. George Logan, for whom Jefferson had written a letter of commendation, took it upon himself to go to Paris and attempt to forge a new agreement with the French Directory.[27] Hamiltonians saw this as a Jefferson-inspired Jacobin conspiracy to undermine administration policy.

Jefferson was innocent, but supporters of the administration would believe almost any accusation against him. The specter of the Mazzei affair still loomed.

Jefferson took solace in his reading and intellectual pursuits. He spent time researching the origins of the Indians in North America and the evolution of their languages and continued to ponder the problem of slavery. He remained convinced that colonization must be connected to emancipation, believing that it behooved the South to prepare for what he deemed an inevitable event.

On August 2, 1797, St. George Tucker sent Jefferson a pamphlet he had written, intended for Virginia's General Assembly, advocating gradual emancipation; such was the opposition to it that the pamphlet was not suffered even to remain on a table outside the assembly's main hall. Tucker asked Jefferson, in a follow-up letter, for his opinion on the ideas expressed therein. Jefferson replied that "the first chapter of this history, which has begun in St. Domingo, and the next succeeding ones which will recount how all the whites were driven from all the other islands, may prepare our minds for a peaceable accommodation between justice, policy and necessity, and furnish an answer to the difficult question Whither shall the coloured emigrants go?" He continued, "And the sooner we put some plan underway, the greater hope there is that it may be permitted to proceed peaceably to it's ultimate effect. But if something is not done, and soon done, we shall be the murderers of our own children." This fear plagued Jefferson, as it did a number of other white southerners. "From the present state of things in Europe and America the day which begins our combustion must be near at hand, and only a single spark is wanting to make that day tomorrow. If we had begun sooner, we might probably have been allowed a lengthier operation to clear ourselves, but every day's delay lessens the time we may take for emancipation."[28] Jefferson did not believe the Virginia legislature yet ready to take up such a cause.

THE SECOND SESSION of the 1797 Congress was scheduled to begin in November, but Jefferson delayed his return to Philadelphia, in part because he was suffering from a debilitating cold. He finally set out for the capital on December 4, taking a room after his arrival, as he had in the spring, at Francis's Hotel, just a few blocks from Congress Hall.[29] Little was happening; as Jefferson described the situation to Edmund Pendleton, "Congress is at present lying on it's oars. there is nothing of the least importance to be taken up."[30] Everyone was waiting to learn the outcome of the attempt by the three special commissioners—Pinckney, Marshall, and Gerry—to resume negotiations with the French government.

Day after frustrating day Jefferson sat in his high-backed red chair, on a slightly raised stage, presiding over the mundane affairs of the Senate. There was more action in the House, but of a dispiriting sort. In February 1798, an angry Republican congressman from Vermont, Matthew Lyon, spit in the face of Roger Griswold, an administration supporter from Connecticut. Several days afterward Griswold attacked Lyon with his cane. As the fight escalated into a brawl, Lyon grabbed a pair of fire tongs and began hitting Griswold with them; others physically dragged the two apart. Hostility was omnipresent. As Jefferson viewed things, "It is now well understood that two political sects have arisen within the U.S. the one believing that the Executive is the branch of our Government which the most needs support: the other . . . incline to the Legislative powers. the former of these are called Federalists, sometimes Aristocrats or mono-crats and Sometimes tories. . . . the latter are Stiled Republicans, Whigs, Jacobins, Anarchists, Disorganisers &c."[31]

Preoccupied as always with fears of creeping monarchism, Jefferson grew even more suspicious of Adams, especially after a dinner conversa-tion on February 15 during which the president stated that, in his opinion, the tenure of senators was much too short and that "trusting to a popular assembly for the preservn. of our liberties was the merest chimaera imag-inable."[32] The Lyon-Griswold scuffle, the constant anxiety about monar-chism, the ongoing silence from Paris, the unwelcome news of break-ins at Monticello, first of his bedroom and then of his meat house—all served to put Jefferson on edge.[33]

Jefferson's and his fellow Republicans' suspicions came to a head on March 5, 1798, when Adams announced to Congress that the first dis-patches from the envoys had arrived. Although there had not been time to decipher them, Adams reported that the last brought news that neu-tral (i.e., US) ships carrying English goods would be seized—and that the French government would not even receive the envoys.[34] Two weeks later, on March 19, Adams again addressed Congress, this time admitting that the original object of the US mission to France was hopeless. He then called for quick passage of measures to protect US commerce, im-prove coastal defenses, strengthen the navy, and authorize new taxes to pay for it all.

At first, in the heat of anger, Adams had actually wanted to declare war against France, but his better judgment prevailed, and he ended up not pushing for the provisional standing army that war would have necessitated. While some in his cabinet judged the president too pacific, even Hamilton was pleased that Adams had not actually beat the drums of war (although he did think Adams should have called for a greatly enlarged army, having himself proposed a regular army of 30,000 men and a backup force of the same size[35]). Hamilton did, however, quickly rush to publish in a friendly newspaper a series of blistering pieces assailing administration opponents for a lack of patriotism.[36] Fearful of rampant Toryism, Jefferson was incensed by, as he put it, Adams's "insane" message to Congress. He was certain war against France was near.[37]

Misunderstanding their opponents, the Republicans took a disastrous next step. Some among them, including Jefferson, thought Adams might be distorting the information in the dispatches. They began to clamor for release of the full texts. Jefferson and those of like mind still did not grasp that, within Federalist circles, Adams was a moderating voice.

Adams turned over the materials. They showed that the French foreign minister, Charles Maurice de Talleyrand-Périgord, had toyed with the envoys for months, never deigning to receive them. Instead, several lower-level agents—the dispatches referred to them as Agents X, Y, and Z—had finally met with the Americans, demanding that the envoys disavow certain passages in President Adams's May 16, 1797, speech that they found derogatory toward France; that the United States make a large loan to the French government; and, what's more, that the United States give the French a *doucer* (a conciliatory gift) as the cost of doing business. The American envoys emphatically refused the blatant demand for a bribe.[38] The Republicans were stunned by these revelations, the Federalists overjoyed. The latter quickly had the dispatches released to the press, and soon a wave of revulsion and anger at France—and its stateside supporters—swept across the nation. Although Jefferson confided to Madison that he thought the actions of the agents "very unworthy of a great nation," the two statesmen decided that addressing the issue publicly would gain nothing.[39] They would try instead to endure and in the meantime do everything possible to oppose the growing popular support for war with France.

ONCE AGAIN, in this period, an insistent correspondent put the question of slavery and emancipation before Jefferson. In June 1798 Jefferson received a long and thoughtful letter from his former Paris associate William Short, who knew Jefferson as well as anyone. The letter is revealing, because it is highly unlikely Short would have sent it if he believed Jefferson not at least somewhat open to the ideas expressed within. After some discussion of his own finances, Short turned to his concern with the so-called slavery problem. Aware of Jefferson's views about African inferiority in *Notes on the State of Virginia*, Short referred his correspondent to the success of a colony of freed slaves in "Sierra Leona": "It gives very encouraging hopes with respect to the perfectibility of the black race," he wrote. Short then said that recent explorations in the interior of Africa had encountered "a city larger than London." This discovery, along with the success of the colony, "leaves no doubt of their susceptibility of all the arts of civilization & gives sanguine hopes that our posterity at least will see improved, populous & extensive nations of the black color." This should "tend to remove the aversion to the mixture of the two colors."

Short proceeded to discuss the lightening of certain members of the black race owing both to their residence in a nontropical region and to intermarriage with whites—an idea to which he displayed no repugnance. In fact, Short pointed to examples of handsome dark-skinned women. Was this a not-so-subtle reference to mulatto Sally Hemings, though she was light skinned? Whatever the case, Short meant to suggest that perhaps the two races could coexist in freedom. He concluded by calling for "the statesman, the philosopher, the philanthrope, in short all who have any regard to the interests of their country or the rights of humanity" to take the lead in seeking this end.[40]

Inexplicably, Jefferson never replied. Short brought the topic up again two years later, in a letter dated September 18, 1800. He remarked how tragic it was that George Washington, who had died the year before and whose will silently freed his slaves following the death of his wife, had not lent his name and influence to the cause.[41] Jefferson apparently never replied to this letter either; his correspondence with Short continued, and in a friendly vein, but it mostly dealt with the financial matters that Jefferson was handling for him. By the time he received the first letter, Jefferson may have thought his primary duty was to protect the future of the constitutional union, which he feared gravely at risk in the late 1790s. He thus would have been unwilling to risk a controversial push for emancipation. Without question, Jefferson cared more about preserving the union than abolishing slavery. This moral failing was not his alone; it characterized the entire political culture. Not a single Founder—not Washington, Jefferson, Madison, Adams, Hamilton, Benjamin Franklin, or even the most radical thinker of them all, Thomas Paine—risked his career to end slavery.

Jefferson had written publicly against the institution until the late 1780s, but after the bitter debate in the First Congress in 1791, he avoided the issue except in private correspondence. And yet none of this explains why he never responded to Short's earnest entreaties.

Jefferson did not completely forsake the cause of emancipation in the late 1790s. Thaddeus Kosciuszko, a Polish-born military engineer and leader active on behalf of the American cause during the revolution, returned to the United States in August 1797 after years of progressive political activities in Europe. In the spring of 1798, fearful of being deported as a result of the various alien bills under consideration, Kosciuszko made plans to flee; Jefferson helped him obtain a passport under an assumed name and return to France.

Immediately before he departed, and surely with Jefferson's assistance, Kosciuszko wrote and signed a will covering his American assets.[42] The will authorized "my friend Thomas Jefferson to employ the whole thereof [Kosciuszko's estate] in purchasing Negroes from among his own or any others and giving them Liberty in my name, in giving them [an] education in trades or otervise and in having them instructed for their new condition. . . . [A]nd I make the said Thomas Jefferson my executor of this."[43]

Alas, this came to no effect. By the time Kosciuszko died on October 15, 1817, he had written three additional wills. Jefferson, then seventy-four years old, had not practiced law in forty-three years. With typical lawyerly caution (and the experience of a private citizen who had lost lawsuits), he felt incompetent to preside over what he could see—once he realized there were competing wills—would be an extraordinarily complicated legal mess. So he asked a trusted younger friend and neighbor, John Hartwell Cocke, a strong supporter of emancipation, to assume the executorship. Cocke, also aware of the difficulties he would face in dealing with Kosciuszko's expectations in the state of Virginia, declined. After seeking the advice of US Attorney General William Wirt, Jefferson had the will entered into the Orphan's Court of the District of Columbia. After many years the complicated case came to the US Supreme Court, which in 1852 decided that Kosciuszko's later will of 1816—which explicitly stated that it superseded any previous wills—did in fact render null and void the 1798 will.[44] Evidently this went against Kosciuszko's intentions. A month before his death in 1817, he had written Jefferson indicating his desire that the latter follow his original will.[45]

ALL THAT LAY in the future. In the summer of 1798, Jefferson's focus was on the war hysteria sweeping across the nation. To Madison, he wrote that, at the most, the peace advocates could try to "prevent war-measures *externally*, consenting to every rational measure of *internal* defence & preparation."[46] Congress, responding to Adams's requests, decided to raise a military of 10,000 regular troops—more than the president had asked for but much less than Hamilton had suggested—as well as a provisional army to be mustered only if France invaded.[47] Congress also went beyond Adams in cutting off all trade with France and nullifying whatever remained of the 1778 Franco-American treaty.

With Adams—now wearing a military uniform and sword—giving bombastic, patriotic speeches, the nation seemed to be barreling toward war, so much so that even Hamilton was worried. Knowing the nation to be militarily unprepared and that political and economic affairs in England were troublesome, he feared taking on France with England in such a weakened condition.[48] Fortunately, enough opposition and good sense remained in the capital for Congress not to declare war on France, which, anyway, had absolutely no intention of invading the United States and forcing the issue.

The High Federalists, with Hamilton at their head, were not satisfied with the enacted military measures; they had in mind a series of laws to suppress their political opponents as well. In the words of Senator Theodore Sedgwick of Massachusetts, the French crisis gave the Federalists "a glorious opportunity to destroy [the Republican] cause."[49] Jefferson was distressed to learn of this campaign and that some regular Republican supporters had gotten swept up in the war hysteria or simply left for home. On April 26 he reported to Madison that a motion had been introduced into the Senate "to send away suspected aliens." Jefferson explained that the motion targeted high-profile people like his friend the Comte de Volney, "but it will not stop there when it gets into a course of execution." He also expected introduction any day of a sedition bill, "the object of which is the suppression of the whig presses" ("whig" referred to a political group in Britain that had favored decreasing the power of the king and increasing that of Parliament).[50] Madison called the alien bill under discussion a "monster that must for ever disgrace its parents" and, acknowledging the absent members of Congress, wrote Jefferson that it was "truly to be deplored that a standing army should be let upon us by the absence of a few sound votes."[51]

Jefferson still trusted that by overreaching, the Federalists would soon lose the support of the people, who, he believed, possessed a great reservoir of common sense. He confided to his son-in-law, "This paroxism will be short, the only fear is of irretrievable injury while it prevails."[52] Jefferson saw no possibility that the Republicans still in the Congress could effectively oppose this torrent of legislation. As he planned to leave for Monticello in June, he could only hope that, after the clamor for war played itself out, the people and their representatives would come to their senses, the Republicans would gain control, and constitutional govern-ment could be restored. As for the current Congress, the alien and sedi-tion bills now under debate were "so palpably in the teeth of the constitution as to shew they mean to pay no respect to it."[53] On June 27, after several of the suppressive measures passed—but before the Sedition Act did—Jefferson left the capital, not to return until December 18.

He remained unaware of the final version of these bills when he wrote to John Taylor, "A little patience and we shall see the reign of witches pass over, their spells dissolve, and the people recovering their true sight, re-store their government to it's true principles."[54] After returning home and learning the full range of the measures history knows as the Alien and Sedition Acts, Jefferson realized that he could not passively await the res-toration of government according to "true principles." He had to shift into a more active political mode.

Of the four acts passed, all signed by Adams, three dealt with aliens and one with so-called internal sedition. The first of the measures, passed on June 18, was the Naturalization Act, which extended from five to four-teen years the period of residence necessary to gain full citizenship. This act rested on the Federalist assumption that most immigrants tended to become Republican supporters. The second measure, known as the Alien Act and passed on June 25, gave the president authority to deport any aliens whose views or activities he believed detrimental to the safety of the nation. The bill was written to allow broad interpretation; Republicans could easily imagine draconian measures against aliens who offered even mildly critical opinions of the administration's policies. Jefferson deemed the bill "worthy of the 8th or 9th century."[55] He feared that Adams planned to deport the chemist and religious radical Joseph Priestley (in addition to Kosciuszko and Volney), although Adams overruled the recommendation of Secretary of State Timothy Pickering that he do so. In fact, Adams would not deport a single person, but, of course, neither Jefferson nor anyone else could have foreseen that in the early summer of 1798.[56]

Only the third of the acts attracted bipartisan support. This was the Alien Enemies Act, passed on July 6 after Jefferson had already left the city; the act, which called for the arrest or deportation of aliens from an enemy power, would only be operative in case of actual war. It never had any effect. The fourth act, however, would be enforced with vigor. This was the Sedition Act. It passed the Senate, ironically, on July 4 but did not pass the House until ten days later. The bill was significantly moderated in the House, where a remnant group of Republican congressmen, led by Albert Gallatin, effectively opposed its most repressive features, and though neither Hamilton nor Adams approved of its every aspect, Adams did sign it into law. (In some respects, Hamilton wanted tougher restrictions against sedition and even stricter enforcement.) The bill as passed primarily targeted "domestic traitors," making it a federal offense, punishable by both fine and imprisonment, for citizens or others to enter into unlawful combinations or conspiracy in opposition to national laws; to try to impede any federal official from carrying out his lawful duties; to publish "any false, scandalous and malicious [read critical] writings" aimed at the US government, the Congress, or the president; or to aid or even attempt "any insurrection, riot, unlawful assembly, or combination" thereof.[57]

Under these broad terms, federal officials, including the president, could harshly suppress all political opposition. The penalty for writing public documents the officials disliked could include a fine of up to $2,000 and imprisonment for up to two years. Nothing like the law had ever existed on the American scene, and its expiration date—the last day of Adams's term of office—revealed its blatantly partisan nature. Jefferson received a letter from Henry Tazewell on July 19 informing him that Washington had been nominated as commander in chief of "the armies raised, and to be raised" and that "Hamilton and ['Light Horse Harry'] Lee are to be the next in command."[58]

With the prospect of the administration raising a powerful army, in part for deployment against domestic enemies, and the realization that Hamilton would effectively be in charge of that army, Jefferson could only hope that public revulsion against Federalist overreach would soon make itself known. Meanwhile, at Monticello, he began to consider the response he, as a vice president who had pledged to remain aloof from most political matters, should offer to these threats to fundamental American liberties.

19

"Reign of Witches"

THROUGHOUT 1798, partisan controversies led Jefferson to ponder the nature of the political system established by the Constitution and to strive to find language to describe it. On at least one occasion he made an analogy to the Copernican model of the solar system. Writing to Peregrine Fitzhugh in Maryland, Jefferson laid out his concern over the distortion of the nation's founding principles. "I do not think it for the interest of the general government itself, & still less of the Union at large, that the state governments should be so little respected as they have been. however I dare say that in time all these as well as their central government, like the planets revolving round their common Sun, acting & acted upon according to their respective weights & distances, will produce that beautiful equilibrium on which our constitution is founded, . . . the enlightened statesman therefore will endeavor to preserve the weight & influence of every part, as too much given to any member of it would destroy the general equilibrium."[1]

Jefferson assumed that when the system malfunctioned, equilibrium should be reestablished. But he did not believe that secession—he used the word "scission," meaning a split or division—was an appropriate response even in hard times. As he counseled another friend, "It is true that in the mean time we are suffering deeply in spirit, and incurring the horrors of a war, & long oppressions of enormous public debt. But who can say what would be the evils of a scission and when & where they would end? better keep together as we are. . . . if the game runs sometimes against us at home, we must have patience, till luck turns, & then we shall have an opportunity of winning back the *principles* we have lost."[2] More than once he made clear his belief that the federal government had the right to employ force to put down potential secessionist movements.[3] Not even in his darkest moments did Jefferson give up on the idea of the union.

He descended into one of those dark moments shortly after the middle of the year. The Alien Acts were not as oppressive as they could have been, in large part because many potentially liable foreigners left before they could be targeted. But the Sedition Act did have a paralyzing effect on the opposition press. Republican editors and printers were singled out, and altogether twenty-five persons were prosecuted, with ten convicted.[4] Jefferson was outraged by the Federalists' flagrant trampling on the rights guaranteed by the First Amendment.

As for the new standing army, of which Alexander Hamilton shared command, it would be months before Jefferson understood its full significance. For one, it was obvious to everyone that George Washington was its commander in chief in name only, but Washington and others essentially forced John Adams to acquiesce to Hamilton's ascension, a backstory not revealed until July.[5] For another, Jefferson also learned, in late July, that new taxes on homes, land, and slaves would pay for the army, with the last two disproportionally affecting the southern states.[6] In Jefferson's view, the nation was at a turning point, with those he termed the "Tories" in an increasingly powerful position.

In theory the division of the government into three branches should prevent any one branch from becoming too powerful, but in reality the Adams administration controlled the legislature and the judiciary and was even reaching into the states to prosecute dissenting publications and individuals. The previous year, when Jefferson perceived attempted prosecution of his local congressman by the federal judiciary, he had sent an anonymous petition to the Virginia House of Delegates proposing its intervention on the grounds that the states could act as "sentinels," protecting the "equilibrium" of the "machine of government."

Although Jefferson cited no specific authority for his assertion that the states could intervene when the federal government overreached, he was surely familiar with *Federalist* 28, ironically penned by none other than Alexander Hamilton (though at the time authorship of specific issues of the *Federalist* was unknown). As Hamilton had written in December 1787,

> It may safely be received as an axiom in our political system, that the State governments will, in all possible contingencies, afford complete security against invasions of the public liberty by the national authority. Projects of usurpation cannot be masked under pretenses so likely to

escape the penetration of select bodies of men, as of the people at large. The legislatures will have better means of information. They can discover the danger at a distance; and possessing all the organs of civil power, and the confidence of the people, they can at once adopt a regular plan of opposition, in which they can combine all the resources of the community. They can readily communicate with each other in the different States, and unite their common forces for the protection of their common liberty.[7]

Jefferson accepted and agreed with this precept.

In the context of perceived threats to the liberty of the people and to the balance of powers, Jefferson drafted a document, probably in August 1798, that offered a means for the states to rein in what he saw as a national government out of control. He may have discussed the issue earlier with James Madison, but they did not go over the draft together, and it is not clear to whom—and to which state legislatures—Jefferson originally intended to send the anonymous document. Because John Breckinridge was around this time passing by Monticello on his way to Kentucky, Jefferson's document was delivered to that state. William Cary Nicholas, to whom Jefferson had first given his draft resolutions on October 4, had informed him that Breckinridge could more promptly introduce the resolutions to the legislature meeting that fall in Lexington. Thus what became known as the Kentucky Resolutions rather accidentally came before the public in that state.[8]

Jefferson opened the document by arguing that the "several states composing the US of America are not united on the principle of unlimited submission to their general government." Rather, the genius of the Constitution was that it gave precise powers to the central government and reserved others for the states. Within its realm, the central government was all powerful, but the fundamental law of the land circumscribed its reach. Therefore, "whensoever the General government assumes undelegated powers, it's acts are unauthoritative, void, & and of no force."[9] The central government could not determine the validity of its own actions alone; instead, the individual states had an "equal right to judge . . . as well of infractions, as of the mode & measure of redress."[10] After establishing that principle, Jefferson addressed the Alien Acts and the Sedition Act, deeming each, because the central government had no authority to pass or enforce them according to the Constitution, "void & of no force." He used that phrase repeatedly.

In the eighth resolution, Jefferson praised the union of the states in some detail, professing how "sincerely anxious" he was "for it's preservation." He said that when unpopular federal laws did not exceed the government's delegated powers, the ultimate and constitutional remedy would be "a change by the people," that is, an election. But "where powers are assumed which have not been delegated, a nullification of the act is the rightful remedy: that every state has a natural right, in cases not in the compact to nullify of their own authority all assumptions of power within their limits."[11] By nullification—a word he apparently coined—Jefferson meant no more than rendering a law, in his oft repeated phrase, "void & of no force."

Jefferson's final remedy was for "this commonwealth [to] call on it's co-states for an expression of their sentiments on the acts." He assumed that the other states, so petitioned, would "concur in declaring these acts void and of no force, & will each take measures of [their] own for providing that neither of these acts, nor any others of the general government, not plainly & intentionally authorized by the constitution, shall be exercised within their respective territories."[12] Nowhere did he hint at secession (as some have claimed since); his purpose was to defend the civil liberties of the citizens of the nation.

When Breckinridge introduced the resolutions to the Kentucky House of Representatives, he did not name their author. And either before introducing the resolutions or while the assembly was considering them, he made several changes to the text, the most important of which were a drastic shortening of resolution eight and excision of the sentences mentioning nullification. The only action called for, other than declaring the acts "void and of no effect," was to convey Kentucky's sentiments to the other states, trusting that they would agree and consequently "unite with this Commonwealth in requesting [the acts'] repeal at the next session of Congress."[13] In such form the Kentucky House passed the resolutions on November 10, 1798. Jefferson never voiced any objections to Breckinridge's emendations.

Jefferson's worried cast of his mind when he wrote the resolutions emerges in a letter he penned just days after showing his draft to Nicholas. Corresponding with Senator Stevens Thomson Mason of Virginia, Jefferson characterized the "Alien & Sedition laws" "as merely an experiment on the American mind to see how far it will bear an avowed violation of the constitution. if this goes down, we shall immediately see attempted another act of Congress declaring that the President shall continue in Office during life, reserving to another occasion the transfer of the succession to his heirs, and the establishment of the Senate for life. . . . that these things are in contemplation I have no doubt."[14] Such a situation, he believed, justified extreme measures.

When Madison had a chance to read Jefferson's resolutions, he was characteristically more cautious. Then preparing a comparable set of anonymous resolutions for the Virginia House of Delegates, he carefully avoided having the legislature explicitly declare the hated acts void. He wanted Virginia to consult with other states; if they agreed, the proper response was for the states' congressmen to take action in the federal Congress. Madison used the ambiguous term "interpose," by which he meant the states should position their authority between their citizens and the disputed federal law. Jefferson tried to stiffen Madison's wording, but the final version passed by the House of Delegates omitted his proposed language.

Madison pushed Jefferson to consider distinguishing between states and state legislatures. A legislature's passing a resolution did not have nearly the force of the state's calling a special convention and in that forum declaring a congressional act void. Jefferson must have accepted the argument; after all, he had made the same one when the Virginia legislature drafted the state's constitution in 1776. And in fact, when the other states came to discuss the so-called Kentucky and Virginia Resolutions, half of them either supported or did not oppose the resolutions. Only Massachusetts explicitly rejected the concept of interposition.[15]

Jefferson came to accept the more moderate Virginia Resolutions with the same equanimity he showed in response to the edited version of his resolutions that passed in Kentucky. He wrote to John Taylor in late November, "I would not do any thing at this moment which should commit us further, but reserve ourselves to shape our future measures or no measures, by the events which may happen."[16] In a narrow sense, then, the vaunted resolutions had no effect, but the lack of opposition to them, especially in the South, showed the strength of the commitment to freedom of the press and speech and, more generally, to the principles Jefferson espoused. And with his authorship of the Kentucky Resolutions, Jefferson surreptitiously launched his candidacy for the presidency in the 1800 election. (Although it would be years before the authorship of the Kentucky and Virginia Resolutions became common knowledge, insiders had almost immediately and correctly guessed the authors' identities.) The resolutions rallied opposition to the Federalists and staked out a position on limiting the power of the national government to what Jefferson argued were its constitutionally defined functions. Within those boundaries, Jefferson accepted a central government that could act with vigor. By limited government, he did not mean weak government.[17]

JEFFERSON SPENT THE remainder of the fall of 1798 at Monticello and during these months wrote few letters on politics, fearing his enemies would steal, read, and publicize his correspondence. With a sense of dread he set forth on December 18 for Philadelphia, prepared to preside once again over the Senate deliberations. Jefferson had learned additional facts about the new standing army, and the more he gleaned about Hamilton's plans, the more he feared for the nation's future. Not only did Hamilton hope to defeat domestic political opposition, but he wanted the nation to seize Spanish Louisiana and possibly help the British conquer Spanish Latin America. He aimed for the United States to become a close partner with the British in the control of the Western Hemisphere—one aspect of a scheme initially proposed by a Venezuelan patriot named Francisco de Miranda, who had also sold it to William Pitt in England.[18] While Jefferson's instincts about Hamilton—he remembered Hamilton's admiration of Caesar—were accurate to a degree, he continued to underestimate John Adams.

Adams had left Philadelphia in July and spent the entire autumn at his family home in Quincy, where he was both overworked and consumed with worry over the health of his dear wife, Abigail. The more he fumed about affairs in the capital, the angrier he grew at the Washington holdovers in his cabinet and Hamilton's power over them. Adams determined to take charge of his administration and, at whatever cost, avoid war with France. He now knew that France did not desire war and would agree to meet with a new American minister. The US minister to The Hague, William Vans Murray, reported a thawing of French opinion, as did his own son, John Quincy, serving in Berlin as the American chargé d'affaires. Elbridge Gerry had finally returned from Paris bearing similar information. Adams, after he returned to Philadelphia in November, had a brief meeting with Dr. George Logan, just arrived from his private mission to France, who told him much the same thing.[19] The Federalists promptly passed legislation outlawing private missions, but Logan's comments confirmed all the others. And, like Jefferson, the more Adams learned about Hamilton's outsize military ambitions, the more he realized that the possibility of war with France gave Hamilton and his fellow High Federalists a rationale for strengthening the army far beyond what Adams thought sensible.

When Adams gave his State of the Union address to the Congress on December 8, 1798, his moderation on the subject of France distressed the High Federalists. He hinted at sending another minister to Paris if unambiguous signals indicated he would be properly received.[20] The High Federalists were incensed, while Jefferson and Madison suspected Adams of disingenuousness,[21] their partisanship still blinding them.

Amid the confusion, Jefferson in January 1799 wrote a long letter to Gerry, a moderate Federalist, seeking not simply to describe his political principles but to woo him to certain Republican positions. The gambit worked, for six months later Gerry was the Republican candidate for governor in Massachusetts. The letter was a work of political art, or a "profession of my political faith," as Jefferson termed it.[22] He opened by suggesting that he and Gerry shared the same sentiments. Because Jefferson said their former correspondence indicated "mutual confidence," he wanted to clarify his positions so as to allay any doubts that could conceivably have arisen in Gerry's mind due to the constant barrage of political attacks on Jefferson.[23] After these introductory words, Jefferson outlined his political philosophy in the context of the partisan tone of the times:

I do then with sincere zeal wish an inviolable preservation of our present federal constitution, according to the true sense in which it was adopted by the states . . . and I am opposed to the monarchising it's features by the forms of it's administration, with a view to conciliate a first transition to a President & Senate for life, & from that to a hereditary tenure of these offices. . . . I am for preserving to the states the powers not yielded by them to the Union, & to the legislature of the Union it's constitutional share in the division of powers: and I am not for transferring all the powers of the states to the general government, & all those of that government to the Executive branch. . . . I am for a government rigorously frugal & simple, applying all the possible savings of the public revenue to the discharge of the national debt. . . . I am for relying, for internal defence, on our militia solely till actual invasion, and for such a naval force only as may protect our coasts and harbours . . . and not for a standing army in time of peace which may overawe the public sentiment. . . . I am for free commerce with all nations, political connection with none . . . and I am not for linking ourselves, by new treaties with the quarrels of

Europe. . . . am for freedom of religion, & against all maneuvers to bring about a legal ascendancy of one sect over another: for freedom of the press, & against all violations of the constitution to silence by force & not by reason the complaints or criticisms, just or unjust, of our citizens against the conduct of their agents. I am for encouraging the progress of science in all it's branches.[24]

Finally, to refute the belief about his supposedly uncritical admiration of the French Revolution and all other things French, he admitted he had been "a sincere wellwisher to the success of the French revolution, and still wish it may end in the establishment of a free & well ordered republic," though he recognized the excesses of late. But as to his Gallic sympathies, "the first object of my heart is my own country. in that is embarked my family, my fortune, & my own existence. I have not one farthing of interest, nor one fibre of attachment out of it, nor a single motive of preference of any one nation to another but in proportion as they are more or less friendly to us." As he concluded to Gerry, "These my friend are my principles; they are unquestionably the principles of the great body of our fellow citizens . . . and I know there is not one of them which is not yours also."[25] If parties had had platforms in 1799, this would have been Jefferson's. Little did he realize that on many of these issues, Adams's positions were nearer to his own than to Hamilton's.

IN THE MEANTIME, Adams was moving closer to reopening negotiations with France. In November word had arrived of Admiral Horatio Nelson's annihilation of Napoleon Bonaparte's fleet at the Battle of the Nile, a major blow to French military ambitions. Adams was also increasingly aware of public opposition to the whole Federalist program, owing in part to the Kentucky and Virginia Resolutions. Without consulting anyone in his party, on February 18, 1799, he made an unexpected announcement in a message to Congress, nominating William Vans Murray as minister to the French republic.[26]

Jefferson was surprised and confused. He still refused to believe that Adams sincerely wanted peace. He considered the appointment a mere gesture and fully expected the Federalist majority to summarily reject it. More than surprised, the High Federalists were outraged, accusing Adams of everything from imbecility to treason. As was typical of the president, as the criticism increased, so did his resolve. His opponents should not have underestimated his stubbornness, especially because on this occasion he was clearly in the right. He had chosen to put the good of the nation ahead of the temporary benefit of his party. The break between the Hamilton faction and Adams was total, and the Federalists descended into internecine warfare.

Jefferson and his supporters were slow to perceive this, but the civil war within the Federalist Party would soon enough propel the Republicans to victory in the elections of 1800. Whereas Hamilton and his backers came to literally hate Adams, Adams grew more and more convinced that Hamilton was the largest threat to the constitutional form of government.[27] Not even Jefferson thought worse of him. Adams, for his part, came to believe that Hamilton had Napoleonic ambitions and to return the hate directed at him. Nevertheless, on the very day Adams nominated Murray, the bill for forming a new regular army of 30,000 men— Hamilton's number—passed the Senate, and Adams signed it.

Moreover, after Adams recognized the scope and intensity of the opposition to his appointment of Murray, he agreed to enlarge the individual mission to a commission. He appointed Chief Justice Oliver Ellsworth and the venerable Patrick Henry of Virginia, then sixty-three years old, to join Murray. The ailing Henry declined appointment, so Adams nominated William R. Davie of North Carolina to replace him.[28] Almost immediately after confirming these appointments, the Congress adjourned. Just as quickly, Adams retreated to Quincy, where he would remain for seven months, causing the members of his administration—most of them Hamilton loyalists—to accuse him of irresponsibility, dereliction of duty, and worse. With the president absent, the dedicated opposition of the High Federalists prevented the commission's departure; Hamilton's faction wanted the threat of war to linger as long as possible, knowing it increased their chances of victory in the coming presidential contest. Jefferson too left Philadelphia, arriving at Monticello on March 8.

Soon after the president and vice president departed the capital, civil unrest, brewing for months in several German-dominated areas northeast of Philadelphia, developed into a mini-rebellion. The cause: the new taxes enacted primarily to pay for the expanded army; the protestors: largely hard-pressed farmers. By January and February 1799, they were taking up arms, intimidating tax assessors, and generally disrupting the normal flow of business. This action culminated in a protest—led by John Fries with about 140 men under his loose control—on March 7 that forced a federal marshal to relinquish a number of suspects he was attempting to take to Philadelphia for questioning. The public disorder worried Adams and frightened the more extreme Federalists. Just before leaving for Quincy, Adams had called for military forces to deal with the unrest, but with Hamilton in charge in his absence, the army moved to crush the protestors. By then the movement had already dissolved, but dozens were arrested and charged with treason, and some Federalists began calling for hangings. Adams came to his senses and eventually pardoned everyone arrested, even Fries, frustrating Hamilton and his allies.

The episode demonstrated to most people, especially to the Republicans, the potential excesses of a standing army.[29] Jefferson interpreted Hamilton's heavy-handedness as indicative of his desire to suppress opposition to his policies. Had Jefferson known more, he would have been even more concerned. Hamilton had written Harrison Gray Otis about the dangers "of internal disorders" and the need for a large military force to restrain them; to Theodore Sedgwick, he had characterized the Kentucky and Virginia Resolutions as "a tendency to destroy the Constitution of the UStates" affording "full evidence . . . of a regular conspiracy to overturn the government." In his view, "the Government must [no]t merely [de]fend itself but must attack and arraign its enemies." Calling for quick expansion of the military to the authorized size, Hamilton recommended, "When a clever force has been collected let them be drawn towards Virginia for which there is an obvious pretext—& then let measures be taken to act upon the laws & put Virginia to the Test of resistance."[30] Jefferson was not paranoid to look so warily at the army under Hamilton's control.[31]

To counter Hamilton's influence, Jefferson was determined from the beginning of 1799 to play a more active role in national politics. While feeling he should not openly work against the Adams administration, of which he was, in some sense, a part, he chose to direct opposition by writing letters, distributing pamphlets, and stealthily motivating and organizing Republicans. He wrote to Madison on February 5, "We are sensible that this summer is the season for systematic energies & sacrifices. the engine is the press. every man must lay his purse & his pen under contribution." He warned that Madison might well receive requests for monetary contributions, but that contributions from his pen would be more essential. "Let me pray & beseech you to set apart a certain portion of every post-day to write what may be proper for the public." He suggested that Madison send his articles to Jefferson (or to whomever he selected) "so that your name shall be sacredly secret."[32] The congenitally optimistic Jefferson worked hard to spread the Republican message, confident that what he called the Tory spell was "dissolving. the public mind is recovering from the delirium into which it has been thrown, and we may still believe with security that the great body of the American people must for ages yet be substantially republican."[33] Despite occasional worry over the course of events, Jefferson never succumbed to fear for long.

As always, Jefferson had concerns closer to home as well. He had become temporarily depressed the moment he arrived back at Monticello: no progress had been made on the roof, which meant another cold winter indeed. "It seems as if I should never get it inhabitable," he lamented to his daughter Maria.[34] But he soon was back to writing and receiving letters, addressing various matters at the plantation and the nailery, and reading and ruminating on everything from Indian languages to wild horses to the meaning of civilizational progress. He also found time to write a kind letter thanking his old teacher George Wythe, stating, "I shall for ever cherish the remembrance of the many agreeable & useful days I have past with you, and the infinite obligations I owe you for what good has fallen to me through life."[35]

For many years Jefferson had been collecting information on Indian languages, seeking thereby to determine the origin of the Native American peoples. His working assumption was that by studying the differences among Indian languages and between them and Euro-Asian languages, one could estimate the length of Indians' separate existence in the New World. His assumptions that the separation went back very far indeed may have received confirmation when one Morgan Brown, a minor government official in Tennessee, wrote to Jefferson in October describing two small marble statues of a man and a woman recently excavated near the Cumberland River. "If you conceive Sir that they will be mat[ters] of Curiosity to you, or worth your Acceptance; they are at your service." Brown had the small statues sent by way of New Orleans to Richmond, where Jefferson took possession them. He put them on display in the entrance hall of Monticello, where they remained for years, labeled by Jefferson as "two busts of Indian figures."[36]

As always, too, Jefferson discovered that his retreat to Monticello did not alleviate his fears about the direction of national politics. The issue that most upset him in the mid and late summer of 1799 was the possibility that the administration would propose the application of common law (borrowed directly from England) in the federal courts. This seemed utterly ridiculous to Jefferson; in high dudgeon he characterized the notion as "the audacious, barefaced and sweeping pretension to a system of law for the U.S. without the adoption of their legislature and so infinitely beyond their power to adopt."[37] Jefferson tended to see many Federalist actions as pushing beyond the bounds of constitutional authority; Federalist judges' advocating the application of common law seemed the most extreme act yet, and he fully concurred with former attorney general Edmund Randolph's public condemnation of the threat of accepting laws not explicitly enacted by the local legislatures.

No doubt it was with all of this in mind that Jefferson wrote a spirited letter to Madison, arguing that he and like-minded patriots should continue to press the principles outlined in the Kentucky and Virginia Resolutions. Jefferson suggested that they should protest "the principle & the precedent" advanced by the administration and insist that the states reserved basic rights to counter "palpable violations of the constitutional compact by the Federal government," by which he meant powers and rights that preceded the ratification of the Constitution. To make clear their ongoing commitment to the Constitution, Jefferson argued that they should "express in affectionate & conciliatory language our warm attachment to union with our sister states." Then came these explosive words:

> We are willing to sacrifice to this every thing except those rights of self government the securing of which was the object of that compact; that not at all disposed to make every measure of error or wrong a cause of scission, we are willing to view with indulgence to wait with patience till those passions & delusions shall have passed over which the federal government have artfully & successfully excited to cover it's own abuses. . . . *but determined, were we to be disappointed in this, to sever ourselves from that union we so much value, rather than give up the rights of self government which we have reserved, & in which we see liberty, safety & happiness.*[38]

The letter was not a public document or intended for wider distribution; rather, as he often did, Jefferson was expressing his frustration in unguarded language to his closest confidant, probably expecting that the more cautious and reserved Madison would—as he often did—successfully cool his hot temper. Madison rode over to Monticello and did precisely that. As Jefferson confided to William Cary Nicholas soon thereafter, Madison cautioned against expressing the idea of a state or region severing itself from the nation, and after hearing him out, Jefferson reported,

"From this I recede readily, not only in deference to his judgment, but because, as we should never think of separation but for repeated and enormous violations" far beyond those now experienced.[39] Jefferson never publicly expressed support of secession and never again mentioned the idea in private. We should view this outburst as a brief moment of passion and anger rather than as an explanation of principle or call to arms.[40]

In late 1799, Madison drafted an elegant defense of the Virginia Resolutions (and by implication the Kentucky Resolutions), which Jefferson so admired that he later had it reprinted in Philadelphia. Madison summarized the intent of both documents as being to promote no specific state action but rather to express principled perspectives "unaccompanied with any other effect than what they may produce on opinion by exciting reflection."[41]

WHILE JEFFERSON WAS at Monticello, Adams was at his farm in Quincy, running the government by means of the postal system. The president was waiting for signals that France would receive a new American commission and come to the table willing to compromise. Both Adams's absence and his patience toward Paris infuriated opponents in his administration. Beside himself, Hamilton pushed the cabinet to seize control of the government, suggesting that he would gladly come to Philadelphia from New York to help govern.[42] As before, this only hardened Adams's resolve to heed his own counsel. Over the course of the summer and early fall of 1799, the president received a steady stream of intelligence that the French government was revising its approach. On August 6 he learned that Talleyrand himself had offered assurances that he would negotiate in good faith with the Americans. Adams wrote a letter to Philadelphia authorizing the commissioners to set off for Paris, but Secretary of State Timothy Pickering, loyal to Hamilton, dithered.

Warned that his cabinet was thwarting his express desires, Adams rushed from Massachusetts on September 30, heading for Trenton, New Jersey, where the government had retreated, fearing another yellow fever outbreak in Philadelphia. He stopped briefly in New York City, where he learned to his disgust that his son Charles was dying, broke, of alcoholism; Adams never spoke to, visited, or wrote Charles again. This sad interlude only darkened Adams's mood, and once he arrived in Trenton, he found his recalcitrant cabinet eager to oppose his decision to send the commissioners to France. When their attempts to forestall Adams proved ineffective, Hamilton himself came down from New York, arguing with, lecturing, and generally infuriating him. Yet the president would not be turned from his course, and on November 3, months after their appointment, the commissioners left for France.[43] In an act of great courage, Adams had risked his popularity and party leadership for the cause of peace.

Jefferson learned of these events later on. He never comprehended the full implications of Adams's principled action to avoid a potentially devastating war with France. Nor did he fully understand the extent of Hamilton's plotting to deprive the Republicans of their influence in national politics. Sometime in October or early November, Hamilton wrote to Senator Jonathan Dayton of New Jersey, outlining his understanding of the political scene, calling on the "supporters of the Government . . . to adopt vigorous measures of counteraction," "calling out the Militia," and advocating the division of the larger states, including Virginia, into several smaller states so as to reduce their power in relation to that of the central government. New "laws for restraining and punishing incendiary and seditious practices" would cap these efforts.[44] Had he seen this letter, Jefferson would have been horrified.

In the final two months of 1799, Jefferson was making preparations to resist a monarchical threat to the existing constitutional government. He began formulating plans to return to Philadelphia at the end of the year, and, as he wrote Madison, he would heed the advice of James Monroe to not tarry at Montpelier (where Madison lived) on the way, because administration spies would make such a visit "a subject of some political slander, & perhaps of some political injury."[45] Four days later he sent a brief letter to Madison—he risked letters only when persons he knew and trusted carried them—to list the critical issues he thought the Republicans should emphasize over the course of the election year: "1. peace even with Gr. Britain. 2. a sincere cultivation of the Union. 3. the disbanding of the army on principles of economy and safety. 4. protestations against violations of the true principles of our constitution." Because he knew that the High Federalists sought an excuse to deploy the army, under Hamilton's control, to squelch any opposition, Jefferson warned that "nothing [should] be said or done which shall look or lead to force, and give any pretext for keeping up the army."[46]

On December 21, 1799, Jefferson set forth from Monticello for his last visit to Philadelphia, as the capital was slated to move to its new location along the Potomac River the next year. He arrived in the rancorous city a week later, expecting to find little seasonal cheer emanating from the

Federalists who dominated the halls of government. He could not yet foresee how the most recent political event—the departure of the diplomatic commissioners to France—would influence the United States' relations with that nation or, for that matter, with Great Britain. Nor could he foresee how the bitter differences between the Hamilton and Adams wings of the Federalist Party would shape domestic politics, the presidential contest, and his role therein. He also probably did not know that a week prior to his departure, George Washington had died of epiglottitis, a severe inflammation and associated swelling that cut off the passage of air through his windpipe, apparently the result of a weakened immune system after he rode about his plantation on horseback for two hours in the middle of a storm of alternating snow, hail, and freezing rain. Washington's body had been placed, on December 18, in a mahogany casket in the family vault at Mount Vernon.[47] Once Jefferson learned of Washington's death, he took great pains to avoid any actions during the formal ceremonies that his political enemies might fashion as hypocrisy. He did not arrive in Philadelphia in time to participate in the day of mourning authorized by Congress; nor did he publish a eulogy. In fact, he appears to have made no public or private remarks about the man Congressman Henry Lee famously called "first in war, first in peace and first in the hearts of his countrymen" during the congressional day of remembrance on December 26 in Philadelphia.[48]

Nor, finally, could Jefferson have imagined that his reputation would be almost fatally injured in the twentieth and twenty-first centuries by the revelation, once Washington's will was probated, that this wealthy man, who had never publicly said a word against slavery and never put his immense prestige behind limiting its spread or eliminating its existence, had ordered that his slaves be freed upon the death of his wife.[49] But Jefferson must have instantly calculated the loss to the Federalist Party that Washington's death entailed, for he had long assumed that the first American president's standing had artificially inflated the popular support for administration policies. With Washington dead and peace with France more or less assured, Jefferson faced the year with renewed optimism.

20

An Attempt to "Strangle the Election"

U NLIKE IN 1796, when he had taken no part in his election as vice president, in 1800 Jefferson eagerly campaigned for the presidency. He would spend much of the year writing occasional guarded letters to associates who could advance his candidacy. Campaigns then bore little resemblance to those today. Openly seeking office for oneself was considered base; rather, the voters summoned one to office. Like his eventual opponents, Jefferson gave no speeches, made no political appearances, and avoided mention in the press. Nevertheless, his ideals and actions informed the efforts of those who did engage, on his behalf, in what we now call retail politics. He was the primary figure within, and symbol of, the Republican Party.

Throughout 1800, Jefferson remained cautious about what he said in his letters and to his confidants. His closest correspondents recognized the need for secrecy; James Monroe even subscribed Jefferson to two newspapers under his own name.[1] As Jefferson explained to his younger daughter, Maria, "I shall write no letters the ensuing year for political reasons."[2] He meant letters sent through the public postal system; he could be more forthcoming in letters hand-delivered by friends. He did believe the prospects for Republican victory in the fall promising, based on letters he received, comments from visitors, and the political gossip that enlivened the shared meals in his Philadelphia boardinghouse, at least until he decamped for Monticello in May.

But the coming election and national politics did not absorb Jefferson totally. In his capacity as president of the American Philosophical Society, for instance, he and three other members drew up a memo proposing to Congress a new and enlarged federal census. They called for enumerating the population by gender and age, tabulating the number of people in various occupations, and listing persons by race as well as by citizenship status. The society wanted the demographic data for scientific purposes, hoping to reveal the factors that determined longevity—and thereby to prove, among other things, the healthfulness of the American climate.[3] Unfortunately the Congress did not adopt the plan, so the 1800 census contained much less data than Jefferson and the others had hoped for.

Closer to Jefferson's heart was a family event: the birth of a new child, which always stimulates hope for the future. Perhaps his receipt, on January 18, of a letter from his son-in-law John Wayles Eppes, reporting the arrival of his and Maria's first child, prodded Jefferson to write a long letter that very day to Joseph Priestley. The eminent British chemist and Unitarian theologian had relocated to Pennsylvania in 1794. Jefferson's ostensible topic was higher education in the state of Virginia. He described the limits of the college in Williamsburg, which he had, of course, attended himself: its "miserable" constitution and its problematic location. He hoped to establish a new college, on a "broad & liberal & *modern*" plan, situated more centrally in the state, that would become a true beacon for learning and scholarship.[4] He would exchange numerous letters with Priestley on this topic, in addition to corresponding with Pierre Samuel Du Pont de Nemours of France on the ideal design of a university.[5] He also wrote Priestley about the importance of teaching foreign languages. In his view, Greek and Latin were especially useful, since they helped one develop an elegant writing style. As he put it, "To read the Latin & Greek authors in their original is a sublime luxury." He continued, "I thank on my knees him who directed my early education for having put into my possession this rich source of delight: and I would not exchange it for any thing."[6]

These pleasant reveries came to an end with the tragic news that Maria's infant had died and Maria herself was terribly ill. She would remain so for months.[7] That was not all: Jefferson's faithful slave Jupiter, mysteriously sick for weeks, had also died, and his wife, Ursula, and their son were at death's door. Distressed over Jupiter's death, Jefferson was devastated by Maria's loss.[8] The day after learning of it, Jefferson wrote to his daughter to profess how deeply he felt for her, adding that he knew only "time & silence" could heal her pain. He tried to comfort her with the fact that she was young and could yet have other children. He made clear his affection for her: "I have felt perpetual gratitude to heaven for having given me, in you, a source of so much pure & unmixed happiness."[9] The domestic circle brought great rewards, intermixed with profound grief, and Jefferson was deeply familiar with both.

He found distraction from his sorrow in, among other things, the drafting of a handbook of parliamentary procedure, which he had begun when first elected vice president.[10] Jefferson drew on his own experience, his wide reading in what he called parliamentary science, and advice from various colleagues. He considered the orderly, fair, and efficient operation of any deliberative body an important aspect of governance, and he labored mightily to finish what he ended up titling his *Manual of Parliamentary Practice*. Published in 1801 and meant for both the Senate and the House, it became the indispensable guide for much of the nineteenth century and, for the Senate, at least, into the mid-twentieth.[11]

THE PRESIDENTIAL CAMPAIGN, such as it was, gained full steam in the spring, though because Jefferson kept his involvement largely concealed, one could hardly glean this from his daily calendar. So careful was he to avoid being seen politicking that he wrote Monroe to say that once Congress had adjourned, he would journey home to Monticello via the eastern shore. He would not announce his route "because I do not wish to beget ceremony anywhere; or have anything to do with it." He cautioned Monroe, "I believe it better to avoid every occasion of the expression of sentiments, which might drag me into the newspapers."[12] He believed showing too much eagerness for votes crass and would accept a call from the citizens rather than grasp for office. When later in the spring Monroe wanted to discuss campaign strategy with Jefferson, he wrote that he would ride over to Monticello to do it in person, fearing that it was "unsafe to repose too much confidence in the fidelity of the post office."[13]

Jefferson knew he must win the electoral votes of either New York or Pennsylvania to capture the presidency; the support of the South alone, which he could count on, would not suffice. Aaron Burr was working with frantic energy and great skill in New York City for the Republican cause, and his successes in attracting strong candidates not only ensured the local election but gained him support for national office. Jefferson learned in the first week of May that the Republican cause had carried the entire state.[14] This news brought such despair to the Federalists that Alexander Hamilton, in desperation, tried to convince the New York legislature, before the newly elected representatives could take their seats, to change the selection process for presidential electors so as to favor the administration. This brazen attempt at subversion had been more than Governor John Jay, a staunch Federalist, could stand, and the Republican victory seemed assured.[15]

BUOYED BY THE New York results, Jefferson prepared to depart Philadelphia on May 15. It would be the last time he ever left the city where, on and off for nearly two decades, he had played such an active role in the affairs of his nation, and his feelings must surely have been mixed as he readied for his journey home. He had especially enjoyed Philadelphia's scientific society, though in the last few years, bitter partisanship had ruptured friendships and soured his experience. As he wrote to William Hamilton, owner of a botanical garden on the western fringe of the city, "I have seen during the late political paroxysm here, numbers whom I had highly esteemed draw off from me, insomuch as to cross the street to avoid meeting me."[16] Was he looking backward nostalgically as his stage pulled away from the city on that day in mid-May, or was he looking forward to Monticello and anticipating with excitement the move to the new federal city?

On the journey to Albemarle County Jefferson tarried in Eppington to visit Francis and Elizabeth Eppes and at Mont Blanco, the home of Maria and her husband John. Maria, fully recovered, joined her father on his way to Monticello, where she stayed for an extended visit. Jefferson remained extremely guarded in his correspondence, but the activity of his supporters throughout the nation had only increased. Republican operatives were busy speaking on his behalf, distributing pamphlets, and organizing. Jefferson did not involve himself in the details of this work, though he was aware of it, and the Republicans—more respectful than the Federalists of the voice of the people—were much more proficient than their opponents in the everyday work of campaigning. Over the late spring and summer, Jefferson received far more letters than he wrote and was circumspect in his replies.

In mid-December he received a letter from William Short in Paris, who pointedly noted that Jefferson had never replied to his letter of February 27, 1798, on black ability, civilization, and emancipation. The news that George Washington's will freed his slaves on Mrs. Washington's death brought the issue back to mind for Short, who believed that the former president's suddenly manumitting all his slaves, without concern for their skills, maturity, and so on, "at least impolitic." Far better to have carefully prepared them for freedom through apprenticeships and other methods. Short believed Washington should have set up a permanent fund to purchase the freedom of his bondspeople as they came of age. Had he done this, Short believed, Washington would have set for other slaveholding men of means an important example that would have done substantial good in the world.[17] Jefferson, of course, did not reply.

One possible explanation is that Jefferson was almost bankrupt. Whatever he might have wished to do, he did not believe himself capable of making such a momentous decision for himself and his many dependents. He was also restrained by a law passed by the Virginia legislature in 1792 allowing creditors to seize freed slaves to settle debts incurred before their emancipation.[18] Any slaves Jefferson manumitted would have been at risk of capture and immediate reenslavement by his creditors.

IF JEFFERSON PREFERRED to stay out of the press, he did expect his correspondents to spread his views by word of mouth. Still upset by the Federalist proposal to impose common law across the nation, for instance, he wrote to Gideon Granger in Connecticut, "If the principle were to prevail of a common law being in force in the US. . . . it would become the most corrupt government on the face of the earth."[19] He knew Granger would share his views widely with other Connecticut Republicans and moderates.

By the end of the summer it seemed increasingly likely that the Republicans would win the majority of seats in the new Congress and that Jefferson would be elected president. Though perhaps not fully aware of the brutal infighting in the Federalist camp, he did know of one outrageous Federalist attempt to steal the election—aside from Hamilton's machinations in New York—that had been thwarted. A Federalist senator from Pennsylvania, James Ross, had introduced a bill in the Senate in January 1800 seeking to establish a new process for counting the votes of the electoral college. Ross's bill would create a committee of thirteen, consisting of six members chosen by the House, six chosen by the Senate, and the chief justice. This committee would determine which votes to count and which to throw out on suspicion of invalidity, and its decisions would be final. Since the Federalists controlled both houses and the chief justice was also a Federalist, the bill would have guaranteed a Federalist victory. The nation only learned about the plan when Republican editor William Duane caught wind of it, obtained a leaked copy of the proposal, and promptly published details of the scheme in his newspaper, the *Aurora*. A firestorm ensued, with even some moderate Federalists like Secretary of

State John Marshall (he would become chief justice of the Supreme Court in January 1801) believing that his colleagues had gone a step too far.[20]

By this time, Jefferson was thinking about how, assuming he won the presidency, he could help scale back the angry rhetoric. People should be able to differ on principle, he believed, without hating one other. As he wrote a political supporter in Virginia, "Our chief object at present should be to reconcile the divisions which have been artificially excited and to restore society to it's wonted harmony. whenever this shall be done it will be found that there are very few real opponents to a government elective at short intervals."[21] He would return to this theme in his inaugural address.

For some unknown reason, Jefferson uncharacteristically committed to paper some self-reflections in the late summer of 1800. Did the anniversary, in mid-August, of his father's death more than four decades earlier prompt him to take the measure of his own life? In any case, the result was a brief document beginning with the sentences "I have sometimes asked myself whether my country is the better for my having lived at all? I do not know that it is. I have been the instrument of doing the following things; but they would have been done by others." He next listed chronologically some of his accomplishments, beginning with improvements to the navigation of the Rivanna River, moving through his authorship of the Declaration of Independence and achievement of disestablishment and religious freedom in Virginia, and continuing on to such matters as the introduction of olive trees to the South and a new species of rice to South Carolina and Georgia. About these latter causes, Jefferson penned one of his more famous aphorisms: "the greatest service which can be rendered any country is to add an useful plant to it's culture."[22]

But on the whole, there was little time for taking stock. On August 30 a slave revolt, led by a man named Gabriel and involving as many as two hundred slaves, was supposed to begin in Richmond; it was foiled by a torrential rainstorm that made several waterways impassable and by the betrayal of the movement by two of its members. The state and local authorities acted quickly and brutally, eventually capturing Gabriel and several other coconspirators, but not before waves of fear and a desire for retribution washed across the state.[23] Once things had calmed a bit, Governor James Monroe—elected the previous year—wrote Jefferson a brief report on the "prospect of an insurrection of the negroes in this city," concluding, "I hope the danger is passed."[24] Six days later another letter arrived from Monroe. "Where to arrest the hand of the Executioner, is a question of great importance," wrote the concerned governor. How could society peacefully reintegrate the would-be rebels? Monroe pointed out that the state had no power to send such slaves abroad. "Nor is it less difficult to say whether mercy or severity is the better policy in this case," he wrote, adding, "I shall be happy to have yr. opinion on these points."[25]

No doubt news of the revolt alarmed Jefferson. And in his cautious election mode, he was not eager to offer an opinion. Nevertheless, he did reply to Monroe, counseling, "There is a strong sentiment that there has been hanging enough. The other states & the world at large will for ever condemn us if we indulge a principle of revenge, or go one step beyond absolute necessity. . . . surely the legislature would pass a law for their exportation, the proper measure on this & all similar occasions?" Then Jefferson, conscious of the political consequences of anything he might say, admonished, "I hazard these thoughts for your own consideration only, as I should be unwilling to be quoted in the case." He urged Monroe to secure a variety of opinions before making a final decision.[26] Ten months later, when Jefferson was president, Monroe wrote again, this time at the legislature's request, asking where to send the convicted slaves. Jefferson did not reply for months, but when he did, he suggested Saint-Domingue, if the present ruler there, François-Dominique Toussaint-Louverture, agreed. Jefferson concluded that foreseeable problems with this plan were "over-weighed" "by the humanity of the measures proposed, & the advantages of disembarrassing ourselves of such dangerous characters."[27] Nothing ever came of this proposed solution. Gabriel and twenty-five other slave rebels were hanged.

BACK IN MAY THE Republicans in Congress had caucused days after the election results in New York State became known, nominating Aaron Burr as their vice presidential candidate. No ballot designated Jefferson and Burr as the presidential and vice presidential candidates, respectively. The Constitution did not provide for tickets. Both men were effectively running for president. The Federalists acted at almost the same time but with less unity. Many of the Hamiltonians continued to despise President John Adams, but they knew an open break would hand the election to Jefferson. So in an elaborately balanced decision, they decided to back Adams, running for a second term, and Charles Cotesworth Pinckney, again with no formal designation of one as the presidential and the other as the vice presidential candidate. The Hamiltonian faction secretly hoped that some of South Carolina's electors would not vote for Adams, thereby throwing the election to Pinckney, whom Hamilton thought far more malleable, thus controllable, than Adams.[28]

Adams had long been aware that most members of his cabinet were more loyal to Hamilton than to him. The acrimony became more widely known in early May, when, shortly after securing the caucus nomination, Adams summarily dismissed Secretary of War James McHenry and Secretary of State Timothy Pickering. Adams had called McHenry in on May 7 for a conference, and a minor disagreement detonated his anger. The president launched into a vitriolic attack on Hamilton, called him "an intriguer—the greatest intriguer in the world—a man devoid of every moral principle—a bastard." Then he pronounced, "Mr. Jefferson is an infinitely better man; a wiser one, I am sure, and, if President, will act wisely." McHenry wrote up a summary of this meeting and sent copies to both Adams and Hamilton, fanning the flames.[29]

A number of events fueled Hamilton's animosity toward Adams. He blamed Adams for the legislature's refusal to keep funding the army that Hamilton commanded; he thought Adams's sending of new delegates to France was misguided and had blunted a Federalist weapon against the Republicans; and he saw Adams's sacking of Pickering and McHenry as depriving him of his rightful power over Adams's faltering administration.[30] Able to contain himself no longer, Hamilton published on October 22, 1800, a fifty-four-page indictment of Adams titled a *Letter from Alexander Hamilton, Concerning the Public Conduct and Character of John Adams*.[31] The Federalist Party was publicly imploding.

Jefferson watched the frenzy from Monticello, taking relatively little notice of the increasingly vicious attacks launched by the Federalists at him. While the Republicans charged the Federalists with monarchical aspirations and support for policies that benefitted only economic elites, the Federalists painted with a broader brush. They revived older allegations that Jefferson was a radical Jacobin, an uncritical supporter of the French Revolution and all things French, as well as critiques of him as a dreamy, impractical philosopher—perhaps a satisfactory temperament for a college professor but certainly not for an elected official. Supposedly, too, he had cheated clients during his years as a lawyer, and while serving as Virginia's governor in 1780, he had fled like a coward from British troops. The small number of southern Federalists attacked him for his antislavery views in *Notes on the State of Virginia*, while northern Federalists criticized his comments about black inferiority in the same publication. Extreme Federalist opponents blamed the aborted slave revolt in Virginia in 1800 on Jefferson's general advocacy of liberty. But perhaps the most common charges concerned Jefferson's supposed atheism or deism; sermon after sermon and pamphlet after pamphlet in the North predicted dire consequences if he became president. According to one clergyman, the effect "would be, to destroy religion, introduce immorality, and loosen all the bonds of society."[32]

Jefferson understood these kinds of diatribes as political propaganda and duly disregarded them. He knew that many of the attacks from clergy stemmed from his fight for religious freedom in Virginia. In fact, he seemed almost to take pride in his vilification by advocates for established religion, for as he wrote Benjamin Rush, "I have sworn upon the altar of god eternal hostility against every form of tyranny over the mind of men." This was "all they have to fear from me," he stated, "& enough too in their opinion."[33]

Throughout the early autumn he received positive news about the election results. He knew that the congressional elections were tilting toward the Republicans as well. While he had great support from the countryside, the artisans, mechanics, small tradesmen, and businessmen in the nation's cities also believed that the party of Jefferson favored them. The general populace viewed the party headed by the Virginia plantation owner as the more supportive of the average man and the Federalists as preferring the economic elites. Charles Pinckney wrote Jefferson about how hard he was working for him in South Carolina; a postscript read merely, "We Have . . . Carried It."[34] Jefferson suspected he would win the electoral vote with relative ease.

JEFFERSON MADE PREPARATIONS to travel to the new capital city, Washington, in late November, planning to arrive shortly after President Adams had addressed the joint meeting of Congress that convened in the middle of that month. Jefferson appeared in the city on November 27 and promptly found quarters in a boardinghouse near the Capitol Building. He had a private room and a "separate drawing-room for the reception of his visitors" and took his meals at a common table that seated up to thirty diners.[35] This table provided him with both sustenance and political intelligence. The boardinghouse commanded a lovely view of the cityscape, at the time consisting only of a scattering of homes among the hills and trees of the gently rolling countryside.

The only building completed so far was that housing the Treasury Department. The president's mansion was still under construction, and both houses of Congress had to crowd into the single chamber in the Capitol ultimately intended for Senate. For Jefferson especially, since he had, along with Washington, been so involved in planning the capital city, it must have been a particularly exciting time.[36] Within days of his arrival, he subscribed to journalist Samuel Harrison Smith's recently founded newspaper, the *National Intelligencer*, and within weeks arranged with Smith to print his *Manual of Parliamentary Practice* in book form.

When Jefferson delivered his manuscript to Smith, he met the printer's vivacious wife, diarist Margaret Bayard Smith, who was taken with Jefferson's gentle nature. "Can this man so meek and mild, yet dignified in his manners, with a voice so soft and low, with a countenance so benignant and intelligent," she asked herself, be that radical Jacobin she had read so much about? She described his voice as "almost femininely soft and gentle," and as they talked at first of mundane things, "before I was conscious of it, he had drawn me into observations of a more personal and interesting nature. I know not how it was, but there was something in his manner, his countenance and voice that at once unlocked my heart, and in answer to his casual enquiries . . . I found myself frankly telling him what I liked or disliked in our present circumstances and abode."[37] It is easy to forget, given all his other qualities and interests and his frequent complaints about the challenges and discord of politics, that Jefferson was, in the most fundamental sense at least, the consummate politician.

On December 3, 1800, the members of the electoral college assembled in their respective state capitals and cast their votes. Within a week interested observers could piece together the likely results. By December 12, Jefferson—after receiving Charles Pinckney's letter—was fairly certain of the outcome. At least, he was certain enough to offer Robert R. Livingston the post of secretary of the navy on December 14.[38] But a potential problem arose. According to the Constitution, of course, electors voted for two men, without selecting one for president and the other for vice president. Everyone seems to have assumed that at least one Republican elector would drop his vote for Burr, giving Jefferson a majority—all based on the expectation that both Jefferson and Burr would have more total votes than either Adams or Pinckney.

But what if, owing to lack of coordination, the two Republicans ended up in a tie? If there were no clear winner, the decision would devolve to the current House of Representatives, not the newly elected House, with its expected Republican majority. The House would choose a president from among the two men with the most electoral votes. Jefferson laid out this scenario to his son-in-law on December 12, with his habitual refusal to begin sentences with capital letters: "it was intended that one vote should be thrown away from Colo. Burr. it is believed Georgia will withhold from him one or two. the votes will stand probably T.J. 73. Burr about 7[o.] mr. Adams 65. Pinckney probably lower than that. it is fortunate that some difference will be made between the two highest candidates; because it is said the Feds here held a Caucus & came to a resolution that in the event of their being equal, they would prevent an election which they could have done, by dividing the H. of R."[39] This was Jefferson's first expression of worry that the Federalists, through their control of the House, might steal the election from him—and, by extension, the people.

Jefferson sent a letter to Burr, surely at least in part to remind his ambitious colleague that, according to what Jefferson understood as the will of the people, Burr would fill the secondary slot. Jefferson wrote, "I understand several of the highflying federalists have expressed their hope that the two republican tickets may be equal, & their determination in that case to prevent a choice by the H. of R." He then explained, "Decency required that I should be so entirely passive during the late contest that I never once asked whether arrangements had been made to prevent so many from dropping votes intentionally as might frustrate the republican wish; nor did I doubt till lately that such had been made."[40] Burr understood the full implications of Jefferson's letter—that the voters intended for Jefferson to be president—and replied on December 23, clarifying that he intended, and had told all his friends, not to "[divert] a single Vote from you."[41]

Jefferson repeated the warning to Judge Hugh Henry Brackenridge, referring to a conspiracy "either to prevent an election altogether, or reverse what has been understood to have been the wishes of the people as to their President & Vice-president."[42] Jefferson's anxiety was growing. He wrote Madison on December 19 that the possibility of a tie between him and Burr was producing "exultation in the federalists, who openly declare they will prevent an election, and will name a President of the Senate pro tem. by what they say would only be a *stretch* of the constitution."[43] He confided to Madison the day after Christmas, "The Feds appear determined to prevent an election, & to pass a bill giving the government to mr. Jay, appointed Chief justice, or to Marshall as Secy. of state."[44] During this brief period of worry came a potentially reassuring letter from Caesar A. Rodney of Philadelphia. Rodney wrote that his friend, James A. Bayard, a Federalist and the only congressman from tiny Delaware, had declared that in the event of a tie vote in the House, "he should not hesitate to vote for you."[45] Jefferson knew that if a single Federalist waivered and changed his vote, that could settle it; but he confessed to son-in-law Thomas Mann Randolph his doubt that even one would actually do so.[46]

In January Monroe wrote from Richmond of rumors that the Federalists were determined not to let the House choose a president but rather to devise some sort of legislative act to declare John Marshall or another prominent Federalist president. Monroe doubted the Federalists would actually go that far, but he broached the ultimate worry: Would the union hold if one party refused to accept the express decision of the people and attempted to steal the election?[47]

From Pennsylvania Thomas McKean wrote Jefferson that while it appeared from the "explicit & honorable conduct of Mr; [sic] Burr there will be no competition on his part," he had also heard that the Federalists would connive to appoint a president of their own choosing until they could arrange for a new national election.[48] That same day, January 10, 1801, Madison wrote of the Federalists' attempt to "strangle the election of the people, and smuggle into the chief Magistracy the creature of a faction,"[49] although he did doubt that Adams would participate. The tone of the letters escalated as the full import of what could possibly happen became better understood.

A few days later a correspondent from Pittsburgh wrote to Jefferson, "The more violent of the ex-federalists protest against an election at all, or declare for Burr as President."[50] Jefferson had probably foreseen this possibility, and perhaps that it might tempt Burr, which may explain his earlier letters to the New Yorker. Burr quickly wrote Jefferson a heartening (if disingenuous) letter: "It was to be expected that the enemy would endeavor to sow tares between us, that they might divide us and our friends. Every consideration satisfies me you will be on your guard against this, as I assure you I am strongly."[51] Jefferson may have begun to question Burr's loyalty and, on February 12, noted that Gouverneur Morris had recently expressed wonderment as to why "Burr who is 400. miles off (at Albany) has agents here at work with great activity, while mr. Jefferson, who is on the spot, does nothing?"[52]

The Federalist Party was in fact doing everything it could to prevent Jefferson's election as president, although neither Adams nor Hamilton participated in the more unsavory maneuvering. Many Federalists realized that they could not simply void the election or contrive to place a

noncandidate like John Marshall into office. The High Federalists, per-
ceiving Burr's relative lack of principles, supported his candidacy, reasoning that he could be bought or manipulated. Burr was known, after all, as
hungry for power and fame. The House passed a set of procedural rules on
February 9 providing for nonstop balloting until a president was chosen.
There was real fear, on all sides, of unrest and violence—or worse. Some
Republicans had conjured the death of the union or even a Federalist attempt to assassinate Jefferson.[53]

As the Federalists began dangling promises before Burr, Hamilton
suddenly put an end to the scheming. He had long opposed Jefferson,
thinking him too impractical, too democratic, and too idealistic, but he
fiercely hated and distrusted Aaron Burr—and Hamilton was a talented
and experienced hater. When faced with the prospect of a man he believed
totally devoid of principle becoming president, Hamilton turned his ferocious energies against Burr, attacking him as dangerous and soliciting support for Jefferson. Hamilton believed Jefferson, despite his faults, an
incorruptible man of character. He was certain that Jefferson could on occasion support energetic executive action and, anyway, that his temporizing nature would make drastic changes unlikely. Clearly, Burr must have
given the High Federalists some reason to think he would go along with
their plot. He never publicly denied his willingness to accept the presidency however he might win it; Jefferson and his supporters never forgave
Burr for this treachery.[54] In addition to Hamilton, neither John Adams
nor John Marshall supported Burr's candidacy in any way.

On February 11, Jefferson, as the sitting vice president, unbound the
certificates bearing the electoral votes and reported the results to the joint
session of Congress. The election totals were as expected: Jefferson and
Burr each had seventy-three; Adams, sixty-five; Pinckney, one less at
sixty-four; and John Jay, one lonely vote. Promptly the members of the
House retired to their hall and, as agreed, began a process of balloting
without formal adjournment or pause for any other business until they
had chosen a president. After the first ballot, with each state casting but
one vote, eight were for Jefferson, six were for Burr, and two were dead-
locked. Victory required nine votes—the support of a majority of the
states. The house voted again and again, eighteen more times, with the final vote coming hours after midnight. In none of these votes did the tally
change.

The representatives were attempting, all along, to extract concessions
from Jefferson in exchange for votes. The Federalist James Bayard of

Delaware believed he had obtained promises from the Republican congressman Samuel Smith that Jefferson would compromise on some of his long-held positions—that he would honor the nation's debt, fund the navy, and not summarily replace all lower-level government employees—but Jefferson flatly denied it (as did Smith). Jefferson wrote Monroe, before the final decision came, "Many attempts have been made to obtain terms & promises from me. I have declared to them unequivocally, that I would not recieve the government on capitulation, that I would not go into it with my hands tied."[55] He stood firm throughout the process, resolved to win the presidency without compromising his principles.

On Tuesday, February 17, the House voted again, for the thirty-seventh time, finally achieving a breakthrough. Bayard abstained, and because he was the sole congressman from Delaware, Jefferson, who still had eight votes, now had a winning majority of the states casting a vote. Bayard's abstention, then, determined the final outcome; the Federalist congressmen from Maryland, Vermont, and South Carolina followed him in abstaining as well. Federalist abstentions in Maryland and Vermont, which each had a Republican senator as well, gave those states to Jefferson. Jefferson now had ten votes. Burr received four votes, from Connecticut, Massachusetts, New Hampshire, and Rhode Island. Jefferson had been elected the nation's third president, but not a single Federalist congressmen ended up voting for him.[56]

THE VOTE DEMONSTRATED the persisting partisan rancor. Though Congress did little in the opening months of the year, on February 3 the Senate had, after some haggling with the High Federalists, ratified a new treaty with France—the Treaty of Môrtefontaine, usually called the Convention of 1800. The commission Adams had sent to Paris in 1799 had borne fruit. Most Federalists opposed the agreement, and the Republicans approved only halfheartedly, believing it insufficiently solved the trade issues between the two nations. But at least, in their view, it eliminated the threat of war.[57]

As for the immediate impact of the election, when on February 11 it became known that Jefferson and Burr had received the most electoral votes, the Federalists acted quickly in an attempt to dominate federal officeholding. On February 13 the Congress passed the Judiciary Act of 1801, reducing the number of seats on the Supreme Court from six to five, to lessen the chance of the Republicans appointing a justice friendly to their philosophy to the highest court. At the same time, the act doubled the number of circuit courts and reorganized the district courts, creating twenty-three new federal judgeships. John Adams instantly set about naming men to these positions, somehow appointing them all in the three weeks left in his administration. Jefferson saw these actions as a means of negating, as much as possible, the consequences of his victory.[58] As he saw it, his most important tasks, after he assumed office, would be to defuse the virulent partisanship dividing the land, prove that he was no radical Jacobin, and convince Americans once again that they shared, and indeed sprang from, the same values.

PART V

WASHINGTON, DC, 1801–1809

21

Political Faith and Presidential Style

IMMEDIATELY AFTER THE House of Representatives elected Thomas Jefferson president on February 17, an artillery piece on the Alexandria courthouse grounds fired sixteen celebratory rounds. Within hours one of that city's newspapers was distributing a handbill announcing the result. Over the next few months, congratulatory letters and proclamations, from both individuals and municipalities, poured in from around the nation. The inauguration was scheduled for March 4, so Jefferson had only two weeks to put together some semblance of an administration before taking office. He also had to staff what was then called either the Presidential Mansion or the President's House. And of course he had to write his inaugural address, recognizing the importance of his first public pronouncements after such a brutal and drawn-out electoral process.

As the inauguration drew near, Jefferson attended to all manner of important details. There was no communication of importance between John Adams and Jefferson, no "transition team," no consultation between the outgoing and incoming administrations. Overall, there was little cooperation of any kind, with two exceptions: Samuel Dexter, whom Adams had appointed interim secretary of the Treasury in December, stayed on for several months until Jefferson's new appointee was available, and Benjamin Stoddert, who lived in Georgetown, did likewise for the secretaryship of the navy.

Other details concerned the inauguration ceremony. As part of his ambition to change the tone and character of the executive office, and with his distaste for everything that smacked of monarchy, Jefferson decided not to ride in a luxurious carriage to his swearing in, as had his predecessors, but rather to walk the several hundred yards from his boardinghouse to the Senate chamber of the Capitol building. Also unlike George Washington and John Adams, he wore relatively plain clothes and no sword. A small parade—headed by a company of artillerymen, followed by a company of riflemen, a delegation of marshals from the District of Columbia, and a small number of Jefferson's friends and Republican congressmen—led him to the Capitol. Jefferson, a tall, lean, long-legged fifty-seven-year old whose powerful stride reflected his lifelong love of walking, came last. This inaugural procession—the first held in the new capital—largely lacked the pomp and pageantry associated with the few other such momentous occasions in the nation's short history.[1]

The ornate Senate chamber, the only completed section of the Capitol building, was full, but no member of Jefferson's family was present, and neither was John Adams, who had left the city that morning at 4:00 a.m., dismayed by the end of his tenure and racked with grief and guilt over the death a few months earlier of his son Charles.[2] When Jefferson entered the room, Vice President Aaron Burr, already having taken his oath, gave him the center chair on the platform and took the one to its left; Chief Justice John Marshall sat to Jefferson's right. After the attendees were seated, Jefferson and Marshall rose, and Jefferson took the presidential oath. Then Jefferson proceeded to address the vast audience, speaking in "so low a tone," as Margaret Bayard Smith recounted, "that few heard it." However, Jefferson had earlier that morning given a copy of his address to her husband, Samuel Harrison Smith, editor of the *National Intelligencer*, and by the time the ceremony had finished, freshly printed copies of the speech were ready and available.[3] The brief address of fewer than 2,000 words proved one of the new president's most elegant attempts to articulate his political principles and unite the nation. Jefferson placed great faith in the power of words carefully composed, and although he had had only a fortnight to prepare his remarks, the result was nevertheless a masterpiece of American political rhetoric.[4]

Jefferson began his address with at once a statement of personal humility and an expansive vision of the future of the nation. Calling his position "the first Executive office," not the presidency, and declaring "a sincere consciousness that the task is above my talents," he described "a rising nation, spread over a wide and fruitful land, traversing all the seas with the rich productions of their industry[.] . . . I shrink from the contemplation & humble myself before the magnitude of the undertaking."[5] But he took heart from the "wisdom" and "virtue" of many of those in his audience, to whom he looked "with encouragement for that guidance and support which may enable us to steer with safety the vessel in which we are all embarked, amidst the conflicting elements of a troubled world."[6]

About the disputatious political campaign the nation had just endured, Jefferson admitted that people "unused to think freely, and to speak and write what they think," would understandably wonder how the nation could heal its recent wounds. As Jefferson optimistically put it, the people would "according to the rules of the constitution of course arrange themselves under the will of the law, and unite in common effort for the common good." Here he began to elaborate on the bedrock of the American system: "All too will bear in mind this sacred principle, that though the will of the majority is in all cases to prevail, that will, to be rightful, must be reasonable; that the minority possess their equal rights, which equal laws must protect, and to violate would be oppression."

Jefferson understood that Federalist partisans who saw him as a wild-eyed French radical feared that he might take actions against them now, and he sought to soothe their anxieties. "Let us then, fellow citizens, unite with one heart and one mind, let us restore to social intercourse that harmony and affection without which liberty, and even life itself, are but dreary things. And let us reflect that having banished from our land that religious intolerance under which mankind so long bled and suffered, we have yet gained little if we countenance political intolerance, as despotic, as wicked, and capable of as bitter and bloody persecutions."[7] In three of the most famous lines he ever wrote, Jefferson continued, "Every difference of opinion is not a difference of principle. We have called by different names brethren of the same principle. We are all republicans: we are all federalists."[8]

Jefferson did not capitalize "republicans" and "federalists" in the written document of the speech, although some later newspaper printings did. He was not referring specifically to the names of the two political parties but rather making the point that practically everyone engaged in the political contest shared two fundamental ideas that the American system held in balance: a strong central government and vigorous state governments, bound together in a federated system that mediated between the two. Some might lean more toward the central government, others toward the state governments, but nearly everyone appreciated and supported the idea that the central and state governments each had constitutionally defined spheres of authority. No one, Jefferson said, suggested abandoning this idea of government, which he called "the world's best hope." Who would possibly want to, on the grounds of some "theoretic and visionary fear," when it had already proved a success in its first thirteen years of existence? Jefferson believed the United States boasted the strongest government in the world and that every citizen would fly to its defense if an enemy, internal or external, ever threatened it.[9]

Having attempted to reassure opponents who feared he aimed to replace the US government with some radical French scheme, Jefferson described his vision of life in America. "Let us then, with courage and confidence, pursue our own federal and republican principles; our attachment to union and representative government. Kindly separated by nature and a wide ocean" from all the turmoil, corruption, and tyranny of Europe, "possessing a chosen country, with room enough for our descendants to the thousandth and thousandth generation," free of aristocratic regimes and able to enjoy the benefits that result from our own merit and actions, "enlightened by a benign religion, professed indeed and practiced in various forms, yet all of them inculcating honesty, truth, temperance, gratitude and the love of man, acknowledging and adoring an overruling providence, which by all its dispensations proves that it delights in the happiness of man here, and his greater happiness hereafter . . . ; with all these blessings, what more is necessary to make us a happy and prosperous people?"[10]

Jefferson then arrived at the principle at the center of his political theory and policy: "Still one thing more, fellow citizens, a wise and frugal government, which shall restrain men from injuring one another, shall leave them otherwise free to regulate their own pursuits of industry and improvement, and shall not take from the mouth of labor the bread it has earned. That is the sum of good government; and this is necessary to close the circle of our felicities."[11] This spare ideal encapsulated Jefferson's reaction to the perceived overreach of the Federalists, with their central bank, laws against free speech, harsh limitations on aliens, and expectation that the Treasury should shape the economy—which could mean, in practice, that the nation's wealth would remain in the hands of the already rich. In fact, Jefferson did expect much more from the central government, including the support of education, science, and exploration, for example. But in this forum, he chose to emphasize that his administration would rein in governmental arrogance and welcome a wider range of viewpoints.

It is imperative to remember the significance to Jefferson of ideas and the words that expressed them; as the primary author of the Declaration of Independence, he perhaps understood more than any other politician of the time the power of ideas upon the mind. The inauguration speech was not mere rhetoric. For him, not narrow self-interest but a set of shared ideals—before laws, convention, and so on—actually held the nation together. To that end he expanded on his conception of what the American government had been, was, and should be. Since he was about to exercise the duties of the nation's chief executive, he explained, it was "proper you should understand what I deem the essential principles of our government." He would attempt to outline them "within the narrowest compass they will bear, stating the general principle, but not all its limitations."[12] Jefferson then provided, in some of his most memorable language, a précis of his political religion.

> Equal and exact justice to all men, of whatever state or persuasion, religious or political:—peace, commerce, and honest friendship with all nations, entangling alliances with none:—the support of the state governments in all their rights . . . :—the preservation of the General government in its whole constitutional vigor, as the sheet anchor of our peace at home, and safety abroad: a jealous care of the right of election by the people, . . . :—absolute acquiescence in the decisions of the majority, the vital principle of republics . . . :—a well disciplined militia, our best reliance in peace, and for the first moments of war, till regulars may relieve them:—the supremacy of the civil over the military authority:— economy in the public expense, that labor may be lightly burthened:—the honest payment of our debts and sacred preservation of the public faith:—encouragement of agriculture, and of commerce as its handmaid:—the diffusion of information, and arraignment of all abuses at the bar of the public reason:—freedom of religion; freedom of the press; and freedom of person, under the protection of the Habeas Corpus:—and trial by juries impartially selected.

These foundational principles should form, he continued, "the creed of our political faith"; should the nation ever wander from them, it should reexamine its history and the "wisdom of our sages" and return to the "touchstone" of these values, "which alone leads to peace, liberty and safety."[13]

Concluding, Jefferson pledged to live, and attempt to govern by, these principles. He claimed that when he erred, as surely he must, as a human being, it would be unintentional, and he would always be open to advice and counsel. With that, he stated, "I advance with obedience to the work." His final words: "And may that infinite power, which rules the destinies of the universe, lead our councils to what is best, and give them a favorable issue for your peace and prosperity."[14] All but his most hardened partisan opponents immediately perceived the inspirational power and political genius of the inaugural address; indeed, its generosity of spirit surprised most Federalists. Thus did Jefferson begin what he much later labeled "the revolution of 1800 . . . as real a revolution in the principles of our government as that of 1776 was in its form."[15]

BY REVOLUTION JEFFERSON meant that the management and personnel of the government would become more democratic and reflective of the entire country and its various interests, not just those of the commercial elite centered in the Northeast.[16] Above all, he venerated the sovereignty of the people. He understood that to be widely accepted and enduring, change would have to take place gradually. It was "difficult . . . to move . . . the great machine of society" because it was "impossible to advance the notions of a whole people suddenly to ideal right. . . . [N]o more good must be attempted than the nation can bear," he wrote to a friend, shortly after his inauguration.[17]

Though determined to make the federal government more reflective of popular opinion, Jefferson also wanted to make his appointments in a careful, deliberative manner, respectful of the other party. He knew that he had control over only a portion of government appointees and that, in pursuit of his goal of national harmony, he could not summarily dismiss all existing Federalist officeholders. The process proved the most intense challenge of his first year as president.

Even before the election was settled, Jefferson had enlisted James Madison as secretary of state, and he also had apparently asked Albert Gallatin to serve as his secretary of the Treasury. With knowledge of finances and banking second only to Alexander Hamilton's, Gallatin was essential to the new administration. The day after the electoral decision in the House of Representatives, Jefferson wrote to General Henry Dearborn of Massachusetts, offering him the secretaryship of war.[18] Jefferson wanted a national, not a sectional, administration, which helps explain this choice. For similar reasons, he appointed as his attorney general a highly respected lawyer from Massachusetts, Levi Lincoln.

Dearborn and Lincoln both took office soon after Jefferson's inauguration.[19] Madison, who became tied up in a complicated tangle of executor duties on the death of his father, had to delay his arrival in the capital until May.[20] Gallatin was also delayed, not wanting to leave the side of his wife who was about to give birth to their third child. Jefferson had to scramble to fill the rest of the posts in his administration. He had sent a feeler to Robert R. Livingston, chancellor of New York, back in December about becoming secretary of the navy, but Livingston declined—although he did accept Jefferson's invitation in February to become minister plenipotentiary to France. Jefferson next offered the appointment to Samuel Smith, a leading Baltimore merchant and trusted Republican, who also demurred. After offering the position, unsuccessfully, to two others and persuading Smith to hold the office temporarily, Jefferson managed to convince a prominent Baltimore maritime lawyer (and Samuel Smith's brother), Robert Smith, to accept the secretaryship. Fortunately, he proved a skilled administrator.[21]

Jefferson's last major appointment, in October, was of Connecticut's Gideon Granger as postmaster general, although this position did not convey cabinet rank. Jefferson's cabinet was young—with an average age in 1801 of forty-seven—and well educated. Aware that a disloyal cabinet often hostile to his policies had crippled John Adams's presidency, Jefferson was pleased to have assembled a group whose competency, cooperativeness, and support he was sure of. From the start, Jefferson decided to manage his cabinet meetings to maximize openness and, ideally, consensus.

Jefferson had lesser appointments to attend to as well. He wanted an accomplished French chef to serve in the President's House, and less than a week after confirmation of his election, he wrote to William Evans, a tavern owner in Baltimore who was in contact with James Hemings, asking him to write Hemings about the position. Even before he heard back, Jefferson got a letter from another previous employee, Francis Say, reporting that he had recently seen Hemings. Jefferson's onetime slave had said that "he was willing to serve you before any other man in the Union" but wanted Jefferson's request in writing, with the details spelled out. Evans eventually reported the same news.

A month later Jefferson replied to Evans that he took Hemings's delays and desire for a written invitation as signs of his unwillingness to come to Washington. Jefferson asked Evans to convey to Hemings that out of deference to what he understood to be the latter's desires, he had hired a chef from Philadelphia.[22] In August Hemings did agree to come to Monticello for several weeks to cook while Jefferson visited; Jefferson paid him well for this. Did Hemings want a letter directly from Jefferson out of pride? Did Jefferson not write one because he believed to do so was beneath him? Other explanations may have had little—or perhaps everything—to do with their relationship. Hemings's drinking (which Evans had mentioned) had apparently gotten worse; the longtime slave, who had lived free for eight years, committed suicide in late October or early November 1801.[23]

Jefferson had more success with another appointment. The entire executive office consisted of one person, the president, with no provision for any staff, so Jefferson decided to hire a private secretary whose salary he would pay out of his own pocket. This individual would do relatively little writing; he would serve more as an aide than a secretary. Jefferson wanted a quick learner whom he trusted implicitly. He also wanted someone who—because Jefferson intended to reduce the size of the army—knew the inner workings of the military establishment and had an informed opinion about the qualifications and merit of various officers. Jefferson turned to twenty-six-year-old Meriwether Lewis from Albemarle County. Jefferson knew him and his family; he also knew that Lewis had served in the army since 1795 in the western and northwestern territories and, in his capacity as a regimental paymaster, had acquired a wide familiarity with the US officer corps. Although the salary was only $500 annually, Jefferson pointed out to Lewis that he would have few expenses because he could live in the President's House.[24] Flattered, Lewis quickly accepted. Jefferson soon came to treat him practically as a son, later writing to his elder daughter that he and Lewis were living alone in the President's House "like two mice in a church."[25]

JEFFERSON DEEMED inappropriate and justly voided the nonjudicial appointments John Adams made after realizing, in mid-December, that he would not be reelected. In fact, Jefferson thought Adams's actions, including his hasty judicial nominations after the passage of the February 1801 Judiciary Act, unconscionable. Jefferson accepted that he could not touch new judges but intended to consider every other Adams appointment null and void.[26] Shortly after he took office Jefferson sent a circular letter to these approximately two dozen officials, informing them that they should consider "the appointment you have received as if never made."[27]

A point of difficulty was that Jefferson's claim in his inaugural address that "we are all republicans: we are all federalists" had led some Federalists to assume that he would not remove certain political appointees. Indeed, many misunderstand Jefferson to have said that he would leave in place every single current (and hence Federalist) officeholder. The Republicans, on the other hand, believed it essential to sweep Federalists from the national government. Representative William Branch Giles of Virginia wrote to Jefferson, "A pretty general purgation of office has been one of the benefits expected by the friends of the new order of things," and the administration's failure to effect one "would produce general and lasting disgusts in its best friends."[28] Even Elbridge Gerry of Massachusetts, a moderate Federalist, urged, "It is therefore incumbent on you, Sir, as expeditiously as circumstances will permit, to clear the Augean stable, of it's obnoxious occupants."[29]

Yet the president firmly believed that while the Federalist Party's leaders were incorrigible—"incurables,"[30] as he put it—the majority of citizens of the Northeast, misled by Federalist propaganda, would flock to the Republican cause if the Republicans acted magnanimously. His was inclined to remove only extreme partisans—and all those included in the "midnight appointments" made by Adams in the waning hours of his administration—but not fair, competent men who simply held political opinions different from his. Yet this policy satisfied no one. The Federalists attacked every single removal, and the Republicans demanded the ouster of most or all Federalists. No wonder Jefferson confessed to George Clinton, "Of all the duties imposed on the Executive head of a government, appointment to office is the most difficult & most irksome."[31]

Jefferson reasoned that if the Republicans could avoid "shocking" the feelings of the Federalist portion of the country, in time they could wean away the average citizens of that region and by that means return "harmony & union . . . to our country."[32] He told Governor Thomas McKean of Pennsylvania, "To restore that harmony which our predecessors so wickedly made it their object to break up, to render us again one people, acting as one nation, should be the object of every man really a patriot."[33] Jefferson knew that patience and moderation would be more effective in winning over his former opponents than an iron fist. As he confided to Madison later that year, although he regarded Noah Webster of Connecticut "as a mere pedagogue of very limited understanding and very strong prejudices & party passions, yet as editor of a paper . . . , he may be worth stroking."[34]

The Connecticut reference was not incidental. The state was inveterately Federalist; Federalists held all public offices, and Republicans were regularly disparaged as unworthy and undeserving of service in the state government. On the death of longtime collector of the port at New Haven, David Austin, on February 5, 1801, President Adams had rushed through his replacement with Elizur Goodrich—one of the appointments Jefferson considered void.

He moved cautiously to find a successor, settling on the seventy-seven-year-old Samuel Bishop, mayor of New Haven and a highly respected judge, though he expected that his far younger son Abraham—a forthright Republican—would perform most of the duties. Unsurprisingly, the city's Federalists were incensed that Jefferson had voided the Goodrich appointment, and on June 18, 1801, eighty merchants signed a protest petition praising Goodrich and excoriating both Bishops, father and son.[35]

Jefferson responded with an emphatic letter on July 1. He began by describing Samuel Bishop's distinguished credentials; by any measure, he was highly qualified for the office. Then he asked, given that the Adams administration had excluded members of the opposing party from all offices, did the New Haven merchants really imagine "that this monopoly of office was still to be continued in the hands of the minority? does it violate their *equal rights* to assert some rights in the Majority also?"[36] Was it not reasonable that the administration of the government reflect the will of the people? If so, there must be some removals.

Jefferson made clear that he regretted the need to consider political affiliation in such matters, but he blamed the Federalists for that reality. He explained that after restoring balance in government offices between the two parties, he would "return with joy to that state of things when the only questions concerning a candidate shall be, is he honest? is he capable? is he faithful to the constitution?"[37]

Naturally, this approach mollified few Federalists. And, pressured as he was by members of his own party, Jefferson did consider party affiliation in many of his appointments. Other than Adams's last-minute appointees and marshals for federal courts, however, he removed only about a third of Federalist officeholders.[38] When Jefferson himself left office in early 1809, many Adams appointees still held their positions. Jefferson did gradually change the profile of government workers, but his thinking about removals was far more moderate than his letter to the New Haven merchants suggested.[39] He was not, in terms of later political practice, "a spoilsman."[40] And his gentle, persuasive, moderate approach to political partisanship proved remarkably effective both electorally and in shaping congressional action.[41]

JEFFERSON'S SCHOLARLY AND unfailingly polite personal style enabled him to maintain a cabinet of unusual stability and effectiveness, and he also proved a master of congressional politics through a combination of personal charm, conversational virtuosity, and the delights of his table.[42] It helped that he genuinely enjoyed living in the District of Columbia; he called the President's House "a very agreeable country residence" and described the small town—its population in 1800 was a mere 3,210—as "free from the noise, the heat, the stench, & the bustle of a close built town." Not every resident found the new capital to their liking, however.[43]

Washington was surely the most unprepossessing capital in the Western world, with its muddy streets interrupted by tree stumps, total absence of great merchant houses, thriving businesses, theaters, and music halls, and lack of the polish and splendor of Philadelphia, much less of London or Paris. It was a dreary place. Most members of Congress only stayed in the "city" for the few months that Congress was in session, leaving their families behind in their hometowns. The congressmen (their numbers grew from 141 to 176 over the course of Jefferson's two terms) mainly lived in boardinghouses, with members from the two parties tending to live separately. No doubt boardinghouse conversation soon became routine, if not boring, and the food was often greasy and monotonous.

In this context an invitation to dine at the President's House was a signal attraction. (Though coated with lime-based whitewash in 1798, the sandstone building was not yet called the White House.) When Congress was in session, Jefferson usually hosted three dinners a week, with the number invited to each ranging from eight to perhaps fifteen; a dozen was normal. Jefferson selected the guests with care, finding that a successful evening required that all be of the same party.[44] He often invited nonpoliticians and ensured that every visitor felt completely welcome. Dinner began at 3:30 p.m. The guests ate at a long, oval table, seated randomly, not by level of distinction.

The food, paired with selections from his unparalleled wine cellar, reflected Jefferson's love of French cuisine—as Margaret Bayard Smith aptly put it, "Republican simplicity was united to Epicurean delicacy."[45] Waiters placed the hot dishes of food in dumbwaiters near the table just before the guests were seated, for Jefferson liked to put the food on the guests' plates himself.[46] And while simple, the menu was remarkably abundant.[47]

Jefferson had a way of putting everyone at ease. His breadth of knowledge allowed him to talk intelligently with all of his guests, and he had a particular knack for reaching out to newcomers, or those who were shy, and easing them into the general conversation. He never dominated the talk, but he shaped the discussion, and though it was never directly about politics or legislation, Jefferson adroitly made his positions known in a manner both nonintimidating and persuasive. Dressing casually to make his guest feel at home, if not unguarded, Jefferson, with his unrivaled gifts as host, made every dinner seem, and every guest feel, special. He had the ability to "draw forth the talents and information of each and all of his guests and to place every one in an advantageous light and by being pleased with themselves, be enabled to please others."[48]

In his second term, explaining the purpose of the dinners to a South Carolina congressman, Jefferson said, "I cultivate personal intercourse with the members of the legislature that we may know one another and have opportunities of little explanations of circumstances, which, not understood might produce jealousies and suspicions injurious to the public interest, which is best promoted by harmony and mutual confidence among its functionaries."[49] Such casual politicking was effective. Federalist legislators who dined with the president were impressed, finding him personally appealing and even, at times, discovering new reasons to go along with his policies. William Plumer, a Federalist senator from New Hampshire, for example, recorded in his diary a congressional dispute over an appointment that resulted in approval of the Republican candidate after initial opposition from a number of senators, because "the President's dinners had silenced them."[50] Jefferson had, as one scholar pithily put it, a "genius for personal politics."[51] Not all dinners at the President's House were implicitly political, however; Jefferson often invited close friends and their wives to dine, and on occasion he invited just one male friend for dinner and a game of chess.

JEFFERSON'S INDUSTRIOUSNESS was a marvel. He wrote to his son-in-law in November 1801 that he spent from ten to twelve or thirteen hours a day at his writing desk.[52] He rose before sunrise, worked for seven or eight hours, took about two hours in the early afternoon for a horseback ride or brisk walk, then ate dinner. After dinner he did not leave the mansion for social visits but rather returned to his desk for another three or four hours, reading and writing. He had hoped, now that he was only three days' travel from Monticello, to return to his home more often, but he found to his dismay that his correspondence and government business followed him there, to a degree he had never before experienced. (Throughout his presidency Jefferson was deluged with correspondence. He wrote Lafayette early in 1804, "I have now a thousand letters before me to each of which I ought to write an answer . . . but to all it is impossible."[53]) In 1801, he escaped to the little mountain for almost three weeks in April and then again later in the summer; this would prove to be his normal practice for the duration of his time in office—he fled the summer humidity and supposed unhealthiness of the Potomac environs for the higher, drier air of Monticello. The postmaster general made special arrangements for mail delivery between Washington and Monticello in two days, so he never fell behind in his official duties. These late-summer or early-autumn visits often lasted about two months. Even so, Jefferson spent far more time in the capital than had Adams, who had often lived more than half the year in Quincy.

Jefferson was especially happy to spend most of August and September 1801 at Monticello; not only did he enjoy two lengthy visits from his daughters and their families, but both daughters gave birth during their time with him. He also managed to vaccinate most of his slave force against smallpox. Jefferson had traveled to New York in 1766 for inoculation, and in 1782 he had had his children similarly treated. Later he did the same for the three slaves closest to him: James, Robert, and Sally Hemings, the last during her time in Paris. By 1801, there was a new technique. Variolation, which involved introducing a tiny bit of live smallpox virus into the body, was dangerous. At the end of the eighteenth century, English doctor Edward Jenner discovered that inoculation with the vaccinia (or cowpox) virus prevented smallpox and was far less risky; thus the term "vaccination." At the time smallpox caused approximately 10 percent of deaths in England, so Jenner's invention was a major breakthrough.[54]

Jefferson kept abreast of Jenner's progress. In 1800, the English doctor sent a booklet describing his discovery to a prominent Philadelphia physician, Dr. Benjamin Waterhouse. Subsequently Waterhouse approached President Adams with it, but Adams was not interested.[55] Waterhouse sent a letter to Jefferson on December 1, 1800, enclosing a pamphlet he had recently published, *A Prospect of Exterminating the Small-pox*, outlining the advantages of the new cowpox vaccine. Jefferson reported to Waterhouse that he read it overnight.[56] Over the course of the next year Jefferson corresponded frequently with Waterhouse and arranged for him to send the new vaccine to Dr. Edward Gantt of Washington. When Gantt's first three trials failed to trigger a minor form of the illness, Jefferson suggested to Waterhouse that perhaps the vaccine had been spoiled in transit. He advised him to try sending it again: this time he should insert the vaccine into a thin vial that, after being securely corked, should be placed in a larger vial filled with water, both to prevent air from getting in and to keep the inner vial cooler.[57] This worked. Jefferson also wrote Waterhouse to ask him to send vials of his vaccine directly to a doctor in Petersburg, who would then give it to Jefferson's family physician in Charlottesville, Dr. William Wardlaw. Jefferson sent Wardlaw several publications on the new procedure and arranged for him to come to Monticello late in the summer of 1801.[58]

Over several weeks, Wardlaw vaccinated twenty of Jefferson's slaves and kept close track of how they reacted, even reporting to Waterhouse the size and shape of the pustules resulting from the injections. Jefferson performed some of the procedures himself, in addition vaccinating some of his white neighbors. Soon thereafter Jefferson's two sons-in-law vaccinated many of their own slaves, and Jefferson extended the program for his, again reporting the results. He also arranged to have the vaccine sent to several other physicians in Virginia. When Waterhouse in 1802 published a medical article on the success of vaccination, it included data on Jefferson's efforts at Monticello.[59] Jefferson's imprimatur helped popularize vaccination among physicians across the nation. Whether Jefferson saw the vaccination of his slaves as a scientific experiment more than an action on behalf of their health, we cannot know.

JEFFERSON SOMEWHAT regretfully returned to Washington on September 30. Nevertheless, he did enjoy the city's bucolic scenery and was still happily engaged with the work of the Board of Commissioners, which laid out streets and designated open spaces. But he became distressed by the destruction of the scattered groves of trees by settlers in need of firewood. At a dinner party with friends—not one of his working dinners—he announced, in self-mocking hyperbole, "How I wish that I possessed the power of a despot." This utterance shocked his guests, but he quickly explained by saying that if he had such power, he would protect the proud, magnificent trees daily falling to the ax. As a mere president, he was helpless to stop their destruction—seventy tall tulip poplars girdled in one night, for instance.[60]

Jefferson was at least able to shape his interactions with his cabinet members. His experience as secretary of state under Washington and his knowledge of both his two predecessors' cabinets guided his approach. He approved of some aspects of Washington's; for example, Washington requested that his secretaries share all meaningful information about their departments with him. Jefferson wanted to avoid the infighting he witnessed among Washington's cabinet members but noted that Washington took advice from them even in difficult times.[61] Adams's relationship with his cabinet, of course, had been little short of disastrous.

Jefferson sat down in November 1801 to formally describe how he wished his cabinet to operate. The resulting "Circular to the Heads of Departments" recommended that cabinet members practice the procedure Washington had pioneered—Jefferson offered a slightly romanticized portrait—of sharing "letters of business" with the president so that he could comment on or suggest revisions as needed and also keep "always in accurate possession of all facts & proceedings in every part of the Union, & to whatsoever department they related." If a letter came directly to the president, he would forward it to the appropriate department head for action. "If a doubt of any importance arose, he reserved it for conference." In this fashion the president "formed a central point for the different branches, preserved a unity of object and action among them, exercised that participation in the gestion of affairs which his office made incumbent upon himself, and met himself the due responsibility for whatever was done."[62]

Perhaps most important to Jefferson was the understanding that he would be the unifying force behind government objectives and actions. Jefferson planned to be an active leader, not a figurehead who delegated most decisions to his cabinet members. He intended to determine and execute policy—a new role for the office. But he also wanted to work closely with and honestly consult his cabinet members, in large part because he knew they shared perspectives and principles with him and were loyal to his purposes. As he told them, "My confidence in those whom I am so happy as to have associated with me, is unlimited, unqualified, & unabated."[63]

In the event, Jefferson had the most stable cabinet in US history, making only one change in his second term, and his consultations with its members were regularly full, frank, and to his benefit. His department secretaries were not afraid to speak their minds, and their advice often caused Jefferson to revise or reject what he had first proposed. He was strong enough to respond to their suggestions, questions, and criticisms professionally and without ill will. It never hurt that Jefferson's irenic personality quelled potential conflicts among the members.[64]

The cabinet operated as Jefferson wished when he began to prepare, in November 1801, what he called his First Annual Message. The Constitution required that the president "from time to time give to the Congress information on the state of the union." Washington and Adams had appeared before Congress and presented oral reports. Jefferson decided to send to both houses a written message, because he fully understood his oratorical abilities were weak and because he and other Republicans believed the president's appearance before Congress smacked of the British practice whereby the monarch annually presented an address to the Parliament.

Washington had asked his cabinet heads for suggestions and ideas and then tasked Hamilton with writing his address. That was not Jefferson's way. He spent upward of two weeks writing a draft, then submitted it, serially, to his cabinet heads for substantive input and stylistic suggestions. After he had their replies—Gallatin was especially thorough—Jefferson prepared a final version.[65] He appears to have completed the message by November 27, but by the time he submitted it to Congress, he had determined to omit a long and controversial passage on the Sedition Act. Eleven days later, on December 8, Meriwether Lewis delivered handwritten copies of the message to both houses of Congress. The document not only assessed the "state of the nation," as had Washington's and Adams's addresses, but looked to the future, to policies Jefferson wished Congress to consider.[66] Jefferson was the intellectual leader of his party, the embodiment of its principles, and its primary political strategist; now he was actively presenting a legislative program to Congress. His conception of the presidency differed quite a bit from either Washington's or Adams's.[67]

ONE OF JEFFERSON'S larger purposes as president was to thwart what he viewed as the monarchical, centralizing tendencies of the previous administrations in favor of his understanding of the nation's foundational principles. Two events at the very end of 1801 made clear that this project was already succeeding. The first was the gift to Jefferson of a huge wheel of cheese, some four feet in diameter and weighing more than 1,200 pounds, prepared by the men and women farmers of Berkshire County, Massachusetts, in the summer of 1801. Federalist wits mocked it as the "mammoth cheese," but its makers soon gladly accepted the moniker, as well as the press attention and acclaim, as the wheel made its way by cart and by boat from western Massachusetts to Washington. It arrived on December 29 and was formally presented to Jefferson at the President's House on January 1, 1802. Among the delegation from Berkshire County was Baptist leader John Leland, who two decades earlier had championed religious liberty in Virginia on behalf of Jefferson's Statute for Religious Freedom.[68]

The delegation stated, "We believe the Supreme Ruler of the Universe, who raises up men to achieve great events, has raised up a *Jefferson* at this critical day, to defend *Republicanism*, and to baffle the arts of *Aristocracy*."[69] This was no lark or advertising stunt but rather a concrete expression of political support by people long deprived by the Federalist majority of a voice in the state's politics.[70] Portions of the cheese were still at the President's House in 1805.

Apparently by happenstance, the day after the mammoth cheese arrived, Jefferson received a letter delivered to him by a committee representing the Danbury Baptist Association, an organization of twenty-three Baptist churches in western Connecticut and three in eastern New York. The committee stated, "Our Sentiments are uniformly on the side of Religious Liberty—That Religion is at all times and places a Matter between God and Individuals." They expressed the hope that "the sentiments of our beloved President, which have had such genial Effect already, like the radiant beams of the Sun, will shine & prevail through all these States and all the world till Hierarchy and tyranny be destroyed from the Earth."[71]

These words, especially since they came from states where religion was still established, gave Jefferson reason to believe that the principles he espoused would in time spread across the land. He sent a reply to the Danbury Baptists on December 31. This brief letter is one of the most consequential in the entire corpus of Jefferson's correspondence. He began by stating that the committee's "affectionate sentiments" gave him "the highest satisfaction" and went on to compare his views with theirs:

> Believing with you that religion is a matter which lies solely between Man & his God, that he owes account to none other for his faith or his worship, that the legitimate powers of government reach actions only, & not opinions, I contemplate with sovereign reverence that act of the whole American people which declared that their legislature should "make no law respecting an establishment of religion, or prohibiting the free exercise thereof," thus building a wall of separation between Church & State. adhering to this expression of the supreme will of the nation in behalf of the rights of conscience, I shall see with sincere satisfaction the progress of those sentiments which tend to restore to man all his natural rights.[72]

Nowhere did he express his long-standing views on religious freedom with more power or eloquence.

Jefferson took great satisfaction in his first year as chief executive; in his view, the domestic political situation had recovered from the low point of the presidential campaign. If he was focused inward in 1801, however, the next year would see him turn his gaze beyond the nation's borders, toward new challenges and opportunities.

22

"We Are Acting for All Mankind"

I N 1797 JEFFERSON HAD referred to the office of the presidency as "a splendid misery," a phrase that he may have recalled once he held the office and found his time devoured by such mundanities as appointing officials.[1] He had far grander ambitions, above all to trim a federal government that he believed had become too powerful under Federalist leadership. Accomplishing that end required a detailed understanding of most government functions. Jefferson may have enjoyed thinking of governance in broad, philosophical terms, but he found that he could not avoid strict attention to the inner workings of the actual federal government—and he showed surprising skill at both the conceptual and the administrative aspects of the job. Yet every president has discovered that events often intervene and his response to them often shapes his administration's nature and legacy. The case proved no different for Jefferson.

WITHIN MONTHS OF taking office Jefferson envisioned two primary goals: "to reduce the government to republican principles & practices; & to heal the wounds of party."[2] By the former he meant not simply that the government should be staffed largely by men who identified with the Republican Party but that its size and expense should reflect republican principles of simplicity and frugality, allowing for a reduction in taxes and a steady decrease in the national debt. In his First Annual Message, the text of which he had delivered to both houses of Congress on December 8, 1801, he staked out his views. As would prove characteristic of his approach to the legislators, he hinted at or suggested rather than dictated the policies he favored. His speech presaged his legislative agenda for the following months, and through his personal contacts with members of Congress, his deft use of the power of persuasion, and the political mandate he enjoyed, Jefferson would accomplish his goals.

He opened by reminding his audience that the European "wars and troubles, which have for so many years afflicted our sister-nations, have at length come to an end."[3] This salutary news had brought about a boom in American commerce, with an accompanying increase in customs duties. Moreover, the census figures for 1800 indicated that the nation's population would double every twenty-two years, and such remarkable fecundity forecast sustained economic growth.[4] These two conditions prompted Jefferson to propose dropping the unpopular internal taxes—"excises [on] stamps, auctions, licenses, carriages and refined sugars . . . [and] postage on newspapers"—that had been in place for ten years. The combined revenue from customs and land sales would suffice "to provide for the support of the government, to pay the interest of the public debts," and at the same time to reduce and then pay off the federal debt. He recognized that a major war would restore a great need for revenue, and other "untoward events may change this prospect of things," but it made no sense now to tax "the industry of our fellow citizens to accumulate treasury for wars to happen we know not when, and which might not perhaps happen but from the temptations offered by that treasure."[5]

By ending internal taxes, Jefferson could abolish the internal revenue service, which meant that four hundred tax collectors, or 40 percent of Treasury employees outside the capital city, would lose their jobs—but this would also reduce the government's costs. The external revenue service, which collected customs, remained in place. Moreover, the president proposed trimming the size of the diplomatic corps in Europe, with similar cuts in the Treasury and State Departments; indeed, by the time Jefferson left office in 1809, the total number of civil service workers in Washington was actually slightly lower than at his inauguration, despite the nation's having doubled in geographical size in the interim.[6] Drawing on the advice of Albert Gallatin, Henry Dearborn, and Samuel Smith, Jefferson proposed drastic cuts to the army and the number of forts throughout the nation, arguing that the first line of defense should be the militia, with the regular army only called upon in a national emergency. Naval reductions had been underway since John Adams's administration. Jefferson thought oceangoing ships necessary only to protect American merchants against the Barbary pirates in the Mediterranean; defending the homeland, in his view, would require nothing more than a fleet of smaller gunboats. Over the course of 1802

Congress enacted Jefferson's policies on all these issues, shrinking government's size and its expenses.

It is difficult to comprehend today just how small the US military was in 1802. Republican legislation lowered the number of officers and enlisted men to only 3,312. The army had one artillery regiment, two regiments of infantry, and a newly authorized corps of engineers stationed at West Point.[7] By the end of 1801, the navy had only six frigates; most had been sold. Eight smaller vessels and some sixty gunboats were in service. All told, naval personnel consisted of 9 captains, 36 lieutenants, and 150 midshipmen. The nation still supported six naval yards but administered them with strict economy.[8]

In other ways, too, Jefferson sought to make real his vision of a "wise and frugal government" that "shall restrain men from injuring one another [and] leave them otherwise free to regulate their own pursuits of industry and improvement."[9] His policy recommendations in his First Annual Message, made concrete by legislation in 1802, largely achieved these aims. Drawing back from the economic centralization of the Hamiltonian years, he described his philosophy in his Annual Message: "Agriculture, manufactures, commerce and navigation, the four pillars of our prosperity, are then most thriving when left most free to individual enterprise."[10] Whether Jefferson's policies had any immediate effect or not, the temporary peace in Europe brought a surge of trade and economic growth, coincidentally winning for the Republicans even broader political support and dooming the Federalist Party.

Jefferson fought what he saw as government assaults on the rights of actual and would-be citizens. The Sedition Act of July 14, 1798, expired on the last day of the Adams administration. As president, Jefferson pardoned those who still suffered under its provisions and forgave their fines; he also dismissed the case against Republican editor William Duane. Strongly opposed to the anti-immigrant feature of the former Alien Act, he argued against the fourteen-year residency requirement. Congress accepted this recommendation, changing it to five years in 1802.[11]

THE DESPISED Judiciary Act of 1801 was still in effect late in the year, and in his address Jefferson offered a deceptively mild statement about it: "The judiciary system of the United States, and especially that portion of it recently erected, will of course present itself to the contemplation of Congress."[12] He developed his case against the Judiciary Act on the grounds of efficiency and economy. He objected to the act's downsizing of the Supreme Court from six justices to five on the grounds that this limited his ability to make appointments to the highest court. And he suggested that, as there existed no heavy press of cases demanding relief, the sixteen new courts the act created were unnecessary. He did not want to remove judges appointed for life but reasoned that if their courts simply ceased to exist, they were not in fact being removed from office.

Due to support for Jefferson in Congress, the Senate repealed the Judiciary Act of 1801 on February 13, 1802, and the House followed suit on March 3.[13] As a complement to this decision, Congress passed an amendatory act on April 29 to address another feature of the Judiciary Act: the latter had expanded federal courts' jurisdictions at the expense of state courts and ended the rule that the Supreme Court justices had to serve on circuit courts across the nation. The amendatory act doubled the number of circuit courts to six and required each Supreme Court justice to serve on one of these courts twice a year. The Supreme Court would meet for one longer session annually (in February) in Washington, DC, as opposed to twice annually, as before. After all, Congress reasoned, the bulk of judicial business occurred at the circuit court level. Still, the amendatory act also represented another small-government response to the Hamiltonian ethos.[14]

As Jefferson was directing his energies against the Judiciary Act, one of the so-called midnight appointees was attempting to force him to honor all of Adams's last-minute appointments. William Marbury of Maryland was one of several new justices of the peace for the District of Columbia, but the commissions had not been delivered before Jefferson took office, and the new president treated them as null. On December 17, 1801, nine days after Jefferson's Annual Message to Congress, Marbury and three of the other would-be justices petitioned the Supreme Court to issue a writ of mandamus—a court order—directing Secretary of State James Madison to deliver the commissions and thereby grant the appointees their positions. Marbury's strategy rested on a provision of the Judiciary Act of 1789 that gave the Supreme Court jurisdiction in cases involving writs against officers of the executive branch. Chief Justice John Marshall, who disliked Jefferson and opposed his policies, wanted to back Marbury, but he was politically astute enough to realize that the Court really had no means to enforce the order.

Marshall's brilliant way out of this dilemma brought no relief to Marbury but set a lasting standard. The chief justice decreed, in a decision delivered on February 24, 1803, that the 1789 act itself violated the

Constitution, so the Court had no authority to issue the desired writ of mandamus. Instead, Marshall criticized Jefferson and his actions toward Marbury and his cohorts. The scolding annoyed Jefferson, but he was gratified that his dismissals stood. The decision—known as *Marbury v. Madison*—later became famous for establishing that the Supreme Court could declare unconstitutional and thus invalidate an act of Congress, although at the time neither Jefferson nor most others disputed that notion.[15] Rather, the Court's decision was widely seen merely as a victory for Jefferson.

AMID THE DAILY political battles, Jefferson never lost sight of his larger project: uniting the nation behind the Republican cause. As he wrote his Parisian friend Pierre Samuel Du Pont de Nemours early in 1802, "I am perfectly satisfied the effect of the proceedings of this session of Congress will be to consolidate the great body of well meaning citizens together, whether federal or republican, heretofore called."[16] Jefferson sometimes sounded like a secular millennialist, so broad were his expectations for the future of the nation and its role as an exemplar for others. In the summer of the same year he wrote to Joseph Priestley, "It is impossible not to be sensible that we are acting for all mankind: that circumstances denied to others, but indulged to us, have imposed on us the duty of proving what is the degree of freedom and selfgovernment in which a society may venture to leave it's individual members."[17] Confident that the mass of the people approved of the policies he was pursuing, Jefferson was determined not to let fanatical Federalist leaders pervert what he saw as the mission of America.

This bedrock confidence helps explains his role in creating the US Military Academy at West Point in 1802—something of an about-face given his opposition almost a decade earlier to then secretary of war Henry Knox's proposal to create such an institution. He had actually interrupted Knox in a cabinet discussion to argue that the Constitution categorically did not allow for one. Jefferson had feared a military academy shaped by Alexander Hamilton, who, he believed, had a Caesar complex and would thus misuse the army, perhaps disastrously. But with the prevailing political winds at his back in 1800, he changed his mind.

Like most Americans, Jefferson was wary of a standing army, particularly one led by an almost hereditary class of aristocratic officers; to Republicans, history showed that an officer corps often posed a threat to civilian government. But now that he was in power, he posited that a military academy, properly administered, could in fact create a corps of *republicanized* army officers.[18] Thus when Secretary of War Dearborn proposed to enlarge the new specialized corps of engineers stationed at West Point into a military school, Jefferson quickly approved the idea,[19] selected Jonathan Williams (a relative of Benjamin Franklin and a scientist in his own right) as superintendent, and began to build support for the proposal in Congress. On March 16, 1802, Congress passed the Military Establishment Act, authorizing Jefferson to appoint a corps of engineers to be stationed at West Point and organized into a military academy. The president would have the power to admit cadets to this academy, and Jefferson planned to draw them from a broad cross section of capable citizens. More specifically, Jefferson, aided by Dearborn, took great care to appoint young men with known Republican credentials.[20] Thus was the US Military Academy established to change the nature of the existing (and, of course, miniscule) officer corps.

Jefferson's approach to the military academy question reveals an often misunderstood facet of his constitutionalism. He did not view the Constitution as a wholly restraining document. Rather, he argued for a narrow interpretation of the powers it granted the federal government. But within that limited sphere—whether it came to the regular army, national commerce, or foreign policy—he believed the government had very great power indeed.[21] And he saw the military academy as a foundation not only for a strong regular army but for increased commercial activity within the nation. Aware of the strong emphasis on engineering in the new French and English military academies, Jefferson recognized the role the school at West Point could play in supplying engineers for the army as well as for civilian purposes in an expanding nation in need of new infrastructure.[22] His vision for the school was even more expansive than that suggests. When in December 1802 superintendent Jonathan Williams formed the United States Military Philosophical Society to promote the study of science at the academy and nominated Jefferson to membership, Jefferson gladly agreed to be a permanent patron.[23] By 1807 the academy was one of the nation's centers for scientific study.[24]

In 1802, Jefferson also played a significant role in the creation of the Library of Congress. There had been proposals for a library to serve the needs of the Congress and other high government officials since 1789, but the capital's original locations, New York and Philadelphia, already had public and private libraries. When the government began preparations to move to Washington, the library became a higher priority. On April 22,

1800, Congress passed a bill providing $5,000 to purchase appropriate books and a room in which to hold them. A committee created for the task ordered 152 works in 740 volumes from a London bookseller, with the books arriving in Baltimore early in 1801 and forwarded to Georgetown in April.[25] But no location had been selected, no rules for the operation of the library had been drafted, and no one had been put in charge.

We do not know what role Jefferson played in the legislation, but on January 26, 1802, the new Congress passed "An Act Concerning the Library for the Use of Both Houses of Congress." It specified a location in the north wing of the Capitol building, authorized the president of the Senate and the Speaker of the House to create the necessary rules, authorized the US president to choose the librarian of Congress, and appropriated additional funds to purchase books and maps. Jefferson promptly appointed John Beckley, a longtime Republican operative and clerk of the House of Representatives, as librarian. That Jefferson did so a mere two days after the bill's passage suggests that he had prior knowledge of it.

Jefferson's actions on the library's behalf did not cease there. As the nation's bibliophile in chief, he selected most of the books purchased while he was president. When Senator Abraham Baldwin, chair of the library committee, asked Jefferson for advice on the matter, Jefferson replied with a long list of titles, explaining that he had "confined the catalogue to those branches of science which belong to the deliberations of the members as statesmen." He omitted classics that he assumed most private libraries already held but did include a variety of encyclopedias and dictionaries. He recommended obtaining "all the travels, histories, accounts &c of America, previous to the revolution," and warned, "It is already become all but impossible to make a collection of these things." "[S]tanding orders should be lodged with our ministers in Spain, France & England, & our Consul at Amsterdam to procure every thing within that description which can be hunted up in those countries."[26] He later arranged with Albert Gallatin to set up accounts for funding book purchases in London and Paris and sent lists of books to be purchased in each city.[27]

Jefferson's work for the library would outlive his presidency. The Library of Congress was destroyed on August 24, 1814, during the War of 1812, when the invading British army used its then 3,000 volumes as kindling to burn the US Capitol. Several weeks later, in despair over Britain's "acts of barbarism," Jefferson wrote a letter to Samuel H. Smith that he wanted his old friend to transmit to Congress. In it he offered to sell his entire library—"I have been 50. years making it, & have spared no pains, opportunity or expence to make it what it is"—to the nation to reconstitute the Library. (As Jefferson wrote to then president Madison, he had "long been sensible that my library would be an interesting possession for the public, and the loss Congress has recently sustained . . . renders this the proper moment for placing it at their service."[28]) Congress could set its own price but had to purchase his library as a whole and keep it together as a single collection. As he explained, "I do not know that it contains any branch of science which Congress would wish to exclude from their collection. there is in fact no subject to which a member of Congress may not have occasion to refer."[29]

Jefferson's library turned out to comprise 6,487 volumes, and the price decided on was $23,950—an incredible bargain. The issue became controversial when the still-diminished Federalist Party began attacking the collection not only for its cost but for containing too many foreign-language titles, too many books of a philosophical nature, and too many works that Federalists deemed deistic or even atheistic in nature.[30] In the end the bill to purchase the library passed on January 26, 1815, with the Federalist minority voting 51–4 against. By May 15 the last of ten heavily laden wagons had left Monticello conveying Jefferson's personal library to its new home, where it formed the foundation of what eventually became the greatest library in the world.[31] As the final wagonload of books left Monticello, Jefferson wrote to Smith, "An interesting treasure is added to your city, now become the depository of unquestionably the choicest collection of books in the US. And I hope it will not be without some general effect on the literature of our country."[32]

ALL THAT LAY FAR in the future. More pressing, early in Jefferson's presidency, than a military academy or national library was the ongoing threat of international conflict, despite the relative quiescence in Europe. He had been in office only six weeks when his attorney general informed him that the bashaw of Tripoli was demanding higher payments. Two months later Jefferson received a letter from an American in Sicily reporting that the bey (bashaw and bey were common titles for rulers in North Africa and the Ottoman Empire) of Tripoli had announced he would declare war against the United States in April if American payments to him did not increase.[33] This was a familiar theme to Jefferson; as American ministers to France and England in the 1780s, he and John Adams had dealt with similar demands and threats from the rulers of the Barbary nations.

Adams and Jefferson had tried diplomacy, but the Barbary nations insisted on payments. At the time, Jefferson believed that sending money to North Africa brought dishonor to the United States. He also believed the amount demanded would constantly increase, arguing that instead of paying off the pirates, the United States should send its navy to bombard the offending city-states. But Adams, on the basis of relative costs, wanted to acquiesce to Barbary demands, and the money-strapped American government agreed with him.[34]

Jefferson convened his cabinet on May 15, 1801, and put the following question to them: Should the small American navy be sent to patrol the Mediterranean? Every cabinet member agreed it should and determined that, if attacked, the vessels could respond without presidential or congressional approval. Five days later the acting secretary of the navy, Samuel Smith, ordered Captain Richard Dale to sail to the Mediterranean.[35] The Barbary powers responded angrily. In late August came confirmation that the bashaw of Tripoli had ordered the US flag at the American consulate cut down, a symbolic declaration of war.[36] By November news arrived that the American ship *Enterprise* had defeated a Tripolitan vessel and killed twenty of its sailors.[37] Jefferson had never asked Congress for a declaration of war, but in his Annual Message to Congress in December, he explained the origins of the crisis and his response. He mentioned the recent success of the men of the *Enterprise*, whose bravery would serve as "a testimony to the world" of the nation's resolve. Jefferson wanted European powers to view his actions against the pirates as evidence that the United States would not be cowed by belligerence. Congress backed Jefferson's policies.

Over the next four years the Jefferson administration prosecuted the Barbary Wars, during which most of the small US fleet, which grew slightly in this period, plied the warm waters of the Mediterranean, sailing from victory to victory.[38] The presence of American ships persuaded the other Barbary states to abandon Tripoli. However, in September 1803 the US frigate *Philadelphia* ran aground while patrolling that port. In a moment of courageousness, Lieutenant Stephan Decatur captured a small Tripolitan boat and snuck into the harbor to burn the *Philadelphia* to prevent its being turned against American ships. The following year, the Tripolitan forces, trapped in the city by the US Navy, finally surrendered.[39] The United States paid $60,000 in ransom to free prisoners from the *Philadelphia* but forced Tripoli to end its demands for tribute. The resulting treaty was widely heralded at home and abroad as a significant American victory; no less an eminence than England's Admiral Horatio

Nelson declared Decatur's raid to burn the *Philadelphia* "the most bold and daring act of the age."[40] Jefferson's policy toward the Barbary pirates was vindicated.

ALMOST SIMULTANEOUSLY with the first reports of impending conflict with Tripoli came news of a potentially much more significant international problem. On August 27, 1801, Jefferson received a private letter written months before by an American citizen in Paris. It contained the intelligence that "Spain has ceded Louisiana to France, & an expedition is preparing to take possession of New Orleans, & to plant a Colony in that country."[41] Rumors had arrived in May from Rufus King, the American minister to England, that such a cession had "in all probability . . . been executed"—and the letter served as confirmation. There was no absolute proof of the transfer—it would take months for US officials to understand what had transpired—but Jefferson was gravely concerned that Napoleon Bonaparte now controlled the trans-Mississippi.[42] If the transfer had occurred, it would be the most serious international incident in the young nation's history, and threatening trade restrictions would not suffice to protect American interests.

Jefferson had long believed that the territory west of the Mississippi was vital to America's future, since free access to Caribbean, Latin American, and European ports via New Orleans was critical to American commerce. He had been pleased that Spain, a weaker nation than France, held the territory, which he assumed that sometime in the distant future the United States would inevitably subsume.[43] In 1790, during the so-called Nootka Sound Controversy, when the government worried that England might try to take Spanish-held Louisiana, Jefferson even considered military intervention to prevent such an outcome.[44] Likewise, Jefferson did not rule out war in 1801, after learning of French actions to acquire the region. But he would conduct his diplomatic maneuvering in secrecy, without involving Congress, as he deemed foreign policy the sole province of the executive branch. In his December 1801 Annual Message, Jefferson made no mention of the rumored cession of Louisiana to France.

Robert R. Livingston was the newly appointed minister to France; Charles Pinckney served as minister to Spain. After consulting with them, Madison and Jefferson concluded that the United States should attempt to convince France that taking over Louisiana was not in her long-term interests: France's Caribbean colonies could freely buy provisions from the United States in peacetime, but if war erupted between France and the

United States, and France blockaded New Orleans, that trade would come to a swift end. If the cession occurred, the United States would not immediately declare war. First it would seek to retain its right to deposit goods in New Orleans, and if France blocked that action, the government would attempt to persuade France to sell a portion of the east bank of the Mississippi and the Florida territories.[45] Jefferson began a correspondence among Livingston, Pinckney, and his friend Du Pont. The last was journeying back to France for private reasons, and Jefferson hoped his letter to him would shape French actions—either as a result of Du Pont's personal relationships with important French officials or because French and Spanish officials would intercept and read his letters to the two ministers.

After a steady drumbeat of reports suggesting a real threat from France, Jefferson sent a long and dramatically worded letter to Livingston by way of Du Pont, filled with information he wanted the French to learn—the envelope was intentionally left unsealed so that Du Pont would read the letter too. Jefferson explained that the cession of Louisiana to France

> completely reverses all the political relations of the US. and will form a new epoch in our political course. . . . There is on the globe one single spot, the possessor of which is our natural & habitual enemy. it is New Orleans, through which the produce of three eights of our territory must pass to market. . . . France placing herself in that door assumes to us the attitude of defiance. Spain might have retained it quietly for years. . . . not so can it ever be in the hands of France. . . . These circumstances render it impossible that France and the US. can continue long friends when they meet in so irritable a position. . . . the day that France takes possession of N. Orleans fixes . . . that moment we must marry ourselves to the British fleet & nation.

The only resolution "would be the ceding to us the island of New Orleans and the Floridas." As if those words were not strong enough, he concluded by writing, "Every eye in the US. is now fixed on this affair of Louisiana. Perhaps nothing since the revolutionary war has produced more uneasy sensations through the body of the nation."[46] Jefferson had thereby made clear that if France went ahead with the cession, it would force the United States into alliance with England, perhaps tipping the balance in a war that France saw as imminent. Meanwhile, Jefferson and Madison went out of their way to make the British chargé d'affaires, Edward Thornton, feel welcome, in the knowledge that the French chargé would notify his superiors in Paris of the United States' apparent change in attitude toward the English.[47]

A little over a week after Jefferson gave Du Pont the letter, he received a response (Du Pont had not yet left New York City for France). Hoping for peaceful relations between France and the United States, Du Pont mentioned, "It is claimed that you have thought of purchasing Louisiana. If there is some truth to it, I think it a salutary and acceptable thought." This pleased Jefferson, although he quickly replied, "Louisiana we do not want. the island of New Orleans & Florida are desireable for the sake of peace; but it must be a very moderate sum of money indeed which we could give for them; we are poor, in debt & anxious to get out of debt."[48] Jefferson's intent was obvious: to scale down possible French expectations of payment. The day before he received Du Pont's letter, Jefferson had sent him another strongly worded missive, explaining that he was writing because "you may be able to impress on the government of France the inevitable consequences of their taking possession of Louisiana. . . . this measure will cost France, & perhaps not very long hence, a war which will annihilate her on the ocean."[49] After receiving this letter, Du Pont replied that he would "argue for their content with all my feeble power," cautioned Jefferson about language that might anger Napoleon, and then suggested that the United States, after considering all the costs of a possible war, offer the very best price it could for Louisiana. Du Pont thought a "financed purchase" would be the best option.[50]

FOR MONTHS THERE was no clear indication of France's response; in July Jefferson admitted, "The affair of Louisiana is still hanging over us," and a month later he indicated that he had "no certain information yet of the definitive resolution of France as to Louisiana."[51] The president believed that France's increasing involvement in attempts to reclaim Saint-Domingue after the slave uprising would likely delay any seizure of Louisiana. Nevertheless, he was on edge, which explains why he reacted quickly to a book newly available in the United States: Scotsman Alexander Mackenzie's account, first published in England in early 1801, of his 1792–1793 trek across Canada, through the Rocky Mountains, to the Pacific coast. Jefferson surely bought the book within days of its Philadelphia publication in May of the same year.[52]

Mackenzie's detailed work was almost a manual for planning another excursion. Its final pages drew Jefferson's particular attention. There Mackenzie remarked on the immense potential for trade with Asia and called for England to colonize the Northwest as a step toward dominating the fur trade of North America.[53] With France already threatening to colonize the Southwest, was England now about to seize the Northwest? Jefferson must have then begun making plans to send an exploratory team—led by his secretary, Meriwether Lewis—to the Northwest, up the Missouri River and from there to the Pacific, with the goal of finding the best route (ideally, on rivers). Jefferson's papers include an undated document, presumably prepared by Lewis before the end of 1802, estimating the cost of such an expedition, assuming only a small group.[54] More concretely, on November 19 Jefferson sent a draft of his Annual Message to Gallatin, and although the draft no longer exists, in his reply Gallatin suggested that he remove a passage about the Missouri River, "as it contemplates an expedition out of our own territory," and submit it to Congress, separately, in the form of a confidential message.[55] Jefferson took this advice.

That same month, Jefferson had a private conversation with Carlos Martinez de Yrujo, the Spanish minister to the United States. According to Yrujo, Jefferson asked him whether the Spanish government would take offense if the United States sent a small "caravan" of travelers to "explore the course of the Missouri River in which they would nominally have the objective of investigating everything which might contribute to the progress of commerce; but that in reality it would have no other view than the advancement of geography." Jefferson explained that the Constitution would allow funding for such an expedition only if it were related to advancing commerce, not science. Yrujo told Jefferson the adventure "could not fail to give umbrage to our Government." Jefferson professed not to understand why, because the explorers would confine themselves to the northern region all the way to the Pacific. Yrujo replied that Mackenzie's recent book made such a journey of exploration unnecessary.

On January 18, 1803, Jefferson sent his confidential message to Congress. The first half reviewed trade relations with various Indian nations in the Midwest. Because the Missouri River flowed into the Mississippi, it behooved the United States, argued Jefferson, to learn more about these Native Americans, their trade goods and possible needs, and how to redirect their trade away from England to the United States. Consequently, the United States should endeavor to chart the transportation potential of the Missouri, from its source all the way to the rivers of the East. And perhaps a short portage could be found linking the Missouri to the Columbia River and thence to the waters of the Pacific. Jefferson maintained that the commercial possibilities resulting from this exploration were sizeable. As he wrote, "An intelligent officer with ten or twelve chosen men, fit for the enterprise and willing to undertake it, taken from our [military] posts, where they might be spared without inconvenience, might explore the entire line, even to the Western ocean, have conferences with the natives on subjects of commercial intercourse, . . . [and] agree on convenient deposits for an interchange of articles." Jefferson took care to indicate the constitutionality of the actions he was proposing: "the interests of commerce place the principal object within the constitutional power and care of Congress." Then, characteristically, he added, "And that it should incidentally advance the geographical knowledge of our own continent, cannot but be an additional gratification." An appropriation of only $2,500 could finance the whole endeavor.[56] On February 28, with one economical sentence, Congress approved that amount "for the purpose of extending the external commerce of the United States."[57]

ALREADY, BY THIS POINT, the Louisiana episode had taken a new turn. Either on or a day or two before November 25, 1802, Madison learned that the acting intendant of New Orleans and West Florida, Juan Ventura Morales, had on October 16 suspended the American right of deposit in New Orleans—a potentially catastrophic blow to the nation's interior commerce. It took weeks for the news to work its way up the Mississippi River, but everywhere it elicited instant outrage. Morales claimed that the decision was his own, made after realizing that the provision in the Treaty of San Lorenzo bestowing the right had expired. A century later historians discovered that he had acted on secret instructions from King Carlos IV.[58] The subject of war was widely broached, and rumors arose that thousands of western farmers were readying to march on New Orleans to, as they might have put it, recover their commercial rights. Federalists in Congress, spoiling for a fight with Spain's ally France, pushed for a military response. Jefferson, though willing to go to war to defend America's most vital interests, always turned to diplomacy first.

An inquiry sent to Spanish minister Yrujo indicated that he had known nothing of the suspension in advance; nor, it turned out, did Louisiana governor Don Manuel Juan de Salcedo. So Jefferson believed the action the result of a rogue functionary, not official Spanish policy. As he and Madison gathered information, the president concluded, "It was not the consequence of any order from Europe, but merely an irregularity of the Intendant." As such, the matter should be resolvable without resort to war.[59] Jefferson wanted to minimize the importance of the event and did not mention the suspension in his Annual Message. But the clamor for war was growing, and the Federalists were eager to open hostilities with both Spain and France. Alexander Hamilton, still hawkish, excoriated Jefferson for his supposedly weak and hesitant leadership.[60]

Though Jefferson could find some relief from politics during evening dinners with his two daughters, who were enjoying their first stay at the President's House, he clearly felt immense pressure to take control of events. If nothing else, he had to buy time for diplomacy to work. Yet he did not want to make public his two approaches: calling on the French to override the Spanish decision and restore American trade rights in New Orleans or possibly purchasing a separate trade depot in Louisiana. In his Annual Message he spoke vaguely about the situation: "The cession of the Spanish province of Louisiana to France, which took place in the course of the late war, will, if carried into effect, make a change in the aspect of our foreign relations, which will doubtless have just weight in any deliberations of the legislature connected with that subject."[61] If this was not outright obfuscation, it was certainly close.

Jefferson hoped the efforts of Livingston and Du Pont in Paris and Pinckney in Madrid would lead to a solution, preferably the purchase of New Orleans. In the meantime, he had to demonstrate firmness, so in January he and Dearborn strengthened US forces at Fort Adams, south of Natchez on the Mississippi River, and communicated with Governor William C. C. Claiborne of the Mississippi Territory about the readiness of the militia.[62] Jefferson then initiated another diplomatic tactic. Knowing that former Virginia governor James Monroe had been liked and trusted in the West since his opposition to the 1785–1786 Jay-Gardoqui negotiations and that, as a result of his service as US minister to France from 1794 to the end of 1796, he was similarly respected in Paris, Jefferson wrote him an urgent letter. "I have but a moment to inform you," the president said, "that the fever into which the Western mind is thrown by the affair at N. Orleans . . . threatens to overbear our peace. in this situation we are obliged to call on you for a temporary sacrifice of yourself, to prevent this greatest of evils in the present prosperous tide of our affairs. I shall tomorrow nominate you to the Senate for an extraordinary mission to France, & the circumstances are such as to render it impossible to decline."[63]

The very next day, January 11, 1803, Jefferson sent a message to the Senate. Referencing the cession of Louisiana and the suspension of the right of deposit in New Orleans, he said that while his confidence in the present US minister in France, Robert R. Livingston, was "entire and undiminished," he would send another diplomat to aid Livingston, "carrying with him the feelings & sentiments of the nation excited on the late occurrence [the suspension]." For that purpose, Jefferson explained, he nominated Livingston as minister plenipotentiary and Monroe as "minister extraordinary & plenipotentiary, with full powers to both jointly, or to either on the death of the other, to enter into a treaty or convention with [Napoleon]" to settle the two contentious matters. The Senate approved the nomination the following day by a vote of 15–12; every Federalist dissented.[64] The appointment of Monroe was an adroit political move by Jefferson; he did indeed have every confidence in Livingston but needed to take public action. As he confided to his son-in-law, "This measure has suppressed all further inflammatory proceedings meditated by the Federalists for instigating the Western country to force on a war between us & the owners of New Orleans. Their confidence in Monroe will tranquilise them on that subject."[65] Nevertheless, Jefferson and Madison made sure that the talk of war in the West and in the Congress was communicated to Spanish and French officials.

By the first month of 1803, Jefferson had thus launched two endeavors—to explore the West and to invigorate negotiations with France over the status of New Orleans—that would eventuate in the two greatest achievements of his administration. But in the moment, he was sufficiently aware of the vagaries of life and of politics not to presume the desired outcomes guaranteed.

23

"Louisiana for a Song"

ALTHOUGH A VERY SOCIAL MAN, after his dinner guests had departed by 6:00 p.m. or so, Jefferson spent his evenings at the President's House alone. He usually had ten or eleven servants at the mansion, most of them white. He employed an accomplished *maître d'hôtel*, Etienne Lemaire, and a skilled *chef de cuisine*, Honoré Julien, both of whom ran the President's House in the French style. He did occasionally employ or lease African American slaves, but usually only one of his own slaves, a young woman apprenticed to Julien to learn French cooking, lived in Washington at a time. A total of three young slave women from Monticello served in this role over the course of his presidency. He did not have a valet, preferring to dress himself.[1]

Thus, early in his presidency Jefferson enjoyed even more than usual the arrival of his two daughters, along with two of Martha's children, Thomas Jefferson Randolph and Ellen Randolph. The trip had been planned far in advance. In early 1801 Jefferson had informed his daughters that the new capital was only a three-day ride from Monticello, and he, Martha, and Maria arranged a visit for the spring of 1802, but an outbreak of measles among the children caused a delay. In June Jefferson sent Martha a detailed itinerary, describing the taverns and fords they would encounter on the roads.[2] At last they arrived on November 21, 1802, and stayed until January 5, 1803, bringing great consolation to Jefferson, particularly in the evenings. He included his daughters in his dinners, leading even the dour Federalist Manasseh Cutler to admit that they "appeared well-accomplished women—very delicate and tolerably handsome."[3] Jefferson's friend Margaret Bayard Smith was kinder. She described Maria as "beautiful, simplicity and timidity personified when in company, but when alone with you of communicative and winning manners." Martha, meanwhile, was "rather homely, a delicate likeness of her father, but still more interesting" than her sister. As Smith put it, Martha was "really one of the most lovely women I have ever met with, her countenance beaming with intelligence, benevolence and sensibility, and her conversation fulfils all her countenance promises."[4] Jefferson adored both daughters, and they almost worshipped him. Both worried about their father living so isolated in Washington; Maria even commented after their visit, "How much pain it gives me to think of the unsafe & solitary manner in which you sleep up stairs."[5]

When his daughters were not there, Jefferson repaired to his study lined with bookshelves; maps, globes, and various scientific and carpentry tools lay scattered across a long table. Here Jefferson worked at night—dressed in comfortable old clothes and shoes—perusing reports and indulging in his avocational reading in science and geography, in the company of a mockingbird. He had long loved these songbirds, and his memorandum book shows him buying several to keep caged in his room beginning in the early 1770s.[6] Of the various ones he owned, his favorite was Dick. The bird would serenade him from its cage, and Jefferson would often let him out so that he could fly about the room, sit on his work desk, and even alight on his shoulder, singing all the while. The bird was so tame that, when perched on Jefferson's shoulder, it would take bits of food from between its master's lips.[7]

Attacked throughout his time in office as too dreamy, too philosophical, and too professorial to be an effective president, Jefferson was in fact an adept administrator. He kept apprised of developments within the various departments of government and personally led, persuaded, and cajoled Congress to do his bidding. So it is one of the ironies of his presidency that the Louisiana Purchase and the Lewis and Clark Expedition took place at a far remove from Washington. He was behind each action, but others executed them. And for most of 1802 and 1803, he waited nervously in the capital to learn whether his goals would be achieved.

The Senate approved James Monroe's assignment to France on January 11, 1803, and authorized Jefferson's proposed exploration of the West on February 28. Yet neither Monroe nor the expedition set forth immediately. Monroe could not depart until Congress authorized $2 million for the purchase of territory in the West; on March 2, it empowered him to offer an additional 50 million francs ($9.375 million), on top of the initial sum. Monroe spent the intervening weeks consulting with both Jefferson and

James Madison about French policy and reading the correspondence from Robert Livingston in Paris and Charles Pinckney in Madrid. Finally, on March 8 Monroe and his family put to sea, arriving in France on April 8. Three days later, he met Livingston in Paris.[8]

JEFFERSON HAD DECIDED, even before delivering his confidential message to Congress, that Meriwether Lewis would head the expedition. But though a talented woodsman and a quick learner, Lewis was no scientist. In late February and early March, Jefferson sent letters to surveyor Andrew Ellicott, botanist and naturalist Benjamin Smith Barton, physician Benjamin Rush, and mathematician Robert Patterson, asking them to tutor Lewis in their respective subjects. To each he explained that "it was impossible to find a character who to a compleat science in botany, natural history, mineralogy & astronomy, joined the firmness of constitution & character, prudence, habits adapted to the woods, & a familiarity with the Indian manners & character, requisite for this undertaking." He said that Lewis was "brave" and, though "not regularly educated, . . . possesses a great mass of accurate observation on all the subjects of nature which present themselves here." Each of his correspondents agreed to the task.[9] By early March Jefferson had already procured passports and safe conduct passes from both the French and English governments for Lewis.[10] He also wrote to Lewis Harvie, who had previously applied for the job as Jefferson's personal secretary in 1801, and offered him the position to replace Lewis; Harvie gladly accepted.[11]

We can only suppose Jefferson's considerable excitement during these weeks of planning; he had envisioned such a trip since 1783. The Lewis initiative seemed full of potential, and Jefferson put the resources of the national government behind it. He began to work on his letter of instruction to Lewis. By this point, he was more knowledgeable about natural history; unlike in his 1793 letter to André Michaux, for example, Jefferson made no reference to looking for mammoths. In his missive to Lewis, Jefferson asked only that he be alert to evidence of animals "which may be deemed rare or *extinct*."[12]

Jefferson sent his initial draft, in succession, to Madison, Albert Gallatin, and Levi Lincoln, and probably also to Henry Dearborn and new secretary of the navy Robert Smith. Madison suggested that Jefferson make more explicit the commercial implications of the exploration of the West. Gallatin provided more extensive advice, calling for investigations of the region that would have required Lewis and his men to roam far beyond the Missouri River, both north toward Canada and south toward Spanish settlements. Gallatin pushed for detailed examinations of the topography, soil, and climate to determine "whether from its extent & fertility that country is Susceptible of a large population." Jefferson did add some questions in this vein but made clear that the expedition's aims had nothing to do with what Gallatin was recommending: the colonization of the territory. Lincoln thought the members of the exploratory party should take kinepox (smallpox) vaccination materials with them, and, anticipating that the soldier in Lewis might take unnecessary risks in the event of disputes with Native Americans, urged Jefferson to tell him to be prudent. Jefferson incorporated both of Lincoln's recommendations.[13]

Jefferson sent an almost final draft to Lewis, who was then in Philadelphia, meeting with mentors and ordering supplies. Jefferson explained that he was sending a draft of the instructions so Lewis would have "time to consider them, & to propose any modifications which may occur to you as useful." Jefferson suggested that he show the letter to Rush, Barton, and Patterson, as well as Caspar Wistar, a physician and anatomist at the University of Pennsylvania, to elicit their reactions.[14] In the final version of the letter, dated June 20, 1803, Jefferson wrote to Lewis and his fellow expedition members, "The object of your mission is to explore the Missouri river, & such principal streams of it, as, by it's course & communication with the waters of the Pacific ocean, may offer the most direct & practicable water communication across this continent, for the purposes of commerce."[15] They were to take precise measurements of the latitude and longitude of the river's notable natural features, and to make multiple copies of these measurements, as a precaution. Since more knowledge of the inhabitants of the West would enhance commerce with these people, Jefferson instructed Lewis to investigate every aspect of the Indian societies the explorers might encounter: their occupations, traditions, clothing, food, laws, and languages.[16] He added an exhaustive list of "other objects worthy of notice": the soils, florae and faunae, minerals, climate, and much more.[17]

Jefferson instructed Lewis to act toward the Indians they encountered in a peaceful and conciliatory manner in order to learn how they conducted trade and what they might want to purchase from and sell to US merchants. He specifically warned Lewis to avoid hostility, even if it meant forsaking the remainder of their trip; on this point, he was emphatic: "we wish you to err on the side of your safety, & to bring back your party safe, even if it be with less information."[18] Upon reaching the Pacific coast, should they come upon seagoing vessels of any nation, they should consider sending not many more than two men, with copies of their journals and data, back to the East Coast by sea.

Months of frustrating delays followed delivery of the letter, to the point that Jefferson was able in July to inform Lewis of the purchase of Louisiana—which meant that Lewis would not be trespassing upon foreign territory. Jefferson must have felt huge relief when Lewis finally wrote that on August 31 he had set forth from Pittsburgh down the Ohio River; the expedition would winter that year near St. Louis and prepare to ascend the Missouri in the spring of 1804.[19]

JEFFERSON SPENT MARCH 1803 at Monticello, where he pondered once more a question that had recurred in his mind and life for four decades or more: the nature of religion generally and Christianity in particular. His views had evolved since the early 1760s, when he had been drawn to the philosophers of antiquity; by the 1790s, after corresponding with minister Richard Price in England and reading Joseph Priestley's Unitarian *History of the Corruptions of Christianity*, Jefferson had reread the Gospels with increasing appreciation. Always reticent publicly about his religious beliefs but stung by harsh Federalist accusations that he was a radical atheist, he may have set out to reconsider and describe his personal creed in order to confide his true sentiments to his family and a handful of close associates. Convinced that New England's ministers—Congregationalists and Presbyterians mainly, Federalists all—opposed him irredeemably, he may have wanted to explore the possibility of a more democratic Christianity, less in thrall to a learned clergy.[20] Nearing sixty, Jefferson may also have begun to think more about death and perhaps to consider the existence of an afterlife, where he might be reunited with his many deceased loved ones.

Toward the end his stay at Monticello, he received a copy of a brief pamphlet by Priestley titled *Socrates and Jesus Compared*. Priestley came down strongly in favor of Jesus, a conclusion Jefferson had arrived at himself, after his youthful infatuation with antiquity. Jefferson read the pamphlet carefully during his final days at Monticello and on the road back to Washington. Then he penned a long and appreciative letter to its author.

Jefferson expressed his "pleasure" "in the perusal of it" and urged Priestley to take up the subject on a grander scale, comparing Jesus to the whole pantheon of ancient philosophers. He said that he had discussed the general topic several years before with Dr. Benjamin Rush, a devout

Christian, and had afterward mentally "sketched" out his own thoughts. Jefferson presented his conclusions: first, on the moral writings of the ancients; second, on the development of the deism (by which he meant monotheism) of the Jewish writers; and finally, on the limitations of both sets of thinkers.[21] To Jefferson, Jesus improved on the earlier Greek philosophers in developing "juster notions of the attributes of god" and by reconciling "moral doctrines to the standard of reason, justice, & philanthropy." In particular, Jesus "inculcate[d] the belief of a future state," which spurred people to better behavior. Jefferson made clear that he saw Jesus as an unrivaled moral guide but not as divine—which, he pointed out, Jesus never claimed to be. He was "the most innocent, the most benevolent, the most eloquent and sublime character that ever has been exhibited to man," but no more than that. Jefferson believed Jesus's disciples had misreported his words, creating the claim to divinity. Although Jesus's beliefs have come down to us in fragments from "unlettered" men who relied on their memory, still his "system of morality was the most benevolent & sublime probably that has ever been taught." Jefferson hoped that Priestley would have time to develop these ideas and expand his view of Jesus's moral stature.[22]

In the days after writing his letter to Priestley, Jefferson began to outline his religious beliefs in a document he called a "Syllabus of an Estimate of the Merit of the Doctrines of Jesus, Compared with Those of Others." Soon after, he sent a carefully crafted letter to Rush, enclosing his so-called syllabus, which he cautioned its recipient not to share; as Jefferson wrote, his enemies would transform his "every word" into "a text for new misrepresentations & calumnies."[23] Jefferson said that the views in the document were "the result of a life of enquiry & reflection, and very different from that Anti-Christian system, imputed to me by those who know nothing of my opinions." He explained, "To the corruptions of Christianity, I am indeed opposed; but not to the genuine precepts of Jesus himself. I am a Christian, in the only sense in which he wished any one to be; sincerely attached to his doctrines, in preference to all others; ascribing to himself every human excellence, & believing he never claimed any other."[24]

The syllabus remarked on the contributions to human ethics made by the ancient philosophers, who taught men to control their personal passions, and the ancient Jews, who developed the concept of a single God. But Jefferson found both these sources of ethics lacking, that of the Jews', in part, because he believed they did not interact with other peoples. Then Jefferson explained his dismal view of Jesus's ministry: he had written nothing, relying on barely literate men to record his sayings, and many later followers had corrupted his teachings, especially churchmen who sought power by claiming that only they could interpret the scriptures. To Jefferson this was a great loss, because Jesus had perfected a system of moral doctrines that extended far beyond his own people "to all mankind." Perhaps most important of all—and Jefferson had said the same in his letter to Priestley—Jesus "taught, emphatically, the doctrine of a future state." Jefferson never used the word "heaven," but that was what he meant, and he saw it as not only a good in itself but "an important incentive, supplementary to the other motives to moral conduct."[25] Jefferson considered himself neither an atheist nor an enemy of Christianity but an authentic Christian, defined as a follower of Jesus, not the church. Still, Jefferson believed that his version of Christianity was his alone; as he later wrote, "I am of a sect by myself, as far as I know."[26] His was a rationalized, minimalist creed: he believed in one all-powerful God, the moral teachings of Jesus, and the afterlife, but he did not believe in the divine inspiration of the Bible, in Jesus's divinity, in the occurrence of miracles, or in Jesus's resurrection and ascension. He strove to live a moral life by Jesus's standards.[27] Jefferson never promoted his own beliefs or attempted to proselytize. He sent copies of his syllabus to a select few, sworn to secrecy, only to assure them of his private faith and relieve their minds against "libels published against me on this, as on every other possible topic."[28]

DURING THE LATE SPRING of 1803 Jefferson heard nothing from Livingston or Monroe. The negotiations depended entirely on Napoleon Bonaparte, who had become first consul of France in 1799. As Livingston wrote Madison (in a coded letter), "There never was a government in which less could be done by negotiation than here. There is no people no legislature no counselors one man is everything—he seldom asks advice and never hears it unasked—his ministers are mere clerks."[29] After losing Egypt to England in 1798, Napoleon had renewed the attempt to subdue the rebelling slaves on Saint-Domingue; in late 1801 he had sent thousands of men under the authority of his brother-in-law, General Charles Victor Emmanuel Leclerc, to regain control of the island. In a secret treaty, Napoleon had indeed convinced Spain to cede Louisiana to France, and his grandiose plans included using that territory as a provisioning base for the restored and lucrative sugar plantations on Saint-Domingue.[30]

The rebels' armies and yellow fever, however, decimated Leclerc's forces. Within a year of their arrival, the French had lost 24,000 men, and as many as 8,000 lay in hospitals. On November 2, 1802, Leclerc himself succumbed to the disease.[31] By the time the news arrived in France, Napoleon had gathered a new fleet at the Dutch port city of Hellevoetsluis under the command of Lieutenant General Claude Perrin Victor, who would lead 3,000 troops to Louisiana and install a new governor, Pierre Clément Laussat. Owing to an uncommonly harsh winter, the harbor had frozen, putting the expedition on hold. Napoleon, never a patient man, was frustrated but helpless. When Leclerc's fate and that of his army reached Paris in January 1803, Napoleon exclaimed, "Damm sugar, damm coffee, damm colonies."[32]

The surviving evidence indicates that within the next couple weeks, Napoleon began to reconsider his strategy in the New World. With Saint-Domingue lost, Louisiana held little value. Instead, Napoleon turned his imperial gaze eastward and began to fantasize about conquering the Middle East and even India. As rumors and then evidence of Napoleon's new ambitions surfaced, the English dispatched a fleet to ensure that Victor remained stuck in the Dutch port even after the thaw.

Napoleon knew that a war with England, which controlled the seas, would compromise any plans for Louisiana. Compounding the matter were warnings from the likes of Pierre Samuel Du Pont de Nemours and Livingston that if New Orleans remained closed to US commerce, the United States would ally with England and perhaps even attack the city. Napoleon's new approach began to take form in March and April 1803. He decided that he needed to prevent a US alliance with England and to build up his war chest. Perhaps there was a way to do both.

In 1802, Livingston had tried to arrange to purchase from France East and West Florida, and if not New Orleans, then a piece of land adjacent to the Mississippi River south of the city, where the United States could construct its own port. Probably in January or early February 1803, Livingston had taken it on himself to propose that in addition to selling Florida and New Orleans to the United States, the French might consider selling the portion of Louisiana west of the Mississippi and above the Arkansas River. He ostensibly sought to secure a buffer colony between French territory to the south and British Canada to the north. Nothing came of this proposal.[33] Still, Livingston may have planted the seed that grew into the Louisiana Purchase.

ON APRIL 12 James Monroe and his family reached Paris. By April 11 Napoleon had informed Talleyrand, his foreign minister, of his decision to sell all of Louisiana; Livingston sent Madison a letter, written that day, describing a strange visit with the French minister (Madison did not receive the letter until June). In conversation Talleyrand had rather casually asked if the United States wanted to have "the whole of Louisiana." Livingston told Madison that he replied no; the United States only wanted to buy New Orleans and the Florida territories—as his instructions stated—unless France would sell the portion north of the Arkansas River.

Pointing out that if the French disposed of New Orleans, then they had little use for the rest of the territory, Talleyrand again asked what the United States would offer for the entirety of Louisiana. Livingston, completely unprepared for such a question, said maybe 20 million francs. Talleyrand thought the number too low. Stalling, Livingston said he expected Monroe in a couple of days and would have to confer with him. Then Talleyrand disingenuously remarked that he wasn't speaking officially, the "idea" of selling the totality of the territory having "struck him" at that moment. Livingston rightfully assumed there was more to the minister's studied casualness.[34] He met the next day with an evasive Talleyrand, who put on a charade by denying that Louisiana was really France's to sell in the first place.[35]

That evening Livingston hosted a dinner for Monroe and several others. At one point he looked out the window and noticed the Marquis François de Barbé-Marbois, Napoleon's minister of the treasury, walking in his garden. Livingston sent his son-in-law (and private secretary) to suggest that the minister return after dinner, which he did. Napoleon, knowing that Talleyrand and Livingston were not on friendly terms, had decided to send Barbé-Marbois to take over the negotiations, a fortuitous move. Barbé-Marbois liked America and was, of course, a friend of Jefferson's. Fluent in English and married to an American, he had served in Philadelphia as secretary to the French legation and later as chargé d'affaires. In the former capacity he had, in 1780, compiled the list of twenty-two questions about the United States that were mailed to the various states—the origin of Jefferson's *Notes on the State of Virginia*. Barbé-Marbois assured Livingston that Napoleon wanted to sell Louisiana to the United States for 100 million francs, which even the French minister admitted was too much. When Livingston pushed back, Barbé-Marbois said that 60 million francs would be a fair offer, assuming the United States added an additional 20 million to reimburse Americans for claims held against the French government. Livingston again demurred. Napoleon had suggested the United States could borrow the funds to pay France quickly, which the minister thought advisable. When Livingston inquired about West and East Florida, Barbé-Marbois protested that these were not France's to sell. The next day Livingston conveyed the content of the negotiations to Monroe; the two men agreed to try to make the deal, believing they needed to move quickly before the mercurial Napoleon changed his mind.

Two days after his informal nighttime discussion with the French minister, Livingston, concerned about exceeding his mandate, wrote to Jefferson. "I think the weal, or woe of our Country lays in our hands, & depends upon the determination of a moment." Mentioning how feverishly busy he and Monroe had been the past two days, Livingston added, "I trust however that we shall concur in opinion, & that your administration will be distinguished, by the acquisition of a territory not less valuable than half the United States." In other words, Livingston was proactively defending their negotiations.[36]

Despite the promising conversation with Barbé-Marbois, much remained to be decided, including the exact price, the structure of the claims, and the precise boundaries of Louisiana. (When Livingston again tried to determine whether the territory included the two Floridas, Talleyrand—in reality, opposed to the whole matter—was typically evasive and, according to Livingston, said only, "You have made a noble bargain for yourselves & I suppose you will make the most of it."[37]) Although Livingston and Monroe were jealous of the other—Livingston believed Monroe's presence unnecessary, and Monroe thought that Livingston, self-importantly, wanted to remain in charge of negotiations—they put aside their differences and worked in tandem with Barbé-Marbois for two weeks to finalize the treaty. They agreed on French as its official language, and on April 28 they consented to the price of 60 million francs ($11.25 million) for the purchase and another 20 million ($3.75 million) for the claims of US citizens on France. At Barbé-Marbois's insistence, Article III of the treaty provided, "The inhabitants of the ceded territory shall be incorporated in the Union of the United States and admitted as soon as possible according to the principles of the federal Constitution to the enjoyment of all these rights, advantages, and immunities of citizens of the United States, and in the mean time they shall be maintained and protected in the free enjoyment of their liberty, property [including slaves] and the Religion which they profess."[38]

Dutch and English banking houses handled the transfer of funds and drew up the terms by which the United States would repay the banks.[39]

According to Barbé-Marbois, as soon as the three negotiators had signed the treaty and associated documents, they shook hands, and Livingston said, "We have lived long, but this is the noblest work of our whole lives. . . . From this day the United States take their place among the powers of the first rank."[40]

Livingston and Monroe sent Madison a copy of the treaty and documents supporting the financial transactions, conveyed by an American friend of Jefferson's returning to the United States. In their accompanying letter, Livingston and Monroe wrote, "An acquisition of so great an extent was, we well Know, not contemplated by our appointment; but we are persuaded that the Circumstances and Considerations which induced us to make it, will justify us, in the measure, to our Government and Country."[41] As this and other letters indicated, the American ministers clearly worried about the deal's reception among the public and in Congress. Some of their letters didn't arrive until in August. On the evening of July 3, however, Jefferson had learned of the deal via a letter from the retiring US minister to England, Rufus King, who had just returned to New York.[42] The ministers needn't have worried: Jefferson was overjoyed by the purchase. What a way to celebrate the anniversary of the nation's birth!

As news of the treaty spread, the Federalists predictably attacked it or grudgingly refused to credit Jefferson and his negotiators. But praise came from most other groups, and many people called the purchase the greatest event in the nation since the end of the American Revolution. As one hero of that conflict, former general Horatio Gates, wrote Jefferson, "Let the Land rejoice, for you have bought Louisiana for a Song."[43]

MUCH WORK REMAINED to formalize the treaty and then to extend American government across the new territory. Jefferson had consulted in January 1803 with Lincoln and Gallatin about the constitutionality of such a purchase, and they had offered rationales approving it, but Jefferson remained hesitant to act without explicit constitutional sanction.[44] He assumed that an appropriate amendment should be adopted, and on or before July 9, he produced two drafts. Jefferson envisioned the amendment as an addition to Article IV, Section 3 of the Constitution, on the admission of new states and the regulation of territories. His drafts' first line ran as follows: "The Province of Louisiana is incorporated with the US. and made part thereof."[45]

Jefferson hoped, through the amendment, to restrict settlement in the territory—at least that portion north of current settlements adjacent to

New Orleans—to Native Americans. This would prevent the nation's existing white population from settling to the west of the Mississippi for years and prohibit southern slaveholders from moving with their slaves to the region. Jefferson proposed exchanging Indian-held land east of the Mississippi for equivalent lands to its west, with the tribes affected moving to the new lands. In short, Jefferson saw the vast Louisiana territory as a preserve for Indians; he believed the current states had sufficient land that opening the purchase to the westward migration of whites would be unnecessary for generations.[46]

This view reflected a long-standing concern of Jefferson's. He believed the Indian nations needed to forsake their traditional hunter-gatherer cultures to survive in a nation increasingly dominated by land-hungry farmers and plantation owners. (Every president from George Washington to John Quincy Adams accepted the general outlines of this view.) Not only whites' desire for their lands but decreasing populations of wild game would inevitably lead to Indian deprivation if they persisted in their ways. The solution, in Jefferson's mind, was to persuade—and if that failed, to pressure—Indians to adopt white attitudes toward landownership and take up agriculture. To give them the necessary time, Jefferson believed it helpful, even philanthropic, to move them to newly available land, assist them in making the agricultural transition, and thereby save them and set them on the path to full assimilation into the American nation. Jefferson believed that Indians, unlike blacks, could become competent citizens, especially after interbreeding with whites—a practice he supported. Blinded by his assumptions about the superiority of European ways, Jefferson did not foresee Indian recalcitrance or the harm this approach would do to their culture.[47]

Around the same time that he was drafting the amendment, Jefferson began to compile a list of questions to send to persons knowledgeable about Louisiana. He anticipated employing the resulting information in considerations of how to govern the new territory and slowly integrate the largely French and Spanish region with the rest of the American nation.[48]

With that, Jefferson left for his annual retreat to Monticello, arriving on July 22 and staying for two months. While at home, he changed his mind about the need to amend the Constitution, because he feared delay would jeopardize the final deal. He learned in mid-August from a letter written by Livingston, originally sent to Madison, that events in France could threaten the treaty. Livingston urged, "I hope in God that nothing will prevent your immediate ratification & without altering a syllable of the terms, if you wish anything changed, ratify unconditionally and set on foot a new negotiation. . . . [T]he slightest pretence will lose you the treaty."[49] Jefferson clearly would have preferred the more orderly process of drafting and winning approval for a constitutional amendment to authorize the purchase, but there was, he believed, no time. Rigid adherence in this case to proper procedure would harm the nation's best interests.

Jefferson wrote to John Breckinridge that he assumed the Congress "will see their duty to their country in ratifying & paying for it [Louisiana], so as to secure a good which would otherwise probably be never again in their power." He allowed that the Constitution did not contain language relevant to this issue. In such cases, Jefferson explained, Congress must cast "behind them Metaphysical subtleties, and risking themselves like faithful servants, must ratify & pay for it, and throw themselves on their country for doing for them unauthorized what we know they would have done for themselves had they been in a situation to do it."[50]

Jefferson wrote another letter on August 18, this time to Madison, saying, "The less we say about constitutional difficulties respecting Louisiana the better, and . . . what is necessary for surmounting them must be done sub silentio."[51] By this point he had substantially shortened his proposed amendment (though he retained the idea of reserving the new territory exclusively for Native Americans). Within a few days, he had pared it down to the latest version of its first sentence: "Louisiana, as ceded by France to the US. is made a part of the US."[52] By this point, he believed it was better to act and, if necessary, to propose an appropriate constitutional amendment justifying such action later on. Upon returning to Washington in late September, Jefferson met with his cabinet members, who agreed that he should ask Congress to gather earlier than usual. Jefferson summoned the body's members to open the session on October 17, 1803. That meant he would need to prepare his Annual Message, which he presented to both houses on that date.

Jefferson began by briefly summarizing recent events, starting with the suspension by Spain of the US right of deposit at New Orleans, continuing through the negotiations in Paris, and culminating with the treaty dated April 30, 1803. With no mention of the Constitution, he continued, "When these [treaty instruments] shall have received the constitutional sanction of the Senate, they will, without delay, be communicated to the House of Representatives." The acquisition of this vast territory "promise[s], in due season, important aids to our treasury, an ample provision for our posterity, & a wide spread for the blessings of freedom and equal laws."⁵³ He addressed several other issues, including the increase in the national debt as a result of the purchase of Louisiana, but focused on the call for approval of the treaty.

The Republican Senate rushed through approval of the treaty in two days, with little debate, though Federalist opposition was almost total. (Alexander Hamilton, however, supported the purchase.) The constitutional question never came up. The English banking firm involved had brought proof to the Unites States that it would advance the needed sums to France, so on October 20 Jefferson exchanged the ratification agreement with the French chargé d'affaires in Washington, Louis-Andrè Pinchon. The next day, Jefferson issued a proclamation announcing the ratification of the purchase treaty. He also sent a message to Congress acknowledging the momentous event and asking its members to begin passing legislation regarding the occupation and governance of the new territory.⁵⁴

There existed some concern in Congress over whether the Spanish officials still in control of New Orleans would agree peacefully to the change in sovereignty. Jefferson and his cabinet made preliminary military preparations in the event force was needed, while Jefferson alone appointed William C. C. Claiborne, territorial governor of Mississippi, governor of the Territory of Orleans. The Spanish in New Orleans, for their part, were more confused than belligerent. They still claimed the city. At the same time, Pierre Clément Laussat had arrived earlier in the year from France, expecting to be governor of France's recently acquired colony of Louisiana. Not yet apprised of the negotiations in Paris, he was stunned to discover, from Pinchon in Washington, that his colony had been sold from underneath him. By now Spain, recognizing its hopelessly weak position, told its representatives in Louisiana to surrender New Orleans. On November 30 Spanish officials, meeting with Laussat in the Cabildo, the seat of colonial government, presented him with a silver tray containing keys to the city's major buildings—thus Spain ceded Louisiana to France, after the United States had already bought it.

On December 20, 1803, in a small ceremony in the Place d'Armes in New Orleans, Laussat officially delivered the territory of Louisiana to Claiborne, who accepted on behalf of the United States. Speaking from a text supplied by Jefferson, Claiborne proclaimed US sovereignty and assured those in the audience that the United States would protect their liberty, property, and religious beliefs. With that, the French tricolor was lowered and the US flag raised.[55] The American nation had doubled in size at a total cost—including the interest payments on the British and Dutch loans—of about four cents an acre.

THE YEAR 1803, marked by signal accomplishments, ended with a comic-opera affair in Washington. It all began when England decided to send a minister to the United States. The man appointed His Majesty's Envoy Extraordinary and Minister Plenipotentiary to the United States was Anthony Merry, who came with no precise instructions from the foreign office about how to interact with the US government other than to "endeavour to cultivate a good Understanding with the several Individuals who compose it."[56] Merry arrived in late November and introduced himself to Madison, who then took him straightaway to Jefferson, apparently having given the president no notice.

Merry, full of self-importance and pomp, dressed for what he thought would be a formal presentation: he arrived in full court attire, wearing a formal blue coat with black trim and gold braid, white breeches, the finest silk stockings, shoes with shiny silver buckles, a dramatic plumed hat, and ceremonial sword.[57] Pity that Madison did not inform this plumed peacock that Jefferson, while working in the private office of his home, usually dressed in the plain clothes of a farmer. Primed to greet Jefferson with a well-prepared speech, Merry was nonplussed to find the president in his everyday garb, including shoes worn down at the heels. Had Jefferson been caught unawares, or was this—as Merry suspected—an intentional act of disrespect? Was Jefferson making a point about American attitudes of democratic equality and simplicity, or was he evoking the time when King George purposely offended John Adams and himself on their presentation to him in 1786? Or was it both at once? In any event, Merry himself was sorely offended.

A week or so later, on December 2, Jefferson, perhaps hoping to make amends, invited the Merrys to the President's House for dinner. Merry assumed, again, that the occasion would be formal—a state dinner in his honor. Jefferson saw it as one of his regular informal gatherings and did not, for that matter, hold state dinners. The Madisons were present, and—because Jefferson wanted to suggest that the United States took a neutral position in European affairs—the president invited the Yrujos and the Pinchons, ignoring the fact that according to European diplomatic protocol, they ranked beneath Merry. One or two congressmen were also present, as was William Short, Jefferson's former secretary in Paris, who was superbly practiced in the etiquette of diplomacy. Merry came in a high state of dress, but his sartorial splendor paled beside that of his wife, who—if Margaret Bayard Smith is to be believed—was always a model of spectacular excess.[58]

Since Jefferson was a widower, it was his custom to ask the wife of one of his cabinet secretaries to serve as his cohost. On this occasion, he took Dolley Madison by the arm when dinner was called and escorted her to the table at his right. She whispered in his ear, "Take Mrs. Merry," but Jefferson would make no exception to his customary practice.[59] Somehow or other Mrs. Yrujo sat on his left, with Yrujo to Dolley Madison's right, then Mrs. Merry. As others hurried to the table, Mr. Merry—befuddled by the bustle to choose a chair at the table—found himself at the far end. Jefferson never seated dinner guests by rank, title, or position, but the Merrys were unaware of this and, having assumed they were the guests of honor, took great umbrage at the final seating arrangements.[60] Jefferson might have adjusted his normal practice in deference to their feelings, but he insisted on making the point that in America rank and privilege counted for nothing. If he hadn't been doing so at their first encounter, here he was certainly using the occasion to teach the Merrys a lesson in democracy: in the United States all (white) persons were theoretically equal. The Merrys never forgave Jefferson for what they interpreted as a rank insult to themselves, their king, and their nation.[61]

Jefferson felt so strongly about the principles underpinning his dinners that he wrote, either in late 1803 or very early 1804, a memorandum to the members of his cabinet on the rules of etiquette at his table. "When brought together in society, all are perfectly equal, whether foreign or domestic, titled or untitled, in or out of office." Another point: "Differences of grade among diplomatic members, gives no precedence." And so on.[62] Alas, this did not exactly solve the problem, especially when a few weeks later he found it necessary to host a dinner for Napoleon's younger brother Jerome, who had been living in Baltimore and recently married the beautiful Elizabeth Patterson of that city, niece of Senator Samuel Smith's wife and cousin of Secretary of the Navy Robert Smith.

Jefferson did not want to insult Napoleon, or the Smith family, and he may not have reflected on how the Merrys might react—now that France and England were at war—to a social event honoring the brother of the French first consul. Mrs. Merry was probably even more incensed when she learned that Jefferson had offered his arm to Betsy Bonaparte—dressed in the new Parisian fashion of scandalously thin cloth draped revealingly over her body—and escorted her to the table. How dare he show more courtesy to this coquette than to the matronly Mrs. Merry! Jefferson had been cornered into hosting this dinner and may have only accidentally ushered Betsy to the table, but the incident ricocheted among Federalist wags and kept the Merrys' animosity burning.[63] Jefferson had foreseen none of these events as he was anticipating the transfer of Louisiana to the United States, but controversy has a way of finding presidents.

24

"Steadily in Her Course"

J EFFERSON, WHO OFTEN USED naval metaphors, must have felt the winds in his sails as he entered the fourth year of his presidency. The momentous issue of Louisiana had been largely solved; what remained was deciding how the new territory would be governed. Meriwether Lewis, now assisted in command by William Clark, was preparing his Corps of Discovery to leave its winter camp near St. Louis and begin its trek up the Missouri River. The Republican Congress's domestic policy of the first three years, backed at every point by Jefferson, had lowered taxes, reduced the size of the government workforce, paid much of the federal debt, and repealed the Judicial Act of 1801. Yet no triumph was without its complications. For one, the ongoing matter of the judges John Adams had appointed raised significant constitutional questions. Presidential fiat could not touch the Federalist judges already seated; the Constitution guaranteed their office for life "during good Behaviour" but did not define what bad behavior might consist of. This imprecision would cause Jefferson new trouble, starting in 1803 with the case of a demonstrably incompetent Federalist judge.

John Pickering, a celebrated jurist in New Hampshire and respected legal authority, had in 1791 been appointed chief justice of that state's highest court. But he became ill, noticeably deranged, and an alcoholic, with the result that citizens in his state began calling for his dismissal. The state's Federalist leaders saw a way to solve the Pickering problem: they convinced President George Washington to appoint him to the federal district court of New Hampshire. Yet Pickering's antics only worsened after the change; his insanity, profanity, and drunkenness while on the bench made a mockery of his judgeship. After Jefferson's election, his secretary of the Treasury, Albert Gallatin, tried to persuade Pickering to resign, and when he did not, Gallatin and the administration pressured several Federalist senators to back them. But they resisted, in the knowledge that Jefferson would appoint a Republican judge to replace him.

Pickering's decisions from the bench became so inappropriate that Jefferson, having received corroborating affidavits from Gallatin,[1] was at last forced to take action. The president was loath to launch proceedings against a sitting judge, because he knew most Federalists assumed he was determined to destroy the existing court system altogether, but Pickering's excesses left him no choice. On February 3, 1803, Jefferson sent a stack of letters and affidavits documenting the situation to the House of Representatives. He wrote, "The constitution has confided a power of instituting proceedings of redress, if [the members of Congress] shall be of the opinion that the case calls for them."[2] Jefferson played no other role in the case. In fact, he wished there was another way to remove justices guilty of incompetence; he wrote Federalist senator William Plumer that, ideally, the Constitution could be amended to allow a president to remove a judge after petition by a majority of both houses of Congress.[3] But Federalists had already dug in to protect Pickering, and members of Jefferson's party were equally determined to remove him—neither side was willing to seek an amendment. The only remedy was impeachment.[4]

Within a month of receiving the materials from Jefferson, the Republican-dominated House voted down party lines to impeach Pickering. The trial in the Senate was scheduled for the next session of Congress in early 1804. Yet as it turned out, many senators from both parties hesitated to remove the judge on the basis of insanity, and the actual illegality of his actions was questionable, despite their outrageousness. Pickering's House critics loosely interpreted his antics as constituting either a misdemeanor or simply bad behavior—they dissembled on the exact interpretation by declaring him guilty without ever specifying the charges. In the end, the Senate debates in the first two weeks of March broke along strictly partisan lines. The result was a narrow vote for impeachment—Pickering was thus the first federal judge in American history to be impeached. The Federalists, predisposed to see Jefferson as a dedicated enemy of the existing judiciary, viewed the vote as proof of the president's perfidy.

In the interval between the House's vote for Pickering's impeachment and the subsequent trial in the Senate, an even more controversial case involving a federal judge arose. Ironically enough, it involved a fellow signer of the Declaration of Independence, Samuel Chase of Maryland.

Chase was a talented jurist but also had an oversized ego, and his irascibility had won him many enemies, including Alexander Hamilton. Yet his ability was undeniable; he had become chief justice of the Maryland General Court in 1791, where he served until President Washington appointed him an associate justice of the US Supreme Court in 1796. By this time Chase had become a redoubtable Federalist, and over the next few years most Republicans came to fear and detest him. From the bench Chase was outspoken, partisan, and strident; he made no attempt to uphold impartial justice. As an imposing man with a gift for invective, he dominated the Court before the appointment of John Marshall as chief justice. Chase became only more outspoken as he aged. On May 2, 1803, he erupted in a tirade in front of a grand jury in Baltimore, railing against the current political situation, demeaning the Republicans and the nation's president.[5]

Jefferson generally preferred to take a moderate approach to the federal courts and had carefully avoided playing a direct role in the ongoing attempt to remove Judge Pickering. But Chase's partisan charge, coming after years of spirited attacks from the bench on men and ideals Jefferson admired, was simply more than he could abide. At the end of a long letter to Republican congressman Joseph H. Nicholson of Maryland, Jefferson, in a moment of incaution, wrote, "You must have heard of the extraordinary charge of Chace [sic] to the grand jury at Baltimore. ought this seditious & official attack on the principles of our constitution, and on the proceedings of a state, to go unpunished? and to whom so pointedly as yourself will the public look for the necessary measures? I ask these questions for your consideration. for myself, it is better that I should not interfere."[6] When Jefferson wrote in this fashion, he had to know his correspondent would take his idle talk as a request, if not a command. Nicholson conferred with Speaker of the House Nathaniel Macon, but both decided to do nothing.[7] For the next several months, Jefferson focused on Louisiana. Apparently he took no other action regarding Chase.

But in the House the highly partisan John Randolph of Roanoke decided to lead an attack on the jurist. Randolph had minimal legal skills, having studied the law but never practiced. A slim, shrill man, he was far better known for his remarkable oratorical talents, especially his capacity for histrionic ridicule and sarcasm. Jefferson surely would not have chosen him for the task. A true believer in Republican ideology, Randolph had begun to criticize the administration for not abolishing all aspects of the Hamiltonian system, including the national bank, and he wanted Jefferson to summarily remove Federalists from every federal office. He disdained moderation and arrogantly assumed leadership of a legal action to remove Chase, ignoring the fact that Chase was an extraordinarily proficient lawyer who moreover would assemble a talented legal team for his defense.

Nevertheless, on January 4, 1804, Randolph demanded that the House mount a formal investigation into Chase's behavior on the bench, and he chaired a committee that rushed to produce a set of charges, delivering them to the full House on March 6. Meanwhile the Senate was debating the fate of Judge Pickering. The simultaneity of the two procedures convinced the Federalists that Jefferson was indeed embarking on a full-scale campaign against the federal judiciary. Randolph drew up a series of seven articles of impeachment against Chase and submitted them to the House on March 26, but the House never acted on them. Instead, the case was moved to the Senate, scheduled to begin its second session in November.[8] Few appreciated at the time the mounting evidence that Randolph was creating his own faction within the Republican Party, to Jefferson's enduring lament.

When the second session of the Congress convened, Randolph headed a select committee formed to prepare the articles of impeachment. Two of the now eight articles claimed procedural errors on Chase's part; the other six alleged criminal behavior. The impeachment charges were reported on December 4, and Chase was scheduled to answer them on January 2, 1805, but he received an additional month to prepare his defense. Finally the Senate impeachment trial began on February 9, with Vice President Aaron Burr supervising Senate proceedings with impressive impartiality. Chase had prepared a masterful defense, aided by adept lawyers, including Robert Goodloe Harper, Luther Martin (possibly the nation's best trial lawyer), and Charles Lee. Chase admitted intemperate behavior and sharp language but made a powerful case that he had done nothing that approached illegality. Randolph was overmatched, and his rhetorical excess stood little chance against the legal expertise of Chase and his team; in fact Luther Martin demolished Randolph's arguments.

When the trial ended on March 1, 1805, the Senate acquitted Chase on every charge. Randolph's prestige suffered a blow from which it never recovered, and the principle was established that the justices of the Supreme Court were safe from partisan removal—even when they themselves acted in a highly partisan manner. It was a major victory for the Court, but Chase had learned a lesson too. Henceforth he controlled his behavior on the bench and never again used his position to badger political opponents.[9] His acquittal was, at least by implication, a defeat for Jefferson, proving exactly how independent of the executive office the Supreme Court justices and federal judges were.

EVEN AMID THE DIFFICULT and sometimes troubling political questions he faced as president, Jefferson managed to indulge his many curiosities. He had begun making copies of his letters in June 1785 with the press invented by James Watt (the Scottish inventor best known for improving the steam engine), which he used for almost two decades.[10] Yet Jefferson was always interested not only in new inventions but in improvements to existing tools. In the seventeenth century, an astronomer had created a device, consisting of four slender rods fixed together in the shape of a parallelogram with two pencils attached at opposite corners. When a person moved one of the pencils, the second traced out an identical design. In the eighteenth century a series of inventors and tinkerers perfected this mechanism, known variously as the pantagraph, pentagraph, or physiognotrace. It was used, primarily, to trace maps and produce silhouette portraits.

A young inventor in Philadelphia, John Isaac Hawkins, produced an improved version for making multiple copies of letters. He became a friend of Charles Willson Peale, who supported his work. In January 1803 Hawkins wrote a letter to James Madison, describing his device and seeking a patent, which he subsequently received on September 4, 1803. Peale, who was quite close to Jefferson, quickly informed him of Hawkins's polygraph, as he called the instrument, a few weeks after Hawkins had applied for a patent. Peale wrote that the polygraph "appears to me to possess many advantages over the copying-press—common Ink, and common paper, without any preparation, such as weting &c—Several originals may be wrote at once, without any considerable labour or restraint on the fingers."[11]

In October 1803 Benjamin H. Latrobe wrote Jefferson to praise the polygraph and subsequently loaned his own to Jefferson, who tried it out, made adjustments, and began a long correspondence with Peale on ways to improve the device.[12] Peale sent Jefferson an improved version, which the president received on March 29, 1804, just before leaving for his annual spring visit to Monticello. Jefferson wrote back almost immediately that this latest iteration represented a major advance over the previous one, although it was still stiff and he was attempting to further adjust it.[13] He almost surely took it with him to Monticello and continued to tinker, sending Peale drawings of and suggestions for a model he believed would

Jefferson's polygraph.
Source: Special Collections, University of Virginia. Used by permission.

be even more useful.[14] Finally, on November 7, Jefferson reported having received two of the latest models, saying, "The improvement in the writing apparatus is indeed precious. I find the pen now as light as a free pen."[15] Jefferson acquired one of the devices for the President's House and another for Monticello. Even today visitors to Monticello marvel at the polygraph on display; it is one of the most remarked-on features of the entire estate.

Less a matter of curiosity than a central aspect of Jefferson's being was his ongoing engagement with broad religious questions. In early 1804, not quite a year after his letter to Joseph Priestley and the drafting of his "Syllabus of an Estimate of the Merits of the Doctrines of Jesus, Compared with Those of Others," which he had sent to Benjamin Rush, Jefferson attempted to carve out of the New Testament the kernels of truth he believed Jesus himself had originally expressed.

Jefferson purchased two identical copies of the New Testament in January 1804; once they arrived, he took a pen knife and carefully removed the verses he believed genuine. Jefferson never explained how he decided which verses represented the actual words of Jesus, other than later saying they were "as easily distinguishable as diamonds in a dunghill."[16] After apparently only several evenings of work, Jefferson pasted the clippings in double columns on a dozen sheets of paper, and in early March he had them bound, calling the "book" *The Philosophy of Jesus of Nazareth*.[17] It was, he later wrote John Adams, "46. pages of pure and unsophisticated doctrines," or, put another way, "the most sublime and benevolent code of morals which has ever been offered to man."[18] Jefferson included no stories of miracles, and as he arranged the quotes, they recommended themselves to the reader's rational analysis. Jefferson did not share his compilation of verses with Rush, Adams, or anyone else and instead used *The Philosophy of Jesus* for his private devotions only. The original no longer exists, although its table of contents does, as do the two Bibles from which he extracted the desired verses.

LATE 1803 AND EARLY 1804 brought permanent visitors into Jefferson's presidential life, as both of his sons-in-law, Thomas Mann Randolph and John Wayles Eppes, newly elected to the House of Representatives, moved into the President's House. Still, Jefferson eagerly anticipated his annual spring visit to Monticello. Perhaps rumors of a group of diehard Federalists talking about seceding from the nation and founding a Northern Confederacy[19] made him even more keen to escape the political scene. Also drawing him home was the fact that his older daughter, Martha, had given birth to another child in November, and his younger daughter, Maria, who wasn't nearly as robust as her sister, was expecting and due sometime in February or early March.

Maria had a difficult pregnancy and on February 15 gave birth prematurely to Maria Jefferson Eppes. The letters exchanged between Jefferson and his daughters reveal how worried all were about Maria's slow recovery. In what turned out to be her last letter to her father, Maria wrote him on February 10 requesting that he commission a profile of himself by the artist Charles Balthazar Julien Févret de Saint-Mémin, who used a physiognotrace.[20] By early April, she had been brought by stretcher from her home at Edgehill to Monticello, where Jefferson arrived on April 4, finding her, as he wrote Madison, "so weak as barely to be able to stand, her stomach so disordered as to reject almost everything she took into it, a constant small fever, and an imposthume [abscess] rising in her breast."[21]

Preoccupied with the health of his beautiful, delicate daughter, Jefferson found odd times to roam his estate, often as a means of calming his nerves; he also saw to the planting of various seeds and a group of

peach and pine trees.[22] Yet this visit to Monticello brought him little solace. In his characteristically laconic style, Jefferson recorded in his memorandum book, "This morning between 8. & 9. aclock my dear daughter
Maria Eppes died." A few days later he recorded that he paid his childhood friend, the Reverend Matthew Maury, for officiating at the funeral
before her interment in the Monticello graveyard.[23] Jefferson was devastated by Maria's death, as was her sister, Martha; his granddaughter Ellen
recalled years afterward that her mother said that she left Jefferson alone in
his room for several hours and, when she returned, found him sitting
"with the Bible in his hands."[24] Perhaps it was the condensed version he
had created for himself. Jefferson's letters over the next few months reveal
the depth of his sorrow. He informed Madison that he would delay his
return to Washington: "On the 17th instant our hopes and fears here took
their ultimate form. I had originally intended to have left this towards the
end of the present week. But a desire to see my family in a state of more
composure before we separate, will keep me somewhat longer."[25] He sent
his childhood friend John Page a sad lament. "Others may lose of their
abundance," he wrote, "but I, of my want, have lost even the half of all I
had. My evening prospects now hang on the slender thread of a single
life. . . . The hope with which I had looked forward to the moment, when,
resigning public cares to younger hands, I was to retire to that domestic
comfort from which the last great step is to be taken, is fearfully blighted."
He went on to muse about the "end of our journey," after which he and
his wife, Martha, would arise "in the midst of the friends we have lost."[26]
The idea of an afterlife brought comfort to Jefferson, especially following
the "inexpressible grief" of losing Maria.[27] Before he left for the capital,
Francis and Elizabeth Eppes—the aunt and uncle with whom Maria had
stayed as a child during her father's first years in Paris and whose son, John
(Jack) Wayles Eppes, Maria had married—arrived at Monticello, ready to
care for Maria's surviving son, Francis, and the infant Maria. The Eppeses
returned to Eppington with the two children, where they lived until their
bereaved father could make other arrangements. Jefferson forever treasured Francis as a link to his daughter; compounding the tragedy, the baby
Maria died in 1806.[28]

Jefferson returned to Washington on May 11 and soon thereafter received a letter out of the past. He and Abigail Adams had been dear friends
during their days and evenings together in France and England, but the
political divisions of the 1790s had ended that friendship and their affectionate, witty correspondence. On May 20, 1804, having heard of

Jefferson's recent loss, Abigail took up her pen. She wrote him that she had "shed the tear of sorrow" over the death of "your beloved and deserving daughter, an event which I most sincerely mourn." Then she recalled her having taken Maria in as a small child when she had arrived in London on her way to rejoin her father and sister in Paris. Abigail had instantly bonded with the child and now commiserated with Jefferson: "I know how closely entwined around a parents heart, are those chords which bind the filial to the parental Bosom, and when snaped asunder, how agonizing the pangs of seperation." Remarking that she too had "tasted the bitter cup," she closed by expressing her hope that Jefferson might "derive comfort and consolation in this day of your sorrow and affliction, from that only source calculated to heal the wounded heart—a firm belief in the Being: perfections and attributes of God, is the sincere and ardent wish of her, who once took pleasure in subscribing Herself your Friend."[29] Moved by this letter, Jefferson, in his reply to Abigail, sought to close the breach between them, but full reconciliation was still several years away.

BACK IN WASHINGTON, Jefferson, despite his grief, found himself quickly caught up in the events of the day. When elected president in 1800, he had intended to serve only one term, but Federalist opposition led him to change his mind. The onrush of urgent matters speeded up his decision to stand for a second term. He reluctantly bowed to the pressure (and what he saw as political necessity) to once more put himself before the voters. As he wrote Elbridge Gerry, "I sincerely regret that the unbounded calumnies of the federal party have obliged me to throw myself on the verdict of my country for trial, my great desire having been to retire, at the end of the present term, to a life of tranquility; and it was my decided purpose when I entered into office. They force my continuance. If we can keep the vessel of State as steadily in her course for another four years, my earthly purposes will be accomplished."[30]

Jefferson met with Aaron Burr in January, and the vice president offered to withdraw from the race, hinting to Jefferson that he would like a plumb appointment in return, but Jefferson was noncommittal.[31] Burr, realizing he had no future in the national Republican Party, given suspicions that he had angled for the presidency in the disputed election of 1800, decided to challenge the George Clinton–dominated Republican Party in New York State, running for governor against the candidate chosen by the state caucus, Morgan Lewis. In the ensuing campaign, Burr's old nemesis, Alexander Hamilton, again attacked him with venom and energy. Burr lost, and the anger that had flared up between them led to their climactic duel. Early in the morning of July 11, 1804, Hamilton and Burr rowed across the Hudson River from New York City and, on the so-called Heights of Weehawken in New Jersey, Burr fatally shot Hamilton.[32] Jefferson did not immediately remark on his old foe's fate. At the time he only made two short references to Hamilton in private letters, both purely factual. Surely Jefferson knew that if he praised Hamilton in eulogy, Federalists would attack him as a hypocrite, and for Jefferson to mention their mutual enmity would seem churlish. Some years later Jefferson, then in retirement, wrote of Hamilton, "We had indeed no personal dissensions. Each of us perhaps thought well of the other as a man. But as politicians it was impossible for two men to be of more opposite principles."[33] Jefferson did, however, keep a bust of Hamilton in the entrance hall of Monticello.

One formidable political enemy was dead, and a potential enemy had forfeited his career by killing him. Shortly after, a constitutional amendment requiring presidential electors to declare one candidate president and the other vice president received the necessary approval by three-quarters of the states (Congress had passed it the previous December).[34] Officially ratified on September 25, 1804, the Twelfth Amendment ensured that there would be no reprise of the electoral debacle of 1800, in which Burr had played so large a role.

IN THE SPRING OF 1804, the exploration of the West was never far from Jefferson's mind. Several letters arrived from Meriwether Lewis, posted from his winter camp across from St. Louis. One described the people and political culture of the city and the surrounding area. Shortly before the Corps of Discovery set off to ascend the Missouri River, on May 22, 1804, Lewis sent another letter. Jefferson would not receive additional news for more than a year.[35]

Meanwhile, he pondered launching other expeditions. On March 13, 1804, he wrote an acquaintance, William Dunbar, a naturalist and planter living near Natchez, proposing that he find good men to explore the western reaches of the Red and Arkansas Rivers. Two abortive efforts, one led by Dunbar and a scientist named George Hunter in the fall of 1805 and another by Thomas Freeman in 1806, resulted from Jefferson's proposal.[36] Little, too, came of the expeditions led by Zebulon Pike in 1805 and 1806, also suggested by Jefferson, one intended to reach the headwaters of the Mississippi, the other to chart the far west of the continent.

Jefferson received an entirely unexpected letter on May 27, 1804, from a far more accomplished explorer, Alexander von Humboldt. Having come to the end of five years traveling throughout Latin America, including Mexico and parts of the Caribbean, Humboldt was visiting the United States. Heartened that the United States was in Jefferson's "enlightened hands," the German scholar expressed "great admiration for your writings, your actions, and the liberalism of your ideals, which have inspired me from my earliest youth." He hoped to meet the president; Jefferson responded enthusiastically, and on June 5, Humboldt, accompanied by Charles Willson Peale, arrived at the President's House.[37] The visit went splendidly, and the following night Jefferson invited Humboldt, Peale, and several other guests to what the last called "a very elegant dinner." As Peale recalled, "Not a single toast was given or called for, or Politicks touched on, but subjects of Natural History, and improvements of the conveniences of Life. Manners of the different nations described, or other agreeable conversation animated the whole company."[38] Fortunately for Jefferson, who spoke no German, Humboldt, as Peale remembered, "spoke English very well, in the German dialect."[39] Dolley Madison said the "charming Prussian Baron" was "the most polite, modest, well-informed, and interesting traveller we have ever met" and "was much pleased with America."[40] Shortly after the dinner, Humboldt gave Jefferson a few pages, translated into French, of one of his earlier works, on the territory between the Rio Grande and the Sabine River.

Though Jefferson was Humboldt's senior by twenty-six years, they were a match intellectually, especially in their disagreement with European theories about the declension of the New World's flora and fauna. Humboldt also admired the liberal institutions of the United States, a subject Jefferson never tired of talking about. He was never swayed from his belief that the United States and the Americas had a special destiny. As he wrote Humboldt in 1813, "The European nations constitute a separate division of the globe; their localities make them part of a distinct system; they have a set of interests of their own in which it is our business never to engage ourselves. America has a hemisphere to itself: it must have it's separate system of interests, which must not be subordinated to those of Europe."[41] These two exemplars of the Enlightenment would continue their correspondence until 1825. Regrettably, they never broached the one topic on which they did disagree: slavery.[42] Humboldt, a strong proponent of emancipation, appeared to recognize and respect that it represented a significant political dilemma for Jefferson.

By MIDSUMMER 1804, many Federalists were almost ready to cede the election to the Jeffersonians. Republicans had founded clubs in many cities across the nation and learned to use parades and celebrations to their benefit. They had established daily newspapers in most of the nation's larger cities and weeklies in most of its small towns.[43] While the Republicans already had a caucus candidate in Jefferson, the Federalists were undecided.[44] Moreover, Jefferson's successes—lower taxes, smaller government, peace, the doubling in size of the nation, and a growing economy—caused even the most hardened Federalists to despair. Hamilton, assessing the reality of American politics in 1802, bemoaned to fellow sufferer Gouverneur Morris, "Every day proves to me more and more that this American world was not made for me."[45] For some the only conceivable solution was secession, but the notion appealed to few beyond the most extreme High Federalists, like Senator Timothy Pickering. Before his death, Hamilton himself had opposed secession as excessive.

Jefferson delivered his Fourth Annual Message to Congress on November 8, 1804, when the election results were still not known. It summarized a nation on the rise. He reported that war in Europe had not deleteriously affected the United States, that the nation's finances exceeded even the most positive forecasts, that there was progress on developing governing procedures for the Louisiana Territory, that solutions were being found for Indian affairs, and that while the navy was expanding, there was no need for a larger army. In his communication Jefferson alluded to the broad agenda he envisioned for the legislature going forward: "Whether the great interests of agriculture, manufactures, commerce, or navigation, can, within the pale of your constitutional powers, be aided in any of their relations; whether laws are provided in all cases where they are wanting; . . . whether anything can be done to advance the general good, are questions within the limits of your functions which will necessarily occupy your attention. In these and other matters which you in your wisdom may propose for the good of our country, you may count with assurance on my hearty co-operation and faithful execution."[46] As president, Jefferson had—perhaps unsurprisingly—come to believe that the power of the federal government was greater than he had initially believed. On this question and many others, his attitudes evolved.

Of particular note was his more positive approach to manufacturing. In early 1805, a publisher approached him about a new, revised edition of *Notes on the State of Virginia*. Jefferson explained that his present duties did not allow him the time to update the book, as much as he wanted to amend the passages disparaging the effect on a citizenry of an economy rooted in manufacturing. He explained that he had meant, "when writing, the manufacturers of the great cities in the old countries, at the time present [the early 1780s], with whom the want of food and clothing necessary to sustain life, has begotten a depravity of morals, a dependence and corruption, which renders them an undesirable accession to a country whose morals are sound. My expressions looked forward to the time when our own great cities would get into the same state." His concern then was not the present reality. "As yet our manufacturers are as much at their ease, as independent and moral as our agricultural inhabitants, and they will continue so as long as there are vacant lands for them to resort to; because whenever it shall be attempted by the other classes to reduce them to the minimum of subsistence, they will quit their trades and go to laboring the earth."[47] In short, the availability of inexpensive land served as a safety valve, offering a release for the social pressures that built up in centers of manufacturing in Europe.

THE FEDERALISTS HAD no caucus, and no obvious frontrunner. They eventually decided on Charles Cotesworth Pinckney of South Carolina as their presidential candidate, and Rufus King of New York—the former minister to England and an associate of Hamilton—as their choice for vice president. The two were no match for Jefferson and his replacement for Burr, the imposing multiterm governor of New York, George Clinton. Jefferson was politically and personally popular; the election was a foregone conclusion. Jefferson carried fourteen states—including even Massachusetts and New Hampshire—while Pinckney won two. The vote in the electoral college was 162–14.

Writing to a correspondent in January 1805, Jefferson praised George Washington for his "voluntary retirement" after eight years, a practice he intended to follow. "And a few more precedents will oppose the obstacle of habit to any one after awhile who shall endeavor to extend his term. Perhaps it may beget a disposition to establish it by an amendment of the Constitution."[48]

Jefferson's second inauguration was scheduled for Monday, March 4, 1805. This time he rode on horseback to the Capitol. Guests crowded the Senate chamber, but no quorum of either body was present. Congress had adjourned the evening before, and many legislators were already on their way home or preparing to leave. Following the acquittal of Justice Samuel Chase by the Senate on March 1 and Aaron Burr's moving farewell address to the Senate the following day, the inaugural was anti-climactic. Again, Jefferson spoke so quietly that no one beyond the front rows could hear a word, and again he had printed copies distributed. The address was less eloquent than his first, less lofty in both style and sentiment; the first was forward-looking, the second more of a recounting of past accomplishments.[49]

Jefferson acknowledged that some Americans feared the acquisition of Louisiana might threaten the integrity of the union, but he discounted the idea that federalism could not be sustained over an even larger territory; and in any case, he asked, wasn't it better that the settlers on the west bank of the Mississippi be "our own brethren and children, than . . . strangers of another family?" As for the peoples living in the new land, the United States was already teaching them agricultural skills, which "humanity enjoins" us to do. He professed great admiration for the Indians, describing them as "endowed with the faculties and the rights of men, breathing an ardent love of liberty and independence."[50]

Jefferson believed the remnant of hidebound Federalists had diminished influence and that a growing majority of the citizenry shared the values of his party. He nonetheless counseled patience toward the opposition, safe in the assurance that "truth, reason, and their own interests, will at length prevail, will gather them into the fold of their country, and will complete their entire union of opinion, which gives to a nation the blessing of harmony, and the benefit of all its strength."[51] He also defended the concept of freedom of the press, while also castigating the "artillery" of the opposition press for its "licentiousness." Yet he did not condemn state actions to punish the publication of "falsehood and defamation." This passage responded to a controversy that had arisen in 1803.

In February of that year, Jefferson received a letter from Thomas McKean, the Republican governor of Pennsylvania and a signer of the Declaration of Independence. McKean complained, "The infamous & seditious libels, published almost daily in our news-papers, are become intolerable. If they cannot be altogether prevented, yet they may be greatly checked by a few prosecutions."[52] He asked Jefferson for his advice on the matter. Jefferson's reply disappoints us today. Perhaps his judgment was temporarily clouded by recent Federalists attacks on him; perhaps his confidence in Governor McKean convinced him that the public's own confidence in the press was legitimately threatened; perhaps he felt the states simply had a more expansive mandate than the federal government, restrained as the latter was by the First Amendment; perhaps he truly believed that punishment of outrageous press abuses would result in a stronger, more trustworthy institution.[53] Whatever his reason, Jefferson's words, though apparently intended as a defense of the press, effectively supported government censorship at the state level. The letter contradicted a basic principle of Jefferson's faith in the free press, elsewhere stated in innumerable letters.

Jefferson insisted to McKean that his note be kept confidential. He reviewed what he assumed to be the Federalist strategy: "The Federalists having failed in destroying the freedom of the press by their gag-law, seem to have attacked it in an opposite form, that is by pushing it's licentiousness and its lying to such a degree of prostitution as to deprive it of all credit." He emphasized, "This is a dangerous state of things, and the press ought to be restored to it's credibility if possible. . . . I have long thought that a few prosecutions of the most eminent offenders would have a wholesome effect in restoring the integrity of the presses, not a general prosecution, for that would look like persecution: but a selective one."[54] His anger at the Federalists led him to betray his belief in the complete and unfettered freedom of the press; this letter, though it did not become public during his lifetime, has endured as a blemish on Jefferson's reputation.

Jefferson concluded his Annual Message with an open appeal to the religiosity of the American people (which serves as evidence of his own religious faith): "I shall need . . . the favor of that Being in whose hands we are, who led our forefathers, as Israel of old, from their native land, and planted them in a country flowing with all the necessaries and comforts of life; who has covered our infancy with his providence, and our riper years with his wisdom and power; and to whose goodness I ask you to join with me in supplications, that he will so enlighten the minds of your servants, guide their councils, and prosper their measures, that whatsoever they do, shall result in your good, and shall secure to you the peace, friendship, and approbation of all nations."[55]

Ten days later, Jefferson departed for Monticello. His mind surely turned to the actions of his first term that remained unfulfilled, including the Lewis and Clark Expedition. The Corps of Discovery, having spent the frigid winter near the Mandan Indians in North Dakota, embarked westward up the Missouri on April 7, 1805. That same day they sent their keelboat back toward St. Louis, loaded with artifacts from their travels (including a live prairie dog) and a letter to Jefferson. Jefferson did not receive Lewis's letter, which brimmed with excitement and confidence about

what lay ahead, until July 13. "I can foresee no material or probable ob-
struction to our progress, and entertain the most sanguine hopes of complete success. . . . At this moment, every individual of the party are in
good health, and excellent sperits; zealously attached to the enterprise, and
anxious to proceed; not a whisper of discontent or murmur is to be heard
among them; but all in unison, act with the most perfect harmony. With
such men I have every thing to hope, and but little to fear."[56]

As Jefferson mulled the welcome letter from the comfort of Monticello,
he could be excused for thinking that one of Lewis's final lines—"all in
unison, act with the most perfect harmony"—could double as Jefferson's
aim for the nation. Little could he foresee the tumult of the final three
years of his presidency.

25

The Collapse of Political Consensus

T HE SUCCESS OF JEFFERSON'S first administration rested on a blend of ideology, personality, and patience. Jefferson clearly spelled out his political philosophy and proposed legislation in his inaugural address and several annual messages to Congress. His personality was on display at his dinner parties for congressmen and other political and cultural leaders, to great effect. As Federalist Supreme Court justice William Patterson once said, "No man can be personally acquainted with Mr. Jefferson and remain his personal enemy." He added, "Few . . . are more opposed to him as a politician than I am," but "there was a mildness and amenity in his voice and manner that at once softened any of the asperities of *party-spirit*."[1] And despite the Federalists' dour predictions, Jefferson was no rigid ideologue. He was genuinely more interested in effective governance than petty politics. He understood that the American system depended upon compromise and believed that moderation would attract to his position many citizens—and, he hoped, lawmakers—who initially opposed his principles. The pragmatic Jefferson understood better than the Federalists that he was president of all Americans, not just those who supported him.

Despite his manifest talents as a leader and administrator, and despite the personal qualities that so endeared him to even some of his opponents, the Republican Party had begun to fracture by the end of Jefferson's first term. Some of his supporters in Congress had expected a wholesale removal of Federalist officeholders, a frontal attack on the national bank, and even constitutional amendments to limit the power of the central government. Jefferson's moderation on these matters had disappointed the extremists in his own party. A handful of Virginia Republicans in particular, led by John Randolph of Roanoke, came to believe that Jefferson had forsaken his own political ideology. Randolph headed a small but vocal faction that, more concerned with ideological purity than matters of governance, would brook no compromise. Randolph was probably the most captivating orator in Congress before Daniel Webster, and his high-pitched voice always attracted a crowd in the House. He would often rush in, still wearing his spurs, with a riding whip at his side and hounds at his feet, and unleash a torrent of words, devastating his opponents and often shocking even his supporters with his excessive ridicule and vituperation.[2]

Randolph openly split with Jefferson for the first time over an arcane land scandal in Georgia. In 1795 the corrupt Georgia legislature—every single member who voted for the deal had taken a bribe—had fraudulently deeded to speculators some 35 million acres of land in the so-called Yazoo region, from the western border of the state all the way to the Mississippi River. The next year, after the scandal became public, the new legislature rescinded the land sale and repudiated every aspect of the transaction. Meanwhile the speculators had sold millions of acres of the Yazoo land to unsuspecting buyers across the nation, many in New England. It was not clear how to solve the problem. Jefferson appointed a commission, consisting of Secretary of State James Madison, Secretary of the Treasury Albert Gallatin, and Attorney General Levi Lincoln, to address the issue.

The three cabinet members ultimately recommended cession of the land in question to the national government, which would pay $1.25 million to the state of Georgia. It would set aside 5 million acres as a reserve that it could either grant directly to the presumably innocent third-party purchasers or sell, using the proceeds to reimburse them.[3] When this plan came before the House of Representatives on February 7, 1804, Randolph and his purist cohorts exploded in outrage. Randolph attacked the Yazoo claims commission deal as the worst kind of speculation, a reward for fraud and corruption. This was proof, according to Randolph and other self-styled Old Republicans, that the administration had chosen expediency over principle. The matter remained unresolved until 1814, after Roanoke voters temporarily ousted Randolph from the House.

In the meantime, Randolph and other southern conservatives—they were not Federalists and did not truly consider themselves Republicans, so they called themselves the Tertium Quid (Latin for the "third something")—complicated Jefferson's life, often delaying passage of legislation and consideration of a range of matters.[4]

RANDOLPH WOULD PROVE troublesome in more serious ways too. The uncertain terms of the original Louisiana Purchase complicated the challenge of governing the territory, a preoccupation of Jefferson's second term. The French negotiator, the Marquis François de Barbé-Marbois, had specified that the purchase included none of the Floridas, but Robert Livingston and James Monroe apparently chose to ignore the statement. France had originally claimed Louisiana proper—the land west of the Mississippi River, including the Isle of New Orleans—transferring it to Spain in 1763. Since Spain also controlled the region that became Texas, confusion arose over the border between French (and then American) Louisiana and Spanish Texas. Jefferson and his advisors wanted to believe that the territory they purchased in 1803 swept west to what they called the Rio Bravo (now the Rio Grande).

Far more valuable at that time was West Florida, a narrow, gulf-hugging swath of land extending from the peninsula to the Mississippi River, including the region surrounding Baton Rouge. The panhandle boasted the best natural port on the Gulf of Mexico, Mobile Bay, and the major rivers of the Mississippi Territory, covering the present-day states of Mississippi and Alabama, flowed through it. West Florida had changed hands several times, but the American negotiators in Paris assumed, despite Barbé-Marbois's words to the contrary, that the pre-1763 boundaries, when French Louisiana included most of the Florida panhandle, defined the Louisiana Purchase. The importance of West Florida had led Jefferson and his advisors, beginning in late 1803, to attempt to secure the territory, claiming it was already US property (that is, included in the purchase agreement with France) while simultaneously approaching Spain about purchasing the region.

Every aspect of the Louisiana issue infuriated Spain: by the terms of the treaty ceding the territory, France could not transfer it to any other nation without Spain's prior approval. Of course, France had done just that. Eager to restrict Louisiana to the narrowest of boundaries, Spanish officials in West Florida sent troops to Nacogdoches in East Texas and several other critical locations. As Jefferson wrote to his friend Pierre Samuel Du Pont de Nemours in November 1803, "At this moment a little cloud hovers in the horizon. the government of Spain has protested against the right of France to transfer; & it is possible she may refuse possession, & that this may bring on acts of force."[5] Jefferson knew that in the latter event, he could expect support at home. Spain soon recognized the futility of protesting and agreed to give up Louisiana but persisted in defending its rights to Texas and West Florida.

During the purchase negotiations, Barbé-Marbois had suggested that France would assist the United States in convincing Spain to approve the transfer of West Florida. But in 1804 the French government reported that Spain was too angry over the Louisiana transfer to discuss other matters, so the United States should delay. Meanwhile the Congress passed the Mobile Act, which brought Louisiana under the nation's revenue laws; the bill assumed that Louisiana included West Florida. A few months later the Senate approved a commission to settle disputes about indemnities Spain owed American citizens arising from its having illegally seized US ships in the late 1790s. But Spain refused to accept the commission's findings.

In February 1805, Jefferson's cabinet drafted three proposals for settling the boundary issues. First, the United States would give up its claim to Texas in exchange for a formal cession of West Florida from the Mississippi to the Perdido River. Second, if Spain would accept a more distant eastern boundary, the United States would close a portion of the western reaches of Louisiana to white settlers for a number of years. Third, in exchange for both West and East Florida, the US would simply pay Spain $1 million. But Spanish attitudes had hardened; in response, Congress stiffened its resolve, persisting in claiming Texas and West Florida. It also sent US troops into Spanish West Florida.[6]

Negotiations in Madrid went nowhere. James Monroe and William Pinkney (the US ministers to England and Spain, respectively) made various other offers.[7] In a joint private letter to Madison, the two concluded that Spain would never cede "one foot of territory" and recommended that the United States simply seize the Floridas and the portion of Texas between the Colorado River and the Rio Grande to force a final settlement.[8]

Neither Madison nor Jefferson was willing to contemplate such an aggressive action in the summer of 1805. Jefferson's initial thought was to threaten France with a US alliance with England in order to prompt France in turn to pressure Spain.[9] Jefferson perhaps recalled how a similar threat in 1802 seemed to have helped persuade Napoleon to sell Louisiana. A month later he learned that Spain had sent five hundred colonists to reinforce San Antonio and a hundred troops to Nacogdoches; he feared they were also constructing a fortification at Matagordo on the Texas coast. To Madison, he wondered if the United States should attempt to "dislodge" these new settlements in Texas, and a few days later he stated that the nation should take actions to "correct the dangerous error that we are a people whom no injuries can provoke to war."[10]

Jefferson called for a cabinet meeting in early October 1805, by which time Madison wanted to secure West Florida without pushing for Texas; for his part, Gallatin said that any claims on territory west of the Sabine River had no legal or historical basis. By this point, Jefferson himself had softened his views, in part because war in Europe appeared imminent. As he wrote to Gallatin, "The war on the Continent of Europe appears now so certain, and that peace is at least one year off, that we are now placed at our ease in point of time. We may make another effort for a peaceable accommodation with Spain." He continued, "Our question now is in what way to give Spain another opportunity of arrangement? Is not Paris the place? France the agent? The purchase of Floridas the means?"[11] Purchase was the key word. At the next cabinet meeting, the president and his secretaries decided on a new proposal: that Spain cede both West and East Florida, the United States pay Spain $5 million, the boundary between Texas and Mexico be set at the Colorado River, the territory between the Colorado and the Rio Bravo remain unsettled for thirty years, and Spain pay $4 million in spoliation claims.[12] Jefferson did not mention the proposal in his Annual Message to Congress, whose text he had delivered on December 3, 1805. Rather, he assumed the delicate diplomatic endeavor would have to take place in secrecy. Jefferson did inform the Congress that he had ordered American troops stationed on the frontier to stand ready to protect American citizens and to "repel by arms any similar aggression in the future." But he said no more. "Other details, necessary for your full information on the state of things between this country and that shall be the subject of another communication."[13]

Three days later Jefferson submitted another letter to Congress along with documents describing some details of the boundary dispute. The tone of this message differed from that of December 3, largely because he did not state the potential need for a military response. Rather, he suggested that France wanted to help settle the dispute and stated that at some point the diplomatic discussions would require federal funds. He did not name an amount or mention who would receive the money. He would leave these questions to the wisdom of Congress, though he expected key congressional leaders to come to him for advice and further information.

To Jefferson's dismay, his proposal had to clear a special select committee of seven congressmen headed by John Randolph of Roanoke, who visited the President's House, where Jefferson explained that he wanted $2 million to pay France for that nation's assistance in making a deal to purchase the Floridas. In Jefferson's mind, the process was identical to that which had resulted in the Louisiana Purchase. But Randolph, though a fervent expansionist, was enraged. In his view, the manly, honorable solution was military force, whereas France's demand for payment was nothing short of a bribe, no less detestable than French actions during the scandalous XYZ Affair of 1797.

In front of Congress, Randolph said he would act to pay for troops but not for payoffs. He attacked the president for cowardliness and corruption, employing terms of abuse so extreme that even longtime observers of Randolph's behavior were shocked. As one member of Congress observed, "Never has the *President* been handled so severely in public debate."[14] Jefferson responded in his usual way. As John Quincy Adams reported on February 25, "I dined at the President's, with a company of fifteen members of both Houses, all federalists."[15] Seeing in Randolph an implacable foe, Jefferson maneuvered to find more cooperative congressmen, identifying one in Barnabas Bidwell, who sat on Randolph's select committee. Bidwell eventually authored a bill on his own, the so-called Two-Million Dollar Act, which, after spirited debate, passed Congress on January 27, 1806, and the Senate on April 14.[16] At that point, Jefferson's break with Randolph was total and permanent.

Meanwhile, Spanish troops had crossed eastward from Texas to Louisiana over the Sabine River, setting up camp just west of Natchitoches, Louisiana. In response, Jefferson bolstered the US military presence in the region. Luckily, the Spanish invaders pulled back into Texas.[17] Jefferson desperately wanted to avoid a military encounter.

Shortly after Bidwell's Two-Million Dollar Act passed, Jefferson appointed John Armstrong, the current American minister to France, and James Bowdoin, the new minister to Spain, to a special commission to broker a deal with Madrid. By the time the two ministers received instructions in the summer of 1806, however, the military situation in Europe had changed significantly: Admiral Horatio Nelson's victory at Trafalgar gave England undisputed control of the seas, and Napoleon Bonaparte's victory at Austerlitz secured French control of the continent. Meanwhile, the US Congress, fearful of French ministers' likely ambition to personally profit from any United States funds ostensibly intended for Spain, had put onerous restrictions on payment of the $2 million; as a consequence, Talleyrand and his operatives lost interest. As for Spain, it turned its focus to Europe, and its American negotiations came to an end.[18] Jefferson's diplomatic efforts to acquire West Florida had utterly failed. The episode was one of the most dismal and disappointing of his presidency. And it would not be the last time he discovered that European events—and European nations—were immune to American threats and demands.

The West Florida question would remain unsettled until after Jefferson left office. In 1810 during the Madison administration, the US finally seized the territory, which by then had—under the leadership of both American and British settlers—become the short-lived Republic of West Florida. Eventually, according to the terms of the Adams-Onís Treaty of 1819, Spain officially ceded all of Florida to the United States, the United States assumed the claims of its citizens against Spain up to $5 million, and the Sabine River was established as the boundary between Louisiana and Spanish Texas.[19]

As JEFFERSON'S FRUSTRATIONS with Randolph's faction and Spain mounted, he found respite in a long visit from his daughter Martha. She arrived on December 2, 1805, about six months pregnant, with her six children and several slaves in tow. Because his daughter and her husband were in financial straits, Jefferson sent her $100 in early November to cover her transportation costs.[20] Once in Washington, Martha and her eldest daughter, sixteen-year-old Anne Cary, made social visits to close friends, and the two on occasion joined Jefferson at his dinners. After she gave birth on January 17, 1806, to another son, whom she named James Madison Randolph—the first child born in the President's House—her role as hostess apparently ended.[21] She and her children stayed until about the beginning of May. It was the last time Martha visited the President's House; she did not, contrary to legend, typically serve as her father's Washington hostess.

Martha, by all accounts gracious and sophisticated, was every bit her father's daughter. When, upon arriving in Washington and receiving a note from the British ambassador's wife, the socially precise Mrs. Merry, inquiring if she wished to be visited "as the wife of a member of congress, or as the daughter of the President," Martha replied as her father would have expected. As Margaret Bayard Smith put it, "She claimed no distinction whatever, but wished only for the same consideration extended to other strangers."[22] Jefferson, often lonely in the large house, treasured the presence of his daughter and grandchildren.

Smith penned a charming portrait of Martha and her father sitting together in the President's House. "While I sat looking at him playing with these infants, one standing on the sopha with its arms round his neck, the two youngest on his knees, playing with him, I could scarcely realize that he was one of the most celebrated men now living, both as a Politician and Philosopher." He was in a remarkably good mood that night, she remembered. On another occasion she described him in the same setting: "His grand-children would steal to his side, while he was conversing with his friends, and climb his knee, or lean against his shoulder, and he without interrupting the flow of conversation would quietly caress them."[23] Jefferson must have found evenings with his precious grandchildren a restorative and much-needed reprieve from his presidential responsibilities.[24]

AARON BURR'S CAREER as a public official had ended with Jefferson's first term, though effectively it was finished the moment he shot Alexander Hamilton. Yet he was only forty-nine years old and remained ambitious, always his most prominent characteristic. No one doubted his ability, though there had always been questions about his scruples, and his political philosophy remained unclear. Long fascinated by the West, following the Louisiana Purchase Burr apparently began to imagine new opportunities for himself in the region. In April 1805, he set off on an unofficial seven-month inspection tour of the new territory, talking to state and local political leaders of all sorts, gauging popular sentiment regarding the union, vaguely suggesting the seizure of additional lands to various people, and insinuating that the Jefferson administration was quietly backing his activities.[25]

Burr was, in short, a troublemaker par excellence. He fell in for a period with General James Wilkinson, governor of the Louisiana Territory and himself a man of uncertain honesty; Wilkinson was, in fact, secretly in the pay of the Spanish Crown. Before he began his westward trip, Burr had contacted English minister Anthony Merry, who, on March 29, 1805, had written his superiors in London to convey Burr's message that the inhabitants of Louisiana, unhappy with the transfer, "seemed determined to render themselves independent of the United States." They only needed the support of a European nation, and Burr, intending to be "the Instrument for effecting such a Connection," came to Merry seeking to unite with England for this secessionist purpose.[26] In late November Merry wrote London again, relating that in a meeting after Burr's return from New Orleans, the latter had told him, "Every thing was in fact completely prepared in every quarter for the execution of his plan."[27]

But the English, likely owing to their preoccupation with events on the Continent, did not respond to Burr's offers. Later, Burr sent similar inquiries to the Spanish minister in Washington, Carlos Martinez de Yrujo, who reported to his superiors that Burr was even contemplating conquering Washington, DC, and seizing the president—with what army, it remained to be seen. But neither Yrujo nor his government gave much credence to these farfetched ideas.[28] The precise dimensions of Burr's plans—whether he hoped to establish a separate government west of the Appalachians, to conquer Mexico, or to combine these two aims and also to take the Floridas—we will probably never know. He said different things to different people and talked expansively, and although he did eventually recruit men to his cause, he was stopped before he could take any significant action. Perhaps the most surprising aspect of the story is how long it took for Jefferson and the administration to recognize the threat Burr posed.

Throughout the autumn months of 1805, Jefferson must have known of rumors and reports from the western states about Burr's activities, but he paid them no attention. Then on December 1 Jefferson received an anonymous letter postmarked with the same date. The communication ominously reported that Burr was "meditating the overthrow of your Administration" and that a "foreign agent, now at Washington knows since February last his plans." Further, the letter warned the president to watch Burr's "connections with Mr. M . . . y and you will find him a British pensioner and agent." A second missive to much the same effect arrived four days later.[29] Jefferson seems to have regarded both as delusional, or simply as fakes. Two months later he received a potentially more credible report from Joseph H. Daveiss, the US attorney for Kentucky. Daveiss described a spreading plot in the West against the union, but he did not name Burr. After consulting with several cabinet members, Jefferson wrote Daveiss requesting additional information. Soon Daveiss replied, implicating both Burr and General Wilkinson; he wrote again listing ten more potential conspirators. Noting that all were prominent Republicans and remembering that Daveiss was the brother-in-law of John Marshall, Jefferson judged the whole affair a Federalist attempt to promote schism within—or simply embarrass—the Republican Party.[30]

But reports of revolt in the West would not die. In the summer of 1806, Philadelphia's *Gazette of the United States*, a Federalist organ, began to print so-called queries that suggested a possible revolutionary conspiracy in the West and plans to set up a rival government there, as well as intentions to attack and subdue Mexico. Republican editors ran editorials claiming that these "queries" were no more than Federalist attempts to sow dissension. Jefferson still evinced no concern. In August a newly established newspaper in Kentucky, the *Western World*, began publishing stories claiming that many of the Republican leaders in the state were plotting conspiracies against the union, but again Jefferson dismissed the reports as Federalist propaganda, aware that the paper's underwriters were Daveiss and Humphrey Marshall, cousin (and brother-in-law) of the chief justice.[31]

Why did Jefferson not perceive that a plot in the West was a real possibility? In addition to his reasonable belief that Federalist intrigues knew few limits, Jefferson was unusually busy in the summer of 1806. The ongoing diplomatic efforts over West Florida aside, in June Jefferson received the staggering news that his mentor, George Wythe, had been murdered, along with a boy named Michael Brown, who may have been Wythe's mulatto son and whom Wythe had asked Jefferson to mentor. The killer was Wythe's grandnephew, George W. Sweeney, who had poisoned them, apparently in response to learning that Wythe had disinherited him because of his dissolute lifestyle and ever-mounting debts.[32]

Later in the year, on October 20, Jefferson reported "with unspeakable joy" the receipt of a letter from Meriwether Lewis, postmarked St. Louis, September 23, 1806. In his first communication in seventeen months, Lewis wrote, "It is with pleasure that I announce to you the safe arrival of myself and party at 12 OClk., today at this place with our paper and baggage. In obedience to your orders we have penetrated the Continent of North America to the Pacific Ocean and sufficiently explored the interior of the country to affirm with confidence that we have discovered the most practicable rout which does exist across the continent."[33] The letter only hinted at the more than two hundred new species of plants and animals the Corps of Discovery had discovered and described in their journals and the difficulties during the two-week portage around the Great Falls of the Missouri, although Lewis did make reference to 140 miles "over tremendious mountains which for 60 mls. are covered with eternal snows."[34] Jefferson replied to Lewis, "The unknown scenes in which you were engaged, & the length of time without hearing from you had begun to be felt awfully." On January 1, 1807, Lewis visited the President's House and regaled Jefferson with tales of his western adventures. Later in the day, the two men spread across the floor one of the expedition's larger maps, drawn by William Clark, and got down on their hands and knees to inspect it.[35]

ALL ALONG, TROUBLING rumors about events in the West continued to trickle in, some from people Jefferson had reason to trust. On September 15, 1805, he received a letter from Colonel George Morgan, who lived a few miles west of Pittsburgh, informing Jefferson that Burr had visited him some months before, tried to recruit his sons for an adventure in the West, and spoken derisively about the national government. A month later, a letter to Madison from two men in Pittsburgh largely confirmed Morgan's story, with additional details. Still, Jefferson took no action. But a letter that arrived on October 20 tipped the balance.[36]

The missive was from the postmaster general, Gideon Granger, a trusted official. Granger related a conversation with a congressman in Massachusetts in which he had learned that General William Eaton—who had played a major role in the Tripolitan War—had told the congressman that Burr had attempted to recruit him to his conspiracy to separate the western states, promising to make Eaton second in command of Burr's forces, after General Wilkinson. Eaton's stepson, meanwhile, had learned that while in Marietta, Ohio, Burr had arranged for the building of flatboats and had tried to sign up young men for his military expedition. Eaton was a complainer, but he was also a patriot, and so on October 22 Jefferson called a meeting of his cabinet.

The cabinet members decided to move a portion of the US troops stationed at Fort Adams to Natchitoches, send eight gunboats to New Orleans, and alert the militia. They considered all the pieces of evidence that had come in over the past few months. According to Jefferson's memorandum of the meeting, "We are of opinion unanimously that confidential letters [should] be written to the Governor of Ohio, Indiana, Mississippi and Orleans, to the district attorney of Kentucky,—of Tennessee,—of Louisiana, to have him [Burr] strictly watched, and on his committing any overt act unequivocally, to have him arrested and tried for treason, misdemeanor, or whatever other offense the act may amount to. And in like manner to arrest and try any of his followers committing acts against the laws." The cabinet also stated that "suspicions of infidelity in Wilkinson being now become very general," they wondered what to do about him.[37]

At a subsequent meeting on October 24, the cabinet unanimously decided to send Captains Edward Preble and Stephen Decatur to take command of US naval forces in New Orleans and to assign seven additional gunboats to the city. Working with Governor William C. C. Claiborne, Preble and Decatur would have "great discretionary powers" to put down an insurrection. The cabinet ordered that John Graham, secretary of the Orleans Territory, "be sent through Kentucky on Burr's trail, with discretionary powers to consult confidentially with the governors, and to arrest Burr if he has made himself liable."[38] The issue of General Wilkinson was postponed again; Secretary of War Henry Dearborn's strong support of Wilkinson may have been decisive. But the next day the cabinet, noting that the mail packet that had arrived the previous day "from the westward" contained no mention whatsoever of any untoward "movements by Col. Burr"—which suggested that their fears that he would commit "overt act[s] against the law" might be unfounded—cancelled the orders to Preble and Decatur and decided to rely on the marines to defend New Orleans. The secretaries also decided that instead of writing the western governors, they would count on John Graham alone to alert them to the potential dangers and to arrest Burr if his actions warranted it.[39]

For the next few weeks the threat of intrigues in the West seemed to diminish, until November 25, 1806, when Jefferson received two letters: one from Wilkinson and the other from an anonymous source, although Wilkinson's authorship of it as well was immediately obvious. The second related details of a large-scale secret operation to invade and seize Mexico; it said that 8,000 or 10,000 men would soon rendezvous in New Orleans prior to embarking for Vera Cruz and suggested that British ships would serve as transports. The letter signed by Wilkinson did not mention Burr, and in it Wilkinson feigned total surprise at the scale of the conspiracy he had supposedly uncovered. Writing that "no doubt the revolt of this Territory [Louisiana], will be made an auxiliary Step to the main design of attacking Mexico,"[40] he went on to propose a number of defensive measures to stop the enterprise before it commenced. Upon receipt of these documents, Jefferson immediately convened his cabinet and prepared a proclamation for release on November 27. If surprisingly slow earlier to react to the flutter of evidence about western conspiracies, Jefferson was now duly alarmed.

In his proclamation, he announced that the government had received information "that sundry persons . . . are conspiring & confederating together to begin & set on foot, provide & prepare the means for a military expedition or enterprise against the dominions of Spain, against which nation war has not been declared by the constitutional authority of the U.S." Such activity, called filibustering (after the Spanish term for piracy), was manifestly illegal. Moreover, in pursuit of their object the leaders of the conspiracy were purportedly gathering provisions and weapons, "deceiving & seducing honest & well meaning citizens under various pretences to engage in their criminal enterprise," and raising troops and designating officers to command them. Jefferson was hereby "warning and enjoining all faithful citizens who have been led to participate in the s[ai]d unlawful enterprises without due knolege or consideration to withdraw from the same without delay & commanding all persons whatsoever engaged or concerned in the same to cease all further proceedings therein [under threat of] prosecution with all the rigors of the law." He then directed all civil and military leaders "to be vigilant," to search out and bring to punishment "all persons engaged or concerned in such enterprise," and to "seize all their arms and supplies"—in short, to prevent such an "expedition or enterprise by all the lawful means within their power." He also requested that all law-abiding citizens help discover and apprehend all perpetrators of the conspiracy.[41]

Jefferson asked Madison—Attorney General John Breckinridge was very sick and died in December—to make sure that the federal government could use regular troops to put down "expeditions having foreign Countries for the object"; they could not, of course, be used to quell domestic insurrections.[42] Jefferson secretly sent a letter to a trusted congressman asking him to introduce a bill authorizing this use of national forces; the bill passed on March 3, 1807.[43]

Just five days later, on December 2, 1806, Jefferson delivered his Sixth Annual Message to Congress. He discussed the issue of the boundary between Louisiana and Texas, the governance of the Orleans Territory and the education of its people in democratic principles, the state of affairs with the Barbary coast nations, and the successful completion of the Lewis and Clark Expedition. So strong were the nation's finances that Jefferson hinted Congress might consider applying the surpluses to "the great purposes of the public education, roads, rivers, canals, and such other objects of public improvement as it may be thought proper to add to the constitutional enumeration of federal powers." He added, however, that the government could advance even these good purposes only if a constitutional amendment made them legal.[44]

In terms of the arc of American history, the single most important passage in this Annual Message came near the end, where Jefferson in his characteristic exercise of presidential leadership strongly suggested that Congress pass legislation to end the transatlantic importation of slaves to the United States. The Constitution stated that the federal government could impose no limitation on the importation of slaves until twenty years after ratification, but it did not require that the trade end in 1808. Because the next Congress would have the opportunity to decide the matter, Jefferson offered the legislators an explicit challenge: "I congratulate you, fellow-citizens, on the approach of the period at which you may interpose your authority constitutionally, to withdraw the citizens of the United States from all further participation in those violations of human rights which have been so long continued on the unoffending inhabitants of Africa, and which the morality, the reputation, and the best interests of our country, have long been eager to proscribe. Although no law you may pass can take prohibitory effect till the first day of the year one thousand eight hundred and eight, yet the intervening period is not too long to prevent, by timely notice, expeditions which cannot be completed before that day."[45] On March 2, 1807, Congress followed Jefferson and acted to forbid the importation of slaves after January 1, 1808. This, perhaps Jefferson's most influential act against slavery, remains practically unremarked upon in most histories of the era. The end of the Atlantic slave trade to the United States did not result automatically from ratification of the Constitution in 1788. It required an act of Congress.

On the day of Jefferson's address, however, of more immediate interest were his words about the growing evidence of a conspiracy underway in the West. Jefferson remarked that, having received information about a "great number of private individuals . . . coming together, arming and organizing themselves contrary to law, to carry on military expeditions against the territories of Spain," he had launched a series of efforts to prevent and suppress the enterprise.[46] He mentioned no names, but Burr was assumed to be the ringleader. The new British minister in the United States, David Erskine, reported to his superiors the "universal" belief that Burr was leading a plot to separate the western states from those on the coast.[47] Jefferson himself had no doubts. As he wrote his old friend the Reverend Charles Clay, "Burr's enterprise is the most extraordinary since the days of Don Quixot. It is so extravagant that those who know his understanding would not believe it if the proofs admitted doubt. He has meant to place himself on the throne of Montezuma, and extend his empire to the Allegany seizing on N Orleans as the instrument of compulsion for our Western States."[48] Slow to recognize Burr's plot for what it apparently was, Jefferson now saw him as a dangerous threat to the nation.

Less than a week after Jefferson delivered his address, a federal grand jury in Frankfurt, Kentucky, failed to indict Burr on charges of conspiracy brought by indefatigable state attorney Joseph Daveiss. (His earlier claims against Burr had not been mere Federalist intrigue—he genuinely believed Burr was up to no good.) Key witnesses had not appeared, and the case fell apart. A few days later, the governor of Ohio seized ten boats belonging to Burr in Marietta, Ohio, although Burr's men managed to escape with several others.[49] Toward the end of December, Burr, who had recently met with potential recruits on Blennerhasset Island, close to Marietta but within the jurisdiction of Virginia, joined a flotilla of boats near the confluence of the Cumberland River and began floating downriver. This activity attracted notice and lent additional credence to the notion of a conspiracy. Congress, impatient to learn more, passed on January 16 a resolution calling on the president to present them with the evidence he had gathered and to inform them about the precautions he had put in place.[50]

IF JEFFERSON NEEDED more documentation, he got it only two days later. On January 18 he received a missive from Wilkinson enclosing, the general claimed, a deciphered letter from Burr. Clearly Wilkinson had decided to save himself. The letter, allegedly written by Burr back in late July, had been tampered with. In 1983, the editors of Aaron Burr's papers argued that the "Cipher Letter to Wilkinson" was fraudulent; more recent evidence suggests that Burr had a major hand in it, even if Wilkinson or another agent made changes.[51] Jefferson himself assumed it was largely legitimate. The letter read, "I have at length obtained funds, and have actually commenced. . . . Naval protection of England is secured. . . . Burr's plan [he was referring to himself in the third person] of operation is to move down rapidly from the falls on the fifteenth November, with the first 500 or 1000 men in light boats." The letter mentioned that Wilkinson was second in command and that Burr had gone to the West with his daughter and grandson, never to return to the United States There was bombastic talk of honor and character. If authentic, the letter proved that Burr had been leading a major conspiracy against the United States.[52]

On January 22, armed with the letter, Jefferson sent a special message to Congress. He explained that within the mass of materials concerning Burr, "little has been given under the sanction of oath, so as to constitute formal and legal evidence. It is chiefly in the form of letters, often containing such a mixture of rumors, conjectures, and suspicions, as render it difficult to sift out the real facts." Thus Jefferson could invoke no names of possible conspirators, except that of the person whose involvement the press had widely trumpeted and "whose guilt" was, on the most recent evidence, "placed beyond question." Jefferson felt justified in stating that the "the prime mover . . . was Aaron Burr."[53]

This was a huge blunder, especially for a man trained in the law. The press had so flagrantly tossed around Burr's name and his involvement was so widely assumed that Jefferson may have felt that to forgo invoking him would have rendered his informational message to Congress farcical. However, his incautious phrasing would play into the hands of Burr's defense lawyers, who argued that a vindictive Jefferson had attempted to persecute an innocent Burr by peremptorily declaring him guilty without a trial.

Needless to say, at the time Jefferson did want Burr and his coconspirators brought before US courts. In New Orleans, Wilkinson, exceeding his authority to suppress the conspiracy, arrested two men—Dr. Justus Erich Bollman and Samuel Swartwout—whom he believed had plotted with Burr. Wilkson sent them to the federal circuit court for the District of Columbia to stand trial for treason. Burr was captured in Wakefield, in the Mississippi Territory, and sent by a district judge, who had learned of Jefferson's proclamation, to Richmond under military escort.[54] Because Burr's effort to launch boats southward—seen as an overt act of conspiracy—had occurred on Blennerhasset Island, which was a part of Virginia, on March 30, 1807, Burr was to be presented to the US Court for the Fifth Circuit and the District of Virginia, where Chief Justice John Marshall would preside.

THE PREVIOUS MONTH, the Supreme Court overruled a district court's conviction of Bollman and Swartwout on the basis that the testimony against them was weak and their alleged crime had not occurred within the lower court's jurisdiction. Yet even though the court freed Bollman and Swartwout, in its decision John Marshall defined treason broadly: "It is not the intention of the court to say that no individual can be guilty of this crime who has not appeared in arms against his country. On the contrary, if war be actually levied, that is, if a body of men be actually assembled for the purpose of effecting by force a treasonable purpose, all those who perform any part, however minute, or however remote from the scene of action, and who are actually leagued in the general conspiracy, are to be considered traitors."[55] The court ruling, issued on February 21, 1807, suggested an obvious strategy to the Richmond district attorney, George Hay, tasked with prosecuting Burr.

In the weeks before the grand jury proceedings in advance of the potential trial, Jefferson, struck down by one of his periodic migraine headaches, was almost unable to perform the duties of his office. This compounded the difficulty of assembling the far-flung evidence and widely scattered witnesses. Jefferson had finally found a replacement for John Breckinridge as attorney general, but Caesar A. Rodney of Delaware, appointed on January 20, 1807, was the sole member of the Justice Department and his position only part-time. Moreover, a family illness meant Rodney had even less time than he would have otherwise, so he ended up playing only a minor part in the greatest legal trial of Jefferson's administration. Jefferson bore much of the burden himself.[56]

Jefferson was not sanguine about the trial's outcome. He and Marshall had long been enemies, and the clerk of the court in Richmond would be William Marshall, the chief justice's brother. When the grand jury was selected, Marshall appointed none other than John Randolph of Roanoke as its foreman. For his part, Burr brought together a talented group of lawyers, led by the best practitioner in the state, John Wickham. Also behind him was the incomparable master of courtroom invective, Luther Martin of Maryland, who had long hated Jefferson. Burr, himself an experienced lawyer, also participated in his own defense. George Hay was competent but no match for these opponents. Nor was another lawyer for the federal government, the ineffective Alexander MacRae. Only the young William Wirt, perhaps Virginia's greatest orator since Patrick Henry, had ability commensurate with that of Burr's team.[57]

Marshall released Burr on $10,000 bail, which he quickly raised, and within a few days, Marshall himself attended a dinner John Wickham hosted for the defendant. Perhaps Marshall did not know that Burr would be there, but Wickham did, and the occasion revealed the camaraderie among Marshall and Burr's defense team.[58] The justice's presence at the dinner or his failure to leave once he found Burr there was, like Jefferson's premature pronouncement of Burr's guilt, a curious lapse of judgment.

When the hearing itself began, the grand jury, at Burr's request, sub-poenaed Jefferson, requesting documents and evidence. Jefferson com-plied, though he did refuse to attend the proceedings, arguing that it was unreasonable to expect the president, given the range of his duties, to do so. Marshall accepted this reasoning, and the principle that the president himself cannot be subpoenaed to attend court proceedings has stood ever since.[59] In the end, on June 24 the grand jury indicted Burr for both mis-demeanor and treason.

The trial proper took place in August, while Jefferson was at Monticello. After the jury was impaneled, Marshall named his brother-in-law and close friend Edward Carrington foreman, which proved influential; Carrington could explain the arcane details of Marshall's redefinition of treason to his fellow jurymen. Burr's defense team portrayed their client as the innocent victim of Jefferson's hateful, vindictive persecution. Luther Martin did not hold back in his diatribes against Jefferson. In a remark-able display of oratorical prowess, Wirt later effectively demonized Burr as the snake in the American Eden. The level of legal discourse was excep-tional, but as it turned out, Marshall, not the lawyers or the jury, deter-mined the outcome.

In reality, the prosecution had a weak case: the evidence was specula-tive, inconclusive, and contradictory; the witnesses were confused, them-selves unsavory (they included Generals Eaton and Wilkinson); and whatever he had been up to, Burr had carefully spoken and acted with lawyerly opaqueness. The prosecution's key problem was that Burr had never been present for the commission of a clearly treasonable event; any-thing he might have had in mind he had not carried forward. Jefferson found himself more involved than he probably wished, discovering and delivering documents, arranging for the testimony of witnesses, and giv-ing Hay general advice. But this extra work stemmed from the lack of Justice Department assistance more than anything else. No evidence sug-gests that Jefferson initiated the action against Burr as a personal vendetta; once the president came to believe, however, that Burr represented a threat to the peace and stability of the nation, his efforts to indict him took on a personal cast.

Listening to the arguments of the learned counsel assembled for Burr and conducting his own reading, Marshall refined the broader definition of treason he had issued the previous February. His new interpretation, stricter in its defense of individual liberty, seemed more appropriate for the United States (the British tradition had influenced his previous definition).

Marshall bore down on the precise meaning of levying war, showing with impeccable logic that it entailed plain acts of force, not simply intention. Obviously nothing like that had occurred on Blennerhasset Island.[60] With this definition communicated to the jury, Marshall effectively ended the trial. No actual acts of war meant no treason, whatever Burr's ambitions.[61]

In the larger sense, Marshall—and the nation—won the trial, and Jefferson lost. The independence of the judiciary was firmly established, and Burr went free. From Jefferson's perspective, though the court's decision brought little comfort, Burr's plans had been thwarted, and the local governments in the West, along with the general public, had combined to defend the national interest. He felt Burr's inability to recruit substantial numbers of men to his cause demonstrated the stability of the union.[62] Neither side in the trial had acted with appropriate neutrality, but the result was probably correct. And though the jury did not convict Burr of treason, as defined by Marshall, it pointedly did not rule him unambiguously not guilty of plotting.

The general public tended to believe Burr guilty, as did the US Senate. That body came within one vote of expelling Senator John Smith for his supposed involvement in Burr's conspiracy, and afterward John Quincy Adams, who had worked mightily for that end as head of the investigative committee, made an observation that probably reflected the sentiment of the majority of the nation's citizens: "Whether the transactions proved against Aaron Burr did or did not amount, in technical language, to an overt act of levying war, your committee have not a scruple of doubt upon their minds that, but for the vigilance and energy of the government, and of faithful citizens under its directions, in arresting their program and in crushing his designs, they would, in a very short lapse of time, have terminated not only in a war, but in a war of the most horrible description, in a war at once foreign and domestic."[63]

After Burr's initial acquittal on several charges in successive trials in Richmond, Jefferson wanted to pursue the case against him in other jurisdictions, but none of his allies supported him. Burr soon receded from Jefferson's range of concern and from active participation in American political life. His plans for the West remain mysterious, as does how this clearly gifted man earned the distrust of nearly every major actor in politics at the time, from John Adams, to Jefferson and Madison, to Alexander Hamilton, who had literally hated him. Governed by ambition rather than principle and with no higher purpose than himself, Burr became a man without a country.[64]

26

"War, Embargo, or Nothing"

A S THE MOST COSMOPOLITAN of American leaders in the nation's early years, Jefferson had international associations that frequently caused and allowed political opponents to doubt his essential loyalties. At no time was Jefferson's international orientation, and his enemies' mistrust thereof, more influential than during his second administration. Jefferson discovered what subsequent presidents would as well: that the broad Atlantic did not insulate the nation from the consequences of European wars. Decisions made in London and Paris in the early nineteenth century gravely affected American commerce and well-being, and the relative weakness of the United States hampered the effectiveness of American responses. Events over which Jefferson had very limited control came to dominate his second term, resulting in frustration, failure, even disillusionment. Not for the last time in our nation's history, a president's second term proved less successful than the first.

England and France had gone to war in 1803, and each desired complete domination of the other. Both trampled on American rights with little concern, treating the neutral United States as incidental to their campaigns. Two great battles in 1805 changed the shape of the war. At Cape Trafalgar, off the southwestern coast of Spain on October 21, a British fleet under the command of Admiral Lord Horatio Nelson defeated the combined fleets of France and Spain. From that point forward, Britain dominated the seas. On December 2, Napoleon Bonaparte's armies emerged victorious against Russian and Austrian forces at the Battle of Austerlitz (in the modern-day Czech Republic), giving France control of the Continent. With supremacy in Europe now clearly at stake, the rights of neutrals meant even less to Britain and France than they had previously. Up until 1805, US merchants depended on their nation's official stance of neutrality, dating to George Washington's Neutrality Proclamation in 1793, to trade with both France and England. One piece of particularly profitable commerce was the carrying trade between the English and French colonies in the West Indies and their homelands. Because it benefitted from this trade, England left American trade with France alone as long as American shippers from the West Indies first landed at any American port and paid duties before then heading forth to European ports (voyages that became known as "broken").

In the context of a total war with France, however, England ruled in the *Essex* case of 1805 that trade relying on the broken voyage principle was illegal. Shippers departing from West Indian colonies for the United States now had to prove that they were heading for a US port as their intended terminus. The principle of so-called continuous voyages ended the long-lucrative practice of broken or interrupted voyages.[1] The British navy began intercepting American ships at sea and inspecting them to determine both their origin and their destination, seizing many of these vessels. The French seized ships too, but almost only those in French ports presumed to be offering British goods. Not only British policy but the size and effectiveness of the British fleet resulted in more numerous interceptions. These were also more upsetting, because they often occurred outside territorial waters, threatening the principle of the freedom of the seas and wounding American national pride.

Jefferson formally brought these matters to the Congress's attention in his Annual Message of December 5, 1805. He knew that military action in direct response to interference with American shipping was within that body's purview, but he did lay out defensive measures he had taken: furnishing cannons to seaport cities, ordering gunboats to patrol the entrances to American harbors, requesting the various states to ready their militias, and gathering building materials for the possible construction of "ships of war of seventy-four guns."[2] A few weeks later he sent Congress a special message calling for the establishment of a naval militia both for service on the high seas and in defense of harbor cities.[3] Some congressmen wanted to ban all imports from England, but Jefferson thought this reaction too strong, and with little or no input from the president, Congress debated that question in late 1805 and early 1806. Finally on March 25, 1806, it passed a watered-down Non-Importation Bill to punish Britain, although it would not go into effect until November 15, 1806, and only banned certain goods, including expensive woolens, glass, and some iron hardware, exempting the most crucial imports such as cotton goods, cheap woolen cloth, and iron and steel.[4]

At least as much as the new trade regulations, the British practice of impressing sailors aboard American vessels into service in the British navy irritated the United States. Laboring conditions and pay in the Royal Navy were atrocious, so thousands of British sailors jumped ship in US ports and ended up working for American captains. At one point, these men made up a third or more of the crew in the nation's international merchant fleet. Britain did not accept the principle that people could change nationalities, and desperate to replenish their naval crews, British captains took it as their right to stop American merchant vessels and seize men they believed had illegally fled the British service. Americans rightfully saw these actions as a grave insult, an arrogant repudiation of the independence of their nation. At the time, citizens still read the Declaration of Independence primarily as a statement of the United States' right to full membership in the community of nations. Nothing rankled this sense of autonomy as much as the British practice of impressment.

An outrageous example of impressment occurred just outside New York City's harbor on April 25, 1806. The captain of a British ship, the *Leander*, fired a shot to stop a US merchant ship, planning to search it for escaped British sailors, and accidently killed an American on another vessel. Jefferson issued a proclamation in May calling for the arrest of the captain, banning the *Leander* and two companion ships from American waters, and forbidding any American from provisioning them.[5] The British government and its naval officers off the coast of the United States simply ignored the proclamation and continued their aggressive practices.

In the late spring of 1806, Jefferson selected William Pinkney of Baltimore to travel to London and, forming a commission with minister James Monroe, negotiate an end to impressment. Monroe (simultaneously involved in the attempted negotiations with Spain over the precise boundaries of Louisiana) initially thought compromise of some sort possible. In reality Britain would never relent on this particular principle, which Jefferson in his instructions had made the sine qua non of any acceptable treaty.

The British negotiators held firm; though they made some minimal concessions, they maintained their current policy.[6] Monroe and Pinkney felt that, given Britain's dependence on its navy in its war against France,

Americans could reasonably expect no more than a slight British reference to greater caution with regard to impressments. When Jefferson finally received the treaty, he did not even submit it to Congress, which he correctly believed would repudiate it.

Other events in 1806 complicated the United States' place in Atlantic commerce. When Nelson's victory at Trafalgar thwarted his hopes of invading England, Napoleon responded by issuing a series of decrees in 1806 and 1807 that sought to block all trade with the island nation. His Berlin Decree of November 1806 interdicted maritime trade with Britain, called for the confiscation of all goods shipped from England or any of its colonies, even when carried by ships of neutral nations, and authorized the seizure of any ship that had merely landed in England or any of its colonies. In reaction, Britain issued a series of toughened orders-in-council that proclaimed a blockade of all ports that excluded British goods and required ships from neutral nations intending to trade at these ports first to stop in England to pay transit duties. In December 1807 Napoleon announced the Milan Decree, which said that French authorities could seize any ship that conformed to Britain's trade requirements as well as any neutral ship that a British search party had boarded in order to examine goods or impress sailors. These policies meant that all American trade (other than trade up and down the East Coast) faced seizure by either British or French naval forces.[7]

Jefferson did not know the full implications of events in Europe when he composed his Annual Message of December 2, 1806. In it, he alerted Congress to the tumult across the Atlantic and called for quickening defensive preparations in port cities, the readying of militia forces, and heightened vigilance.[8] Most of this 1806 message dealt, of course, with the efforts to resolve the borders of Louisiana, the supposed threat posed by Aaron Burr, the success of the Lewis and Clark Expedition, and the transatlantic slave trade. Clearly the warring nations in Europe could affect American citizens and interests even more than they already had, but Jefferson could not tell what the new year would bring. He decided to wait and see.

IN JUNE 1807, when Burr was indicted for treason in the much publicized trial in Richmond, Jefferson was at least momentarily focused on the court proceedings. Meanwhile at Norfolk, British naval vessels sat in the broad harbor and in the outer bay. Some months earlier three reputedly British sailors had escaped from the HMS *Melampus* and subsequently joined the crew of the American naval frigate USS *Chesapeake*. Incensed by rumors of their flight, Vice Admiral George Cranfield Berkeley, stationed at Halifax, sent an order to the various British captains under his authority to be on the lookout for the *Chesapeake* and, if they came across it, to request permission to board and search for the deserters. In Norfolk, *Chesapeake* commander James Barron believed (correctly) that any deserters aboard were Americans—not impressed British citizens—and hence not properly subject to seizure.

On the morning of June 22, 1807, the *Chesapeake* left its mooring and began to sail past the entrance to the harbor. Suddenly it sighted the *Leopard*, which maneuvered into a threatening position, then sent word to the *Chesapeake* to heave to and let men from the *Leopard* search it. Barron denied the presence of any escaped British citizens aboard his ship, and after additional communication (Barron later claimed to misunderstand exactly what was asked), the *Leopard* fired one warning shot into the completely unprepared *Chesapeake* and then, for ten minutes or more, subjected it to a furious bombardment. The *Chesapeake* lowered its flag in surrender, whereupon officers of the *Leopard* boarded and searched her, taking four men. The crippled American vessel, having suffered three dead and sixteen injured and taking on water, limped back to port at Hampton Roads. By any measure, this instance of unprovoked hostility by the British could easily have been deemed an act of war.[9]

The outrage in Norfolk was immediate. A mob destroyed casks of water intended for a British ship, British sailors on land were assaulted, and there were calls for retaliation. Word of the *Chesapeake-Leopard* incident reached Washington on June 25, alarming and angering both Jefferson and Congress. Several weeks later Jefferson wrote, "Never since the battle of Lexington have I seen this country in such a state of exasperation as at present."[10] Yet for all his indignation and accumulated dislike of Britain, the president recognized that the United States was in no position for war. At the same time, he understood that he could use the clamor for it to motivate Congress to make the necessary preparations should open conflict become unavoidable.

In his official, public response to the incident, Jefferson made clear that he was not against using military force, but that was neither his initial nor his sole recourse. And while respecting Congress's central role in that decision, he also perceived that how the nation reacted could affect the warring nations of Europe positively. "This will leave Congress free to decide whether war is the most efficacious mode of redress in our case, or whether, having taught so many other useful lessons to Europe, we may not add that of showing them that there are peaceable means of repressing injustice, by making it the interest of the aggressor to do what is just, and abstain from future wrong."[11] The lesson would start with a sharply worded proclamation written by Jefferson and sent directly to Britain. Dated July 2, 1807, it began by describing how the United States had tried to observe all the conventions of neutrality toward the belligerent nations, including by offering its harbors to the ships of France and Britain when they needed provisions or medical or other kinds of assistance, despite repeated abuses by the commanders of British ships.[12]

"At length," Jefferson wrote, "a deed transcending all we have hitherto seen or suffered brings the public sensibility to a serious crisis and our forbearance to a necessary pause." A heavily armed British vessel had without cause attacked an American ship, resulting in deaths and injuries. In what he considered a justifiable response to this affront, Jefferson's proclamation required all British ships to leave US ports and forbade others from entering.[13] If any hesitated to depart or successfully entered, he forbade any intercourse with them or their officers and crew, as well as any attempt to provide them with supplies or aid. He called on all American civil and military officials to exercise their authority to ensure that British ships received no assistance, unless the ships entered a port bringing official dispatches from England or, after a proper request, showed that they were in distress.[14] An armed US schooner, the *Revenge*, would travel to England with a copy of the proclamation and with instructions to the American ministers there to immediately demand from the British a formal "disavowal of the act and of the principle of searching a public armed vessel," a return of the men seized, and the recall of Vice Admiral Sir George Berkeley, whose name Jefferson misspelled "Barclay."[15]

Again demanding disavowal of impressment practically guaranteed that Britain would not respond positively, even in light of the *Chesapeake-Leopard* affair. Jefferson also sent an order to all the ships of the American merchant fleet in the Mediterranean to return to Boston, lest the British navy capture them in the event of war.[16] Over the next few weeks Jefferson sent letters to Secretary of War Henry Dearborn and others to ready defensive measures at the various seaports, and he alerted governors yet again to the need to prepare their militias. By the end of July he took notes on plans for a possible invasion of British-held Canada should warfare erupt.[17]

DESPITE JEFFERSON's prodding, preparations for war moved slowly, probably because the prospect still seemed remote. In August 1807 Jefferson began to receive discouraging news from Monroe about the likelihood that Britain would disavow impressments. British foreign secretary George Canning, curt and dismissive, made clear that the United States could expect no apologies. Rather than free the men seized from the *Chesapeake*, British officials in Halifax court-martialed three of them and hanged the fourth (the only one who was not an American citizen). New orders from London, largely a reaction to American complaints following the attack on the *Chesapeake*, specifically allowed sailors on British naval vessels to board the warships of neutral nations for the purpose of impressment—Britain would not retreat one step from the practice. Around the same time, word arrived in the United States that a British fleet had cruelly bombarded Copenhagen, in neutral Denmark, to destroy the Dano-Norwegian fleet there, which the British believed Napoleon would force to help provision France.

The more Jefferson learned of British actions, the angrier he grew. Although he had long since moved beyond his almost inveterate sympathy for France, in late August he wrote in frustration from Monticello to an old friend, "I say, 'down with England.'"[18] No longer an ideological Francophile, he now took a more pragmatic stance. Yet for his entire adult life, Jefferson had sought to establish American independence of British control, and this long experience colored his reaction to recent events. Meeting with his cabinet on July 4, 1807, Jefferson decided to issue a call on August 24 for the new session of Congress to open early, on October 26.[19]

Jefferson worked to prepare his Seventh Annual Message, which he would send to the members of Congress the day after the new session opened. It had a decidedly anti-British tone. Jefferson referred to the outrage visited upon the *Chesapeake* and its crew and then to another "violation of maritime rights . . . of very extensive effect." Britain had just issued the order that essentially prevented trade on the part of neutral and unfriendly nations, and because, in Jefferson's words, Britain was "now at war with nearly every nation on the Atlantic and Mediterranean seas," this new order shut down practically all American maritime commerce.[20]

Importantly, Jefferson did not raise the specter of war with Britain. He simply stated that as soon as he received news concerning the efforts of ministers Monroe and Pinkney, he would pass it along to Congress.

Recognizing that body's constitutional role, should further actions be necessary, he assured its members, "Nothing shall be wanting on my part which may give information or dispatch to the proceedings of the legislature in the exercise of their high duties, and at a moment so interesting to the public welfare."[21]

Not until November did Jefferson learn of Foreign Secretary Canning's official response to the US demands. Canning, as shrewd as he was arrogant, admitted that the attack on the *Chesapeake* was unauthorized and reparations were appropriate, but he added that Americans had also committed many hostile acts—he included among them, amazingly, Jefferson's July 2 *Chesapeake* Proclamation—which should also be addressed before consideration of any payments. He categorically denied, however, that the principle of impressment was subject to reconsideration. This ended the prospects for any kind of negotiation compatible with Jefferson's wishes. Canning said he would send a special envoy, one George Rose, to the United States to discuss a range of issues.[22] Just weeks later, Jefferson received news from the American minister to France, John Armstrong, that Napoleon had applied his Berlin Decree to the United States, thereby cutting off trade between Britain and the Continent even on neutral ships containing goods from England. And Jefferson also learned that King George III—the same monarch he had first opposed in 1774—had determined to pursue the policy of impressment "even more vigorously."[23] The unrelenting warfare between Britain and France threatened all American maritime commerce and all American ships.

In a private letter to son-in-law Thomas Mann Randolph, Jefferson had written that Congress would have to decide between "War, Embargo, or Nothing."[24] But the president was surprisingly noncommittal when, on December 7, he submitted to Congress duplicates of the dispatches from London, showing Canning's refusal to back down from impressment and his insistence on tying a whole series of issues together before broaching the subject of reparations for the *Chesapeake* attack. Jefferson made no recommendations in his short accompanying message, though by suggesting that negotiations were ongoing, he hinted that no immediate decision was called for.[25] Still, he was aware of what British and French policies and actions meant for the safety of American seamen and merchant ships. Eleven days later, Jefferson submitted another short, special communication to Congress.

Titled "Special Message on Commercial Depredations," it accompanied other documents that demonstrated "the great and increasing

dangers with which our vessels, our seamen, and merchandise, are threatened on the high seas and elsewhere, from the belligerent powers of
Europe."[26] Because it was essential to keep these resources safe, he wrote,
"I deem it my duty to recommend the subject to the consideration of
Congress, who will doubtless perceive all the advantages which may be
expected from *an inhibition of the departure of our vessels from the ports of
the United States*." He knew that the "wisdom" of Congress "will also see
the necessity of making every preparation for whatever events may grow
out of the present crisis."[27] With no further explanation to either Congress
or the public, Jefferson (with his cabinet's support) recommended a total
embargo of all American shipping to ports outside the United States itself—the most fateful decision of his second term.[28]

Jefferson suggested no end date; he did not expect the embargo to last
for long. He seems to have seen it as a temporary and primarily defensive
measure that would buy time for diplomacy, safeguard American ships
and seamen, and allow for developments in Europe that could potentially
advantage neutrals. His desire for peace, his prior successes with procrastination in solving problems, and his long-held belief that commercial pressure was an efficacious substitute for war all led him to support an embargo
that, to be effective, had to be almost total. The embargo ultimately failed.
It also preoccupied Jefferson in the final year of his second administration
like no other issue in his entire presidency. It consumed him, harmed the
nation, and distressed his closest advisors as much as it did him.

JEFFERSON INCLUDED no members of Congress in the drafting of diplomatic initiatives or in the shaping of embargo policy because he believed
such matters—unlike the decision to go to war—solely within the purview of his office. In retrospect he surely should have attempted to explain
and justify both, especially the rationale for the embargo, to the public.
Long accustomed to following Jefferson's suggestions, the Republican
Congress did so again. The very day it received his message, the Senate
approved the embargo overwhelmingly, followed three days later by almost two-to-one approval in the House; Jefferson signed the act into law
the next day, December 22, 1807. The embargo stopped all international
exports from the United States. By preventing US ships from engaging in
international trade, Jefferson eliminated the risk of their capture or detain-
ment for the purpose of impressment, either of which he believed could
escalate tensions to the point that a declaration of war became politically
irresistible.

Almost as important as the embargo itself was the need to delay any further action. As in earlier moments during his public career, procrastination was a policy decision. During the Nootka Sound incident of 1790 and the closure of the port of New Orleans in 1802, the mere passage of time had led to peaceful resolutions. Jefferson could hope that something similar might happen now if neither side acted precipitously. As he wrote in January 1808, "Time prepares us for defense; time may produce peace in Europe that removes the ground of difference with England."²⁹ Because Jefferson had seen commercial pressure as an aspect of diplomacy, he may have thought from the beginning that cutting English and French markets off from American agricultural products would influence the policies of the belligerent nations. If so, he overestimated their need for American goods and underestimated the other factors driving European policies.³⁰

The embargo's initial broad popular support began to evaporate as the trade restrictions were felt. An effective embargo required extensive efforts to patrol ports and prevent the many actions merchants took to evade restrictions. Trade purportedly limited to the American coast could be diverted to West Indian islands; coastal vessels could rendezvous with British merchant ships just beyond territorial waters; merchants could practice a variety of subterfuges to get their products to European markets. Bonds had to be posted, cargoes searched, manifests prepared. American residents along the Canadian border or adjoining the Great Lakes could smuggle in goods. As Jefferson and Congress learned, for many merchants, particularly in New England, the desire for profits quickly overcame respect for the law, and for those New Englanders who had long favored strengthening ties with Britain, it became almost a matter of principle to try to circumvent the embargo, which they interpreted as an anti-British policy anyway. Many Federalists remained suspicious of Jefferson's reputed Francophilia.

It quickly became clear that the original legislation was inadequate to address all the issues involved, which meant that Congress found it necessary to pass supplementary embargo bills.³¹ Already Jefferson perceived that enforcing the acts would require a degree of government interference that was antithetical to traditional Republican principles, and he foresaw that the fact of this interference, on top of the harm done to the American economy, would further whittle away public support for the embargo. As he wrote James Madison on March 11, "I take it to be an universal opinion that war will become preferable to a continuance of the embargo after a certain date."³²

Most of the enforcement efforts fell to Albert Gallatin and the staff of the Treasury Department, although from the beginning the Treasury secretary had doubts about the policy. He warned Jefferson, when the cabinet initially began discussing the issue, about the dangers of a permanent embargo and the need to constantly expand the restrictions. He wrote, "A restrictive measure of the nature of the embargo applied to a nation under such circumstances as the United States cannot be enforced without the assistance of means as strong as the measure itself."[33] Jefferson found himself in precisely that dilemma. As he saw it, to protect the liberty of the United States, he had to assume—at least temporarily—near dictatorial powers.

The series of enforcement acts aimed at prohibiting all export trade entailed surveillance of every port city, navigable river, bay, and so on—an almost impossible task. The first enforcement act, passed April 25, 1808, required presidential permission for any voyage to a port adjacent to a foreign territory, which dragged Jefferson into closer involvement in the embargo than he originally expected.[34] Merchants connived to avoid the embargo, stretching gunboats, soldiers, and treasury officials to the breaking point, and the more effective the embargo became, the more economic hurt it caused. The second enforcement act, passed January 9, 1809, entailed unprecedented interference in trade and commerce along with a degree of government supervision and oversight never seen, or even imagined, in the young nation.[35]

Jefferson's willingness to expand his authority (and that of his administration) to enforce the embargo is yet another reminder that he never opposed energetic government conducted within the limits of the Constitution, and in this case, which concerned matters of commerce and international affairs, he deemed the central government supreme. Moreover, Jefferson had long believed that on occasions of national emergency or exceptional opportunity, the executive could temporarily move beyond narrowly legalistic normal restrictions on his authority. As he later wrote, "A strict observance of the written laws is doubtless *one* of the high duties of a good citizen: but it is not *the highest*. the laws of necessity, of self-preservation, of saving our country when in danger, are of higher obligation. to lose our country by a scrupulous adherence to a written law, would be to lose the law itself, with life, liberty, property & all those who are enjoying them with us; thus absurdly sacrificing the ends to the means."[36] But he made clear that this responsibility to act beyond the literal law only obtained in matters of the largest importance: "It is incumbent on those only who accept of great charges, to risk themselves on great occasions, when the safety of the nation, or some of it's very high interests are at stake."[37] He had felt, in 1808, that enforcement of the embargo met that high bar.

NEVERTHELESS, PUBLIC backing of the embargo continued to fall away, although support stemming from ideological and patriotic principles lasted longest in the southern states that were, because their economies depended on exporting their agricultural products, actually most affected by the act. Ideology was also the primary cause of the violent opposition to the embargo in New England. The issue resurrected the most vituperative of the High Federalists, who hated Jefferson in the first place. Pro-British from the era of Alexander Hamilton, New England leaders bitterly ridiculed and attacked the embargo and wrote supportive letters to British officials stating that it could not last long, that it was hurting the United States more than it was Britain, and that the public had completely turned against it and administration policy generally. Jefferson complained that the Federalists "were endeavoring to convince England that we suffer more by the embargo than they do, and if they will but hold out awhile, we must abandon it."[38] In the late spring of 1808, committed Anglophile and bitter anti-Jeffersonian Timothy Pickering sent letters to envoy George Rose and friends in England that in retrospect seem almost treasonous.

The merchant class in many New England towns flooded Jefferson with petitions against the embargo. As in 1804, there was again talk in New England of disunion. If anything, this opposition strengthened Jefferson's resolve to see the embargo through. He refused to accept the opposition as genuine, started to defend the embargo on the grounds that it was promoting an increase in American manufacturing, and more and more began justifying it in private correspondence as an experiment in nonmilitary and nonlethal diplomacy, the ultimate use of commercial policy in place of a resort to arms. He became fixated on the embargo to a degree that, again in retrospect, is inexplicable. Even harder to understand is Jefferson's never embarking on a concerted campaign of public education to buttress public support for the policy. He seemed to think the rationale self-evident. And in truth, a substantial degree of support for the embargo persisted far longer than one might have expected.

Jefferson delivered his last Annual Message to Congress on November 8, 1808. He announced, "It would have been a source, fellow citizens, of much gratification, if our last communications from Europe had enabled me to inform you that the belligerent nations . . . had become awakened to the duty and true policy of revoking their unrighteous edicts."[39] But alas, he could not offer such a report, and his language suggested how deeply he felt about these issues. After describing the inability to convince either Britain or France to respect the neutral rights of the United States, he admitted, "This candid and liberal experiment [the embargo] having thus failed, and no other event having occurred on which a suspension of the embargo by the executive was authorized, it necessarily remains in the extent originally given to it." It had saved "our mariners and our vast mercantile property," but it had not resolved the precipitating and underlying problem of European restraint on American maritime trade. Jefferson then figuratively threw up his hands in exasperation: "it will rest with the wisdom of Congress to decide on the course best adopted to such a state of things."[40]

IN A REMARKABLE TURN of events that no one foresaw, Jefferson practically abdicated responsibility for policy in the final four months of his presidency. He decided to give no direction to the new Congress that was assembling. In a letter to his former attorney general and present lieutenant governor of Massachusetts, Levi Lincoln, Jefferson wrote that Congress's agenda would include the decision between "1. Embargo. 2. War. 3. Submission and tribute." He made no recommendations. "On this occasion, I think it is fair to leave to those who are to act on them, the decisions they prefer; being to be [sic] myself but a spectator."[41] His retreat is one of the puzzles of his presidency. Some have suggested that, remembering his anger at John Adams's raft of last-minute actions and appointments in early 1801, Jefferson was determined not to interfere with the freedom he wanted his successor, James Madison, to enjoy as he began his administration several months later. But this seems an insufficient reason by itself, given the pressure on Jefferson to stay involved.

Jefferson simply refused to lead the Congress, or the public, in a discussion of what the nation should do next, and his inactivity frustrated both Madison and Gallatin (at the time the latter was widely expected to become Madison's secretary of state; in fact he continued as secretary of the Treasury through Madison's two terms). Because Jefferson made no policy recommendations after delivering his Annual Message, Gallatin, on behalf of himself and Madison, wrote the president that the two of them "concur in opinion that . . . it would be eligible to point out to them some precise and distinct course." Gallatin suggested delicately, "Perhaps the knowledge of the various feelings of the members [of Congress] and of the apparent public opinion may on consideration induce a revision of your own." Gallatin said he was not quite sure exactly where he himself came down on the issue of continuing the embargo, "but I think that we must (or rather you must) decide the question absolutely, so that we may point out a decisive course either way to our friends."[42] Congressman Nathaniel Macon of North Carolina complained on December 4 to former Maryland congressman Joseph H. Nicholson that Congress was adrift: "The President gives no opinion as to the measures that ought to be adopted. It is not known whether he be for war or peace."[43] Meanwhile, Jefferson wrote to Doctor George Logan that he was "chiefly an unmeddling listener to what others say."[44] He advisors wanted and expected more of him.

During this period of drift, the tide turned against the embargo, the key moment being when Republicans in the northern states decided enough was enough. Jefferson was uninvolved in these final developments. He even stopped making presidential appointments that could be delayed until the next administration. With no presidential leadership, and with Congress in disarray, its members floundered in an attempt to stop what Jefferson had euphemistically labeled an experiment. Finally Congress decided that the embargo should end on March 4, 1809, the day Jefferson left the presidency and Madison was inaugurated.[45] In an attempt to save face, Congress passed in late February, and Jefferson signed into law on March 1, a Non-Intercourse Act that opened trade with all nations other than Britain and France and authorized the president to reopen trade to either (or both) of the belligerent nations contingent on their ceasing their infringement of America's neutral rights.[46] With Jefferson's withdrawal from executive direction, Congress by default had taken up the governmental reins, which it would hold for the next five presidential administrations. Not until Andrew Jackson took office in 1833 did another president work so effectively to set the federal agenda.

EARLY IN 1808 THERE had been a flurry of support for Jefferson's standing for reelection for a third term, but he quickly quashed that idea. It proved a terrible year for him. Still dismayed by the outcome of the Burr trial, he was sorely afflicted by migraine headaches. Then a persistent toothache caused fevers and the development of a large knot on his jawbone that eventually required painful bone surgery and kept him indoors for six weeks. He worried to the point of distraction about the difficulty of enforcing the embargo. Jefferson could find no exit from the problems facing him.[47] The frustrations were by no means only political. Jefferson had appointed Meriwether Lewis governor of the Louisiana Territory on February 28, 1807, replacing General James Wilkinson, but Lewis proved a poor administrator and an even poorer correspondent. He seemed to be suffering from writer's block: tasked with publishing the journals of the Corps of Discovery, he was making no progress on the project. Jefferson politely complained to Lewis in July 1808, mentioning that since seeing him in Albemarle County in September of the previous year, "I have never had a line from you," and commenting, "We have no tidings yet of the forwardness of your printer. I hope the first part will not be delayed much longer."[48] Lewis would not live to see the publication of the journals of his and Clark's expedition to the West.

Family issues and financial worries greatly added to Jefferson's troubles. He had no one to whom he could vent his frustrations in complete privacy and confidentiality. He was not living alone in the President's House, but his cohabitants provided little relief. Although Jefferson loved his son-in-law Thomas Mann Randolph like a biological son, Randolph was a difficult, troubled man, filled with self-doubt. He once had confessed to Jefferson feeling unworthy of the company of his father-in-law and the talented Martha and Maria; as he put, he could not "like the proverbially silly bird feel at my ease in the company of the Swans."[49] Jefferson knew Randolph required treatment with special care. In the early summer of 1806 Randolph, then a congressman living with Jefferson in the President's House, felt that a comment on the floor of Congress by his irascible cousin, John Randolph, had insulted his honor, and he thereupon challenged the arrogant man to a duel. Jefferson ultimately succeeded in persuading his son-in-law to back down.[50]

Another crisis developed early the next year. Jefferson's other son-in-law, John Wayles Eppes, was also a congressman and also—with his young son Francis—lived in the President's House; somehow Randolph took an innocent invitation to Eppes from Jefferson as an indication that Jefferson favored the latter. In a fit of anger, Randolph moved out and took lodging in a boardinghouse. This upset Jefferson considerably, for he put great importance on family peace and proximity. He assured Randolph that his love and respect for each son-in-law was equal, and when Randolph came down with a debilitating fever, Jefferson had him brought back to the President's House and tenderly nursed him back to health.[51] Meanwhile, Jefferson still hoped Eppes would continue to visit Monticello and bring Francis, for Jefferson wanted to maintain the tie with his grandson; he wrote Eppes in July 1807 that little Francis "will ever be to me one of the dearest objects in life."[52] But for that year and the next, Eppes—feeling Randolph's hostility—did not visit Monticello or allow Francis to, much to Jefferson's regret. Eppes treated Jefferson almost as a father and wanted Francis to benefit from Jefferson's kindness and mentoring, but he feared that Randolph in his animosity might try to wean Francis's affections away from his father. Eventually Jefferson worked out some kind of rapprochement, and Francis did visit Monticello after 1809.[53]

Although Jefferson had long recorded his daily expenditures in his memorandum books, he seems never to have added up all the figures and related them to his annual income. Hard as it is to believe, this meticulous man and fanatical record keeper was largely unaware of how precarious his financial situation was. Somehow he had convinced himself that his presidential salary, combined with his plantation income, would allow him even to pay down his debts and bolster his financial ledger. Suddenly, at the beginning of 1808, however, he recognized his plight. As he wrote to his daughter after his economic epiphany, "I have now the gloomy prospect of retiring from office loaded with serious debts, which will materially affect the tranquility of my retirement."[54] Martha, who saw her most important life's work to be the love and care of her father, quickly responded, "Let not the tranquility of your old age be disturbed and we shall do well. I never could enjoy happiness to see you deprived of those comforts you have allways been accustomed to and which habit has rendered necessary to your health and ease."[55]

Yet another minor issue flared up just before Jefferson left the presidency. It had already been decided that reliable Martha, her husband Thomas, and their eight children would move to Monticello. Jefferson suggested that perhaps his youngest sister, Anna Marks, could move in as well and serve as manager of the household. But Martha objected. She wrote to her father that Anna simply wouldn't do. At Monticello the previous summer it had become clear to Martha that Anna was "totally incompetent to the business. . . . [T]he servants have no sort of respect for her."[56] Martha, an extremely skilled manager and smart as a whip, knew her father better than anyone and was totally devoted to him; she took over the daily management. Jefferson now understood (at least in theory, if not in practice) the importance of close attention to expenditures and that this was not a personal strength of his. He knew that he needed someone like Martha, with a good business head, to take over and supervise his household.[57] By the time Jefferson got home to

Martha Jefferson Randolph,
by Thomas Sully, 1836.
Source: Thomas Jefferson Foundation at Monticello.
Used by permission.

Monticello in mid-March, Martha had the situation fully in hand, and she managed the Monticello household for the rest of her father's life with consummate skill.

FOR REASONS BOTH personal and political, by the last few months of his second term Jefferson was intellectually and physically exhausted, confessing to his longtime friend James Monroe, "Five weeks more will relieve me from a drudgery to which I am no longer equal, and restore me to a scene of tranquility, amidst my family and friends, more congenial to my age and natural inclinations."[58] He seemed more and more to be looking ahead to the future. After years of almost constant construction, the enlarged and completely redesigned Monticello was now almost complete, just in time for Jefferson's retirement. Throughout 1808 he instructed his builders and slaves to rush through the final improvements—to finish the floors and the terraces, level out the large garden plot, construct winding walkways along the flower beds in the expansive west lawn.[59] He had already planned and begun to build a smaller house, called Poplar Forest, on his Bedford County property about ninety miles southwest of Monticello, and after its completion in 1809, Jefferson used it as his private retreat. He was counting the days until he could leave the cockpit of government, buying packing boxes and thinking longingly about having time to read "for amusement only." He had begun shipping trunks of books from the President's House to Monticello.[60] Even more pleasant to contemplate was the time he would spend with his "daughter and numerous family of grandchildren, [who] will furnish me great resources of happiness."[61]

Unanswerable political and policy questions had plagued him for months. How draconian would enforcement need to be to make for a leakproof embargo? Could the nation stand that? Was giving up and suffering the humiliation of bowing to England's every demand acceptable? Would not war with either England or France, or—worse still—both, be extremely damaging? He could see no good options, and neither could anyone else. It is important not to overemphasize the opposition he encountered to the embargo, despite the vehemence of the High Federalists. Through the end of 1808, nationwide, the embargo was still moderately accepted, and in the election that fall, which in many ways proved a referendum on the embargo, Jefferson's candidate, James Madison, won handily. The embargo did bring economic hardship, but the lurid tales of ships rotting in harbors and grass growing on wharfs were mainly the stuff of partisan exaggeration (even so, such stories have lived on in textbooks). And recent econometric analysis suggests that the embargo did in fact hurt Britain more than it did the United States. In other words, perhaps in the end it failed for want of political will—including on the part of Jefferson, who never launched a public campaign for it—more than anything else.[62] Support for the embargo did actually collapse in early 1809, soon after which Congress brought it to its ignominious end.

A wearied Jefferson could hardly wait to hand over the reins of power. Preparing to leave office, he wrote to Pierre Samuel Du Pont de Nemours, "Nature intended me for the tranquil pursuits of science, by rendering them my supreme delight. But the enormities of the times in which I have lived, have forced me to take a part in resisting them, and to commit myself on the boisterous ocean of political passions." He could at least depart in good conscience because he had confidence in the men who would follow him.⁶³ On March 4, Jefferson rode on horseback, accompanied by his oldest grandson, Thomas Jefferson Randolph, to attend Madison's inauguration.

That same day Jefferson issued a farewell message to the citizens of Washington, the emerging city he had done so much to establish. He began with a paean to the nation itself: "the only monument of human rights and the sole depository of the sacred fire of freedom and self-government, from hence it is to be lighted up in other regions of the earth, if other regions of the earth shall ever become susceptible of its benign influence." Jefferson still saw the nation as the best hope of the world. To preserve that sacred cause, he asked rhetorically, "To what sacrifices of interest, or convenience, ought not these considerations animate us? To what compromises of opinion and inclination, to maintain harmony and union among ourselves, and to preserve from all danger this hallowed ark of human hope and happiness[?]" With that call for unity and faithful commitment to the larger project the United States represented, Jefferson bade the city good-bye. He had a premonition that he would never again see the "seat of government."⁶⁴

James and Dolley Madison patiently waited a few days before moving into the President's House as Jefferson struggled to pack up (assisted by his Monticello overseer, Edmund Bacon, who spent sixteen days helping him), settle his accounts, say farewell to his many friends, and finally depart Washington on March 11. Five days later Jefferson arrived, utterly fatigued, at Monticello, having ridden in his phaeton through a raging snowstorm over execrable roads—never again, as he suspected, to visit the nation's capital.⁶⁵ Thomas Jefferson's public career was over.

PART VI

MONTICELLO, 1809–1826

27

"Returning to the Scenes of My Birth and Early Life"

J EFFERSON ARRIVED AT Monticello on March 15, 1809, soon before the convoy of three wagons sent by Edmund Bacon. He was already planning new work on the estate; Monticello's fields and gardens had fallen into dismal condition during the busy years of his presidency, despite his best efforts from the capital. As always Jefferson contemplated not just repairs but improvements—one of Bacon's wagons carried bushes and shrubs for replanting around Monticello and in its orchards.¹ Just after leaving office he had written to John Armstrong, the minister to France, "I retire from scenes of difficulty, anxiety & of contending passions to the elysium of domestic affections & the . . . direction of my own affairs."² Jefferson's affection for Monticello and indeed Albemarle County was widely known, and his neighbors reciprocated his esteem. Shortly after his return he received a proclamation "From the Inhabitants of Albemarle County," stating that they "hope[d] to see realized those sweets of retirement for which you have often sighed, and to which they are now anxious personally to contribute." A local Baptist congregation, thankful for Jefferson's work to establish religious freedom, sent congratulations on "your Return home, from your labour and painful Servis of eight years[,] now to take some Sweet hours of retirement and rest."³

Jefferson was delighted to be surrounded at last by his family, his farm, and his books. Many wonderful moments of pleasure and comfort lay ahead, though heartbreak, tragedy, and financial worry would intrude on his retirement. At first, however, there was little darkness in his life. On the contrary, he was simply content, again looking forward to the beauty of the region in the spring, when dogwoods blossomed wild, in the autumn, when the leaves were resplendent in their color, and on warm summer days, when looming clouds created shadows on the plains below and occasionally one could watch thunderstorms move across the terrain below, with streaks of rain reaching to the ground. Responding appreciatively to the proclamation of the county residents, Jefferson remarked that on "Returning to the scenes of my birth & early life, to the society of those with whom I was raised, & who have been ever dear to me, I receive, fellow citizens & neighbors, with inexpressible pleasure, the cordial welcome you are so good to give me." Having been "long absent on duties which the history of a wonderful aera made incumbent on those called to them" and confident in the new administration in Washington, he was ready to "gladly lay down the distressing burthen of power, & seek, with my fellow citizens, repose & safety."[4] The final phase of his life, now begun, would be eventful beyond his expectations.

JEFFERSON IMMEDIATELY focused on his gardens. Before he arrived the garden plot had been plowed, manured, and readied for planting, and within days he had various kinds of peas, beans, celery, carrots, parsnips, beets, squash, pumpkins, and other vegetables and herbs planted. The latter included his latest agricultural infatuation, the benne, or sesame, a plant brought from Africa, whose seed, when processed, produced an oil useful in cooking. (Despite his efforts to promote it over the years, the benne never became widely cultivated in the South.[5]) He maintained a seed cabinet in his study, its several shelves filled with containers of different varieties, each carefully labeled. His grandchildren later commented on his love of measuring out his garden plots and flower beds, keeping detailed records of the progress of the various plants, and recording with precision when they first flowered or brought forth fruit. He once again began making notations in his Garden Book, which had lain almost forgotten during his political years. And he rhapsodized about the pleasures of domestic agriculture in a letter to artist Charles Willson Peale. "I have often thought," he wrote, "that if heaven had given me a choice of my position & calling, it should have been on a rich spot of earth, well watered, and near a good market for the productions of the garden. no occupation is so delightful to me as the culture of the earth, & no culture comparable to that of the garden. such a variety of subjects, some one always coming to perfection, the failure of one thing repaired by the success of another, & instead of one harvest a continued one thro' the year." Writing in his sixty-eighth year, Jefferson continued, "Under a total want of demand except for our family table I am still devoted to the garden. but tho' an old man, I am but a young gardener."[6]

Most of the produce from his gardens Jefferson intended for household consumption, and to ensure preparation of his food in the manner that he preferred, he hired his chef from the President's House, Etienne Lemaire, to visit Monticello for about two weeks in late March and early April to finalize the training of Edy Hern Fossett and Fanny Gillette Hern—two young slave women who had already spent several years in Washington learning from Lemaire—in the art of French cuisine.[7] Jefferson loved vegetables, especially peas, and always tried to have fresh greens available, for which he insisted on salad oils. He asked Lemaire to bring bottles with him from Washington; a year later, having exhausted that supply, Jefferson wrote to his nephew Thomas Jefferson Randolph in Richmond, "We are out of salad-oil, and you know it is a necessary of life here, can any be had in Richmond?" If yes, he asked his nephew to send a few bottles.[8] Although Jefferson recognized the need for frugality, he was unwilling to forgo salad oil. He was able, however, to have Congress extend to him free postage for both outgoing and incoming mail, and given the volume of his correspondence, that represented a significant saving.[9]

Since his childhood at Shadwell, Jefferson had been accustomed to company; once his retirement began, Monticello hosted an almost constant stream of visitors: close family, distant kin, friends, dignitaries touring America, those merely wishing to pay homage to the Sage of Monticello, and casual travelers hoping to catch sight of the former president. The first official visitors to leave a detailed portrait of Jefferson during his early retirement years were his old Washington friends Margaret Bayard Smith and her husband, Samuel H. Smith. They arrived on August 1, 1809, climbing the little mountain and noting its "sublime scenery." Jefferson, on horseback, met their carriage and accompanied them along the final portion of the road that circled up to the leveled-off top. Martha, preoccupied with the care of an ill son, soon came out to welcome the Smiths. They enjoyed a plain but delicious meal late that afternoon, complemented, after the table was cleared, by a variety of French and Italian wines. Jefferson then took the Smiths on a brief walking tour of Monticello and its grounds, finishing up the evening with tea, after which Jefferson retired to his private chambers for reading. The next day offered the Smiths insight into a typical day for Jefferson.

He rose very early, and at about 9:00 a.m. the table was set for family breakfast, during which the younger and older grandchildren were arrayed

around the table; Margaret Smith remarked on their unusually good behavior. The menu consisted of tea and coffee, hot muffins along with
wheat and cornbread, and cold ham and butter. After the meal, Jefferson
always excused himself and either went to his study or rode about the
plantation, while the others began their daily chores or lessons. Martha
Randolph spent much of her own time teaching the children. Generally
Jefferson was astride his horse supervising his plantation till about 3:30
p.m., when he came in for dinner, normally served between 4:00 and 5:00.
This was the most social time of the day; after a leisurely meal with des-
sert, the dishes were cleared and the adults enjoyed wine and conversation.
Jefferson relished these hours, and whoever the dinner guests, his conversational skills still shone. Martha and the older children sat at the table for
the actual meal, with Martha's evident social grace and manifest intelligence a perennial reminder of her Parisian education.

Margaret Smith commented on Jefferson's private quarters, which everyone who visited the house found fascinating. They took up the entire
south wing of Monticello. Jefferson's bedroom, with a large window to the
west, was right off the entrance hall. His bed was set in an alcove that divided the bedroom proper from what he called his cabinet, or study, where
he wrote and kept his several scientific instruments, along with his polygraph. To the east of the cabinet were two rooms that comprised his library; movable wooden cases rather than built-in bookshelves contained
his approximately 6,000 books. In several cabinets, lined with shelves and
fronted by locked doors, he kept his extensive files of correspondence.
What he called the South Square Room, between the easternmost library
room and the entrance hall, housed yet more books and also served as
Martha's sitting room, where she often instructed the children.

Jefferson's rooms were considered absolutely private; no one entered
without his permission, and he was not to be disturbed when at his desk
or in his reading chair. After 1809, following completion of the outdoor
south terrace, Jefferson discovered to his dismay that utter strangers would
walk right up and peer in at him sitting at his writing table. One insistent
tourist even used her parasol to poke out a pane of glass in order to get a
better view of the great man. To protect his privacy, Jefferson had two un-
attractive louvered porticos constructed on the east and west sides of the
piazza; one also doubled as an aviary for several of his beloved mockingbirds. With only a doorway from the entrance hall and a small internal
stairway down to the slave quarters below, Jefferson's quarters afforded
him an ideal retreat for reading and research.

Many visitors saw Jefferson's situation as idyllic, especially when they experienced his table and conversation, and they typically commented on his sweet nature, gentle tone, and playful grandparenting. Of course Jefferson was not the first to discover the joys of grandchildren, but he did truly relish his time with them. As Margaret Smith observed, "He seems to have transposed his hopes and anticipations into the existence of his children. It is in them he lives."[10] She described a scene one day after dinner, when the children ran up to him and proposed a race. He obliged by marking out starting spots for each child, adjusted according to age. Off they ran across the west lawn and back to him, falling joyously into his waiting arms, while he smothered them in kisses. Then they suggested he race them, which he did for a short distance, giving them fits of laughter. When Smith commented on the amusement provided by grandchildren, Jefferson replied, "Yes, it is only with them that a grave man can play the fool."[11] On an earlier evening she noticed that throughout an hour-long visit that included his daughter—who had not been feeling well—Jefferson sat the whole time tenderly holding Martha's hand.

Jefferson's grandchildren left commentary on him in their correspondence with his mid-nineteenth-century biographer Henry S. Randall, who had solicited their stories.[12] Several mentioned the foot races that Smith had described, adding that Jefferson would give little fruits like figs or dates as rewards. After dinner, when the family sat about the parlor reading by candlelight, Jefferson occasionally put down his book—likely a familiar Greek or Latin classic, which he loved reading in the original language—and, smiling contentedly, looked around the room at his whole family with their own books in their hands. Jefferson always loved nurturing younger minds or seeing them nurtured by others such as Martha. Another grandchild recalled climbing up on Jefferson's knees and playing with his watch chain, being taught games by him, and accompanying him about his flower beds, watching and helping him plant seeds or insert tender slips into the soft soil. The children were always very careful not to step into one of the prepared beds. They could all remember occasions of his thoughtfulness in providing them with a little saddle, or a watch, or a new silk dress upon having heard them mention a desire for one. When they were slightly older, he often invited one or two granddaughters to accompany him on a visit to Poplar Forest, and he took care to provide warm robes for the carriage drive and packed picnic lunches. Jefferson, remarkably didactic with his own daughters three decades earlier, seemed much more relaxed now—as perhaps all grandparents are—and seldom scolded the children.[13]

As these stories suggest, loved ones surrounded Jefferson at Monticello. A census he took in 1810 listed twenty white people living at the house; in addition to Martha Randolph and eight of her nine children at the time— Thomas Jefferson (always called Jeff), Ellen Wayles, Cornelia Jefferson, Virginia Jefferson, Mary Jefferson, James Madison, Benjamin Franklin, and Meriwether Lewis—her husband, Thomas Mann Randolph, was sometimes there too. Jefferson often hosted his sisters Martha (whose husband, Dabney Carr, had died in 1773) and Anna Marks, as well as various nephews and nieces. Anne, the first child of Jefferson's daughter Martha, had married in 1808, so no longer lived at home. Jefferson's grandson Francis Eppes was often present from 1809 on.[14] (Subsequently Martha had two more children, Septima Anne and George Wythe, for a total of eleven who lived until adulthood.) As the patriarch, Jefferson saw it as his sacred obligation to take in and care for needy members of his extended family.

But guests, both expected and unannounced, drained his resources. Every day for about eight months a year, Monticello had visitors, who usually expected food and a place to sleep, both for themselves and their horses, there being no tavern nearby. The federal government at the time provided no pension or financial assistance of any kind to former presidents (except free postage for Jefferson). Moreover, owing to the number of visitors, in 1810 Jefferson employed twenty-five of his slaves in Monticello itself, rather than in a more financially productive manner.[15] The glut of visitors drove Jefferson to spend more and more time as the years went by at Poplar Forest, the octagonal retreat he had finished in 1809 on his Bedford County property, where he could escape the hoards who so consumed his time and energy (and provisions) at Monticello.

Even in his late sixties Jefferson stood straight and tall, with his white hair cut shorter than, for instance, when as a diplomat in France he wore it powdered, in a queue. He still wore knee britches, holding off on trousers—a relatively new and more democratic fashion—until about 1818, when he was seventy-five; he was surprised to find how comfortable they were.[16] Jefferson had long been an indefatigable walker, but now, often slowed by painful attacks of arthritis, he got around Monticello on horseback. His longtime overseer, Edmund Bacon, described him as "an uncommonly fine rider [who] sat easily upon his horse and always had him in the most perfect control."[17] Because he found Monticello run down upon arriving to begin his retirement in 1809, he felt it necessary to spend more time riding about and supervising its operations than perhaps he wanted; he certainly had less time for correspondence and reading than he had expected. As he wrote in 1811, his existence was "at present more a life of riding than reading. I am on horseback among my farms from breakfast to dinner."[18] Later, when he was much older and more enfeebled, a slave accompanied Jefferson about his farms and carried a little campstool so the old man could sit while supervising his workers' and slaves' chores.

As a farmer, Jefferson had several passions. One that arose during his early retirement years was merino sheep.[19] Since at least the early 1790s, he had been interested in various breeds of sheep, having received in 1792, courtesy of Robert Morris, a ram and ewe closely related to the famous merino breed from Spain. Off and on from that time forward, Jefferson acquired sheep of what he called the Iceland, Barbary, and Senegal breeds, but he maintained his fascination with merinos because of the fineness of their wool. So convinced was he that this breed would significantly upgrade the sheep population in Virginia that he chose purebred rams from his own flock and gave one to each county in the state.[20] Incidentally, Jefferson hoped that an increase in wool production and cloth manufacturing would render the United States more self-sufficient and less dependent on trade with England. Despite his best efforts, however, Virginia farmers did not take to the merinos: they produced less wool, which was too fine for the mills and markets in the state. Moreover, early on in the process, a disease the farmers called the scab afflicted many of the merinos, so by 1812 it was becoming clear that the merino craze would be short-lived.[21] Jefferson wrote comparatively little of sheep after about 1815.

A secondary aspect of Jefferson's temporary passion for sheep was his admiration for French shepherd dogs, beginning with the "chienne bergere big with pup" that he had purchased just before leaving France with his family on October 7, 1789.[22] Into the nineteenth century he owned descendants of this dog and then French shepherd dogs sent to him by friends, including the Marquis de Lafayette.[23] Jefferson liked them for their "wonderful sagacity & never ceasing attention to what they are taught to do."[24] While he prized this breed because it adapted so well to the herding of sheep, he also realized that roving packs of uncontrolled dogs were a significant danger to sheep and other small animals. In general he despised canines and participated in several efforts to control the population of feral dogs that marauded through the countryside.[25]

BY ALL ACCOUNTS Jefferson was a patient man, but by 1809 he was anxious to read the journals that Meriwether Lewis and William Clark had produced during their two-year journey through the West. Jefferson had seen enough of their content—Lewis had sent him an early version in the spring of 1805 and shown him other materials at the President's House in early January 1807—to recognize the scientific riches that lay within. People interested in geography and the flora and fauna of America asked him repeatedly about when the journals would be published. Finally, in the summer of 1809, no longer able to restrain himself, he wrote to Lewis, then governor of the Territory of Louisiana.[26] Jefferson could not have known the state of Lewis's mind; indeed, those closer to the governor were not fully aware of his mental condition. But severely depressed over his inability to find a wife, monetary and accounting problems, and the difficulties of managing Indian affairs, Lewis had turned to drink. His resultant inability to make progress toward publication of the expedition's paper surely only added to the strain, for he knew by his delay he was letting down Jefferson, whom he revered. In the early fall, while traveling by horseback (with his journals) back to Washington, DC, he committed suicide in Tennessee. Jefferson heard the tragic news in late November. Local officials reported that they were prepared to send Lewis's belongings wherever Jefferson directed, which they assumed would be Monticello.[27]

Jefferson was initially at a loss about how to proceed. He had just received a letter from Lewis's prospective publisher in Philadelphia, C&A Conrad & Company, informing him of its contract to publish the journals and reporting, "Lewis never furnished us with a line of the M.S. nor indeed could we ever hear any thing from him respecting it tho frequent applications to that effect were made to him."[28] Jefferson promptly replied to say that William Clark would soon be coming to Monticello; Jefferson would consult with him about what to do. After all, Clark had written many of the journal entries—more, in fact, than Lewis, although Jefferson did not know that. Jefferson assured the publisher that he would "spare no pains to secure the publication of [the] work, and when it may be within my sphere to take any definitive step respecting it, you shall be informed."[29] He wrote again in December to inform the publisher that Clark was proceeding to Washington, where Jefferson had directed the papers be sent, then proceed with them directly to Philadelphia "to do whatever is necessary to the publication."[30]

In the following weeks, Clark, after first inquiring if lawyer William Wirt was available to work with him on the journals (he was not), came to an agreement with Nicholas Biddle of Philadelphia. Biddle, who would do the actual editorial work, visited Clark in Virginia and went over the papers with him in some detail, asking questions for clarification and background information. Biddle kept careful notes, and his emendations in red pencil in the original journals show the results of this research.[31] Later Clark sent George Shannon, a member of the Corps of Discovery, to assist Biddle in Philadelphia.[32] We do not know how much of this preparatory work Jefferson knew about, but he did receive a comforting letter from the publisher in mid-April, stating, "We have now the pleasure to inform you that Genl. Clarke has engaged Professor Barton & Mr. Nicholas Biddle to write his book and that it is likely to be published without any further unnecessary delay."[33] Jefferson must have felt enormous relief from this news. He could not have known the liberties Biddle would take with the original texts.

In July 1812 Biddle informed Clark that C&A Conrad & Company had collapsed; a month later he reported that the firm of Bradford and Inskeep had taken over the project.[34] But the press of outside events led Biddle to withdraw from the project the following year, and he asked a young journalist and Brown University graduate, Paul Allen, to see the manuscript through to press. Biddle had already completed most of his editing—almost completely rewriting the original texts. He did, at least, leave the original manuscripts intact. Dismayed by what he deemed Lewis and Clark's rude, colorful prose, Biddle had wanted to render their story in an English more in keeping with the literary standards of the day.[35] Allen believed that the resulting narrative would benefit from a biographical sketch of Lewis, so he wrote Jefferson on May 25, 1813, soliciting one. Jefferson willingly accepted the assignment and, after corresponding with various people who could supplement what he already knew, completed the essay on August 18. He sent it to Allen by way of Biddle, whom Jefferson must have still considered in charge of the project.[36]

The book was published in 1814 in two volumes under the formal title *History of the Expedition Under the Command of Captains Lewis and Clark* . . . . The title page read, in part, "Prepared for the Press by Paul Allen, Esquire"—Biddle had not wanted his name on the book. A literary paraphrase written mostly by Biddle, the book emphasized the adventurous nature of the travels, omitting most of the scientific data Lewis and Clark recorded. Jefferson never appears to have commented on the published version, though he did lament the absence of the astronomical observations, Indian vocabularies, and other purely scientific papers that were left out. He wrote Clark in 1816 inquiring about the location of those materials and wondering whether somehow they could be published separately.[37]

Despite the fame of the expedition and the fascination with the West it helped engender among American citizens, as a scientific endeavor it was largely a failure because its results remained unpublished for decades. This must have been a profound disappointment for Jefferson. Jefferson's own contribution, his biographical sketch of Lewis, did appear as the introduction to the first volume of the 1814 publication, along with a reprinting of his original letter of instruction to Lewis. The sketch has shaped all subsequent interpreters' view of the man. Jefferson described Lewis's youth and proclivity to outdoor life, his skill at observation, his subsequent military career, and, in words that became famous, the attributes that made Lewis such an exceptional leader:[38] "of courage undaunted, possessing a firmness & perseverance of purpose nothing but impossibilities could divert from it's direction, careful as a father of those committed to his charge . . . intimate with the Indian character, . . . guarded by exact observation of the vegetables and animals of his own country against losing time in the description of objects already possessed; . . . of sound understanding, and a fidelity to truth so scrupulous that whatever he should report would be as certain as if seen by ourselves."[39]

Having to account, in some way, for the tragedy of the younger man's death, Jefferson wrote that Lewis "had, from early life, been subject to hypocondriac affections. it was a constitutional disposition in all the nearer branches of the family."[40] He hypothesized that the frustrations of Lewis's sedentary position as governor brought "some symptoms of a derangement of mind," leading him to do "the deed which plunged his friends into affliction, and deprived his country of one of her most valued citizens." With these words about "this melancholy close of the life of one, whom posterity will declare not to have lived in vain," Jefferson ended his account.[41] His judgment both of Lewis's genetic predisposition toward depression and his suicide have stood up to the inquiries of subsequent research.

A HUGELY UPSETTING issue interrupted Jefferson's retirement in 1810, and for more than eighteen months it commanded much of his attention. The problem began with a letter Jefferson received on May 18 from attorney John Wickham (who had been one of Aaron Burr's lawyers), alerting him that, without prior notice, Edward Livingston of New Orleans had asked Wickham to institute an action against Jefferson in the federal district court of Richmond. Wickham did not indicate what the case might involve, and Jefferson—probably suspecting it had something to do with a land dispute in New Orleans—quickly wrote back inquiring if Wickham might be available to represent him alongside his own lawyers from the Burr trial, William Wirt and George Hay. Wickham replied that since Livingston had approached him about entering the suit, it would be inappropriate for him now to represent Jefferson.[42] Jefferson did engage Wirt and Hay and soon added Littleton Waller Tazewell of Norfolk, another accomplished attorney. (Although Jefferson initially assumed the government would cover all his court costs, he himself ended up personally paying—on April 12, 1812—his legal fees, which amounted to only $100 for each of his three lawyers.[43]) Within days Jefferson read in the newspapers that Livingston was indeed suing him for actions taken several years before concerning a land controversy. Livingston sought a staggering $100,000 in damages, an amount Jefferson knew would ruin him financially[44]—which explains the intensity of his response.

Jefferson assumed, as did his lawyers, that Livingston had chosen the Richmond federal court because John Marshall still presided over it. As Jefferson wrote to James Madison, "It is little doubted that his knolege of Marshall's character, has induced him to bring this action."[45] Jefferson's hatred of Marshall led him to assume that the justice would ensure Livingston's winning, regardless of the merits of the case.

Jefferson's expressed fears of Marshall have led Federalist-oriented historians ever since to argue that his next act—his attempt to convince President Madison to stack the court in his favor—was a direct result thereof.[46] While Jefferson no doubt understood that the careful appointment of another judge to the court could protect him from Marshall's animus, his suggestion to Madison of a court appointee had a far longer pedigree.

For a decade, Jefferson had believed that Federalist appointees unfairly dominated the entire federal judiciary, and he had long wished for opportunities to bring more balance to the courts. On May 16, 1810—two days before he received the fateful letter from Wickham—Jefferson had received a letter from John Tyler Sr., a prominent jurist and then governor of Virginia. Tyler asked Jefferson to persuade Madison to appoint him to the federal district court of Richmond, should a sitting judge who had grown quite feeble, Cyrus Griffin, pass away, as he did later that year.[47] Jefferson respected Tyler and thought he had the substance and character to stand up to Marshall on the court (at the time, the justices spent more time sitting on district courts than they did on the Supreme Court in Washington).

Jefferson seized the opportunity to recommend Tyler to Madison because he believed it would be "difficult to find a character of firmness enough to preserve his independence on the same bench with Marshall. Tyler, I am certain, would do it. He is an able and well read lawyer . . . [of] incorruptible integrity."[48] Madison obviously agreed, and after Griffin's death, the president appointed Tyler to the federal district court of Richmond on January 2, 1811. Despite his long-standing complaints about the Federalist-dominated judiciary, given that he had a case pending in that court, Jefferson's urging of the appointment of a judge he could expect would side with him does appear unseemly. As it turned out, he did not need Tyler's support.

The case itself involved a property dispute over a sandbank (*batture* in French) that had built up on a bend of the Mississippi River between the levee and the river. When the river was up, the sandbank was underwater, and small boats anchored there to unload; when the river was down, the area, averaging about two hundred yards in width, formed a bank from which New Orleanians often took sand to build up roads and fill in lots.[49]

A prominent New York lawyer, Livingston, after being charged with malfeasance in that state and subjected to a large property settlement owed to the federal government, moved to New Orleans, where he prospered. He came to represent a New Orleanian who claimed a portion of the *batture* and apparently gave Livingston a portion of the disputed territory as his fee. Livingston hired men to develop the site, and when city officials did not intervene to stop irate citizens from driving the workers away, Livingston appealed to a territorial court, which sided with him. City officials then appealed to federal authorities.

Jefferson had first become vaguely aware of the matter in October 1807, but caught up at the time in the Burr trial and the *Chesapeake-Leopard* affair, he paid little attention to a quarrel over a sandbank in New Orleans. His attorney general, Caesar A. Rodney, advised him that the disputed land was federal property, and Jefferson's cabinet agreed. Jefferson, without extensive research into the matter, asked Secretary of State Madison to order the federal marshal in New Orleans to claim jurisdiction. Jefferson later shifted the issue to the Congress, which neglected to rule either way. The president seemed to assume, under the authority of the attorney general's reasoning and the absence of further congressional action, that the local authorities were in control, and he gave the issue no additional consideration. But Livingston was nothing if not determined and launched his suit, expecting less to win the money demanded than to advance his claims to obtain a legal grant to the disputed land. For his part, Jefferson was appalled to discover that in making a good-faith decision on behalf of the public good, based on the advice of the attorney general and with the approval of the cabinet, he could later find himself potentially liable for such an impossible amount.

Wickham had immediately concluded that Livingston had no case due to jurisdiction; the land under dispute was in Louisiana, and the district court of Richmond had no power there regarding a matter of trespass against property.[50] Both Wirt and Hay advised Jefferson similarly, and when the case came to court, on December 5, 1811, Marshall agreed (as did John Tyler Sr.). Marshall would have liked the case to proceed to a higher court, but because of the established jurisdictional principle and the concurrence of the other judge, the trial ended there.

Jefferson, who was at Poplar Forest, did not learn the outcome for several weeks. Still, the news, when he received it, did not satisfy him: he wanted the public to know that beyond the legal technicality, the case, had it come to trial, would have been decided in his favor on substantial legal grounds.[51] To prepare for a trial, Jefferson had spent months poring over legal volumes and quoting sources in French, Latin, Spanish, and even Greek to argue that the *batture*, according to French law, belonged to the king and hence formed part of the federal purchase of Louisiana in 1803. Moreover, according to long-established riparian law, the *batture* was actually a portion of the bed of the river and, as such, could not be alienated or legally conveyed to an individual. Jefferson submitted to his lawyers numerous materials, arguments, and precedents that he had accumulated (although the case had already been dismissed) because he wanted to solidly establish in law the public's ownership of the land and explain the basis of the public's claim. The result was a pamphlet of ninety-one pages that Jefferson had printed in New York in a run of 250 copies, under the long title *The Proceedings of the Government of the United States, in Maintaining the Public Right to the Beach of the Missisipi, Adjacent to New-Orleans, Against the Intrusion of Edward Livingston. Prepared for the Use of Counsel, by Thomas Jefferson.*[52]

Although Jefferson never liked the disputation involved in courtroom pleadings, he loved legal research and writing, and the pamphlet displayed not only his sharpness of thought but his passion for argument. John Adams later called it "as masterly a pamphlet as ever I have read . . . [in] every way worthy of the Mind that composed and the pen which committed it to writing."[53] As far as Jefferson was concerned, the pamphlet ended the matter, but Livingston continued to push versions of his case in a variety of jurisdictions, finally, more than a decade and a half later, acquiring title to a portion of the *batture*. By then he and Jefferson had reconciled, and Livingston had gained deserved fame for his drafting of the Louisiana Civil Code of 1825, an adaptation of the Napoleonic Code by which the state is still governed.[54]

ALTHOUGH THE SURPRISING letter that Jefferson had received from John Wickham in May 1810 heralded a season of controversy and worry, not all unexpected correspondence had the same effect. Early the next year, a missive arrived from his old friend Benjamin Rush, dated January 2, 1811. Although the letter began with Rush's description of the depressed state of his eldest son, it ended with an attempt to effect a reconciliation between Jefferson and "your and my old friend Mr. Adams." Rush recalled Jefferson's "early attachment to Mr. Adams, and his to you," as well as how their work together helped achieve American independence. Rush remarked on the current similarity of their views on most major political questions and stated how "ardently" he wished that the two venerable revolutionaries could revive their affections. Imagining Jefferson's hesitance, Rush wrote, "I am sure an advance on your side will be a cordial to the heart of Mr. Adams. Tottering over the grave, he now leans wholly upon the shoulders of his old Revolutionary friends."[55] (Rush had reached out to Adams in late 1809, artfully describing an imaginary dream of his wherein Adams and Jefferson had smoothed out their differences and entered upon an extensive correspondence.[56] But Rush's letter did not spur Adams to initiate a rapprochement with Jefferson.)

Jefferson in due time sent a detailed reply to Rush, stating that he too regretted the breach in his correspondence with Adams, for he recalled the "high degree of mutual respect & esteem" they had once enjoyed. Then Jefferson related the differences that emerged amid the members of George

Washington's administration, Adams's and Alexander Hamilton's preference for a more British-type system, and Hamilton's admiration for Julius Caesar. He also mentioned how the attacks of the High Federalists had succeeded somewhat in swaying Adams against him, and he commented on the impropriety of Adams's so-called midnight appointments. Still, after Abigail Adams's letter on the death of his beloved daughter Maria, he had tentatively tried to effect a more general reconciliation with her, but she had shown no interest; Jefferson had given up. Nevertheless, he wrote, "I have the same good opinion of mr Adams which I ever had."[57] Knowing Adams to be vain and suspicious, he needed some evidence that were he to reach out, the initiative would not be rebuffed.

Fortuitously he soon received an encouraging sign. During the summer of 1811, Edward Coles, then private secretary to President Madison, was visiting Massachusetts along with his brother John, and the brothers spent most of their two days there conversing with John Adams. When Adams complained to them of his past ill treatment by Jefferson, the Coleses told Adams that his attitude toward Jefferson did not match the many positive statements they had personally heard Jefferson make about Adams. As they continued to talk, Adams mellowed and began to "display . . . kind feelings to Mr. Jefferson, and an exalted admiration of his character, and appreciation of his services to his country." Adams ended up exclaiming, "'I always loved Jefferson, and still love him.'" The Coles brothers, returning to Virginia, visited Jefferson and told him this story.[58] This was the signal Jefferson needed. He reported to Rush in December 1811 that "a late incident had satisfied" him. "I only needed this knolege to revive towards him all the affection of the most cordial moments of our lives." He did not quite know how to proceed from there.[59]

Rush immediately replied, saying that he had just written Adams and quoted to him "such passages from your letter as contained the kindest expressions of regard for mr Adams."[60] Rush had implored Adams "to receive the olive branch which has thus been offered to you by the hand of a man who still loves you. Fellow laborers in erecting the great fabric of American independence! . . . embrace—embrace each other! . . . Bury in silence all the causes of separation."[61] Adams wrote back in good humor. "I perceive plainly enough, Rush, that you have been teasing Jefferson to write me, as you did me some time ago to write to him." And then he disingenuously stated that they had nothing to write about, except to wish each other "an easy journey to heaven," while expressing a desire that the journey be delayed. Still, Adams said enigmatically, "Time and chance,

however, or possibly design, may produce ere long a letter between us."[62]
Design it would be, and on January 1, 1812, Adams postmarked from
Quincy the first letter he'd written to his old ally since 1801.[63] Thus began
the most remarkable body of correspondence between two politicians in
American history.

28

"We Ought Not to Die
Before We Have Explained Ourselves"

JOHN ADAMS, BENEATH whose gruff and prickly exterior resided a robust sense of humor, opened his correspondence with a pun that Jefferson did not at first grasp. Because you are a "Friend to American Manufacturers," Adams wrote, he was sending "two pieces of Homespun lately produced in this quarter by One who was honoured in his youth with some of your Attention and much of your kindness." Jefferson should have picked up on this clue. Adams added that his daughter was staying with them after "a perilous and painful Operation"—she had had a tumorous breast removed, without anesthesia, with the bleeding staunched by means of a red-hot iron—then concluded by pronouncing his "long and sincere Esteem" and himself "your Friend and Servant."[1]

Jefferson promptly answered, noting that the additional package had not arrived yet and reporting on the rise of cloth manufacturing in his neighborhood as well. With more frankness than Adams had shown, Jefferson wrote, "A letter from you calls up recollections very dear to my mind. It carries me back to the times when, beset with difficulties and dangers, we were fellow laborers in the same cause, struggling for what is most valuable to man, his right of self-government." They would return often to this theme. With his usual grace, Jefferson recalled, "Laboring always at the same oar, with some wave ever ahead threatening to overwhelm us and yet passing harmless under our bark, we knew not how, we rode through the storm with heart and hand, and made a happy port."[2]

Not wishing to raise old disagreements, Jefferson announced that of "politics . . . I have taken final leave. I think little of them, and say less. I have given up newspapers in exchange for Tacitus and Thucydides, for

Newton and Euclid; and I find myself much the happier." While most of their old friends had passed away, he and Adams still enjoyed comparably good health, and Jefferson reported that he still spent three or four hours daily on horseback, though he walked little. He described himself surrounded by grandchildren and lately a great grandchild and said he would be happy to learn more about Adams's "health, your habits, occupations and enjoyments."[3] The two old revolutionaries would exchange 158 letters over the next fourteen years, with Adams sending 109 to Jefferson's 49 (Abigail and Jefferson also corresponded, though much less frequently). Two days after Adams's first letter arrived, Jefferson received the enclosures, which, to his embarrassment, were not pieces of cloth but two volumes of lectures written by Adams's son John Quincy.

THE CORRESPONDENCE between Jefferson and Adams is revealing about both men. Jefferson was far busier than Adams and simply did not have time to write as often or at such length, for he was fully absorbed in the effort to turn Monticello into a profitable enterprise. In part because of the wider range of his interests and, no doubt, his "friendly warmth," as Adams put it, Jefferson also received far more letters from others than did Adams and felt an obligation to reply to most of them.[4] Jefferson told Adams that in 1820 he received 1,267 letters, all of which he answered; in reply, Adams said he doubted that he had been sent one-twelfth that number.[5] As he said to Jefferson, "Answer my Letters at Your Leisure. . . . Give yourself no Concern. I write as for a refuge and protection against Ennui."[6] While the two covered a range of topics, Adams was more interested in theology, in resurrecting old political matters, and in clarifying comments in old letters from Jefferson. Adams also had scores to settle, though Jefferson was not immune to the same, excoriating John Marshall several times, especially for "twist[ing] Burr's neck out of the halter of treason."[7] Adams's rambling letters showed signs of hurried writing, but they always evinced his scholarship, quality of mind, and depth of feeling.

Adams was more impulsive, Jefferson more reticent. Both obviously enjoyed having a learned, lively friend with whom to correspond in complete confidence. Jefferson's letters were usually briefer, far better written—often they were carefully considered short essays—and demonstrated his lifelong distaste of contentiousness and personal disputation (aside, again, from his attacks on Marshall and a few other exceptions). Both men critiqued, to one another, the public exposure of private correspondence and demonstrated an astonishing breadth of reading and familiarity with classical sources. They wrote frankly of their health, movingly about the past, profoundly about religion, sadly about the tragedy in their personal lives, and worriedly about such ongoing issues as banks, European affairs, and the survival of the union. They shared opinions on books, philosophers, and political thinkers. They differed on a few important issues, especially aristocracy. The letters are a rich repository of Jefferson's considered thoughts on many subjects. A grateful Adams recognized the eloquence of Jefferson's writing. "Never mind it, my dear Sir, if I write four Letters to your one; your one is worth more than my four."[8]

When Adams acknowledged Jefferson's first letter in their renewed correspondence, he remarked on a concern that he knew Jefferson shared: "The Union is still to me an Object of as much Anxiety as ever Independence was." He also apologized to Jefferson for his shaky handwriting, caused by his palsy. Eventually he would have to dictate his letters to an amanuensis. A few months later he received from Jefferson "a piece of homespun in return," a copy of Jefferson's legal justification for his actions concerning the *batture* case in New Orleans. Adams already disliked Edward Livingston, and incensed by his suit against Jefferson, he blurted, "Great God!" "Is a President of U.S. to be Subject to a private Action of every Individual," making up in his use of capital letters for Jefferson's relative parsimony. In a subsequent letter Adams praised Jefferson's legal treatise and concluded, "My better half charges me to present you her ancient respect and regards," the first indication that Abigail had forgiven Jefferson for the political controversies of the past.[9]

While the two occasionally carried a thread of discussion across several letters, now and then one or the other would introduce a new subject. Or one would mention a book, and the other would discourse on its theme. In a letter on June 11, 1812, Jefferson discussed in detail his interest in and admiration of Indians. He repeated his belief in urging them to adopt settled agriculture, praising the Creeks, who now were "far advanced in civilization" and had "good Cabins, inclosed fields, large herds of cattle and hogs, spin and weave their own clothes, . . . write and read, are on the increase in numbers."[10] Jefferson's general views on Indians never changed. Adams asked if he knew of any books on Indian religion, described seeing Indians in Massachusetts as a boy, and stated his "Commiseration for them from my Childhood," but he offered no ideas about how to integrate them into American society.[11]

The two men shared similar sentiments when lamenting the death of Benjamin Rush in May 1813, but early the next month Adams came across a letter Jefferson had written in 1801 charging that he looked backward, not forward, and did not welcome advances in science. The touchy Adams promptly wrote Jefferson, "I totally disclaim and demand in the French sense of the word demand of you the proof. It is totally incongruous to every principle of my mind and every Sentiment of my heart for Threescore Years at least." Jefferson wrote back tactfully, explaining that he had really meant those around Adams, who, he added, were secretly Adams's enemies. Jefferson did not want to revive the political passions of that era, recognizing that they were bound to differ. A few weeks later Jefferson emphasized his position: "The renewal of these old discussions, my friend, would be . . . useless and irksome."[12]

Adams, though, could not quit the subject of what he called "Politicks." In a series of letters he dredged up old topics, vented his resentment against Timothy Pickering, George Washington, and especially Alexander Hamilton, and taunted Jefferson for his early support of the French Revolution. "Where are now in 1813," he wrote, "the Perfection and perfectability of human Nature?" Then came a heartfelt line: "You and I ought not to die, before We have explained ourselves to each other."[13]

In the next several letters Adams talked mainly about religion. He repeatedly invoked the work of Joseph Priestley, even chiding Jefferson for what Adams incorrectly charged was his insufficient attention to Priestley's *History of the Corruptions of Christianity*. Meanwhile, at the foot of Adams's letter of July 15, Abigail wrote that she had been waiting for enough space on one of her husband's pages to "add the regards of an old Friend, which are still cherished and preserved through all the changes and v[ic]issitudes which have taken place." Jefferson replied on August 22, finally reconciled with both John and Abigail. Yet tragedy again struck the Adamses. Just days before Jefferson replied, Adams had written in great sadness that his daughter (whom Jefferson had gotten to know so well in Paris and London) had died, though Jefferson did not receive this letter until mid-September.[14]

Because Jefferson trusted Adams not to turn his letters over to others, he revealed his heterodox religious ideas to his correspondent. He wrote that "priests" (as he always called them) had overly complicated the message of Jesus "in the Platonic mysticisms" because this "constitutes the craft, the power and the profit of the priests. Sweep away their gossamer fabrics of factitious religion, and they would catch no more flies." As Jefferson argued, one should not talk about things no one can believe or understand—here he meant the concept of the Trinity—"for I suppose belief to be the assent of the mind to an intelligible proposition." He wrote that he was sending Adams a copy of "a Syllabus" that summed up his beliefs, the document he had originally written and sent to Benjamin Rush in April 1803 and had shared with no one else except Priestley. He urged Adams to show it only to Abigail and then return it.[15] Adams did so, but requested that Jefferson send him a copy to keep. Jefferson was glad to know that Adams (a theological liberal) approved of his views, and that he shared his most private religious beliefs with Adams was a measure of his respect and trust for him. Adams had read much more extensively in theology and church history and often sent Jefferson detailed discussions of esoteric texts, to which Jefferson never explicitly replied.

On September 20, 1813, a grieving Abigail sent Jefferson a letter describing the death of her only daughter, writing, "You sir, who have been called to seperations of a similar kind, can sympathize with your bereaved Friend." Jefferson, at the end of a long letter on religion to her husband three weeks later, said to both of them that he would remain silent on the subject of their daughter, knowing full well "the depth of the affliction it has caused" and that nothing he could say would lessen the pain. By hard experience he had "ever found time and silence the only medecine, and these but assuage, they never can suppress, the deep-drawn sigh which recollection for ever brings up, until recollection and life are extinguished together."[16]

In the same letter he reiterated his views on the Bible. To get at the heart of Jesus's message, one had first "to strip off the artificial vestments in which they have been muffled by priests" by removing everything except the "very words only of Jesus." Jefferson believed, "There will be found remaining the most sublime and benevolent code of morals which has ever been offered to man." Then he admitted that he had "performed this operation for my own use by cutting verse by verse out of the printed book, and arranging, the matter which is evidently his, and which is as easily distinguishable as diamonds in a dunghill. The result is a [pamphlet] of 46. pages of pure and unsophisticated doctrines."[17] He emphasized the following year the simplicity of Jesus's instructions, remarking, "The doctrines which flowed from the lips of Jesus himself are within the comprehensions of a child."[18]

Around this time, Jefferson found that his hurriedly compiled 1804 collection of scriptural verses no longer fully satisfied him. In 1816, he mentioned to his old friend Charles Thomson that while his first attempt to select the authentic words of Jesus sufficed for his original purposes, he wished to augment the compilation with one that compared key fragments of the Gospels across various languages.

Although Jefferson had never attempted to prove the point, he did say to Thomson that his 1804 pamphlet constituted "a document in proof that I am a <u>real Christian</u>, that is to say, a disciple of the doctrines of Jesus."[19] But Jefferson realized that his exact set of beliefs were his alone, not necessarily congruent with any established religion. He wrote in 1819, "I am of a sect by myself," and he thought anyone should be able to say the same, assuming they read the Gospels according to their own reason.[20] Concerns such as these, and perhaps the urging in 1819 of his old friend and former secretary in France, William Short, that he resume and complete his early work on abstracting the Gospel teaching of Jesus, finally led Jefferson, sometime in early 1820, to finish that project.[21]

Jefferson acquired two copies each of the Gospels in English, French, Latin, and Greek. From these he selected the verses that he believed to be the authentic words of Jesus, then arranged them—in four parallel columns by language—in such fashion as to create a chronological life of Jesus. (The 1804 compilation had been thematic.) Jefferson titled this collection "The Life and Morals of Jesus of Nazareth, Extracted Textually from the Gospels in Greek, Latin, French & English." The result was a rationalist interpretation of the Gospel story, with no virgin birth, no miracles, no resurrection, no claims of divinity on Jesus's part, and no references to anything that smacked of the Trinity. For Jefferson, the simple, unadorned ethical principles of Jesus were sufficient and sublime. He meant this collection, which he had bound, for his private devotional use; he never intended to spread his views, even though the book, published in the twentieth century, would become widely known as *The Jefferson Bible*. Jefferson did not accept the Bible as divinely inspired or as the sole guide to faith. When he used the word "God," he usually attached "Nature," as in "Nature's God." In a long 1823 letter to Adams, he wrote, "I hold (without appeal to revelation) that when we take a view of the Universe, in it's parts general or particular, it is impossible for the human mind not to perceive and feel a conviction of design, consummate skill, and indefinite power in every atom of it's composition. . . . it is impossible, I say, for the human mind not to believe that there is, in all this, design, cause, and effect, up to an ultimate cause, a fabricator of all things from matter and motion, their preserver and regulator. . . . We see, too, evident proofs of the necessity of a superintending power to maintain the Universe in it's course and order."[22] This proof of God's existence and the evident superiority of Jesus's moral teachings formed the basis of Jefferson's religion, a personal faith quite similar to Adams's Unitarianism.

ON NO OTHER ISSUE did Adams and Jefferson diverge more than on the question of what Jefferson called monarchism. Ever since learning of the proposed constitution in 1787, Jefferson had feared the American president wielded too much power and could be reelected for life, whereas Adams had wished to give the office even more power and its holder a longer term. When Jefferson joined George Washington's cabinet, he took exception to Adams's attempts to magnify the pomp and power of the office of the president, to the point of having him addressed, essentially, as royalty. In the hard-fought political conflicts of the 1790s, Jefferson feared Adams and Alexander Hamilton's pro-British, pro-monarchical preferences, and Jefferson knew that Adams, at various points, had disparaged democracy and promoted aristocratic influence. Jefferson, whose background, far more than Adams's, suggested an aristocratic orientation, nevertheless was the most emphatic proponent of democracy among the Founding Fathers, the strongest believer in electoral politics as the ultimate decider of national policy. Once they renewed their correspondence as old men, Adams tried to correct Jefferson's view of him as an uncritical devotee of aristocracy. Jefferson responded with a long letter that laid out his views on that form of government and illustrated his faith in the common man.

Jefferson, who always sought common ground even with opponents, began this letter by agreeing with Adams "that there is a natural aristocracy among men. The grounds of this are virtue and talents." But "there is also an artificial aristocracy founded on wealth and birth, without either virtue or talents. . . . The natural aristocracy I consider as the most precious gift of nature for the instruction, the trusts, and government of society." Jefferson assumed that the natural aristocracy reflected God's will. He posited, "May we not even say that that form of government is best which provides the most effectually for a pure selection of these natural aristoi into the offices of government?"[23] In short, democratically elected government was the natural and rational outcome of the very logic of creation. Adams accepted the existence of "a natural aristocracy" but differed with Jefferson in his belief that members of this natural—as opposed to artificial—aristocracy were also susceptible to corruption and a desire for power. In his view, the false or artificial aristocracy often emerged from the natural aristocracy.[24]

Jefferson suggested that perhaps the differences between Massachusetts and Virginia explained his and Adams's views on natural and artificial aristocracies. Since the late 1770s, Virginia (but not Massachusetts) had disallowed the practices of entail and primogeniture, striking a blow against artificial aristocracy. Also, the Virginia Statute for Religious Freedom, which ended taxpayer support of churches, had vitiated the concept of a clerical aristocracy, which still existed in Massachusetts. Jefferson took pride in his role in these two achievements but lamented his ultimate inability to create free public education in the state. Had the bill he had proposed passed, "Worth and genius would . . . have been sought out from every condition of life, and completely prepared by education for defeating the competition of wealth and birth for public trusts."[25] He saw education as the guarantor of democracy.

Jefferson did not expect Adams to always agree. "I have thus stated my opinion on a point on which we differ, not with a view to controversy, for we are both too old to change opinions which are the result of a long life of inquiry and reflection, but on the suggestion of a former letter of yours, that we ought not to die before we have explained ourselves." To the end Jefferson sought to avoid contention.[26]

ONE SURPRISING ASPECT of Jefferson and Adams's correspondence is how little they commented on contemporary politics and, more specifically, the war raging between the United States and England. Somehow they focused, for the most part, on either the past or the future, on intellectual matters that floated above mundane daily affairs, on the ultimate questions of life and death. They were increasingly aware of their own mortality; having heard that Adams had been ill, Jefferson wrote, "Our machines have now been running for 70. or 80. years, and we must expect that, worn as they are, here a pivot, there a wheel, now a pinion, next a spring, will be giving way, and however we may tinker them up for awhile, all will at length surcease motion."[27]

Adams responded, "I am sometimes afraid that my 'Machine' will not 'surcease motion' soon enough; for I dread nothing so much as 'dying at top' and expiring like . . . Sam. Adams, a Grief and distress to his Family, a weeping helpless Object of Compassion for Years." Anxiety about what we today call dementia was a recurrent theme in their letters. "Bodily decay is gloomy in prospect," noted Jefferson in the summer of 1816, "but of all human contemplations the most abhorrent is body without mind."[28] Fortunately, both maintained vital intellects to the very end.

In another letter, from 1816, Adams asked his correspondent, "Would you go back to your Cradle and live over again Your 70 years?" Jefferson responded, "Yea. I think with you that it is a good world on the whole, that it has been framed on a principle of benevolence, and more pleasure than pain dealt out to us." He understood that others had a less positive view of their lives, but "my temperament is sanguine. I steer my bark with Hope in the head, leaving Fear astern. My hopes indeed sometimes fail; but not oftener than the forebodings of the gloomy."[29] Whatever he may have thought in the deepest, most private recesses of his mind, Jefferson never expressed regrets about his life.

Both men had endured the deaths of family members, Jefferson more often than Adams, and both saw great value in the Christian expectation of life after death. At this late point, the afterlife now meant primarily a reunion with loved ones. Contemplating his eventual existence "in the future World," Adams in 1818 wrote that in that heavenly abode he hoped to "meet my Wife [though Abigail was still alive at this time] and Friends, Ancestors and Posterity, Sages ancient and modern." Then turning humorous, he said, "I believe I could get over all my Objections to meeting Alex Hamilton and Tim Pick[ering], if I could perceive a Symptom of sincere Penitence in either." Upon receiving Adams's heartbroken letter of October 20, 1818, announcing his grief upon the death of the "dear Partner of my Life for fifty four Years as a Wife," Jefferson sent a characteristic response, suggesting that "time and silence are the only medecines." He added, "It is of some comfort to us both that the term is not very distant at which we are to deposit, in the same cerement, our sorrows and suffering bodies, and to ascend in essence to an ecstatic meeting with the friends we have loved and lost and whom we shall still love and never lose again. God bless you and support you under your heavy affliction."[30]

As do all older people in full command of their memories, Adams and Jefferson often thought back to those stirring times before and during the American Revolution, and both feared that the true nature of those events would fade when they and their few like-minded contemporaries were no longer around. "Who shall write the history of the American revolution?" Adams asked in 1815. "Who can write it? Who will ever be able to write it? The most essential documents, the debates and deliberations in Congress from 1774 to 1783 were all in secret, and are now lost forever." Jefferson shared Adams's concern. To the first question, he answered, "Nobody; except it's external facts. All it's councils, designs and discussions, having been conducted by Congress with closed doors, no member, as far as I know, having even made notes of them, these, which are the life and soul of history must for ever be unknown."[31] Three years later Jefferson wrote, "It would moreover be as difficult to say at what moment the revolution began, and what incident set it in motion." Adams agreed: "In my Opinion it began as early as the first Plantation [settlement] of the Country."[32] Later Adams told Jefferson, "I hope one day your letters will all be published in volumes; they will not always appear Orthodox," he allowed, "or liberal in politicks; but they will exhibit a Mass of Taste, Sense, Literature and Science, presented in a sweet simplicity and a neat elegance of Stile, which will be read with delight in future ages."[33]

LOOKING BACK OVER the history of the still-young nation, Jefferson and Adams remained mostly optimistic about the future. Speaking primarily about the influence of the American example on Europe, Jefferson revealed in 1821, "I shall not die without a hope that light and liberty are on a steady advance. . . . the flames kindled on the 4th. of July 1776. have spread over too much of the globe to be extinguished by the feeble engines of despotism."[34] Yet he wrote these words after the nation had survived a dire threat to its survival, the combined crises of the Panic of 1819 and the controversy over slavery in Missouri. Here Jefferson and Adams did not forgo talk of contemporary politics. Jefferson had long been an opponent of banks, which he thought led to inflation, speculation, and corruption, and he blamed them for the severe economic recession. From his perspective, the "bubble" had burst, with "disastrous effects." He reported that land prices collapsed to such an extent that acreage could not fetch the equivalent of a year's rent. His personal finances had been affected, especially because he had planned on land sales to reduce his debt and put Monticello back on a profitable footing. But far more was at stake than his own interests; all of the "Southwardly and Westwardly" states were in economic distress.[35]

The simultaneous controversy over the admission of the Missouri Territory as a state greatly magnified these worries. The sticking point was over the extension of slavery. There were eleven slave states and eleven free states, and with the more populous free states dominating the House of Representatives, the control of Congress hung in the balance. Jefferson, who had committed his life to the creation and continuation of the union, was extraordinarily upset over the possible consequences of the debate. Adams had written in late November about a number of threats—the "Clouds look Black and thick," he had said—including the Spanish treaty, import duties, a proposed bankruptcy act, and the issue of "Missouri Slavery." The tone of Jefferson's reply conveys real fear. "The banks, bankrupt law, manufacturers, Spanish treaty are nothing. These are occurrences which like the waves in a storm will pass under the ship. But the Missouri question is a breaker on which we lose the Missouri country by revolt, and what more, God only knows."[36] A contemporary visitor to Monticello in November 1820, Maryland Quaker Isaac Briggs, recalled how Jefferson seemed preoccupied with the possibility that the union would fracture and the "horrors of civil war" would sweep the land.[37]

Jefferson, along with Adams and most of the Founding Fathers, had long feared that slavery would tear the nation asunder, and as a southerner Jefferson had personally witnessed the violent passions of those who defended the institution. Adams responded to Jefferson's letter with the hope that the Missouri issue would pass like "the other Waves under the Ship" but admitted that he was "Cassandra enough to dream that another Hamilton, another Burr might rend this mighty Fabric in twain."[38] The Compromise of 1820 ended the crisis, but Jefferson continued to fear the possible dangers of slavery, including slave revolt. So did Adams, who wrote, "I have been so terrified with this Phenomenon that I constantly said in former times to the Southern Gentlemen that I cannot comprehend this object; I must leave it to you. I will vote for forcing no measure against your judgements."[39]

BECAUSE JEFFERSON and Adams realized that most of the history of the American Revolution resided only in the minds of the few remaining Founders, they believed it was important that they talk to members of the younger generations. Each sent young men to visit the other. Indeed, Jefferson's last letter to Adams asked him to permit a visit from Jefferson's grandson, Thomas Jefferson Randolph. "Like other young people," Jefferson wrote just weeks before his death, "he wishes to be able, in the winter nights of old age, to recount to those around him what he has heard and learnt of the Heroic age preceding his birth, and which of the Argonauts particularly he was in time to have seen."[40] Adams once explained to Jefferson, "All the Literary Gentlemen of this part of the Country have an Ambitious Curiosity to see the Philosopher and Statesman of Monticello—and they all apply to me for Introductions."[41]

Two of the literary gentlemen Adams recommended were Francis C. Gray and George Ticknor. Traveling together in February 1815, Gray and Ticknor visited Jefferson, and each left memorable portraits of the man

Adams was already calling the Sage of Monticello.[42] Jefferson greatly enjoyed their company, especially that of Ticknor, who, as Jefferson told Adams, was "the best bibliograph I have met with." Having just sold his great library to the United States to replace the Library of Congress recently burned by the British army, Jefferson was already buying replacement books and had commissioned young Ticknor to seek out particular titles. "I cannot live without books," Jefferson said to Adams, "but fewer will suffice where amusement, and not use, is the only future object."[43]

Gray described the quality of Jefferson's library, deeming the collection of works on North and South America as undoubtedly the finest in the world. He also remarked on the chairs in Jefferson's parlor. "They had leather bottoms stuffed with hair, but the bottoms were completely worn through and the hair sticking out in all directions."[44] Jefferson might have been scrimping on décor and his personal attire, but in addition to planning to purchase new books, he still served good wine. Ticknor was fascinated by the museum-like entrance hall to Monticello, its walls filled with "curiosities," including artifacts from the Lewis and Clark Expedition, an Indian map drawn on leather, mammoth bones, and European paintings. Surprised by Jefferson's height, he commented on the "dignity in his appearance, and ease and graciousness in his manners." Ticknor acknowledged that he enjoyed the dinner with members of Jefferson's family: "I assure you I have seldom met a pleasanter party." Jefferson was pleased to learn that Ticknor would soon travel in Europe, telling him that he had once expected to spend more time in Italy and in fact proceed to Sicily and Greece, but his mission to France had ended earlier than expected. Ticknor believed the former president was "an extraordinary character."[45]

THE PANIC OF 1819, the Missouri Compromise, the arrival in their homes of young men eager to learn the history of the American nation—all prompted Jefferson and Adams to ponder the future. Yet remarkably, in their correspondence they did not discuss slavery itself, despite the clear threat it posed to the union. Jefferson had thought and written about slavery his entire life. In the 1820s, he owned more than two hundred slaves. Except for several brief comments during the Missouri Crisis, the two most thoughtful of the Founding Fathers did not examine the subject. Publicly, Adams did say that he would leave the issue to so-called southern gentlemen to settle, but in the privacy of his correspondence with Jefferson, Adams—not known for avoiding controversy—strangely never raised it. Jefferson could not be expected to discuss his relationship with

Sally Hemings, but why did he not broach the practical difficulties presented by emancipation, or a procedure to effect colonization, or even the moral complexities of the issue? Had Jefferson decided, at this stage in his life, that such a conversation served little purpose? Why did he not seek to explain to Adams his decision not to manumit his own slaves? As much as Jefferson wrote and revealed about himself, in the end aspects of his character, personality, and beliefs remain inscrutable.

29

Living with Paradox

T HOMAS JEFFERSON'S FIRST and last memories involved both a
slave and a pillow. His first was of being carried on a pillow by one
of his family's bondsmen, who was riding on horseback, transporting him in 1746 to Tuckahoe, the plantation home of William
Randolph, where Jefferson's family resided for several years. His final conscious moment occurred at about 10:00 a.m. on July 4, 1826, when trusted
slave Burwell Colbert alone recognized Jefferson's attempt to communicate and adjusted his head on his pillow. Jefferson, one of three surviving
signers of the Declaration of Independence, died shortly before 1:00 p.m.
that afternoon, just hours before John Adams, who was about six hundred
miles away, in Quincy.[1] Contemporaries heralded the coincidental death
of the two patriarchs and signers on the fiftieth anniversary of congressional approval of the declaration as a sign from God of the special destiny of
the nation. But authorship of that document proclaiming liberty and
equality for all raises profound questions about Jefferson, who simultaneously both abhorred and benefited from the institution of slavery.

More than any other major Founder, Jefferson spoke and acted against
slavery. During his first session in the Virginia House of Burgesses in 1769,
he had tried, along with a much older delegate, Richard Bland, to make
manumission easier; the other members only excoriated them. In 1770
Jefferson represented a mulatto named Samuel Howell, who was pleading
for his freedom; Jefferson attempted to argue that all men were born free,
but the judge summarily threw the case out and ruled against Howell.[2]
Jefferson attacked slavery in 1774 in his *A Summary View of the Rights of
British America* and in his draft of the Declaration wrote of the "sacred
rights of life & liberty" denied to Africans—but Congress excised the passage. In 1784 Jefferson had proposed the abolition of slavery after 1800 in

all the newly gained territory west of the Appalachians and to the Mississippi, including the southern portion, but Congress defeated that proposal by one vote. The 1787 (English) publication of his *Notes on the State of Virginia*, which contained derogatory (but also commonplace) remarks on the supposed inferiority of blacks, nevertheless made a blistering attack on slavery so provocative that Jefferson attempted to restrict the book's release in the United States. And in 1806, in his second term as president, he successfully lobbied Congress to pass legislation to ban the importation of slaves. In many private letters Jefferson attacked slavery as a moral evil. In short, his contemporaries knew him primarily as an enemy of the institution.

Yet Jefferson owned many slaves, buying and selling them and freeing only six favored ones during his lifetime. In his will, he freed five more, all members of one extended slave family. For more than three decades he had an intimate relationship with a slave woman from this family, Sally Hemings. Slaves largely built and maintained Monticello, and the profits of their labors supported Jefferson and his dependents. Jefferson, in short, was an antislavery slave owner, an often personally kind master who nevertheless did not manumit the vast majority of his slaves upon his death. Other than by rendering a simplistic and presentist charge of hypocrisy, how are we to make sense of this Jeffersonian paradox?

JEFFERSON INHERITED slightly more than 30 slaves from his father, and by "natural increase" that number had grown to 52 in 1774, when he inherited another 135 from his father-in-law, John Wayles. Suddenly Jefferson was among the largest slaveholders in Virginia. Over the years the number of bondspeople he owned fluctuated, but averaged about two hundred, over half of them living at Monticello. The rest lived and toiled at his Bedford County property, with its better soil for tobacco cultivation. For his entire life—including the short period when he was a practicing lawyer—Jefferson's income depended primarily on the labor of his slaves. He may have often expressed opposition to slavery and always supported widening democratic opportunities for the white population, but he lived as a slave-owning southern aristocrat.

Jefferson seems to have been quite removed from the farm labor performed by his slaves until 1794, when he resigned his position as secretary of state and returned to Monticello for, he believed, the rest of his life. Just as he had been largely an armchair traveler before going to Paris in 1784, Jefferson had been mostly an armchair farmer, employing overseers to manage the agricultural operations at Monticello and his Bedford County property. He had read widely about agricultural reform. During his abortive first retirement, however, he began to theorize about and put into practice a system of crop rotation to increase his income. He took even more interest in his new nail factory, in part because he could apply his fascination with measuring productivity more easily to the regularity of a factory than to the vagaries of agriculture. Moreover, he saw the nail factory as a place to instill discipline, industriousness, and trustworthiness in his slaves, using it as a filter for identifying talented, dutiful young bondsmen whom he then had trained for artisanal positions. Many of his skilled slaves were central to the demolishing and rebuilding of the main house at Monticello, another project he undertook at the time.

Jefferson gave up on crop rotation. He also embarked on and soon after abandoned wheat cultivation, returning to tobacco, even though, as he admitted in 1801, "I never saw a leaf of tobo. packed in my life."[3] Not until he retired from the presidency in March 1809 and returned to Monticello for good did Jefferson become much more interested in and knowledgeable about, in an experiential sense, the agricultural work on his plantations.

As the newly retired Jefferson rode around his property, he tended to defer to his various overseers on anything pertaining to his crops, but not when it came to punishing his slaves. He demanded minimal physical discipline and, when away from Monticello, always cautioned his overseers against harsh treatment. He was, by the standards of the day, a lenient owner. We have no credible evidence that he himself ever administered physical discipline, though some overseers clearly used the whip on his behalf more than Jefferson cared to acknowledge.[4] Instead of threatening violence, he preferred to incentivize his slaves, holding out the carrots of what he called "premiums" (bonuses) and increased autonomy. He provided more or less the standard rations of food and clothing, paid for the services of doctors and midwives when needed, regularly mended the slave dwellings, and after the 1790s moved away from larger, dormitory-type quarters to family-sized cabins. He allowed his slaves to rest on Sundays, though they used the time to do their laundry, cultivate their garden plots, and care for their poultry or hogs. Jefferson typically purchased vegetables, eggs, poultry, and hog meat from his slaves, providing them a source of income. He gave them four days off for Christmas. Evidently many of the slaves at Monticello practiced Christianity; though Jefferson did not actively promote religion among them, neither did he forbid it. Monticello's slaves, like bondspeople elsewhere, also sang, played musical instruments, and danced, all ways to add meaning and a modicum of pleasure to their lives.[5]

Jefferson never doubted that well-treated slaves were more productive, so a good measure of self-interest underlay his relative benevolence. In fact, he believed that in general—not just with regard to slavery—Providence had ordered the world so that doing good was to one's economic advantage. His insistence that slaves be adequately fed and not overworked and that pregnant women receive close attention embodied his beliefs: this treatment was both moral and conducive to higher productivity and profits. Jefferson worried that slave overseers often did not see the long-term benefits of leniency. As he confided to one correspondent in 1819, he feared "that the overseers do not permit the women to devote as much time as is necessary to the care of their children: that they view their labor as the 1st object and the raising their child but as secondary. I consider the labor of a breeding woman [that is, one young enough to be pregnant] as no object, and that a child raised every 2. years is of more profit than the crop of the best laboring man. in this, as in all other cases, providence has made our interest & our duties coincide perfectly."[6] On occasion he moved slaves between Monticello and Poplar Forest, though he concentrated the skilled artisans among them at Monticello.

For Jefferson, owning slaves was a means to an end—improving and sustaining Monticello—and never an end in itself. Unlike some other planters, including his father-in-law, John Wayles, Jefferson did not buy and sell slaves speculatively in search of profits. Over the course of his adult life, he bought about 20 slaves, usually to keep slave families intact, and although he sold or transferred over 150 slaves over several decades, he did so during financial emergencies or to help various family members, usually his daughters, by giving them bondspeople. When he did disperse slaves, he did not divide husbands and wives or separate children under twelve from their mothers.[7] Enduring and intact slave families were the norm at Monticello.

At the time, limiting sales to moments of perceived economic necessity was the hallmark of a benevolent slaveholder. As was common among planters of the age, Jefferson used the word "family" to denote all the members of his household—his biological family as well as the slaves he owned and considered dependents. Likewise he occasionally used the word "servant" to refer to a slave, in small measure because the King James Bible employed that usage. Jefferson envisioned his familial role as that of the biblical patriarch, responsible for caring for everyone else. To him, this was the duty of a man of his social position.

OTHER THAN URSULA and George Granger, both of whom Jefferson had purchased in 1773 because his wife, Martha, had wanted her former favorite house slave with her again, all the other slaves in favorable positions were members of the extended Elizabeth (Betty) Hemings clan. Until her death, Ursula ruled the kitchen, smokehouse, and wash house (laundry), and her husband, known as Great George after he and Ursula had a son also named George, handled most agricultural matters at the estate, even serving as the overseer at Monticello from 1791 until his death in November 1799. Their son ran both the blacksmith shop and the nailery, while Ursula was the wet nurse for at least several of Martha's children.

John Wayles had owned Betty Hemings, born in 1735, and after the death of his third wife, he took Betty as his concubine—at the time the term merely referred to a substitute wife and had no particularly derogatory or salacious connotation. With her, Wayles fathered at least six children, including Sally, born in 1773.[8] The children of Hemings and Wayles, all slaves because of their mother's legal status, were the half siblings of Jefferson's wife, Martha. All seem to have recognized, but never commented on, Wayles's second family. This practice was quite common at the time, and indeed white men who were discreet about their second families were not criticized.[9] After Betty and her family became Jefferson's property in 1774, her son Bob quickly replaced Jupiter as Jefferson's personal attendant and traveling companion, and Bob's older brother Martin became essentially the butler of Monticello. Betty's son James accompanied Jefferson to France, where he learned French cooking.

Over the following decades, all the skilled slaves at Monticello—with the exception of the Grangers—were Hemingses, who numbered almost fifty by the time of Jefferson's death in 1826. Jefferson's wife Martha clearly approved of the ascendency of the Hemings family, appreciating their competency and personally comfortable with Betty and her children. Visitors commented that most of the slaves they came into contact with were light skinned, not necessarily realizing that they all belonged to the same large family. The Duc de La Rochefoucauld-Liancourt, after his stay at Monticello in 1796, wrote that he had seen "at Mr. Jeffersons, slaves, who, neither in point of colour nor features, shewed the least trace of their original descent."[10]

Treated as a caste above the other slaves, members of the Hemings clan enjoyed slightly better housing and more generous clothing allowances.[11] Unlike the domestic slaves at George Washington's Mount Vernon, Jefferson's house servants did not wear livery but rather had substantial freedom of attire, although he expected them to be neat and clean.[12] The Hemings women were exempted from the harvest-time labor expected of all other slaves. Several of the skilled Hemings men could even hire themselves out when Jefferson was away from Monticello for more than a few weeks. An unusual number of the Hemingses were literate; Jefferson's grandchildren apparently tutored them, and he never objected.[13] He saw the convenience of having literate bondspeople who could read letters of instruction and correspond with him about plantation needs. By all accounts, the members of the Hemings clan recognized and enjoyed their elevated status. Perhaps the most privileged of all was Betty Hemings's grandson, Burwell Colbert, who later served as Monticello's butler and overall house manager, holding all the keys; toward the end, he was also Jefferson's personal servant. Starting in his twenties Colbert received an annual gratuity of $20, a large sum at that time.[14]

Jefferson, in daily contact with the Hemingses, appears to have read their comparative contentment as validation of his style as a slave master. Believing emancipation to be decades away, since the younger generation of southern political leaders was not rejecting the institution as he had hoped—he wrote in 1805, "I have long since given up the expectation of any early provision for the extinguishment of slavery among us"—Jefferson was sure that improving the status of his slaves, however slightly, was the hallmark of benevolence.[15] But he seems to have experienced relatively little of the conflict between slave workers, on the one hand, and owners and overseers, on the other, that characterized many plantations, and he seems to have seldom—possibly never—realized that even slaves living in better conditions resented their bondage and wanted their freedom. In a sense, Jefferson had created a plantation environment that largely insulated him from the common instances of slave resistance and thus from the inhumanity of the institution. Surrounded mostly by the skilled, motivated Hemings slaves, Jefferson may have subtly backed away from some of the more negative judgments of African Americans he had expressed in *Notes on the State of Virginia* in 1787, while at the same time arriving at a slightly more positive assessment of slavery as an institution.

Jefferson never came to accept blacks as the equals of whites, but he became somewhat more tentative in his appraisal, moving away from his initially harsh and rigid conclusions. In 1809 he wrote, "No person living wishes more sincerely than I do, to see a complete refutation of the doubts I have myself entertained and expressed on the grade of understanding allotted to them by nature, and to find that in this respect they are on a par with ourselves." Showing more awareness of what slavery actually meant for slaves, he explained, "My doubts were the result of personal observation on the limited sphere of my own State, where the opportunities for the development of their genius were not favorable. I expressed them therefore with great hesitation." He offered a forthright statement on the inalienable rights of black men and women, though his prejudice was still manifest: "whatever be their degree of talent it is no measure of their rights. Because Sir Isaac Newton was superior to others in understanding, he was not therefore lord of the person or property of others."[16]

Though this letter did not suggest it, Jefferson did revise upward his view of the mental capabilities of African Americans, likely due to his increased interactions and familiarity with the Hemingses (and the Grangers); his daily proximity to them surely had a greater impact on his attitudes than had his famous epistolary exchange with black mathematician Benjamin Banneker. Yet, as he moderated his judgments of African Americans, he did the same for the institution that trapped them. By the nineteenth century, he certainly was no longer the man who had written in 1786 that slaves suffered "a bondage, one hour of which is fraught with more misery than ages of that which [white American revolutionaries] rose in rebellion [against England] to oppose."[17] One may be prompted to wonder whether Jefferson saw the Hemingses' evident ability as the result of the "white blood" coursing through their veins. We simply do not know. We should at least recall that he also had great confidence in the competency of the Grangers, who were not mulatto.

NONE OF JEFFERSON's slave interactions could have been more important to him than his intimate relationship with Sally Hemings, which started when she joined his Parisian household in 1787 and spanned almost the final four decades of his life. Sometime in the latter months of her stay in Paris, Sally and Jefferson became close, probably even intimate. It seems that by mutual agreement, she agreed to forgo life as a free woman in France to return with Jefferson to Virginia, having apparently extracted from him a promise to treat her well and eventually free any children they might have. The testimony of one of their younger children suggests that Sally was pregnant when she arrived back in Virginia, but that child, if indeed born in 1790, apparently was either stillborn or died very soon after birth. (A diverging family tradition holds that one Thomas C. Woodson was that child, but late-twentieth-century scientific investigation of his bloodline suggests no genetic link between him and Jefferson.)

Shortly after Jefferson returned to Virginia with his family in November 1789, he learned that he had been appointed secretary of state and quickly discovered that his daughter Patsy (Martha) had become engaged to Thomas Mann Randolph. Even though she had served as Patsy's maid in Paris, Jefferson did not include Sally when he gave his newly married daughter twenty-seven slaves on February 21, 1790.[18] Nor later, in 1797, when his younger daughter, Maria, married, was Sally among the thirty-one slaves included in her dowry, which is perhaps more surprising since Sally had gone to Eppington in 1784 to serve as Maria's childhood maid.[19] Normally Sally would have been given to Maria as the latter began her married life. Jefferson defied convention by ensuring that the young slave remained at Monticello.

However and whenever their relationship started, it does appear that by the early 1790s Sally had become Jefferson's concubine. Interracial, unofficial "marriages" were hardly unknown in Albemarle County; indeed, Sally's own parentage is evidence of the practice. One of her siblings ended up in a similar relationship. In 1792, her older sister Mary had asked Jefferson to sell her to a white Charlottesville merchant, Thomas Bell, who had previously leased her. Jefferson agreed, and Mary lived with Bell until his death in 1800 and bore him two children. Bell freed Mary and their offspring, bequeathing to them all his property. Neither Sally nor Jefferson would have thought their own relationship in any way unusual. Sally's official duties at Monticello were light; she probably minded Jefferson's private rooms and wardrobe. In Paris she had stayed with his laundress for five weeks, learning how to wash delicate and fine clothing, and she already had the skills of a seamstress. Both would have prepared her perfectly for her Monticello duties. Jefferson resigned his position as secretary of state on the last day of 1793, so he was living at Monticello throughout 1794 and 1795 and presumably fathered Sally's child born in 1795, though this infant died in 1797.

Over the next thirteen years Sally gave birth to five children, four of whom survived to adulthood. Jefferson was demonstrably present at Monticello nine months prior to each of these births, and Sally had no other children. (Sally was with Jefferson only at Monticello—she never joined him in Philadelphia, New York City, or Washington, DC, or at

Poplar Forest.) The four children who survived—Beverley, Harriet, Madison, and Eston—all later held privileged positions in the household. Jefferson eventually freed all of them, the latter two in his will, Beverley and Harriet by simply allowing them to run away; he even arranged a stage ticket for Harriet.[20] Since Sally was three-fourths white, by Jefferson's own calculations, any children that she had would be white, although in Virginia and elsewhere in the South, not color but the status of the mother determined a child's legal status.[21] Jefferson never commented on the preposterousness of this situation. At least one of their sons bore an uncanny resemblance to his father, so much so that, according to Jefferson's grandson, Thomas Jefferson Randolph, at a distance he might have been mistaken for him.[22] The white Jefferson household never spoke of these matters.

For the first decade and a half of their relationship, Sally seems to have lived in one of the stone houses along Mulberry Row originally built for white artisans working on Monticello. After the completion of the south terrace about the time of Jefferson's retirement from the presidency, Sally apparently moved into one of the three slave rooms built underneath it and directly connected to Monticello.[23] She could easily move along the underground corridor and up the steps of the private stairway directly to Jefferson's quarters. Since she took care of his wardrobe, this might not have raised suspicions, though it strains credulity to think that Jefferson's daughter Martha, living permanently at Monticello after 1809, was unaware of the situation. Perhaps the sexual intimacy between Jefferson and Sally ceased after Martha and her children moved permanently to Monticello in 1809; Sally bore no more children after that date.

We can never know the exact nature of the relationship between Jefferson and Sally Hemings. All the evidence indicates that it was monogamous, and since Sally's kin surrounded Jefferson at Monticello, any mistreatment of her would likely have drawn repercussions of some kind: Hemingses would have shown disgruntlement, run away, or asked to be sold. Indeed, Annette Gordon-Reed, the closest student of their relationship, argues that Thomas Jefferson and Sally Hemings, as unlikely as it might seem, probably had genuine mutual affection.[24] Despite their drastically unequal educational backgrounds, they shared memories of Paris, and Jefferson was a gentle, kind, unfailingly polite man. We know nothing of Sally's personality, but she was reputedly pretty, if not beautiful, by the standards of white society (in 1847, the slave Isaac Jefferson recalled her as being "mighty near white" and "very handsome, long straight hair down her back"[25]). She also bore a striking resemblance to her half sister, Jefferson's deceased wife.

In *Notes on the State of Virginia* Jefferson had famously disparaged Africans for the "eternal monotony" of their blackness, which veiled blushing, and their kinky hair and inelegant form. Surely Sally's beauty must have caused him to rethink those hateful passages, even though she was mulatto. He had also cast doubt on Africans' ability to truly love: "love seems with them to be more an eager desire, than a tender delicate mixture of sentiment and sensation."[26] He could not have believed this of Sally unless, again, he thought her status as a mulatto set her apart from most other blacks. How did he live with such contradictions? Of course, they could not publicly acknowledge their feelings, so in a sense, he did not really have to—except perhaps privately. Even though Jefferson doted on his white children and grandchildren, he scrupulously avoided acknowledging paternity of Sally's offspring and showed them no special affection. Perhaps they always stayed in the slave quarters and never had the run of Monticello, a distance Jefferson wanted to maintain. In 1798, William Short had written to suggest that racial amalgamation would result in lighter-skinned slaves whose attractiveness and similarity to whites would lessen racial prejudice and ease the path toward emancipation.[27] Though Jefferson never responded, in the final months of his life he wrote to Short that he still harbored "great aversion" to race mixing.[28] Did he believe Sally was so nearly white that his relationship with her was not truly an instance of miscegenation? He had written to Edward Coles in 1814 that blacks' "amalgamation with the other colour produces a degradation to which no lover of his country, no lover of excellence in the human character can innocently consent."[29] How could he honestly think this? Was racial ideology trumping his own life experience? Did he even recognize the apparent contradiction? We simply cannot know, but it is clear enough why Jefferson has been charged with hypocrisy.

At his death Jefferson, in a codicil to his will, freed Sally's two children who still lived at Monticello (Madison and Eston) and successfully petitioned the Virginia legislature to exempt them from the 1806 law that required manumitted slaves to leave the state within one year. By the same codicil he also freed butler and valet Burwell Colbert, John Hemings (Sally's brother), and Joe Fossett (one of Sally's nephews). He did not legally free Sally, but he orally arranged with Martha to unofficially free her (and her nephew, Wormley Hughes). This allowed Sally to remain in the state and spared Jefferson the possible embarrassment of petitioning the legislature for her to remain in Albemarle County. Of course, Sally was probably not terribly worried about Jefferson's personal embarrassment in this situation. She moved to a small house near the University of Virginia and lived there with Madison and Eston, who worked in Charlottesville as carpenters. Census documents indicate that Sally was later considered free. After her death in 1835, her two sons moved to Ohio.[30]

Despite Jefferson's discretion, the claim that he had an improper relationship with one of his slaves became widely known as a result of newspaper attacks begun in 1802 by James Callender, out of anger that Jefferson had not granted him a government sinecure in Richmond. Callender likely picked up the story from gossip in Charlottesville, for some had probably noticed that Sally's children always came within nine months of Jefferson's presence. Or perhaps slaves at Monticello who were not of the privileged Hemings caste spread rumors about Sally's secret relationship with her master. Political enemies of the president ballyhooed the charges, wrote doggerel about "Black Sally," sang off-color songs about a scandalous relationship, and did everything in their power to besmirch Jefferson's reputation. The charges upset and humiliated Jefferson's daughters and other family members, but Jefferson coolly ignored them, never replying or offering a denial, and acted as though no suspicions had ever surfaced. He did not end his relationship with Sally, and in fact her last two sons were born after Callender's initial exposé. Jefferson's immediate family did not deny that mixed-race people lived on the mountain, but they suggested that others—temporary workmen at Monticello, perhaps one of the Carr brothers (Jefferson's nephews), or random visitors—had fathered Sally's children. No one in Jefferson's white family ever admitted to his long-term relationship with Sally, which only gained widespread acceptance among scholars at the turn of the twenty-first century.[31]

NOTHING ABOUT JEFFERSON upsets modern readers more than his failure to emancipate his own slaves or work actively to end slavery completely. How can we explain these failures? As he saw it, the law and his personal finances limited his range of action. Jefferson believed wholeheartedly that only the electoral vote, not the moral dictate of elites, could effect lasting societal change, and though he had hoped earlier in his career that the generation after his—reared in an atmosphere of political liberty—would expand the concept of liberty to include general emancipation, that did not occur. If anything, slavery was more firmly entrenched in 1800 or 1820 than it had been in 1770. While a good number of slaveholders had personally experienced a political or religious conversion in the two decades after the American Revolution and had voluntarily freed some if not all of their slaves, a 1792 Virginia law, allowing creditors to confiscate slaves freed by their debtors, limited Jefferson's ability to do the same: Jefferson still shouldered the obligations inherited from John Wayles.[32] When Jefferson became president, he initially assumed he could live on his government salary and use the profits from his plantations to pay off his creditors. Once he had "dischare[d]" his debts and could "accumulate property," he wrote to his son-in-law Thomas Mann Randolph, enigmatically, "on my retirement . . . I may be subjected to an expence the more difficult to be controuled on account of the motives which will subject me to it. I must leave to the day to provide it's own remedy."[33] Might he have been referring to his future expectation of emancipating his slaves at considerable expense, perhaps because he believed the vast majority should be colonized and supplied the wherewithal to support themselves in earnest endeavor?

If the eventual emancipation of his slaves had been a fleeting or inchoate plan in Jefferson's mind, his expectations were thwarted, at least on the grounds of financial necessity. The expenses of the President's House, including the dinners that were essential to his ability to govern, completely consumed his salary. Moreover, his plantation income was less than anticipated; absent his close supervision, for instance, his nail factory did not produce regular profits. The situation only worsened with time, as his own embargo policies restricted tobacco sales, as did the eventual War of 1812, and renewed infestations of Hessian flies reduced output in the years following that conflict. His soils were depleted, and there were bad crop years, especially in 1816, when Jefferson complained repeatedly that it had been extraordinarily cold and dry, with "the summer . . . as cold as a moderate winter."[34] Still, through it all, he maintained his various indulgences, including wine and salad oils.

He had written earlier in 1816 that the weather "baffled" him because the "spring has been unusually dry and cold"; to that point the month of May had been, on average, ten degrees colder than normal.[35] Crop yields fell accordingly. Later Jefferson analyzed six years of his own meteorological data and discovered that the overall annual temperature for 1816 was one degree colder than normal, with the July mean a full four degrees less than usual.[36] He did not know that the previous year, on April 10, 1815, the volcano Tambora in Indonesia had erupted with incredible fury, killing as many as 100,000 nearby islanders and tossing thousands of tons of volcanic ash and dust into the upper atmosphere. The result was three years of extravagantly red sunsets, lower global temperatures, and famines that killed hundreds of thousands of people across the planet.[37]

Another law, passed in 1806, drastically circumscribed Jefferson's ability to free his slaves, even had his finances improved. Fearing the growing population of free blacks due to manumission, the Virginia House of Delegates required all slaves freed after May 1, 1806, to leave the state or forfeit their freedom.[38] Jefferson had long believed that it was morally irresponsible to free slaves without giving them land, tools, draft animals, and enough financial backing to sustain themselves for the first year or two. He appears never to have abandoned the hope that the federal government would underwrite the immense cost of emancipation and colonization; nor did he ever seem to realize that this was not remotely probable. Jefferson was not completely consistent in his belief that all emancipated slaves must be mandatorily colonized outside the United States. He may have come to believe that a tiny minority of skilled, mulatto slaves—like the Hemingses—could be exempted. If he did, it would have been because of their light skin, not their potentially greater contributions to the nation's society and economy.

Even if Jefferson could have paid off his debts, the new law meant that he could not distribute his land even to a few of his freed people. To responsibly emancipate his slaves, he would have to help almost all of them leave the state and purchase land elsewhere. Where would he find the necessary funds? He owned a good amount of land, but the persisting economic decline in Virginia meant that there were no buyers, and prices had collapsed. Absent government funding, Jefferson did not have the resources to establish freed slaves as productive farmers on their own land in the Midwest, much less somewhere in the West Indies, which until the end of his life he considered the best home for those colonized: "greatly preferable," he wrote, "to the mixture of colour here."[39] Of course, he could have accepted the possibility of a mixed-race society to begin with, given that he was already living in one.

Financial constraints arose from within Jefferson's own (white) family too. He believed profoundly that heads of families had an obligation to care for their dependents, and by the time he retired from the presidency, his daughter Martha's marriage to Thomas Mann Randolph was falling to pieces. Randolph suffered from depression and other undiagnosed afflictions, and always moody, he could become unpredictably angry and violent. He found it difficult to maintain friendships, in marked contrast with his father-in-law. Overseer Edmund Bacon called Randolph a "strange" and "very eccentric" man.[40] In 1809, with her marriage faltering and Randolph in financial difficulty, Martha brought her eight children to live at Monticello, and Jefferson took responsibility for their care from then on. He also had two widowed sisters, and others also expected the family patriarch to support them. Jefferson did not hesitate to assume what he considered his sacred duty to his family. Given this sense of responsibility and the 1792 and 1806 Virginia laws, Jefferson likely believed himself caught in a vise with no escape.

OTHERS, HOWEVER, could do what Jefferson could not, including people he knew well. Edward Coles, born in Albemarle County on December 15, 1786, into a wealthy slaveholding family, grew up on Enniscorthy, the elegant plantation where Jefferson and his own family had rested overnight in 1781 when fleeing the British troops who had rushed up Monticello Mountain. Coles attended William & Mary College, where he first encountered serious antislavery views, and later, around 1806 or 1807, he came to oppose slavery personally. That year, upon his father's death, Coles inherited a small plantation of 782 acres and about twenty slaves, whom he soon considered moving to the Midwest and freeing there (by the 1806 Virginia law, if freed in that state, they would have had to leave). His family and other matters—including an appointment in 1810 as President James Madison's private secretary and the War of 1812—intervened, and Coles remained a reluctant slave owner. By 1814 he decided that he had to act to end slavery, not just in his own life but in the South as a whole.[41] Knowing and admiring Jefferson and considering him the preeminent spokesman for liberty and antislavery among the Founders, Coles screwed up his courage, took pen in hand, and wrote a passionate letter to Jefferson on July 31, 1814.

After opening with some words about his trepidation in writing, Coles arrived at his concern: "a general emancipation of the Slaves of Virginia." Saying there was no need to tell Jefferson about the rights of all men, he stated, "My object is to entreat and beseech you to exert your knowledge and influence, in devising, and getting into operation, some plan for the gradual emancipation of Slavery." Coles believed that such a task could be performed "more successfully . . . by the revered Fathers of all our political and social blessings" than by any current leaders, and "it is a duty that devolves particularly on you, from your known philosophical and enlarged view of subjects, and from the principles you have professed and practiced through a long and useful life, preeminently distinguished." Though Jefferson no longer held office, Coles emphasized, "in the calm of this retirement you might, most beneficially to society, and with much addition to your own fame, avail yourself of that love and confidence to put into complete practice these hallowed principles contained in that renowned Declaration, of which you were the immortal author."[42]

Aware that Jefferson had previously tried to end slavery, Coles hoped "that the fear of failing, at this time, will have no influence in preventing you from employing your pen to eradicate this most degrading feature of British Colonial Policy, which is still permitted to exist."[43] Referring to the "irresistible influence" that he believed the opinions Jefferson expressed would have on his contemporaries, Coles begged Jefferson, "Permit me then, my dear Sir, again to intreat you to exert your great powers of mind and influence, and to employ some of your present leisure, in devising a mode to liberate one half of our Fellowbeings from an ignominious bondage to the other; either by making an immediate attempt to put in train a plan to commence this goodly work, or to leave human Nature the invaluable Testament—which you are so capable of doing—how best to establish its rights."[44] Coles concluded by mentioning that in order to free his own slaves, he had determined to leave Virginia and settle with them elsewhere.

Jefferson received Coles's letter on August 3. He sent his reply on August 25—speedy for him, at least on this subject—but it was not the reply Coles had hoped for. Jefferson said he had read Coles's original letter with pleasure, and its "sentiments" did "honor to both the head and heart" of its author. Jefferson explained that his sentiments on the topic "have long since been in possession of the public, and time has only served to give them stronger root." As he wrote, "The love of justice & the love of country plead equally the cause of these people, and it is a mortal reproach to us that they should have pleaded it so long in vain, and should have produced not a single effort, nay I fear not much serious willingness to relieve them & ourselves from our present condition of moral and political reprobation." Jefferson made clear his view that nothing could be expected from his own generation, which had been educated to believe that slavery was natural, that slaves were mere property, and that the institution was immutable—he recalled his 1769 attempt with Richard Bland to make personal manumission easier, which the Virginia assembly had squashed.[45]

Jefferson mentioned his earlier expectation "that the younger genera-tion, recieving their early impressions after the flame of liberty had been kindled in every breast, and had become as it were the vital spirit of every American, . . . would have sympathized with oppression wherever found."[46] But alas, Jefferson's involvement with this next generation had not convinced him "that they had made towards this point the progress I had hoped." In fact, he told Coles, "your solitary but welcome voice is the first which has brought this sound to my ear; and I have considered the general silence which prevails on this subject as indicating an apathy unfa-vorable to every hope." Yet Jefferson, ever optimistic, believed "the hour of emancipation is advancing in the march of time. It will come," although he did not know if by sensible policy decisions or the result of a bloody insurrection.[47] Jefferson had long believed that issues of great moment took years to resolve. As he wrote in 1808, "There is a snail-paced gait for the advance of new ideas on the general mind, under which we must ac-quiesce. . . . If too hard pushed, they baulk, & the machine retrogrades."[48]

Jefferson expressed his continuing support for the policy idea that slaves born after a preannounced date would be emancipated upon attain-ing a certain degree of education and skill. To free everyone immediately, he believed, when their status as bondspeople had not given them experi-ence in self-control and discipline, would release them "as incapable as children of taking care of themselves," and he felt that a policy of coloni-zation would have to accompany emancipation to prevent undesirable and degrading amalgamation.[49]

As to Coles's urging that Jefferson himself lead a campaign to generate public support for emancipation, Jefferson pled old age, writing that his correspondent was in effect "bidding old Priam to buckle the armour of the [deceased] Hector." He added, "I have overlived the generation with which mutual labors and perils begat mutual confidence and influence. This enterprise is for the young; for those who can follow it up, and bear it through to it's consummation. It shall have all my prayers, and these are the only weapons of an old man."[50] It sounds as though Jefferson had given up on the project, but although he thought his active role was over, he genuinely believed emancipation to be a viable project for the coming generation.

For that reason he argued against Coles's moving with his handful of slaves to the Northwest. Single, with no dependents to support and unen-cumbered with debt, Coles could afford to do so. Yet Jefferson suggested that because most slaveholders simply could not, it was best for owners to "feed & clothe" the slaves among them, "protect them from ill usage," require only reasonable labor of them, and do all "our duties to them." He hoped Coles would not abandon his home state and instead become a spokesman there for his views, that he would take an active role in "public councils, become the Missionary of this doctrine truly Christian, [and] insinuate & inculcate it softly but steadily." When, finally, a phalanx of supporters came together, they should "bring on & press the proposition perseveringly until it's accomplishment. . . . no good measure was ever proposed which, if duly pursued, failed to prevail in the end." In this process, Jefferson argued, "you will be supported by the religious precept 'be not wearied in well doing.'"[51]

Coles responded carefully. After thanking Jefferson for his kind words, he said he would never have considered leaving Virginia if he thought he could somehow be "instrumental" in ending slavery in the state. And he begged to differ with Jefferson that the latter's only weapon as an old man was prayer. "To effect so great and difficult an object great and extensive powers both of mind and influence are required," and no one more than Jefferson possessed these attributes of persuasion. Unassisted public opinion could not be depended on, and the general citizenry should not be expected to "lead" in such momentous matters; rather it needed to be "led." Only people like Jefferson, who did have the power "effectually to arouse and enlighten the public sentiment," could play the role of leader; with them, Coles argued, the "subject of emancipation must originate." And of these elders, Coles considered Jefferson the worthiest and looked to him for leadership. Coles closed by reiterating his respect and regard for the man he considered the greatest of the Founders.[52] Coles and Jefferson did not correspond again on the matter. Against all odds, Jefferson remained hopeful. In 1819 Coles and his freed slaves resettled in Illinois, and Coles later invoked Jefferson's name to pass antislavery legislation in the state.

As JEFFERSON'S RESPONSE to Coles suggests, his faith led him to believe that Providence would eventually see to the end of slavery. In March 1815 he received a letter from David Barrow, a former Virginia Baptist minister who had freed his slaves and in 1798 moved to Kentucky, where he remained a voice for emancipation. Barrow sent Jefferson some antislavery writings, perhaps including his own. Six weeks later Jefferson replied, thanking Barrow for his thoughtfulness and repeating what had become his mantra: the minds of planters had to be changed, and slaves had to be prepared for freedom. As always, he gave no indication of when these changes would bear fruit but restated his faith that ultimately they would. Slavery "will yield in time to temperate & steady pursuit, to the enlargement of the human mind, and it's advancement in science. we are not in a world ungoverned by the laws and the power of a superior agent. our efforts are in his hand, and directed by it; and he will give them their effect in his own time."[53]

Jefferson's confidence that Providence, as he would say, controlled world events was sincere; this belief, along with his relatively benign relations with the Hemings caste of slaves at Monticello, allowed him to face the issue of emancipation with a surprising degree of equanimity. (Of course, it was perhaps easy enough: he was white.) As he wrote to a correspondent in 1817, he still had seen no signs of moral growth in the generation following his, no sign of emancipationist sentiment, and "no symptoms inform me that it will take place in my day. I leave it therefore to time, and not at all without hope, that the day will come."[54] After the Missouri Crisis of 1819, Jefferson feared increased agitation of the issue would imperil the union—and preservation of the union was the preeminent passion of his life. From this position Jefferson never wavered. In one of the last letters he ever sent, addressed to James Heaton on May 20, 1826, six weeks before his death, he briefly summarized his lifetime of writings on emancipation: "A good cause is often injured more by ill-timed efforts of its friends than by the arguments of its enemies. Persuasion, perseverance, and patience are the best advocates on questions depending on the will of others. The revolution in public opinion which this cause requires, is not to be expected in a day, or perhaps in an age; but time, which outlives all things, will outlive this evil also. My sentiments have been forty years before the public. Had I repeated them forty times, they would only have become the more stale and threadbare. Although I shall not live to see them consummated, they will not die with me; but living or dying, they will ever be in my most fervent prayer."[55]

Activists in Jefferson's time like Edward Coles, much less the abolitionists who emerged soon after his death, could not accept such a patient approach; nor can modern readers. Jefferson's willingness to wait tells us a great deal about his character and also about his era, his race, and his class. As a wealthy white man, he saw little need for urgency; he believed, rather, that in God's good time, emancipation would somehow be effected. In no other aspect of his life does Jefferson seem more distant from us or more disappointing.

30

One Last Crusade

THE WORD "AUTODIDACT" came into use in 1748, five years after
Jefferson's birth, almost as if it were invented to describe him.
Throughout his life, he maintained a rigorous program of per-
sonal study, and his erudition became the best-known aspect of his character. President John F. Kennedy's widely known quip that a 1962 meeting of
Nobel Prize winners "was the most extraordinary collection of talent, of
human knowledge, that has ever been gathered together at the White
House, with the possible exception of when Thomas Jefferson dined
alone," reflects the popular understanding of the third president. Yet to
Jefferson himself, just as central to his life's mission as his own self-
education was his devotion to public education. It was the chief goal of his
final years, and by the end of his life, he viewed the creation of the
University of Virginia as one of the three accomplishments for which he
most wanted to be remembered.[1]

IN THE LATE 1770S, Jefferson had been on a committee tasked with revising the laws of Virginia, and he was particularly proud of Bill No. 79, titled "A Bill for the More General Diffusion of Knowledge." This bill called
for tax-supported elementary schools in Virginia that would offer three
years of basic education to each county's white children (boys and girls)
and for twenty free grammar schools (which today we would call high
schools) throughout the state; one superior student chosen annually would
attend the College of William & Mary for four more years of learning.
This one meritorious student—a "natural genius"—would be educated for
state leadership at public expense.[2] Two other bills Jefferson proposed
would have created a state research library and remade the College of

William & Mary into a more modern university. But his fellow lawmakers approved none of these measures.

Jefferson's ideas on education, as on most matters, evolved over time as he became more experienced and learned more about the world. In 1794 he toyed with a proposal from Europe that the total faculty of the University of Geneva move to America; in 1800 he corresponded with Joseph Priestley and Pierre Samuel Du Pont de Nemours about higher education, further developing his ideas; and during his presidency Jefferson acted to create the US Military Academy at West Point, which trained officers in engineering and scientific skills.

On Christmas Eve 1804, Littleton Waller Tazewell, a member of Virginia's General Assembly, informed the president that rising state income suggested there might be sufficient interest to revisit the idea of a state university (these hopes proved ill founded), spurring Jefferson to write Tazewell a long letter several days later spelling out in some detail his latest thinking about higher education. Jefferson was thrilled to learn that the state might be ready to consider establishing a genuine university, for he was "convinced that the people are the only safe depositories of their own liberty, & that they are not safe unless enlightened to a certain degree."[3] He believed that the education requisite for liberty was of two kinds. First, the mass of the people should, in local schools, be taught to read and thus be able "to judge and to vote understandingly." Second, the state must provide an "institution where science [meaning knowledge generally] in all it's branches is taught, and in the highest degree to which the human mind has carried it." In other words, a system of primary education should be available to the masses, along with a university of the highest grade to educate the natural aristocracy.

Jefferson suggested a range of questions to consider, such as location, the method of funding, the general governance of the university, and the number of professors necessary. He supposed that ten professors, teaching a broad range of courses, could cover the core subject matter, although he admitted at the beginning the university might have to make do with only six. These professors, he insisted, should be scholars of distinction; he hoped the state could attract faculty from Europe. He emphasized that the professors and students should not live in one large central building. Instead each professor should have his own house (called a pavilion), with his living quarters above a first-floor classroom, and a covered walkway should connect nearby student rooms to the various professorial houses.

Thus expansion would be easier; a university, he wrote, "should not be an house but a village."[4] This was apparently the first time Jefferson articulated the concept that he would eventually expand into the phrase "academical village."

In 1810 several men in Tennessee wrote Jefferson asking for suggestions about their idea of founding a college. In his reply Jefferson amplified his plan for the layout of a university, a plan apparently without antecedents:

> [It would be] infinitely better to erect a small and separate lodge for each separate professorship, with only a hall below for his class, and two chambers above for himself; joining these lodges by barracks for a certain portion of the students, opening into a covered way to give a dry communication between all the schools. The whole of these arranged around an open square of grass and trees, would make it, what it should be in fact, an academical village, instead of a large and common den of noise, of filth and fetid air. It would afford that quiet retirement so friendly to study, and lessen the danger of fire, infection and tumult. Every professor would be the police officer of the students adjacent to his own lodge.[5]

At the time of writing, Jefferson held no office, political or otherwise; nor was he directly involved in educational schemes, except in his always fertile mind. As he explained in a letter to his old friend Thomas Cooper, written on January 16, 1814, "I have long had under contemplation, & been collecting materials for the plan of an university in Virginia which should comprehend all the sciences useful to us."[6]

Jefferson had met with Virginia governor John Tyler in 1809 and urged him to do something on behalf of education in the state; the following year Tyler won approval in the General Assembly for a Literary Fund expressly dedicated to education for Virginia's poor white families who could not afford to send their sons to a private academy.[7] Initially the funds available were quite limited, so the Literary Fund had little effect. Meanwhile, the Albemarle Academy, in theory the school for Jefferson's home county chartered by the General Assembly in 1803, had never opened. On March 25, 1814, for unclear reasons, five prominent citizens of the county met to consider how to breathe life into the dormant academy. According to legend, Jefferson was out on his horse and happened to ride by, whereupon one of the five men hallooed for him to join them.[8] No firm evidence establishes this story as true or that Jefferson attended the meeting. We do know, however, that the five men present voted to expand the size of the academy's board of trustees, and that Jefferson was among the thirteen new members chosen.[9]

AT THE FIRST REGULARLY scheduled meeting of the expanded board, Jefferson was appointed to a committee that would draft "rules and regulations for the government of the board of Trustees."[10] At a subsequent meeting on May 3, 1814, his committee presented its report. After stating that their purpose was the establishment "within the county of Albemarle, of a seminary of instruction of youth already well grounded in the knowledge of reading and writing and Common Arithmetic . . . and Such useful Sciences as shall be within the competence of the means they may provide," the committee members said they had a duty "to enquire into and report the ways and means of carrying the institution into effect." To that end the trustees elected Jefferson, Peter Carr (Jefferson's nephew), and Thomas Mann Randolph to yet another committee, this one charged with drafting a petition to the state's next General Assembly. In its final form, the petition asked that the state appropriate to the academy money resulting from the sale of the glebe lands once owned by the former state-supported church.[11]

The War of 1812 was ongoing, and the British had just sacked the nation's capital, so many of the younger men in the state were either joining the militia or otherwise preparing to defend the nation. Jefferson, meanwhile, sent a comprehensive letter to Carr, now president of the Albemarle Academy's board, laying out his mature ideas about what the academy might enable them to accomplish. Jefferson explained to Carr that he was writing because he had promised the board a plan for education, an issue he had been studying and considering for years, but worried that he might not be able to attend future meetings.

Jefferson believed the first step was to "ascertain with precision the object of our institution" by surveying the potential benefits of education.[12] The white population comprised two basic groups, "the laboring & the learned." It was the government's responsibility to provide the great majority of the people with "education to qualify them for their pursuits and duties." It should do this by means of elementary schools developed on a very local level as outlined in Jefferson's 1779 Bill for the More General Diffusion of Knowledge. After three years of basic education, the future learned class—that is, talented boys—would then proceed "to College," which Jefferson now said should consist of both general schools and professional schools.[13] He was not specific about how many years students would attend.

The general schools would provide a broad education in languages, mathematics, and philosophy, by which he meant ethics, law, government, and the traditional range of sciences and belles lettres. This second tier of instruction would prepare men for practically every profession, equipping them for public and private life. Those who were wealthy and motivated enough could then enter the third level of education, the professional schools, in effect departments in a university, where "each science is to be taught in the highest degree it has yet attained."[14] Jefferson believed Albemarle Academy should have at least a second-tier general school, which could become the flagship university at the apex of a statewide system.

Jefferson did not envision similar educational opportunities for women and blacks. His original proposal provided women with no more than basic literacy, although he did not oppose families sending their daughters to private academies for additional education, as he himself had done in Paris with Patsy and Polly. And although he had written Quaker Robert Pleasants in 1796 admitting that it would require only "very small alterations" to his original support of public elementary schools to include similar educational opportunities for blacks, nothing ever came of this suggestion.[15]

Sometime in the fall of 1814, the full board of the academy must have met to consider Jefferson's proposal, which it later sent to the state legislature with the previously prepared petition regarding glebe lands, along with draft legislation in Jefferson's hand to change the name of Albemarle Academy to Central College. After unexpected delays, on February 14, 1816, Central College was finally created by law.

Jefferson, realizing Richmond would not be sending enough money to support both elementary schools and a university, made a strategic decision: assuming that counties would be more apt to support local schools—less so a distant university or college—he tried to siphon all the money from the Literary Fund and similar sources for the support of Central College. This policy decision, made in the face of miserly state support for all education, in no way indicated hostility to the concept of state-supported public elementary schools, as some have suggested. Governor William Cary Nicholson, a longtime friend of Jefferson's, appointed a board of visitors (trustees) for the new college and accepted the full list proposed by the secretary of the former Albemarle Academy board. That list included Jefferson, James Madison, James Monroe (the sitting US president), David Watson, Joseph C. Cabell, and John Hartwell Cocke, all close associates of Jefferson and firm supporters of higher education.[16]

Still, finances especially worried Cabell, because he was aware of the popular support for using the Literary Fund to educate the children of poor parents, and from his position in the state capital, he knew the College of William & Mary would continue to oppose funding another institution of higher learning in the state. The 1816 bill had authorized Central College, not the creation of a new state university. Yet the possibility was in the air, and the College of William & Mary wanted to hold onto that mantle. In addition, tiny Washington College in Lexington also hoped to win the designation, and boosters in Staunton, who aspired to make their city the state capital, came to see creation of a state university as a step toward that goal. Cabell, in a sense representing Jefferson and his vision, knew he would be waging a multifront battle. When the board of visitors of Central College met in May 1817, they began the process of choosing a site in Charlottesville for the construction of the new institution. The board soon purchased two tracts of land just west of the center of Charlottesville, and the members present at the meeting each (including Jefferson) pledged $1,000 toward the campaign to finance construction of at least a portion of the campus, whose design Jefferson had proposed.[17]

Jefferson sent letters describing his plans and enclosing his sketches to architects Dr. William Thornton and Benjamin Henry Latrobe, with whom he had worked on the designs for the new capital city of Washington, DC. Jefferson's striking new concept of collegiate design excited both men, each of whom independently suggested placing a dominant building at the center of the north side of the square. Jefferson accepted this suggestion, and from it grew his design for the Rotunda, based on drawings of the Pantheon in Rome. Jefferson proposed that each of the professors' homes should differ in design, offering to students visible examples of numerous architectural styles.[18] With the assistance of his trusted overseer, Edmund Bacon, and master carpenter James Dinsmore, Jefferson took stakes and a ball of twine and began laying out the boundaries of the first building, which became Pavilion VII.[19] The campus of Central College was underway, the initial cornerstone being laid on October 6, 1817.[20]

CENTRAL COLLEGE was still only a local institution, not the state university, and Jefferson almost surely had his mind set on changing that. Over the next few years he and the board of visitors struggled to secure the necessary state funds to construct the campus. Even so, Jefferson insisted on the highest-quality materials and even hired stonecutters from Italy to finish the Carrara marble capitals for the columns of the pavilions and the Rotunda. Jefferson believed distinguished architecture would help establish the reputation of the institution and enable it to recruit faculty from the best universities in Europe and the North. Critics portrayed him as unrealistic, but Jefferson could be firm when necessary, and for years he fought tenaciously to realize his vision. Jefferson made enemies in this struggle, but time would prove him right.

Cabell and others worked hard in Richmond to overcome opposition from the competing sites and from legislators opposing either any state funding whatsoever for education or a shift from free public elementary schools to a capstone state university. After much controversy, the Senate first passed a bill to create a state university, which the House then passed on February 21, 1818. It instructed the governor to appoint a committee of twenty-four members who would meet on August 1 of that year at Rockfish Gap (thirty miles west of Charlottesville) to determine the location of the new university, along with its structure and curriculum. Jefferson had not wanted to sit on the committee (or so he protested), but friends pushed him, and the governor appointed him anyway, along with Madison and other notables.

Jefferson prepared for the meeting—to be held at the Mountain House, a resort inn at Rockfish Gap—by drafting a comprehensive report and arming himself with demographic data and a map of the state. He had sent a wagon ahead bearing a mattress and a stand for supporting it, in the belief that the meeting might take multiple days. He knew this was a gathering of great import, dealing with a matter central to his life for decades. As he had written Cabell in late 1817, hoping to hear about the progress of the bill to establish a university, "I have only this single anxiety in the world. It is a bantling [young child] of 40. years birth & nursing, & if I can once see it on its' legs, I will sing with sincerity & pleasure my nunc dimittas."[21]

Soon after the meeting began at Rockfish Gap, the committee unanimously elected Jefferson its president. He acted judiciously and said little unless prompted. When questioned on the matter of choosing a location, he used a map of the state, with strings drawn across it in various locations to indicate distances, to demonstrate that Charlottesville was more centrally located in terms of population than any other competing site. After two rounds of voting, Charlottesville was the unanimous choice. As discussion turned to questions of the purpose, structure, and curriculum of a state university, Jefferson brought forth his already prepared report. With only minor changes, the Rockfish Gap committee accepted it as its official report. Jefferson asked Cabell to prepare a fair copy of the final document—one of the most impressive statements of educational vision in American history—which Jefferson submitted in November to the Speakers of the Virginia Senate and House of Delegates.[22]

THE REPORT FIRST explained the chosen location of the state university and then presented the "plan for its buildings," which reflected Jefferson's notion of an academical village. It suggested that in time a larger building at the northern end of the two parallel series of pavilions and associated student rooms could perhaps provide a venue for religious services or public lectures and also house a library as well as schools for music, art, and similar purposes.[23] As for when university-level education would begin, the report stated that the state should provide for the primary education of the white children of Virginia. This primary level should "give to every citizen the information he needs for the transaction of his own business; to enable him to calculate for himself, and to express and preserve his ideas, contracts and accounts, in writing," and so perform a variety of practical, everyday functions. A crucial aim of primary education was to enable each and every citizen "to know his rights" and perform his civic duties as a responsible citizen.[24] Higher education had a narrower purpose: education in the professions (law, medicine, the church, and so on) and preparation for government office. Higher education, as the report made clear, was open only to white males.

The report went into some detail on the role of higher education in the state. Its purpose was to "form the statesmen, legislators and judges" essential for good governance and to "expound the principles and structure of government, the laws . . . [and] a sound spirit of legislation" that would defend each individual's rights and inculcate respect for the rights of others. Higher education was necessary "to harmonize and promote the interests of agriculture, manufactures and commerce . . . to develop the reasoning faculties of our youth, enlarge their minds, cultivate their morals, and instill into them the precepts of virtue and order." Moreover, it would "enlighten [the youth] with mathematical and physical sciences, which advance the arts, and administer to the health, the subsistence, and comforts of human life."[25] University education was essential for character formation, for developing the faculties of reason, and for gaining other skills considered aspects of the foundation of meaningful, productive lives.

Higher education thereby served a larger social purpose: the "advantages of well-directed education, moral, political and economical, are truly above all estimate. Education generates habits of application, of order, and the love of virtue." It was a means of promoting social happiness, moving society beyond barbarism, training "able counselors to administer the affairs of our country in all its departments . . . [and] advancing the prosperity, the power and the happiness of a nation."[26] Of course, however inspiring readers may have found the opening statement, its vision of social harmony through "collective" education did not include the majority of people in the state.

Following the broadly philosophical statement came a precise listing of recommended "branches of learning," complete with related subfields.[27] The document called for instruction in ancient and modern languages, including Anglo-Saxon, or Old English, though the report assumed that students would have acquired the rudiments of the classic languages before matriculation at the university. Jefferson made strenuous arguments for the teaching of French ("the language of general intercourse among nations, and as a depository of human science, . . . unsurpassed by any other language"). He deemed Spanish important because so many people in the Western Hemisphere spoke it, while he prized Italian as a model of "the finest taste in style and composition."[28]

By contrast, Jefferson at first thought that the school should not teach medicine because Charlottesville had no large general hospital. In conformity with a US Constitution that mandated freedom of religion and a Virginia Statute for Religious Freedom that prohibited exclusive state support for any one religion, there would be no professor of theology. Jefferson assumed that morality would be taught under the rubric of ethics, and that instruction in the ancient languages would assist those who on their own wanted to pursue biblical studies. The report discussed matters including tuition, student government and discipline, and "honorary excitements" in detail. Student governance was left primarily to the pupils themselves; Jefferson included an appeal to their character and honor. Corporal punishment was forbidden. Again and again, Jefferson emphasized character, since the university would be training future voters and civil servants and politicians.[29] According to the report, entrance requirements, the scheduling of exams, awards given for merit, the bestowal of honorary degrees, and similar topics were best left to the discretion of the board of visitors, as were faculty appointments, the courses of instruction, the erection and maintenance of buildings, tuition fees, and dorm rates. The board of visitors would choose from among themselves the university rector, and all aspects of university governance should conform to state law.[30]

The legislature received the report on December 8, and if either Jefferson or Cabell thought its internal logic would ensure quick acceptance, they were mistaken. Again, however, Cabell defended Jefferson's vision adroitly, fending off delegates from the western sections of the state who argued against Charlottesville as the site of the university and others who still felt the state had no obligation to support higher education. After overwhelming approval of the entire report on January 25, 1819, the governor promptly appointed a new board of visitors, which, in addition to two members from the Shenandoah Valley and one from the Tidewater region, also included Jefferson, Madison, Cabell, and Cocke. At their first meeting on March 29, to no one's surprise, they elected Jefferson rector. Jefferson had his new university, located where he wished, with the freedom (and support) to shape it according to his decades-long dream.[31]

Jefferson aimed all his efforts on behalf of a state university at educating young men. He admitted in early 1818, "A plan of female education [that is, beyond the elementary level] has never been a subject of systematic contemplation with me. It has occupied my attention so far only as the education of my own daughters occasionally required."[32] Aware that they could not enter the professions, he had them well educated privately, both because he treasured learning in itself and because he knew they would likely play the primary role in educating any children they had. When asked by Nathaniel Burwell for a reading list for young women, Jefferson replied with several dozen substantial titles on history, philosophy, literature, sermons, and poetry.[33]

ONE COULD BE forgiven for assuming that 1819 and the years that followed were nothing but fulfilling for Jefferson as he watched what he later called his "Hobby," the University of Virginia, take form. That did eventually happen, but a series of crises characterized this period in Jefferson's life and in that of the nation. Illness, family violence, and devastating economic news brought despair and colored his response to the momentous national issue of the time, the Missouri Crisis. Jefferson's fatalistic response to that event grew out of his low state of mind at the end of 1819, and in his attempt to convince the Virginia House of Delegates to fund the new university, he exaggerated his fears of what that political crisis meant and how the university offered a potential solution.[34] Perhaps the immediate aftermath of the meeting at Rockfish Gap in August 1818 augured the misfortune to come. Jefferson, accompanied by General James Breckinridge, journeyed westward to Virginia's famed Warm Springs, hoping the mineral waters there would relieve his recurrent rheumatism (osteoarthritis). In a cruel irony, Jefferson instead came down with what appears to have been a debilitating staphylococcus infection. A series of abscesses and boils developed on his buttocks, making his trip home, accomplished in a number of short segments, excruciating. As he explained to his grandson, Francis Eppes, "the torment of the journey back reduced me to the last stage of weakness and exhaustion." He wouldn't recover fully for months.[35]

By that point, Jefferson had worried terribly for several years over the plight of his first granddaughter, Anne Cary Randolph Bankhead, who had been Jefferson's favorite in part because she shared his love of gardening. But her husband, Charles Bankhead, proved a hopeless alcoholic who battered Anne, to Jefferson's immeasurable anguish. As early as 1815 he had written Bankhead's father seeking help in curbing the son's violence and drunkenness, to no effect. Jefferson tried to convince Anne to leave her husband, but she did not, whether out of loyalty or fear.[36] On February 1, 1819, Jefferson's favorite male grandson, Thomas Jefferson Randolph (Jeff)—Jefferson had made him manager of the Monticello plantation in 1815 and of the Bedford County property in 1821—rode into Charlottesville, apparently to confront Bankhead after his most recent assault on Anne. A wildly drunk Bankhead stabbed Jeff in his left arm and above the hip, serious wounds that bled profusely. Jeff was carried into a nearby store, and someone hurried to Monticello to inform Jefferson. The almost seventy-six-year-old man rode his horse "at full gallop" through the nighttime to see his beloved grandson. Jeff later preserved the moment in his handwritten memoirs: "I had been laid on a bail of blankets in the crating Room of a store and had borne myself with proper fortitude; but when he entered and knelt at my head and wept aloud I was unnerved."[37] Jeff, a strong, healthy youth, recovered from his injuries, but his grandfather was truly shaken.

Shortly after this disturbing episode, on April 9, 1819, a fire of unknown origin broke out in Monticello's North Pavilion and, driven by fierce winds, threatened the main building. Jefferson himself helped fight the fire, falling and painfully scraping a shin in the process. Thankfully the fire was extinguished; yet it was frightening to consider what could have happened.[38] Later in the year, Jefferson fell seriously ill twice, once with a bout of colic and then with what was called a "stricture of the ilium," the largest bone of the pelvis.[39] Another severe blow to Jefferson's sense of well-being was economic. Due to three successive poor harvests, his farm income already lagged far behind expectations, when the nationwide economic contraction known as the Panic of 1819 struck him hard. The Bank of the United States began to call in loans from state banks, which responded by drastically curtailing the loans they extended to private citizens, significantly impacting Jefferson. As he put it, this year was "the gloomiest in his financial history so far."[40] But still more devastating was the consequence of a good deed he had performed the year before.

Former Virginia governor Wilson Cary Nicholas, an old and dear friend, became even closer to Jefferson after his daughter married Jefferson's grandson Jeff. As a prominent Richmond banker, Nicholas had often provided Jefferson the loans he needed to avoid bankruptcy. Then in 1818 Nicholas himself got into economic difficulty and came to Jefferson, asking him to cosign notes for two loans of $10,000 each that the banker had taken out. Jefferson was assured the notes were for no more than a year's duration, and since Nicholas's net worth was estimated at $350,000, the loans seemed risk-free for Jefferson—Nicholas even said, "This request wou'd not be made but under the most entire confidence, that you can never suffer the slightest inconvenience from complying with it"—who in any case felt he could not honorably refuse this request from an old friend and now family member.[41]

But later that summer, with his own crops afflicted by a hailstorm and then drought, Jefferson learned that Nicholas had defaulted, leaving Jefferson with an additional $20,000 of debt, with annual interest of $1,200, and crushing all hope that he might one day finish paying off his creditors. As Jefferson confided to James Madison seven years later, "Our friend W.C.N. gave me the *coup de grace*."[42] Jefferson's outlook in the immediate aftermath of learning about Nicholas's default was bleak indeed.

Soon enough, national events again dimmed Jefferson's outlook. In 1817, the residents of Missouri launched the process of transforming the territory into a state. The enabling legislation came to Congress in early 1819. On February 13 of that year, Congressman James Tallmadge Jr. of New York proposed an amendment to prohibit the introduction of additional slaves into Missouri and to free all slaves born in the territory (after its admission as a state) at the age of twenty-five. The South erupted in anger, fearing the amendment jeopardized the region's future prosperity. This was the first time in the young nation's history that the federal government was called upon to limit the expansion of slavery, and the controversy lingered for months until finally settled by the so-called Missouri Compromise, which maintained the balance between free and slave states in the Senate by admitting Maine among the former and Missouri among the latter. The compromise also called for prohibiting slavery in the remaining portion of the Louisiana Purchase north of the southern boundary of Missouri.

Perhaps too preoccupied early in the year with his personal and family difficulties to focus on the issue, Jefferson panicked when he finally did. According to a visitor, Quaker Isaac Briggs, on the second day of November, Jefferson lamented, "The Union will be broken. All the horrors of civil war . . . will ensue. Bloodshed, rapine and cruelty will soon roam at large. . . . Out of such state of things will naturally grow a war of extermination toward the African in our land."[43] In addition to John Adams, Jefferson wrote other correspondents to express his utter despondency. In early 1820, he wrote to a friend that the Missouri issue "is the most portentous one which ever yet threatened the Union. In the gloomiest moment of the revolutionary war I never had any apprehensions equal to what I feel from this source."[44] But that assertion looked tame compared with a letter he wrote in April 1820.

Addressed to John Holmes, a congressman representing the Maine district of Massachusetts, and penned after Congress had passed the compromise, the letter made clear Jefferson's concern that northern politicians were using the controversy to gain political power. In retrospect, the letter seems a vast overreaction, if he was not writing at least in part for political effect. Although prophetic, Jefferson appears almost hysterical, writing, "This momentous question, like a fire bell in the night, awakened and filled me with terror. I considered it at once as the knell of the Union. . . . A geographical line, coinciding with a marked principle, moral and political, once conceived and held up to the angry passions of men, will never be obliterated; and every new irritation will mark it deeper and deeper."[45]

These words came from a man mired in a deep malaise. Suffering from his chronic rheumatism, enduring distress and violence within his own family, his economic plight worsened by Nicholas's default, Jefferson must have felt that everything dear to him was falling apart. And now the union—in a sense, his life's work—suddenly seemed threatened. He saw the proposed restriction against new slaves coming into Missouri not as a way to end slavery but rather as a measure that would make more difficult the eventual demise of the institution, as slaves' "diffusion over a greater surface would make them individually happier, and proportionally facilitate the accomplishment of their emancipation, by dividing the burthen on a greater number of coadjutors."[46] Jefferson had long feared the division of the nation into competing sections and believed that the resolution of the slavery issue would result only from a nationwide commitment, not one made by the South alone.[47]

With a note of self-pity he concluded his letter to Holmes, "I regret that I am now to die in the belief, that the useless sacrifice of themselves by the generation of 1776, to acquire self-government and happiness to their country, is to be thrown away by the unwise and unworthy passions of their sons, and that my only consolation is to be, that I live not to weep over it."[48] But we can view his letters penned during the crisis as more than the jeremiad of a disillusioned old man. Though distraught by the political situation, Jefferson always knew the power of words, and he may have intended these letters, to some extent, to persuade politicians to step back from the precipice of disunion.[49] We do know, at least, that he did use the crisis to persuade the Virginia General Assembly to fund his ambitious proposals for a great university in the state.

WITHIN A COUPLE YEARS of these various crises, both familial and national, Jefferson regained his balance. Already by the end of 1820 he was writing his old compatriot the Marquis de Lafayette, "The boisterous sea of liberty indeed is never without a wave, and that from Missouri is now rolling towards us, but we shall ride over it as we have over all others."[50] And even when his spirits were at their lowest, he managed to focus on the issues he believed most important. In 1819 and over the next several years, Jefferson primarily employed his energies to advance the cause of the University of Virginia. The state had approved the founding of a university but was unwilling to provide the funds Jefferson thought necessary. He was unrelenting, and with effective colleagues like Cabell in the legislature, he squeezed money out of the parsimonious legislature. Jefferson tried to shame the state by comparing its educational weakness with superior programs from New York to Kentucky.[51] We are threatening to become the "Barbary of the Union," he wrote to Cabell, with a state educational establishment so underdeveloped that "the little we have we import, like beggars, from other States." He pointed out how this backwardness affected every aspect of society.[52]

When appeals to state pride failed, Jefferson turned to sectional rivalries, and here he used the Missouri Crisis to pressure the delegates. He spelled out the dangers of the state's sending its sons north for an education in a letter to General James Breckinridge, a longtime member of the House of Delegates from Botetourt County, and he wrote Cabell the same day that Breckinridge should show the letter, with discretion, to those delegates it might influence.[53] To Breckinridge, Jefferson wrote, "We are now trusting to those who are against us in position and principle, to fashion to their own form the minds and affections of our youth." Jefferson may have feared the vestiges of Federalist political ideas as much as precipitous actions on behalf of emancipation. He estimated the state was spending $300,000 annually to send upward of five hundred of its sons to colleges in the northern states for their university educations. "This canker is eating on the vitals of our existence, and if not arrested at once, will be beyond remedy."[54] Unless the state created a university that kept these students at home, it risked losing its future leadership class to alien political views—if Virginia's best sons returned to the state at all. As Jefferson argued, it was absolutely necessary to Virginia's future that the legislature generously fund the new state university.

JEFFERSON'S APPEALS TO state pride and self-defense were only partially effective, but gradually the funds did become available, and the pavilions and Rotunda of his university went up between 1820 and 1825. Members of the public pressured Jefferson to begin classes before these buildings were finished, and many critics thought the Rotunda in particular an extravagance, but he persisted against all opposition in making sure that the school did not open until the buildings met his specifications. Jefferson rode down from his mountaintop nearly every day to inspect the site; he could also see the campus from a telescope perched on the north terrace of Monticello. The final results surpassed even his high expectations. As the young Harvard scholar George Ticknor wrote in 1824, the emerging campus was "more beautiful than anything architectural in New England, and more appropriate to an university than can be found, perhaps, in the world."[55] That same year, during his visit to Monticello, Ticknor noted that Jefferson talked "without the least restraint, very pleasantly, upon all subjects[.] In politics, his interest seems nearly gone." He had moved past his fixation on the Missouri Crisis.[56] And Jefferson's insistence on

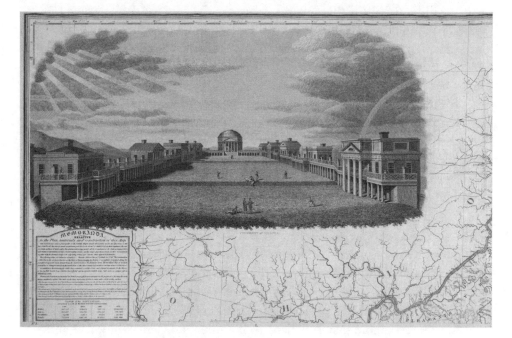

Rotunda and Lawn of the University of Virginia.
F. Tanner engraving from Boye's Map of Virginia.

Source: Albert and Shirley Small Special Collections Library, University of Virginia.

architectural distinction for the new university became one of his most enduring legacies. In 1976 a poll of members of the American Institute of Architects revealed that the overwhelming favorite nominee for the label of "the proudest achievement of American architecture over the past 200 years" was the original campus of the University of Virginia, and it and Monticello were two of the first World Heritage Sites designated in the United States.[57]

In Jefferson's conception, the university would comprise various academic schools or departments, each headed by a professor. The teaching would be done through lectures, not the recitation system that prevailed at most other universities, and Jefferson wanted to test students' progress by means of occasional written exams rather than daily oral quizzes.[58] Both were novel ideas. The rigid curriculum encountered by his grandson Francis Eppes in the early 1820s at the University of South Carolina had frustrated Jefferson. As he put it, the new university will "teach to every particular student the branches of science which those who direct him think will be useful in the pursuits proposed for him, and . . . waste his time on nothing which they think will not be useful to him. . . . the fundamental law of our University [will be] to leave every one free to attend whatever branches of instruction he wants, and to decline what he does not want."[59]

In fact, there would be no required courses of any kind—it was the ultimate elective system, radically innovative at the time. A student could progress through the available (and desired) courses at his own pace. The university initially did not even offer bachelor's degrees. Rather, after a period of study, the content and duration of which depended on each individual's skills and choices, students would receive a certificate of graduation. Additional study could result in either a doctoral degree or a "graduate" degree. In effect, Jefferson was designing an institution akin to a modern research university. Variations on these practices would not become common at other American universities for years.

An initially intractable problem was the selection of faculty, an effort complicated by a major political mistake Jefferson made, one so stupendous and preventable that it is hard to comprehend. Jefferson knew and greatly admired the scientist and religious radical Thomas Cooper, considering him the most learned man in America. This admiration seems to have blinded him to political reality, for he pushed the board of visitors to offer Cooper a position. Religious leaders across the state—many already suspicious of Jefferson's heterodoxy—took umbrage at this apparent affront to their faiths. They knew that he had not provided for a professor of theology at the new university. A wave of opposition soon arose, and the leading Presbyterian minister in Virginia, the Reverend John Holt Rice of Richmond, mounted a statewide protest (and thereby earned Jefferson's everlasting antipathy).[60] This controversy cost the university support in the General Assembly and only came to an end when Cooper, having the good sense to recognize that his appointment could compromise the entire university project, withdrew.[61] Jefferson later tried to assuage the clerical opposition by proposing that the various religious denominations could establish theological schools adjacent to the university—he privately hoped that the university would influence them and their students—but none took up the offer. Most would remain largely suspicious of Jefferson's university.

Jefferson tried to attract other major American scholars to Charlottesville, offering positions to both George Ticknor of Harvard and the nation's foremost mathematician, Nathaniel Bowditch, but neither

New Englander accepted. Finally, in the spring of 1824 the board of visitors, following Jefferson's advice, sent Francis Walker Gilmer, a young Charlottesville lawyer of genuine scholarly promise himself, on a faculty recruiting trip to England. The salary he could offer did not attract the very top academics, but in time he found five reputable scholars who agreed to help launch the fledgling Virginia university. For his part, Jefferson worried as Gilmer's trip seemed to go on for months without results.

JEFFERSON WROTE HIS last public address for an event on November 8, 1824, linking two great periods of his career, as he saw it: the era of the American Revolution and the creation of the University of Virginia. While his despair over the Missouri Crisis had passed, his health difficulties had not. He had fallen through partially rotten steps leading down from a terrace at Monticello in late 1822, breaking his left arm. It healed slowly, and forever afterward he was plagued by not one but two ailing wrists, the first a result of his tumble decades before in Paris during his flirtation with Maria Cosway. His osteoarthritis remained chronic, and in October 1824 he had such a severe abscess on his jaw that he had to take nourishment through a straw.

Within days of overcoming that painful inconvenience, there occurred a wonderful reunion at Monticello. The aged (and significantly more obese) General Lafayette was making a triumphant return tour of the United States, and Jefferson had invited his old revolutionary friend (and colleague in Paris) to visit. After many delays, Lafayette's entourage reached the little mountain late in the afternoon of November 4, his arrival announced with a trumpet fanfare. Lafayette was helped down from his carriage and laboriously made his way across the lawn toward the entrance of Monticello; Jefferson—walking slowly at first but quickening his stride—rushed to embrace the old general; both shed tears of joy at seeing one another again.[62]

Lafayette enjoyed Jefferson's famous hospitality at Monticello for several days. On Friday, November 8, at 10:00 a.m., the two rode in a carriage to Charlottesville, where they made a brief public appearance at the Central Hotel. About noon another procession began, and the two old revolutionaries made their way to the university grounds, climbed the steps of the unfinished Rotunda, and at 3:00 p.m. began a long dinner. This was the first event held in the building and on the campus overall. Many dignitaries were present, including James Madison. Thirteen toasts had been prepared, and when his turn came, the eighty-one-year-old Jefferson professed to be too weak to deliver it, so the presiding official read aloud his remarks. An obviously moved Lafayette grasped Jefferson's hand. Jefferson affectionately acknowledged the crowd, among whose fathers, as he put it, he had grown up. There followed respectful, appreciative words about the honored guest from France, "our ancient and distinguished leader and benefactor . . . [who] made our cause his own." Jefferson modestly stated that, while serving his country in Paris, "I only held the nail, he drove it."[63] This was Jefferson's paean to the past. Now he turned to the future.

> My friends I am old, long in the disuse of making speeches, and without voice to utter them. In this feeble state, the exhausted powers of my life leave little within my competence for your service. If, with the aid of my younger and able coadjutors, I can still contribute anything to advance the Institution, within whose walls we are now . . . , it will be, as it ever has been, cheerfully and zealously bestowed. And could I live to see it once enjoy the patronage and cherishment of our public authorities with undivided voice, I should die without a doubt of the future fortunes of my native State, and in the consoling contemplation of the happy influence of this institution on its character, its virtue, its prosperity, and safety.[64]

Almost forty years after first imagining a university for his home state, Jefferson, by force of intellect and will—and often through sheer stubbornness—had realized one of his oldest dreams.

HE COULD NOT KNOW, as those words were read, that a few days later he would receive a letter from Francis Walker Gilmer announcing the hiring of five faculty members.[65] In early 1825 the board of visitors approved the appointment of two additional faculty, both Americans. There was criticism of the European—not to mention English—character of the faculty, and Jefferson and Madison were determined to find an accomplished native scholar to hold the critical professorship of law. Representing the board of visitors and with the advice of Madison, Jefferson offered the professorship to John T. Lomax, a prominent lawyer in Fredericksburg, more than a year after the university opened to students. Jefferson and Madison had been particularly careful about this position, because they wanted someone fully competent who also firmly shared their politics.

Jefferson even went so far as to suggest a set of readings to include in the law professor's classes; Madison modified the list to include George Washington's first inaugural address and his farewell message. This act seems to contradict what later became known as Jefferson's famous statement of academic freedom from 1820: "This institution will be based on the illimitable freedom of the human mind. For here we are not afraid to follow truth wherever it may lead, nor tolerate any error so long as reason is left free to combat it."[66] Perhaps Jefferson and Madison thought that the professors from England necessitated a counterweight, though it had been their choice to hire them. Perhaps they would argue that they were only creating a list of certain readings, not banning others. But one suspects that their memories of the bitter political controversies of the 1790s simply overwhelmed their commitment to complete intellectual freedom. Madison admitted as much four months after Jefferson's death when he stated that they intended to make the university "a nursery of Republican patriots, as well as genuine scholars."[67]

With a surprising lack of ceremony, the University of Virginia opened on March 7, 1825, with only about thirty students. More trickled in weekly, and by May the number was almost eighty.[68] Not all the professors had arrived in Charlottesville, and three of the pavilions stood empty. Almost no books were yet available—years earlier Jefferson had planned on donating his library, but he had since sold his books to the government to replace the first Library of Congress. The students proved less prepared and less disciplined than Jefferson had imagined, and within months some of the headstrong sons of planters rioted. They made noise, threw a bottle of urine through the window of the one of the professor's homes, and shouted, "Damn the European professors." When the board of visitors met to consider the situation, Jefferson was too upset to speak.[69] The visitors and faculty restored order and strengthened the disciplinary machinery. With the university stabilized, it grew in repute and students, and by 1860 it was among the largest in the nation. Jefferson considered it one of the three major achievements of his life, alongside the Declaration of Independence and the Virginia Statute for Religious Freedom.

The Sage of Monticello

FORTUNATELY FOR LATER HISTORIANS, several visitors to Monticello in the last years of Thomas Jefferson's life recorded their impressions of their host. When future senator Daniel Webster arrived in December 1824, he found Jefferson "of an ample, long frame, rather thin and spare . . . with hair, which having been once red, and now turning gray, is an indistinct sandy color." Webster thought his eyes small, "now neither brilliant nor striking." He noted that Jefferson still had all his teeth, and while "strongly compressed," his lips bore "an expression of contentment and benevolence." Webster described his dress in some detail, commenting on its informality and characterizing it as "very much neglected, but not slovenly." He concluded that his "general appearance indicates an extraordinary degree of health, vivacity, and spirit. His sight is still good, for he needs glasses only in the evening. His hearing is generally good, but a number of voices in animated conversation confuses it." For that reason, when numerous guests joined him for dinner—"served in half Virginian, half French style"—Jefferson preferred to converse in smaller groups, ideally of no more than two, after the meal.[1]

One of Jefferson's granddaughters, Ellen Wayles Coolidge, later objected to Webster's depiction of her grandfather's attire and wrote the nineteenth-century biographer Henry S. Randall a correction that seems justified. According to Coolidge, Jefferson's "dress was simple, and adapted to his ideas of neatness and comfort. He paid little attention to fashion, wearing whatever he liked best, and sometimes blending the fashions of several periods. He wore long waistcoats when the mode was for very short, white cambric stocks fastened behind with a buckle, when cravats were universal. He adopted the pantaloon very late in life, because he found it more comfortable and convenient, and cut off his queue for the same reason. [He did] nothing to be in conformity with the fashion of the day. He considered such independence as the privilege of his age."[2] That description fits how we would think an older man, in the confines of his rural home and secure in his position in life, would approach a quotidian task like dressing himself in the morning.

Even though his osteoarthritis and other problems often severely afflicted Jefferson in his final decade, he could pull himself together and find the energy to engage meaningfully with visitors. In November 1825 a German prince touring the United States, Bernhard of Saxe-Weimar-Eisenach, came to Monticello right at dinnertime. The courtly Jefferson arose and insisted the unexpected visitors come to the table and share the meal with his family. The prince described Jefferson as an "old man of eighty-six [sic] years of age, of tall stature, plain appearance, and long white hair. In conversation he was very lively, and his spirits, as also his hearing and sight, seemed not to have decreased at all with his advancing age. I found in him a man who retained his faculties remarkably well in his old age, and one would have taken him for a man of sixty."[3] With such a small dinner party, Jefferson's ears could distinguish each conversation.

Jefferson's ability and desire to entertain guests lasted to the very end. Henry Lee went to Monticello just six days before Jefferson's death, seeking details as he prepared to issue a new edition of the memoirs of his father, Henry (Light Horse Harry) Lee, a Revolutionary War statesman. Martha informed Lee that Jefferson was too weak to see him. But when Jefferson learned that Lee had arrived, he insisted he be admitted to his bedroom. The younger man was greatly moved as he approached Jefferson, lying in his bed. "There he was," Lee later wrote, "extended, feeble, prostrate; but the fine and clear expression of his countenance not [at] all obscured. At the first glance he recognized me, and his hand and voice at once saluted me. The energy of his grasp, and the spirit of his conversation, were such as to make me hope he would yet rally—and that the superiority of mind over matter in his composition, would preserve him yet longer."[4]

Not until the final months of his life was Jefferson actually "feeble," however; for instance, one marvels at the volume and range of his correspondence over his last decade. Of course, the work he did between the 1818 Rockfish Gap report and the opening of the University of Virginia in 1825 alone belies the idea that he had sunk into infirmity. He remained alert to and involved in many other issues as well, including his own faith and that of others. Since his collegiate days he had been on a religious journey, from orthodoxy to doubt to, finally, creation of his own version

of the Gospels in 1820. Jefferson continued to write to various correspondents about religion, although he carefully avoided taking a proselytizing
tone. He wrote to the Reverend Thomas Whittemore on June 5, 1822, that
he was pleased to learn of the growing popularity of antitrinitarianism,
but as always Jefferson refrained from specifying the exact beliefs he
thought others should accept. As he said, "I have never permitted myself
to meditate a specified creed. These formulas have been the bane and ruin
of the Christian church."[5]

Later that month Jefferson corresponded with Dr. Benjamin
Waterhouse, with whom he had worked years before on a vaccination
against small pox, and again Jefferson reported his pleasure to learn that
the doctrine of one God (rather than a triune deity) was gaining traction.
He also summarized his basic interpretation of Christianity: "1. That there
is one only God, and He all perfect. 2. That there is a future state of rewards and punishments. 3. That to love God with all thy heart and thy
neighbor as thyself, is the sum of religion."[6] With his typical optimism, he
wrote, "I rejoice that in this blessed country of free inquiry and belief . . .
the genuine doctrine of one only God is reviving, and I trust that there is
not a young man now living in the United States who will not die as
Unitarian."[7] Since evangelicalism was in ascendance in the South, Jefferson
perhaps did not mean the literal triumph of the Unitarian Church but
rather the success of a vastly simplified theology that resulted in more of a
folk religion than a hierarchal and rigid system of belief and practice. He
could hardly wait to witness the declining influence of the clergy, especially the Presbyterians. This prediction turned out to be entirely wrong.
But Jefferson never departed from his insistence on the simplicity of the
Gospels, truly read. "Christians," he said in 1824, should "rally to the
Sermon in [sic] the mount, make that the central point of Union in religion, and the stamp of genuine Christianity."[8]

ANOTHER PERENNIAL MATTER was his concern that the national government was growing too strong and exceeding its proper constitutional limits. He had carefully outlined his understanding of the genius of the
American system in a letter to Joseph C. Cabell in 1816. "The way to have
good and safe government," he wrote, "is not to trust it all to one; but to
divide it among the many, distributing to every one exactly the functions
he is competent to. let the National government be entrusted with the
defence of the nation, and it's foreign & federal relations; the State governments with the civil rights, laws, police & administration of what

concerns the state generally."[9] Jefferson's worry about the tendency of the federal government to expand in power related closely to his antipathy for John Marshall and how he believed Marshall controlled and ran the Supreme Court. Jefferson interpreted the dispute over slavery in Missouri as part of the trend toward increasing the dominance of the national government over state governments.

Jefferson's fear that the national government—with a rogue Marshall-dominated Supreme Court at the forefront—was arrogating the rights of the states became a motif of his correspondence in the final years of his life. We see him remarking in 1821 that he was "sensible of the inroads daily [made] by the federal, into the jurisdiction of its co-ordinate associates, the State governments. . . . The judiciary branch is the instrument which, working like gravity, without intermission, is to press us at last into one consolidated mass."[10] Two months later he wrote, "The great object of my fear is the federal judiciary. That body, working like gravity, ever acting, with noiseless foot, and unalarming advance, gaining ground step by step[.] . . . Let the eye of vigilance never be closed."[11] Jefferson did not—as later southerners would—deem the state governments more important than or rightfully superior to the national government. Nor was he invoking "states' rights" as a means of defending the institution of slavery.

He never could free himself from abstract concern about the theoretical balance between state and federal powers, which made him—oddly for a person who had so eloquently protested against the dead hand of the past—a cautious and conservative political thinker in his final years, in the sense that he simply could not accept a more powerful federal government. This explains why Jefferson attacked President John Quincy Adams's call, in December 1825, for a strongly nationalistic—and progressive—program of internal improvements, including canals, roads, and a national university and astronomical observatory. On a gloomy Christmas Eve, days after first reading about this proposal, Jefferson wrote a highly negative response. He sent this document to James Madison, who wisely suggested that Jefferson bury it; as usual Jefferson took Madison's advice.

But he did not suggest separation or secession as a possible and justified response to Adams's proposals. Even when the states believed their rights were being trampled, he argued that they should not question the very foundation of American government, because they "owe every other sacrifice to ourselves, to our federal brethren, and to the world at large, to pursue with temper and perseverance the great experiment which shall prove that man is capable of living in society, governing itself by laws self-imposed, and securing to its' members the enjoyment of life, liberty, property and peace." If the federal government seemed to be moving beyond its constitutional limits, we should not despair but instead wait for the citizenry, in their "watchfulness," to recognize the problem and "reform it's aberrations. . . . And these are the objects of this Declaration and Protest," which Madison had counseled him to bury. Thus one solution to Adams's proposal would be to pass a constitutional amendment making internal improvements a federal responsibility. After all, Jefferson did not oppose improvements in themselves; on the contrary, he had long advocated fervently not only for new and renovated infrastructure that would directly promote internal trade and commerce but also, of course, for new institutions of learning and science. He simply believed the federal government should not act without constitutional authorization[12]—except in moments of extraordinary danger or opportunity, such as the Louisiana Purchase; then a president should do what was necessary, turning to the people afterward for forgiveness or approbation.

Jefferson never believed the Constitution a rigid, immutable document; rather, he thought it should evolve as the nation matured. "Some men look at constitutions with sanctimonious reverence, and deem them, like the arc of the covenant, too sacred to be touched," he wrote, an idea he repudiated. While he did not believe in constant and casual change, he argued, "The laws and institutions [of the nation] must go hand in hand with the progress of the human mind." The nation's legislators had to abide by the Constitution, but the Constitution itself provided a method for revision when the people thought it advisable.[13]

But in normal circumstances, in the absence of such an amendment, citizens should "pay full obedience at all times to the Acts" under protest.[14] In the document attacking Adams's proposals, Jefferson called not for secession but for patience and for a search to challenge alleged incorrect interpretations of the Constitution. This episode does lead one to doubt that had Jefferson lived until 1861, he "would have gone with the Confederacy," as one prominent modern scholar has suggested.[15] Despite his (infrequent) fulminations and hyperbolic rhetoric, the bedrock of Jefferson's mature political thought was the doctrine that "nothing then is unchangeable but the inherent and unalienable rights of man."[16] And the union guaranteed those rights.

As he wrote in 1820, an act of secession was an act of "treason against the hopes of the world."[17] When invited in 1826 to attend a celebration in

Washington, DC, of the fiftieth anniversary of the Declaration of Independence, Jefferson—in the next-to-the-last letter he ever composed—respectfully declined on the grounds of his poor health. Still, with hands crippled by rheumatism, he wrote ten days before his death that, regarding the declaration, "May it be to the world, what I believe it will be . . . the signal of arousing men to burst the chains under which monkish ignorance and superstition had persuaded them to bind themselves, and to assume the blessings and security of self-government. That form which we have substituted, restores the free right to the unbounded exercise of reason and freedom of opinion. All eyes are opened, or opening, to the rights of man. . . . the mass of mankind has not been born with saddles on their backs, nor a favored few booted and spurred, ready to ride them legitimately, by the grace of God. These are the grounds of hope for others."[18] These words represented Thomas Jefferson's political valedictory. He still believed, as he had stated in his first inaugural address a quarter century earlier, that the American government established by the Constitution was "the world's best hope."[19]

NOR DID JEFFERSON ever stop thinking about a related dilemma, slavery, though he continued to ponder it more in the context of the nation's future than of his own life. By now he believed that his financial woes made it impossible for him to free his slaves. Even if he managed to sell all his land in Virginia's depressed economy, doing so would not bring in enough funds to allow him to purchase land for his slaves in a state that permitted free black migration and also provide them the means to start a prosperous life in freedom. While he did not neglect the potential benefits for the enslaved that general emancipation would bring, he seems to have been more interested in the positive influence of abolitionism on the (white) nation, if the elimination of slavery was tied to colonization. He never ceased believing that slavery was evil, but he never succeeded in working out a politically or economically viable way to end it. He remained convinced that immediate and wholesale emancipation, with no provision for colonization, would likely lead to a genocidal war between whites and blacks. He appears to have resigned himself to his personal failure to emancipate his own slaves, but he clung to a kind of mystical hope that the nation could overcome sectional differences, fund emancipation, subsidize the transport of slaves to another location—ideally in the West Indies—and furnish them with the supplies, tools, and skills to succeed as citizens in their own distinct nation. For many years, he never explained how the United States would find the political will to effect this massive act of expatriation.

In an 1824 letter to Jared Sparks, editor of the *North American Review*, Jefferson finally presented a plan to emancipate and colonize America's slaves. He admitted that limited colonization in Africa could "introduce among the aborigines the arts of cultivated life, and the blessings of civilization and science. By doing this, we may make to them some retribution for the long course of injuries we have been committing on their population." This was a common argument of colonizationists during the first three decades of the nineteenth century, and like many of the ministerial supporters of the colonization movement, Jefferson thought such a relocation of freed slaves to Africa could "in the long run . . . render them perhaps more good than evil." Thus the colonization movement "could be considered as a missionary society."[20]

Yet, though Jefferson supported the idea of "send[ing] the whole population from among us, and establish[ing] them under our patronage and protection, as a separate, free, and independent people, in some country and climate friendly to human life and happiness," he did not think Africa was such a place.[21] He believed it too unhealthy and the transport costs involved too high. As always, he believed the West Indies the far more promising site. He proposed a multiyear program whereby after a certain date, slave children would be taken from their mothers, trained in various occupations, and ultimately sent to their new home; he thought the sale of public lands in the various states could underwrite the effort. He believed that purchasing newborns for later training might be economically feasible, because the babies would be significantly cheaper. He also believed that the black rulers of Haiti, now "independent, and with a population of that color only," were ready to "receive them as free citizens, and to provide for their employment."[22] Perhaps surprisingly for a relatively benevolent slave owner, Jefferson deemed the cruelty of separating infants and toddlers from their mothers insignificant in comparison to the great and lasting good of emancipation.

In July of the following year, 1825, Jefferson learned of the plan of Fanny Wright, a British freethinker, feminist, and abolitionist, to establish an interracial colony near Memphis, Tennessee, where slaves could work and earn money to purchase their own freedom, after which they would migrate to either Africa or Haiti. Jefferson offered only moral support, no practical plans of his own. The cause of emancipation, he wrote to Wright, "has been through life [one] of my greatest anxieties. The march of events has not been such as to render its completion practicable within the limits of time allotted to me; and I leave its accomplishment as the work of another generation."[23] He told her that he was "cheered" by the current effort and the people promoting it, counseling, "The abolition of the evil is not impossible; it ought never therefore to be despaired of. Every plan should be adopted, every experiment tried, which may do something towards the ultimate object. That which you propose is well worthy of trial." He mentioned several other projects underway, offering that even if her plans did not work out exactly as hoped, still "it may yet, in its development, lead to happy results. These, however," he said, repeating himself, "I must leave to another generation."[24]

In other words, Jefferson remained suspended between reality and hope until his death. Just weeks before the end, in his penultimate letter, he wrote once again about slavery and his hesitancy to take a more aggressive stand for emancipation. Addressing James Heaton, a correspondent from Ohio, he counseled caution, saying that "persuasion, perseverance, and patience" were always necessary when trying to change public opinion, and such efforts should not be expected to produce quick results: "but time, which outlives all things, will outlive this evil also."[25] Within a few years, new advocates of immediate emancipation would revolt against this gradualist approach. Jefferson did not live to see that day and was content to simply wait patiently for the necessary change in public opinion. It only came, of course, as the result of the bloodiest war in American history, an event that would have horrified him.

ON THE QUESTION OF Europe and, specifically, whether the United States should involve itself in foreign affairs, Jefferson remained cautious. He spelled out his ideas to German explorer Alexander von Humboldt in some detail in 1813. Imagining a nation no "longer to be involved in the never-ceasing broils of Europe," he described the geographical division of the world. "The European nations constitute a separate division of the globe; their localities make them part of a distinct system; they have a set of interests of their own in which it is our business never to engage ourselves. America has a hemisphere to itself. It must have its separate system of interests, which must not be subordinated to those of Europe. The insulated state in which nature has placed the American continent, should so far avail it that no spark of war kindled in the other quarters of the globe should be wafted across the wide oceans which separate us from them. And it will be so."[26] Jefferson repeated this sentiment several years later in a letter to William Short, remarking, "The day is not distant, when we may formally require a meridian of partition through the ocean which separates the two hemispheres, on the hither side of which no European gun shall ever be heard, nor an American on the other."[27]

Beginning in the second decade of the nineteenth century, one Spanish colony after another in South America revolted and declared its independence. Meanwhile, in Europe, the monarchist powers of Russia, Austria, and Prussia in 1815 arranged the so-called Holy Alliance (or Grand Alliance) to suppress revolutionary, progressive tendencies in Europe, and soon France had joined them. France invaded Spain to prop up the country's monarch and put down a liberal movement that had recently drafted a constitution. When in the early summer of 1823 President James Monroe sent Jefferson a letter recounting recent events in Europe, France's interference in Spanish affairs appalled the former president, who responded that the "presumption of dictating to an independent nation the form of its government, is so arrogant, so atrocious, that indignation, as moral sentiment, enlists all our partialities and prayers in favor of one, and our equal execrations against the other." He was clearly outraged. "But farther than this," he wrote, "we are not bound to go; . . . I have ever deemed it fundamental for the United States, never to take active part in the quarrels of Europe."[28]

A more serious question quickly arose. Would Spain now, individually or in coordination with the Holy Alliance, try to stamp out the revolutionary movements in Latin America? England, enjoying profitable trade with the former Spanish colonies, strongly opposed any intervention in South American affairs that might jeopardize its commerce. George Canning, the English foreign minister, approached the American ambassador to England, Richard Rush, with a proposal: the United States should join England, whose navy would act as enforcer, in preventing any intervention by the Holy Alliance in the American hemisphere. Rush communicated this proposal to President Monroe, who on October 16 wrote to Jefferson for advice on the issue (and asking him to forward the president's letter on to Madison for his response too). Monroe allowed, "My own impression is that we ought to meet the proposal of the British government."[29] On October 24 Jefferson replied.[30]

He started by characterizing the issue as "the most momentous which has ever been offered to my contemplation since that of Independence."

That event made the American colonies into a nation; this new proposal "points the course which we are to steer through the ocean of time opening on us." Jefferson restated the position Monroe probably already knew he would take: "Our first and fundamental maxim should be, never to entangle ourselves in the broils of Europe. Our second, never to suffer Europe to intermeddle with cis-Atlantic affairs. America, North and South, has a set of interests distinct from those of Europe."[31] While Europe seemed once again to be leaning toward despotism, "our endeavor," Jefferson stated, "should surely be, to make our hemisphere that of freedom." Then, displaying the pragmatic streak that had shaped his foreign policy as president, and using words that may have surprised Monroe, Jefferson continued, "By acceding to her proposition, we . . . bring her mighty weight into the scale of free governments, and emancipate a continent at one stroke, which might otherwise linger long in doubt and difficulty. . . . with her on our side we need not fear the whole world."[32]

That Jefferson backed an accord with England might seem strange, but he remained centrally committed to the United States and had always been willing to trade and otherwise cooperate with other nations if doing so benefited the cause of American freedom. And in this case, he believed that joining England would "prevent rather than provoke war." He supported a declaration that the United States did not aim "at the acquisition of any of those [formerly Spanish] possessions, that we will not stand in the way of any amicable arrangement between them and the mother country; but that we will oppose, with all our means, the forcible interposition of any other power . . . and most especially, their transfer to any power by conquest, cession, or acquisition in any way."[33]

Monroe also received support from Madison, although he surely expected his two predecessors to agree with one another. After much discussion in his cabinet, where he had the strong support of Secretary of State John Quincy Adams, Monroe issued what eventually became known as the Monroe Doctrine, declaring US noninterference in European affairs and warning Europe against interference in the Americas. Diverging from Jefferson, Monroe decided that an independently drafted proclamation would double as a signal of US autonomy and power. He knew that, in any case, it was in England's interest to support an American policy with its strong navy. Canning, seeing that Monroe had outplayed him, was annoyed. The doctrine would shape European-American affairs for the next century and beyond.

OVER THE COURSE of his adult life, Jefferson was committed to maintaining a record of his correspondence. While in France he began using a letterpress to make copies of his outgoing correspondence, and during his presidency he switched to the polygraph. His Monticello study contained a series of cabinets in which he carefully filed his incoming and outgoing mail—he kept a log of each letter received and the date—and from an early age he also collected copies of the laws of Virginia, various documents, and records of other sorts. He understood that later historians would need a documentary record to build on.[34] In 1823 he expressed to a correspondent his agreement "that it is the duty of every good citizen to use all the opportunities which occur to him, for preserving documents relating to the history of our country."[35]

So it is surprising that Jefferson did not seek to publish any portion of his private letters, state papers, or other addresses during his lifetime. Despite leaving modern historians an incomparable trove of primary sources, he produced no formal history of his era. He gathered together notes he had taken on his years as secretary of state and had them privately bound in what he called his "anas," an archaic term for a collection of materials on a particular subject. But he went no further. Comments he made in private letters about Patrick Henry and, more famously, about George Washington reveal that he could produce brilliant character sketches, but except for his biographical portrait of Meriwether Lewis, he did not set his hand to such tasks. And but for a letter from his intimate friend William Short, Jefferson may not have written even the partial, private autobiography that he began in 1821. We must be grateful for the little we know about Jefferson that comes from the man himself.

After rereading Benjamin Franklin's autobiography, William Short wrote to Jefferson in March 1820, "I have lately read over again Dr. Franklin's plain and simple narration of the events of his own life. It has renewed my desire to see the same kind of work from yourself." Short said he would not press Jefferson to do something against his will, "notwithstanding the great gratification it would give to your invariable and faithful friend."[36] Perhaps the letter caught Jefferson at just the right moment, for his rheumatism and other ailments may have led him at least temporarily to think about leaving a document for his family, if no one else. Still, he may have had difficulty overcoming his desire to keep his inner life private. Nevertheless, on January 6, 1821, Jefferson began to write his autobiography, although the very first sentence suggested it would not be a personal reflection on his life. Rather, Jefferson began by announcing his intention to "make some memoranda and state some recollections of dates & facts concerning myself, for my own ready reference & for the information of my family."[37]

While the resulting partial autobiography provides otherwise unavailable information about Jefferson's time at the College of William & Mary, it gives nothing more than the essentials about his parents and tells us only slightly more about several of his early tutors. He does point out the value of his interactions with his professors at college and with the royal governor, but his entire experience at William & Mary takes up less than one page. He records nothing about how he met and came to marry Martha Wayles Skelton, although he does say that, upon her death, he "lost the cherished companion of my life, in whose affections, unabated on both sides, I had lived the last ten years in unchequered happiness."[38] That is the most intimate comment in the entire autobiography, which Jefferson did not intend as a personally revealing memoir.

Notwithstanding these limitations, and though the book contains few colorful anecdotes, he did leave valuable comments about his role in pre-revolutionary Virginia, in the Continental Congress, and in other events before 1791. He took the liberty of correcting alleged misunderstandings, including, for example, John Marshall's crediting Massachusetts—rather than Virginia—with the idea of creating committees of correspondence between the colonies.[39] Showing his enduring sensitivity about Congress's changes to his original text of the Declaration of Independence, he reproduced his version, with the excisions underlined and additions included as marginalia.[40] He wanted his full draft preserved. In addition, he offered several critical comments about Patrick Henry, though Jefferson credited him for his role in bringing attention to the revolutionary cause and said of him that he appeared "to speak as Homer wrote."[41] Jefferson included brief but remarkably insightful sketches of George Mason and James Madison, praising the latter's "pure and spotless virtue" and his "luminous and discriminating mind."[42] Then there are examples of the aphoristic language that often makes Jefferson's writing so memorable. For instance, while narrating the occasion when he and others planned to add an amendment to a proposed law in Virginia that would have ended slavery, he added, "Nothing is more certainly written in the book of fate than that these people are to be free."[43]

His discussion of the lead-up to revolution in France is disproportionately long and involved, but he thought Americans were interested in the topic and knew little about it—and he had firsthand insights. This section ends, in essence, with a love note to France, even though its leaders and policies since Jefferson's time there had often infuriated and disappointed him. He concluded that any well-traveled person, if asked where in the world he would choose to live outside his native land, would reply, "France."[44] And then, three pages later, having just reached the spring of 1791, when he was assuming the office of secretary of state, he quit. His last words were "So far July 29.[18]21."[45] He never picked up the story again.

JEFFERSON WAS NOT a morbid man, but by 1825 his unremitting health problems led him to surmise that he did not have long to live and would be in frequent pain until his death. He said as much to his personal physician, Dr. Robley Dunglison, who made a number of visits to Monticello that year. Finally Jefferson admitted to him in late November, "The fragment of life remaining to me is likely to be past in sickness and suffering."[46] Persistent diarrhea weakened him considerably, and Dr. Dunglison had him on a regular regimen of opiates to relieve the pain. Given as laudanum, a tincture of opium, the drug did alleviate the symptoms, though Jefferson had to take heavier doses as time passed.[47] He could no longer take the lengthy walks so central to his daily life, and he could barely ride. The slave stable master would lead his favorite horse, Eagle, a handsome bay with a white star on his forehead and white hind feet, up to the side of the terrace outside Jefferson's room, and Jefferson would be gently lowered down into the saddle, with the reins placed in his arthritic hands. To the very end he insisted on riding alone, despite the protests of Martha and other family members.[48]

He had outlived most of his contemporaries, observing to John Adams some years before that anywhere they looked, they could see "the graves of those we have known."[49] His family, too, was diminished. By now his only living sibling was his youngest sister, Anna, who was known as Aunt Marks and lived at Monticello; her twin, Randolph, had died in 1815. Jefferson's first and favorite grandchild, Anne Cary Bankhead, was also living at Monticello, and Jefferson had long grieved over her suffering at the hands of her alcoholic and abusive husband. Jefferson was greatly saddened when another of his favorites, granddaughter Ellen Wayles Randolph, married Joseph Coolidge Jr. of Boston in May 1825 and soon after moved to Massachusetts. She had been quite close to her grandfather, and he never recovered from her departing Monticello; he wrote her that summer, "We did not know, until you left us, what a void it would make in our family."⁵⁰ When Jefferson discovered that the ship carrying all her papers, belongings, and other goods to Massachusetts had been lost at sea—taking with it a much-beloved writing box made for her by John Hemings, who Jefferson had had trained as a carpenter—he sent her the writing box he had used in Philadelphia in 1776 when composing the Declaration of Independence,⁵¹ an act typical of the generosity that so endeared Jefferson to all his grandchildren.

A freak accident in early October almost killed Jefferson. A sculptor named John H. I. Browere came to Monticello to take a plaster cast of his head, from which he would make a life mask. This involved coating Jefferson's face and head with layers of wet plaster, which would be removed as soon as it had set. Jefferson was laying back in a chair, and the family went on about its business. But probably because of the sculptor's incompetence, the plaster hardened quicker than expected. Unable to breath and too weakened to summon help, Jefferson almost suffocated. Fortunately, he managed to lift an adjacent chair and slam it to the floor, whereupon his slave valet, Burwell Colbert, sprang to his side and began trying to remove the plaster. Browere soon frantically joined in. As Jefferson later explained the scene to Madison, "He was obliged to use freely the mallet and chisel to break it into pieces and cut off a piece at a time. These thumps of the mallet would have been sensible almost to a loggerhead [a large sea turtle]. The family became alarmed, and he confused, till I was quite exhausted, and there became a real danger that the ears would separate from the head sooner than from the plaister. I now bid adieu for ever to busts."⁵² It was quite a trial for an octogenarian.

THOUGH ON THE DECLINE, Jefferson suffered the train of visitors who continued to come up his little mountain simply to see or, if they were lucky, converse with the man now often called—after John Adams's coinage—the Sage of Monticello. Even though the visitors sapped his energy and emptied his cupboard, he was too polite to turn them away. He remained engaged, too, in the university, a project no doubt good for his morale and health. But ever-looming financial concerns wore him down, robbed him of sleep, and led him to worry about Martha and her children now that Thomas Mann Randolph was bankrupt and mostly separated from the family. The state's economy was in decline, land sales were stagnant, and property values were declining. What could be done?

As his daughter related it, he had a revelation one sleepless night. In early January 1826, Martha wrote to Ellen Coolidge that he was "lying awake one night from painful thoughts" when an idea suddenly hit him "like an inspiration from the realms of bliss."[53] The next morning Jefferson promptly confided the idea to his grandson Jeff, who thought it a possible solution to the family's situation. The idea was for a lottery: for a small, manageable sum, people could buy a raffle ticket that would give them a chance of winning items from his Monticello property. There existed much opposition in the state—especially among evangelicals—to anything that hinted of gambling or games of chance, and Jefferson himself had previously opposed such schemes. Any lottery had to secure legislative approval to go forward. Jefferson managed to satisfy his scruples in this case, rationalizing that charities had resorted to similar methods to raise funds. Jefferson arranged for Jeff and close supporters, including Joseph C. Cabell, to take the issue to the General Assembly. In his explanation of the proposed lottery, Jefferson said that if successful the sale of the tickets would "pay my debts and leave a living for myself in my old age, and leave something for my family. . . . To me it is almost a question of life and death."[54]

When his proposal met with principled opposition, Jefferson fretted and feared the worst. Humiliated, he wrote to Jeff, "It is a part of my mortification to perceive that I had so far overvalued myself, as to have counted on it with too much confidence. I see, in the failure of this hope, a deadly blast of all my peace of mind, during my remaining days."[55] He was most concerned about providing for Martha and her children. And at that moment, his beloved granddaughter Anne, whose abusive marriage had troubled him for years, had just had another baby and was not recovering; his own health had not allowed him to journey to her bedside. Amid this sadness Jefferson realized anew how much Jeff meant to him, writing to him in this same letter, "Yourself particularly, dear Jefferson, I consider as the greatest of the god-sends which heaven has granted me."[56] When, three days later, Jefferson finally visited Anne, he found her "speechless and insensible." Dr. Dunglison, who witnessed the scene, recorded that it was "impossible to imagine more poignant distress than was exhibited by him. He shed tears, and abandoned himself to every evidence of intense grief."[57] Anne died later that day.

By late February he learned, at least, that the General Assembly had approved his lottery. The legislature limited the total amount of the sales to the value of Monticello plantation in order to guarantee that the lottery was not a for-profit scheme. But the offerings would have to include the house of Monticello itself. With this news, Jefferson's face noticeably blanched, according to a witness. Stunned, he said he would need to consult with Martha, who he had imagined would continue to live in the house after his death. Jeff assured him that Martha would be able to remain at Monticello for years.[58] Jefferson gave his consent.

Yet the lottery came together slowly (raffle tickets had to be printed), and meanwhile Jeff toured several eastern cities and came across groups organizing to raise funds for Jefferson now that his plight was becoming better known. Money flowed in from Baltimore, Philadelphia, and New York; later, the legislatures of South Carolina and Louisiana appropriated sums to give directly to Jefferson. The gifts seemed to render the lottery unnecessary but soon proved insufficient. Jefferson died believing that the voluntary contributions would cover his debts, but that was not to be.

By THE TIME THE General Assembly was considering his lottery proposal, Jefferson seemed to accept his impending death with composure. Henry Lee, who visited him on June 29, 1826, recalled that he "alluded to the probability of his death—as a man would to the prospect of being caught in a shower—as an event not to be desired, but not to be feared."[59] Jefferson wrote Madison a valedictory letter in mid-February, remarking, "The friendship which has subsisted between us, now half a century, and the harmony of our political principles and pursuits, have been sources of constant happiness to me through that long period." He told Madison how pleased he was that the university would be in Madison's care. Then, thinking about his afterlife in the pages of history books, Jefferson continued, "It has also been a great solace to me, to believe that you are engaged in vindicating to posterity the course we have pursued for preserving to them, in all their purity, the blessings of self-government, which we had assisted too in acquiring for them. . . . To myself you have been a pillar of support though life. Take care of me when dead, and be assured that I shall leave you with my last affections."[60] To the very end, Jefferson was concerned about his reputation and fearful that political opponents would misrepresent his ideas and policies.

Almost a month later Jefferson turned to a final piece of business: his will. In it, he left to grandson Francis Eppes his lands (very precisely described) at Poplar Forest. All his other property would go to paying his debts. Assuming there would be something left after that, he designated three trustees—his grandson Jeff, grandson-in-law Nicholas P. Trist, and

Alexander Garrett, the bursar of the University of Virginia—as the executors of his residual estate, to be used solely for the support and benefit of his daughter, Martha, and her heirs. He excluded her husband, Thomas Mann Randolph, from any and all executive functions. (After Randolph's death, the other two executors would step aside, leaving Jeff as the sole executor.) In a series of codicils Jefferson recommended that Martha care for Jefferson's sister Anna Scott Marks for the remainder of her life; gave his gold-mounted walking stick to Madison; donated his books to the University of Virginia; bequeathed gold watches to those of his grandchildren who had not already received one; and granted freedom to five "servants," as he labeled them, all members of the Hemings family: Burwell Colbert, John Hemings, Joe Fossett, Madison Hemings, and Eston Hemings. The latter two would gain emancipation at the age of twenty-one; in the meantime, they were to serve John Hemings as his apprentices. Jefferson also called for the construction of log cabins for the first three men, along with $200 for Colbert to purchase the tools of his trade, glaziery. To the ever-dependable Jeff, Jefferson gave not only a watch but his business papers (necessary for Jeff's duties as executor), and "all others of a literary or other character I give to him as of his own property." Included were the thousands of letters, neatly stacked in wooden cabinets.[61] Thus was the invaluable archive preserved for posterity.

During the spring of 1826 Jefferson noticeably declined in stamina, and on top of all of his previous ailments, he had developed prostate problems. He no longer took rides on Eagle, and in April he attended (via carriage) his last meeting of the board of visitors of the university. He had hoped to establish a botanical garden at the university, but his plans foundered. Though visitors continued to stream to Monticello to see the honored sage, his family members now spared him from meeting them. Dr. Dunglison was called to visit Madison in Montpelier in late June, but on July 1 he wrote Madison to decline the invitation, saying that Jefferson was suffering so severely that the doctor's "worst apprehensions must soon be realized."[62] Jefferson had always insisted on taking care of himself, but he no longer could. Now bedridden but still conscious, he spoke with each of his grandchildren, admonishing them "to pursue virtue, be true and truthful."[63] Martha sat with him during the day, sometimes with grandson-in-law Nicholas P. Trist and often with Dr. Dunglison; Jeff spent nights in his room. There were always slaves about, including Jefferson's favorite, Burwell Colbert. On July 2 Jefferson handed Martha a little box; when she opened it after his death, she found a poem he had composed and written himself.

> I go to my fathers, I welcome the shore
> Which crowns all my hopes or which buries my cares.
> Then farewell, my dear, my lov'd daughter, adieu!
> The last pang of life is in parting from you!
> Two seraphs await me long shrouded in death;
> I will bear them your love on my last parting breath.[64]

Still later she discovered, in a drawer in his room, several small envelopes that contained snippets of the hair of her sister, Maria, and of the two infants named Lucy, as well as what her father had labeled "some of my dear, dear wife's writing."[65] The two seraphs in the poem were, of course, Jefferson's wife Martha and his daughter Maria.

He hovered between consciousness and unconsciousness on July 3, his mind wandering back to the days of the American Revolution; hearing the name of the Reverend Frederick Hatch mentioned, Jefferson said, "I have no objection to see him, as a kind and good neighbor." The family took that as a sign to invite Hatch to officiate at the funeral. Sometime early that morning Jefferson had mistakenly uttered, "This is the fourth of July."[66] No one corrected him. At about 7:00 p.m. he awoke and asked, "Is it the Fourth?" Dr. Dunglison answered, "It soon will be."[67] Later that evening, upon being awakened for another dose of laudanum, Jefferson said clearly, "No, Doctor, nothing more." Still later, Jefferson was obviously trying to communicate with Jeff about something, but to no avail, until Burwell Colbert finally grasped his wish and adjusted his pillow. Now it was after midnight, and July 4 had arrived. Jefferson was barely conscious, but when Jeff put a wet sponge to his lips, he smacked them in satisfaction. He did not speak again, though his eyes opened intermittently in the morning. Hours later, at 12:50 p.m., he ceased breathing, and Jeff leaned over and closed his eyelids.[68]

The funeral on July 6 was, according to Jefferson's wishes, private, with the Reverend Hatch officiating. The day was gloomy and pouring with rain, but still a small crowd of townspeople attended, church bells having announced his death two days before. Placed in a wooden casket crafted by John Hemings, Jefferson was interred between the graves of Martha and Maria in the Monticello family cemetery. Madison, who knew Jefferson best, did not attend because he only learned the news on the day of the funeral. His letter written that day to Nicholas P. Trist revealed his estimation of Jefferson's full worth: "We are more than consoled for the loss by the gain to him, and by the assurance that he lives and will live in the memory and gratitude of the wise and good, as a luminary of science, as a votary of liberty, as a model of patriotism, and as a benefactor of the human kind."[69]

In 1833 an unadorned obelisk designed by Jefferson was erected atop his grave, with a modest inscription:

HERE WAS BURIED
THOMAS JEFFERSON
AUTHOR OF THE
DECLARATION
OF
AMERICAN INDEPENDENCE
OF THE
STATUTE OF VIRGINIA
FOR
RELIGIOUS FREEDOM
AND FATHER OF THE
UNIVERSITY OF VIRGINIA
BORN APRIL 2, 1743. O.S.
DIED JULY 4, 1826

It was a simple marker for a man of vast accomplishments and complexities, the supreme spokesman of America's promise. Ironically, today he is often found wanting for not practicing the principles he articulated best. Yet Jefferson, despite his limitations, more than anyone else was the intellectual architect of the nation's highest ideals. He will always belong in the American pantheon.

Postscript

O N HIS DEATH IN 1826, Thomas Jefferson left behind a daughter and numerous grandchildren and great grandchildren, a home in decay, and unresolved debts amounting to more than $100,000. He believed that a combination of gifts and the proceeds of a lottery of his effects would settle his financial problems, but the lottery fizzled, leaving his executor—his grandson, the dependable Jeff Randolph—saddled with his financial burdens. Jefferson had long worried about supporting his daughter Martha, who had separated from her contentious and depressive husband, but soon she would lose not only the assistance her father had offered but his estate—Monticello—itself. It was fortunate for Jefferson that he did not witness the sad denouement of his affairs: the dispersal of his family and slaves, the sale of his beloved home, and the stressful indebtedness Jeff endured for the rest of his life.

Accepting with reluctance that she could no longer afford to reside at Monticello itself, Martha decided to travel to Boston and live—at least for a while—with her daughter Ellen and son-in-law Joseph Coolidge. Before she left for New England, the family, after much discussion, decided to sell everything except the physical structure of Monticello—the slaves, farm animals and equipment, household furnishings, and various memorabilia—keeping only Jefferson's art collection and books for a later sale in Boston, where they might fetch more. Luckily Martha would be staying with Ellen when the household auction occurred, on January 19, 1827.

Jeff recalled in his memoirs, "The breaking up [of Jefferson's] estate, sale and dispersion of his slaves was a sad scene. I had known all of them from childhood and had strong attachments to many." Of course, it was a much sadder day for the slaves themselves, even if, as Jeff wrote, "they were sold in families."[1] Jeff's memory was not exactly correct: one slave woman's children were sold in six different lots. The auction brought in almost $49,000, most of which went to paying down Jefferson's debt; about $13,000 went to covering accrued interest. The Boston sale brought practically nothing.

In late May 1828 Martha returned to Albemarle County only to find Thomas Mann Randolph, from whom she had been estranged for years, near death in his solitary room in Monticello's North Pavilion. In his last weeks he reached out to seek forgiveness from Martha, his children, and especially his son Jeff, whom he had often unfairly blamed for his own plight. Martha was relieved that in his final days, a family reconciliation did occur; Randolph died on June 20.[2] Martha stayed very briefly in the now bare Monticello, then moved to Jeff's recently enlarged home at Edgehill; for the next few months, however, she lived mostly with friends and other relatives. In the spring she returned to Edgehill. Though she was very close to Jeff and his affectionate wife, Jane, the home must have brought back memories both pleasant and sad: looking westward, she could see in the foreground the original site of the Shadwell house where her father had been born in 1743, and farther in the distance loomed the little mountain he had long ago named Monticello.

For the remainder of her life, Martha eked out a living, staying most of the time in rented homes in Washington, DC, with occasional lengthy visits to her children and other relatives. Although she lived in genteel poverty, Martha was something of a celebrity in Washington, often finding herself invited to dinners hosted by Andrew Jackson, Martin Van Buren, and others. She died on October 10, 1836, while visiting Jeff and his family at Edgehill. She was buried in the family cemetery at Monticello, her tomb lying perpendicular to those of her mother, father, and sister.

Jeff continued in his role as the family's patriarch, working to provide for his own immediate (and large) family and for extended family. He was always paying back his grandfather's debt. Jeff served six terms in the Virginia House of Delegates, where in 1832 he introduced a bill for the gradual emancipation of Virginia's slaves, followed by their colonization outside the borders of the United States, a plan likely inspired by those of his grandfather. But in the aftermath of the 1831 Nat Turner slave insurrection, the bill failed to pass. With the delegates, the state, and the South overall suddenly on edge, harsh repression of the slaves rather than their emancipation became the rage.[3] As for another of his grandfather's legacies, not until after Jeff's death on October 8, 1875, and the settlement of his own estate three years later were Thomas Jefferson's debts extinguished.[4]

The family had finally agreed in the fall of 1828 to sell the house at Monticello. Jefferson had not been able to afford its upkeep, and over the years the weather, as well as thousands of guests, had reduced it to a poor state. Jeff had hoped Monticello, along with surrounding acreage, would attract an offer of approximately $10,000, but since the state was mired in an economic depression, no buyers at that level emerged. Finally, in 1831 a pharmacist in Charlottesville named James Turner Barclay offered $4,500, plus a house in Charlottesville, for Monticello and 552 acres of surrounding land. The sale was finalized on November 1, 1831, and shortly thereafter the Barclays furnished the house and moved in. Barclay's wife improved Monticello's condition, while he himself planted mulberry trees in the fields, hoping to raise silkworms. But his plans for Monticello soon foundered, in part as a result of the ongoing hordes of tourists. By October 1833 the Barclays had had enough and put the house back on the market.[5]

An unlikely buyer appeared: Uriah P. Levy, a Philadelphia-born Jewish lieutenant in the US Navy who greatly admired Jefferson for his efforts on behalf of religious freedom. Levy visited and on April 5, 1834, made an offer of $2,700 for the house and 218 acres of surrounding land. The deal was consummated on May 20, 1836, and thereafter, when his naval career would allow, Lieutenant Levy spent a month or more annually at Monticello. He spent thousands of dollars rehabilitating the home itself: fixing broken window panes, repainting, replacing rotted wooden shutters, and so on; he also planted new trees and shrubs. Levy's efforts stabilized the house and prevented further deterioration. Toward the end of his life, in 1858, Levy drew up a will proposing to bequeath Monticello and its nearby acreage to "the People of the United States," but Congress did not know how the Constitution could allow the government to accept the property (or pay for its renovation).[6] As a result, Monticello lingered in domiciliary purgatory for several years.

After the start of the Civil War, the Confederate government, under the terms of the Alien Enemies Act of 1861, seized Monticello on the grounds that an officer of the US Navy owned it. After a great deal of legal wrangling, the Levy estate regained the property in 1873. Meanwhile the house had fallen into ruin: windows were broken, the roof leaked, the terraces had rotted through, graffiti defaced the front of the house, souvenir hunters had chipped away at Jefferson's burial shaft, any remaining furnishings had been stolen, and even shrubs had been pulled up as keepsakes. Some of the rooms had stored grain; the basement had stabled horses. Bats and rats gamboled and searched for food throughout the empty dwelling.[7] Uriah Levy's nephew, the aptly named Jefferson Monroe Levy, who shared his uncle's reverence for Jefferson, stepped in to rescue the home. In the late 1870s he began buying acreage and shares of the house from other members of his family, and by 1879, when the Virginia courts decreed a public sale to settle lingering disputes over ownership, Jefferson Monroe Levy was the sole proprietor of Monticello.

The new owner had the intent and the resources to return Jefferson's home to its former glory. Over the next few decades Levy restored and modernized the house, adding bathrooms and eventually electrical wiring. He furnished it with the heavy Victorian furniture of the era but did not change its internal structure. From 1880 to 1922, the Levy family spent about four months there annually, and once again the house attracted visitors and guests. We can credit Jefferson Monroe Levy with saving Monticello.

By the second decade of the twentieth century, a group of American citizens had launched a movement to purchase the home from the Levy family and transform it into a house museum open to the public. Out of sincere love for the house, Levy resisted. Eventually, however, he sustained financial losses and found it necessary to sell. In 1923 the newly formed Thomas Jefferson Memorial Foundation raised funds to purchase Monticello.[8] In subsequent years the home was completely renewed: steel beams replaced rotted floor joists, modern heating and cooling were added, and architects and preservationists meticulously restored the house. The result, by the early 1950s, was a better Monticello than Jefferson himself ever saw. It has since become one of the most treasured house museums in America. Joining the giant bust of Jefferson carved into Mount Rushmore in 1939, the Jefferson Memorial dedicated in 1943 in Washington, DC, and the original campus of the University of Virginia, Monticello completed the quartet of permanent physical tributes to the architect of American liberty.

Acknowledgments

I am indebted to the teachers who introduced me, half a century ago, to Thomas Jefferson, S. W. Higginbotham, Bernard Mayo, and Merrill D. Peterson, as well as, obliquely, Dumas Malone; to the past two generations of scholars who have written about Jefferson; to the various editors associated with the projects to publish his papers; to the librarians of Fondren Library at Rice University; to my colleagues, especially Randal L. Hall and Bethany Johnson; to Suzanne Scott Gibbs; and to my graduate research assistant, Cara J. Rogers. Rice University, from my first day as a freshman to the present day, has been the center of my academic life, even when I was not here. Dan Gerstle at Basic Books pushed me to find the more concise biography lurking within my original, much longer manuscript and has edited the result with care, intelligence, and enormous patience. The entire team at Basic Books has been ideal to work with: Hélène Barthélemy, Meg Peck, Michelle Welsh-Horst, copyeditor Jennifer Kelland Fagan, indexer Catherine Bowman, and publicist Carrie Majer. My wife, Nancy, has accommodated my work habits for decades, and friends Michael and Donna Kay Farr and Jim and Nancy Lomax have put up with listening to me talk endlessly about Jefferson. Our sons, David and Matthew, and their wives, Stephanie and Janica, have contributed immensely to our sense of fulfillment, and their children—Parker, Bailey, Sonia, and Nicolas—are not only the joyful center of our lives but offer hope for the future. This book is lovingly dedicated to them.

Abbreviations in Notes

Bergh	*The Writings of Thomas Jefferson*, ed. Albert Ellery Bergh, 20 vols. (Washington, DC, 1907)
DL	Sarah N. Randolph, *The Domestic Life of Thomas Jefferson* (1871; rpt. Charlottesville, 1978)
FB	Edwin Morris Betts, ed., *Thomas Jefferson's Farm Book* (Charlottesville, 1987)
FL	*The Family Letters of Thomas Jefferson*, ed. Edwin Morris Betts and James Adam Bear Jr. (1966; rpt. Charlottesville, 1986)
GB	Edwin Morris Betts, ed., *Thomas Jefferson's Garden Book* (Monticello, 2012)
JMB	James A. Bear Jr. and Lucia C. Stanton, eds., *Jefferson's Memorandum Books: Accounts, with Legal Records and Miscellany, 1767–1826* (Princeton, 1997)
Notes	*Notes on the State of Virginia*, ed. William Peden (Chapel Hill, 1954)
PJMSSS	*The Papers of James Madison, Secretary of State Series*, ed. David B. Matten et al., 10 vols. To date (Charlottesville, 1986–)
PTJ	*Papers of Thomas Jefferson*, ed. Julian P. Boyd (Princeton, 1950)
PTJRS	*Papers of Thomas Jefferson, Retirement Series*, ed. J. Jefferson Looney (Princeton, NJ, 2011)
VTM	*Visitors to Monticello*, ed. by Merrill D. Peterson (Charlottesville, 1989)

Notes

A NOTE ON CAPITALIZATION

1. Julian P. Boyd, ed., *Papers of Thomas Jefferson*, 42 vols. (Princeton, 1950–).

1:
"A HARD STUDENT"

1. Marie Kimball, *Jefferson: The Road to Glory, 1743–1776* (New York, 1943), 8.

2. Thomas Jefferson, "Autobiography," in *Thomas Jefferson, Writings: Autobiography; a Summary View of the Rights of British America; Notes on the State of Virginia; Public Papers; Addresses, Messages, and Replies; Miscellany; Letters*, ed. Merrill D. Peterson (New York, 1984), 3.

3. Jefferson, "Autobiography," 3; Kimball, *Jefferson: The Road to Glory*, 9–12; Dumas Malone, *Jefferson and His Time*, 6 vols. (Boston, 1948–1981), 1:6–9.

4. Henry S. Randall, *The Life of Thomas Jefferson*, 3 vols. (New York, 1858), 1:13–14.

5. Kimball, *Jefferson: The Road to Glory*, 14–16; Malone, *Jefferson and His Time*, 1:12–13.

6. Susan Kern, *The Jeffersons at Shadwell* (New Haven, 2010), 19.

7. Malone, *Jefferson and His Time*, 1:15–16.

8. Randall, *The Life of Thomas Jefferson*, 1:7.

9. Jefferson, "Autobiography," 4.

10. John Hammond Moore, *Albemarle: Jefferson's County, 1727–1976* (Charlottesville, 1976), 21–22.

11. Kimball, *Jefferson: The Road to Glory*, 26.

12. Malone, *Jefferson and His Time*, 1:20; Kimball, *Jefferson: The Road to Glory*, 27–28.

13. Jefferson, "Autobiography," 4; Malone, *Jefferson and His Time*, 1:22n4.

14. Malone, *Jefferson and His Time*, 1:23–26; Kimball, *Jefferson: The Road to Glory*, 29–30. Jefferson cited "Fry and Jefferson's Map of Virginia" in *Notes on the State of Virginia*, ed. William Peden (Chapel Hill, 1954), 18 [hereafter *Notes*].

15. See Joel Kovarsky, *The True Geography of Our Country: Jefferson's Cartographic Vision* (Charlottesville, 2014), 10, passim.

16. Randall, *The Life of Thomas Jefferson*, 1:17.

17. Jefferson, "Autobiography," 4.

18. Kimball, *Jefferson: The Road to Glory*, 31.

19. Kern, *The Jeffersons at Shadwell*, 159–60.

20. The settlement of Peter's will is described by Kimball, *Jefferson: The Road to Glory*, 32–33; Kern, *The Jeffersons at Shadwell*, 109–12; Malone, *Jefferson and His Time*, 1:31–32. Kern suggests the quasi-parenting role perhaps played by Sawney on 111.

21. Jefferson, "Autobiography," 4.

22. Malone, *Jefferson and His Time*, 1:44–48, has a detailed discussion of Jefferson at Maury's school, as does Kimball, *Jefferson: The Road to Glory*, 34–38. See also Randall, *The Life of Thomas Jefferson*, 1:18. For Maury's emphasis on reason, see Thomas E. Buckley, SJ, "Placing Thomas Jefferson and Religion in Context, Then and Now," in *Seeing Jefferson Anew: In His Time and Ours*, ed. John B. Boles and Randal L. Hall (Charlottesville, 2010), 133. For the tenor of Maury's mind as reflected in his sermons, see the ten sermons reprinted in Edward L. Bond, ed., *Spreading the Gospel in Colonial Virginia: Sermons and*

Devotional Writings (Lanham, MD, 2004), 272–347.

23. Buckley, "Placing Thomas Jefferson and Religion in Context," 132.

24. Douglas L. Wilson, ed., *Jefferson's Literary Commonplace Book* (Princeton, 1989), 16.

25. Jefferson to John Harvie, January 14, 1760, in *Papers of Thomas Jefferson*, ed. Julian P. Boyd (Princeton, 1950), 1:3 (hereafter *PTJ*).

26. Kevin J. Hayes, *The Road to Monticello: The Life and Mind of Thomas Jefferson* (New York, 2008), 48.

27. Jenny Uglow, *The Lunar Men: Five Friends Whose Curiosity Changed the World* (New York, 2002), 84.

28. Jefferson, "Autobiography," 4.

29. Merrill D. Peterson, *Thomas Jefferson and the New Nation: A Biography* (New York, 1970), 12. For Jefferson and Small generally, see also Hayes, *The Road to Monticello*, 50–56; Malone, *Jefferson and His Time*, 1:51–55.

30. Jefferson to Louis H. Girardin, January 15, 1815, in *Papers of Thomas Jefferson, Retirement Series*, ed. J. Jefferson Looney (Princeton, NJ, 2011), 8:200 (hereafter *PTJRS*).

31. Ibid.

32. Imogene E. Brown, *American Aristides: A Biography of George Wythe* (Rutherford, NJ, 1981), 87–89; Malone, *Jefferson and His Time*, 1:68–74; Hayes, *The Road to Monticello*, 57–60.

33. Frank L. Dewey, *Thomas Jefferson, Lawyer* (Charlottesville, 1986), 121.

34. I draw my discussion of Fauquier from Malone, *Jefferson and His Time*, 1:75–78; Hayes, *The Road to Monticello*, 60–62; and Peterson, *Thomas Jefferson and the New Nation*, 14–15.

35. Jefferson, "Autobiography," 4.

36. Randall, *The Life of Thomas Jefferson*, 1:22.

37. Quoted in Kimball, *Jefferson: The Road to Glory*, 45.

38. Quoted in Malone, *Jefferson and His Time*, 1:56.

39. Randall, *The Life of Thomas Jefferson*, 1:24.

40. Jefferson to Dr. Vine Utley, March 21, 1819, in Peterson, *Thomas Jefferson, Writings*, 1416.

41. Jefferson to John Page, December 25, 1762, *PTJ*, 1:3–6 (quotations on 5).

42. See H. Trevor Colbourn, "Thomas Jefferson's Use of the Past," *William and Mary Quarterly*, 3rd ser., 15 (January 1958): 56–70; Trevor Colbourn, *The Lamp of Experience: Whig History and the Intellectual Origins of the American Revolution* (Chapel Hill, 1965), 158–84.

43. Jefferson to Page, January 20, 1763, in *PTJ*, 1:7–9 (quotation on 7).

44. This schedule is often described; for a convenient summary, see Peterson, *Thomas Jefferson and the New Nation*, 18–19.

45. Jefferson to Page, October 7, 1763, in *PTJ*, 1:11–12 (quotation on 12).

46. For Jefferson's dependence upon Jupiter, see Kern, *The Jeffersons at Shadwell*, 73–74, 252. Robert Hemings replaced Jupiter as Jefferson's manservant in the early 1770s.

47. See the purchases recorded throughout *The Virginia Gazette Daybooks, 1750–1752; 1764–1766* (microfilm, Charlottesville, 1967); Hayes, *The Road to Monticello*, 71.

48. For Jefferson's devotion to his sister Jane, see Randall, *The Life of Thomas Jefferson*, 1:41.

49. Jefferson to Thomas Cooper, February 10, 1814, in *PTJRS*, 7:190–91 (quotation on 191).

50. Wilson, *Jefferson's Literary Commonplace Book*, entry #6, p. 25.

51. Ibid., entries #20, p. 31; #44, pp. 42–43; and #56, p. 50 (quotation).

52. Ibid., entry #28, p. 35.

53. Rosalie Edith Davis, transcriber and ed., *Fredericksville Parish Vestry Book*,

1742–1787 (Manchester, MO, 1978), 86, 88, 89, 92, 93, 94, 96.

54. Edwin Morris Betts, ed., *Thomas Jefferson's Garden Book* (Monticello, 2012), 1 (hereafter *GB*).

55. Malone, *Jefferson and His Time*, 1:98–100; Randall, *The Life of Thomas Jefferson*, 1:46.

56. Jefferson to John Page, May 25, 1766, in *PTJ*, 1:18–20 (quotations on 19).

57. Ibid., 20.

2:
YOUNG LEGISLATOR

1. Jefferson, "Autobiography," 6.

2. Thomas Jefferson to William Wirt, August 14, 1814, in *PTJRS*, 7:544–50 (quotation on 547).

3. Ibid., 548; Malone, *Jefferson and His Time*, 1:91–97.

4. Jefferson, "Autobiography," 9; Jefferson to William Wirt, August 5, 1815, in *The Works of Thomas Jefferson*, ed. Paul Leicester Ford (New York, 1904), 11:415n ("idle disposition" quote).

5. Thomas Jefferson, "A Memorandum" [c. 1800], in Peterson, *Thomas Jefferson, Writings*, 702.

6. *GB*, 6.

7. James A. Bear Jr. and Lucia C. Stanton, eds., *Jefferson's Memorandum Books: Accounts, with Legal Records and Miscellany, 1767–1826* (Princeton, 1997), 1:[3] (hereafter *JMB*); see Dewey, *Thomas Jefferson, Lawyer*, 26, 28. See the table of the results of Jefferson's 1767 cases on 34.

8. Dewey, *Thomas Jefferson, Lawyer*, chaps. 9–11.

9. Ibid., chap. 6.

10. Jefferson lays out the essentials of the case. See Ford, *The Works of Thomas Jefferson*, 1:471n. The entire document, titled "Argument in the Case of Howell vs. Netherland," is reprinted on 470–81.

11. Ibid., 474.

12. Ibid., 471. See also the notation in Jefferson's legal account book: *JMB*, 1:174.

13. Jefferson, "Autobiography," 5. See also Randall, *The Life of Thomas Jefferson*, 1:58, which makes clear it was during his first session.

14. The law is quoted in Annette Gordon-Reed, *The Hemingses of Monticello: An American Family* (New York, 2008), 109.

15. Jefferson to Edward Coles, August 25, 1814, in Peterson, *Thomas Jefferson, Writings*, 1344. See also *PTJ*, 2:23n–24n.

16. Precisely between these two actions in 1769 and 1770, when one of his slaves, a mulatto named Sandy, ran away, Jefferson placed an ad in the *Virginia Gazette* offering a reward to anyone who captured and returned him. The ad from the September 7, 1769, *Virginia Gazette* is reproduced in *PTJ*, 1:33.

17. *GB*, 12; see also *JMB*, 1:23n8.

18. *JMB*, 1:147, 150, 150n.

19. Ibid., 145.

20. See *GB*, 15, on transplanting the trees.

21. *JMB*, 1:212. Jefferson did not move to his own home because he had become disaffected from his mother; after all, he was twenty-seven years old and a practicing lawyer.

22. Malone, *Jefferson and His Time*, 1, and esp. Kimball, *Jefferson: The Road to Glory*, have useful chapters on the building of Monticello, but see also Jack McLaughlin, *Jefferson and Monticello: The Biography of a Builder* (New York, 1988). As suggested in the text, Jefferson's memorandum books and Garden Book contained, sprinkled throughout their pages, many notices about every aspect of Monticello and its gardens.

23. See Malone, *Jefferson and His Time*, 1:128–30; Kimball, *Jefferson: The Road to Glory*, 187, 196.

24. *JMB*, 1:84, 139.

25. Ibid., 70–84, passim (illustrating Jefferson's activities for 1768).

26. Quoted in Kimball, *Jefferson: The Road to Glory*, 198.

27. "Resolutions for an Answer to Governor Botetourt's Speech," [May 8, 1769], in *PTJ*, 1:26, 27.

28. See Jefferson's account in Jefferson to William Wirt, August 5, 1815, in Ford, *The Works of Thomas Jefferson*, 2:414.

29. The wording of each of the resolutions is provided by Kimball, *Jefferson: The Road to Glory*, 201–2.

30. Found most conveniently in Malone, *Jefferson and His Time*, 1:136.

31. The "Virginia Nonimportation Resolutions, 1769" are reprinted in *PTJ*, 1:27–31 (quotations on 29).

32. Quoted in Malone, *Jefferson and His Time*, 1:154. See appendix 3, "The Walker Affair," 447–51.

33. Jefferson to John Page, February 21, 1770, in *PTJ*, 1:36.

34. Ibid., 1:34. Luckily, he appears to have had his commonplace book with him at Monticello. Malone, *Jefferson and His Time*, 1:125, quotes the *Virginia Gazette* news item of February 22 that gave notice of the Shadwell fire.

35. In his memorandum book for October 6, 1770, Jefferson records a payment to a blacksmith "at Wayles." This is the first recorded visit to the Forest. See *JMB*, 1:209.

3:
"INSPIRE US WITH FIRMNESS"

1. Jefferson, "Autobiography," 5. The indispensable work on Martha Wayles Skelton Jefferson is Virginia Scharff, *The Women Jefferson Loved* (New York, 2010), chaps. 5–12.

2. Wayles's name appears in the records of the *Virginia Gazette Daybook, 1750–1752, 1764–1766* (microfilm, Charlottesville, 1967); the signatories to the Nonimportation Agreement appear in *PTJ*, 1:46–47.

3. These comments by Martha's children and grandchildren are from Sarah N. Randolph, *The Domestic Life of Thomas Jefferson* (1871; rpt. Charlottesville, 1978), 43–44 (hereafter *DL*); Randall, *The Life of Thomas Jefferson*, 1:63–64. See also another contemporary, Isaac Jefferson, "Memoirs of a Monticello Slave," in *Jefferson at Monticello*, ed. James A. Bear (Charlottesville, 1967), 5. See Gordon-Reed, *The Hemingses of Monticello*, 107, for her discussion of the meaning of the word "concubine" in eighteenth-century Virginia. It carried no pejorative connotation and simply signified a substitute wife.

4. Malone, *Jefferson and His Time*, 1:159.

5. *JMB*, 1:212–13, 251–66.

6. Story recounted in Randall, *The Life of Thomas Jefferson*, 1:64.

7. Jefferson to James Ogilvie, February 20, 1771, in *PTJ*, 1:63; Mrs. Drummond to Jefferson, March 12, [1771], in ibid., 65–66 (quotation on 66).

8. Jefferson to Thomas Adams, June 1, 1771, in ibid., 71.

9. Ibid., 72.

10. McLaughlin, *Jefferson and Monticello*, 160, says, "By architect, he meant a master builder or a housewright; this was the way the term was used in the eighteenth century."

11. Skipwith to Jefferson, July 17, 1771, and Jefferson to Robert Skipwith, August 3, 1771, in *PTJ*, 1:74–75, 76–81 (quotations on 78).

12. Skipwith to Jefferson, September 20, 1771, in ibid., 83–84 (quotation on 84).

13. *JMB*, 1:264.

14. Ibid., 265. The curtains were purchased on December 12 and the bed on December 16, 1771.

15. Ibid., 285, with details for various days in January 1772.

16. Jefferson, "Autobiography," 46.

17. Randall, *The Life of Thomas Jefferson*, 1:64 (first quotation), 65 (second quotation).

18. *GB*, 33.

19. Jefferson copied her original 1772 account book at the end of his notations for 1772 in his memorandum book. See *JMB*, 1:299–301. For the brewing casks of beer, see Martha Wayles Skelton Jefferson, "Household Accounts," [1772], Library of Congress, accessed on August 5, 2015, http://hdl.loc.gov/loc.mss/mtj.mtjbib 026572.

20. Quoted in Scharff, *The Women Jefferson Loved*, 105.

21. *JMB*, 1:290.

22. See the photograph of the leaf of Jefferson's prayer book where he has recorded Martha's birth. Reproduced in Scharff, *The Women Jefferson Loved*, [235].

23. See Malone, *Jefferson and His Time*, 1:160; Cynthia A. Kierner, *Martha Jefferson Randolph, Daughter of Monticello* (Chapel Hill, 2012), 15. On Ursula, see Lucia Stanton, *Free Some Day: The African-American Families of Monticello* (Charlottesville, 2000), 33–34. The enslaved man Isaac Jefferson, one of Ursula's sons, recalled that Martha "was suckled part of the time" by his mother. See Isaac Jefferson, "Memoirs of a Monticello Slave," quotations on [3]. Ursula's purchase by Jefferson is recorded in *JMB*, 1:334.

24. Jefferson, "Autobiography," 6.

25. Ibid., 6, 7.

26. *DL*, 47.

27. Randall, *The Life of Thomas Jefferson*, 1:83–84.

28. The entire complicated issue of this inheritance and its associated debt is laid out in Malone, *Jefferson and His Time*, 1, appendix 2, B:3 (441–45).

29. *JMB*, 1:369, 370, 370n.

30. Ibid., 370.

31. *GB*, 55.

32. Quoted in Kimball, *Jefferson: The Road to Glory*, 234.

33. Quoted in T. H. Breen, *Tobacco Culture: The Mentality of the Great Tidewater Planters on the Eve of Revolution* (Princeton, 1985), 196–97; Breen

brilliantly interprets the meaning of debt in colonial Virginia.

34. All the quotations are from Jefferson, "Autobiography," 8.

35. The resolution is reprinted in *PTJ*, 1:105–6.

36. Ibid., 106n.

37. This document, whose precise authorship is unknown, is reprinted in ibid., 107–9.

38. See "Proceedings of a Meeting of Representatives in Williamsburg, 30th May 1774," reprinted in ibid., 109–11.

39. See the letter "From Peyton Randolph and Others, to Members of the Late House of Burgesses," in ibid., 111–12.

40. "Thomas Jefferson and John Walker to the Inhabitants of the Parish of St. Anne," [before July 23, 1774], in ibid., 116–17 (quotation on 117n).

41. Jefferson, "Autobiography," 9.

42. *PTJ*, 1:117n.

43. "Resolutions of the Freeholders of Albemarle County," [July 26, 1774], in ibid., 117–19 (quotation on 117).

44. Jefferson, "Autobiography," 9; for Jupiter's probable role, see *JMB*, 1:376n.

45. Bernard Mayo, *Myths and Men: Patrick Henry, George Washington, Thomas Jefferson* (Athens, GA, 1959), 49, quoting Hugh Blair Grigsby.

4:
"THESE ARE OUR GRIEVANCES"

1. Edmund Randolph, *History of Virginia*, ed. Arthur H. Shaffer (Charlottesville, 1970), 205.

2. Jefferson, "Autobiography," 10 (first quotation); Randall, *The Life of Thomas Jefferson*, 1:90 (second quotation).

3. See "Instructions by the Virginia Convention to Their Delegates in Congress, 1774," in *PTJ*, 1:141–44 (quotations on 141).

4. The printing history is conveniently laid out in appendix 1, "Historical and Bibliographical Notes on A Summary

View of the Rights of British America," in
ibid., 1:669–76.

5. Randolph, *History of Virginia*, 181.

6. Two very helpful discussions of the
larger meaning of *A Summary View* are
Kristofer Ray, "Thomas Jefferson and *A
Summary View* of the Rights of British
North America," in *A Companion to
Thomas Jefferson*, ed. Francis D. Cogliano
(Sussex, UK, 2012), 32–43; and Brian
Steele, *Thomas Jefferson and American
Nationhood* (Cambridge, UK, 2012),
chap. 1.

7. Thomas Jefferson, "Draft of
Instructions to the Virginia Delegates in
the Continental Congress (MS Text of A
Summary View, &c.)," in *PTJ*, 1:121.

8. Ibid.

9. Ibid., 1:123–25.

10. Ibid., 125.

11. Ibid., 127–28.

12. See Pauline Maier, *American
Scripture: Making the Declaration of
Independence* (New York, 1997), 51–54.

13. *PTJ*, 1:126–29. Jefferson did not
expect the king to accept his suggestion.

14. Ibid., 130.

15. Ibid., 130, 132.

16. Ibid., 134.

17. Ibid.

18. Ibid., 1:135.

19. The text of the "Continental
Association of 20 October 1774" is
reprinted in ibid., 149–54 (first quotation
on 150, other quotations on 149).

20. Jefferson was concerned that many
in Parliament were held in the grip of
this miscomprehension. See Jefferson to
John Randolph, August 25, 1775, in ibid.,
240–43.

21. Randolph, *History of Virginia*, 212.

22. Henry quoted in Kimball, *Jefferson:
The Road to Glory*, 258–59.

23. See "Report of a Committee to
Prepare a Plan for a Militia," [March 25,
1775], in *PTJ*, 1:160.

24. See "Resolution on Land Grants,"
[March 27, 1775], in ibid., 162–63.

25. For the Virginia convention, see
ibid., 256–59; Malone, *Jefferson and His
Time*, 1:193–96; Randolph, *History of
Virginia*, 208–16.

26. Quoted in Michael A. McDonnell,
*The Politics of War: Race, Class, and
Conflict in Revolutionary Virginia* (Chapel
Hill, 2007), 55.

27. Jefferson to William Small, May 7,
1775, in *PTJ*, 1:165–67 (quotation on 165).
Unbeknownst to Jefferson, Small had died
on February 18, 1775.

28. Jefferson, "Autobiography," 11; the
text is reprinted as "Virginia Resolutions
on Lord North's Conciliatory Proposal,"
[June 10, 1775], in *PTJ*, 1:170–74.

29. See James Corbett David,
Dunmore's New World (Charlottesville,
2013), 94.

30. "Virginia Resolutions on Lord
North's Conciliatory Proposal," *PTJ*,
1:170–74 (first and second quotations
on 171, third quotation on 172, fourth
quotation on 173).

31. Jefferson to Francis Eppes, June 26,
1775, in ibid., 174–75 (quotation on 175).

32. The evolution of the "Declaration
of the Causes and Necessity of Taking
Up Arms" is discussed in careful detail
in ibid., 187–219. The version of the
declaration ultimately accepted is on
213–19.

33. Jefferson, "Autobiography," 12.

34. See the final text, along with
Jefferson's original draft, in *PTJ*, 1:225–33.

35. See entries in *JMB*, 1:403.

36. For the military details, see John E.
Selby, *The Revolution in Virginia, 1775–1783*
(Charlottesville, 2007 [first published in
1988]), 51–52.

37. *GB*, 66; Kern, *The Jeffersons at
Shadwell*, [235] (photocopy of Jefferson's
handwritten listing of births and deaths of
family members).

38. Jefferson to John Randolph, August
25, 1775, in *PTJ*, 1:240–43 (quotation on
242).

5:
"PEN OF THE
AMERICAN REVOLUTION"

1. Jefferson to Francis Eppes, November 7, in *PTJ*, 1:252 (quotation).

2. Selby, *The Revolution in Virginia*, 58ff. Quotation on 66.

3. Jefferson to Francis Eppes, November 21, 1775, in *PTJ*, 1:264.

4. Jefferson to John Randolph, November 29, 1775, in ibid., 268–70 (quotation on 269).

5. The text is at "The Crisis, by Thomas Paine," UShistory.org, accessed July 29, 2013, http://www.ushistory.org/Paine/crisis/singlehtml.htm.

6. Thomas Nelson to Jefferson, February 4, 1776, in *PTJ*, 1:285–86.

7. Thomas Paine, "Common Sense," in *The Life and Works of Thomas Paine*, ed. William M. Van der Weyde, 5 vols. (New Rochelle, NY, 1925), 2:150.

8. Paine, "Common Sense," 122 (second quotation), 147 (third quotation).

9. On the popularity of Paine, see Kimball, *Jefferson: The Road to Glory*, 281–83; McDonnell, *The Politics of War*, 198–200; for the burning of Norfolk, see Selby, *The Revolution in Virginia*, 81–84.

10. *JMB*, 1:415. For Dabney Carr, see ibid., 340; for his wife, see ibid., 521; for his daughter, see ibid., 2:1125.

11. On this issue, see Kern, *The Jeffersons at Shadwell*, 68–72; see esp. Scharff, *The Women Jefferson Loved*, 48–57. Scharff explains that Jefferson's almost curt mention of his mother's death in a letter of June 1776 to her brother, Tory William Randolph, was meant as a reprimand to William for forsaking both his country and his sister, implying, "As if you cared, your sister died."

12. For his illness, see Jefferson to Thomas Nelson, May 16, 1776, in *PTJ*, 1:292. He paid the Reverend Carr more than a year after the funeral. See *JMB*, 1:444.

13. Jefferson to Nelson, May 16, 1776, in *PTJ*, 1:292.

14. See Maier, *American Scripture*, 47–96.

15. Their resolution is reprinted in *PTJ*, 1:290–91.

16. Jefferson to Nelson, May 16, 1776, in ibid., 292.

17. The formal resolution as moved and seconded is reprinted in ibid., 298–99.

18. John Adams to Timothy Pickering, August 6, 1822, in *The Works of John Adams*, ed. Charles Francis Adams, 10 vols. (Boston, 1850–1856), 2:513–14.

19. Edmund Pendleton to Thomas Jefferson, May 24, 1776, in *PTJ*, 1:296–97 (quotation on 296).

20. The wording of the enumeration of grievances against the king varies slightly in each of the three versions, which are reprinted in ibid. The first draft is on 337–47, the second draft is on 347–55, and the third draft is on 356–65; quotations are on 357.

21. Previously one had to own a minimum of one hundred acres of uncultivated land, or twenty-five acres with a house on it, or a house and a lot in a town in order to be eligible to vote. See Eva Sheppard Wolf, "Natural Politics: Jefferson, Elections, and the People," in Boles and Hall, *Seeing Jefferson Anew*, 49.

22. The quotations are from Jefferson's third draft, in *PTJ*, 1, with the first quotation from 358, the last from 364, and all the others from 363.

23. On the deliberations in Williamsburg, see the careful and detailed discussions in McDonnell, *The Politics of War*, 216–44, esp. 223–31, for the impact of petitions; Selby, *The Revolution in Virginia*, 100–123.

24. Quoted in Selby, *The Revolution in Virginia*, 101.

25. See the editorial note in Robert A. Rutland, ed., *The Papers of George Mason, 1725–1792*, 3 vols. (Chapel Hill, 1970), 1:274–76.

26. For the discussion and approval of the Declaration of Rights, see Selby, *The Revolution in Virginia*, 101–7.

27. See "Committee Draft of the Virginia Declaration of Rights," reprinted in Rutland, *Papers of George Mason*, 1:282–85 (quotation on 283).

28. See "Final Draft of the Virginia Declaration of Rights," in ibid., 287–89 (quotation on 287), 289n. See also, for discussion of the debate that led to this revision, Randolph, *History of Virginia*, 250–53.

29. Rutland, *Papers of George Mason*, 1:277.

30. Ibid., 278.

31. Ibid., 289, 289n.

32. On the number of committees Jefferson served on, see *PTJ*, 1:404n–405n. The reports mentioned are reprinted in ibid., 389–404.

33. Jefferson to Edmund Pendleton, [c. June 30, 1776], in ibid., 408.

34. Lyman H. Butterfield, ed., *Diary and Autobiography of John Adams*, 4 vols. (Cambridge, MA, 1962), 3:336.

35. My general discussion of Jefferson's role in writing the Declaration of Independence is shaped by the documents in *PTJ*, 1:413–33; Maier, *American Scripture*, chap. 3; Robert G. Parkinson, "The Declaration of Independence," in Cogliano, *A Companion to Thomas Jefferson*, 44–59; and Garry Wills, *Inventing America: Jefferson's Declaration of Independence* (Garden City, NY, 1978).

36. Jefferson to Benjamin Franklin, [June 21?, 1776], in *PTJ*, 1:404.

37. This is the central point of Carl L. Becker, *The Declaration of Independence: A Study in the History of Political Ideas* (New York, 1922).

38. Danielle Allen, *Our Declaration: A Reading of the Declaration of Independence in Defense of Liberty* (New York, 2015), has significantly shaped my view of the Declaration.

39. See Jefferson's draft, reprinted in *PTJ*, 1:426.

40. Jefferson, "Autobiography," 18.

41. Ari Helo, *Thomas Jefferson's Ethics and the Politics of Human Progress* (Cambridge, UK, 2014), 42. See also Eric Slauter, "The Declaration of Independence and the New Nation," in *The Cambridge Companion to Thomas Jefferson*, ed. Frank Shuffelton (Cambridge, UK, 2009), 22.

42. Adams to Timothy Pickering, August 6, 1822, in Adams, *The Works of John Adams*, 2:514.

43. Quoted in Kimball, *Jefferson: The Road to Glory*, 300.

44. The citations to the final Declaration are easily found in any printed version of the same.

45. Jefferson to Henry Lee, May 8, 1825, in Ford, *The Works of Thomas Jefferson*, 12:408–9 (quotation on 409).

46. *JMB*, 1:420, 420n; *GB*, 69.

6:
REVOLUTIONARY LAWMAKER

1. Edmund Randolph to Jefferson, June 23, 1776, in *PTJ*, 1:407; Jefferson to Edmund Pendleton, [ca. June 30, 1776], in ibid., 408 (quotations).

2. Jefferson to Francis Eppes, July 23, 1776, in ibid., 472–73 (quotation on 473).

3. Jefferson to Richard Henry Lee, July 29, 1776, in ibid., 477.

4. See "Report of the Committee to Draw Up Rules of Procedure in Congress," [before July 10, 1776], in ibid., 456–58.

5. See "From Edmund Pendleton to the Virginia Delegates in Congress," July 15, 1776, in ibid., 462–65; John Page to Jefferson, July 20, 1776, in ibid., 468–70; Jefferson to John Page, July 30, 1776, in ibid., 482–84; Adam Stephen to Jefferson, July 29, 1776, in ibid., 480–82.

6. Edmund Pendleton to Jefferson, July 22, 1776, in ibid., 471–72; Pendleton to

Jefferson, August 10, 1776, in ibid., 488–91 (quotation on 489).

7. John Adams to Abigail Adams, August 14, 1776, in *Adams Family Correspondence*, ed. L. H. Butterfield, 11 vols. (Cambridge, MA, 1963), 2:95–97 (quotation on 96). The best description of the effort to create a seal is in Marie Kimball, *Jefferson: War and Peace, 1776 to 1784* (New York, 1947), 5–6.

8. See his complicated chart, reprinted in *PTJ*, 1:511–14, and "Draft Report on the Value of Gold Coins," [September 2, 1776], in ibid., 515–18.

9. *JMB*, 1:424, 425, 428, 447.

10. Jefferson, "Autobiography," 45.

11. John Hancock to Jefferson, September 30, 1776, in *PTJ*, 1:523–24 (quotations on 523); "Resolution of Congress, Appointing Franklin, Deane, and Jefferson as Commissioners to France," in ibid., 521–22; Richard Henry Lee to Jefferson, September 27, 1776, in ibid., 522–22 (quotation on 522).

12. Jefferson to John Hancock, October 11, 1776, in ibid., 524.

13. Jefferson to Edmund Pendleton, August 26, 1776, in ibid., 503–7 (quotations on 503, 504).

14. For the eighteenth-century model of the gentleman, see Gordon S. Wood, *Revolutionary Characters: What Made the Founders Different* (New York, 2006), 15.

15. See "Bill to Enable Tenants in Fee Tail to Convey Their Lands in Fee Simple," [October 14, 1776], in *PTJ*, 1:560–62.

16. Peterson, *Thomas Jefferson and the New Nation*, 111.

17. *PTJ*, 1:133, 362, 363; "A Bill Declaring Who Shall Be Deemed Citizens of This Commonwealth," in ibid., 2:476–79 (quotation on 477).

18. "A Bill for the More General Diffusion of Knowledge," in ibid., 2:526–35 (quotations on 526–27).

19. Ibid., 529–33.

20. See "A Bill for Amending the Constitution of the College of William and Mary, and Substituting More Certain Revenues for Its Support," in ibid., 535–43.

21. "A Bill for Proportioning Crimes and Punishments in Cases Hithertofore Capital," in ibid., 492–507 (quotations on 492).

22. Jefferson to George Wythe, November 1, 1778, in ibid., 229–31 (quotation on 230).

23. Selby, *The Revolution in Virginia*, 158.

24. "A Bill Concerning Slaves," in *PTJ*, 2:470–73. It was feared that freedmen would exert a dangerous influence on slaves.

25. Jefferson, "Autobiography," 43–44 (quotation on 44).

26. See "A Bill Concerning the High Court of Chancery," in *PTJ*, 2:566–69; "A Bill Constituting the General Court," in ibid., 569–71; "A Bill Constituting the Courts of Admiralty," in ibid., 572–75; "A Bill Constituting the Court of Appeals," in ibid., 575–78; "A Bill Constituting Justices of the Peace and County Courts," in ibid., 578–82.

27. See "Bill for the Removal of the Seat of Government of Virginia," [November 11, 1776], in ibid., 1:598–602, along with Jefferson's "Notes Concerning the Bill for the Removal of the Seat of Government of Virginia," in ibid., 602–3, and "Bill for the Removal of the Seat of Government of Virginia," [May 29, 1779], in ibid., 2:271–72.

28. James Monroe to William Bradford, January 24, 1774, in *The Papers of James Madison*, ed. William T. Hutchinson and William M. E. Rachal, 18 vols. (Chicago, 1962), 1:104–6 (quotation on 106).

29. See "Petition of Dissenters in Albemarle and Amherst Counties," [before November 1, 1776], in *PTJ*, 1:586–89 (quotation on 587); "Declaration of the Virginia Association of Baptists," [December 25, 1776], in ibid., 660–61.

30. See Rhys Isaac, "'The Rage of Malice of the Old Serpent Devil': The Dissenters and the Making and Remaking of the Virginia Statute for Religious Freedom," in *The Virginia Statute for Religious Freedom: Its Evolution and Consequences in American History*, ed. Merrill D. Peterson and Robert C. Vaughn (Cambridge, MA, 1988), 139–69, esp. 159.

31. Jefferson, "Autobiography," 34.

32. "Final Draft of the Virginia Declaration of Rights," [June 12, 1776], in Rutland, *The Papers of George Mason*, 1:289.

33. "Third Draft by Jefferson," [before June 13, 1776], in *PTJ*, 1:363.

34. Joseph Priestley to Benjamin Franklin, February 13, 1776, in *The Papers of Benjamin Franklin*, ed. William B. Willcox, 39 vols. (New Haven, 1982), 22:348; Alfred Owen Aldridge, *Benjamin Franklin and Nature's God* (Durham, NC, 1967), 207 (quotation).

35. Richard Price, *Observations on the Nature of Civil Liberty, the Principles of Government, and the Justice and Policy of the War with America* (London, 1776), 3.

36. "Notes on Locke and Shaftsbury," in *PTJ*, 1:544–51 (quotations on 544, 545, 547, 548).

37. See ibid., 525–58, passim. For Jefferson's readings in early Saxon history, see Colbourn, *The Lamp of Experience*, 169.

38. The funeral sermon preached by the Reverend Charles Clay for Jefferson's mother on April 6, 1776, contained many allusions to heaven and "everlasting life." See the sermon in the Charles Clay Papers, Virginia Historical Society, Mss C579a, Sermons, folder 12–13.

39. The phrase appears in Jefferson, "Autobiography," 8.

40. All three quotations are taken from the drafts of the relevant documents as printed in *PTJ*, 1:135, 202, 423.

41. See the discussion in Peterson, *Thomas Jefferson and the New Nation*, 133–34; Selby, *The Revolution in Virginia*, 145–46; John Ragosta, *Religious Freedom: Jefferson's Legacy, America's Creed* (Charlottesville, 2013), 64–67; Malone, *Jefferson and His Time*, 1:277–78.

42. "Jefferson's Outline of Argument in Support of His Resolutions," in *PTJ*, 1:536, 537, 538 (quotations).

43. See Ralph Ketcham, *James Madison: A Biography* (Charlottesville, 1990; first published in 1971), 77.

44. The text of the bill and its legislative history is in *PTJ*, 2:545–53.

45. Ibid., 545. In his "Autobiography," 40, Jefferson made clear that he intended by his refusal to put the name of Jesus Christ after the phrase "holy author of our religion" to extend the protection of religious freedom to "the Jew and the Gentile, the Christian and Mahometan, the Hindoo, and infidel of every denomination."

46. *PTJ*, 2:545.

47. Ibid., 546.

48. Ibid.

49. See the extensive discussion in Denise A. Spellberg, *Thomas Jefferson's Qur'an: Islam and the Founders* (New York, 2013), 100–20. When rewriting Virginia's naturalization bill, Jefferson revised it explicitly so it would not exclude Jews, Catholics, and Muslims from immigrating to the state. Ibid., 108–9. See also note 45 above.

50. *PTJ*, 2:547.

51. James Madison to Jefferson, January 22, 1786, in ibid., 9:194–209.

52. *JMB*, 1:437–80, passim.

53. *GB*, 70–89, passim.

54. See Jacob Rubsamen to Jefferson, December 1, 1780, in *PTJ*, 4:174, quoting a letter, published in a Hamburg newspaper, from a German officer describing the interior of Monticello. On Jefferson's love of singing, see Ann Lucas Birle and Lisa A. Francavilla, eds., *Thomas*

Jefferson's Granddaughter in Queen Victoria's England: The Travel Diary of Ellen Wayles Coolidge, 1838–1839 (Charlottesville, 2011), 73n.

55. Jefferson to Giovanni Fabbroni, June 8, 1778, in *PTJ*, 2:195–98 (quotation on 196).

56. *JMB*, 1:447, 468. See also the facsimile of Jefferson's list of the births and deaths of his children, in Kern, *The Jeffersons at Shadwell*, 235. Mary later in effect changed her name to Maria and so signed her letters.

7:
THE FIGHT FOR INDEPENDENCE

1. Moore, *Albemarle*, 57.

2. Malone, *Jefferson and His Time*, 1:293.

3. John Harvie to Thomas Jefferson, September 15, 1778, in *PTJ*, 2:211–13.

4. Ibid., 242.

5. Jefferson to Richard Henry Lee, April 21, 1779, in ibid., 2:255; Richard Henry Lee to Jefferson, May 22, 1779, in ibid., 270–71; Malone, *Jefferson and His Time*, 1:295.

6. *JMB*, 1:478, 479, 483, 485.

7. *JMB*, 1:482.

8. For the trip to Berkeley Springs, see Phillips to Jefferson, June 18, 1779, in *PTJ*, 3:3; Jefferson to Phillips, June 25, 1779, in ibid., 14–15; Jefferson to Riedesel, July 4, 1779, in ibid., 24–25; Jefferson to Riedesel, [July 1779], in ibid., 59–60; for the theater invitation, see Phillips to Jefferson, August 12, 1779, in ibid., 66.

9. "Message Accepting Election as Governor," June 2, 1779, in ibid., 2:277–78 (quotation).

10. Jefferson to Richard Henry Lee, June 17, 1779, in ibid., 298.

11. Jefferson to Baron von Riedesel, July 4, 1779, in ibid., 3:24.

12. The Constitution of 1776 is reprinted in ibid., 1:377–83 (quotation on 380).

13. Jefferson to Richard Henry Lee, July 17, 1779, in ibid., 3:39.

14. The best accounts of Virginia's plight are John E. Selby, *The Revolution in Virginia*, and Michael Kranish, *Flight from Monticello: Thomas Jefferson at War* (New York, 2010), though a persistent animosity toward Jefferson mars the latter. Essential for anyone attempting to assess Jefferson's role as wartime governor is Emory G. Evans, "Executive Leadership in Virginia, 1776–1781: Henry, Jefferson, and Nelson," in *Sovereign States in an Age of Uncertainty*, ed. Ronald Hoffman and Peter J. Albert. Perspectives on the American Revolution (Charlottesville, 1981), 185–225.

15. Patrick Henry to Jefferson, February 15, 1780, in *PTJ*, 3:293–94 (quotation on 293).

16. George Washington to Jefferson, December 11, 1779, in ibid., 3:217.

17. A memorandum Jefferson apparently prepared for himself outlines his efforts to buttress the defenses. See his "Notes on Threatened British Invasion," [December 1779], in ibid., 252–53.

18. Jefferson to George Rogers Clark, March 19, 1780, in ibid., 316–17 (quotation on 317).

19. James Madison to Jefferson, March 27, 1780, in ibid., 335–36.

20. "Resolution of the General Assembly Appointing Jefferson Governor," June 2, 1780, in ibid., 410; [Jefferson], "To the General Assembly," June 4, 1780, in ibid., 417–18 (quotation).

21. Jefferson to George Washington, June 11, 1780, in ibid., 432–34 (quotation on 433).

22. Martha Wayles Skelton Jefferson to Eleanor Conway Madison, August 8, 1780, in ibid., 532. This is one of the very few extant letters from Martha Jefferson.

23. Jefferson to Richard Henry Lee, September 13, 1780, in ibid., 642–43 (quotation on 643).

24. See the itemized to-do list, "Steps to Be Taken to Repel General Leslie's Army," October 22, 1780, in ibid., 4:61–63.

25. Jefferson to James Wood, October 26, 1780, in ibid., 72–75; Selby, *The Revolution in Virginia*, 220–21.

26. George Washington to Jefferson, December 9, 1780, in *PTJ*, 4:195.

27. Jefferson himself provided a careful account of these fateful days; see his anonymously published piece in the *Virginia Gazette* for January 13, reprinted in ibid., 269–70.

28. I base my account on Malone, *Jefferson and His Time*, 1:336–41; Peterson, *Thomas Jefferson and the New Nation*, 205–9; Selby, *The Revolution in Virginia*, 221–25; and Kranish, *Flight from Monticello*, 166–82, 187–99.

29. Kimball, *Jefferson: War and Peace*, 134.

30. Isaac Jefferson tells this story colorfully in Isaac Jefferson, "Memoirs of a Monticello Slave," 8–9.

31. See Selby, *The Revolution in Virginia*, 260; Lafayette to Jefferson, March 3, 1781, in *PTJ*, 5:49–51.

32. See, for example, Jefferson to Garret Van Meter, April 27, 1781, in ibid., 565–66 (quotation on 565).

33. Jefferson to John Banister, January 30, 1781, in ibid., 4:477.

34. Jefferson to Steuben, February 12, 1781, in ibid., 592–94 (quotation on 593).

35. Jefferson to Lafayette, March 10, 1781, in ibid., 5:113–14 (quotation on 113).

36. "From Samuel Huntington, Enclosing a Resolution of Congress Adopting the Articles of Confederation," March 2, 1781, in ibid., 5:41–42; "From the American Philosophical Society," February 7, 1781, in ibid., 4:544.

37. *JMB*, 1:508.

38. Jefferson to David Jameson, April 16, 1781, in *PTJ*, 5:468–69 (quotation on 468).

39. Selby, *The Revolution in Virginia*, 286–300.

40. Jefferson to Speaker of the House, May 28, 1781, in *PTJ*, 6:28–29 (quotation on 28).

41. Jefferson to George Washington, May 28, 1781, in ibid., 32–33.

42. See Francis D. Cogliano, *Emperor of Liberty: Thomas Jefferson's Foreign Policy* (New Haven, 2014), 34–41.

43. Selby, *The Revolution in Virginia*, 279–81; Malone, *Jefferson and His Time*, 1, 354–55.

44. This whole episode is clearly narrated in Malone, *Jefferson and His Time*, 1:356–58, and Kranish, *Flight from Monticello*, 275–84. Practically every Jefferson biography tells a version of this event. Jefferson does not mention it in his brief autobiography, although he recorded in his account book for June 4, 1781, "British horse came to Monticello." See *JMB*, 1:510. In 1816 Jefferson gave his account of the raid on Monticello and his escape; see "The 1816 Version of the Diary and Notes of 1781," in *PTJ*, 4:262–66.

45. Kranish, *Flight from Monticello*, 283.

46. To say of Jefferson's escape from the grasp of the British that he "had cravenly fled into the woods before the advancing British troops" (Ron Chernow, *Alexander Hamilton* [New York, 2004], 450) is so one-sided and biased as to constitute intellectual dishonesty.

47. The original version of this story is in Randall, *The Life of Thomas Jefferson*, 1:337–39 (quotation on 338).

48. *PTJ*, 13:362–64 (quotation on 363–64).

49. *JMB*, 1:511, for payment on June 30.

50. Selby, *The Revolution in Virginia*, 283.

51. Quoted in Selby, *The Revolution in Virginia*, 283–85.

52. Jefferson to James Monroe, May 20, 1782, in *PTJ*, 6:184–87 (quotation on 185).

53. Jefferson to George Nicholas, July 28, 1781, in ibid., 104–5; Nicholas to Jefferson, July 31, 1781, in ibid., 105–6.

54. Jefferson suggests that Nicholas was being used "by another hand" in a letter

to Isaac Zane, December 24, 1781, in ibid., 143–44 (quotation on 143).

55. Jefferson to George Rogers Clark, November 26, 1782, in ibid., 204–5 (quotation on 205). On the enmity between Jefferson and Henry in general, see the discussion in Andrew Burstein, *The Inner Jefferson: Portrait of a Grieving Optimist* (Charlottesville, 1995), 198–202.

56. Jefferson to Thomas McKean, August 4, 1781, in *PTJ*, 6:113. He got another letter from McKean later that month and again declined.

57. Jefferson to Edmund Randolph, September 16, 1781, in ibid., 117–18 (quotation on 118).

58. "From John Harvie, Enclosing a Resolution to Inquire into the Conduct of the Executive," November 27, 1781, in ibid., 133–34 (quotation on 133).

59. Malone, *Jefferson and His Time*, 1:366; "Resolution of Thanks to Jefferson by the Virginia General Assembly," December 12, 1781, in *PTJ*, 6:135–36. This judgment accords with that of the most acute present-day scholar of the era, Evans, "Executive Leadership in Virginia, 1776–1781," 202. Moreover, "Under the circumstances the conclusion must be that he [Jefferson] did remarkably well" (ibid., 218).

8:
A CONGRESS "LITTLE NUMEROUS, BUT VERY CONTENTIOUS"

1. Jefferson to Barbé-Marbois, March 4, 1781, in *PTJ*, 5:58–59 (quotation on 58).

2. Jefferson to Barbé-Marbois, December 20, 1781, in ibid., 6:141–42 (quotation on 142). Barbé-Marbois had sent similar inquiries to other states but only received one other response. See Kimball, *Jefferson: War and Peace*, 275, 383n34.

3. Jefferson to Charles McPherson, February 25, 1773, in *PTJ*, 1:96–97 (quotation on 96). On Jefferson's

infatuation with Ossian, see Hayes, *The Road to Monticello*, 133–38, 142–46; Amanda Johnson, "Thomas Jefferson's Ossianic Romance," *Studies in Eighteenth-Century Culture* 45 (2015–2016): 19–35.

4. Chastellux's long account is reprinted in *Visitors to Monticello*, ed. by Merrill D. Peterson (Charlottesville, 1989), 10–17 (quotations on 11–12) (hereafter *VTM*).

5. Ibid., 12.

6. Ibid., 13–15 (quotation on 13).

7. Ibid., 17.

8. *GB*, entries for February 12, February 28, and September 11, 1782, 94, 95.

9. The birth is recorded in the leaf of Jefferson's prayer book. See photograph in Kern, *The Jeffersons at Shadwell*, [235].

10. Jefferson to James Monroe, May 20, 1782, in *PTJ*, 6:184–87 (first quotation on 186, second on 184).

11. Ibid., 184–85. Wood, *Revolutionary Characters*, 23–25.

12. *JMB*, 1:521.

13. Martha Jefferson Randolph's reminiscences are quoted in Randall, *The Life of Thomas Jefferson*, 1:382.

14. Bacon's memoirs are reprinted as "Jefferson at Monticello: The Private Life of Thomas Jefferson," in Bear, *Jefferson at Monticello*, 27–137 (quotations on 99–100). Actually, at the time of her death Mrs. Jefferson had only three surviving children.

15. Randall, *The Life of Thomas Jefferson*, 1:380.

16. "Lines Copied from Tristram Shandy by Martha and Thomas Jefferson," in *PTJ*, 6:196.

17. In Randall, *The Life of Thomas Jefferson*, 1:382.

18. Quoted in ibid.

19. Ibid., 384.

20. Edmund Randolph to James Madison, September 20, 1782, in Hutchinson and Rachal, *The Papers of James Madison*, 5:150–51.

21. Jefferson to Elizabeth Wayles Eppes, October 3[?], 1872, in *PTJ*, 6:198–99.

22. Gaillard Hunt, ed., *Journals of the Continental Congress, 1774–1789*, 34 vols. (Washington, 1914), 23:720.

23. "Notes of Debates in the Continental Congress, by James Madison," entry for November 12, 1782, in ibid., 848.

24. See Robert R. Livingston to Jefferson, November 13, 1782, in *PTJ*, 6:202; Jefferson to Livingston, November 26, 1782, in ibid., 206.

25. Jefferson to Marquis de Chastellux, in ibid., 203–4 (quotations on 203); Jefferson to Elizabeth Blair Thompson, January 19, 1787, in *PTJ*, 11:56–58 (quotation on 57).

26. Robert R. Livingston to Jefferson, April 4, 1783, in *PTJ*, 6:259–60 (quotation on 259).

27. Edmund Randolph to James Madison, in Hutchinson and Rachal, *The Papers of James Madison*, 7:200–1 (quotation on 201).

28. Jefferson to James Madison, June 17, 1783, in *PTJ*, 6:277–78.

29. See "Jefferson's Draft of a Constitution for Virginia," in ibid., 294–305 (quotation on 299). The original text of the proposed constitution was printed in both the 1785 and 1787 editions of Jefferson's *Notes on the State of Virginia* in ibid., 305n.

30. Ibid., 298.

31. Arthur Zilversmit, *The First Emancipation: The Abolition of Slavery in the North* (Chicago, 1967), 128.

32. Jefferson to James Madison, August 31, 1783, in *PTJ*, 6:335–36.

33. *JMB*, 1:536–37; Jefferson to Isaac Zane, November 8, 1783, in *PTJ*, 6:347–49; *Notes*, 19–24.

34. See Kierner, *Martha Jefferson Randolph*, 43–48.

35. Jefferson to Barbé-Marbois, December 5, 1783, in ibid., 373–74 (quotation on 374).

36. Jefferson to Martha [Patsy] Jefferson, November 28, 1783, in ibid., 359–60.

37. Jefferson to Barbé-Marbois, December 5, 1783, in *PTJ*, 6:373–74 (quotation on 374).

38. Jefferson to Martha Jefferson, December 22, 1783, in ibid., 416–17 (quotation on 417).

39. As in Jefferson to Martha Jefferson, January 15, 1784, in ibid., 465–66 (quotation on 466).

40. The best discussion of her affection for her father is in Kierner, *Martha Jefferson Randolph*.

41. Kimball, *Jefferson: War and Peace*, 331.

42. Jefferson, "Autobiography," 47, 52.

43. Jefferson to Benjamin Harrison, November 11, 1783, in *PTJ*, 6:351–53. On the advantages of having the capital at the falls of the Potomac, see "Notes and Calculations by Jefferson," [November ?, 1783], in ibid., 364–65.

44. Hunt, *Journals of the Continental Congress*, 25:812.

45. Ibid., 818–20 (quotation on 818).

46. Ibid., 837. It is also reprinted as "Washington's Address to Congress Resigning His Commission," December 23, 1783, in *PTJ*, 6:411–12.

47. *PTJ*, 6:405n.

48. Hunt, *Journals of the Continental Congress*, 25:413; also reprinted in *PTJ*, 6:413 (emphasis in the original).

49. Jefferson to George Washington, April 16, 1784, in *PTJ*, 7:105–8 (quotation on 106–7).

50. Hunt, *Journals of the Continental Congress*, 26:15–17, 22–23.

51. See Jefferson, "Autobiography," 50–54.

52. The original report of December 16 is printed as "Report on the Definitive Treaty of Peace and the Letter from the American Commissioners," December 16, 1783, in *PTJ*, 6:384; the final documents are "Ratification of the Definitive Treaty of Peace," January 14, 1784, in ibid., 456–61, and "Proclamation Announcing

Ratification of Definitive Treaty," January 14, 1784, in ibid., 462–63.

53. Bernard Bailyn, *To Begin the World Anew: The Genius and Ambiguities of the American Founders* (New York, 2003), 45.

54. Jefferson to Martha Jefferson, January 15, 1784, in *PTJ*, 6:465–66 (quotation on 466); Jefferson to William Short, March 1, 1784, in ibid., 569–70 (quotation on 570).

55. For the entire story, see Robert F. Berkhofer Jr., "Jefferson, the Ordinance of 1784, and the Origins of the American Territorial System," *William and Mary Quarterly*, 3d ser., 29 (1972): 231–62, and the detailed explanatory material in *PTJ*, 6:571–74, 581–600. See also Hunt, *Journals of the Continental Congress*, 26:112–17.

56. The report is printed in Hunt, *Journals of the Continental Congress*, 26:118–21, and also reprinted in *PTJ*, 6:603–5. Citations will be to the *PTJ* version.

57. *PTJ*, 6:603–5 (quotation on 604). The delay until 1800 was intended—by giving slaveholders time to adjust to the change—to make the ending of slavery more politically acceptable. The northern states that soon acted to end slavery within their boundaries followed a similar procedure—not instant but gradual abolition. See Zilversmit, *The First Emancipation*. By proposing such a gradual scheme of emancipation, in other words, Jefferson sought wider support for the concept, not to postpone it indefinitely. Cf. Paul Finkelman, "Jefferson and Slavery: 'Treason Against the Hopes of the World,'" in *Jeffersonian Legacies*, ed. Peter S. Onuf (Charlottesville, 1993), 181–221, esp. 199.

58. For passage of the ordinance, see Hunt, *Journals of the Continental Congress*, 26:275–79; for the motion to remove the antislavery clause, see ibid., 247.

59. Jefferson to James Madison, April 25, 1784, in *PTJ*, 7:118–21 (quotation on 118).

60. Hunt, *Journals of the Continental Congress*, 26:356; 27:446–53; 28:114, 264, 298–302, 375–81.

61. See Peter S. Onuf, *Statehood and Union: A History of the Northwest Ordinance* (Bloomington, 1987).

62. Jefferson to George Washington, March 15, 1784, in *PTJ*, 7:25–27 (quotations on 26).

63. See Washington to Jefferson, April 8, 1784, in ibid., 88–89; Jefferson to Washington, April 16, 1784, in ibid., 105–10.

64. Quoted by Boyd in ibid., 109n. See Jefferson's account of the dinner with Washington in Franklin B. Sawvel, ed., *The Complete Anas of Thomas Jefferson* (New York, 1903), 27–28.

65. See Jefferson's notes and the report, reprinted in *PTJ*, 1:511–18.

66. See the discussion in Peterson, *Thomas Jefferson and the New Nation*, 275–78.

67. See Michael Schwarz, "The Origins of Jeffersonian Nationalism: Thomas Jefferson, James Madison and the Sovereignty Question in the Anglo-American Commercial Disputes of the 1780s," *Journal of Southern History* 79 (August 2013): 569–92.

68. For an analysis of Jefferson's nationalism tied to his commercial concerns, see ibid.

69. Hunt, *Journals of the Continental Congress*, 25:821–36 (quotation on 821).

70. Ibid., 822.

71. Ibid., 26:355, 356, 357–62 (quotation on 356, emphasis added).

72. Jefferson to William Short, May 7, 1784, in *PTJ*, 7:229; "Power of Attorney to Francis Eppes and Nicholas Lewis," May 9, 1784, in ibid., 239; "List of Books Sold to James Monroe" and "Statement of Account with James Monroe," May 10, 1784, in ibid., 240–41; "Jefferson's Account of Expenses, with Order on Treasurer," [May 10, 1784], in ibid., 243–44.

73. *JMB*, 1:548–49.

74. See "From Charles Thomson, with Instructions and Commissions," May 16, 1784, reprinted in *PTJ*, 7:261–71.

75. Charles Thomson to Jefferson, May 19, 1784, in ibid., 272–73 (quotation on 272); Samuel Hardy to Jefferson, May 21, 1784, in ibid., 278–79.

76. Peterson, *Thomas Jefferson and the New Nation*, 292 (quotation).

77. Jefferson to Edmund Pendleton, May 25, 1784, in *PTJ*, 7:292–93 (quotation on 292).

78. See his queries and the replies as reprinted in ibid., 324–46.

79. Jefferson to [unknown] Cabot, July 24, 1784, in ibid., 383; see also *JMB*, 1:551, 551n43.

80. "Extract from the Diary of Ezra Stiles," in *PTJ*, 7:302–3 (quotation on 303). See also Jefferson to Stiles, June 10, 1784, in ibid., 304–5.

81. See the notations in *JMB*, 1:551–54; Peterson, *Thomas Jefferson and the New Nation*, 293–94; Kimball, *Jefferson: War and Peace*, 359–62; Edward Dumbauld, *Thomas Jefferson: American Tourist* (Norman, OK, 1946), 58–59.

82. Jefferson noted that they reached the Scilly Isles on July 24 and then came ashore at Cowes on July 26. See *JMB*, 1:554–55.

9:
"ON THE VAUNTED SCENE OF EUROPE"

1. Martha Jefferson to Eliza House Trist, [after August 24, 1785], in *PTJ*, 8:436–38 (quotation on 436).

2. *JMB*, 1:555.

3. Ibid., 556.

4. Martha Jefferson to Eliza House Trist, [after August 24, 1785], in *PTJ*, 8:436–37.

5. Ibid., 437.

6. *JMB*, 1:556–57.

7. Martha Jefferson to Eliza House Trist, [after August 24, 1785], in *PTJ*, 8:437.

8. St. John de Crèvecoeur to Jefferson, July 15, 1784, in ibid., 7:376–77.

9. See the notations for August 6, 10, and 13 in *JMB*, 1:558–59. For the rise of fashion in Paris and the importance of fashionable dress, see Joan DeJean, *How Paris Became Paris: The Invention of the Modern City* (New York, 2014), 38, 115–20, 144–69.

10. *Journal and Correspondence of Miss Adams, Daughter of John Adams, Second President of the United States. Written in France and England, in 1785*, ed. by her daughter (New York, 1841), 14.

11. Jefferson to Lucy Ludwell Paradise, June 1, 1789, in *PTJ*, 15:162–63 (first quotation on 163); Jefferson to Samuel H. Smith, September 21, 1814, in *PTJRS*, 7:681–83 (second quotation on 682).

12. See Chastellux to Jefferson, [August 24, 1785], in *PTJ*, 7:410–11, esp. 411n.

13. Jefferson to Ralph Izard, September 26, 1785, in ibid., 8:552–54 (quotation on 552).

14. Martin Clagett, *Scientific Jefferson Revealed* (Charlottesville, 2009), 70–80, describes this system of code.

15. Silvio A. Bedini, *Thomas Jefferson and His Copying Machines* (Charlottesville, 1984), 10–22.

16. *JMB*, 1:565; Howard C. Rice, *Thomas Jefferson's Paris* (Princeton, 1976), 37–42.

17. *Letters of Mrs. Adams, the Wife of John Adams, with an Introductory Memoir*, ed. Charles Francis Adams (Boston, 1841), 45–46 (quotation on 46). She describes the number of servants and so forth on 47–49.

18. *Journal and Correspondence of Miss Adams*, 71.

19. Jefferson to James Monroe, November 11, 1784, in *PTJ*, 7:508–13 (quotation on 512). For background on Jefferson's debt problems, see Steven H. Hochman, "Thomas Jefferson: A Personal Financial Biography" (PhD diss., University of Virginia, 1987), 123–88.

20. Jefferson to John Adams, May 25, 1785, in *PTJ*, 8:163–64 (quotation on 164).

21. Abigail Adams to Jefferson, June 6, 1785, in ibid., 178–80 (quotation on 178).

22. *Letters of Mrs. Adams*, 94.

23. For descriptions of the house, see Rice, *Thomas Jefferson's Paris*, 51–52; William Howard Adams, *The Paris Years of Thomas Jefferson* (New Haven, 1997), 52–56; George Green Shackelford, *Thomas Jefferson's Travels in Europe, 1784–1789* (Baltimore, 1995), 11–12.

24. *JMB*, 1:698 (waffle irons), 740 (macaroni machine). See "Jefferson's Notes on Macaroni," in *PTJ*, 14:544. For the French cookware at Monticello, see Justin A. Sarafin, "Like Clockwork: French Influence in Monticello's Kitchen," in Damon Lee Fowler, ed., *Dining at Monticello: In Good Taste and Abundance* (Chapel Hill, 2005), 19–26.

25. For ice cream being served and Jefferson's recipe, see Fowler, *Dining at Monticello*, 172–73.

26. DeJean, *How Paris Became Paris*, 97–100.

27. Quoted in *DL*, 73.

28. For this exciting era in Paris's history, see Rice, *Thomas Jefferson's Paris*; Adams, *The Paris Years of Thomas Jefferson*.

29. DeJean, *How Paris Became Paris*, chaps. 2 and 5. See Stephene Kirkland, *Paris Reborn: Napoléon III, Baron Hausmann, and the Quest to Build a Modern City* (New York, 2013), 4, 8.

30. Jefferson belonged to the chess club only briefly because he quickly realized it made little sense to try to play competitively with leisured men who spent two or more hours daily at the chess board. See *JMB*, 1:610n.

31. Beatrix Cary Davenport, ed., *A Diary of the French Revolution, by Gouverneur Morris, 1752–1816* (Boston, 1939), 83; Robert J. Taylor et al., eds., *Diary of John Quincy Adams* (Cambridge, MA, 1981), 238; *Journal and Correspondence of Miss Adams*, 39–40; [John Trumbull], *Autobiography, Reminiscences and Letters of John Trumbull* (New York, 1841), 100. Later in the evenings, as Gouverneur Morris revealed when he described two married women trying to pick him and his friend up for an "intrigue," the Palais Royal promenades could become somewhat risqué. Davenport, *A Diary of the French Revolution*, 83–84.

32. See Rice, *Thomas Jefferson's Paris*, 18–21; Adams, *The Paris Years of Thomas Jefferson*, 62–64; Shackelford, *Thomas Jefferson's Travels in Europe*, 21. Jefferson characterized it so in a letter to Maria Cosway, October 12, 1786, in *PTJ*, 10:443–53 (quotation on 445).

33. *JMB*, 1:587, records his paying a "subscription" for seats at the Tuileries, similar to the lawn chairs one still finds there.

34. See Rice, *Thomas Jefferson's Paris*, 62; Adams, *The Paris Years of Thomas Jefferson*, 64–65; Shackelford, *Thomas Jefferson's Travels in Europe*, 19–20.

35. Jefferson to Madame de Tessé, March 20, 1787, in *PTJ*, 11:226–28 (quotation on 226).

36. Davenport, *A Diary of the French Revolution*, 83.

37. "Jefferson's Hints to Americans Travelling in Europe," [June 19, 1788], in *PTJ*, 13:264–75 (quotation on 269).

38. Jefferson to Pierre Charles L'Enfant, April 10, 1791, in ibid., 20:86.

39. Jefferson to James Madison, September 20, 1785, in ibid., 8:534–35.

40. Jefferson to Madame de Tessé, March 20, 1787, in ibid., 11:226–28 (quotation on 226).

41. Jefferson to Madison, September 20, 1785, in ibid., 534–35 (both quotations on 535).

42. Rice, *Thomas Jefferson's Paris*, 30; Shackelford, *Thomas Jefferson's Travels in Europe*, 25.

43. Jefferson to Charles Bellini, September 30, 1785, in *PTJ*, 8:568–70 (quotation on 569).

44. Adams, *The Paris Years of Thomas Jefferson*, 68–71; Rice, *Thomas Jefferson's Paris*, 68–70.

45. *Journal and Correspondence of Miss Adams*, 36–37 (quotation on 36).

46. Jefferson to Charles Bellini, September 30, 1785, in *PTJ*, 8:568–70 (quotation on 568).

47. Rice, *Thomas Jefferson's Paris*, 31–35; Shackelford, *Thomas Jefferson's Travels in Europe*, 22–25, 163–67.

48. Shackelford, *Thomas Jefferson's Travels in Europe*, 165–66.

49. On this point, see Randall, *The Life of Thomas Jefferson*, 1:421.

50. Thomas Shippen's letter to his father is printed as a footnote in *PTJ*, 12:502–4 (quotation on 504).

51. See Judith Poss Pulley, "Thomas Jefferson at the Court of Versailles: An American Philosophe and the Coming of the French Revolution" (PhD diss., University of Virginia, 1966), 1–58.

52. *Letters of Mrs. Adams*, 55–56.

53. Gouverneur Morris to Robert Morris, July 21, 1789, in Davenport, *A Diary of the French Revolution*, 159n.

52. Jefferson to William Shippen, May 8, 1788, in *PTJ*, 13:146–47 (quotations on 146).

10:
AT HOME IN PARIS

1. A good description of the school is in Rice, *Thomas Jefferson's Paris*, 65–68.

2. Martha Jefferson to Eliza House Trist, [after August 24, 1785], in *PTJ*, 8:436–38 (quotation on 437).

3. Ibid., 438.

4. Martha Jefferson to Jefferson, March 25, 1787, in ibid., 11:238.

5. Jefferson to Martha Jefferson, March 28, 1787, in ibid., 250–52 (quotation on 250).

6. Martha Jefferson to Jefferson, April 9, 1787, in ibid., 281–82 (quotations on 282).

7. Martha Jefferson to Jefferson, May 3, 1787, in ibid., 333–34 (quotation on 334).

8. James Currie to Jefferson, November 20, 1784, in ibid., 7:538–39.

9. Francis Eppes to Jefferson, September 16, 1784, in ibid., 15:615–16.

10. Jefferson to Martha Jefferson Carr, August 20, 1785, in ibid., 15:620–21 (quotation on 620).

11. Jefferson to Francis Eppes, February 5, 1785, in ibid., 7:635–36 (quotation on 635).

12. Ibid., 636.

13. Elizabeth Wayles Eppes to Jefferson, October 13, 1784, in ibid., 441; Francis Eppes to Jefferson, October 14, 1784, in ibid., 441–42 (quotation).

14. The summary of the letter is reprinted in ibid., 8:141.

15. Jefferson to Francis Eppes, August 30, 1785, in ibid., 451.

16. George Washington to Jefferson, June 2, 1784, in ibid., 7:300–1.

17. See Jefferson to William Short, May 7, 1784, in ibid., 7:229; Short to Jefferson, May 14, 1784, in ibid., 253–55.

18. See Yvon Bizarde and Howard C. Rice Jr., "'Poor in Love Mr. Short,'" *William and Mary Quarterly*, 3rd ser., 21 (October 1964): 516–33.

19. See "To the Prévôt des Marchands et Echevins de Paris, with Enclosure," in *PTJ*, 10:407–9; George Green Shackelford, *Jefferson's Adoptive Son: The Life of William Short, 1759–1848* (Lexington, KY, 1993), 27.

20. Irma B. Jaffe, *John Trumbull: Patriot-Artist of the American Revolution* (Boston, 1975), 96.

21. [Trumbull], *Autobiography, Reminiscences and Letters of John Trumbull*, 95.

22. Jefferson to Ezra Stiles, September 1, 1786, in *PTJ*, 10:316–17 (quotation on 317).

23. Oswaldo Rodriguez Roque, "Trumbull's Portraits," in *John Trumbull: The Hand and Spirit of a Painter*, ed. Helen A. Cooper (New Haven, 1982), 94–177, esp. 117.

24. See Jaffe, *John Trumbull*, 104–17.

25. This initial encounter is discussed in many places, but see Rice, *Thomas Jefferson's Paris*, 20. For the larger affair with Cosway, see Helen Duprey Bullock, *My Head and My Heart: A Little History of Thomas Jefferson and Maria Cosway* (New York, 1945); Malone, *Jefferson and His Time*, 2:70–74; Marie Kimball, *Jefferson: The Scene of Europe, 1784 to 1789* (New York, 1950), 159–83; Jon Kukla, "Maria Cosway," chap. 5 in *Mr. Jefferson's Women* (New York, 2007), 86–114; Scharff, *The Women Jefferson Loved*, 204–8; Fawn M. Brodie, *Thomas Jefferson: An Intimate History* (New York, 1974), 199–215; Burstein, *The Inner Jefferson*, 78–95, passim.

26. For where Jefferson and Cosway went and what they saw, see Kimball, *Jefferson: The Scene of Europe*, 161–68. Gouverneur Morris, who had plenty of experience with women, called Maria Cosway "vastly pleasant." See Davenport, *A Diary of the French Revolution*, 197.

27. The best discussion of this tumble and its precise date is in *PTJ*, 10:432n–33n.

28. Jefferson to Charles Bellini, September 30, 1785, in ibid., 8:568–70 (quotation on 568–69).

29. Jefferson to John Bannister Jr., October 15, 1785, in ibid., 635–37 (quotation on 636).

30. Jefferson to Anne Willing Bingham, February 7, 1787, in ibid., 11:122–23 (quotations on 122–23).

31. The definitive text, based on the letterpress version that Jefferson kept, is in ibid., 10:443–53.

32. Ibid., 446.

33. Jefferson to Eliza House Trist, December 15, 1786, in ibid., 599–600 (quotation on 600).

34. Jefferson, "Autobiography," 61–62 (quotation on 61).

35. Jefferson to William Carmichael, March 4, 1789, in *PTJ*, 14:615–17 (quotation on 616).

36. "Jefferson's Hints to Americans Travelling in Europe," in ibid., 13:264–75.

37. See Archibald Bolling Shepperson, *John Paradise and Lucy Ludwell of London and Williamsburg* (Richmond, 1942).

38. Mary Jefferson to Jefferson, ca. September 13, 1785, in ibid., 8:517.

39. Jefferson to Mary Jefferson, September 20, 1785, in ibid., 532–33.

40. Jefferson to Elizabeth Wayles Eppes, September 22, 1785, in ibid., 539–40.

41. Jefferson to Francis Eppes, January 24, 1786, in ibid., 9:211–12 (emphasis in the original).

42. John Wayles Eppes to Jefferson, May 22, 1786, in ibid., 560; Mary Jefferson to Jefferson, [May 22, 1786], in ibid., 560–61.

43. Jefferson to Elizabeth Wayles Eppes, December 14, 1786, in ibid., 10:594.

44. Francis Eppes to Jefferson, August 31, 1786, in ibid., 15:631–32.

45. Jefferson to Francis Eppes, December 14, 1786, in ibid., 10:594–95.

46. Mary Jefferson to Jefferson, March 31, 1787, in ibid., 11:260.

47. Martha Jefferson Carr to Jefferson, January 2, 1787, in ibid., 15:632–34 (quotation on 633).

48. Jefferson to Martha Jefferson, April 7, 1787, in ibid., 11:277–78 (quotations on 278).

49. Elizabeth Wayles Eppes to Jefferson, May 7, 1787, in ibid., 356.

50. See *DL*, 125.

51. Abigail Adams to Jefferson, June 26, 1787, in *PTJ*, 11:501–2; Andrew Ramsey to Jefferson, July 6, 1787, in ibid., 556; Abigail Adams to Jefferson, June 27, 1787, in ibid., 502–3.

52. See the two letters from Abigail in the preceding note. Quotations from the June 27 letter on 502 and 503.

53. Jefferson to Abigail Adams, July 1, 1787, in ibid., 11:514–15.

54. According to his account books, Jefferson had arrived back in Paris on June 10. See *JMB*, 1:670.

55. Abigail Adams to Jefferson, July 6, 1787, in *PTJ*, 11:550–52 (quotations on 551).

56. Ibid., 551–52.

57. John Adams to Jefferson, July 10, 1787, in ibid., 575; "From Abigail Adams, with List of Purchases for Mary Jefferson," in ibid., 572–74.

58. Jefferson to Abigail Adams, July 16, 1787, in ibid., 592.

59. Jefferson to Mary Jefferson Bolling, July 23, 1787, in ibid., 612–13 (first quotation on 612); Jefferson to Elizabeth Wayles Eppes, July 28, 1787, in ibid., 634–35 (second and third quotations on 634).

60. "Passports Issued by Jefferson, 1785–1789," in ibid., 15:483–87, entry for July 1, 1787 ("Petit, Polly J. & Sally Hemings 2.m"), 485.

61. See the expense, dated November 7, 1787, as noted in *JMB*, 1:684. A few pages earlier, on 681, Jefferson noted (on October 1, 1787) the first of what became regular monthly salary payments to James Hemings of twenty-four francs. For an insightful discussion of Sally's inoculation, see Gordon-Reed, *The Hemingses of Monticello*, 213–23; for James and Bob, see 214.

62. For Jefferson's stopping payment for a French chef, see *JMB*, 1:673n80; for the beginning of regular salary payments to James, see ibid., 681, for October 1787.

63. Ibid., 542 (entries for February 3, 10, and 13, 1784). For the background on Bob remaining in the United States and James coming to France, see Gordon-Reed, *The Hemingses of Monticello*, 154–56.

64. Gordon-Reed, *The Hemingses of Monticello*, 230. Gordon-Reed, in part 2, "The Vaunted Scene of Europe," 153–392, brilliantly discusses every aspect of Sally Hemings's stay in Paris.

65. Ibid., 309–11.

66. Jefferson to Maria Cosway, April 24, 1788, in *PTJ*, 13:103–4 (quotation on 103).

67. See the discussion in Brodie, *Thomas Jefferson*, 230–31; Gordon-Reed, *The Hemingses of Monticello*, 281–83.

68. The final payment is noted in *JMB*, 1:730, 730n–31n.

11:
TOURIST

1. Jefferson to Martha Jefferson Randolph, December 23, 1790, in *PTJ*, 18:350.

2. Jefferson to Marquis de Chastellux, with enclosure, September 2, 1785, in ibid., 8:467–70 (quotations on 468).

3. John Adams to Jefferson, February 21, 1786, in ibid., 9:295.

4. Jefferson to the Comte de Vergennes, February 28, 1786, in ibid., 307; Jefferson to John Jay, March 12, 1786, in ibid., 325–26, indicating Vergennes's quick approval.

5. American Commissioners [Adams and Jefferson] to John Jay, March 28, 1786, in ibid., 357–59 (quotation on 358).

6. Spellberg, *Thomas Jefferson's Qur'an*, 126. See her extended discussion on 124–57.

7. Jefferson, "Autobiography," 57–58.

8. Jefferson to John Page, May 4, 1786, in *PTJ*, 9:444–46 (quotation on 446).

9. Jefferson to Abigail Adams, September 25, 1785, in ibid., 8:547–49 (quotation on 548–49).

10. For Siddons, see Kimball, *Jefferson: The Scene of Europe*, 135–36.

11. For examples of Jefferson's shopping, see the notations in *JMB*, 1:614–23.

12. Ibid., 618.

13. See E. Millicent Sowerby, ed., *Catalogue of the Library of Thomas Jefferson*, 5 vols. (Washington, DC, 1955), 4:386–88, 486, item numbers 4227, 4228, and 4431. For Jefferson's background in gardening, see Andrea Wulf, *Founding Gardeners: The Revolutionary Generation,*

Nature, and the Shaping of the American Nation (New York, 2011), 35–57.

14. [Notes on a Tour of English Country Seats, &c., with Thomas Jefferson, 4–10 April 1786], in Butterfield, *Diary and Autobiography of John Adams*, 3:184–86 (quotation on 186).

15. Jefferson, "Notes of a Tour of English Gardens," in *PTJ*, 9:369–73 (quotation on 369).

16. Ibid., 370.

17. See the discussion in Wulf, *Founding Gardeners*, 46–47; Andrea Wulf and Emma Gieben-Gamal, *This Other Eden: Seven Great Gardens and Three Hundred Years of English History* (London, 2005), 87–130.

18. Ibid., 53–54.

19. See, for example, Jefferson to John Bartram with enclosure, January 27, 1786, in *PTJ*, 9:228–30; Jefferson, "To Antonio Giannini, with a List of Seeds Wanted," February 5, 1786, in ibid., 252–55; Jefferson to Richard Cary, August 12, 1786, in ibid., 10:226–28; Jefferson to John Banister Jr. with enclosure, February 7, 1787, in ibid., 11:121–22; Benjamin Hawkins to Jefferson, June 9, 1787, in ibid., 11:413–14.

20. Adams, [Notes on a Tour of English Country Seats], in Butterfield, *Diary and Autobiography of John Adams*, 3:185.

21. Jefferson to Madame de Corny, June 30, 1787, in *PTJ*, 11:509–10 (quotation on 509).

22. See Jefferson to John Banister Jr., September 7, 1786, in ibid., 10:332 (first quotation); Jefferson to John Trumbull, October 13, 1786, in ibid., 460; Jefferson to William Stephens Smith, October 22, 1786, in ibid., 478–79 (second quotation on 479); Jefferson to James Madison, December 16, 1786, in ibid., 602–6 (third quotation on 602); Jefferson to James Monroe, December 18, 1786, in ibid., 611–13 (final quotation on 612).

23. Jefferson to William Short, March 15, 1787, in ibid., 11:214–15 (quotation on 214).

24. Jefferson to William Short, March 27, 1787, in ibid., 246–48 (quotation on 247), writing from Aix en Provence.

25. Jefferson to Maria Cosway, July 1, 1787, in ibid., 519–20 (quotation on 519).

26. See Jefferson, "Notes of a Tour into the Southern Parts of France, &c.," in ibid., 415–64.

27. See James M. Gabler, *Passions: The Wines and Travels of Thomas Jefferson* (Baltimore, 1995), 75, 289–92.

28. Jefferson to George Wythe, September 16, 1787, in *PTJ*, 12:127–30 (first quotation on 127); Jefferson to William Drayton, July 30, 1787, in ibid., 11:644–50, esp. 648.

29. These examples are scattered throughout his "Notes of a Tour into the Southern Parts of France, &c.," in ibid., 11:415–64.

30. Ibid., 415, 435, 446, 458, 424, respectively. Jefferson was appalled at seeing white women, not slaves, employed at such hard labor.

31. Gordon S. Wood, *The Americanization of Benjamin Franklin* (New York, 2004), 35. For how his experiences may have led Jefferson to see US slavery as comparatively less oppressive, see Annette Gordon-Reed and Peter S. Onuf, *"Most Blessed of the Patriarchs": Thomas Jefferson and the Empire of the Imagination* (New York, 2016), esp. 148.

32. Jefferson to Lafayette, April 11, 1787, in *PTJ*, 11:283–85 (quotation on 285).

33. Jefferson to William Short, March 29, 1787, in ibid., 253–55 (quotation on 254).

34. Jefferson to John Jay, May 4, 1787, in ibid., 338–43 (quotation on 341).

35. Jefferson to Madame de Tesse, March 20, 1787, in ibid., 226–28 (first two quotations on 226).

36. Jefferson to Edward Rutledge, July 14, 1787, in ibid., 587–89; Jefferson to John Jay, May 4, 1787, in ibid., 338–39.

37. "Jefferson's Hints to Americans Travelling in Europe," in ibid., 13:264–75 (quotation on 272).

38. See L. T. C. Rolt, *From Sea to Sea: The Canal du Midi* (Miami, OH, 1973).

39. Jefferson to Martha Jefferson, May 21, 1787, in *PTJ*, 11:369–70 (quotation on 369).

40. Ibid., 370.

41. Abigail Adams to Jefferson, February 26, 1788, in ibid., 12:624–25; Jefferson to John Adams, March 2, 1788, in ibid., 637–38.

42. Jefferson to John Jay, March 16, 1788, in ibid., 671–76.

43. See "Notes of a Tour Through Holland and the Rhine Valley," in ibid., 13:8–10.

44. "Notes of a Tour Through Holland and the Rhine Valley," 13–15.

45. Jefferson to William Short, April 9, 1788, in *PTJ*, 13:48–49 (quotation on 48).

46. Jefferson to William Short, April 9, 1788, in ibid., 48–49.

47. *JMB*, 1:23.

48. Jefferson to Maria Cosway, April 24, 1788, in *PTJ*, 13:103–4 (quotation on 104).

49. "Notes of a Tour Through Holland and the Rhine Valley," 24, 35n21 (quotation).

50. "Hints on European Travel," 267.

51. "Notes of a Tour Through Holland and the Rhine Valley," 18 (the ladder), 27 (the plow), 27 (women in the fields), 13 (the fear of being a slave).

12:
"A POWERFUL OBSTACLE . . . TO EMANCIPATION"

1. Jefferson to Charles Bellini, September 30, 1785, in *PTJ*, 8:568–70 (quotation on 568).

2. See Jefferson to Monroe, June 17, 1785, in ibid., 227–33.

3. This favorable view of the Order of Cincinnati is in "Jefferson's Observations on Démeunier's Manuscript," in ibid., 48–52; Jefferson to George Washington, November 14, 1786, in ibid., 531–33 (first two quotations on 532, third quotation on 533).

4. For the widespread worry that slavery would stain the reputation of the United States, see François Furstenberg, "Atlantic Slavery, Atlantic Freedom: George Washington, Slavery, and Transatlantic Abolitionist Networks," *William and Mary Quarterly*, 3d ser., 68 (April 2011): 262–63.

5. Jefferson, "Answers to Démeunier's First Queries," January 24, 1786, in *PTJ*, 10:11–20 (quotations on 18).

6. On this widespread expectation, see Wood, *Revolutionary Characters*, 27.

7. See Zilversmit, *The First Emancipation*.

8. See Helo, *Thomas Jefferson's Ethics*, 27; Peter S. Onuf, "Thomas Jefferson and American Democracy," in Boles and Hall, *Seeing Jefferson Anew*, 24; Mark D. McGarvie, "'In Perfect Accordance with His Character': Thomas Jefferson, Slavery, and the Law," *Indiana Magazine of History* 95 (June 1999): 142–77, esp. 145–46, 149, 166.

9. See Brissot de Warville to Jefferson, February 10, 1788, and Jefferson to Brissot de Warville, February 11, 1788, in *PTJ*, 12:577–78 (quotation on 578). This hesitancy to connect his name as an official of the United States to anything that could be considered advocacy without the approval of his government may be why, on the title page of his 1785 edition of *Notes on the State of Virginia*, he indicated incorrectly that he had written it in 1782, before he was an agent of the nation.

10. See Furstenberg, "Atlantic Slavery, Atlantic Freedom," 281.

11. Merrill D. Peterson, "Thomas Jefferson's *Notes on the State of Virginia*," *Studies in Eighteenth-Century Culture* (Madison, 1978), 7:49–62.

12. For background, see Alexander O. Boulton, "The American Paradox:

Jeffersonian Equality and Racial Science," *American Quarterly* 47 (September 1995): 467–92.

13. George Rogers Clark to Jefferson, February 20, 1782, in *PTJ*, 6:159–60; Jefferson to Clark, November 26, 1782, in ibid., 204–5; Arthur Campbell to Jefferson, November 7, 1782, in ibid., 201; Jefferson to Campbell, November 29, 1782, in ibid., 208.

14. For more on bones, see Jefferson to George Rogers Clark, January 6 and December 4, 1783, in ibid., 218–19, 371; Jefferson to Thomas Walker, September 25, 1783, in ibid., 339–40; Archibald Cary to Jefferson, October 12, 1783, in ibid., 342–44.

15. Jefferson to Marquis de Chastellux, January 16, 1784, in ibid., 466–67 (quotations on 467).

16. Jefferson explained all this in a letter to Charles Thomson, May 21, 1784, in ibid., 7:281–82.

17. Jefferson to James Monroe, December 10, 1784, in ibid., 7:563; Jefferson to James Madison, May 11, 1785, in ibid., 8:147.

18. In his presentation copies to trusted associates, Jefferson penned a message identical or very similar to what he wrote in Benjamin Franklin's copy: "Unwilling to expose these sheets to the public eye, he asks the favor of Doctr. Franklin to put them into the hands of no person on whose care and fidelity he cannot rely to guard them against publication." Quoted in Coolie Verner, "Mr. Jefferson Distributes His Notes: A Preliminary Checklist of the First Edition," *Bulletin of the New York Public Library* 56 (April 1952): 163.

19. Jefferson to James Monroe, June 17, 1785, in *PTJ*, 8:227–33 (quotation on 229).

20. Jefferson to C. W. F. Dumas, February 2, 1786, in ibid., 9:243–44 (quotation on 244); Jefferson, "Autobiography," 56.

21. Jefferson to James Madison, February 8, 1786, *PTJ*, 9:264–67 (quotation on 265).

22. Ibid.

23. James Madison to Jefferson, May 12, 1786, in ibid., 517–22 (quotations on 517).

24. John Stockdale to Jefferson, August 8, 1786, in ibid., 10:201–2 (quotation on 201).

25. Jefferson to Stockdale, February 1, 1787, in ibid., 11:107–8 (quotations on 107).

26. See Kovarsky, *The True Geography of Our Country*, 38–40, 48–49.

27. Stockdale to Jefferson, February 13, 1787, in *PTJ*, 11:143; Jefferson to Stockdale, February 27, 1787, in ibid., 183–84 (quotation on 183).

28. Terry L. Meyers, "Thinking About Slavery at the College of William and Mary," *William & Mary Bill of Rights Journal* 21, no. 4 (2013): 1253–54.

29. Charles Thomson to Jefferson, March 6, 1785, in *PTJ*, 8:15–16 (quotation on 16). Thomson based his remarks on a near-final manuscript version that he had seen several years earlier.

30. On Jefferson's rearrangement of Barbé-Marbois's queries, see David Tucker, *Enlightened Republicanism: A Study of Jefferson's* Notes on the State of Virginia (Lanham, MD, 2008), 3–18. The best account of the composition of *Notes* and its impact on the next generation of Virginians is Cara J. Rogers, "Jefferson's Sons: Notes on the State of Virginia and Virginian Antislavery, 1760–1832" (unpublished diss., Rice University, in progress).

31. Jefferson to Maria Cosway, October 12, 1786, in *PTJ*, 10:443–53 (quotation on 447).

32. *Notes*, 19.

33. Ibid., 24–25.

34. Ibid., 45 (first quotation), 47 (second quotation), 53–54 (third quotation).

35. Elizabeth Kolbert, *The Sixth Extinction: An Unnatural History* (New York, 2014), 28–29, 33, 37–38.

36. *Notes*, 58 (first two quotations), 59 (third quotation), 60 (fourth quotation). This section of *Notes* was part of a chapter titled "Productions Mineral, Vegetable and Animal."

37. Ibid., 55.

38. Ibid., 64 (quotation), 65.

39. Ibid., 98–100. For a consideration of the nature of Jefferson's archaeological report, see Clagett, *Scientific Jefferson Revealed*, 17–23 (quotation on 19); Silvio A. Bedini, *Thomas Jefferson: Statesman of Science* (New York, 1990), 102–6; Jeffrey Hantman and Gary Dunham, "The Enlightened Archaeologist," *Archaeology* 46 (May–June 1993): 46–49.

40. The section titled "Constitution" is in *Notes*, 110–29.

41. Ibid., 128 (first quotation), 129 (final quotation).

42. See ibid., 100–101.

43. See Peter S. Onuf, "'To declare them a free and equal people': Race, Slavery, and National Identity in Jefferson's Thought," *Journal of the Early Republic* 18 (spring 1998): 1–46.

44. *Notes*, 138.

45. Ibid.

46. Ibid., 139. Jefferson's language here reflected what David Brion Davis, in *The Problem of Slavery in the Age of Emancipation* (New York, 2014), 15–35, called the widespread effort among European thinkers to "animalize" Africans in the late eighteenth century.

47. *Notes*, 140.

48. Ibid., 139 (first two quotations), 142 (third and fourth quotations), 143 (final four quotations).

49. Ibid., 137–38.

50. See Eric Foner, "Lincoln and Colonization," in *Our Lincoln: New Perspectives on Lincoln and His World*, ed. Eric Foner (New York, 2008), 135–66, esp.,

136, 138; Davis, *The Problem of Slavery in the Age of Emancipation*, 83.

51. Davis, *The Problem of Slavery in the Age of Emancipation*, 149. See his discussion of the influential 1823 "Report on Colonization" by the well-known New Haven Congregationalist minister Leonard Bacon (ibid., 144–63). Jefferson to Edward Bancroft, January 26, 1788, in *PTJ*, 14:492–94 (quotation on 492).

52. See Suzanne Cooper Guasco, *Confronting Slavery: Edward Coles and the Rise of Antislavery Politics in Nineteenth-Century America* (De Kalb, IL, 2013); Beverly C. Tomek, *Colonization and Its Discontents: Emancipation, Emigration, and Antislavery in Antebellum Pennsylvania* (New York, 2011).

53. For Jefferson's unchanging views, see, for example, Peter Thompson, "'I have known': Thomas Jefferson, Experience, and Notes on the State of Virginia," in Cogliano, *A Companion to Thomas Jefferson*, 61. In 1809 Jefferson insisted that he had intended his words of 1787 as a tentative evaluation of blacks' abilities and said that even if they were lacking in understanding or talent, that did not mean they held no rights. See Jefferson to Henri Gregoire, February 25, 1809, in Ford, *The Works of Thomas Jefferson*, 11:99–100.

54. Most of his friends had only positive comments about *Notes*. See John Adams to Jefferson, May 22, 1785, in *PTJ*, 8:159–60; Richard Price to Jefferson, July 2, 1785, in ibid., 258–59; James Madison to Jefferson, November 15, 1785, in ibid., 9:38–39; Ezra Stiles, April 30, 1788, in ibid., 13:118. However, David Ramsay of South Carolina wrote, "I admire your generous indignation at slavery; but think you have depressed the negroes too low"; he went on to mention, in an environmentalist vein, that he thought in the future the "negroes will lose their black color." David Ramsay to

Jefferson, May 3, 1786, in ibid., 19:440–41 (quotations on 441).

55. Quoted in Douglas L. Wilson, "The Evolution of Jefferson's *Notes on the State of Virginia,*" *Virginia Magazine of History and Biography* 112, no. 2 (2004): 124.

56. See Winthrop D. Jordan, *White over Black: American Attitudes Toward the Negro, 1550–1812* (Baltimore, 1969), 29–35, 216–65; Davis, *The Problem of Slavery in the Age of Emancipation,* 26–35; Andrew S. Curran, *The Anatomy of Blackness: Science and Slavery in an Age of Enlightenment* (Baltimore, 2011). The orangutan was actually a native of Borneo and Sumatra, not Africa, but here it referred generically to any large primate.

57. Curran, *The Anatomy of Blackness,* 167–215, shows that in the final decade of the eighteenth century, a more positive view of blacks emerged and contributed to the rise of abolitionism in France, but Jefferson had left France by then and had less leisure to keep abreast of French scholarship.

58. *Notes,* 159 (all quotations).

59. Ibid., 159 (first quotation), 160 (second quotation).

60. Ibid., 160 (first quotation), 161 (final quotation).

61. Jefferson to George Wythe, August 13, 1786, in *PTJ,* 10:243–45 (quotations on 244).

62. *Notes,* 162.

63. Ibid., 162 (first quotation), 163 (remaining quotations).

64. Ibid., 163. This belief in the efficacy of changed attitudes to effect such large social issues as slavery was common to that phalanx of late-eighteenth and early-nineteenth-century ministers who developed a powerful religious critique of slavery and thought that religious conversion of slaveholders would inevitably lead to their emancipating their slaves. See, for example, Ben Wright, "Gospel of Liberty: Antislavery and American Salvation" (PhD diss., Rice University, 2014).

65. See Eva Sheppard Wolf, *Race and Liberty in the New Nation: Emancipation in Virginia from the Revolution to Nat Turner's Rebellion* (Baton Rouge, 2006), xiii.

66. *Notes,* 164–65. In 1805, when asked about a revised edition of the *Notes on the State of Virginia,* Jefferson remarked that if he should ever prepare one, he would "certainly qualify several expressions in the nineteenth chapter. . . . I had under my eye when writing, the manufactures of the great cities of the old countries, at the present time [i.e., 1784], with which the want of food and clothing necessary to sustain life, has begotten a depravity of morals, a dependence and corruption." But he pointed out that such conditions did not develop in the United States, whose manufacturing workers were "as independent and moral as our" farmers, "and they will continue so long as there are vacant lands for them to resort to; because whenever it shall be attempted by the other classes to reduce them to the minimum of subsistence, they will quit their trades and go to laboring the earth." Jefferson to [?] Lithgow, January 4, 1805, in Ford, *The Works of Thomas Jefferson,* 4:86–87n.

13:
"LIBERTY IS TO BE GAINED BY INCHES"

1. These instructions are reprinted in *PTJ,* 7:265–71.

2. "Draft of a Model Treaty," in ibid., 479–88.

3. Ibid., 482.

4. Jefferson, "Autobiography," 57.

5. Merrill D. Peterson, "Thomas Jefferson and Commercial Policy, 1783–1793," *William and Mary Quarterly* 22 (October 1965): 596–98.

6. For background on Americans captured and enslaved, see Christin E. Sears, *American Slaves and African Masters* (New York, 2012).

7. Jefferson to James Monroe, November 11, 1784, in *PTJ*, 7:508–13 (quotations on 511–12).

8. Jefferson to John Page, August 20, 1785, in ibid., 8:417–19 (quotation on 419). See also Cogliano, *Emperor of Liberty*, 67 (for the whole issue of dealing with the Barbary pirates, see 42–75.)

9. See Walter Lafeber, "Jefferson and an American Foreign Policy," in Onuf, *Jeffersonian Legacies*, 377–80; Cogliano, *Emperor of Liberty*, 8–9.

10. Jefferson to Montmorin, June 20, 1778, in *PTJ*, 14:121–25 (first quotation on 124, second quotation on 125).

11. Jefferson, "Autobiography," 78.

12. See the text of the Consular Convention of 1778, reprinted as "The Official Text as Ratified," in *PTJ*, 14:171–77 (quotation on 177).

13. Ibid., 88–90.

14. Jefferson to the Speaker of the House of Delegates, May 11, 1784, in ibid., 7:244.

15. Charles Thomson to Jefferson, May 19, 1784, in ibid., 272–73 (quotation on 272).

16. James Monroe to Jefferson, April 12, 1785, in ibid., 8:75–80 (quotation on 76); Jefferson to James Monroe, June 17, 1785, in ibid., 227–33 (quotation on 231).

17. James Madison to Jefferson, October 3, 1785, in ibid., 579–82.

18. Jefferson to Madison, October 28, 1785, in ibid., 681–83 (quotation on 682).

19. Jefferson, "Answers to Démeunier's First Queries," January 24, 1786, in ibid., 10:11–20 (quotation on 14).

20. Jefferson to Eliza House Trist, August 18, 1785, in ibid., 8:403–5 (quotation on 404).

21. John Jay to Jefferson, August 18, 1786, in ibid., 10:271–72 (quotation on 272); Jay to Jefferson, October 27, 1786,

in ibid., 488–89 (first and third quotations on 488, second quotation on 489).

22. John Adams to Jefferson, November 30, 1786, in ibid., 556–57 (quotations on 557).

23. Jefferson to James Madison, January 30, 1787, in ibid., 11:92–97 (quotation on 93). His letter a few weeks later to Abigail Adams should be read in the same light: "The spirit of resistance to government is so valuable on certain occasions, that I wish it to be always kept alive. It will often be exercised when wrong, but better so than not to be exercised at all. I like a little rebellion now and then. It is like a storm in the atmosphere." Jefferson to Abigail Adams, February 22, 1787, in ibid., 174–75 (quotation on 174). Again, he was looking at the Massachusetts disturbance from the perspective of France, where the total passivity of the people allowed an oppressive monarchical government to endure.

24. James Madison to Edmund Pendleton, February 24, 1787, in Hutchinson and Rachal, *The Papers of James Madison*, 9:294–95 (quotations on 294).

25. James Madison to Edmund Randolph, February 25, 1787, in ibid., 299.

26. Jefferson to James Madison, January 30, 1787, in *PTJ*, 11:92–97 (quotation on 93). For background on the Jay-Gardoqui negotiations, see Malone, *Jefferson and His Time*, 2:174; Peterson, *Thomas Jefferson and the New Nation*, 357–58; Richard B. Morris, ed., *Encyclopedia of American History* (New York, 1965), 114.

27. James Madison to Jefferson, March 19, 1787, in *PTJ*, 11:219–23 (quotations on 219).

28. James Madison to Jefferson, June 6, 1787, in ibid., 400–402 (quotation on 401). Jefferson received this letter on July 14.

29. Jefferson to David Hartley, July 2, 1787, in ibid., 525–26; Jefferson to Edward

Carrington, August 4, 1787, in ibid., 678–80 (quotation on 678); Jefferson to Benjamin Hawkins, August 4, 1787, in ibid., 683–84; Jefferson to David Ramsay, August 4, 1787, in ibid., 686–85; Jefferson to George Washington, August 14, 1787, in ibid., 12:36–38.

30. Jefferson to John Adams, August 30, 1787, in ibid., 12:66–69 (quotation on 69).

31. James Madison to Jefferson, September 6, 1787, in ibid., 102–4 (quotations on 102–3).

32. Jefferson to C. W. F. Dumas, September 10, 1787, in ibid., 113.

33. James Madison to Jefferson, October 24, 1787, in ibid., 270–84.

34. Jefferson to John Adams, November 13, 1787, in ibid., 349–51 (quotation on 350–51).

35. Jefferson to George Washington, May 2, 1788, in ibid., 13:124–28 (quotation on 128).

36. Jefferson to John Adams, November 13, 1787, in ibid., 12:351.

37. Jefferson to William Stephens Smith, November 13, 1787, in ibid., 355–57 (quotations on 356–57).

38. John Adams to Jefferson, November 10, 1787, in ibid., 334–35 (quotation on 335).

39. See Jefferson to Carmichael, December 15, 1787, in ibid., 423–27 (quotation on 425).

40. John Adams to Jefferson, December 6, 1787, in ibid., 396–97 (quotation on 396).

41. Jefferson to James Madison, December 20, 1787, in ibid., 438–42 (first quotation on 439, all others on 440).

42. Ibid., 442.

43. Edward Carrington to Jefferson, April 24, 1788, in ibid., 13:100–103 (quotation on 101).

44. Jefferson to James Madison, February 6, 1788, in ibid., 12:568–70 (quotation on 569–70).

45. See Jefferson to Alexander Donald, February 7, 1788, in ibid., 571; Jefferson to James Monroe, August 9, 1788, in ibid., 13:490.

46. Jefferson to Edward Carrington, May 27, 1788, in ibid., 13:208–9 (quotation on 208).

47. Jefferson to James Madison, July 31, 1788, in ibid., 440–43 (first quotation on 442, second quotation on 443).

48. Jefferson to William Carmichael, August 12, 1788, in ibid., 502–3 (quotation on 502).

49. George Washington to Jefferson, August 31, 1788, in ibid., 554–57 (quotation on 556–57).

50. Jefferson to David Humphreys, March 18, 1789, in ibid., 14:676–79 (quotations on 678).

51. See William Doyle, *The French Revolution: A Very Short Introduction* (Oxford, UK, 2002), 34–35.

52. Jefferson to John Jay, January 9, 1787, in *PTJ*, 11:29–33; Jefferson to Edward Carrington, January 16, 1787, in ibid., 48–50 (first quotation on 48); Jefferson to William Stephens Smith, February 19, 1787, in ibid., 168–69 (second quotation on 169).

53. Jefferson to John Jay, February 23, 1787, in ibid., 179–80 (quotation on 179); Jefferson to Madame de Tesse, March 20, 1787, in ibid., 226–28.

54. Jefferson to John Adams, August 30, 1787, in ibid., 66–69 (quotations on 67).

55. Jefferson explained his views in a long letter to John Jay, August 6, 1787, in ibid., 11:693–99, esp. 696.

56. Doyle, *The French Revolution*, 35.

57. Jefferson to Anne Willing Bingham, May 11, 1788, in *PTJ*, 13:151–52 (first quotation on 151); Jefferson to John Brown, May 28, 1788, in ibid., 211–13 (second quotation on 212); Jefferson to Bishop James Madison, July 19, 1788, in ibid., 379–82 (third quotation on 382).

58. Jefferson to John Brown Cutting, July 24, 1788, in ibid., 403–7 (quotations on 406).

59. Jefferson to John Banister Jr., August 9, 1788, in ibid., 483–84 (first quotation on 483); Jefferson to James Monroe, August 9, 1788, ibid., 488–90 (second quotation on 489).

60. Jefferson to David Humphreys, March 18, 1789, in ibid., 676–79 (quotation on 677).

61. Jefferson to Nicholas Lewis, December 16, 1788, in ibid., 362–63 (quotation on 363); Jefferson to Madame de Brehan, March 14, 1789, in ibid., 655–56.

62. Quote from Jefferson to Richard Price, July 12, 1789, in *PTJ*, 15:271–72 (quotation on 272).

63. Jefferson to Thomas Paine, July 17, 1789, in ibid., 279; Jefferson to James Madison, July 22, 1789, in ibid., 299–301 (quotation on 300).

64. Lafayette to Jefferson, August 25, 1789, in ibid., 354. Shortly following this dinner Jefferson wrote what became a letter sent to Madison several months later in which he used the famous phase "the earth belongs in usufruct [trust] to the living" and argued that no one generation had a right to bind future generations. This radical letter, probably originally written as a brief essay, perhaps to justify the actions of the Dutch Patriots, seems more to address French realities than American ones. And although Jefferson always believed that future generations had the right to revise by legal process the laws under which they lived, he never tried to put into force the formulation developed in the letter. Madison later refuted his tendentious accounting of the lifespan of generations. Much of the letter discusses the unfairness of burdening one generation with the debts of a previous generation, which clearly Jefferson felt personally. See Jefferson to James Madison, September 6, 1789, in ibid., 392–97; Madison to Jefferson, February 4, 1790, in ibid., 16:147–54.

For an early and still useful discussion of this exchange between Jefferson and Madison, see Adrienne Koch, *Jefferson and Madison: The Great Collaboration* (New York, 1950), 62–96. See also Herbert Sloan, "The Earth Belongs in Usufruct to the Living," in Onuf, *Jeffersonian Legacies*, 281–315. Jefferson always remained open to learning new things and felt that most issues, both scientific and political, were not settled for all time but subject to revision as new information became available. See, for instance, Jefferson to "Henry Tompkinson" [Samuel Kercheval], July 12, 1816, in *PTJRS*, 10:222–28.

65. Jefferson to Thomas Paine, September 13, 1789, in *PTJ*, 15:424.

66. Jefferson to John Jay, September 19, 1789, in ibid., 454–60.

67. Jefferson to Charles Clay, January 27, 1790, in ibid., 16:129.

68. Jefferson to Elizabeth Wayles Eppes, July 28, 1787, in *PTJ*, 11:634–34 (quotation on 634).

69. Jefferson to Elizabeth Wayles Eppes, July 12, 1788, in ibid., 13:347–48 (quotation on 347).

70. "George Ticknor's Account of a Visit to Monticello," [February 4–7, 1815], in *PTJRS*, 7:238–42 (quotation on 240).

71. See *DL*, 146.

72. Quoted in Catherine Kerrison, "French Education of Martha Jefferson Randolph," *Early American Studies* 10 (spring 2013), 349–94 (quotation on 364).

73. John Jay to Jefferson, June 19, 1789, in *PTJ*, 15:202–3, 203n.

74. See Kierner, *Martha Jefferson Randolph*, 67–69; Kerrison, "French Education of Martha Jefferson Randolph," 376.

75. Gordon-Reed, *The Hemingses of Monticello*, 348. I base my entire discussion of James and Sally Hemings' options on ibid, 343–52.

76. Ibid., 286.

14:
FROM PARIS TO NEW YORK

1. *JMB*, 1:745.

2. Jefferson to William Short, October 17, 1789, in *PTJ*, 15:524–25 (quotation on 524).

3. Malone, *Jefferson and His Time*, 2:243n.

4. Jefferson to John Trumbull, November 25, 1789, in *PTJ*, 15:559–60 (quotation on 560); Martha Jefferson gave a more detailed description in her reminiscences, quoted in ibid., 560n–561n.

5. "Address of Welcome of the Officials of Norfolk," in ibid., 556; "Jefferson's Reply to the Foregoing Address of Welcome," ibid., 556–57 (quotation).

6. Jefferson to William Short, December 14, 1789, in ibid., 16:24–28 (quotations on 26).

7. George Washington to Jefferson, November 30, 1789, in ibid., 8–9 (first quotation on 9); Washington to Jefferson, October 13, 1789, in ibid., 15:519–20 (second quotation on 519).

8. Jefferson to George Washington, December 15, 1789, in ibid., 16:34–35 (quotations on 35).

9. Martha's and Wormeley's accounts are reprinted in *DL*, 152–53, and Randall, *The Life of Thomas Jefferson*, 1:552–53; they first appeared in print in the latter. Randall had actually interviewed the aged Wormeley about the occasion.

10. James Madison to George Washington, January 4, 1790, in *PTJ*, 16:118n.

11. "The Response," reprinted in ibid., 178–79 (quotation on 179).

12. Ibid.

13. George Washington to Jefferson, January 21, 1790, in ibid., 116–17 (quotations on 117, emphasis in the original).

14. Jefferson to George Washington, February 14, 1790, in ibid., 184.

15. See Kierner, *Martha Jefferson Randolph*, 76–81.

16. Jefferson to Madame de Corny, April 2, 1790, in *PTJ*, 16:289–90 (first quotation on 290); Jefferson to Richard Gem, April 4, 1790, in ibid., 297 (second quotation).

17. It has been suggested that Patsy's quick marriage was a response to Sally Hemings's pregnancy, but there is no incontrovertible evidence that she was pregnant then or, if she was, that she was showing. See Gordon-Reed, *The Hemingses of Monticello*, 422, who argues Hemings was pregnant. For more on their courtship, see William H. Gaines Jr., *Thomas Mann Randolph: Jefferson's Son-in-Law* (Baton Rouge, 1966), 25–30.

18. This is suggested by Nathaniel Cutting to Martha Jefferson, March 30, 1790, in *PTJ*, 16:207n.

19. *JMB*, 1:750.

20. Jefferson to Martha Jefferson Randolph, April 4, 1790, in *PTJ*, 16:300; Martha Jefferson Randolph to Jefferson, April 25, 1790, in ibid., 384–85.

21. "Address of Welcome from the Mayor of Alexandria," March 1790, in ibid., 224; "Response to the Address of Welcome," March 11, 1790, in ibid., 225.

22. The journey is described in Jefferson to William Fitzhugh, March 11, 1790, in ibid., 223.

23. Sawvel, *The Complete Anas of Thomas Jefferson*, 30.

24. Malone, *Jefferson and His Time*, 2:260 (first quotation); Stanley Elkins and Eric McKitrick, *The Age of Federalism: The Early American Republic, 1788–1800* (New York, 1993), 129 (second quotation).

25. "Final State of the Report on Weights and Measures," July 4, 1790, in *PTJ*, 16:650–73.

26. James Madison to Jefferson, February 4, 1790, in ibid., 183–84 (quotation on 184).

27. Jeffrey H. Matsuura, *Jefferson vs. the Patent Trolls: A Populist Vision of Intellectual Property Rights* (Charlottesville, 2008), 79–94; Malone, *Jefferson and His Time*, 2:281–85.

28. Edgar S. Maclay, ed., *The Journal of William Maclay, United States Senator from Pennsylvania, 1789–1791* (New York, 1890), 272.

29. John Rutledge to Jefferson, May 6, 1790, in *PTJ*, 16:413–15. Jefferson received the letter on June 18. William Short to John Jay, May 11, 1790, in ibid., 425–26.

30. "Jefferson's Outline of Policy Contingent on War Between England and Spain," in ibid., 17:109–10 (quotation on 109).

31. Julian P. Boyd indicts Hamilton in *Number 7: Alexander Hamilton's Secret Attempts to Control American Foreign Policy* (Princeton, 1964). For a defense of Hamilton's actions (in this case and practically every other), see Elkins and McKitrick, *The Age of Federalism*, 222–23.

32. Malone, *Jefferson and His Time*, 2:310–15, covers the Nootka Sound controversy in detail; Peterson, *Thomas Jefferson and the New Nation*, 415–18; Noble E. Cunningham Jr., *In Pursuit of Reason: The Life of Thomas Jefferson* (Baton Rouge, 1978), 141–47.

33. Elkins and McKitrick, *The Age of Federalism*, 67–74.

34. Ibid., 115–23, 136–45; James Roger Sharp, *American Politics in the Early Republic: The New Nation in Crisis* (New Haven, 1993), 34–35.

35. Elkins and McKitrick, *The Age of Federalism*, 146–50; Sharp, *American Politics in the Early Republic*, 36.

36. See Richard S. Newman, "Prelude to the Gag Rule: Southern Reaction to Antislavery Petitions in the First Federal Congress," *Journal of the Early Republic* 16 (winter 1996): 571–99.

37. The best description of this episode in Congress is in Donald L. Robinson, *Slavery in the Structure of American Politics, 1765–1820* (New York, 1971), 302–12. See also Elkins and McKitrick, *The Age of Federalism*, 151–52; Irving Brant, *James Madison: Father of the Constitution, 1787–1800* (Indianapolis, 1950), 308–9. As Chernow, *Alexander Hamilton*, 307, says of Hamilton's response, "He certainly couldn't push through his controversial funding program if he stirred up the slavery question, which was probably a futile battle anyway. So this man of infinite opinions grew mute on that all important matter."

38. James Madison to Benjamin Rush, March 20, 1790, in Hutchinson and Rachal, *The Papers of James Madison*, 13:109.

39. James Madison to Edmund Randolph, March 21, 1790, in ibid., 110.

40. Adam Stephen to James Madison, April 25, 1790, in ibid., 176.

41. Maclay, *The Journal of William Maclay*, 222.

42. Jefferson to Thomas Mann Randolph Jr., April 18, 1790, in *PTJ*, 16:351–52; Jefferson to Henry Lee, April 26, 1790, in ibid., 385–86; Jefferson to Thomas Mann Randolph Jr., May 30, 1790, in ibid., 448–50.

43. "Jefferson's Account of the Bargain on the Assumption and Residence Bills," [1792], in ibid., 17:205–7; Sawvel, *The Complete Anas of Thomas Jefferson*, 33–35.

44. "Jefferson's Account of the Bargain on the Assumption and Residence Bills," 205 (first quotation); Sawvel, *The Complete Anas of Thomas Jefferson*, 33 (second and third quotations).

45. "Jefferson's Account of the Bargain on the Assumption and Residence Bills," 207 (quotation); Sawvel, *The Complete Anas of Thomas Jefferson*, 34.

46. Jefferson to James Monroe, June 20, 1790, in *PTJ*, 16:536–38 (quotation on 537).

47. Most scholars accept Jefferson's account of the dinner and the compromises, with the exception of

Joseph Ellis, in *Founding Brothers: The Revolutionary Generation* (New York, 2001), who is loath to give Jefferson much credit. See, by contrast, Elkins and McKitrick, *The Age of Federalism*, 156.

15:
JEFFERSON VERSUS HAMILTON

1. Finally a contract was worked out in 1792 so that Martha and Thomas could live at Edgehill, practically adjacent to Monticello.

2. "Jefferson's Deed of Gift of Certain Slaves," in *PTJ*, 18:12.

3. See ibid., 33n–39n; *JMB*, 1, 769.

4. See *GB*, 172–73.

5. For quick summaries of these issues, see Bedini, *Thomas Jefferson: Statesman of Science*, 218, 221.

6. "The Secretary of State to Gouverneur Morris," December 17, 1790, in *PTJ*, 18:303–4.

7. "Report of the Secretary of State to the President," January 18, 1791, in ibid., 565–70. See the discussion of this report in Malone, *Jefferson and His Time*, 2:328–30; Peterson, *Thomas Jefferson and the New Nation*, 422–23.

8. "Report on American Trade in the Mediterranean," in *PTJ*, 18:423–30.

9. "Report on the American Fisheries by the Secretary of State," February 1, 1791, in ibid., 19:206–22. See the discussion of this report in Malone, *Jefferson and His Time*, 2:332–33, and Peterson, *Thomas Jefferson and the New Nation*, 426.

10. Elkins and McKitrick, *The Age of Federalism*, 225–26.

11. Ibid., 226; Sharp, *American Politics in the Early Republic*, 38.

12. Elkins and McKitrick, *The Age of Federalism*, 227.

13. Ibid., 226–27; Peterson, *Thomas Jefferson and the New Nation*, 432.

14. Sharp, *American Politics in the Early Republic*, 39.

15. See Elkins and McKitrick, *The Age of Federalism*, 229–32.

16. Peterson, *Thomas Jefferson and the New Nation*, 434–37.

17. "Opinion on the Constitutionality of the Bill for Establishing a National Bank," February 15, 1791, in *PTJ*, 19:275–80 (quotation on 276).

18. Ibid., 280.

19. Elkins and McKitrick, *The Age of Federalism*, 232–33.

20. See Jefferson to Jonathan B. Smith, April 26, 1791, in *PTJ*, 20:290.

21. Malone, *Jefferson and His Time*, 2:363–64.

22. Jefferson to George Washington, May 8, 1791, in *PTJ*, 20:291–92 (first two quotations on 291, final quotation on 292).

23. See Jefferson to John Adams, July 17, 1791, and John Adams to Jefferson, July 29, 1791, in ibid., 302–3, 305–7.

24. The itinerary is well covered in Dumbauld, *Thomas Jefferson: American Tourist*, 172–77. James Hemings accompanied Jefferson and Madison and took Jefferson's horses and phaeton along. See *JMB*, 2:819n49.

25. See Noble E. Cunningham Jr., *The Jeffersonian Republicans: The Formation of Party Organization, 1789–1801* (Chapel Hill, 1957), 11–12.

26. Jefferson to Phillip Freneau, February 28, 1791, in *PTJ*, 19:351.

27. For the dates of his journey, see *JMB*, 2:832, 835, 836. Jefferson got news of the birth of his granddaughter from Mary Walker Lewis. See Lewis to Jefferson, January 23, 1791, in *PTJ*, 18:594.

28. Jefferson to Martha Jefferson Randolph, January 15, 1792, in ibid., 23:44–45 (quotation on 44).

29. "Notes of a Conversation with Alexander Hamilton," August 13, 1791, in ibid., 22:38–39 (quotations on 38).

30. Jefferson to Benjamin Rush, January 16, 1811, in *PTJRS*, 3:304–8 (quotations on 305). On 308n the editor

dates the dinner to probably the spring of 1791.

31. Jefferson to Thomas Paine, June 19, 1792, in *PTJ*, 20:312.

32. See *JMB*, 2:836n18, 837n21.

33. Silvio A. Bedini, *The Life of Benjamin Banneker* (New York, 1972), 108–9.

34. Benjamin Banneker to Jefferson, August 19, 1791, in *PTJ*, 22:49–52 (quotations on 49).

35. Ibid., 51.

36. *Notes*, 142–43.

37. Jefferson to Benjamin Banneker, August 30, 1791, in *PTJ*, 22:97–98 (quotation).

38. Jefferson to Marquis de Condorcet, August 30, 1791, in ibid., 98–99 (quotation).

39. See Richard Newman, "'Good Communications Corrects Bad Manners': The Banneker-Jefferson Dialogue and the Project of White Uplift," in *Contesting Slavery: The Politics of Bondage and Freedom in the New American Nation*, ed. John Craig Hammond and Matthew Mason (Charlottesville, 2011), 79. Unfortunately Nelson's view of Jefferson is more reductionist than nuanced.

40. See *PTJ*, 22:54n; Bedini, *The Life of Banneker*, 280–83; Gordon-Reed, *The Hemingses of Monticello*, 475–77.

41. Jefferson to Joel Barlow, October 8, 1809, in *PTJRS*, 1:588–89 (quotation).

42. See Tim Matthewson, *A Proslavery Foreign Policy: Haitian-American Relations During the Early Republic* (Westport, CT, 2003), 20, 24–25. For the revolt generally, see Laurent Dubois, *Avengers of the World: The Story of the Haitian Revolution* (Cambridge, MA, 2004).

43. Jefferson to Lafayette, June 16, 1792, in *PTJ*, 24:85–86 (quotations on 85). See also Tim Matthewson, "Jefferson and Haiti," *Journal of Southern History* 61 (May 1995): 209–48, in which he cautions against Michael Zuckerman's rather knee-jerk assumption that racism shaped Jefferson's Haitian policy ("Zuckerman provides no documentation to support his claims," [210]). Matthewson was referencing the chapter "The Power of Blackness: Thomas Jefferson and the Revolution in St. Domingue," in Zuckerman's *Almost Chosen People: Oblique Biographies in the American Grain* (Berkeley, 1993), 175–218. For a defense of Jefferson's policies toward the Haitian rebellion, including a convincing demonstration that Jefferson never called the rebels "cannibals," see Arthur Scherr, *Thomas Jefferson's Haitian Policy: Myths and Realities* (Lanham, MD, 2011).

44. Peterson, *Thomas Jefferson and the New Nation*, 451; Elkins and McKitrick, *The Age of Federalism*, 244–45.

45. Peterson, *Thomas Jefferson and the New Nation*, 451; Elkins and McKitrick, *The Age of Federalism*, 246–51; Malone, *Jefferson and His Time*, 2:398–99.

46. Peterson, *Thomas Jefferson and the New Nation*, 456–58, and Malone, *Jefferson and His Time*, 2:406–19, describe the effort briefly and clearly.

47. See Elkins and McKitrick, *The Age of Federalism*, 440.

48. Ibid., 258–60; Peterson, *Thomas Jefferson and the New Nation*, 458–59.

49. "Memorandum of Conversations with the President," March 1, 1792, in *PTJ*, 23:184–87 (first quotation on 184, second and third on 185).

50. For background, see Michael Lienisch, "Thomas Jefferson and the American Democratic Experience: The Origins of the Partisan Press, Popular Political Parties, and Public Opinion," in Onuf, *Jeffersonian Legacies*, 316–39, esp. 320–24; Todd Estes, "Jefferson as Party Leader," in Cogliano, *A Companion to Thomas Jefferson*, 128–44, esp. 132–36; and, more generally, Jeffrey L. Pasley, *"The Tyranny of Printers": Newspaper Politics in the Early American Republic* (Charlottesville, 2001).

51. Jefferson to George Washington, May 23, 1792, in *PTJ*, 23:535–40 (quotations on 536).

52. Ibid. (first quotation on 537; second, third, and fourth quotations on 538; fifth quotation on 539).

53. "Notes of a Conversation with George Washington," July 10, 1792, in ibid., 24:210–11 (quotations on 210).

54. Alexander Hamilton to George Washington, August 18, 1792, in *The Papers of Alexander Hamilton*, ed. Harold C. Syrett, 27 vols. (New York, 1961–1987), 12:228–58.

55. George Washington to Jefferson, August 23, 1792, in *PTJ*, 24:315–18 (all quotations on 317).

56. Jefferson to George Washington, September 9, 1792, in ibid., 351–59 (quotation on 353).

57. See Alexander Hamilton to George Washington, September 1, 1792, in Syrett, *The Papers of Alexander Hamilton*, 12:311–12; George Washington to Jefferson, September 15, 1792, in *PTJ*, 24:383–84, esp. 384n–385n; Jefferson to George Washington, September 18, 1792, in ibid., 403–4.

58. Ibid. (first quotation on 434, second and third quotations on 435).

59. See Jefferson to George Washington, October 17, 1792, in ibid., 494, with the enclosures described at 495n.

60. George Washington to Jefferson, October 18, 1792, in ibid., 499.

61. Jefferson to Thomas Pinckney, December 3, 1792, in ibid., 696–97 (quotation on 696).

62. For the story of the design of the capital city, see Malone, *Jefferson and His Time*, 2:371–87; Peterson, *Thomas Jefferson and the New Nation*, 447–49; Elkins and McKitrick, *The Age of Federalism*, 163–93; Frederick Doveton Nichols and Ralph E. Griswold, *Thomas Jefferson: Landscape Architect* (Charlottesville, 1978), 38–75. Saul K. Padover, ed., *The Complete Jefferson: Containing His Major Writings, Published and Unpublished, Except His Letters* (New York, 1943), conveniently gathers together all the relevant documents, but see the Jefferson materials scattered throughout the relevant volumes of *PTJ* for the extensive and extremely helpful footnotes.

63. "Jefferson's Draft of Agenda for the Seat of Government," August 29, 1790, in *PTJ*, 17:460–61.

64. Malone, *Jefferson and His Time*, 2:373–74.

65. See Pierre Charles L'Enfant to Thomas Jefferson, April 4, 1791, in *PTJ*, 20:83–84 (quotation on 83); Jefferson to L'Enfant, April 10, 1791, in ibid., 86.

66. Commissioners to L'Enfant, September 9, 1791, in *Thomas Jefferson and the National Capital . . . 1783–1818*, ed. Saul K. Padover (Washington, DC, 1946), 74–75.

67. For L'Enfant's firing, see Jefferson to L'Enfant, February 27, 1792, in *PTJ*, 23:161.

68. The phrase is a term of art meaning a supervisor of building works in progress. Thornton was responsible for the exterior design of the capitol, but he was no experienced architect, as was Hallet, so Hallet was hired to do the drawings and make such adjustments as necessary to Thornton's design to make construction practicable.

69. Malone, *Jefferson and His Time*, 2:384–87. The Executive Mansion or President's House, as it was known before the name "White House" became official in 1901, was not finished until 1833, and the capitol dome was completed during the Civil War.

16:
THE SPECTER OF
THE FRENCH REVOLUTION

1. I base my discussion of Jefferson's cipher wheel on the discussions in Bedini, *Thomas Jefferson: Statesman of Science*, 233–43; Clagett, *Scientific Jefferson*

Revealed, 79–86; and David Kahn, *The Codebreakers* (New York: Signet Books, 1973), 114–16 (quotation on 116). For strong evidence that this "cipher wheel" was invented during Jefferson's presidency, see "Description of a Wheel Cipher," [before March 22, 1802], in *PTJ*, 37:102–4, and the helpful note on 104n–107n.

2. See "Jefferson and André Michaux's Proposed Western Expedition," editorial note, in *PTJ*, 25:75–81; Jefferson to Paul Allen, August 18, 1813, in *PTJRS*, 6:418–24 (quotation on 420).

3. Benjamin Smith Barton to Jefferson, January 4, 1793, in *PTJ*, 25:17–18, esp. 18n.

4. "American Philosophical Society's Subscription Agreement for André Michaux's Western Expedition," in ibid., 81–84.

5. David Rittenhouse to Jefferson, April 10, 1793, in ibid., 527.

6. "American Philosophical Society's Instructions to André Michaux," ca. April 30, 1793, in ibid., 624–26 (quotations on 624).

7. Ibid., 625.

8. Ibid.

9. Ibid., 625–26 (quotations on 626).

10. Marquis de Condorcet to Jefferson, December 21, 1792 [received on May 8, 1793], in ibid., 24:760–62; Thomas Pinckney to Jefferson, January 3, 1793 [received April 12, 1793], in ibid., 25:11–12.

11. Jefferson to Brissot de Warville, May 8, 1793, in ibid., 679.

12. Jefferson to William Short, January 3, 1793, in ibid., 14–16 (quotation on 14).

13. Jefferson to Thomas Mann Randolph Jr., July 14, 1793, in ibid., 26:503–4 (quotation on 504). Until almost the end of his life, Jefferson maintained hope that the southern states would eventually come to their senses and free (and colonize abroad) their slaves. This contradicts the argument of Henry Wiencek, in *Master of the Mountain: Thomas Jefferson and His Slaves* (New York, 2012), 8–9, that Jefferson

drastically backed away from his earlier antislavery stance after he realized in June 1792 that the institution was profitable in part because slaves reproduced themselves. Wiencek draws this farfetched conclusion from a comment Jefferson made—in response to a request from President Washington—that he reply to some queries put to Washington by eminent British agricultural writer Arthur Young. Jefferson subsequently wrote, considering Virginia as a whole, that the slave population doubled every twenty-five years, representing a 4 percent annual increase in their value. Wiencek mistakenly believes Jefferson was referring specifically to the slaves at Monticello. It simply strains credulity to argue that Jefferson, with his compulsively quantitative state of mind (he was constantly measuring, counting, calculating) and his lifelong familiarity with the institution of slavery, did not realize the profitability of slave reproduction until he was forty-nine years old. Nevertheless, for Wiencek, this supposed eureka moment in 1792 was a turning point in Jefferson's attitude toward slavery. For Washington's request to Jefferson for assistance and Jefferson's hurried and brief comments on Young's questions, see George Washington to Jefferson, June 17, 1792, in *PTJ*, 24:95; Jefferson's "Notes on Arthur Young's Letter to George Washington," June 18, 1792, in ibid., 95–98.

14. Jefferson to Thomas Leiper, December 9, 1792, in *PTJ*, 24:714.

15. Jefferson to Martha Jefferson Randolph, January 26, 1793, in ibid., 25:97–98.

16. "Note of a Conversation with George Washington," February 7, 1793, in ibid., 153–55 (quotation on 154).

17. *JMB*, 2:892, 892n; Jefferson to Martha Jefferson Randolph, March 10, 1793, in *PTJ*, 25:352–53; Jefferson to Francis Eppes, April 7, 1793, in ibid., 515;

Jefferson to Martha Jefferson Randolph, July 7, 1793, in ibid., 26:445–46.

18. The background to all this is clearly laid out in Elkins and McKitrick, *The Age of Federalism*, 295–302, and "Jefferson and the Giles Resolutions," in *PTJ*, 25:280n–292n.

19. In addition to the sources in the previous note, see Malone, *Jefferson and His Time*, 3:17–26; Peterson, *Thomas Jefferson and the New Nation*, 477–79; Cunningham, *The Jeffersonian Republicans*, 51–54.

20. "Jefferson and the Giles Resolutions," 290n.

21. See Jefferson to Thomas Mann Randolph Jr., March 3, 1793, in *PTJ*, 25:313–14.

22. Jefferson to George Washington, September 9, 1792, in ibid., 24:351–59 (quotation on 358).

23. James Madison to Jefferson, May 27, 1793, in ibid., 26:133; Jefferson to James Madison, June 9, 1793, in ibid., 239–42 (quotation on 240).

24. "Notes on Conversations with William Stephens Smith and George Washington," February 20, 1793, in ibid., 25:243–45 (quotations on 244).

25. Jefferson to Gouverneur Morris, March 12, 1793, in ibid., 25:367–69 (quotation on 367).

26. Gouverneur Morris to George Washington, January 6, 1793, quoted in Malone, *Jefferson and His Time*, 3:91.

27. "Notes on the Reception of Edmond Charles Genet," in *PTJ*, 25:469–70 (quotation on 469).

28. Hamilton to Edward Carrington, May 26, 1792, in Syrett, *The Papers of Alexander Hamilton*, 11:426–45 (quotation on 439, emphasis in the original).

29. George Washington to Cabinet, April 18, 1793, in *PTJ*, 25:568.

30. "Jefferson's Opinions on the Treaties with France," in four parts, with long explanatory editorial note, in ibid., 597–619. James Madison agreed with Jefferson

that Congress should decide matters of neutrality as well as war, not the executive alone. See James Madison to Jefferson, June 13, 1793, in ibid., 26:272–74, esp. 273.

31. For Genet's background, see Harry Ammon, *The Genet Mission* (New York, 1973), 2–9.

32. Ibid., 44–45, 51–54.

33. Ibid., 52–54.

34. Quoted in Malone, *Jefferson and His Time*, 3:94.

35. Jefferson to James Madison, May 19, 1993, in *PTJ*, 26:61–62 (quotations on 62).

36. Jefferson to Harry Innes, May 23, 1793, in ibid., 99–100 (quotation on 100).

37. "Notes of a Conversation with George Washington," May 23, 1793, in ibid., 101–2.

38. Genet's antics are well described in Ammon, *The Genet Mission*, 65–131, and Elkins and McKitrick, *The Age of Federalism*, 344–62.

39. Jefferson to James Madison, July 7, 1793, in *PTJ*, 26:443–44 (quotations on 444).

40. "Notes of Cabinet Meeting on Edmond Charles Genet," July 23, 1793, in ibid., 553–55.

41. Jefferson to George Washington, July 31, 1793, in ibid., 593–94 (quotation on 593).

42. "Notes of Cabinet Meeting on Edmond Charles Genet," August 2, 1793, in ibid., 601–3 (first quotation on 602, second and third quotations on 603).

43. "Notes of a Conversation with George Washington," August 6, 1793, in ibid., 627–30 (quotation on 628).

44. Jefferson to George Washington, August 11, 1793, in ibid., 659–60; Washington to Jefferson, August 12, 1793, in ibid., 660.

45. Jefferson to James Madison, August 11, 1793, in ibid., 651–53 (quotation on 652).

46. See "The Recall of Edmond Charles Genet," in ibid., 685–715; "Cabinet Opinions of Edmond Charles Genet,"

August 23, 1793, in ibid., 745; Jefferson to Gouverneur Morris, August 23, 1793, in ibid., 747–48.

47. See Catherine A. Herbert, "The Genet Element in Pennsylvania in the 1790s: The Francophone Immigrants' Impact," *Pennsylvania Magazine of History and Biography* 108 (October 1984): 451–69, esp. 455.

48. Ammon, *The Genet Mission*, 159–60.

49. Josef Ignacio de Viar and Josef de Jaudenes to Jefferson, August 27, 1793, in *PTJ*, 26:771–73, Jefferson to Isaac Shelby, August 29, 1793, in ibid., 785.

50. See J. H. Powell, *Bring Out Your Dead: The Great Plague of Yellow Fever in Philadelphia in 1793* (Philadelphia, 1949).

51. Jefferson to James Madison, September 1, 1793, in *PTJ*, 27:6–8 (quotations on 7).

52. Jefferson to James Madison, September 8, 1793, in ibid., 61–63 (quotations on 62).

53. Jefferson to James Madison, September 12, 1793, in ibid., 102.

54. *JMB*, 2:901–3.

55. George Washington to Jefferson, October 7, 1793, in *PTJ*, 27:218–19 (first quotation on 219), which Jefferson received on October 15; Jefferson to James Madison, November 2, 1793, in ibid., 297–98.

56. See "Notes of Cabinet Meetings on Edmund Charles Genet and the President's Address to Congress," November 18, 1793, in ibid., 399–401, 401n.

57. See "Notes of Cabinet Meeting on the President's Address and Messages to Congress," November 28, 1793, in ibid., 453–55.

58. Jefferson to Martha Jefferson Randolph, December 22, 1793, in ibid., 608–9; Jefferson to Thomas Mann Randolph Jr., December 8, 1793, in ibid., 496–97.

59. Jefferson to Mary Jefferson, December 15, 1793, in ibid., 523–24 (quotation on 524).

60. See Peterson, *Thomas Jefferson and the New Nation*, 508–16; Peterson, "Thomas Jefferson and Commercial Policy, 1783–1793," 584–610.

61. Jefferson to George Washington, December 31, 1793, in ibid., 656.

62. George Washington to Jefferson, January 1, 1974, in ibid., 27:3.

63. See *JMB*, 2:908–12.

17:
"TOTALLY ABSORBED IN MY RURAL OCCUPATIONS"

1. Jefferson to Caleb Lownes, December 18, 1793, in *PTJ*, 27:586; *JMB*, 2:910.

2. *JMB*, 2:909.

3. Jefferson to Edmund Randolph, February 3, 1794, in *PTJ*, 27:15–16 (quotation on 15).

4. Jefferson to James Madison, April 3, 1794, ibid., 28:49–50 (quotation on 50).

5. Jefferson to John Adams, April 25, 1794, in ibid., 57.

6. Jefferson to George Wythe, October 23, 1794, in ibid.,181.

7. Jefferson to James Madison, February 15, 1794, in ibid., 21–22.

8. *GB*, 208–12.

9. Edwin Morris Betts, ed., *Thomas Jefferson's Farm Book* (Charlottesville, 1987), 87–89, 109–112, 143–44 (hereafter *FB*).

10. Lucia Stanton, *"Those Who Labor for My Happiness": Slavery at Thomas Jefferson's Monticello* (Charlottesville, 2012), 125.

11. *Notes*, 167–68.

12. Jefferson to George Washington, May 14, 1794, in *PTJ*, 28:74–75 (quotations on 75). See the document titled "Farming. Rotation," in *FB*, 314–17.

13. On his giving up on wheat, see Malone, *Jefferson and His Time*, 3:205.

14. Jefferson to Sir John Sinclair, March 23, 1798, in *PTJ*, 30:198–99; Jefferson to

John Taylor, March 25, 1798, in ibid., 217–18.

15. See Lewis Cecil Gray, *History of Agriculture in the Southern United States to 1860*, 2 vols. (Washington, DC, 1933), 1:171, 2:798–99.

16. Edwin Morris Betts has gathered the relevant excerpts of all Jefferson's correspondence dealing with the threshing machine in *FB*, 69–76. Jefferson noted in his diary, reprinted in *GB*, 246, the exact day he began using the machine.

17. See the complicated listing of slaves and their assigned tasks, with notations on how much labor was performed by day, in *GB*, 228–29.

18. "Notes of a Tour Through Holland and the Rhine Valley," in *PTJ*, 13:27. For a succinct collection of fragments of correspondence concerning the moldboard plow, see *FB*, 49–64.

19. For his use of the calculus, see I. Bernard Cohen, *Science and the Founding Fathers: Science in the Political Thought of Thomas Jefferson, Benjamin Franklin, John Adams, and James Madison* (New York, 1995), 101, 293–95.

20. Jefferson to John Taylor, December 29, 1794, in *PTJ*, 28:230–34 (quotation on 233).

21. Jefferson to Sir John Sinclair, March 23, 1798, in ibid., 30:197–207 (see 207n for the publication in *Transactions*).

22. "Potash," Wikipedia, accessed August 7, 2014, wikipedia.org/wiki/Potash.

23. See the facsimile of the page in Jefferson's hand on the requirements of potash production. Facsimile of original memorandum book reproduced in *FB*, 117.

24. See Hochman, "Thomas Jefferson: A Personal Financial Biography," 231–38.

25. See Bedini, *Thomas Jefferson: Statesman of Science*, 253; Gordon-Reed, *The Hemingses of Monticello*, 510.

26. Stanton, *"Those Who Labor for My Happiness,"* 11.

27. *JMB*, 2:914, 915.

28. Jefferson to John Adams, May 27, 1795, in *PTJ*, 28:363.

29. See Isaac Jefferson, "Memoirs of a Monticello Slave," in Bear, *Jefferson at Monticello*, 23.

30. Jefferson in 1803 wrote to Thomas Mann Randolph to sell a slave named Cary, to set "an example . . . in terrorem to others," because Cary had used a hammer to smash in the head of another worker in the nailery, breaking his skull and necessitating an emergency operation that somehow saved his life. Jefferson to Thomas Mann Randolph, June 8, 1803, quoted in *FB*, 19. For Jefferson's management techniques, see Lucia Stanton, "Jefferson's People: Slavery at Monticello," in Shuffelton, *The Cambridge Companion to Thomas Jefferson*, 83–100, esp.88–90.

31. Stanton, *"Those Who Labor for My Happiness,"* 15, 86.

32. Jefferson to Bowling Clark, September 21, 1782, in *PTJ*, 24:408–9.

33. See Jefferson to Archibald Stuart, January 3, 1796, in ibid., 28:572–74, complaining of the action of the Richmond merchants.

34. Jefferson to Edward Rutledge, November 30, 1795, in ibid., 541–42 (quotation on 541).

35. Jefferson to Martha Jefferson Randolph, July 31, 1795, in ibid., 429.

36. Edmund Randolph to Jefferson, August 28, 1794, in ibid., 117–19; Jefferson to Randolph, September 7, 1794, in ibid., 148 (first quotation); Jefferson to Randolph, November 6, 1794, in ibid., 187 (second quotation). Because Jefferson always called it rheumatism, I will follow his usage.

37. Jefferson to Martha Jefferson Randolph, January 22, 1795, in ibid., 249–50 (quotations on 249). Jefferson to

Thomas Mann Randolph, January 29, 1795, in ibid., 251–52; Jefferson to Martha Jefferson Randolph, February 5, 1795, in ibid., 260–61.

38. *JMB*, 2:930.

39. Jefferson to Thomas Mann Randolph, August 7, 1794, in *PTJ*, 28:111–12 (quotation on 111); Jefferson to Thomas Mann Randolph, January 18, 1796, in ibid., 592–93 (quotation on 592).

40. Cynthia A. Kierner ably recounts this tragic series of events in *Scandal at Bizarre: Rumor and Reputation in Jefferson's Virginia* (New York, 2004). Bizarre was the name of Richard and Judith Randolph's plantation.

41. Martha Jefferson Randolph to Jefferson, November 18, 1808, in *FL*, 359–61 (first quotation on 360); Ellen Wayles Randolph Coolidge to Virginia Jefferson Randolph Trist, March 20, 1827, in Coolidge Correspondence, University of Virginia (second quotation). Cynthia A. Kierner brought this letter to my attention.

42. Jefferson to Mary Jefferson, June 14, 1797, in *PTJ*, 29:429–30.

43. *JMB*, 2:972.

44. The most detailed and nuanced treatment of every aspect of the Jefferson–Sally Hemings relationship is Gordon-Reed, *The Hemingses of Monticello*. See also Scharff, *The Women Jefferson Loved*, 218–20. Jon Kukla, in *Mr. Jefferson's Women*, 125–27, 200, argues that the sexual relationship between the two began in 1793 or 1794. Gordon-Reed convincingly refutes the assumption that all such relationships were based in rape, forced on the essentially helpless black women by their white owners, thereby denying any agency to all slave women in such relationships. No doubt this was true in most situations but not in every one.

45. See Joshua D. Rothman, *Notorious in the Neighborhood: Sex and Families Across the Color Line in Virginia, 1787–1861* (Chapel Hill, 2003).

46. Jefferson to Edmund Randolph, September 7, 1794, in *PTJ*, 28:148 (first quotation); Jefferson to Benjamin Carter Waller, October 9, 1794, in ibid., 180–81 (third quotation on 180); Jefferson to James Madison, October 30, 1794, in ibid., 182 (second quotation).

47. Jefferson to James Madison, April 27, 1795, in ibid., 338–40 (quotation on 339).

48. See the abbreviated listing in James Gilreath and Douglas L. Wilson, eds., *Thomas Jefferson's Library: A Catalog with the Entries in His Own Order* (Washington, DC, 1989), 40–43.

49. Sowerby, *Catalogue of the Library of Thomas Jefferson*, 1:405–6.

50. Andrew Burstein, *Jefferson's Secrets: Death and Desire at Monticello* (New York, 2005), 34–37, 156–58; see also Kukla, *Mr. Jefferson's Women*, 129–32.

51. Jefferson to Angelica Schuyler Church, November 27, 1793, in *PTJ*, 27:449–50 (quotation on 449).

52. Jefferson to Thomas Mann Randolph, January 22, 1797, in ibid., 29:272. Slightly later she fell out of a door and sprained her ankle. Malone, *Jefferson and His Time*, 3:240.

53. Quoted in *VTM*, 21.

54. Jefferson to John Brown, April 5, 1797, in *PTJ*, 29:345–46.

55. Jefferson to Martha Jefferson Randolph, February 14, 1796, in ibid., 28:609–10 (quotation on 609).

56. Jefferson to Compte Constantin de Volney, April 9, 1797, in ibid., 29:352–53 (quotation on 352).

57. Jefferson to Benjamin Hawkins, March 22, 1796, in ibid., 29:42–43 (quotation on 43).

58. Diary entry of Anna Thornton, September 22, 1802, in *VTM*, 33.

59. Jefferson to Volney, April 10, 1796, in *PTJ*, 29:61.

60. See the informative booklet by Frederick D. Nichols and James A. Bear Jr., *Monticello* (Charlottesville, 1967);

Jack McLaughlin's useful *Jefferson and Monticello*; and the definitive studies by Frederick D. Nichols, [Thomas Jefferson's] *Architectural Drawings* (Boston, 1961); and Fiske Kimball, *Thomas Jefferson, Architect* (Cambridge, MA, 1916).

61. From the memoirs of Isaac Shelby, as quoted in Bear, *Jefferson at Monticello*, 17–18.

62. Jefferson to Mary Jefferson Eppes, March 3, 1802, in *PTJ*, 36:676–77 (quotation on 676).

63. Thomas P. Slaughter, *The Whiskey Rebellion: Frontier Epilogue to the American Revolution* (New York, 1986). But see also the discussions in Elkins and McKitrick, *The Age of Federalism*, 461–63, 478–83; Sharp, *American Politics in the Early Republic*, 92–98.

64. Jefferson to William Branch Giles, December 17, 1794, in *PTJ*, 28:218–19 (quotation on 219).

65. Jefferson to Madison, December 28, 1794, in ibid., 228–30 (first quotation on 228, second quotation on 230).

66. For the Jay Treaty and its political implications generally, see Jerald A. Combs, *The Jay Treaty: Political Battleground of the Founding Fathers* (Berkeley, 1970).

67. Jefferson to James Madison, September 21, 1795, in *PTJ*, 28:475–76 (quotation on 475).

68. Jefferson to Edward Rutledge, November 30, 1795, in ibid., 28:541–42 (quotation on 542).

69. "Notes on the Letter of Christoph Daniel Ebeling," [after October 15, 1795], in ibid., 506–10, esp. 509.

70. On the gradual emergence of parties, see Sharp, *American Politics in the Early Republic*, 133–42; see esp. Cunningham, *The Jeffersonian Republicans*, chaps. 4–5. For a commonsense and persuasive discussion of the whole idea of party, see Jeffrey L. Pasley, *The First Presidential Election: 1796 and the Founding*

of American Democracy (Lawrence, KS, 2013), 3–15.

71. John Stuart to Jefferson, April 11, 1796, in *PTJ*, 29:64.

72. Jefferson to John Stuart, May 26, 1796, in ibid., 113–14.

73. Jefferson to David Rittenhouse, July 3, 1796, in ibid., 138–39 (quotation on 139).

74. John Stuart to Jefferson, July 13, 1796, in ibid., 152–53.

75. Benjamin Smith Barton to Jefferson, August 1, 1796, in ibid., 165–66; Archibald Stuart to Jefferson, August 19, 1796, in ibid., 171–72; Jefferson to John Stuart, November 10, 1796, in ibid., 205–6 (quotation on 206).

76. "Memoir on the Megalonyx," [February 10, 1797], in ibid., 291–99, with helpful notes on 299–304. By the time Jefferson submitted his piece, he had become familiar with similar bone remains in Europe described by Cuvier, who demonstrated that the claw came not from a lion-like creature but rather from a prehistoric ground sloth. See Bedini, *Thomas Jefferson: Statesman of Science*, 267–72; Clagett, *Scientific Jefferson Revealed*, 40–44. In 1822 the French naturalist Anselm Desmarest gave Jefferson's finding the name *Megalonyx jeffersonii*, by which it has been called ever since. Bedini, *Thomas Jefferson: Statesman of Science*, 272.

77. William Cocke to Jefferson, August 17, 1796, in *PTJ*, 29:169.

78. Jefferson to William Cocke, October 21, 1796, in ibid., 199.

79. Consult Andrew Burstein and Nancy Isenberg, *Madison and Jefferson* (New York, 2010), 312, for the details of this 1796 stealth campaign for Jefferson. For practically every aspect of the election, however, the definitive account is Jeffrey L. Pasley's *The First Presidential Election*, which is essential for understanding the election and the surprisingly passive role Jefferson (and John Adams) played in it.

80. James Madison to Jefferson, December 5, 1796, in *PTJ*, 29:214.

81. James Madison to Jefferson, December 10, 1796, in ibid., 218.

82. Jefferson to Madison, December 17, 1796, in ibid., 223–24 (quotations on 223).

83. Madison to Jefferson, December 19, 1796, in ibid., 226–27 (quotation on 226, emphasis in the original); Madison to Jefferson, December 25, 1796, in ibid., 227–28.

84. Jefferson to Madison, January 1, 1797, in ibid., 247–48.

85. "From the American Philosophical Society," January 7, 1797, in ibid., 254 (Jefferson received the letter on January 21); Jefferson to the American Philosophical Society, January 28, 1797, in ibid., 276–77 (quotation on 276).

18:
THE VICE PRESIDENCY

1. Jefferson to Elbridge Gerry, May 13, 1797, *PTJ*, 29:361–64 (quotation on 362).

2. Jefferson to John Adams, December 28, 1796, in ibid., 235.

3. James Madison to Jefferson, January 15, 1797, in ibid., 263–65 (quotation on 264). According to Edmund S. Morgan, *The Meaning of Independence: John Adams, George Washington, and Thomas Jefferson* (Charlottesville, 1976), 9, "John Adams was one of the vainest men who ever lived."

4. Jefferson to Madison, January 22, 1797, in *PTJ*, 29:270–72 (quotation on 271).

5. Jefferson to George Wythe, January 22, 1797, in ibid., 275–76 (quotation on 276).

6. Wythe to Jefferson, February 1, 1797, in ibid., 283.

7. Jefferson to James Sullivan, February 6, 1797, in ibid., 289–90 (first quotation on 289, other quotations on 290).

8. Malone, *Jefferson and His Time*, 3:296–97; Peterson, *Thomas Jefferson and the New Nation*, 561.

9. Jefferson, "Address to the Senate," March 4, 1797, in *PTJ*, 29:310–11 (quotations on 311).

10. Jefferson to Thomas Mann Randolph, March 11, 1797, in ibid., 315–16 (quotation on 316).

11. "Notes on Conversations with John Adams and George Washington," [after October 13, 1797], in ibid., 551–52 (quotation on 552).

12. See the various notations in *JMB*, 2:955–57; Peterson, *Thomas Jefferson and the New Nation*, 563–64.

13. Timothy Pickering to Jefferson, March 26, 1797, *PTJ*, 29:325.

14. Jefferson to Philip Mazzei, April 24, 1796, in ibid., 81–83 (quotations on 82).

15. The best short summary of the letter and the furor it evoked is the editorial note that proceeds the publication of the letter in ibid., 73–81.

16. Jefferson to Elbridge Gerry, May 13, 1797, in ibid., 361–64 (quotation on 362).

17. Ibid.

18. Ibid., 363.

19. Ibid.

20. Ibid., 364.

21. Sharp, *American Politics in the Early Republic*, 165–68; Peterson, *Thomas Jefferson and the New Nation*, 564–65; Malone, *Jefferson and His Time*, 3:314–16; John Ferling, *Adams vs. Jefferson: The Tumultuous Election of 1800* (New York, 2004), 99–104.

22. Jefferson to Thomas Mann Randolph, May 19, 1997, in *PTJ*, 29:385–86 (quotation on 385).

23. Jefferson to Martha Jefferson Randolph, June 8, 1797, in ibid., 424–26 (quotation on 424); Jefferson to Mary Jefferson, June 14, 1797, in ibid., 429–30.

24. Jefferson to John Gibson, December 31, 1797, in ibid., 599–600 (quotation on 600).

25. "Revised Petition to the Virginia House of Delegates," August 7–September 7, 1797, in ibid., 499–504 (first quotation on 499, second quotation on 501, third

quotation on 504). For an excellent brief background on the Cabell matter, see the editorial note in ibid., 491–93.

26. Sharp, *American Politics in the Early Republic*, 171.

27. Peterson, *Thomas Jefferson and the New Nation*, 602–3, 617–18.

28. Jefferson to St. George Tucker, August 28, 1797, in *PTJ*, 29:519–20 (quotations on 519).

29. *JMB*, 2:974, 975.

30. Jefferson to Edmund Pendleton, January 14, 1798, in *PTJ*, 30:35.

31. Jefferson to John Wise, February 12, 1798, in ibid., 98–99 (quotation on 98).

32. "Notes on a Conversation with John Adams," February 15, 1798, in ibid., 113.

33. For the break-ins at Monticello, see Thomas Mann Randolph to Jefferson, February 3, 1798, in ibid., 78–80; Martha Jefferson Randolph to Jefferson, February 26, 1798, in ibid., 144.

34. Malone, *Jefferson and His Time*, 3:369–70; Peterson, *Thomas Jefferson and the New Nation*, 594–95.

35. See Elkins and McKitrick, *The Age of Federalism*, 584.

36. Hamilton's pieces, titled "The Stand," were published in the March 30 and April 4, 7, 12, 16, 19, and 21, 1798, issues of the [New York] *Commercial Advertiser*. They are reprinted under the appropriate date in Syrett, *The Papers of Alexander Hamilton*, 21:21.

37. See Jefferson to James Madison, March 21, 1798, in *PTJ*, 30:189–90 (quotation on 189); Jefferson to James Monroe, March 21, 1798, in ibid., 191–92 (quotation on 191).

38. See Malone, *Jefferson and His Time*, 3:371–72; Peterson, *Thomas Jefferson and the New Nation*, 596.

39. Jefferson to James Madison, April 6, 1798, in *PTJ*, 30:250–51 (quotation on 250).

40. William Short to Jefferson, February 27, 1798, in ibid., 146–53 (first four quotations on 149, fifth quotation on 149–50, sixth quotation on 151).

41. William Short to Jefferson, September 18, 1800, in ibid., 32:147–58, esp. 155–56.

42. See ibid., 195n–96n; James S. Pula, "The American Will of Thaddeus Kosciuszko," *Polish American Studies* 34 (spring 1977): 16–18; Gordon-Reed and Onuf, *"Most Blessed of the Patriarchs,"* 288–91.

43. "Will of Tadeusz Kosciuszko," in *PTJ*, 30:332–33.

44. The decision of the Court is discussed in ibid., 333n, and Pula, "The American Will of Thaddeus Kosciuszko," 19–22.

45. The relevant portion of this letter is quoted in Pula, "The American Will of Thaddeus Kosciuszko," 24.

46. Jefferson to Madison, April 12, 1798, in *PTJ*, 31:268–69 (quotations on 268).

47. See John C. Miller, *Alexander Hamilton and the Growth of the New Nation* (New York, 1959), 467–68.

48. Ibid., 471–72, 495–98; Sharp, *American Politics in the Early Republic*, 176; Peterson, *Thomas Jefferson and the New Nation*, 600–1.

49. Quoted in Ferling, *Adams vs. Jefferson*, 111.

50. Jefferson to James Madison, April 26, 1789, in *PTJ*, 31:299–300 (quotations on 300).

51. James Madison to Jefferson, May 20, 1798, in ibid., 358–60 (quotations on 359).

52. Jefferson to Thomas Mann Randolph, April 26, 1798, in ibid., 304–5 (quotation on 305).

53. Jefferson to James Madison, June 7, 1798, in ibid., 393–94 (quotation on 393).

54. Jefferson to John Taylor, June 4, 1798, in ibid., 387–89 (quotations on 389).

55. Jefferson to Thomas Mann Randolph, May 9, 1798, in ibid., 341.

56. See Morris, *Encyclopedia of American History*, 129; Peterson, *Thomas Jefferson and the New Nation*, 603–4; Malone, *Jefferson and His Time*, 3:385–86.

57. Elkins and McKitrick, *The Age of Federalism*, 700 (first quotation); Morris, *Encyclopedia of American History*, 129 (second quotation).

58. Henry Tazewell to Jefferson, July 5, 1798, in *PTJ*, 30:440–42 (quotation on 440).

19:
"REIGN OF WITCHES"

1. Jefferson to Peregrine Fitzhugh, February 23, 1798, in *PTJ*, 30:129–31 (quotation on 130).

2. Jefferson to John Taylor, June 4, 1798, in ibid., 387–89 (quotation on 389).

3. Brian Steele makes this point persuasively in "Thomas Jefferson, Coercion, and the Limits of Harmonious Union," *Journal of Southern History* 73 (November 2008): 823–54, which, among other contributions, refutes the facile idea that had Jefferson been alive in 1861, he would have supported the Confederacy. See ibid., 824n3.

4. See Sharp, *American Politics in the Early Republic*, 218–19; Ferling, *Adams vs. Jefferson*, 122; Morris, *Encyclopedia of American History*, 129–30. Once Jefferson became president, he pardoned these individuals, and Congress eventually reimbursed their fines, with interest.

5. Richard H. Kohn, *Eagle and Sword: The Federalists and the Creation of the Military Establishment in America, 1783–1802* (New York, 1975), 237.

6. This information came to him in a letter from Henry Tazewell, dated July 12, 1798, which Jefferson received on July 30. See *PTJ*, 30:447–50.

7. "The Federalist No. 28," in *The Federalist*, ed. Jacob E. Cooke (Middleton, CT, 1961), 176–90 (quotations on 179–80).

8. The best and most concise description of this drafting is in the editorial note in *PTJ*, 30:529–35, but also see Adrienne Koch and Harry Ammon, "The Virginia and Kentucky Resolutions: An Episode in Jefferson's and Madison's Defense of Civil Liberties," *William and Mary Quarterly* 5 (April 1948): 145–76.

9. "Jefferson's Fair Copy [of the Kentucky Resolutions]," [before October 4, 1798], in *PTJ*, 30:543–49 (quotations on 543–44).

10. Ibid., 544.

11. Ibid., 547.

12. Ibid., 548 and 549.

13. "Resolutions Adopted by the Kentucky General Assembly," in ibid., 550–55 (first quotation on 551, second quotation on 555).

14. Jefferson to Stevens Thomson Mason, October 11, 1798, in ibid., 559–60 (first quotation on 559, second quotation on 560).

15. See Sharp, *American Politics in the Early Republic*, 197–203; Elkins and McKitrick, *The Age of Federalism*, 719–21; and Burstein and Isenberg, *Madison and Jefferson*, 339–41. My view is largely shaped by Wendell Bird, "Reassessing Responses to the Virginia and Kentucky Resolutions," *Journal of the Early Republic*, 35 (Winter 2015): 519–51.

16. Jefferson to John Taylor, November 26, 1798, in *PTJ*, 30:588–90 (quotation on 589).

17. See Richard Ellis, "Constitutionalism," in *Thomas Jefferson: A Reference Biography*, ed. Merrill D. Peterson (New York, 1986), 126.

18. See Kohn, *Eagle and Sword*, 253–54; Miller, *Alexander Hamilton and the Growth of the New Nation*, 495–96; Sharp, *American Politics in the Early Republic*, 214–15.

19. For a convenient summary, see Ferling, *Adams vs. Jefferson*, 115–18.

20. See Elkins and McKitrick, *The Age of Federalism*, 610–12.

21. Jefferson to James Madison, January 3, 1799, in *PTJ*, 30:610–11 (first quotation

on 610); Madison to Jefferson, December 29, 1798, in ibid., 605–6 (second and third quotations on 606).

22. Jefferson to Elbridge Gerry, January 26, 1799, in ibid., 645–50 (quotation on 646).

23. Ibid., 645.

24. Ibid., 645–47.

25. Ibid., 647.

26. Quoted in Elkins and McKitrick, *The Age of Federalism*, 618.

27. Quoted in ibid., 617.

28. For Henry's declining health, see Thomas S. Kidd, *Patrick Henry: First Among Patriots* (New York, 2011), 241.

29. See Elkins and McKitrick, *The Age of Federalism*, 620–21, 696–700; Sharp, *American Politics in the Early Republic*, 209–10.

30. Hamilton to Harrison Gray Otis, December 27, 1798, in Syrett, *The Papers of Alexander Hamilton*, 20:393–95 (first quotation on 394); Hamilton to Theodore Sedgwick, February 2, 1799, in ibid., 452–53 (second and third quotations on 452, final quotation on 453).

31. Both Washington and Hamilton had insisted that all officers be politically safe from their viewpoint (i.e., Federalist in orientation).

32. Jefferson to James Madison, February 5, 1799, in *PTJ*, 31:9–10 (quotations on 10).

33. Jefferson to Robert R. Livingston, February 23, 1799, in ibid., 56–57 (quotation on 57).

34. Jefferson to Mary Jefferson Eppes, March 8, 1799, in ibid., 75.

35. Jefferson to George Wythe, May 29, 1799, in ibid., 118.

36. Morgan Brown to Jefferson, October 1, 1799, in ibid., 195–96 (first quotation on 195–96, second quotation on 196n). See Jefferson to Morgan Brown, January 16, 1800, in ibid., 309; Jefferson to Daniel Clark, January 16, 1800, in ibid., 309–10; Jefferson to James Wilkerson, January 16, 1800, in ibid., 312.

37. Jefferson to Edmund Randolph, August 18, 1799, in ibid., 168–71 (quotation on 169). For more on Jefferson's fear of the intrusion of common law, see Peterson, *Thomas Jefferson and the New Nation*, 607, 623–24.

38. Jefferson to James Madison, August 23, 1799, in *PTJ*, 31:172–74 (first three quotations on 173, fourth quotation on 173–74, emphasis added).

39. Jefferson to Wilson Cary Nicholas, September 5, 1799, in ibid., 178–79 (quotation on 179).

40. See Koch and Ammon, "The Virginia and Kentucky Resolutions," 168.

41. Quoted in ibid., 173.

42. See Miller, *Alexander Hamilton and the Growth of the New Nation*, 500–501.

43. This story is told in most accounts of the era, but convenient summaries are Ferling, *Adams vs. Jefferson*, 122–24, and Sharp, *American Politics in the Early Republic*, 212–13. For a description of the pitiful status of Charles Adams, see Page Smith, *John Adams*, 2 vols. (Garden City, NY, 1962), 2:1037, 1049.

44. Alexander Hamilton to Jonathan Dayton, [October–November 1799], in Syrett, *The Papers of Alexander Hamilton*, 23:599–604 (first quotation on 599, second quotation on 600, third quotation on 600–601, fourth quotation on 602, fifth and sixth quotations on 603, seventh quotation on 604).

45. Jefferson to James Madison, November 22, 1799, in *PTJ*, 31:240–41 (quotation on 240).

46. Jefferson to James Madison, November 26, 1799, in ibid., 243.

47. For Washington's final illness and burial at Mount Vernon, see John Alexander Carroll and Mary Wells Ashworth, *George Washington*, 7 vols. (New York, 1957), 7:617–34. This is the final volume of the seven-volume biography, the first six volumes of which were written by Douglas Southall Freeman.

48. On Jefferson's silence, see Malone, *Jefferson and His Time*, 3:442–44; for Lee's remarks, see Carroll and Ashworth, *George Washington*, Appendix VIII-3, 651.

49. See Dorothy Twohig, "'That Species of Property': Washington's Role in the Controversy over Slavery," in *George Washington Reconsidered*, ed. Don Higginbotham (Charlottesville, 2001), 114–38, esp. 116.

20:
AN ATTEMPT TO "STRANGLE THE ELECTION"

1. James Monroe to Jefferson, January 4, 1800, in *PTJ*, 31:289–90.

2. Jefferson to Mary Jefferson Eppes, January 17, 1800, in ibid., 314–15 (quotation on 315).

3. "American Philosophical Society Memorial to U.S. Congress," [January 7–10, 1800], in ibid., 293–94.

4. John Wayles Eppes to Jefferson, January 1, 1800, in ibid., 286; Jefferson to Joseph Priestley, January 18, 1800, in ibid., 319–22 (quotation on 320, emphasis in the original). See Priestley's long, thoughtful response: Joseph Priestley to Jefferson, May 8, 1800, with enclosure, in ibid., 567–70.

5. See Jefferson to Pierre Samuel Du Pont de Nemours, April 12, 1800, in ibid., 495–96; Du Pont de Nemours to Jefferson, April 21, 1800, in ibid., 527–30.

6. Jefferson to Joseph Priestley, January 27, 1800, in ibid., 339–41 (quotations on 340).

7. Martha Jefferson Randolph, January 30, 1800, in ibid., 347–48.

8. Jefferson to Thomas Mann Randolph, February 4, 1800, in ibid., 359–61 (quotation on 360). Jupiter was apparently poisoned by a black practitioner of folk medicine.

9. Jefferson to Mary Jefferson Eppes, February 12, 1800, in ibid., 367–68 (first quotation on 367, second quotation on 368).

10. Jefferson to George Wythe, February 28, 1800, in ibid., 400–401; Jefferson to Edmund Pendleton, April 19, 1800, in ibid., 520–21; Jefferson to Wythe, April 7, 1800, in ibid., 486. Pendleton replied with useful comments; see Pendleton to Jefferson, June 17, 1800, in ibid., 32:21–28.

11. See Peterson, *Thomas Jefferson and the New Nation*, 634; Malone, *Jefferson and His Time*, 3:456–58.

12. Jefferson to Philip Norborne Nicholas, April 7, 1800, in *PTJ*, 31:485; Jefferson to James Monroe, March 26, 1800, in ibid., 461–62 (quotations on 462).

13. James Monroe to Jefferson, April 23, 1800, in ibid., 537.

14. Edward Livingston to Jefferson, [before May 3, 1800], in ibid., 554–55; Aaron Burr to Jefferson, [before May 5, 1800], in ibid., 557.

15. For a good discussion of this plot, see Edward J. Larson, *A Magnificent Catastrophe: The Tumultuous Election of 1800, America's First Presidential Campaign* (New York, 2007), 104–9.

16. Jefferson to William Hamilton, April 22, 1800, in *PTJ*, 30:533–35 (quotation on 534).

17. William Short to Jefferson, September 18, 1800, in ibid., 147–58 (quotation on 155). The previous letter to which Short referred is in ibid., 30:146–53.

18. See Samuel Shepherd, *The Statutes at Large of Virginia: From October Session 1792, to December Session of 1806 . . .*, 3 vols. (Richmond, 1835–1836), 1:128.

19. Jefferson to Gideon Granger, August 13, 1800, in *PTJ*, 32:95–97 (quotation on 96).

20. See Larson, *A Magnificent Catastrophe*, 78–83; Sharp, *American Politics in the Early Republic*, 219–20;

much discussion of this bill in correspondence is reprinted in *PTJ*, 31.

21. Jefferson to John Vanmetre, September 4, 1800, in *PTJ*, 32:126–27 (quotation on 127).

22. "Summary of Public Service," [after September 2, 1800], in ibid., 122–24 (first quotation on 122, second quotation on 124).

23. See Douglas R. Egerton, *Gabriel's Rebellion: The Virginia Slave Conspiracies of 1800 and 1802* (Chapel Hill, 1993); James Sidbury, *Ploughshares into Swords: Race, Rebellion, and Identity in Gabriel's Virginia, 1730–1810* (Cambridge, UK, 1997).

24. James Monroe to Jefferson, September 9, 1800, in *PTJ*, 32:131.

25. James Monroe to Jefferson, September 15, 1800, in ibid., 144–45 (quotations on 145).

26. Jefferson to James Monroe, September 20, 1800, in ibid., 160. Sidbury, *Ploughshares into Swords*, 127, quotes this letter but says of it that Jefferson "displayed his characteristic timidity with regard to slavery by asking that his opinion be kept secret." It is just as likely that Jefferson's concern was with politics and the possibility that anything he said would be used against him. It bears remembering that Jefferson spoke, wrote, and acted far more often and openly against slavery than did George Washington, James Madison, John Marshall, or any other major southern political personality.

27. Jefferson to James Monroe, November 24, 1801, in *PTJ*, 35:718–21 (quotation on 720).

28. For this background, see Larson, *A Magnificent Catastrophe*, 115–23; Ferling, *Adams vs. Jefferson*, 130–32; Sharp, *American Politics in the Early Republic*, 237–39.

29. Adams quoted in Ferling, *Adams vs. Jefferson*, 132–33.

30. Elkins and McKitrick, *The Age of Federalism*, 739.

31. Miller, *Alexander Hamilton and the Growth of the New Nation*, 520–23; Ferling, *Adams vs. Jefferson*, 140–43; Larson, *A Magnificent Catastrophe*, 216–23.

32. [William Linn], *Serious Considerations of the Election of a President: Addressed to the Citizens of the United States* (New York, 1800), 24.

33. Jefferson to Benjamin Rush, September 23, 1800, in *PTJ*, 32:167–68 (quotations on 168).

34. Charles Pinckney to Jefferson, November 22, 1800, in ibid., 256–57 (quotation on 257).

35. See the description in [Margaret Bayard Smith], *The First Forty Years of Washington Society*, ed. Gaillard Hunt (New York, 1906), 12.

36. For the uncompleted state of Washington, see Ferling, *Adams vs. Jefferson*, 138–39; Larson, *A Magnificent Catastrophe*, 139–41. For the bucolic nature of the scene, see [Smith], *The First Forty Years*, 10–11.

37. [Smith], *The First Forty Years*, 6 (first two quotations), 7 (final quotation).

38. See Jefferson to Robert R. Livingston, December 14, 1800, in *PTJ*, 32:302–4.

39. Jefferson to Thomas Mann Randolph, December 12, 1800, in ibid., 300.

40. Jefferson to Aaron Burr, December 15, 1800, in ibid., 306–7.

41. Aaron Burr to Jefferson, December 23, 1800, in ibid., 342–43 (quotation on 343).

42. Jefferson to Hugh Henry Brackenridge, December 18, 1800, in ibid., 318. Jefferson apparently first used the word "conspiracy" in a letter to James Monroe, December 20, 1800, in ibid., 330.

43. Jefferson to James Madison, December 19, 1800, in ibid., 321–23 (quotation on 322).

44. Jefferson to James Madison, December 26, 1800, in ibid., 358.

45. Caesar A. Rodney to Jefferson, December 28, 1800, in ibid., 368–71 (quotation on 369).

46. Jefferson to Thomas Mann Randolph, January 9, 1801, in ibid., 417–18.

47. James Monroe to Jefferson, January 6, 1801, in ibid., 32:403–4 (quotations on 404).

48. Thomas McKean to Jefferson, January 10, 1801, in ibid., 432–35 (quotations on 432).

49. James Madison to Jefferson, January 10, 1801, in ibid., 436–39 (quotation on 436).

50. Hugh Henry Brackenridge to Jefferson, January 19, 1801, in ibid., 483–87 (quotation on 483). For the Federalist/Burr interactions, see Nancy Isenberg, *Fallen Founder: The Life of Aaron Burr* (New York, 2007), 208–20.

51. Aaron Burr to Jefferson, February 1, 1801, in *PTJ*, 32:528.

52. "Note on a Conversation with Gen. John Armstrong," [probably February 12, 1801], in ibid., 590.

53. See Larson, *A Magnificent Catastrophe*, 247–52, 261; Ferling, *Adams vs. Jefferson*, 182–84; Elkins and McKitrick, *The Age of Federalism*, 744–48.

54. Miller, *Alexander Hamilton and the Growth of the New Nation*, 526–29; Isenberg, *Fallen Founder*, 211–13. The three books in the previous note all discuss this election maneuvering, as does Sharp, *American Politics in the Early Republic*, 250–62.

55. Jefferson to James Monroe, February 15, 1801, in *PTJ*, 32:594.

56. For the complicated story of the balloting, see Ferling, *Adams vs. Jefferson*, 187–94; Sharp, *American Politics in the Early Republic*, 271–73; Larson, *A Magnificent Catastrophe*, 262–68.

57. The most detailed description of the negotiations, both in Paris and in Washington, is in Elkins and McKitrick, *The Age of Federalism*, 662–90.

58. See Ferling, *Adams vs. Jefferson*, 198–99; see esp. Kathryn Turner, "Federalist Policy and the Judiciary Act of 1801," *William and Mary Quarterly*, 3d ser., 22 (January 1965): 3–32, showing that there had been a concern since 1798 about enlarging the federal judiciary.

21:
POLITICAL FAITH AND PRESIDENTIAL STYLE

1. See the description in Samuel Harrison Smith's *National Intelligencer*, March 6, 1801.

2. Charles Adams died from alcoholism; his sad state had disgusted his father, who refused to either visit or correspond with his son during his last year. John Adams soon came to regret this lack of fatherly concern; he wrote Jefferson a few weeks after the inauguration of "the Funeral of a Son who was once the delight of my Eyes and a darling of my heart, cutt off in the flower of his days . . . by causes which have been the greatest Grief of my heart and the deepest affliction of my Life." John Adams to Jefferson, March 24, 1801, in *PTJ*, 33:426.

3. [Smith], *The First Forty Years*, 26 (quotation).

4. See the various drafts as reprinted in *PTJ*, 33:139–52, along with the illuminating introductory note on 134–38. All quotations come from the third and final draft, as originally printed in the *National Intelligencer*, March 4, 1801, and here reprinted on 148–52.

5. Ibid., 148 (both quotations).

6. Ibid., 148–49.

7. Ibid., 149.

8. Ibid.

9. Ibid., 149–50 (quotations on 149).

10. Ibid., 150 (all quotations).

11. Ibid.

12. Ibid.

13. Ibid., 150–51 (all quotations).

14. Ibid., 152.

15. Jefferson to Spencer Roane, September 6, 1819, in Peterson, *Thomas Jefferson, Writings*, 1425–28 (quotation on 1425).

16. See Jeffrey L. Pasley, "1800 as a Revolution in Political Culture: Newspapers, Celebrations, Voting, and Democratization in the Early Republic," in *The Revolution of 1800: Democracy, Race, and the New Republic*, ed. James Horn, Jan Ellen Lewis, and Peter S. Onuf (Charlottesville, 2002), 121–52; Joyce Appleby, "Thomas Jefferson and the Psychology of Democracy," in ibid., 155–72; Gordon S. Wood, *Empire of Liberty: A History of the Early Republic, 1789–1815* (New York, 2009), 278, 286, 301–2.

17. Jefferson to Dr. Walter Jones, March 31, 1801, in *PTJ*, 33:506 (all quotations).

18. Jefferson to Henry Dearborn, February 18, 1801, in *PTJ*, 33:13. For the earlier appointments of Madison and Gallatin, see Noble E. Cunningham Jr., *The Process of Government Under Jefferson* (Princeton, 1978), 4.

19. Cunningham, *The Process of Government Under Jefferson*, 5, 19.

20. James Madison to Jefferson, February 28, 1801, in *PTJ*, 33:99–100; Madison to Jefferson, March 7, 1801, in ibid., 207; Jefferson to Madison, March 12, 1801, in ibid., 255–56.

21. Cunningham, *The Process of Government Under Jefferson*, 3, 5, 13, 14; Jefferson to Robert Livingston, February 24, 1801, in *PTJ*, 33:61.

22. See series of letters from Jefferson to William Evans, February 22, 1801, in *PTJ*, 33: 38–39; Francis Say to Jefferson, February 23, 1801, in ibid., 53 (quotation); William Evans to Jefferson, February 27, 1801, in ibid., 91–92; Jefferson to William Evans, March 31, 1801, in ibid., 505.

23. William Evans reported Hemings's suicide to Jefferson. See Evans to Jefferson, November 5, 1801, in ibid., 35:569–70. On this whole matter, see the subtle discussion in Gordon-Reed, *The Hemingses of Monticello*, 544–51.

24. Jefferson to Meriwether Lewis, February 23, 1801, in *PTJ*, 33:51.

25. Jefferson to Martha Jefferson Randolph, May 28, 1801, in ibid., 34:200–201 (quotation on 200).

26. Jefferson to Benjamin Rush, March 24, 1801, in ibid., 436–38 (quotation on 436–37).

27. "Circular Letter to Midnight Appointees," [after March 4, 18901], in ibid., 172–73 (quotations on 173).

28. William Branch Giles to Jefferson, March 16, 1801, in ibid., 310–12 (quotation on 311).

29. Elbridge Gerry to Jefferson, May 4, 1801, in ibid., 34:21–23 (quotation on 21).

30. Jefferson to John Dickinson, July 23, 1801, in ibid., 615–16 (quotation on 616).

31. Jefferson to George Clinton, May 16, 1801, in ibid., 127–28 (quotation on 127).

32. Jefferson to William Branch Giles, March 23, 1801, in ibid., 413–14 (quotations on 414).

33. Jefferson to Thomas McKean, July 24, 1801, in ibid., 34:625–27 (quotation on 626).

34. Jefferson to James Madison, August 13, 1801, in ibid., 35:80–81 (quotation on 80).

35. See "Remonstrance of the New Haven Merchants," June 18, 1801, in ibid., 381–83. For son Abraham Bishop's Republican bona fides, see David Waldstreicher and Stephen B. Grossbart, "Abraham Bishop's Vocation; or, the Mediation of Jeffersonian Politics," *Journal of the Early Republic* 18 (winter 1998): 617–57.

36. Jefferson, "To the New Haven Merchants," July 12, 1801, in *PTJ*, 34:554–56 (quotations on 555–56).

37. Ibid., 556.

38. Carl E. Prince, in "The Passing of the American Aristocracy: Jefferson's

Removal of the Federalists, 1801–1805," *Journal of American History* 57 (December 1970): 653–75, argues that Jefferson was more partisan than do other scholars, but he includes in his figures all those last-minute Adams appointees that Jefferson did not think were legitimate.

39. See Cunningham, *The Process of Government Under Jefferson*, 171–82; Appendix I of *PTJ*, 33:663–79.

40. See Leonard D. White, *The Jeffersonians: A Study in Administrative History, 1801–1829* (New York, 1951), 347–54, 379 (quotation on 354).

41. For Jefferson's moderate removal policy and partisan appointment policy, see Noble E. Cunningham Jr., *The Jeffersonian Republicans in Power: Party Operations, 1801–1809* (Chapel Hill, 1963), chaps. 1–2, 12–70.

42. See the classic discussion in James Sterling Young, *The Washington Community, 1800–1818* (New York, 1966), 167–70.

43. Jefferson to Thomas Mann Randolph, June 4, 1801, in *PTJ*, 34:256–57 (quotation on 257). For the population, see Constance Mc Laughlin Green, *Washington: Village and Capital, 1800–1878* (Princeton, 1962), 21.

44. See Merry Ellen Scofield, "The Fatigues of His Table: The Politics of Presidential Dining During the Jefferson Administration," *Journal of the Early Republic* 26 (fall 2006): 449–69.

45. [Smith], *The First Forty Years*, 391–92.

46. See Lucia Stanton, "'A Well-Ordered Household': Domestic Servants in Jefferson's White House," *White House History* 17 (winter 2006): 14.

47. See Senator Cutler's description of a typical menu in William Parker Cutler and Julia Cutler, eds., *Life, Journals, and Correspondence of Rev. Manasseh Cutler, LL.D.*, 2 vols. (Cincinnati, 1888), 2:71–72.

48. [Smith], *The First Forty Years*, 389.

49. Jefferson to David R. Williams, January 31, 1806, quoted in Charles T. Cullen, "Jefferson's White House Dinner Guests," *White House History* 17 (winter 2006): 29.

50. Quoted in White, *The Jeffersonians*, 33.

51. Fred I. Greenstein, "Presidential Difference in the Early Republic: The Highly Disparate Leadership Styles of Washington, Adams, and Jefferson," *Presidential Studies Quarterly* 36 (September 2006): 373–90 (quotation on 381).

52. Jefferson to Thomas Mann Randolph, November 16, 1801, in *PTJ*, 35:677–78 (quotation on 677).

53. Jefferson to Lafayette, [January 31, 1804], in ibid., 42:376.

54. For background, see Clagett, *Scientific Jefferson Revealed*, 54–58; Bedini, *Thomas Jefferson: Statesman of Science*, 309–15. The word "vaccinia" comes from the Latin word for cow, *vacca*.

55. See Robert H. Halsey, *How the President, Thomas Jefferson, and Doctor Benjamin Waterhouse Established Vaccination as a Public Health Procedure* (New York, 1936), 16.

56. Benjamin Waterhouse to Jefferson, December 1, 1800, in *PTJ*, 32:264; Jefferson to Waterhouse, December 25, 1800, in ibid., 355.

57. Jefferson to Benjamin Waterhouse, June 26, 1801, in ibid., 34:462; Jefferson to Waterhouse, July 25, 1801, in ibid., 640–41.

58. Jefferson to William Wardlaw, July 16, 1801, in ibid., 581–82. For this whole occasion, see Clagett, *Scientific Jefferson Revealed*, 56–58; Bedini, *Thomas Jefferson: Statesman of Science*, 311–15.

59. See Benjamin Waterhouse to Jefferson, January 11, 1802, in ibid., 34:359–61, 361n.

60. The story is told in [Smith], *The First Forty Years*, 11–12 (quotation on 11). Anthony F. C. Wallace quotes these

eleven words in his attempt to prove that Jefferson had authoritarian tendencies and a "deeply controlling temperament." See Anthony F. C. Wallace, *Jefferson and the Indians: The Tragic Fate of the First Americans* (Cambridge, MA, 1999), 14.

61. The best evaluation of Jefferson's use of his cabinet is Cunningham, *The Process of Government Under Jefferson*, 48–71, 318–20.

62. "Circular to the Heads of Departments," November 6, 1801, in *PTJ*, 35:576–78 (quotations on 577).

63. Ibid., 577.

64. Cunningham, *The Process of Government Under Jefferson*; Malone, *Jefferson and His Time*, 4:51, 62–63; White, *The Jeffersonians*, 8–9, 77–80.

65. See Cunningham, *The Process of Government Under Jefferson*, 25, 72–78; Peterson, *Thomas Jefferson and the New Nation*, 684–87; editorial note in *PTJ*, 35:612–17; foreword in *PTJ*, 36:vii.

66. The first printed version, exactly what Jefferson sent over to Congress (omitting the section on the Sedition Act in the final draft), dated December 8, 1801, is reprinted in *PTJ*, 36:58–65.

67. See Robert M. Johnstone Jr., "The Presidency," in Peterson, *Thomas Jefferson: A Reference Biography*, 352–53, 368; Greenstein, "Presidential Difference in the Early Republic," 380–82.

68. C. A. Browne, "Elder John Leland and the Mammoth Cheshire Cheese," *Agricultural History* 18 (October 1944): 145–53; for Leland's career, see Lyman H. Butterfield, "Elder John Leland, Jeffersonian Itinerant," *Proceedings of the American Antiquarian Society* 62 (1952): 155–242.

69. "From the Committee of Cheshire, Massachusetts," [December 30, 1801], in *PTJ*, 36:249–50 (quotation on 249, emphasis in the original).

70. Jeffrey L. Pasley, "The Cheese and the Words: Popular Political Culture and Participatory Democracy in the Early

Republic," in *Beyond the Founders: New Approaches to the Political History of the Early American Republic*, ed. Jeffrey L. Pasley, Andrew W. Robertson, and David Waldstreicher (Chapel Hill, 2004), 31–78, esp. 39–45.

71. "From the Danbury Baptist Association," [after October 7, 1801], in ibid., 35:407–8 (quotations on 408).

72. "To the Danbury Baptist Association," January 1, 1802, in ibid., 36:258. A large body of scholarship discusses Jefferson's letter to the Danbury Baptists and the influence of the "wall of separation" phrase on American judicial opinions. See, for example, Johann N. Neem, "Beyond the Wall: Reinterpreting Jefferson's Danbury Address," *Journal of the Early Republic* 27 (spring 2007): 139–54; Johann N. Neem, "A Republican Reformation: Thomas Jefferson's Civil Religion and the Separation of Church from State," in Cogliano, *A Companion to Thomas Jefferson*, 91–109; Richard Samuelson, "Jefferson and Religion: Private Belief, Public Policy," in Shuffelton, *The Cambridge Companion to Thomas Jefferson*, 143–54.

22:
"WE ARE ACTING FOR ALL MANKIND"

1. Jefferson to Elbridge Gerry, May 13, 1797, in *PTJ*, 29:361–64 (quotation on 362).

2. Jefferson to William Hylton, June 5, 1801, in ibid., 34:262.

3. "First Annual Message to Congress," in ibid., 36:58–65 (quotation on 58).

4. Ibid., 59–60.

5. Ibid., 60.

6. Ibid., 60–63. See the extensive Jefferson correspondence with Gallatin, Dearborn, and the two Smiths in ibid., vols. 33–37. For a general discussion of these expected economies, see Cunningham, *The Process of Government*

Under Jefferson, 87–133 (for the 40 percent reduction in Treasury officials, see 98).

7. Cunningham, *The Process of Government Under Jefferson*, 124; Norman K. Risjord, *Jefferson's America, 1760–1815* (Madison, 1991), 245.

8. Cunningham, *The Process of Government Under Jefferson*, 128–33.

9. Jefferson, "First Inaugural Address," March 4, 1801, in *PTJ*, 38:148–52 (quotation on 150).

10. Jefferson, "First Annual Message to Congress," in ibid., 36:58–65 (quotation on 63).

11. Jefferson, "First Annual Message to Congress," in ibid., 64.

12. Ibid., 63.

13. Richard E. Ellis, *The Jeffersonian Crisis: Courts and Politics in the Young Republic* (New York, 1971), 45–51, outlines the debate and the votes.

14. See Malone, *Jefferson and His Time*, 4:130–34.

15. See Ellis, *The Jeffersonian Crisis*, 43–44, 65–68.

16. Jefferson to Pierre Samuel Du Pont de Nemours, January 18, 1802, in *PTJ*, 36:390–92 (quotation on 390).

17. Jefferson to Joseph Priestley, June 19, 1802, in ibid., 37:625–26.

18. See Theodore J. Crackel, "The Military Academy in the Context of Jeffersonian Reform," in *Thomas Jefferson's Military Academy*, ed. Ronald M. S. McDonald (Charlottesville, 2004), 99–117, esp. 111–12.

19. See "Henry Dearborn's Report on the War Department," May 12, 1801, in *PTJ*, 34:84, 87n; "Henry Dearborn's Plan for Reorganizing the Army," December 7, 1801, in ibid., 35:44, 47n–48n.

20. See Theodore J. Crackel, *Mr. Jefferson's Army: Political and Social Reform of the Military Establishment, 1801–1809* (New York, 1987), 71.

21. For Jefferson's consistency of constitutional interpretation, see David N. Mayer, "'Necessary and Proper': West Point and Jefferson's Constitutionalism," in McDonald, *Thomas Jefferson's Military Academy*, 54–76.

22. See Jennings L Wagoner Jr. and Christine Coalwell McDonald, "Mr. Jefferson's Academy: An Educational Interpretation," in ibid., 118–53; Stephen E. Ambrose, *Duty, Honor, Country: A History of West Point* (Baltimore, 1966), 3–6, 18, 97.

23. See Jonathan Williams to Jefferson, December 12, 1802, in *PTJ*, 39:145–46; Jefferson to Jonathan Williams, December 25, 1802, in ibid., 220–21.

24. Ambrose, *Duty, Honor, Country*, 32–32.

25. This early history comes from David C. Mearns, *The Story Up to Now: The Library of Congress, 1800–1946* (Washington, DC, 1947), 1–10; Edmund Berkeley and Dorothy Smith Berkeley, *John Beckley: Zealous Partisan in a Nation Divided* (Philadelphia, 1973), 237–38.

26. Jefferson to Abraham Baldwin, April 14, 1802, in *PTJ*, 37:227–28, with attached "List of Books for the Library of Congress," 229–33 (first quotation on 227, other quotations on 232–33).

27. See Jefferson to Albert Gallatin, July 9, 1802, in ibid., 38:42; Jefferson to William Duane, July 16, 1802, in ibid., 75, with attached list of books for booksellers in London and Paris, in ibid., 76–80.

28. Jefferson to James Madison, September 24, 1814, in *PTJRS*, 7:691–93 (quotations on 693).

29. Jefferson to Samuel H. Smith, September 21, 1814, in ibid., 681–83 (first two quotations on 682, third quotation on 683).

30. See Mearns, *The Story Up to Now*, 18–20; see also Peter Manseau, "How a Christian Congress Embraced Jefferson's 'Atheistical' Library," *Boston Globe*, January 30, 2015.

31. For the congressional vote, see Mearns, *The Story Up to Now*, 24; for the shipping, see *PTJRS*, 7:680n.

32. Jefferson to Samuel H. Smith, May 8, 1815, in *PTJRS*, 8:476.

33. Joseph Barnes to Jefferson, March 19, 1801, in *PTJ*, 33:363–64; Jefferson received the letter on June 24, 1801.

34. See the discussion in detail in Chapter 13 in this volume.

35. "Notes on a Cabinet Meeting," May 15, 1801, in *PTJ*, 34:114–15; for Dale's orders, see ibid., 115n.

36. Jacob Wagner to Jefferson, August 31, 1801, in ibid., 188.

37. Jefferson to Thomas Newton, November 9, 1801, in ibid., 588; Samuel Smith to Jefferson, November 14, 1801, in ibid., 663.

38. See James R. Sofka, "The Jeffersonian Idea of National Security: Commerce, the Atlantic Balance of Power, and the Barbary War, 1786–1805," *Diplomatic History* 21 (fall 1997): 519–44.

39. See Sofka, "The Jeffersonian Idea of National Security," 539–41; Robert J. Allison, *The Crescent Obscured: The United States and the Muslim World, 1776–1815* (New York, 1995), 26–28, 31.

40. Quoted in Sofka, "The Jeffersonian Idea of National Security," 539.

41. Joseph Allen Smith to Jefferson, March 22, 1801, in *PTJ*, 33:404–5 (quotation on 404).

42. Alexander DeConde, *This Affair of Louisiana* (New York, 1976) (quotation on 108).

43. See Jefferson to Archibald Stuart, January 25, 1786, in *PTJ*, 9:217–19; Jefferson to James Monroe, November 24, 1801, in ibid., 34:718–21.

44. See Chapter 14 in this volume.

45. See the discussion in James E. Lewis Jr., *The Louisiana Purchase: Jefferson's Noble Bargain?* (Chapel Hill, 2003), 32–33; DeConde, *This Affair of Louisiana*, 110.

46. Jefferson to Robert R. Livingston, April 18, 1802, in *PTJ*, 37:263–66 (first five quotations on 264, sixth quotation on 265, seventh quotation on 266).

47. See Harry Ammon, *James Monroe: The Quest for National Identity* (New York, 1971), 206.

48. Du Pont to Jefferson, April 24, 1802, in *PTJ*, 37:320–22 (translated quotation on 321); Jefferson to Du Pont, April 30, 1802, in ibid., 365–66 (quotation on 365).

49. Jefferson to Du Pont, April 25, 1802, in ibid., 332–34 (quotations on 333).

50. Du Pont to Jefferson, April 30, 1802, in ibid., 367–75, esp. 375 (first translated quotation on 372, second on 375).

51. Jefferson to Nathan Macon, July 17, 1802, in ibid., 38:89–91 (quotation on 90); Jefferson to John Brown, August 14, 1802, in ibid., 214–15 (quotation on 214).

52. John Vaughan to Jefferson, May 8, 1802, in ibid., 37:431–33.

53. See the key paragraph as reprinted in Donald Jackson, *Thomas Jefferson and the Stony Mountains: Exploring the West from Monticello* (Norman, OK, 2002), 95.

54. "Meriwether Lewis: Estimated Costs of Missouri River Expedition," [before January 18, 1803], in *PTJ*, 39:342.

55. "Gallatin's Remarks on the Draft," [November 19–21, 1802], in ibid., 18–22 (quotation on 20).

56. "To the Senate and the House of Representatives," [January 18, 1803; marked confidential], in *PTJ*, 39:350–53 (first two quotations on 352, third quotation on 352–53).

57. Ibid., 354n.

58. For background on the suspension, see DeConde, *This Affair of Louisiana*, 119–24; Lewis, *The Louisiana Purchase*, 42–44; Jon Kukla, *A Wilderness So Immense: The Louisiana Purchase and the Destiny of America* (New York, 2003), 245–49.

59. Jefferson to James Garrard, December 16, 1802, in *PTJ*, 39:179.

60. DeConde, *This Affair of Louisiana*, 128; Lewis, *The Louisiana Purchase*, 47.

61. "Annual Message to Congress," [December 15, 1802], in *PTJ*, 39:162–68 (quotation on 163–64).

62. DeConde, *This Affair of Louisiana*, 132.

63. Jefferson to James Monroe, January 10, 1803, in *PTJ*, 39:306.

64. "To the Senate," January 11, 1803, in ibid., 312–13 (first two quotations on 312, third quotation on 313).

65. Jefferson to Thomas Mann Randolph, January 17, 1803, in ibid., 341.

23:
"LOUISIANA FOR A SONG"

1. See Stanton, "'A Well-Ordered Household,'" 6–23.

2. See the letters from Jefferson to his daughters on January 4, 1801; January 16, 1801; April 28, 1801; March 3, 1802; April 24, 1802; and June 3, 1802, in *The Family Letters of Thomas Jefferson*, ed. Edwin Morris Betts and James Adam Bear Jr. (1966; rpt. Charlottesville, 1986), 190–91, 191–92, 203, 218–20, 224–25, 226–28, and 228–31 (hereafter *FL*). It has been suggested that Jefferson brought his daughters to the capital to counter the first appearance, on September 1, 1802, of James Callender's charges in a Richmond newspaper that Jefferson had a black mistress, Sally Hemings. Obviously their visit was in the works long before these charges were published, which Jefferson never responded to; neither did he change his behavior in any way.

3. Cutler and Cutler, *Life, Journals, and Correspondence of Rev. Manasseh Cutler, LL.D.*, 2:113.

4. [Smith], *The First Forty Years*, 34.

5. Mary [Maria] Jefferson Eppes to Jefferson, January 11, 1803, in *PTJ*, 39:309–10.

6. See the notations in *JMB*, 1:297 (November 4, 1772), 343 (July 9, 1773), and 508 (April 5, 1781).

7. See the elaborate description in [Smith], *The First Forty Years*, 385.

8. Ammon, *James Monroe*, 205–7.

9. See Jefferson to Benjamin Smith Barton, February 27, 1803, in *PTJ*, 39:588–89 (first quotation on 589); Jefferson to Benjamin Rush, February 28, 1803, in ibid., 598–600 (second and third quotations on 599); Jefferson to Robert Patterson, March 2, 1803, in ibid., 618. Jefferson's letter to Andrew Ellicott, listed in Jefferson's Journal of Letters but not existent, was written on February 26. See ibid., 640. Ellicott replied in the affirmative on March 6, 1803, ibid., 40:15–16.

10. See Louis André Pichon to Jefferson, March 4, 1803, in ibid., 8, and esp. 8n–9n.

11. Jefferson to Lewis Harvie, February 28, 1803, in ibid., 39:597–98; Harvie to Jefferson, [before March 12], 1803, in ibid., 40:33.

12. See [Jefferson], "American Philosophical Society's Instructions to Andre Michaux," April 30, 1793, in ibid., 25:625. For Cuvier's discovery, see Kolbert, *The Sixth Extinction*, 23–30; Jefferson, "Instructions for Meriwether Lewis," April 13, 1803 [postdated June 20, 1803, when given to Lewis], in *PTJ*, 40:176–81 (quotation on 178, emphasis added).

13. See "From James Madison" [before April 13, 1803], in *PTJ*, 40:172; "From Albert Gallatin" [on or before April 13, 1803], in ibid., 173–74 (quotation on 174); "From Levi Lincoln," April 17, 1803, in ibid., 175–76.

14. Jefferson to Meriwether Lewis, April 27, 1803, in ibid., 277–78 (quotations on 278); see also Jefferson to Lewis, May 16, 1803, in ibid., 377.

15. "Instructions for Meriwether Lewis" [dated June 20, 1803], in ibid., 176–81 (quotation on 177).

16. Ibid., 178.

17. Ibid.

18. Ibid., 179–80 (quotation on 180).

19. Jefferson to Meriwether Lewis, July 15, 1803, in ibid., 41:57; Meriwether Lewis to Jefferson, September 8, 1803, in ibid., 351–52.

20. See Eugene R. Sheridan, "Introduction," in *Jefferson's Extracts from the Gospels: "The Philosophy of Jesus" and "The Life and Morals of Jesus,"* ed. Dickinson W. Adams (Princeton, 1983), 3–42; Peter Onuf, "Jefferson's Religion: Priestcraft, Enlightenment, and the Republican Revolution," in *The Mind of Thomas Jefferson* (Charlottesville, 2007), 139–68.

21. Jefferson to Joseph Priestley, April 9, 1803, in *PTJ*, 40:157–59 (first two quotations on 157, third quotation on 158).

22. Ibid., 158 (all quotations).

23. Jefferson to Benjamin Rush, April 21, 1803, in ibid., 251–52 (quotations on 252).

24. Ibid., 252.

25. Ibid., 255.

26. Jefferson to Ezra Stiles Ely, January 25, 1819, in *The Writings of Thomas Jefferson*, ed. Albert Ellery Bergh, 20 vols. (Washington, DC, 1907), 15:202–4 (quotation on 203) (hereafter Bergh).

27. In addition to Sheridan and Onuf, cited above, for an estimate of Jefferson's Christianity, see Burstein, *Jefferson's Secrets*, 237–63; Paul K. Conkin, "The Religious Pilgrimage of Thomas Jefferson," in Onuf, *Jeffersonian Legacies*, 19–49. For a strongly dissenting view of Jefferson's religion, one that denies his belief in the afterlife, see Arthur Scherr, "Thomas Jefferson Versus the Historians: Christianity, Atheistic Morality, and the Afterlife," *Church History* 83 (March 2014): 60–109.

28. See, for example, Jefferson to Mary [Maria] Jefferson Eppes, April 25, 1803, in *PTJ*, 30:270–71 (quotation on 270).

29. Robert R. Livingston to James Madison, September 1, 1802, in *The Papers of James Madison, Secretary of State Series*, ed. David B. Matten et al., 10 vols. to date (Charlottesville, 1986–), 3:536–37 (quotation on 536) (hereafter *PJMSSS*).

30. For a succinct version of Napoleon's changing plans for Louisiana, see Eberhard L. Faber, *Building the Land of Dreams: New Orleans and the Transformation of Early America* (Princeton, 2016), 43–46.

31. For background, see Kukla, *A Wilderness So Immense*, 218–24; DeConde, *This Affair of Louisiana*, 100–104, 149.

32. From the diary of an eyewitness to the occasion, following a dinner party, as quoted in DeConde, *This Affair of Louisiana*, 151.

33. See Robert R. Livingston to James Madison, February 18, 1803, in *PJMSSS*, 4:328–31. On the potential influence of this offer on later events, see Ammon, *James Monroe*, 218.

34. Robert R. Livingston to Madison, April 11, 1803, in *PJMSSS*, 4:500–502 (first quotation on 500, second and third on 501).

35. See Livingston to Madison, April 13, 1803, in ibid., 511–15.

36. Livingston to Jefferson, April 14, 1803, in *PTJ*, 40:198–200 (first two quotations on 198, third quotation on 199). Jefferson received this letter on June 9, 1803.

37. Livingston to Madison, May 20, 1803, in *PJMSSS*, 5:18–20 (quotation on 19).

38. Cited in Kukla, *A Wilderness So Immense*, 280.

39. See DeConde, *This Affair of Louisiana*, 172.

40. François Barbé-Marbois, *The History of Louisiana, Particularly the Cession of That Colony to the Unites States of America . . .* (Philadelphia, 1830), 310–11.

41. Livingston and Monroe to Madison, May 13, 1803, in *PJMSSS*, 4:601–6.

42. Jefferson to Thomas Mann Randolph, July 5, 1803, in *PTJ*, 40:660–61.

43. Horatio Gates to Jefferson, July 18, 1803, in ibid., 41:87–88 (quotation on 87).

44. Gallatin thought the act presupposed by virtue of the United States' nationhood. See Levi Lincoln to Jefferson, January 10, 1803, in ibid.,

39:302–5; Albert Gallatin to Jefferson, January 13, 1803, in ibid., 324–27.

45. "Revised Amendment," [ca. July 9, 1803], in ibid., 40:686–88 (quotation on 686). The first draft had an identical first line.

46. Both drafts of the proposed amendment outline these provisions. See ibid., 685–88.

47. See Bernard W. Sheehan, *Seeds of Extinction: Jeffersonian Philanthropy and the American Indian* (Chapel Hill, 1973).

48. See Jefferson to William C. C. Claiborne, July 17, 1803, in *PTJ*, 41:71; Jefferson to Daniel Clark, July 17, 1803, in ibid., 72; Jefferson to William Dunbar, July 17, 1803, in ibid., 73–74.

49. Robert R. Livingston to James Madison, June 25, 1803, in *PJMSSS*, 5:119–21 (quotation on 120).

50. Jefferson to John Breckinridge, August 12, 1803, in *PTJ*, 41:185–86 (quotation on 186).

51. Jefferson to James Madison, August 18, 1803, in ibid., 219.

52. "Resolution for Introduction of Constitutional Amendment," [August 1803?], in ibid., 305.

53. "Annual Message to Congress," [October 17, 1803], in ibid., 534–39 (quotation on 535).

54. See "Proclamation on the Ratification of the Louisiana Purchase Treaty and Conventions," [October 21, 1803], in ibid., 582; "To the Senate and the House of Representatives," October 21, 1803, in ibid., 583.

55. The details of the final transfer are presented in DeConde, *This Affair of Louisiana*, 193–207, and Kukla, *A Wilderness So Immense*, 312–22. For the text Jefferson supplied Claiborne to proclaim on December 20, 1803, see "Draft of a Proclamation for the Temporary Government of Louisiana," [on or before October 31, 1803], in *PTJ*, 41:639–40. For the rest of the story over the coming decade, see Eberhard Farber,

Building the Land of Dreams: New Orleans and the Transformation of Early America (Princeton, 2016).

56. Lord Hawkesbury [British foreign secretary] to Anthony Merry, September 16, 1803, in *Instructions to the British Ministers to the United States, 1791–1812*, ed. Bernard Mayo (Washington, 1941), 197.

57. See the description of Merry and the occasion of his meeting with the president in Malcolm Lester, *Anthony Merry Redivivus: A Reappraisal of the British Minister to the United States, 1803–6* (Charlottesville, 1978), 31.

58. See [Smith], *The First Forty Years*, 46.

59. [Dolly Madison], *Memoirs and Letters of Dolly Madison . . .*, edited by her grandniece (Boston, 1886), 49.

60. Malone, *Jefferson and His Time*, 4:378–92, carefully describes this famous encounter. Every biography of Jefferson gives a variant of the tale, but the most famous and artful version—though not the fairest—is that provided by Henry Adams in *History of the United States of America During the First Administration of Thomas Jefferson*, 9 vols. (1889; rpt. New York, 1962), 2:360–88. For Jefferson's account of the dinner, in which he primarily blamed Mrs. Merry for the uproar—"she has . . . disturbed our harmony extremely"—see Jefferson to James Monroe, January 8, 1804, in *PTJ*, 42:245–50 (quotation on 249), and Jefferson to William Short, January 23, 1804, in ibid., 331–34.

61. See Richard Beale Davis, ed., *Jeffersonian America: Notes on the United States of America Collected in the Years 1805–06–07 and 11–12 by Sir Augustus John Foster* (San Marino, CA, 1954), 52–53.

62. "A Memorandum (Rules of Etiquette)," reprinted in Peterson, *Thomas Jefferson, Writings*, 705.

63. For more on the incident, see Malone, *Jefferson and His Time*, 4:383–84; see esp. Peterson, *Thomas Jefferson*

and the New Nation, 732–73; Lester, *Anthony Merry*, 38; Charlene M. Boyer Lewis, *Elizabeth Patterson Bonaparte: An American Aristocrat in the Early Republic* (Philadelphia, 2012), 33.

24:
"STEADILY IN HER COURSE"

1. Albert Gallatin to Jefferson, January 31, 1803, in *PTJ*, 39:422; also see the extensive notes on 422n–25n.

2. Jefferson, "To the House of Representatives," February 3, 1803, in ibid., 443.

3. See Ellis, *The Jeffersonian Crisis*, 71–72.

4. See the classic analysis of the case in Lynn W. Turner, "The Impeachment of John Pickering," *American Historical Review* 54 (April 1949): 485–507.

5. For background, see Ellis, *The Jeffersonian Crisis*, 76–80; Malone, *Jefferson and His Time*, 4:464–67.

6. Jefferson to Joseph H. Nicholson, May 13, 1803, in *PTJ*, 40:371–72 (quotation on 372).

7. See ibid., 372–73n.

8. See the careful account in Ellis, *The Jeffersonian Crisis*, 81–90.

9. Ibid., 96–107; see esp. James Haw et al., *Stormy Patriot: The Life of Samuel Chase* (Baltimore: Maryland Historical Society, 1980), 209–41.

10. See *JMB*, 2:1222.

11. Charles Willson Peale, January 28, 1803, in *PTJ*, 39:406–7 (quotation on 407). For the definitive history of Jefferson and the polygraph, see Bedini, *Thomas Jefferson and His Copying Machines*.

12. Benjamin H. Latrobe, October 2, 1803, in ibid., 460–61 (quotation on 461). According to Bedini, Latrobe had bought the first polygraph Peale and Hawkins offered for sale in September 1803. Bedini, *Thomas Jefferson and His Copying Machines*, 51.

13. Jefferson to Charles Willson Peale, March 30, 1804, in Horace W. Sellers,

"Letters of Thomas Jefferson to Charles Willson Peale, 1796–1825," *Pennsylvania Magazine of History and Biography* 28, no. 2 (1904): 143.

14. Jefferson to Charles Willson Peale, April 23, 1804, in ibid., 144–46.

15. Jefferson to Charles Willson Peale, November 7, 1804, in ibid., 151–52 (quotation on 151). For the June payment, see *JMB*, 2:1128.

16. Jefferson to John Adams, October 12, 1813, in *PTJRS*, 6:548–51 (quotation on 549).

17. See Sheridan, "Introduction," 27, 27n. Jefferson described this effort to Priestley: Jefferson to Joseph Priestley, January 29, 1804, in Peterson, *Thomas Jefferson, Writings*, 1141–43.

18. Jefferson to Adams, October 12, 1813, in *PTJRS*, 6:549.

19. See Peterson, *Thomas Jefferson and the New Nation*, 793–94; Jefferson to Gideon Granger, April 16, 1804, in Bergh, 11:24–26.

20. Mary Jefferson Eppes to Jefferson, February 10, 1804, in *FL*, 256–57. Jefferson had the physiognotrace done in November, months after Maria's death.

21. Jefferson to Madison, April 9, 1804, in *The Republic of Letters: The Correspondence Between Thomas Jefferson and James Madison, 1776–1826*, ed. James Morton Smith, 3 vols. (New York, 1995), 2:1303–4 (quotation on 1304).

22. *GB*, 291.

23. *JMB*, 2:1125.

24. The undated letter from Ellen W. Coolidge is reprinted in *DL*, 299–302 (quotation on 300).

25. Jefferson to Madison, in Smith, *The Republic of Letters*, 2:1322–23 (quotation on 1323).

26. Jefferson to John Page, June 25, 1804, in Bergh, 11:30–32 (quotations on 31).

27. Jefferson to Philip Mazzei, July 18, 1804, in ibid., 38–42 (quotation on 41).

28. See Malone, *Jefferson and His Time*, 4:417.

29. Abigail Adams to Jefferson, May 20, 1804, in *The Adams-Jefferson Letters: The Complete Correspondence Between Thomas Jefferson and Abigail and John Adams*, ed. Lester J. Cappon (1959; rpt. Chapel Hill, 1987), 268–69 (quotations on 269).

30. Jefferson to Elbridge Gerry, March 3, 1804, in Bergh, 11:15–16 (quotation on 16). See also Jefferson to Philip Mazzei, July 18, 1804, in ibid., 38–42, esp. 40.

31. Jefferson privately noted that Burr's ambition and conduct "inspired me with disgust." Jefferson, "Notes on a Conversation with Aaron Burr," January 26, 1804, in *PTJ*, 42:346–49 (quotation on 348).

32. For a detailed and colorful account, see Thomas Fleming, *The Duel: Alexander Hamilton, Aaron Burr, and the Future of America* (New York, 1999); Malone, *Jefferson and His Time*, 4:425–27.

33. Jefferson to Joel Barlow, January 24, 1810, in *PTJRS*, 2:176–77 (quotation on 177).

34. See Malone, *Jefferson and His Time*, 4:393–94; Manning Dauer, "Election of 1804," in *History of American Presidential Elections, 1789–1968*, ed. Arthur M. Schlesinger Jr., 5 vols. (New York, 1971), 1:163–64.

35. See Meriwether Lewis to Jefferson, December 17, 1803; December 28, 1803; and March 26, 1804, in *Letters of the Lewis and Clark Expedition, with Related Documents, 1783–1854*, ed. Donald Jackson, 2nd ed., 2 vols. (Urbana, IL, 1978), 1:145–47, 148–55, 170–71.

36. Jackson, *Thomas Jefferson and the Stony Mountains*, 223–33.

37. See Alexander von Humboldt to Jefferson, May 24, 1804, in Sandra Rebok, *Humboldt and Jefferson: A Transatlantic Friendship of the Enlightenment* (Charlottesville, 2014), 143–45 (quotation on 143); Jefferson to Alexander von Humboldt, May 28, 1804, in ibid., 145.

38. Charles Willson Peale, "Diary 20. Part 1: A Journey to Washington, D.C., and Return, Including Baltimore and Annapolis, Maryland," May 29–June 24, 1804, in *The Selected Papers of Charles Willson Peale and His Family*, ed. Lillian B. Miller, 11 vols. (New Haven, 1983), 2: Part 2: 693.

39. Peale, "Diary," 683.

40. [Madison], *Memoirs and Letters of Dolly Madison*, 45.

41. Jefferson to Alexander von Humboldt, December 6, 1813, in Rebok, *Humboldt and Jefferson*, 154–57 (quotation on 155).

42. Rebok, *Humboldt and Jefferson*, 61–63.

43. For the Republican use of the press, see Pasley, *"The Tyranny of Printers,"* 172–75.

44. Dauer, "Election of 1804," 164–65.

45. Alexander Hamilton to Gouverneur Morris, February 29, 1802, in Syrett, *The Papers of Alexander Hamilton*, 25:544.

46. Jefferson, "Fourth Annual Message," November 8, 1804; Padover, *The Complete Jefferson*, 406–10 (quotation on 410).

47. Jefferson to Mr. Lithson, January 4, 1805, in Bergh, 11:55–56 (quotation on 55).

48. Jefferson to John Taylor [of Caroline], January 6, 1805, in Bergh, 11:56–58 (quotations on 57).

49. See "Second Inaugural Address," March 4, 1805, in Peterson, *Thomas Jefferson, Writings*, 518–23.

50. Ibid., 519 (first quotation), 520 (second and third quotations).

51. Ibid., 522–23.

52. Thomas McKean to Jefferson, February 7, 1803, in *PTJ*, 39:471–74 (quotation on 473).

53. For an excellent discussion of this issue, see Pasley, *"The Tyranny of Printers,"* 264–65.

54. Jefferson to Thomas McKean, February 19, 1803, in *PTJ*, 39:552–53 (quotations on 553). Over the next two years, the Republicans prosecuted one editor in Pennsylvania and one in New

York for libelous publications; Jefferson had no role in either case.

55. Peterson, *Thomas Jefferson, Writings*, 523.

56. Meriwether Lewis to Jefferson, April 7, 1805, in Jackson, *Letters of the Lewis and Clark Expedition*, 1:231–34 (quotation on 234).

25:
THE COLLAPSE OF POLITICAL CONSENSUS

1. Quoted in [Smith], *The First Forty Years*, 406 (second quotation, emphasis in the original), 407 (first quotation).

2. His most recent biographer, David Johnson, presents a vivid portrait in *John Randolph of Roanoke* (Baton Rouge, 2012), 2–45.

3. See ibid., 77–79; Peterson, *Thomas Jefferson and the New Nation*, 820–21; Norman K. Risjord, *The Old Republicans: Southern Conservatism in the Age of Jefferson* (New York, 1965), 40–42.

4. The most detailed treatment of the influence of the Quids is Risjord, *The Old Republicans*, but see also Johnson, *John Randolph*, 88–105.

5. Jefferson to Pierre Samuel Du Pont de Nemours, November 1, 1803, in *PTJ*, 41:647–48 (quotation on 647). On Spanish deployments, see DeConde, *This Affair of Louisiana*, 198.

6. Ammon, *James Monroe*, 231, 233–37.

7. Ibid., 237–42.

8. Ibid., 243.

9. Jefferson to James Madison, August 4, 1805, in Smith, *The Republic of Letters*, 3:1375.

10. Jefferson to Madison, September 16, 1805, in ibid., 1386–87 (first quotation on 1387); Jefferson to Madison, September 18, 1805, in ibid., 1387–88 (second quotation on 1387).

11. Jefferson to Albert Gallatin, October 23, 1805, in Ford, *The Works of Thomas Jefferson*, 10:178–79 (first quotation on 178, second quotation on 179).

12. "Jefferson, Madison, and the Cabinet's Decision on Spain," November 14, 1805, in Smith, *The Republic of Letters*, 3:1396.

13. "Fifth Annual Message," December 3, 1805, in Padover, *The Complete Jefferson*, 417 (all quotations).

14. Quoted in Cunningham, *The Process of Government Under Jefferson*, 44.

15. Charles Francis Adams, ed., *Memoirs of John Quincy Adams*, 13 vols. (Philadelphia, 1874), 1:415.

16. Malone, *Jefferson and His Time*, 5:70–77; DeConde, *This Affair of Louisiana*, 232–35.

17. See Thomas Perkins Abernethy, *The Burr Conspiracy* (New York, 1954), 47–48.

18. See DeConde, *This Affair of Louisiana*, 235; Malone, *Jefferson and His Time*, 5:92–94; Cunningham, *In Pursuit of Reason*, 282–83.

19. For the best treatment of this treaty, see Ammon, *James Monroe*, 426–28.

20. *JMB*, 2:1166; Jefferson to Martha Jefferson Randolph, November 7, 1805, in *FL*, 280–81 (quotation on 281).

21. Kierner, *Martha Jefferson Randolph*, 131.

22. [Smith], *The First Forty Years*, 404–5.

23. Ibid., 50 (first quotation), 405 (second quotation).

24. Jefferson used this phrase in his letter to Elbridge Gerry, May 13, 1797, in *PTJ*, 29:367.

25. There is an enormous literature on the so-called Burr Conspiracy. Most historians believe that whatever exactly Burr had in mind, he was up to no good. Abernethy, *The Burr Conspiracy*, is very critical of Burr but largely persuasive. Malone, *Jefferson and His Time*, 5:216–88, provides a careful, judicious account that also assumes Burr's guilt. Nancy Isenberg's *Fallen Founder* is a full-throated defense of Burr—she believes him guilty of nothing nefarious—but I do not find her central thesis persuasive. A more convincing

account, arguing that Burr was clearly guilty of conspiring against the interests of the United States, is David O. Stewart, *American Emperor: Aaron Burr's Challenge to Jefferson's America* (New York, 2011).

26. Anthony Merry to Lord Harrowby, March 29, 1805, in *Political Correspondence and Public Papers of Aaron Burr*, ed. Mary-Jo Kline, 2 vols. (Princeton, 1983), 2:927–30 (quotations on 928).

27. Merry to Lord Mulgrave, November 25, 1805, in ibid., 943–47 (quotation on 943–45).

28. See Abernethy, *The Burr Conspiracy*, 39–40.

29. Ibid., 38–39 (quotation on 38).

30. Ibid., 90–92; see also Malone, *Jefferson and His Time*, 5:223–25.

31. Malone, *Jefferson and His Time*, 5:238.

32. Ibid., 135–40.

33. Jefferson to Meriwether Lewis, October 20, 1806, in Ford, *The Works of Thomas Jefferson*, 10:295–96 (quotation on 295); Meriwether Lewis to Jefferson, September 23, 1806, in Jackson, *Letters of the Lewis and Clark Expedition*, 1:319–24 (quotation on 319–20).

34. Lewis to Jefferson, September 23, 1806, in Jackson, *Letters of the Lewis and Clark Expedition*, 1:320. For the portage, see Gary E. Moulton, ed., *The Definitive Journals of Lewis & Clark*, 13 vols. (Lincoln, 1987), 4:323–52; for the hazardous trip over the Bitterroot Mountains, see ibid., 5:185–229.

35. See Jefferson's description of the event in Jefferson to José Corrèa de Serra, April 26, 1816, in Jackson, *Letters of the Lewis and Clark Expedition*, 2:611–13.

36. See Malone, *Jefferson and His Time*, 5:239–40; Abernethy, *The Burr Conspiracy*, 84, 184; Isenberg, *Fallen Founder*, 303–4.

37. Sawvel, *The Complete Anas of Thomas Jefferson*, 246–47.

38. Ibid., 247–48.

39. Ibid., 248. Malone, *Jefferson and His Time*, 5:244, suggests that funds were insufficient to pay for sending the gunboats.

40. Meaty portions of the supposedly anonymous document and Wilkinson's letter are reprinted in Abernethy, *The Burr Conspiracy*, 151–52 (quotation on 151).

41. "Proclamation Against Burr's Plot," November 27, 1806, in Ford, *The Works of Thomas Jefferson*, 10:300–301 (first four quotations on 300, last two on 301).

42. See the memo from James Madison to Jefferson (and Jefferson's note on it), October 30, 1806, in Smith, *The Republic of Letters*, 3:1454.

43. See Malone, *Jefferson and His Time*, 5:253.

44. "Sixth Annual Message," in Peterson, *Thomas Jefferson, Writings*, 524–31 (quotation on 529.

45. Ibid., 528.

46. Ibid., 525.

47. Quoted in Malone, *Jefferson and His Time*, 5:255. See Malone's discussion of Erskine's views, 255–56.

48. Jefferson to Charles Clay, January 11, 1807, in Ford, *The Works of Thomas Jefferson*, 10:338–39 (quotation on 339).

49. Abernethy, *The Burr Conspiracy*, 106–9.

50. Malone, *Jefferson and His Time*, 5:261–62.

51. See editorial note in Kline, *Political Correspondence and Public Papers of Aaron Burr*, 2:973–86; "Appendix 1" in Stewart, *American Emperor*, 309–12.

52. Aaron Burr to James Wilkinson, [July 22–29, 1806], in Kline, *Political Correspondence and Public Papers of Aaron Burr*, 2:986–87. (Stewart, *American Emperor*, 310, points out that Burr occasionally referred to himself in the third person.)

53. "Special Message on the Burr Conspiracy," January 22, 1807, in Peterson, *Thomas Jefferson, Writings*, 532–38 (quotations on 532).

54. For this background, see Abernethy, *The Burr Conspiracy*, 219–26.

55. Quoted in R. Kent Newmyer, *The Treason Trial of Aaron Burr: Law, Politics, and the Character Wars of the New Nation* (Cambridge, UK, 2012), 63.

56. See, for example, Jefferson (writing from Monticello) to James Madison, April 4, 1807, asking the secretary of state's assistance in making government funds available to cover the travel expenses of witnesses asked to come to Richmond; as Jefferson stated, he asked Madison on account of "Mr. Rodney not being at Washington." In Smith, *The Republic of Letters*, 3:1466–67 (quotation on 1466).

57. See Malone, *Jefferson and His Time*, 5:296, 310; Newmyer, *The Treason Trial of Aaron Burr*, 76–81.

58. See Newmyer, *The Treason Trial of Aaron Burr*, 146–48; Malone, *Jefferson and His Time*, 5:301–2.

59. Jefferson to William Branch Giles, April 20, 1807, in Peterson, *Thomas Jefferson, Writings*, 1173–76 (quotation on 1174).

60. See Newmyer, *The Treason Trial of Aaron Burr*, 154–66.

61. On this point, see Wood, *Empire of Liberty*, 439.

62. See Jefferson to Monsieur Du Pont de Nemours, July 14, 1807, and to the Marquis De La Fayette, July 14, 1807, in Bergh, 11:274–76, 276–80.

63. Quoted in Malone, *Jefferson and His Time*, 5:361. Federalist James Bayard, who voted against John Quincy Adams on the expulsion of John Smith, also felt that Burr was guilty of conspiracy and believed that "scarcely a man in the United States doubts it" (ibid).

64. Gordon S. Wood, in "The Real Treason of Aaron Burr," *Proceedings of the American Philosophical Society* 143 (June 1999): 280–95, argues that Burr's failure to share the other Founders' idealism was his "real treason" and what distanced him from them. In 1863 American writer Edward Everett Hale wrote a short story titled "The Man Without a Country" inspired by Burr's alleged conspiracy.

26:
"WAR, EMBARGO, OR NOTHING"

1. Wood, *Empire of Liberty*, 640, explains this briefly but lucidly; for a more detailed explanation, see Bradford Perkins, *Prologue to War: England and the United States, 1805–1812* (Berkeley, 1961), 79–82.

2. Jefferson, "Fifth Annual Message," December 3, 1805, in Padover, *The Complete Jefferson*, 417–18 (quotation on 418).

3. See "A Bill for Establishing a Naval Militia," [December 1805], in Ford, *The Works of Thomas Jefferson*, 10:206–13.

4. See Perkins, *Prologue to War*, 112.

5. See "Draft of Proclamation Concerning 'Leander,'" May 3, 1806, in Ford, *The Works of Thomas Jefferson*, 10:256–59.

6. See Ammon, *James Monroe*, 248–69 (quotations on 260–61); Malone, *Jefferson and His Time*, 4:395–405.

7. See Perkins, *Prologue to War*, 69, 71; Wood, *Empire of Liberty*, 646.

8. "Sixth Annual Message," December 2, 1806, in Padover, *The Complete Jefferson*, 421–26.

9. There are many accounts of the incident; Malone, *Jefferson and His Time*, 5:415–22, offers a convenient and judicious version.

10. Jefferson to Pierre Samuel Du Pont de Nemours, July 14, 1807, in Ford, *The Works of Thomas Jefferson*, 10:460–62 (quotation on 460).

11. Ibid., 433.

12. "Jefferson's Proclamation About the *Chesapeake* Affair," July 2, 1807, in Smith, *The Republic of Letters*, 3:1477–79.

13. Ibid., 1478.

14. Ibid., 1478–79.

15. Quotation in Burton Spivak, *Jefferson's English Crisis: Commerce,*

Embargo, and the Republican Revolution (Charlottesville, 1979), 91.

16. Sawvel, *The Complete Anas of Thomas Jefferson*, 254–55.

17. Ibid., 256–57.

18. Jefferson to Thomas Leiper, August 21, 1807, in ibid., 482–84 (quotation on 484).

19. Sawvel, *The Complete Anas of Thomas Jefferson*, 255.

20. "Seventh Annual Message," October 27, 1807, in Padover, *The Complete Jefferson*, 434–39 (quotation on 436).

21. Ibid. (quotation on 439).

22. See Malone, *Jefferson and His Time*, 5:464–68. While Perkins and Spivak have books on the embargo generally, Malone's is the most judicious and convincing treatment.

23. Ibid., 479–81 (quotation on 481).

24. Quoted in Cunningham, *In Pursuit of Reason*, 310.

25. "Confidential Message to the Senate & House of Representatives of the United States," December 7, 1807, in Ford, *The Works of Thomas Jefferson*, 10:528–29.

26. "Special Message of Commercial Depredations," December 18, 1807, in ibid., 530–31.

27. Ibid., 531 (emphasis added).

28. Albert Gallatin to Jefferson, December 18, 1807, in *The Writings of Albert Gallatin*, ed. Henry Adams, 3 vols. (Philadelphia, 1879), 1:368.

29. Jefferson to Charles Thomson, January 11, 1808, in Ford, *The Works of Thomas Jefferson*, 11:6–7 (quotation on 7).

30. See Spivak, *Jefferson's English Crisis*, 111–13.

31. See Malone, *Jefferson and His Time*, 5:563; White, *The Jeffersonians*, 427–29.

32. Jefferson to Madison, March 11, 1808, in Ford, *The Works of Thomas Jefferson*, 11:12–18 (quotation on 12).

33. Gallatin to Jefferson, July 29, 1808, in Adams, *The Writings of Gallatin*, 1:396–99 (quotations on 398).

34. White, *The Jeffersonians*, 431–32.

35. For details on these enforcement acts, see ibid., 453–73.

36. Jefferson to John B. Colvin, September 20, 1810, in *PTJRS*, 3:99–101 (quotations on 99, emphasis added).

37. Ibid., 101.

38. Jefferson to Dr. Thomas Leib, June 23, 1808, in Bergh, 12:76–77 (quotation on 77).

39. "Eighth Annual Message," November 8, 1808, in Padover, *The Complete Jefferson*, 441–47 (quotation on 441).

40. Ibid., 442.

41. Jefferson to Levi Lincoln, November 13, 1808, in Ford, *The Works of Thomas Jefferson*, 11:73–75 (quotations on 74–75).

42. Gallatin to Jefferson, November 15, 1808, in Adams, *The Writings of Gallatin*, 1:428.

43. Quoted in Cunningham, *In Pursuit of Reason*, 317.

44. Jefferson to Dr. George Logan, December 27, 1808, in Bergh, 12:219–20 (quotation on 220).

45. See ibid., 317–19; Wood, *Empire of Liberty*, 657–58; Spivak, *Jefferson's English Crisis*, 180–97.

46. See Morris, *Encyclopedia of American History*, 137.

47. For the problem with his tooth, see Jefferson to Martha Jefferson Randolph, December 29, 1807, in *FL*, 317, 317n; Jefferson to Martha Jefferson Randolph, January 5, 1808, in ibid., 319–20.

48. Jefferson to Meriwether Lewis, July 17, 1808, in Jackson, *Letters of the Lewis and Clark Expedition*, 2:444–45 (first quotation on 444, second quotation on 445).

49. Thomas Mann Randolph to Jefferson, October 29, 1802, in *PTJ*, 38:601–2.

50. Quoted in Malone, *Jefferson and His Time*, 5:131.

51. The episode is described both in ibid., 141–43, and in Kierner, *Martha Jefferson Randolph*, 135. See Jefferson's letters to Martha Jefferson Randolph dealing with his care of her husband in *FL*, 297–306.

52. Jefferson to John W. Eppes, July 12, 1807, in Ford, *The Works of Thomas Jefferson*, 10:45–59 (quotation on 457).

53. Kierner, *Martha Jefferson Randolph*, 155–56. For Eppes's concern about the possible effect of Randolph's hostility on Francis, see John Wayles Eppes to Jefferson, July 10, 1809, in *PTJRS*, 1:336–37. In 1809 Eppes married Martha Burke Jones of North Carolina and moved (with his son) to Buckingham County, just south of Albemarle County.

54. Jefferson to Martha Jefferson Randolph, January 5, 1808, in *FL*, 319.

55. Martha Jefferson Randolph to Jefferson, January 16, 1808, in ibid., 322–23 (quotation on 322).

56. Martha Jefferson Randolph to Jefferson, March 2, 1809, in ibid., 386–88 (quotation on 388).

57. Jefferson, settling his affairs in Washington, first fully realized the extent to which he had been living beyond his means. See *JMB*, 2:1238n13.

58. Jefferson to James Monroe, January 28, 1809, in Ford, *The Works of Thomas Jefferson*, 11:93–96 (quotation on 96).

59. *GB*, 359–60.

60. *JMB*, 2:1215 (shipping books), 1228 (packing boxes).

61. Jefferson to Charles Thomson, December 25, 1808, in Ford, *The Works of Thomas Jefferson*, 11:83–84 (quotation on 84).

62. See Jeffrey A. Frankel, "The 1807–1809 Embargo Against Great Britain," *Journal of Economic History* 42 (June 1982): 291–308. Frankel argues that the embargo "failed through a lack of the political will and perseverance to use it, rather than

through a lack of economic power" (ibid., 291–92).

63. Jefferson to Pierre Samuel Du Pont de Nemours, March 2, 1809, in Peterson, *Thomas Jefferson, Writings*, 1203–4 (quotation on 1203).

64. "To the Citizens of Washington," March 4, 1809, in Padover, *The Complete Jefferson* 252–53.

65. See Bear, *Jefferson at Monticello*, 104 (quoting Bacon's memoirs); *JMB*, 2:1243; Jefferson to James Madison, March 17, 1809, in Smith, *Republic of Letters*, 3:1576.

27:
"RETURNING TO THE SCENES OF MY BIRTH AND EARLY LIFE"

1. For the shrubs, see Bear, *Jefferson at Monticello*, 106, from Edmund Bacon's memoirs.

2. Jefferson to John Armstrong, March 6, 1809, in *PTJRS*, 1:19–20 (quotation on 20).

3. "From the Inhabitants of Albemarle County," [ca. March 1809], in ibid., 46–47 (quotation on 46); "From the Albemarle Buckmountain Baptist Church," March 19, 1809, in ibid., 63.

4. "To the Inhabitants of Albemarle County," April 3, 1809, in ibid., 102–3.

5. See the notations in *GB*, 385–87.

6. Jefferson to Charles Willson Peale, August 20, 1811, in *PTJRS*, 4:93 (all quotations).

7. See Jefferson to Etienne Lemaire, April 25, 1809, in *PTJRS*, 1:161–62, 162n; see also the April 7, 1809, entry in *JMB*, 2:1244, 1244n. The best treatment of Jefferson's food and dining preferences is Fowler, *Dining at Monticello*.

8. Jefferson to Etienne Lemaire, April 25, 1809, in *PTJRS*, 1:161–62; Jefferson to Thomas Jefferson Randolph, April 16, 1810, in ibid., 2:335.

9. Jefferson to Wilson Cary Nicholas, June 12, 1809, in ibid., 2:276–77; Nicolas to Jefferson, July 18, 1809, in ibid., 349–50.

10. [Smith], *The First Forty Years*, 75.

11. Ibid., 76.

12. Randall, *The Life of Thomas Jefferson*, vol. 3, offers a goldmine of primary evidence through such letters.

13. Ibid., 342–51. Several slaves also always made the journey to Poplar Forest with him.

14. See "Census of Inhabitants and Supplies at Monticello," November 8, 1810, in *PTJRS*, 3:202.

15. See the facsimile of his slave census reprinted in *FB*, 135. Altogether there were about one hundred slaves at Monticello, but many of them were artisans or employed in the nail factory. The farm in Bedford County was more productive than Monticello.

16. "Memoirs of Thomas Jefferson Randolph," MSS 5454-c, in Albert and Shirley Small Special Collections Library, University of Virginia (transcribed by James A. Bear), 3.

17. Bear, *Jefferson at Monticello*, 60.

18. Jefferson to Thomas Law, April 23, 1811, in *PTJRS*, 3:578–79 (quotation on 579).

19. Jefferson's interest in sheep is best illustrated by the discussion in *FB*, 111–42, which reprints all the relevant Jefferson correspondence. For the sake of convenience, I will cite this volume for the correspondence rather than the respective volumes in *PTJRS*.

20. Jefferson to Joseph Dougherty, May 24, 1810, in *FB*, 130–31; Jefferson to William Thornton, May 24, 1810, in ibid., 131–32.

21. See Jefferson to George Jefferson, March 11, 1811, and George Jefferson to Jefferson, March 15, 1811, in ibid., 136; Jefferson to John H. Cocke, July 28, 1811, in ibid., 137; Jefferson to Joseph Dougherty, December 25, 1812, in ibid., 139; Jefferson to George Washington Jeffreys, June 12, 1817, in ibid., 141.

22. See *JMB*, 1:745.

23. On dogs sent by Lafayette, see Jefferson to George Jefferson, August 22, 1809, in *PTJRS*, 1:457.

24. See Jefferson to William Thornton, April 27, 1810, in *FB*, 126–27 (quotation on 127).

25. Jefferson to Peter Minor, September 14, 1811, in *FB*, 138; "Petition of Albemarle County Residents to Virginia General Assembly," [before December 19, 1811], in *PTJRS*, 4:346–48, 348n.

26. Jefferson to Meriwether Lewis, August 16, 1809, in *PTJRS*, 1:435–36 (quotations on 436).

27. Brahan to Jefferson, October 18, 1809, in ibid., 602 (first quotation), 603 (second quotation).

28. C. & A. Conrad & Company to Jefferson, November 13, 1809, in ibid., 668–69 (quotation on 669).

29. Jefferson to C. & A. Conrad & Company, November 23, 1809, in ibid., 2:30–31 (quotation on 31).

30. Jefferson to C. & A. Conrad & Company, December 11, 1809, in ibid., 72. President Madison's private secretary, Isaac A. Coles, wrote Jefferson in January to inform him that Clark had picked up the papers relevant "to the Expedition." Coles to Jefferson, January 5, 1810, in ibid., 123.

31. Biddle's extensive notes are reprinted in Donald Jackson, ed., *Letters of the Lewis and Clark Expedition, with Related Documents, 1783–1854*, 2nd ed., 2 vols. (Urbana, IL, 1978), 2:497–545.

32. See Lester J. Cappon, "Who Is the Author of the *Expedition under the Command of Captains Lewis and Clark* (1814)," *William and Mary Quarterly*, 19 (April 1962), 259.

33. C. & A. Conrad & Company to Jefferson, [received April 15, 1810), in *PTJRS*, 2:332.

34. See the correspondence between Biddle and Clark, dated July 4, 1812, August 6, 1812, September 5, 1812, and February 23, 1813, in Jackson, *Letters of the Lewis and Clark Expedition*, 2:577–82.

35. See the discussion in Cappon, "Who Is the Author," 261, 263–64.

36. See Jefferson to Paul Allen, August 5, 1813, in *PTJRS*, 6:357, replying to Allen's nonextant letter of May 25; Jefferson to Paul Allen, August 18, 1813, in ibid., 418–24; Jackson, *Letters of the Lewis and Clark Expedition*, 2:594.

37. See Jefferson to Clark, September 8, 1816, in Jackson, *Letters of the Lewis and Clark Expedition*, 2:619.

38. Jefferson's original version is reprinted in *PTJRS*, 6:418–24.

39. Ibid., 421.

40. Ibid., 423.

41. Ibid., 423 (first quotation), 424 (second and third quotations).

42. See the series of letters reproduced in *PTJRS* 2: John Wickham to Jefferson May 16, 1810 (395); Jefferson to Wickham, May 18, 1810 (398); Jefferson to William Wirt and George Hay, May 19, 1810 (401–2); Wickham to Jefferson, May 22, 1810 (406–7).

43. See Jefferson to Wirt and Hay, May 19, 1810, in ibid., 401–2; Albert Gallatin to Jefferson, September 10, 1810, in ibid., 3:68–69; *JMB*, 2:1276.

44. See Jefferson to James Madison, May 25, 1810, in *PTJRS*, 2:416–17.

45. Ibid., 417 (quotation). A modern legal scholar agrees that Livingston was indulging in judge shopping. See Ronan E. Degnan, "Livingston v. Jefferson—a Freestanding Footnote," *California Law Review* 75 (January 1987): 126.

46. For a flagrant example of such bias, see Albert J. Beveridge, *The Life of John Marshall*, 4 vols. (1819; rpt. Boston, 1947), 4:103–16.

47. John Tyler to Jefferson, May 12, 1810, in *PTJRS*, 2:384–87.

48. Jefferson to Madison, May 25, 1810, in ibid., 416–17 (both quotes on 416).

49. This background material is based on Malone, *Jefferson and His Time*, 6:55–60.

50. See John Wickham to Edward Livingston, May 16, 1810, quoted in Edward Dumbauld, *Thomas Jefferson and the Law* (Norman, OK, 1978), 37 (see also 186n8).

51. See Jefferson to George Hay, December 28, 1811, in *PTJRS*, 4:367.

52. See the bibliographical details with much supporting data in Sowerby, *Catalogue of the Library of Thomas Jefferson*, 3:404–13.

53. John Adams to Jefferson, May 3, 1812, in *PTJRS*, 5:11–13 (quotation on 11–12).

54. For Jefferson's reconciliation with Livingston, see Burstein, *Jefferson's Secrets*, 232–34.

55. Benjamin Rush to Jefferson, January 2, 1811, in *Letters of Benjamin Rush*, ed. L. H. Butterfield, 2 vols. (Princeton, 1951), 2:1073–76 (first four quotations on 1075, last quotation on 1076). The letter is also reprinted in *PTJRS*, 3:276–78.

56. See Rush to John Adams, October 17, 1809, in Butterfield, *Letters of Benjamin Rush*, 2:1021–22 (quotations on 1022).

57. Jefferson to Benjamin Rush, January 16, 1811, in *PTJRS*, 3:304–8 (first quotation on 304, second quotation on 307).

58. Edward Coles to Henry S. Randall, May 11, 1857, reprinted as Appendix XXV in Randall, *The Life of Thomas Jefferson*, 3:639–40 (quotations on 640).

59. Jefferson to Benjamin Rush, December 5, 1811, in *PTJRS*, 4:312–14 (first quotation on 312, other quotations on 313).

60. Benjamin Rush to Jefferson, December 17, 1811, in ibid., 338–40 (quotation on 338).

61. Benjamin Rush to John Adams, December 16, 1811, in Butterfield, *Letters of Benjamin Rush*, 2:1110–11 (all quotations on 1110).

62. Quoted in L. H. Butterfield, "The Dream of Benjamin Rush: The Reconciliation of John Adams and Thomas Jefferson," *Yale Review* 40 (December 1950): 314.

63. John Adams to Jefferson, January 1, 1812, in *PTJRS*, 4:390.

28:
"WE OUGHT NOT TO DIE BEFORE WE HAVE EXPLAINED OURSELVES"

1. John Adams to Jefferson, January 1, 1812, in Cappon, *The Adams-Jefferson Letters*, 290.

2. Jefferson to Adams, January 21, 1812, in ibid., 290–92 (quotations on 291).

3. Ibid. (first and second quotations on 291, third quotation on 292).

4. Adams to Jefferson, July 8, 1813, in ibid., 350–52 (quotation on 351).

5. Jefferson to Adams, June 27, 1822, in ibid., 580–81; Adams to Jefferson, July 12, 1822, in ibid., 581–82.

6. Adams to Jefferson, December 25, 1813, in ibid., 409–13 (quotations on 409).

7. Jefferson to Adams, January 14, 1814, in ibid., 421–25 (quotations on 423).

8. Adams to Jefferson, July 15, 1813, in ibid., 357–58 (quotation on 357).

9. Adams to Jefferson, February 3, 1812, in ibid., 293–96 (quotation on 295); Jefferson to Adams, April 20, 1812, in ibid., 298–300 (quotation on 298); Adams to Jefferson, May 1, 1812, in ibid., 300–1 (quotation on 301); Adams to Jefferson, May 3, 1812, in ibid., 302–4 (quotation on 304).

10. Jefferson to Adams, June 11, 1812, in ibid., 305–8 (quotation on 307).

11. Adams to Jefferson, June 28, 1812, in ibid., 308–11 (quotation on 310).

12. Jefferson to Adams, May 27, 1813, in ibid., 323–25; Adams to Jefferson, May 29, 1813, in ibid., 325–26; Adams to Jefferson, June 10, 1813, in ibid., 326–27 (first quotation on 327); Jefferson to Adams, June 15, 1813, in ibid., 331–33; Jefferson to Adams, June 27, 1813, in ibid., 335–38 (quotation on 337).

13. Adams to Jefferson, June 28, 1813, in ibid., 338–40 (first quotation on 338); Adams to Jefferson, June 30, 1813, in ibid., 346–48; Adams to Jefferson, July [3], 1813, in ibid., 349–50; Adams to Jefferson, July 15, 1813, in ibid., 357–58 (last two quotations on 358)

14. For Abigail's note, see Adams to Jefferson, July 15, 1813, in ibid., 358; Jefferson to Abigail Adams, August 22, 1813, in ibid., 366–67. For the announcement of the death of the Adamses' daughter, see Adams to Jefferson, [August 16, 1813], in ibid., 365–66. For the date of Jefferson's receipt of this letter, see *PTJRS*, 6:388n.

15. Abigail Adams to Jefferson, September 20, 1813, in Cappon, *The Adams-Jefferson Letters*, 377–78 (quotation on 377); Jefferson to Adams, August 22, 1813, in ibid., 367–70 (quotations on 368).

16. Jefferson to Adams, October 12, 1813, in ibid., 383–86 (quotations on 386).

17. Ibid., 384.

18. Jefferson to Adams, July 5, 1814, in ibid., 430–34 (quotation on 433).

19. Jefferson to Charles Thomson, January 9, 1816, in *PTJRS*, 9:340–42 (quotations on 341).

20. Jefferson to Ezra Stiles Ely, June 25, 1819, in Adams, *Jefferson's Extracts from the Gospels*, 386–87 (quotation on 387).

21. The letter from Short, December 1, 1819, is quoted in ibid., 37.

22. Jefferson to Adams, April 11, 1823, in Cappon, *The Adams-Jefferson Letters*, 591–94 (quotations on 592).

23. Jefferson to Adams, October 28, 1813, in ibid., 387–92 (quotations all on 388).

24. Adams to Jefferson, November 15, 1813, in ibid., 397–402.

25. Jefferson to Adams, October 28, 1813, in ibid., 390.

26. Ibid., 391.

27. Jefferson to Adams, July 5, 1814, in ibid., 430–34 (quotation on 430–31).

28. Adams to Jefferson, July 16, 1814, in ibid., 434–39 (quotation on 435); Jefferson to Adams, August 9, 1816, in ibid., 485–87 (quotation on 485).

29. Adams to Jefferson, March 2, 1816, in ibid., 464–66 (quotation on 464); Jefferson to Adams, April 8, 1816, in ibid., 466–69 (quotations on 467).

30. Adams to Jefferson, May 29, 1818, in ibid., 525–26 (first three quotations on 526); Adams to Jefferson, October 20, 1818, in ibid., 528–29 (fourth quotation on 529); Jefferson to Adams, November 13, 1818, in ibid., 529 (all remaining quotations).

31. Adams to Jefferson, July 30, 1815, in ibid., 451; Jefferson to Adams, August 10[–11], 1815, in ibid., 452–54 (final quotation on 452). Jefferson did go on to say that James Madison had taken detailed notes on the Constitutional Convention (ibid., 453).

32. Jefferson to Adams, May 17, 1818, in ibid., 523–25 (quotation on 524); Adams to Jefferson, May 29, 1818, in ibid., 525–26 (quotation on 525).

33. Adams to Jefferson, July 12, 1822, in ibid., 581–82 (quotation on 582).

34. Jefferson to Adams, September 12, 1821, in ibid., 574–76 (quotation on 575).

35. Jefferson to Adams, November 7, 1819, in ibid., 546–47 (first two quotes on 546, all others on 547).

36. Adams to Jefferson, November 23, 1819, in ibid., 547–48 (first two quotations on 548); Jefferson to Adams, December 10, 1819, in ibid., 548–50 (third quotation on 548–49).

37. See Briggs's account in "A Cordial Return in 1820," reprinted in *VTM*, 80–92 (quotation on 90).

38. Adams to Jefferson, December 21, 1819, in Cappon, *The Adams-Jefferson Letters*, 550–51 (quotations on 551).

39. Jefferson to Adams, January 22, 1821, in ibid., 569–70; Adams to Jefferson, February 3, 1821, in ibid., 571–72 (quotation on 571).

40. Jefferson to Adams, March 25, 1826, in ibid., 613–14 (quotations on 614).

41. Adams to Jefferson, May 21, 1819, in ibid., 540–41 (quotation on 540).

42. See Adams letters recommending both to Jefferson: Adams to Jefferson, December 11, 1814, in ibid., 440; Adams to Jefferson, December 20, 1814, in ibid., 441. Adams called Jefferson Monticello's "sage" in the letter of December 20.

43. Jefferson to Adams, June 20, 1815, in ibid., 441–43 (quotations on 443).

44. Gray's account is titled "Boston Comes to Monticello," in *VTM*, 55–60 (quotation on 57).

45. Ticknor's account is titled "Old Books and Young Society," in ibid., 61–65 (first two quotations on 62, third quotation on 63, fourth quotation on 64, final quotation on 65).

29:
LIVING WITH PARADOX

1. Charles Carroll of Carrollton was the longest surviving Signer; he died on November 14, 1832, at the age of ninety-two.

2. Jefferson was not attacking the entire institution of slavery here but rather arguing that in the case of the mulatto Howell, the lack of positive law defining the heritable status of indentured servitude meant that natural law determined Howell's case. See David T. Konig, "Thomas Jefferson and the Practice of Law," Encyclopedia Virginia, accessed October 12, 2015, http://www.encyclopediavirginia.org/Jefferson_Thomas_and_the_Practice_of_Law.

3. Jefferson to Thomas Leiper, February 23, 1801, in *PTJ*, 33:50.

4. According to Edmund Bacon, Jefferson's longtime overseer at Monticello, "Mr. Jefferson was always very kind and indulgent to his servants. He would not allow them to be at all overworked, and he would hardly ever allow one of them to be whipped." See Bear, *Jefferson at Monticello*, 97. Jefferson specified to various overseers that none of the Hemings slaves was ever to be physically disciplined.

5. See Stanton, *Free Some Day*, 131–32.

6. Jefferson to Joel Yancey, January 17, 1819, in *FB*, 42–44 (quotation on 43).

7. Stanton, *"Those Who Labor for My Happiness,"* 4, 6, 59, 67. Stanton's work is the definitive scholarship on Jefferson as a slave owner.

8. For the meaning of concubine at this time, see Gordon-Reed, *The Hemingses of Monticello*, 107.

9. See Rothman, *Notorious in the Neighborhood*, esp. chap. 1, 14–52.

10. "A Frenchman Views Jefferson the Farmer," in *VTM*, 30.

11. See Jefferson's directions to his overseer that Martha Randolph herself would attend to "the clothing for the house servants [and other Hemingses]" (quoted in *FB*, 25).

12. For Washington's slaves, see Ron Chernow, *Washington: A Life* (New York, 2010), 118. For members of the Hemings caste picking out their own clothing, see, for example, Jefferson's note to his Charlottesville merchant, James Leitch, authorizing "any clothing which the bearer Burwell [Colbert] may chuse for himself." Jefferson to James Leitch, March 25, 1815, in *PTJRS*, 8:380.

13. Stanton, *"Those Who Labor for My Happiness,"* 23.

14. Stanton, *Free Some Day*, 121. Several other members of the Hemings families also received regular gratuities.

15. Jefferson to William A. Burwell, January 28, 1805, in Ford, *The Works of Thomas Jefferson*, 10:126–27 (quotation on 126); Stanton, *"Those Who Labor for My Happiness,"* 19, 72.

16. Jefferson to Henri Gregoire, February 25, 1809, in Ford, *The Works of Thomas Jefferson*, 11:99–100 (first quotation on 99, subsequent quotations on 100).

17. Jefferson to Jean Nicolas Démeunier, June 26, 1786, in *PTJ*, 10:61–63 (quotation on 63).

18. "Marriage Settlement for Martha Jefferson," [February 21, 1790], in ibid., 16:189–91.

19. "Marriage Settlement for Mary Jefferson," [October 12, 1797], in ibid., 29:549–50.

20. See the genealogy chart for the Hemings family printed as an unpaged appendix to Stanton, *Free Some Day*.

21. See Jefferson to Francis C. Gray, March 4, 1815, in *PTJRS*, 8:10–12, wherein Jefferson employs mathematical and proportional calculations to discuss heredity and determine how many "mixtures" it required to produce a white person from African ancestry.

22. Related by Henry S. Randall to James Parton, June 1, 1868, quoted in Annette Gordon-Reed, *Thomas Jefferson and Sally Hemings: An American Controversy* (Charlottesville, 1997), 254–57 (quotation on 254).

23. Henry S. Randall wrote in a letter to James Parton, June 1, 1868, that some years before Thomas Jefferson Randolph, Jefferson's nephew, had shown him "a smoke blackened and sooty room in one of the collonades, and informed me that it was Sally Hening's [*sic*] room" (quoted in ibid., 254).

24. The definitive account is Gordon-Reed, *The Hemingses of Monticello*.

25. Bear, *Jefferson at Monticello*, 4.

26. *Notes*, 138 (first quotation), 139 (second quotation).

27. William Short to Jefferson, February 27, 1798, in *PTJ*, 30:140–53, esp. 150–51.

28. Jefferson to William Short, January 18, 1826, in Founders Online, National Archives, accessed October 12, 2015, http://founders.archives.gov/?q=William%20Short%20Recipient%3A%22Short%2C%20William%22&s=1111311111&sa=&r=340&sr=.

29. Jefferson to Edward Coles, August 25, 1814, in *PTJRS*, 7:603–5 (quotation on 604).

30. Stanton, *Free Some Day*, 143, 148.

31. This is the substance of Gordon-Reed's pathbreaking *Thomas Jefferson and*

Sally Hemings: An American Controversy. There is substantial scholarship on this topic today.

32. Wolf, *Race and Liberty in the New Nation*, 116, 117n. See this book also for the rise of manumissions after 1780.

33. Jefferson to Thomas Mann Randolph, November 16, 1801, in *PTJ*, 35:677–78 (quotation on 678).

34. Jefferson to Albert Gallatin, September 8, 1816, in ibid., 10:379–80 (quotation on 379).

35. Jefferson to David Bailie Warden, May 17, 1816, in ibid., 64–65 (quotations on 64).

36. "Analysis of Weather Memorandum Book," January 1817, in ibid., 11:33–40.

37. William K. Klingaman and Nicholas P. Klingaman, *The Year Without Summer: 1816 and the Volcano That Darkened the World and Changed History* (New York, 2013), 159–60, 174–75; Gillen D'Arcy Wood, *Tambora: The Eruption That Changed the World* (Princeton, 2014), 199–228.

38. Wolf, *Race and Liberty in the New Nation*, 125.

39. Jefferson to William Short, January 18, 1826, in Founders Online, National Archives, accessed October 12, 2015, http://founders.archives.gov/?q=William%20Short%20Recipient%3A%22Short%2C%20William%22&s=1111311111&sa=&r=340&sr=. He had more specifically recommended St. Domingo as a location for settling colonized freedmen in a letter to Jared Sparks, February 4, 1824, in Peterson, *Thomas Jefferson, Writings*, 1484–87.

40. Bear, *Jefferson at Monticello*, 90, 89.

41. For Coles's background, see Guasco, *Confronting Slavery*, 10–64.

42. Edward Coles to Jefferson, July 31, 1814, in *PTJRS*, 7:503–4 (all quotations on 503).

43. Ibid., 503–4.

44. Ibid., 504 (all quotations).

45. Jefferson to Edward Coles, August 25, 1814, in ibid., 603–5 (quotations on 603).

46. Ibid., 603.

47. Ibid., 604.

48. Jefferson to Joel Barlow, December 10, 1807, in Ford, *The Works of Thomas Jefferson*, 10:529–30 (quotation on 530).

49. Jefferson to Edward Coles, August 25, 1814, in *PTJRS*, 7:604.

50. Ibid.

51. Ibid., 605. The quote is a reference to Galatians 6:9: "And let us not be weary in well doing: for in due season we shall reap, if we faint not." Historian Paul Finkelman, a ferocious and unrelenting critic of Jefferson, in discussing Jefferson's reply to Coles's letter, simply has Jefferson telling Coles to take good care of his slaves without mentioning Jefferson's appeal to Coles to lend his influence to ending the institution. See Finkelman, "Jefferson and Slavery: 'Treason Against the Hopes of the World,'" 209. David Brion Davis, in *The Problem of Slavery in the Age of Revolution, 1770–1823* (Ithaca, 1975), makes the same omission.

52. Edward Coles to Jefferson, September 26, 1814, in *PTJRS*, 7:702–4 (quotations on 703).

53. David Barrow to Jefferson, March 20, 1815, in ibid., 8:364–65; Jefferson to David Barrow, May 1, 1815, in ibid., 454–55 (quotation on 455).

54. Jefferson to Thomas Humphreys, February 8, 1817, in ibid., 11:60–61 (quotation on 61).

55. Jefferson to James Heaton, May 20, 1826, in Peterson, *Thomas Jefferson, Writings*, 1516.

30:
ONE LAST CRUSADE

1. See John F. Kennedy, "161—Remarks at a Dinner Honoring Nobel Prize Winners of the Western Hemisphere, April 29, 1962," The American Presidency

Project, accessed September 29, 2015, www.presidency.ucsb.edu/ws/?pid=8623.

2. See "A Bill for the More General Diffusion of Knowledge," in *PTJ*, 2:526–33.

3. Jefferson to Littleton Waller Tazewell, January 5, 1805, in Peterson, *Thomas Jefferson, Writings*, 1149–53 (quotation on 1149).

4. Ibid. (first and second quotations on 1149, third quotation on 1152).

5. Jefferson to Messrs. Hugh L. White and others, May 6, 1810, ibid., 1222–1223.

6. Jefferson to Thomas Cooper, January 16, 1814, in *PTJRS*, 7:124–29 (quotation on 127).

7. See Cameron Addis, *Jefferson's Vision for Education, 1760–1845* (New York, 2003), 35; Jennings L. Wagoner Jr., *Jefferson and Education* (Charlottesville, 2004), 75–76.

8. See Philip Alexander Bruce, *History of the University of Virginia, 1819–1919: The Lengthened Shadow of One Man*, 5 vols. (New York, 1920), 1:121; Wagoner, *Jefferson and Education*, 79–80.

9. See *PTJRS*, 7:264n–66n.

10. "Minutes of the Albemarle Academy Board of Trustees," [April 5, 1814], in ibid., 282–83 (quotation on 283).

11. "Minutes of the Albemarle Academy Board of Trustees," [May 3, 1814], in ibid., 335–40 (first quotation on 336, second quotation on 337, third quotation on 340).

12. Jefferson to Peter Carr, September 7, 1814, in ibid., 636–41 (quotation on 636–37).

13. Ibid., 637.

14. Ibid., 637–41 (quotation on 639).

15. Jefferson to Robert Pleasants, August 27, 1796, in *PTJ*, 29:177–78 (quotation on 177).

16. Wagoner, *Jefferson and Education*, 90–92.

17. Ibid., 93–97.

18. For a detailed discussion, see Richard Guy Wilson, ed., *Thomas Jefferson's Academical Village: The Creation of an Architectural Masterpiece*, rev. ed. (Charlottesville, 2009), 13–27. The relevant correspondence with Thornton and Latrobe is in *PTJRS*, vol. 11.

19. Edmund Bacon's memoirs are printed in Bear, *Jefferson at Monticello*; for the story of laying out the campus, see ibid., 32–33.

20. On the cornerstone, see Malone, *Jefferson and His Time*, 6:265.

21. Jefferson to Joseph C. Cabell, December 18, 1817, in *PTJRS*, 12:263. The *nunc dimittas*, a canticle drawn from the second chapter of the Gospel of Saint Luke, is often used as the final song in a religious service. For the meeting site at Mountain House, see *JMB*, 2:1346n86.

22. Wagoner, *Jefferson and Education*, 115–21, and Malone, *Jefferson and His Time*, 6:277–82, narrate all of this succinctly.

23. "Report of the Commissioners for the University of Virginia," August 4, 1818, in Peterson, *Thomas Jefferson, Writings*, 457–73 (first quotation on 457, second quotation on 458).

24. Ibid., 459.

25. "Report of the Commissioners," 459–60 (first two quotations on 459, all other quotations on 460).

26. Ibid., 461 (first quotation), 462 (last quotation).

27. Ibid., 462–63 (quotation on 462).

28. Ibid., 465.

29. Ibid., 468–69 (quotation on 468).

30. Ibid., 469–73.

31. See Wagoner, *Jefferson and Education*, 119–21; Malone, *Jefferson and His Time*, 6:280–82, 365–66.

32. Nathaniel Burwell, March 14, 1818, in *PTJRS*, 12:532–33 (quotation on 532).

33. "Enclosure," in ibid., 534.

34. Jefferson to Adams, October 12, 1823, in Cappon, *The Adams-Jefferson Letters*, 599–601 (quotation on 599).

35. Jefferson to Francis Walker Eppes, September 11, 1818, in *FL*, 426–27 (quotation on 427); Malone, *Jefferson and*

His Time, 6:279; Wagoner, *Jefferson and Education*, 119.

36. Anne Z. Cockerham, Arlene W. Keeling, and Barbara Parker, "Seeking Refuge at Monticello: Domestic Violence in Thomas Jefferson's Family," *Magazine of Albemarle County History* 64 (2006): 34–51.

37. "Memoirs of Thomas Jefferson Randolph," MSS 5454-c, in the Albert and Shirley Small Special Collection Library, University of Virginia (transcribed by James A. Bear), 46.

38. For the fire, see Alan Pell Crawford, *Twilight at Monticello: The Final Years of Thomas Jefferson* (New York, 2008), 174. See also *JMB*, 2:1353.

39. Malone, *Jefferson and His Time*, 6:373; Randall, *The Life of Thomas Jefferson*, 3:453 (quotation).

40. Malone, *Jefferson and His Time*, 6:308 (quotation). See also Peterson, *Thomas Jefferson and the New Nation*, 989–90.

41. Wilson Cary Nicholas to Jefferson, April 19, 1818, in *PTJRS*, 12:649.

42. Jefferson to James Madison, February 17, 1826, in Smith, *The Republic of Letters*, 3:1964–67 (quotation on 1964).

43. Isaac Briggs, "A Cordial Reunion in 1820," in *VTM*, 80–92 (quotation on 90).

44. Jefferson to Hugh Nelson, February 7, 1820, in Ford, *The Works of Thomas Jefferson*, 12:157.

45. Jefferson to John Holmes, April 22, 1820, in ibid., 158–60 (quotations on 158).

46. Ibid. (quotations on 159).

47. See Peter S. Onuf, "Thomas Jefferson, Missouri, and the 'Empire for Liberty,'" in *Thomas Jefferson and the Changing West*, ed. James P. Ronda (St. Louis, 1997): 111–53, esp. 118–22.

48. Jefferson to John Holmes, in Ford, *The Works of Thomas Jefferson*, 12:158–61 (quotation on 159–60).

49. See Stuart Leibiger, "Thomas Jefferson and the Missouri Crisis: An Alternative Interpretation," *Journal of the Early Republic* 17 (spring 1997): 121–30.

50. Jefferson to Lafayette, December 26, 1820, in Ford, *The Works of Thomas Jefferson*, 12:189–91 (quotation on 191). See also Jefferson to Gallatin, December 26, 1826, in ibid., 185–89, esp. 186–87.

51. Addis, *Jefferson's Vision for Education*, 93–94.

52. Jefferson to Joseph C. Cabell, November 28, 1820, in Ford, *The Works of Thomas Jefferson*, 12:169–74 (quotations on 170).

53. For the letter to Cabell suggesting the potential political use of the Breckinridge letter, see Leibiger, "Thomas Jefferson and the Missouri Crisis," 127, which quotes the Cabell letter.

54. Jefferson to General James Breckinridge, February 15, 1821, in Peterson, *Thomas Jefferson, Writings*, 1452–54 (quotation on 1452).

55. George Ticknor to W. H. Prescott, December 16, 1824, in *Life, Letters, and Journals of George Ticknor*, [ed. George S. Hillard], 2 vols. (Boston, 1876), 1:346–49.

56. Ibid. (quotation on 349).

57. *AIA Journal* 65 (July 1976): 91. For the World Heritage Site, see www.worldheritagesite.org, accessed October 2, 2015.

58. See Joseph F. Kett, "Education," in Peterson, *Thomas Jefferson: A Reference Biography*, 246–47.

59. See the series of letters between Jefferson and Francis Epps in *FL*, 433–54. The quotation is from Jefferson to Francis Epps, December 13, 1820, 436–37 (quotation on 436).

60. See David E. Swift, "Thomas Jefferson, John Holt Rice, and Education in Virginia, 1815–1825," *Journal of Presbyterian History* 49 (spring 1971): 32–58. In the midst of the controversy with Rice over the appointment of Cooper, Jefferson erupted in anger to the Portuguese botanist Correa that Presbyterians "dread the advance of

science as witches do the approach of day." Jefferson to Jose Francisco Correa de Serra, April 11, 1820, in Jefferson Papers, Library of Congress, https://www.loc.gov/resource/mtj1.051_1213_1213.

61. Wagoner, *Jefferson and Education*, 102–3, 141; Malone, *Jefferson and His Time*, 6:368–69, 376–80.

62. For Lafayette's visit to Albemarle County generally, see Malone, *Jefferson and His Time*, 6:404–8. Randall, *The Life of Thomas Jefferson*, 3:503, provides a vivid description of Lafayette's arrival at Monticello.

63. "Speech on Lafayette," October 1824 [presumably when Jefferson had written it out], in Padover, *The Complete Jefferson*, 447–48 (quotations on 448).

64. Ibid., 448.

65. Malone, *Jefferson and His Time*, 6:409.

66. Jefferson to William Roscoe, December 27, 1820, in Bergh, 15:302–4 (quotation on 303).

67. Quoted in Ralph Ketcham, *The Madisons at Montpelier: Reflections on the Founding Couple* (Charlottesville, 2009), 90.

68. See Addis, *Jefferson's Vision for Education*, 117.

69. Jennings L. Wagoner Jr., "Honor and Dishonor at Mr. Jefferson's University: The Antebellum Years," *History of Education Quarterly* 26 (summer 1986): 155–80, esp. 175–77 (quotation on 175).

31:
THE SAGE OF MONTICELLO

1. Daniel Webster, "A Yankee Congressman Pens a Portrait," in *VTM*, 97 (first three quotations), 97–98 (fourth quotation), 98 (fifth and sixth quotations), 99 (final quotation).

2. Randall, *The Life of Thomas Jefferson*, 3:507.

3. "A German Prince Climbs the Mountain," in *VTM*, 105.

4. "A Visit to the Dying Sage," in ibid., 109.

5. Jefferson to Rev. Thomas Whittemore, June 5, 1822, in Bergh, 15:373–74 (quotation on 373).

6. Jefferson to Dr. Benjamin Waterhouse, June 26, 1822, in ibid., 383–85 (quotation on 384).

7. Ibid., 385.

8. Jefferson to George Thacher, January 26, 1824, in Adams, *Jefferson's Extracts from the Gospels*, 414–15 (quotation on 414).

9. Jefferson to Joseph C. Cabell, February 2, 1816, in *PTJRS*, 9:435–38 (quotations on 436–37).

10. Jefferson to Archibald Thweat, January 19, 1821, in Bergh, 15:306–7 (quotation on 307).

11. Jefferson to Judge Spencer Roane, March 9, 1821, in ibid., 325–26 (quotation on 326).

12. Enclosure in Jefferson to James Madison, December 24, 1825, in Smith, *The Republic of Letters*, 3:1944–46 (quotation on 1946).

13. Jefferson to Samuel Kercheval, July 12, 1816, in Peterson, *Thomas Jefferson, Writings*, 1395–1403 (quotations on 1401).

14. Ibid.

15. Historian Joseph Ellis in a talk at the Massachusetts Historical Society once said that if he had lived, "Jefferson would have gone with the Confederacy." Quoted in Steele, *Thomas Jefferson and American Nationhood*, 238.

16. Jefferson to Major John Cartwright, June 5, 1824, in Peterson, *Thomas Jefferson, Writings*, 1490–96 (quotation on 1494).

17. Jefferson to John Holmes, April 22, 1820, in ibid., 1433–35 (quotation on 1435).

18. Jefferson to Roger C. Weightman, June 24, 1826, ibid., 1516–17 (quotations on 1517).

19. "First Inaugural Address," March 4, 1801, in ibid., 492–96 (quotation on 493).

20. Jefferson to Jared Sparks, February 4, 1824, in Peterson, *Thomas Jefferson, Writings*, 1484–87 (quotations on 1484). For an insightful discussion of conversion

and abolition, see Wright, "Gospel of Liberty."

21. Jefferson to Jared Sparks, February 4, 1814, in Peterson, *Thomas Jefferson, Writings*, 1484.

22. Ibid., 1485–86 (quotations on 1486).

23. Jefferson to Fanny Wright, August 7, 1825, in Bergh, 16:119–21 (quotation on 120).

24. Ibid. (first two quotations on 120, third quotation on 121).

25. Jefferson to James Heaton, May 20, 1826, in Peterson, *Thomas Jefferson, Writings*, 1516.

26. Jefferson to Alexander von Humboldt, December 6, 1813, in ibid., 1311–14 (quotations on 1312).

27. Jefferson to William Short, August 4, 1820, in ibid., 1435–40 (quotation on 1439).

28. Jefferson to James Monroe, June 11, 1823, in Bergh, 15:435–39 (first quotation on 435, second quotation on 436).

29. Quoted in Dexter Perkins, *A History of the Monroe Doctrine*, rev. ed. (Boston, 1955), 46. Perkins is still the best overall account of the origins and formation of the doctrine, though one should also consult Ammon, *James Monroe*, chap. 27.

30. Jefferson to James Madison, October 24, 1823, in Smith, *Republic of Letters*, 3:1878–79.

31. Jefferson to James Monroe, October 24, 1823, in Peterson, *Thomas Jefferson, Writings*, 1481–83 (quotations on 1481).

32. Ibid., 1482.

33. Ibid., 1483.

34. Jefferson to John Adams, August 10, 1815, in Cappon, *The Adams-Jefferson Letters*, 453–54. Jefferson knew (and commented to Adams) that Madison had kept detailed notes on the deliberations at the 1787 Constitutional Convention in Philadelphia (ibid., 453).

35. Jefferson to Hugh P. Taylor, October 4, 1823, in Bergh, 15:471–74 (quotation on 473).

36. William Short to Jefferson, March 27, 1820, in Jefferson Papers, Founders Online, National Archives, accessed October 29, 2015, http://founders.archives.gov/?q=%20Author%3A%22Short%2C%20William%22&s=1111311121&sa=&r=457&sr=.

37. "Autobiography," in Peterson, *Thomas Jefferson, Writings*, 3–101 (quotation on 3).

38. Ibid., 46.

39. Ibid., 7.

40. Ibid., 19–24.

41. Ibid., 6.

42. Ibid., 37.

43. Ibid., 44.

44. Ibid., 98.

45. Ibid., 101.

46. Jefferson to Robley Dunglison, November 26, 1825, in *The Jefferson-Dunglison Letters*, ed. John M. Dorsey (Charlottesville, 1960), 44–45 (quotation on 44).

47. See Crawford, *Twilight at Monticello*, 209–10.

48. For Jefferson's purchase and description of Eagle, see *JMB*, 2:1371 (November 6, 1820). For his getting on the horse, see Randall, *The Life of Thomas Jefferson*, 3:538.

49. Jefferson to John Adams, October 14, 1816, in Cappon, *The Adams-Jefferson Letters*, 490–93 (quotation on 490).

50. Jefferson to Ellen Wayles Randolph Coolidge, August 27, 1825, in *FL*, 457–58 (quotation on 457).

51. Jefferson to Ellen Wayles Randolph Coolidge, November 14, 1825, in ibid., 460–63.

52. Jefferson to James Madison, October 18, 1825, in Smith, *The Republic of Letters*, 3:1942–43 (quotation on 1942). For the event, see Randall, *The Life of Thomas Jefferson*, 3:540.

53. Martha Randolph to Ellen Wayles Randolph Coolidge, April 5, 1826, quoted in Malone, *Jefferson and His Time*, 6:473.

54. Jefferson to Joseph C. Cabell, January 20, 1826, quoted in Randall, *The Life of Thomas Jefferson*, 3:527.

55. Jefferson to Thomas Jefferson Randolph, February 8, 1826, in *FL*, 469–70 (quotation on 469).

56. Ibid.

57. Jefferson to Thomas Jefferson Randolph, February 11, 1826, in *FL*, 470 (first quotation); Dunglison quoted in *DL*, 416 (second quotation).

58. Crawford, *Twilight at Monticello*, 232. Actually, Martha would be allowed to live at Monticello for only two years after her father's death. See Malone, *Jefferson and His Time*, 6:479n.

59. "A Visit to the Dying Sage," in *VTM*, 109.

60. Jefferson to James Madison, February 17, 1826, in Peterson, *Thomas Jefferson, Writings*, 1512–15 (quotations on 1515).

61. "Jefferson's Will," [March 16, 1826], in Ford, *The Works of Thomas Jefferson*, 12:478–83 (quotation on 482). The codicil was dated March 17, 1826.

62. Dr. Robey Dunglison to James Madison, July 1, 1826, in Dorsey, *Jefferson-Dunglison Letters*, 66–67 (quotation on 67).

63. Thomas Jefferson Randolph to Henry S. Randall, [n.d.], in Randall, *The Life of Thomas Jefferson*, 3:543–44 (quotation on 544).

64. *DL*, 429.

65. Ibid., 431.

66. Thomas Jefferson Randolph to Henry S. Randall, [n.d.], in Randall, *The Life of Thomas Jefferson*, 3:543 (first quotation), 544 (second quotation).

67. "Dr. Dunglison's Memoranda, Resumed," in ibid., 548.

68. Randolph to Randall, in ibid., 544.

69. Quoted in *DL*, 430.

POSTSCRIPT

1. "Memoirs of Thomas Jefferson Randolph," MSS 5454-c, in Albert and Shirley Small Special Collections Library, University of Virginia (transcribed by James A. Bear), 54.

2. Kierner, *Martha Jefferson Randolph*, 228–29. I draw most of my discussion of Martha's life following the death of her father from Kierner's definitive account.

3. Ibid., 249–50. Malone, *Jefferson and His Time*, 6:511, gives the precise amount of Jefferson's debt upon his death.

4. Hochman, "Thomas Jefferson: A Personal Financial Biography," 287–88.

5. See Melvin I. Urofsky, *The Levy Family and Monticello, 1834–1923* (Charlottesville, 2000), 42–44; James A. Bear Jr., "Monticello," in Peterson, *Thomas Jefferson: A Reference Biography*, 445–46.

6. Urofsky, *Levy Family and Monticello*, 86 (quotation).

7. Bear, "Monticello," 447–49.

8. Urofsky, *Levy Family and Monticello*, 120–92.

Bibliographical Essay

The first biography of Thomas Jefferson of real substance was the three-volume work published by Henry S. Randall in the mid-nineteenth century and titled simply *The Life of Thomas Jefferson* (New York, 1858). Randall interviewed people who had known Jefferson and quoted many letters, so the volumes serve as a primary source as well as an interpretative biography, and Randall presented a very favorable portrait. Many of the memorable anecdotes about Jefferson come from this volume, especially in the letters of his grandchildren. But the foundational scholarly biography of Jefferson remains Dumas Malone's six volume *Jefferson and His Time* (Boston, 1948–1981); each volume has its own title. Malone published volume one in 1948, and, working for decades, did not finish the sixth until thirty-three years later. Totaling more than 3,100 pages of text, this rather old-fashioned life-and-times biography is as comprehensive as its length suggests, and Malone is judicious and protective of Jefferson's reputation, though the later volumes are more critical. Still, every serious student of Jefferson must begin with these deeply researched volumes.

The best one-volume life is Merrill D. Peterson's *Thomas Jefferson and the New Nation: A Biography* (New York, 1970), which has more than 1,000 pages of text, and unlike Malone, Peterson included no notes. Peterson is more interpretative than Malone, more interested in Jefferson's ideas, but overall is also quite sympathetic. Both Malone and Peterson offer criticism where they think it is needed, so theirs are by no means uncritical studies, but their books both appeared before the newer revelations about Jefferson and Sally Hemings and before the issue of slavery loomed so large in American historical scholarship.

Fawn M. Brodie's *Thomas Jefferson: An Intimate History* (New York, 1974), with its strong emphasis on Jefferson's relationship with Sally Hemings, drastically altered the popular image of Jefferson. There was a simultaneous upsurge of remarkably innovative scholarship on slavery. As a result, Jefferson scholarship took a critical, primarily negative turn after the early 1970s, and both Malone and Peterson now read as artifacts of another age. While some books on Jefferson today are mostly dismissive and intemperately critical, one can still find careful, balanced biographies and a vast literature of narrower studies—monographs—of great quality. The best short biographies are Noble E. Cunningham Jr.'s *In Pursuit of Reason: The Life of Thomas Jefferson* (Baton Rouge, 1987), an outgrowth of the author's important earlier monographs on the political history of the Jefferson era; Richard B. Bernstein's excellent, brief *Thomas Jefferson* (New York, 2003); and Joyce Appleby's even shorter, though perceptive, volume, also titled *Thomas Jefferson* (New York, 2003). An important newer and more comprehensive biography is Jon Meacham's *Thomas Jefferson: The Art of Power* (New York, 2012), which has a welcome focus on Jefferson's political skills. Kevin J. Hayes's lengthy *The Road to Monticello: The Life and Mind of Thomas Jefferson* (New York, 2008), by contrast, focuses more on Jefferson's reading and ideas. Merrill D. Peterson offers a different approach in his edited volume *Thomas Jefferson: A Reference Biography* (New York, 1986), wherein chapters by twenty-five separate authors cover the key periods and aspects of Jefferson's life, creating a collective biography that incorporates varying perspectives.

There are books on every aspect of Jefferson life, but all recent work builds upon the foundation of Jefferson's correspondence and other writings. While there were earlier editions of his works, modern Jefferson scholarship began with the *Papers of Thomas Jefferson*, the first volume of which Julian P. Boyd edited and Princeton University Press published in 1950. This series is a landmark in the editing and publishing of the papers of major figures in American history; Boyd established a standard of accurate and meticulous transcription, with elaborate explanatory footnotes, that revolutionized the publication of such materials. Luckily, Boyd also established the convention of including correspondence from and to Jefferson, so one can fully understand the context of each letter. Subsequent editors have restrained the complexity and depth of Boyd's footnoting style, but still these volumes—as of 2016 numbering forty-two, by several editors—are a wonderful resource for scholars. To date, even after more than six decades, the editors have only gotten to March 1804 of Jefferson's massive correspondence. Luckily a second series, titled *Papers of Thomas Jefferson, Retirement Series*, began publication in 2004 under the editorship of J. Jefferson Looney, and these volumes, of which there are twelve so far, include the correspondence from March 1809 through April 1818. All subsequent Jefferson scholarship will depend on these two series. I have found them absolutely indispensable. Few people will have the time to read though fifty-four volumes and counting of correspondence, but luckily Merrill D. Peterson selected a wonderful sampling of Jefferson's most important letters, along with his most important public papers and addresses, for the Library of America volume titled *Thomas Jefferson, Writings: Autobiography; a Summary View of the Rights of British America; Notes on the State of Virginia; Public Papers; Addresses, Messages, and Replies; Miscellany; Letters* (New York, 1984). The best edition of Jefferson's *Notes on the State of Virginia* is that edited by William Peden and published in 1954 by the University of North Carolina Press.

A moving portion of Jefferson's correspondence has been collected and published as *The Family Letters of Thomas Jefferson* (Columbia, MO, 1966), edited by Edwin Morris Betts and James Adam Bear Jr., reprinted in 1986 by the University Press of Virginia. The most famous subset of Jefferson's correspondence is that with John Adams, and these letters, especially those written after the renewal of their friendship and correspondence in 1812, constitute an epistolary masterpiece. Lester J. Cappon collected and edited the whole corpus in 1959, though it has been reprinted several times. The best modern version of *The Adams-Jefferson Letters: The Complete Correspondence Between Thomas Jefferson and Abigail and John Adams* (Chapel Hill, 1987) is the reprinting by the University of North Carolina Press. This should be seen as a contribution to American literature as well as history. Jefferson also had a fifty-year collaboration with James Madison, and James Morton Smith has collected their many letters—the most important correspondence between any two Founders—and provided helpful interpretive introductions in three meaty volumes collectively titled *The Republic of Letters: The Correspondence Between Thomas Jefferson and James Madison, 1776–1826* (New York, 1995). A classic book in the Jeffersonian bibliography, *The Domestic Life of Thomas Jefferson*, compiled in 1871 by his great granddaughter Sarah N. Randolph, includes many of the best-known Jefferson letters. The University Press of Virginia conveniently reprinted this volume in 1978, and though modern editors have subsequently published most of the letters more authoritatively, Randolph's connective language remains valuable.

Jefferson was a compulsive record keeper. One of the most fascinating aspects of this resulted in a two-volume work that his modern editors, James A. Bear Jr. and Lucia C. Stanton, titled *Jefferson's Memorandum Books: Accounts, with Legal Records and Miscellany,*

1767–1826 (Princeton, 1997), wherein Jefferson recorded every expenditure and countless other details of his daily life. These volumes allow an almost daily reconstruction of his adult life. Two other books reflect Jefferson's infatuation with record keeping: *Thomas Jefferson's Garden Book* (Monticello, 2012), edited by Edwin Morris Betts, and *Thomas Jefferson's Farm Book* (Charlottesville, 1987), also edited by Betts, both conveniently reprinted. The Garden Book focuses on the gardens and orchards in the immediate vicinity of Monticello, and the Farm Book covers the agricultural operations of the entire plantation.

The biographies listed above cover the whole of Jefferson's life, but many volumes use a biographical approach to focus on selected aspects, with no claim to comprehensiveness. A particularly insightful example of this kind of limited study is *"Most Blessed of the Patriarchs": Thomas Jefferson and the Empire of the Imagination* (New York, 2016) by today's leading Jefferson scholars, Annette Gordon-Reed and Peter S. Onuf. Similar studies are Andrew Burstein's *The Inner Jefferson: Portrait of a Grieving Optimist* (Charlottesville, 1995), which includes a penetrating analysis of Jefferson's correspondence and reading, and *Jefferson's Secrets: Death and Desire at Monticello* (New York, 2005). More critical of Jefferson and far less sympathetic is Joseph J. Ellis, *American Sphinx: The Character of Thomas Jefferson* (New York, 1997). Daniel J. Boorstin's older *The Lost World of Thomas Jefferson* (New York, 1948) remains useful despite the changes in historiography; it compares Jefferson's worldview with those of several contemporaries and emphasizes that they all lived in a pre-Darwinian age.

Many other important books emphasize particular aspects of Jefferson's life, such as Alan Crawford Pell, *Twilight at Monticello: The Final Years of Thomas Jefferson* (New York, 2008); Michael Knox Beran, *Jefferson's Demon's: Portrait of a Restless Mind* (New York, 2003); Jack McLaughlin's *Jefferson and Monticello: The Biography of a Builder* (New York, 1998); Carl Lehmann, *Thomas Jefferson: American Humanist* (New York, 1947); and Albert Jay Nock's essay-like *Jefferson* (New York, 1916). There is also the highly critical account by Leonard Levy, *Jefferson and Civil Liberties: The Darker Side* (Cambridge, MA, 1963). Susan Kern's archeologically informed *Jeffersons at Shadwell* (New Haven, 2010) transformed how we think about Jefferson's youth and his parents' household and, as such, is immensely important. The best intellectual histories of Jefferson are the carefully nuanced essays in Peter S. Onuf, *The Mind of Thomas Jefferson* (Charlottesville, 2007), and his *Jefferson's Empire: The Language of American Nationalism* (Charlottesville, 2000). The images of Jefferson have long fascinated historians, both the image he created and the one historians created of him. The essential book on this topic is Merrill D. Peterson's magisterial *Jeffersonian Image in the American Mind* (New York, 1960), but see also the very able studies by Francis D. Cogliano, *Thomas Jefferson: Reputation and Legacy* (Edinburgh, 2006), and Robert M. S. McDonald, *Confounding Father: Thomas Jefferson's Image in His Own Time* (Charlottesville, 2016). See as well the essays in the volume coedited by John B. Boles and Randal S. Hall, *Seeing Jefferson Anew: In His Time and Ours* (Charlottesville, 2010).

Several other collections of essays on varied Jefferson topics offer terrific insights into this complex man. The most significant of these is Peter S. Onuf, ed., *Jeffersonian Legacies* (Charlottesville, 1993). Originally papers presented at the University of Virginia on the 250th anniversary of Jefferson's birth, the fourteen essays represent an impressive summary of Jefferson scholarship. The Library of Congress likewise celebrated Jefferson's 250th birthday with another set of lectures, eighteen in total, usefully published as *Thomas Jefferson and the Education of a Citizen* (Washington, DC, 1999), which include material on Jefferson's role in the creation of the library. Jefferson was so multifaceted that essay collections have proven useful ways to assess him. Two valuable recent volumes are Frank Shuffelton, ed., *The Cambridge Companion to Thomas Jefferson* (Cambridge, UK, 2009), with fourteen diverse essays, and Francis D. Cogliano, ed., *A Companion to Thomas Jefferson* (Malden, MA, 2012), one of a series of "companion" books published by Blackwell. The thirty-three essays in this volume have an explicitly bibliographical focus, making them unusually helpful to the student or beginning scholar.

Two splendid museum catalogs offer glimpses into the aesthetic Jefferson: William Howard Adams, ed., *The Eye of Jefferson* (Washington, DC, 1976), featuring an exhibition at the National Gallery of Art, and Susan R. Stein, *The Worlds of Thomas Jefferson at Monticello* (New York, 1993), which brought together items scattered near and far to reproduce for the nonce the Monticello that Jefferson would have known. Related to these volumes is a large bibliography on Jefferson as architect. Of the many relevant volumes, useful introductions are Hugh Howard, *Thomas Jefferson, Architect: The Built Legacy of Our Third President* (New York, 2003); Frederick Doveton Nichols and Ralph E. Griswold, *Thomas Jefferson, Landscape Architect* (Charlottesville, 1978); and Richard Guy Wilson, ed., *Thomas Jefferson's Academical Village: The Creation of an Architectural Masterpiece* (Charlottesville, 2009).

Any consideration of Jefferson and the arts leads a reader to his five years in Paris. The most general study of Jefferson abroad is George Green Shackelford, *Thomas Jefferson's Travels in Europe, 1784–1789* (Baltimore, 1995), which traces his complete itinerary. More detailed analyses focus on his experiences in Paris: Howard C. Rice, *Thomas Jefferson's Paris* (Princeton, 1976), and William Howard Adams, *The Paris Years of Thomas Jefferson* (New Haven, 1997). One should also read Jefferson's correspondence for these years—much of it conveniently collected in Douglas L. Wilson and Lucia Stanton, eds., *Thomas Jefferson Abroad* (New York, 1999)—and the notations in his memorandum books.

A number of monographs focus on discrete episodes in Jefferson's career. Much has been written about Jefferson's authorship of the Declaration of Independence, but indispensable is Pauline Maier's *American Scripture: Making the Declaration of Independence* (New York, 1997). Her book should be complemented by Gary Wills, *Inventing America: Jefferson's Declaration of Independence* (New York, 1978), and Danielle Allen, *Our Declaration: A Reading of the Declaration of Independence in Defense of Liberty* (New York, 2015). Lance Banning brilliantly analyzes Jefferson's political ideology in *The Jeffersonian Persuasion: Evolution of a Party Ideology* (Ithaca, 1978).

Three works by Noble E. Cunningham Jr. best illustrate Jefferson's reaction to opposing views and the resulting development of an oppositionist party: *The Jeffersonian Republicans: The Formation of Party Organization, 1789–1801* (Chapel Hill, 1957), *The Jeffersonian Republicans in Power: Party Operations, 1801–1809* (Chapel Hill, 1963), and *The Process of Government Under Jefferson* (Princeton, 1978). Of course, one should consult the major biographies of the other actors, including Alexander Hamilton, George Washington, John Adams, and James Madison. The bibliography on the politics of the era is massive, but the best introductions are James Roger Sharp, *American Politics in the Early Republic: The New Nation in Crisis* (New Haven, 1993), and Stanley Elkins and Eric McKitrick's very substantial *The Age of Federalism: The Early American Republic, 1788–1800* (New York, 1993), which offers a Federalist-tinged interpretation of events. Meacham's biography, cited above, highlights Jefferson's political career.

One should also consult several volumes that focus on particular aspects of Jefferson's political thought and practice: Jeremy D. Bailey, *Thomas Jefferson and Executive Power* (New York, 2007); Robert M. Johnstone Jr., *Jefferson and the Presidency: Leadership in the*

Young Republic (Ithaca, 1978); David N. Mayer, *The Constitutional Thought of Thomas Jefferson* (Charlottesville, 1994); and Brian Steele's especially perceptive *Thomas Jefferson and American Nationalism* (New York, 2012). Three books are essential for understanding the controversial election of 1800: Edward J. Larson, *A Magnificent Catastrophe: The Tumultuous Election of 1800, America's First Presidential Campaign* (New York, 2008); John Ferling, *Adams vs. Jefferson: The Tumultuous Election of 1800* (New York, 2004); and Susan Dunn, *Jefferson's Second Revolution: The Election Crisis of 1800 and the Triumph of Republicanism* (Boston, 2004). All three evaluate the consequences of the election, but the sixteen essays gathered in James Horn, Jan Ellen Lewis, and Peter S. Onuf, eds., *The Revolution of 1800: Democracy, Race, and the New Republic* (Charlottesville, 2002), are necessary for understanding the larger issues at stake.

For the Burr controversy that marred the second term of Jefferson's presidency, see the indictment of Aaron Burr in Thomas Perkins Abernethy, *The Burr Conspiracy* (New York, 1954), and the careful study of Burr's trial in R. Kent Newmyer, *The Treason Trial of Aaron Burr: Law, Politics, and the Character Wars of the New Nation* (Cambridge, UK, 2012). For Burr himself, David O. Steward provides a critical but credible portrayal in *American Emperor: Aaron Burr's Challenge to Jefferson's America* (New York, 2011). The Embargo, which even more significantly marred Jefferson's second term, is the focus of Burton Spivak, *Jefferson's English Crisis: Commerce, Embargo, and the Republican Revolution* (Charlottesville, 1979), but there is no better treatment than that provided in Dumas Malone's sixth volume.

Central to Jefferson scholarship over the past few decades has been the issue of race. One's reading on Jefferson and slavery should begin with five books that provide the necessary background. First is the classic study by Winthrop Jordan, *White over Black: American Attitudes Toward the Negro, 1550–1812* (Chapel Hill, 1968), which places Jefferson's thought in the context of Western Christendom in the early modern era. For the Virginia background, Eva Sheppard Wolf's *Race and Liberty in the New Nation: Emancipation in Virginia from the Revolution to Nat Turner's Rebellion* (Baton Rouge, 2006) is essential, as is Joshua D. Rothman, *Notorious in the Neighborhood: Sex and Families Across the Color Line in Virginia, 1787–1861* (Chapel Hill, 2003). Andrew S. Curran's *The Anatomy of Blackness: Science and Slavery in an Age of Enlightenment* (Baltimore, 2011) suggests the impact of contemporary scientific thought in France on Jefferson's racial views. For Jefferson as slaveholder, Lucia Stanton, *"Those Who Labor for My Happiness": Slavery at Thomas Jefferson's Monticello* (Charlottesville, 2012), is absolutely indispensable.

Annette Gordon-Reed examines the once controversial topic of Jefferson and Sally Hemings with extraordinary care and sophistication in two books. The first, *Thomas Jefferson and Sally Hemings: An American Controversy* (Charlottesville, 1997), persuaded most historians that they indeed did have a long-term relationship. The second, *The Hemingses of Monticello: An American Family* (New York, 2008), not only looks at the larger group of Hemings slaves at Monticello but discusses the Paris years, when Jefferson and Sally Hemings's relationship apparently began, with stunning detail and insight. Together these books have superseded Fawn Brodie's above-mentioned earlier work. See also Jan Ellen Lewis and Peter S. Onuf, eds., *Sally Hemings and Thomas Jefferson: History, Memory and Civic Culture* (Charlottesville, 1999). Alert to historical context, balanced, and perhaps surprisingly sympathetic to Jefferson, these three recent volumes are triumphs of historical scholarship. In contrast are two unrelenting attacks on Jefferson: Paul Finkelman's *Slavery and the Founders: Race and Liberty in the Age of Jefferson* (3rd ed., Armonk, NY, 2014), and Henry Wiencek's reductionist *Master of the Mountain: Thomas Jefferson and His Slaves* (New York, 2012).

The fields of women's history and religious history have offered new perspectives on Jefferson's life. On Jefferson and women, one must begin with Jan Lewis's *The Pursuit of Happiness: Family and Values in Jefferson's Virginia* (Cambridge, UK, 1983), as well as her articles in the above-cited collections edited by Onuf, *Jeffersonian Legacies*, and Boles and Hall, *Seeing Jefferson Anew*. Also insightful is Virginia Scharff, *The Women Jefferson Loved* (New York, 2010). More critical of Jefferson is Jon Kukla, *Mr. Jefferson's Women* (New York, 2007). Cynthia A. Kierner's subtle *Martha Jefferson Randolph, Daughter of Monticello* (Chapel Hill, 2012), is indispensable, as is her more narrowly focused *Scandal at Bizarre: Rumor and Reputation in Jefferson's America* (New York, 2004).

There is a growing literature on Jefferson and religion, but the starting point remains W. Dickingson Adams Jr., *Jefferson's Abstracts from the Gospels: "The Philosophy of Jesus" and "The Life and Morals of Jesus"* (Princeton, 1983). The best overall treatment in book form is Edwin S. Gaustad, *Sworn on the Altar of God: A Religious Biography of Thomas Jefferson* (Grand Rapids, MI, 1996), but again some of the best work is in articles. See those by Thomas E. Buckley Jr. in the previously cited collection edited by Boles and Hall, *Seeing Jefferson Anew*; by Paul K. Conkin in Onuf, *Jeffersonian Legacies*; and by Richard Samuelson in Shuffelton, *Cambridge Companion*. Also see Peter S. Onuf's "Jefferson's Religion: Priestcraft, Enlightenment, and the Republican Revolution," reprinted in his *The Mind of Thomas Jefferson* (Charlottesville, 2007). Thomas E. Buckley, *Establishing Religious Freedom: Jefferson's Statute in Virginia* (Charlottesville, 2013), and Denise A. Spellberg, *Thomas Jefferson's Qur'an: Islam and the Founders* (New York, 2013), discuss different aspects of the topic.

Readers rightly associate Jefferson with the Louisiana Purchase, and among a substantial literature on this topic, the three key books are Alexander DeConde, *This Affair of Louisiana* (New York, 1976); Jon Kukla, *A Wilderness So Immense: The Louisiana Purchase and the Destiny of America* (New York, 2003); and Peter J. Kastor, *The Nation's Crucible: The Louisiana Purchase and the Creation of America* (New Haven, 2004). For Jefferson and the West, see, generally, Charles A. Miller, *Jefferson and Nature: An Interpretation* (Baltimore, 1988); Donald Jackson, ed., *Thomas Jefferson and the Stony Mountains: Exploring the West from Monticello* (Urbana, IL, 1981); and the popular account by Stephen E. Ambrose, *Undaunted Courage: Meriwether Lewis, Thomas Jefferson, and the Opening of the American West* (New York 1996). The best study of Jefferson and the Indians is Bernard W. Sheehan, *Seeds of Extinction: Jeffersonian Philanthropy and the American Indian* (Chapel Hill, 1973).

Jefferson's last crusade was the creation of the University of Virginia. Several histories of the university portray his role, but see volume one of Philip Alexander Bruce, *History of the University of Virginia, 1819–1919: The Lengthened Shadow of One Man* (5 vols., New York, 1920), and Jennings L. Wagoner Jr., *Jefferson and Education* (Charlottesville, 2004). Dumas Malone also carefully explores this topic in volume six of his *Jefferson and His Time*. Jefferson's role in the foundation of West Point is relevant to his later efforts to create the University of Virginia, and on this earlier story, see Robert M. S. McDonald, *Thomas Jefferson's Military Academy: Founding West Point* (Charlottesville, 2004).

Jefferson, of course, had varied interests and made contributions across a range of endeavors, all of which have inspired books. Representative titles include Silvio Bedini, *Thomas Jefferson, Statesman of Science* (New York, 1990); Francis D. Cogliano, *Emperor of Liberty: Thomas Jefferson's Foreign Policy* (New Haven, 2014); Helen Cripe, *Thomas Jefferson and Music* (Charlottesville, 1974); Frank L. Dewey, *Thomas Jefferson, Lawyer* (Charlottesville, 1986); James M. Gabler, *Passions: The Wines and Travels of Thomas Jefferson* (Baltimore, 1995); Damon Lee Fowler, ed., *Dining at Monticello: In Good Taste and Abundance*

(Charlottesville, 2005); and Peter J. Hatch, *"A Rich Spot of Earth": Thomas Jefferson's Revolutionary Garden at Monticello* (New Haven, 2012). Still, the best introduction to Jefferson is a hearty sampling of his correspondence, along with the Declaration of Independence, his first inaugural address, and *Notes on the State of Virginia*, all conveniently found in the previously cited Peterson, *Thomas Jefferson, Writings*.

Index

John B. Boles is the William P. Hobby Professor of History at Rice University and former editor of the *Journal of Southern History*. He lives in Houston, Texas.